Tourism and Opportunities for Economic Development in Asia

Patricia Ordóñez de Pablos
University of Oviedo, Spain

Zeyar Myo Aung
Ministry of Hotels and Tourism, Myanmar

A volume in the Advances in Hospitality, Tourism, and the Services Industry (AHTSI) Book Series

IGI GLOBAL
DISSEMINATOR OF KNOWLEDGE
www.igi-global.com

Published in the United States of America by
IGI Global
Business Science Reference (an imprint of IGI Global)
701 E. Chocolate Avenue
Hershey PA, USA 17033
Tel: 717-533-8845
Fax: 717-533-8661
E-mail: cust@igi-global.com
Web site: http://www.igi-global.com

Library of Congress Cataloging-in-Publication Data

Names: Ordóñez de Pablos, Patricia, 1975- editor. | Aung, Zeyar Myo, 1973- editor.
Title: Tourism and Opportunities for Economic Development in Asia / Patricia Ordóñez de Pablos and Zeyar Myo Aung, Editors.
Description: Hershey PA : Business Science Reference, 2017. | Includes bibliographical references and index.
Identifiers: LCCN 2016053744| ISBN 9781522520788 (hardcover) | ISBN 9781522520795 (ebook)
Subjects: LCSH: Tourism--Asia. | Tourism--Southeast Asia. | Economic development--Asia. | Economic development--Southeast Asia.
Classification: LCC G155.A74 T656 2017 | DDC 338.4/7915--dc23
LC record available at https://lccn.loc.gov/2016053744

This book is published in the IGI Global book series Advances in Hospitality, Tourism, and the Services Industry (AHTSI) (ISSN: Pending; eISSN: Pending)

British Cataloguing in Publication Data
A Cataloguing in Publication record for this book is available from the British Library.

For electronic access to this publication, please contact: eresources@igi-global.com.

Advances in Hospitality, Tourism, and the Services Industry (AHTSI) Book Series

ISSN:Pending
EISSN:Pending

MISSION

Globally, the hospitality, travel, tourism, and services industries generate a significant percentage of revenue and represent a large portion of the business world. Even in tough economic times, these industries thrive as individuals continue to spend on leisure and recreation activities as well as services.

The Advances in Hospitality, Tourism, and the Services Industry (AHTSI) book series offers diverse publications relating to the management, promotion, and profitability of the leisure, recreation, and services industries. Highlighting current research pertaining to various topics within the realm of hospitality, travel, tourism, and services management, the titles found within the AHTSI book series are pertinent to the research and professional needs of managers, business practitioners, researchers, and upper-level students studying in the field.

COVERAGE

- Sustainable Tourism
- Cruise Marketing and Sales
- Casino Management
- Tourism and the Environment
- Health and Wellness Tourism
- Travel Agency Management
- Destination Marketing and Management
- Service Management
- Service Design
- Leisure & Business Travel

IGI Global is currently accepting manuscripts for publication within this series. To submit a proposal for a volume in this series, please contact our Acquisition Editors at Acquisitions@igi-global.com or visit: http://www.igi-global.com/publish/.

The Advances in Hospitality, Tourism, and the Services Industry (AHTSI) Book Series (ISSN Pending) is published by IGI Global, 701 E. Chocolate Avenue, Hershey, PA 17033-1240, USA, www.igi-global.com. This series is composed of titles available for purchase individually; each title is edited to be contextually exclusive from any other title within the series. For pricing and ordering information please visit http://www.igi-global.com/book-series/advances-hospitality-tourism-services-industry/121014. Postmaster: Send all address changes to above address.

Titles in this Series

For a list of additional titles in this series, please visit: www.igi-global.com

Handbook of Research on Holistic Optimization Techniques in the Hospitality, Tourism, and Travel Industry
Pandian Vasant (Universiti Teknologi PETRONAS, Malaysia) and Kalaivanthan M. (Rasa Sayang Resort and Spa, Malaysia & Golden Sands Resort, Malaysia)
Business Science Reference • copyright 2017 • 515pp • H/C (ISBN: 9781522510543) • US $235.00 (our price)

Opportunities and Challenges for Tourism and Hospitality in the BRIC Nations
Mohinder Chand Dhiman (Kurukshetra University, India)
Business Science Reference • copyright 2017 • 426pp • H/C (ISBN: 9781522507086) • US $205.00 (our price)

Strategic Place Branding Methodologies and Theory for Tourist Attraction
Ahmet Bayraktar (Bozok University, Turkey) and Can Uslay (Rutgers University, USA)
Business Science Reference • copyright 2017 • 394pp • H/C (ISBN: 9781522505792) • US $205.00 (our price)

Global Place Branding Campaigns across Cities, Regions, and Nations
Ahmet Bayraktar (Bozok University, Turkey) and Can Uslay (Rutgers University, USA)
Business Science Reference • copyright 2017 • 368pp • H/C (ISBN: 9781522505761) • US $205.00 (our price)

Global Dynamics in Travel, Tourism, and Hospitality
Nikolaos Pappas (The University of West London, UK) and Ilenia Bregoli (University of Lincoln, UK)
Business Science Reference • copyright 2016 • 372pp • H/C (ISBN: 9781522502012) • US $205.00 (our price)

Corporate Social Responsibility in the Hospitality and Tourism Industry
Lipika Kaur Guliani (Panjab University, India) and Syed Ahmad Rizwan (Tourism Recreation Research, CTRD, India)
Business Science Reference • copyright 2016 • 356pp • H/C (ISBN: 9781466699021) • US $190.00 (our price)

Strategic Tools and Methods for Promoting Hospitality and Tourism Services
Alexandru-Mircea Nedelea (Stefan cel Mare University of Suceava, Romania) Maximiliano Korstanje (University of Palermo, Argentina) and Babu George (Fort Hays State University, USA)
Business Science Reference • copyright 2016 • 326pp • H/C (ISBN: 9781466697614) • US $195.00 (our price)

Handbook of Research on Global Hospitality and Tourism Management
Angelo A. Camillo (Woodbury University, USA)
Business Science Reference • copyright 2015 • 621pp • H/C (ISBN: 9781466686069) • US $345.00 (our price)

Editorial Advisory Board

Table of Contents

Preface xvi

Chapter 1
Impact of Advertising and Public Relations on Tourism Development in Da Nang, Vietnam 1
Xuan Tran, University of West Florida, USA
Minh Nguyen, Duy Tan University, Vietnam
Ha Kieu Tan Luu, Duy Tan University, Vietnam
Ny Ngo, Duy Tan University, Vietnam
My Tran, Duy Tan University, Vietnam
Ngoc Bich Nguyen, Duy Tan University, Vietnam
Hai Tran, Duy Tan University, Vietnam

Chapter 2
Environmental protection and Tourism: Tourism in the Protected Area in Mongolia 17
Navchaa Tugjamba, University of the Humanities, Mongolia
Amarbayasgalan Gantumur, University of the Humanities, Mongolia

Chapter 4
Implication of SASEC Tourism Initiatives on North Eastern States of India: A Descriptive Analysis – SASEC Tourism 34
Supriya Dam, Govt. Degree College, India

Chapter 5
Mastering Sustainable Tourism and Rural Tourism in the Global Economy 53
Kijpokin Kasemsap, Suan Sunandha Rajabhat University, Thailand

Chapter 6
Sustainable Tourism Development in Asia: Evaluation of the Potential and Challenges: 77
Gamini Herath, Monash University, Malaysia

Chapter 7
Prioritization of Eco-Tourism Forms at Sikkim, India 101
Ajeya Jha, Sikkim Manipal Institute of Technology, India
Sherap Shenga, Government of Sikkim, India
Somnath Mishra, Sikkim Manipal University, India
Manjushree Mishra, Sikkim Manipal University, India

Chapter 8
Can Educational Tourism Spur Economic Growth in Malaysia? Evidence from Neoclassical Growth Model 120
Hylmee Matahir, Universiti Teknologi MARA Cawangan Sabah, Malaysia
Chor Foon Tang, Universiti Sains Malaysia, Malaysia

Chapter 9
Changing Behavioural of Patterns of Travelers to Urban Ecotourism Sites of Kuala Lumpur 132
Sudipta Kiran Sarkar, Berjaya University College of Hospitality, Malaysia

Chapter 10
Critical Review of Tourism in India 149
Neeta Baporikar, Namibia University of Science and Technology, Namibia & University of Pune, India

Chapter 11
The Life Cycles of Destination Life Cycle Models: A Critical Comparison and Synthesis in the Context of Destinations in Asia 170
Sudipta Kiran Sarkar, Berjaya University College of Hospitality, Malaysia
Babu P. George, Fort Hays State University, USA

Chapter 12
The Relevance of the Tourism-Led Growth Hypothesis to Malaysia: A View Through Rolling-Samples and Disaggregated Tourism Markets 188
Chor Foon Tang, Universiti Sains Malaysia, Malaysia
Eu Chye Tan, University of Malaya, Malaysia

Chapter 13
Tourism Development and Rural Tourism in Taiwan: A Literature Review 203
I-Ting Chen, Sheffield Hallam University, UK
Konstantin Karl Weicht, Vienna University of Economics and Business, Austria

Chapter 14
Tourism-Led Growth Hypothesis and Foreign Direct Investment in ASEAN 224
Praopan Pratoomchat, Bates College, USA

Chapter 15
UNESCO World Heritage Designation: An Opportunity or a Threat to Hoi An Ancient Town (Vietnam)? 250
Huong T. Bui, Ritsumeikan Asia Pacific University, Japan
Tuan-Anh Le, Southern Cross University, Australia
Chung H. Nguyen, Vietnam National University, Vietnam

Chapter 16
Actor Network Theory in Tourism 261
Xuan Tran, University of West Florida, USA

Chapter 17
Adequacy of Government Policy on Ecotourism: A Case Study of Sikkim 270
Ajeya Jha, Sikkim Manipal Institute of Technology, India
Sherap Shenga, Government of Sikkim, India
Somnath Mishra, Sikkim Manipal University, India
Manjushree Mishra, Sikkim Manipal University, India

Compilation of References 287

About the Contributors 334

Index 339

Detailed Table of Contents

Preface xvi

Chapter 1
Impact of Advertising and Public Relations on Tourism Development in Da Nang, Vietnam 1
Xuan Tran, University of West Florida, USA
Minh Nguyen, Duy Tan University, Vietnam
Ha Kieu Tan Luu, Duy Tan University, Vietnam
Ny Ngo, Duy Tan University, Vietnam
My Tran, Duy Tan University, Vietnam
Ngoc Bich Nguyen, Duy Tan University, Vietnam
Hai Tran, Duy Tan University, Vietnam

An exploratory study was conducted to determine the impact of advertising and public relations on the visit intention of tourists in Da Nang, Vietnam. In 2015, Trip Advisor and New York Times selected Da Nang, Vietnam as one of the top Asia tourist destinations. This study sought to address the relationship between advertising or public relations and tourists' intention to visit based on the theory of planned behavior. Structure Equation Modeling was conducted to predict the impact of advertising and public relations on the visit intention of tourists in Da Nang. Findings indicate that an increased favorable attitude and control of advertising would increase tourist arrivals. Surprisingly, an increased positive attitude and control of public relations did not significantly affect tourists' intention to visit. Instead, the social norms of public relations were effective in driving the decision to visit but the social norms of advertising were not. The findings have contributed to destination brand through advertising and public relations. Implications are discussed.

Chapter 2
Environmental protection and Tourism: Tourism in the Protected Area in Mongolia 17
Navchaa Tugjamba, University of the Humanities, Mongolia
Amarbayasgalan Gantumur, University of the Humanities, Mongolia

Mongolia is a unique and relatively unexplored tourism and leisure travel destination. In the world tourism market, the tourism sector offers a great combination of wild natural features, a wide variety of untouched landscapes, historical heritage reserves, and nomadic life style and culture. The Protected Area Network of Mongolia cover over 14.5 percent of the country's territory and has become major destinations for rapidly growing tourism and recreational activities for its natural beauty, rare species of wildlife and historical and cultural heritage sites. Orkhon valley National Park (OVNP) is one of Mongolian main tourism destinations regarding to natural beautiful landscape and including numerous cultural and historical remains and sites. Thus, promoting sustainable tourism development to improve local livelihoods based on the nomadic lifestyle and protection of land with natural wilderness, watersheds, important biodiversity, historical and cultural heritage and rare remains is challenging in the national park.

Chapter 4
Implication of SASEC Tourism Initiatives on North Eastern States of India: A Descriptive Analysis – SASEC Tourism 34
Supriya Dam, Govt. Degree College, India

India's North Eastern Region (NER) stretches from the foothills of the Himalayas in the eastern range and is surrounded by international borders with countries like Bangladesh, Bhutan, China (Tibet Autonomous Region), Nepal, and Myanmar. The landlocked region is constrained by a brief spell of insurgency, and dismal unemployment has affected the region's progress since 1947. The advent of the Look East Policy coupled with a number of South Asia sub-regional arrangements with neighboring countries opened a "Pandora's Box" for this region. The SASEC initiatives of ADB helped to improve the status of tourism and infrastructure, including roads, air connectivity, and also opened cross-border land routes and roads within the North East (NE). The present study takes stock of tourism development from a sustainability perspective and examines the implementation of the SASEC tourism project in eight NE States of India with a view to suggest priority areas for action for promotion of tourism in this region.

Chapter 5
Mastering Sustainable Tourism and Rural Tourism in the Global Economy 53
Kijpokin Kasemsap, Suan Sunandha Rajabhat University, Thailand

This chapter explains the overviews of tourism, sustainable development, sustainable tourism, and rural tourism; the perspectives on rural tourism destination; rural tourism and entrepreneurship; the importance of sustainable tourism in the global economy; and the importance of rural tourism in the global economy. The fulfillment of sustainable tourism and rural tourism is necessary for modern tourism organizations that seek to serve suppliers and customers, increase business performance, strengthen competitiveness, and achieve continuous success in the global economy. Therefore, it is essential for modern tourism organizations to promote their sustainable tourism and rural tourism and develop a strategic plan to regularly check their practical advancements toward satisfying customer requirement. The chapter argues that promoting sustainable tourism and rural tourism has the potential to enhance organizational performance and gain sustainable competitive advantage in the global economy.

Chapter 6
Sustainable Tourism Development in Asia: Evaluation of the Potential and Challenges: 77
Gamini Herath, Monash University, Malaysia

Sustainable Tourism as a concept respects both local people, the traveler, cultural heritage and the environment. It should meet the needs of and opportunity for the future. But operationalizing sustainable tourism is problematic due to analytical weaknesses, conceptual criticisms and the need to redefine better perspectives. Asia faces many challenges in promoting sustainable tourism including political leadership, poor participation by all stakeholders, adverse environmental and social impacts. Another challenge is to ensure social sustainability and creating opportunities to transfer income to the poorer. The empirical study of island tourism in Malaysia shows that Marine Parks regulations are not adequately enforced and Malaysian coral reefs can suffer from increasing degradation. Water pollution, overfishing, beach erosion, coral bleaching and damage, fishing, snorkeling and poor recycling and sewage disposal all are still significant challenges to the Marine Park in in Tioman Island in Malaysia.

Chapter 7
Prioritization of Eco-Tourism Forms at Sikkim, India 101
Ajeya Jha, Sikkim Manipal Institute of Technology, India
Sherap Shenga, Government of Sikkim, India
Somnath Mishra, Sikkim Manipal University, India
Manjushree Mishra, Sikkim Manipal University, India

Sikkim is the one of the smallest states in India. The state government is promoting eco-tourism as a primary sector of economy. Natural and cultural attributes make Sikkim an ideal destination for Cultural, wildlife, adventure and religious tourism. The objective of the paper is to prioritize these four identified forms of tourism with a view to measure their relative appropriateness in the context of Sikkim. The methodology is based on three tools based on continuous scale, Analytical Hierarchy process (AHP) and Quality Function Deployment (QFD) respectively. The data has been collected from 40 respondents (senior civil service officers) The paper concludes that that in terms of appropriateness cultural tourism emerges as best followed by religious, adventure and wildlife tourism in that order. Also the three tools appear valid as they arrive at matching conclusions. Our contribution is that prioritization of forms of tourism has been done for the first time and that too using a comprehensive methodology utilizing AHP, QFD and continuous scale.

Chapter 8
Can Educational Tourism Spur Economic Growth in Malaysia? Evidence from Neoclassical
Growth Model 120
Hylmee Matahir, Universiti Teknologi MARA Cawangan Sabah, Malaysia
Chor Foon Tang, Universiti Sains Malaysia, Malaysia

This paper employs the neoclassical growth model to investigate empirically the role of educational tourism in Malaysia's economic growth during the period of 2002:Q1 to 2014:Q4. The present study finds that all determinants including educational tourism have a significant positive impact on economic growth in Malaysia, especially in the long-run. In terms of Granger causality, our results show that educational tourism and economic growth are Granger-cause each other in both the short- and long-run. In light of this, educational tourism can be an effective stimulator of Malaysia's economic growth. Moreover, the generalised variance decomposition analysis also affirms that educational tourism explained most of the long-run variation in economic growth compared to other determinants. Therefore, educational tourism is found to be a new and reliable source for Malaysia's economic growth. For the sake of brevity, any macroeconomic policies that heading toward promoting inbound educational tourism will probably spur the growth of the Malaysian economy, especially in the long-run.

Chapter 9
Changing Behavioural of Patterns of Travelers to Urban Ecotourism Sites of Kuala Lumpur 132
Sudipta Kiran Sarkar, Berjaya University College of Hospitality, Malaysia

This underlying motivation behind this chapter is to examine and understand the changing patterns of travel behaviour of travellers to urban nature attractions of 2010 and 2015 (5 year gap period) in the context of Kuala Lumpur. Kuala Lumpur, the capital of Malaysia offers a major potential for the growth and development of urban ecotourism given the natural hotspots in both inside and on the peripheries of the city. The results emanating from the descriptive statistics employed in this study demonstrate that changes have occurred in terms of benefits of urban ecotourism, ecotourism activity, source of ecotourism knowledge and in terms of more female ecotourists than male. These results put forth a range of implications from the perspectives of understanding the evolving tourist behaviour in urban spaces and significance of urban eco-travel in Malaysia. In light of challenges and prospects faced in terms of survival of nature-based areas in and around Kuala Lumpur, the findings of the study have been discussed.

Chapter 10
Critical Review of Tourism in India 149
Neeta Baporikar, Namibia University of Science and Technology, Namibia & University of Pune, India

Tourism plays a pivotal role in socio-economic development. It fosters international understanding, trust among people and brings many social benefits. According to United Nations World Tourism Organization, travel and tourism can be part of the solution to world problems of poverty employment and sustainability. Today, tourism has grown to become a major social and economic force and it is a well-known fact. Hence, it certainly is an activity of global importance and significance. With abundant nature's gift, one of the oldest culture and civilization India as tourist destination is in an envious position to locus itself as one of the best global destination by adopting innovative and holistic tourism policies. Through exploratory and descriptive examination and in depth literature review of policy documents and reports, the aim of this chapter is review critically the tourism policies and intends to suggest new avenues and innovations in tourism.

Chapter 11
The Life Cycles of Destination Life Cycle Models: A Critical Comparison and Synthesis in the Context of Destinations in Asia 170
Sudipta Kiran Sarkar, Berjaya University College of Hospitality, Malaysia
Babu P. George, Fort Hays State University, USA

Product Life Cycle (PLC) has always been a hot topic in the tourism literature. Butler's Tourism Area Lifecycle model and Plog's destination life cycle model have both been applied and analysed extensively in tourism destination development and lifecycle studies. This study attempts to offer a critical conversation on the similarities and differences as well as the strengths and weaknesses of these two widely referred generic models of destination life cycle. It also identifies some recent socio-political, economic, and technological developments that have changed the nature of tourism destination development in many parts of the world and in particular to Asia and the implications of these developments upon life cycles. Based on more recent research, the present authors suggest that the reality of destination development lies somewhere in between, as a resultant of interaction with the processes laid out by Plog and Butler.

Chapter 12
The Relevance of the Tourism-Led Growth Hypothesis to Malaysia: A View Through Rolling-Samples and Disaggregated Tourism Markets 188
Chor Foon Tang, Universiti Sains Malaysia, Malaysia
Eu Chye Tan, University of Malaya, Malaysia

This paper explored whether the tourism-led growth (TLG) hypothesis is empirically relevant to Malaysia based upon both full sample and rolling sample analyses. Data from January 1995 to December 2010 have been utilised for the purpose. Instead of relying upon aggregated data of tourist arrivals, disaggregated data of arrivals from 12 major tourism markets are relied upon for more insightful and accurate findings. The empirical results suggest that there was cointegration between Malaysia's economic growth and tourist arrivals from these tourism markets. However, the results of the full sample Granger causality test indicate that only 2 out of 12 tourism markets contributed to economic growth in the short-run. The TLG hypothesis is only supported in the long run by tourist arrivals from 10 out of the 12 tourism markets. The rolling-based Granger causality test shows that it is also these 10 markets situated mostly in developed countries that could provide a stable support for the TLG hypothesis.

Chapter 13
Tourism Development and Rural Tourism in Taiwan: A Literature Review 203
I-Ting Chen, Sheffield Hallam University, UK
Konstantin Karl Weicht, Vienna University of Economics and Business, Austria

Although tourism plays an increasingly important role in Taiwan's economy, and despite increasing government and academic interest in tourism development and rural tourism in Taiwan, the literature currently lacks of a concise review that brings together the various aspects of tourism development in Taiwan. The present chapter aims to contribute to closing this gap. It does so in six concise sections: a brief overview of Taiwan; the development of tourism in Taiwan; tourism and the economy in Taiwan; tourism and politics in Taiwan; rural tourism development; and small hotels in Taiwan. It is hoped that this account would serve as an important context specific prerequisite for future and more in-depth studies on tourism development and rural tourism in Taiwan.

Chapter 14
Tourism-Led Growth Hypothesis and Foreign Direct Investment in ASEAN 224
Praopan Pratoomchat, Bates College, USA

This study tests the relationships of visitor spending, foreign direct investment in the tourism sector, and the gross domestic product (GDP) per capita among members of the Association of Southeast Asian Nations (ASEAN) during the period of 1988 to 2011 to prove the tourism-led growth hypothesis. The results of panel regression show that tourism-led growth hypothesis is valid for the ASEAN countries. Factors determining the GDP per capita in these countries are visitor spending, foreign investment and government consumption in tourism sector, human capital and trade openness. The results from this study suggest that the governments of the ASEAN countries are able to have effective growth policies by encouraging foreign direct investment in the tourism sector and improving their human capital. Therefore, ASEAN Economic Community (AEC) which will strengthen and facilitate investment cooperation and human capital developments in the tourism sector among ASEAN countries will have a significant benefit to economic growth in the region.

Chapter 15
UNESCO World Heritage Designation: An Opportunity or a Threat to Hoi An Ancient Town (Vietnam)? 250
Huong T. Bui, Ritsumeikan Asia Pacific University, Japan
Tuan-Anh Le, Southern Cross University, Australia
Chung H. Nguyen, Vietnam National University, Vietnam

The chapter analyzes the impacts of World Heritage List designation on the local economy, residents, and environment in the Vietnamese site of Hoi An Ancient Town. Findings from the study raise concerns about managing heritage tourism in developing countries. While Hoi An successfully attracts a large number of tourists and enjoys economic success from tourism, social and environmental sustainability are in question. This case study demonstrates that management of tourism at World Heritage-listed sites is facing challenges of land speculation, inflation, commodification of local culture, and environmental degradation.

Chapter 16
Actor Network Theory in Tourism 261
Xuan Tran, University of West Florida, USA

The purpose of this study is to use actor network theory to explore the short-term and long-term relationships between two Asian countries: Malaysia and China, the two most visited countries in Asia in 2012. The Actor Network theory explains the roles of two actors China and Malaysia in tourism as mobility and performativity, respectively. The tourism in China is composed of culture differences whereas the tourism in Malaysia focuses on business concentration. Vector Auto Regressive, Vector Error Correction, and Granger analysis were conducted to explore the time series data of tourism receipts. Findings indicate that both Malaysia and China do not have short-term influence of tourism development. Interestingly, the long-term tourism of Malaysia will depend on the disequilibrium of tourism receipts between China and Malaysia but not vice versa. The findings have contributed to supporting the Actor Network Theory in developing tourism of China and Malaysia.

Chapter 17
Adequacy of Government Policy on Ecotourism: A Case Study of Sikkim........ 270
Ajeya Jha, Sikkim Manipal Institute of Technology, India
Sherap Shenga, Government of Sikkim, India
Somnath Mishra, Sikkim Manipal University, India
Manjushree Mishra, Sikkim Manipal University, India

Sikkim is known as a natural and ideal destination for the tourists looking for exotic and varied experiences. The study explores the adequacy of the policy in the context of eco-tourism principles espoused by eco-tourism society (TES) which are - minimize physical, social and psychological impact, Build environmental and cultural awareness, Provide positive experiences for both visitors and hosts, Produce direct financial benefits for conservation, and Recognize the rights and spiritual beliefs of the Indigenous People. Methodology used is case study for based on a structured questionnaire with 55 statements (on

Likert scale) responded by the civil officers of the state government involved with eco-tourism policy and its implementation. To make it more meaningful one sample t-test has been conducted to test hypotheses. It concludes that the policy document has areas with distinct adequacies and inadequacies. The purpose of the study is to identify inadequacies that need to be addressed to make the policy document holistic and help in facilitating its proper implementation.

Compilation of References 287

About the Contributors 334

Index 339

Preface

INTRODUCTION

The subject area of the book focuses on tourism priorities, challenges and trends in Asia as well as on the role of information technologies in tourism management.

The book offers a collection of 17 chapters on key topics in the fields of tourism in the globalized economy. It aims to be an international platform to bring together academics, researchers, lecturers, decision makers, policy makers, and practitioners to share new theories, research findings, and case studies, to enhance understanding and collaboration in issues of tourism and know key tourism priorities now and in the future. The book will focus on tourism in Asia, with a special attention to South East Asian nations.

The target audience of the book is wide, from professors in academia, deans, heads of departments, director of masters and students (undergraduate and postgraduate level), to politicians, policy makers, corporate heads of firms, senior general managers, managing directors, information technology directors and managers, libraries, etc.

CONTENTS OF THE BOOK

The editors of the book chose chapters covering a wide variety of interesting manuscripts in the field of tourism with emphasis on empirical studies, examples and case studies. Among other topics, the chapters discuss advertising and public relations in tourism, environmental protection and economic development and tourism, rural tourism, ecotourism, urban ecotourism, economic growth and tourism, etc. The chapters analyse tourism, economic development and opportunities in Asia, with a special focus on India, Malaysia, Mongolia, Taiwan, and Vietnam.

Organization of the Book

The book presents a collection of 17 chapters written by leading experts on tourism in Asia. A brief description of each of the chapters follows.

Thus, Chapter 1, "Impact of Advertising and Public Relations on Tourism Development in Da Nang, Vietnam" (by Xuan Tran Tran, University of West Florida, USA; Minh Nguyen, Duy Tan University, Vietnam; Ha Kieu Tan Luu, Duy Tan University, Vietnam; Ny Ngo, Duy Tan University, Vietnam; My Tran, Duy Tan University, Vietnam; Ngoc Bich Nguyen, Duy Tan University, Vietnam; and Hai Tran, Duy Tan University, Vietnam), presents an exploratory study was conducted to determine the impact of advertising and public relations on the visit intention of tourists in Da Nang, Vietnam. In 2015, Trip Advisor and New York Times selected Da Nang, Vietnam as one of the top Asia tourist destinations. This study sought to address the relationship between advertising or public relations and tourists' intention to visit based on the theory of planned behavior. Structure Equation Modeling was conducted to predict the impact of advertising and public relations on the visit intention of tourists in Da Nang. Findings indicate that an increased favorable attitude and control of advertising would increase tourist arrivals. Surprisingly, an increased positive attitude and control of public relations did not significantly affect tourists' intention to visit. Instead, the social norms of public relations were effective in driving the decision to visit but the social norms of advertising were not. The findings have contributed to destination brand through advertising and public relations. Implications are discussed.

Chapter 2, "Environmental Protection and Tourism: Tourism in the Protected Area in Mongolia" (by Navchaa Tugjamba, University of the Humanities, Mongolia and Amarbayasgalan Gantumur, University of the Humanities, Mongolia), suggests that Mongolia is a unique and relatively unexplored tourism and leisure travel destination. In the world tourism market, the tourism sector offers a great combination of wild natural features, a wide variety of untouched landscapes, historical heritage reserves, and nomadic life style and culture. The Protected Area Network of Mongolia cover over 14.5 percent of the country's territory and has become major destinations for rapidly growing tourism and recreational activities for its natural beauty, rare species of wildlife and historical and cultural heritage sites. Orkhon valley National Park (OVNP) is one of Mongolian main tourism destinations regarding to natural beautiful landscape and including numerous cultural and historical remains and sites. Thus, promoting sustainable tourism development to improve local livelihoods based on the nomadic lifestyle and protection of land with natural wilderness, watersheds, important biodiversity, historical and cultural heritage and rare remains is challenging in the national park.

Chapter 4, "Implication of SASEC Tourism Initiatives on North Eastern States of India: A Descriptive Analysis – SASEC Tourism" (by Supriya Dam, Govt. Degree College, Dharmanagar, North Tripura, India), discusses that India's North Eastern Region (NER) stretches from the foothills of the Himalayas in the eastern range and is surrounded by international borders with countries like Bangladesh, Bhutan, China (Tibet Autonomous Region), Nepal, and Myanmar. The landlocked region is constrained by a brief spell of insurgency, and dismal unemployment has affected the region's progress since 1947. The advent of the Look East Policy coupled with a number of South Asia sub-regional arrangements with neighboring countries opened a "Pandora's Box" for this region. The SASEC initiatives of ADB helped to improve the status of tourism and infrastructure, including roads, air connectivity, and also opened cross-border land routes and roads within the North East (NE). The present study takes stock of tourism development from a sustainability perspective and examines the implementation of the SASEC tourism project in eight NE States of India with a view to suggest priority areas for action for promotion of tourism in this region.

Chapter 5, "Mastering Sustainable Tourism and Rural Tourism in the Global Economy" (by Kijpokin Kasemsap, Suan Sunandha Rajabhat University, Thailand), describes the overviews of tourism, sustainable development, sustainable tourism, and rural tourism; the perspectives on rural tourism destination; rural tourism and entrepreneurship; the importance of sustainable tourism in the global economy; and the importance of rural tourism in the global economy. The fulfillment of sustainable tourism and rural tourism is necessary for modern tourism organizations that seek to serve suppliers and customers, increase business performance, strengthen competitiveness, and achieve continuous success in the global economy. Therefore, it is essential for modern tourism organizations to promote their sustainable tourism and rural tourism and develop a strategic plan to regularly check their practical advancements toward satisfying customer requirement. The chapter argues that promoting sustainable tourism and rural tourism has the potential to enhance organizational performance and gain sustainable competitive advantage in the global economy.

Chapter 6, "Sustainable Tourism Development in Asia: Evaluation of the Potential and Challenges" (by Gamini Herath, Monash University, Malaysia), proposes Sustainable Tourism as a concept respects both local people, the traveler, cultural heritage and the environment. It should meet the needs of and opportunity for the future. But operationalizing sustainable tourism is problematic due to analytical weaknesses, conceptual criticisms and the need to redefine better perspectives. Asia faces many challenges in promoting sustainable tourism including political leadership, poor participation by all stakeholders, adverse environmental and social impacts. Another challenge is to ensure social sustainability and creating opportunities to transfer income to the poorer. The empirical study of island tourism in Malaysia shows that Marine Parks regulations are not adequately enforced and Malaysian coral reefs can suffer from increasing degradation. Water pollution, overfishing, beach erosion, coral bleaching and damage, fishing, snorkeling and poor recycling and sewage disposal all are still significant challenges to the Marine Park in Tioman Island in Malaysia.

Chapter 7, "Prioritization of Eco-Tourism Forms at Sikkim, India" (by Ajeya Jha, Sikkim Manipal Institute of Technology, India; Sherap Shenga, Government of Sikkim, India; and Somnath Mishra, Sikkim Manipal University, India), focuses on Sikkim, one of the smallest states in India. The state government is promoting eco-tourism as a primary sector of economy. Natural and cultural attributes make Sikkim an ideal destination for Cultural, wildlife, adventure and religious tourism. The objective of the paper is to prioritize these four identified forms of tourism with a view to measure their relative appropriateness in the context of Sikkim. The methodology is based on three tools based on continuous scale, Analytical Hierarchy process (AHP) and Quality Function Deployment (QFD) respectively. The data has been collected from 40 respondents (senior civil service officers) The paper concludes that that in terms of appropriateness cultural tourism emerges as best followed by religious, adventure and wildlife tourism in that order. Also the three tools appear valid as they arrive at matching conclusions. Our contribution is that prioritization of forms of tourism has been done for the first time and that too using a comprehensive methodology utilizing AHP, QFD and continuous scale.

Chapter 8, "Can Educational Tourism Spur Economic Growth in Malaysia? Evidence from Neoclassical Growth Model" (by Hylmee Matahir, Universiti Teknologi MARA Sabah, Malaysia; and Chor Foon Tang, Universiti Sains Malaysia), presents the results of a study that employs the neoclassical growth model to investigate empirically the role of educational tourism in Malaysia's economic growth during the period of 2002:Q1 to 2014:Q4. The present study finds that all determinants including educational tourism have a significant positive impact on economic growth in Malaysia, especially in the long-run. In terms of Granger causality, our results show that educational tourism and economic growth are Granger-cause each other in both the short- and long-run. In light of this, educational tourism can be an effective stimulator of Malaysia's economic growth. Moreover, the generalised variance decomposition analysis also affirms that educational tourism explained most of the long-run variation in economic growth compared to other determinants. Therefore, educational tourism is found to be a new and reliable source for Malaysia's economic growth. For the sake of brevity, any macroeconomic policies that heading toward promoting inbound educational tourism will probably spur the growth of the Malaysian economy, especially in the long-run.

Chapter 9, "Changing Behavioural of Patterns of Travelers to Urban ecotourism Sites of Kuala Lumpur" (by Sudipta Kiran Sarkar, Berjaya University College of Hospitality, Malaysia), indicates that his motivation was to examine and understand the changing patterns of travel behaviour of travellers to urban nature attractions of 2010 and 2015 (5 year gap period) in the context of Kuala Lumpur. Kuala Lumpur, the capital of Malaysia offers a major potential for the growth and development of urban eco-tourism given the natural hotspots in both inside and on the peripheries of the city. The results emanating from the descriptive statistics employed in this study demonstrate that changes have occurred in terms of benefits of urban ecotourism, ecotourism activity, source of ecotourism knowledge and in terms of more female ecotourists than male. These results put forth a range of implications from the perspectives of understanding the evolving tourist behaviour in urban spaces and significance of urban eco-travel in Malaysia. In light of challenges and prospects faced in terms of survival of nature-based areas in and around Kuala Lumpur, the findings of the study have been discussed.

Chapter 10, "Critical Review of Tourism in India" (by Neeta Baporikar, University of Pune, India), agrees in that tourism plays a pivotal role in socio-economic development. It fosters international understanding, trust among people and brings many social benefits. According to United Nations World Tourism Organization, travel and tourism can be part of the solution to world problems of poverty employment and sustainability. Today, tourism has grown to become a major social and economic force and it is a well-known fact. Hence, it certainly is an activity of global importance and significance. With abundant nature's gift, one of the oldest culture and civilization India as tourist destination is in an envious position to locus itself as one of the best global destination by adopting innovative and holistic tourism policies. Through exploratory and descriptive examination and in depth literature review of policy documents and reports, the aim of this chapter is review critically the tourism policies and intends to suggest new avenues and innovations in tourism.

Chapter 11, "The Life Cycles of Destination Life Cycle Models: A Critical Comparison and Synthesis in the Context of Destinations" (by Sudipta Kiran Sarkar, Berjaya University College of Hospitality, Malaysia; and Babu P George, Fort Hays State University, USA), indicates that Product Life Cycle (PLC) has always been a hot topic in the tourism literature. Butler's Tourism Area Lifecycle model and Plog's destination life cycle model have both been applied and analysed extensively in tourism destination development and lifecycle studies. This study attempts to offer a critical conversation on the similarities and differences as well as the strengths and weaknesses of these two widely referred generic models of destination life cycle. It also identifies some recent socio-political, economic, and technological developments that have changed the nature of tourism destination development in many parts of the world and in particular to Asia and the implications of these developments upon life cycles. Based on more recent research, the present authors suggest that the reality of destination development lies somewhere in between, as a resultant of interaction with the processes laid out by Plog and Butler.

Chapter 12, "The Relevance of the Tourism-Led Growth Hypothesis to Malaysia: A View Through Rolling-Samples and Disaggregated Tourism Markets" (by Chor Foon Tang, Universiti Sains Malaysia, Malaysia; and Eu Chye Tan, University of Malaya, Malaysia), explores whether the tourism-led growth (TLG) hypothesis is empirically relevant to Malaysia based upon both full sample and rolling sample analyses. Data from January 1995 to December 2010 have been utilised for the purpose. Instead of relying upon aggregated data of tourist arrivals, disaggregated data of arrivals from 12 major tourism markets are relied upon for more insightful and accurate findings. The empirical results suggest that there was cointegration between Malaysia's economic growth and tourist arrivals from these tourism markets. However, the results of the full sample Granger causality test indicate that only 2 out of 12 tourism markets contributed to economic growth in the short-run. The TLG hypothesis is only supported in the long run by tourist arrivals from 10 out of the 12 tourism markets. The rolling-based Granger causality test shows that it is also these 10 markets situated mostly in developed countries that could provide a stable support for the TLG hypothesis.

Chapter 13, "Tourism Development and Rural Tourism in Taiwan: A Literature Review" (by I-Ting Chen, Sheffield Hallam University, Taiwan; and Konstantin Karl Weicht, Vienna University of Economics and Business, Austria), proposes that although tourism plays an increasingly important role in Taiwan's economy, and despite increasing government and academic interest in tourism development and rural tourism in Taiwan, the literature currently lacks of a concise review that brings together the various aspects of tourism development in Taiwan. The present chapter aims to contribute to closing this gap. It does so in six concise sections: a brief overview of Taiwan; the development of tourism in Taiwan; tourism and the economy in Taiwan; tourism and politics in Taiwan; rural tourism development; and small hotels in Taiwan. It is hoped that this account would serve as an important context specific prerequisite for future and more in-depth studies on tourism development and rural tourism in Taiwan.

Chapter 14, "Tourism-Led Growth Hypothesis and Foreign Direct Investment in ASEAN" (by Praopan Pratoomchat, Bates College, USA), presents the results of a study that tests the relationships of visitor spending, foreign direct investment in the tourism sector, and the gross domestic product (GDP) per capita among members of the Association of Southeast Asian Nations (ASEAN) during the period of 1988 to 2011 to prove the tourism-led growth hypothesis. The results of panel regression show that tourism-led growth hypothesis is valid for the ASEAN countries. Factors determining the GDP per capita in these countries are visitor spending, foreign investment and government consumption in tourism sector, human capital and trade openness. The results from this study suggest that the governments of the ASEAN countries are able to have effective growth policies by encouraging foreign direct investment in the tourism sector and improving their human capital. Therefore, ASEAN Economic Community (AEC) which will strengthen and facilitate investment cooperation and human capital developments in the tourism sector among ASEAN countries will have a significant benefit to economic growth in the region.

Chapter 15, "UNESCO World Heritage Designation: An Opportunity or a Threat to Hoi An Ancient Town (Vietnam)?" (by Huong T. Bui, Ritsumeikan Asia Pacific University, Japan; Tuan Anh Le, Southern Cross University, Australia; and Chung H. Nguyen, Vietnam National University, Vietnam), analyzes the impact of World Heritage List designation on the local economy, residents, and environment in the Vietnamese site of Hoi An Ancient Town. Findings from the study raise concerns about managing heritage tourism in developing countries. While Hoi An successfully attracts a large number of tourists and enjoys economic success from tourism, social and environmental sustainability are in question. This case study demonstrates that management of tourism at World Heritage-listed sites is facing challenges of land speculation, inflation, commodification of local culture, and environmental degradation.

Chapter 16, "Actor Network Theory in Tourism" (Xuan Tran Tran, University of West Florida, USA), analyses the use actor network theory to explore the short-term and long-term relationships between two Asian countries: Malaysia and China, the two most visited countries in Asia in 2012. The Actor Network theory explains the roles of two actors China and Malaysia in tourism as mobility and performativity, respectively. The tourism in China is composed of culture differences whereas the tourism in Malaysia focuses on business concentration. Vector Auto Regressive, Vector Error Correction, and

Granger analysis were conducted to explore the time series data of tourism receipts. Findings indicate that both Malaysia and China do not have short-term influence of tourism development. Interestingly, the long-term tourism of Malaysia will depend on the disequillibrium of tourism receipts between China and Malaysia but not vice versa. The findings have contributed to supporting the Actor Network Theory in developing tourism of China and Malaysia.

And finally, Chapter 17, "Adequacy of Government Policy on Ecotourism: A Case Study of Sikkim" (by Ajeya Jha, Sikkim Manipal Institute of Technology, India; Sherap Shenga, Director, Commerce & Industries, Govt. of Sikkim, India; and Somnath Mishra, Sikkim Manipal University, India), indicates that Sikkim is known as a natural and ideal destination for the tourists looking for exotic and varied experiences. The study explores the adequacy of the policy in the context of eco-tourism principles espoused by eco-tourism society (TES) which are - minimize physical, social and psychological impact, Build environmental and cultural awareness, Provide positive experiences for both visitors and hosts, Produce direct financial benefits for conservation, and Recognize the rights and spiritual beliefs of the Indigenous People. Methodology used is case study for based on a structured questionnaire with 55 statements (on Likert scale) responded by the civil officers of the state government involved with eco-tourism policy and its implementation. To make it more meaningful one sample t-test has been conducted to test hypotheses. It concludes that the policy document has areas with distinct adequacies and inadequacies. The purpose of the study is to identify inadequacies that need to be addressed to make the policy document holistic and help in facilitating its proper implementation.

This collection of chapters will definitely contribute to understand current challenges and trends in the tourism in Asia and define strategies and actions to be taken in this economic region. The book will be a valuable source of updated information and knowledge for students, academics, policy makers and general readers interested in getting new insights on the Asian tourism industry, to how develop effective strategies for economic and social growth, for sustainable development, for preserving cultural heritage, etc.

Patricia Ordóñez de Pablos
University of Oviedo, Spain

Zeyar Myo Aung
Ministry of Hotels and Tourism, Myanmar

Chapter 1
Impact of Advertising and Public Relations on Tourism Development in Da Nang, Vietnam

Xuan Tran
University of West Florida, USA

Ny Ngo
Duy Tan University, Vietnam

Minh Nguyen
Duy Tan University, Vietnam

My Tran
Duy Tan University, Vietnam

Ha Kieu Tan Luu
Duy Tan University, Vietnam

Ngoc Bich Nguyen
Duy Tan University, Vietnam

Hai Tran
Duy Tan University, Vietnam

ABSTRACT

An exploratory study was conducted to determine the impact of advertising and public relations on the visit intention of tourists in Da Nang, Vietnam. In 2015, Trip Advisor and New York Times selected Da Nang, Vietnam as one of the top Asia tourist destinations. This study sought to address the relationship between advertising or public relations and tourists' intention to visit based on the theory of planned behavior. Structure Equation Modeling was conducted to predict the impact of advertising and public relations on the visit intention of tourists in Da Nang. Findings indicate that an increased favorable attitude and control of advertising would increase tourist arrivals. Surprisingly, an increased positive attitude and control of public relations did not significantly affect tourists' intention to visit. Instead, the social norms of public relations were effective in driving the decision to visit but the social norms of advertising were not. The findings have contributed to destination brand through advertising and public relations. Implications are discussed.

DOI: 10.4018/978-1-5225-2078-8.ch001

INTRODUCTION

Failure to appropriately understand the impact of advertising and public relations on visit intention for tourist destinations creates critical issues for tourism development in Vietnam. In 2015, Trip Advisor and New York Times selected Da Nang, Vietnam as one of the top Asia tourist destinations. However, in 2016, Da Nang tourism is threatened by difficulties such as the latest incident of shipwreck on the Han River and the problem of polluted water due to toxic waste water from a steel factory in Vietnam. This ultimately resulted in the decreased number of visitors to Da Nang. Although the factory compensated USD500 million for the environmental violation, suggesting solutions proposed to strengthen the confidence of tourists to the image of tourism in the city of Da Nang is essential. The combination of the advertisement and public relations is the most optimal solution to improve the image of Da Nang.

Effects of public relations and advertising on consumer decision making have been studied by recent research. Gretzel, Yuan, and Fesenmaier (2000) and Kotler and Armstrong (2005) report the importance of public relations and advertising on destination image. Pratt, McCabe, Cortes-Jimenez, and Blake (2010), Pike and Page (2014), and Gretzel, Fesenmaier, Formica, and O'Leary (2006) report that marketing through public relations and advertising can stimulate consumer demand effectively. Little research has focused on predicting consumer buying intention by advertising and public relations. The purpose of this study is thus to examine the model of tourist visit intention predicted by advertising and public relations.

The assumptions of the study are if there are significant relationships between advertising or public relations and tourists' visit intention which is predicted by attitudes, social norms, and controls. Tourists with a high attitude often visit a certain destination because they believe that they can get benefits from the destination visit. Tourists with a high social norm often visit a destination because they believe that their visit would be approved and respected by other people. Tourists with a high control often visit a place where they can control the access to that place; they trust in certain online travel agents (OTA) so they use the OTA as the access to that place. The survey questions based on the theory of planned behavior (Ajzen & Fishbein, 1980) were distributed to a random sample of 100 tourists in Da Nang in mid-June 2016. Responses to were analyzed in structure equation modeling to find key factors for destination brand development.

LITERATURE

Advertising and Public Relations

Advertising creates an awareness of product or service to influencing a buying decision, Public relations would create an awareness of the business contribution to social environment, rather than its products or services (Gretzel, Yuan, & Fesenmaier, 2000; Kotler & Armstrong, 2005). Both advertising and public relations focus on the transmission of information about products or services and the business itself in order to increase the decision of the customer's buying process as well as business' selling products.

Advertising is one of the five tools that companies use to provide some persuading information to customers. The strong development with various forms of advertising makes itself becoming the tool to get the attention of the companies. The advertising includes the following basic criteria: (1) Be a pre-defined media, (2) Be transferred from a certain advertiser, (3) Use the mass media, and (4) Persuade target customers. Advertising is the use of the indirect media that aimed to inform, persuade or get influence on your target customers in a certain time. Therefore, advertising has 3 types of function (1) informing, (2) convincing, and (3) reminding. Kim, Hwang, and Fesenmaier (2005), Mok (1990), Pitgoff and Smith (2003) report the relationships of advertising.

Kim, Hwang, and Fesenmaier (2005) indicate characteristics of advertising in tourism including publicity, extensive, and expressiveness. Advertising is a form of one-way communication so businesses can use advertising to create one image that makes sense for the product, position it in customer's mind, build strong brands, or stimulate consumption. In addition, "word of mouth advertising" is considered as an efficient form of advertising in the large range due to reliability of verbal communications and cost savings. Public relation is a business that has good relationships with not only the customers, suppliers, sale agents, but also the wide publicity in general because they can create advantages achieving the business's goal. Public relations are thus one form of communication between businesses and publicity which provides knowledge to the customers, ensures the publicity's understanding and encourages, builds reputation and image as well as handling bad publicity.

Thieke (2007) and Tidball (1988) report the basic activities of public relations including updating valuable information on the media to attract the attention of people, promotion of products promotion of cooperation and advising. Public relations help create positive comments from customers, build a favorable environment making mixed marketing activities easier and more efficient. The main tools of public relations are publications: businesses can rely on traditional materials to reach and get influence on the target customer groups. Such examples include annual reports, magazine and newspaper articles, audiovisual material, and public events such as charity events or press conferences.

Shields (2006) and Tyrrell and Johnston (2003) indicate the importance of public relations. It is considered as the basic tool which can support the success of other tools. Public relations can introduce specific descriptions of products and businesses, create high reliability for customers. Public relations differ from advertising as follows. First, public relations are more objective because it often uses intermediaries to bring messages to consumers and do not have monologues like advertising. Second, the messages of the public relations are less commercial and more informative than advertising. Finally, public relations activities bring more detailed information. Because of these reasons, we cannot separate the public relations and advertising activities, they must always be carried out simultaneously to provide the best efficient communication for businesses

Tourism advertising is regarded as one of the most influential information sources for prospective and current visitors (Gretzel, Yuan, & Fesenmaier, 2000; Kim, Hwang, & Fesenmaier, 2005; USTA, 2011). If the information about advertising is misleading or inaccurate, it will cause negative images for tourists and lead to reduce their visit intention. Therefore, when a business advertises, it is required to provide information accurately, completely and focuses on consumers' demand. Unlike advertising, public relations (PR) can help customers understand the duty of a business in developing a good environment for the community. The PR is thus credited for its contributions to the bottom line by applying the strategic elements of marketing The mix between advertising and public relations for a tourist destination creates a destination marketing (Balakrishman, 2009; Ballman, Burke, Blank, & Korte, 1984; Ekinci, Sirakaya-Turk, Preciado, 2013) Destination marketing is an important tool for stimulating demand (Pratt, McCabe, Cortes-Jimenez, & Blake, 2010; Pike & Page, 2014; Gretzel, Fesenmaier, Formica, & O'Leary, 2006; WTO, 2009; USTA, 2011). Woodside and Dubelaar (2002) propose a general theory of tourism consumption that advertising forms positive perceptions of the destination for tourists and increases their expenditures in the destination. Woodside and King (2001) argue that advertising are often catalysts to activate tourists' selections that ultimately affect their destination decisions. Kim et al. (2005), Wober and Fesenmaier (2004), Woodside and Reid (1974), and Woodside and Motes (1980) have recognized the impact of destination advertising. Due to their importance in developing a tourist destination, advertising and public relations were used as predictors to forecast the visit intention of tourists in Da Nang, Vietnam. The present study used the theory of planned behavior (Ajzen & Fishbein, 1980) to build a model of visit intention of tourists in Da Nang predicted by their attitudes, social norms, and control beliefs toward advertising and public relations.

Theory of Planned Behavior

According to the theory, consumer behavior is guided by three beliefs: (1) the consequences of the behavior (behavioral beliefs), (2) expectations of others (normative beliefs), and (3) the impede performance of the behavior (control beliefs) (Ajzen, 2008). Behavior belief is a positive attitude about a certain behavior. Tourists' frequent visits of a certain destination indicate that tourists have a positive attitude about benefits of this place and believe that they would be pleased and satisfied with their visit. Normative belief is a positive norm of society about a certain behavior. Tourists often visit a certain destination because they believe their visit is beneficial for their society and other people would approve and admire for the visit. Control belief is a belief of some facilitator that can make it easy for a certain behavior. Tourists often travel to a certain place because their facilitator such as online travel agents recommends this place. All three behavioral beliefs are aggregated to produce a favorable or unfavorable attitude toward the behavior and lead to the formation of a behavioral intention. "As a general rule, the more favorable the attitude and subjective norm, and the greater the perceived control, the stronger should be the person's intention to perform the behavior in question." (Ajzen, 2008, p. 20).

In the present study, we suggested the following model (Figure 1) of visit intention of tourists in Da Nang, Vietnam:

Figure 1. Visit intention of tourists in Da Nang, Vietnam

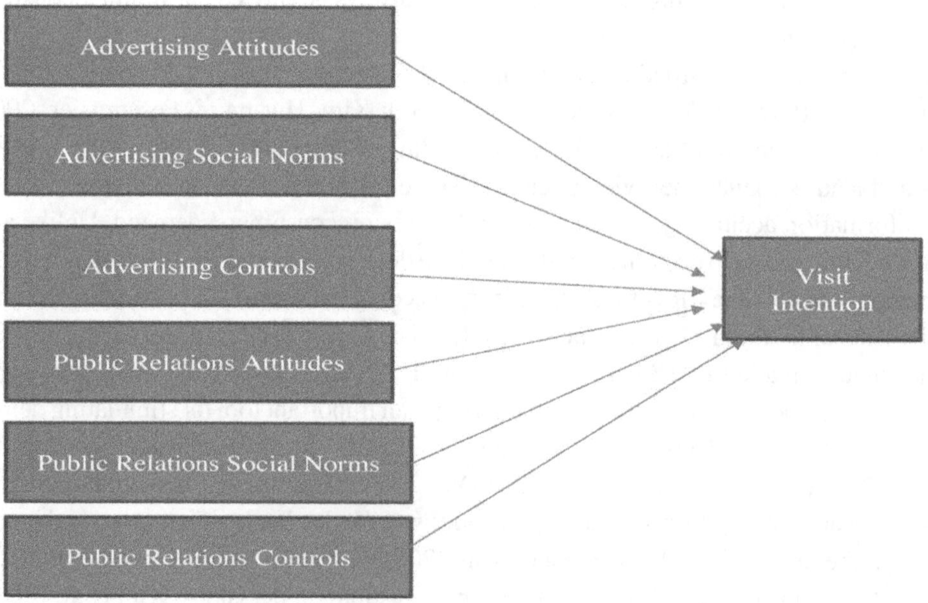

Hypotheses:

Hypothesis 1: There would be a significant effect of tourists' attitudes on their visit intention by advertising.
Hypothesis 2: There would be a significant effect of tourists' social norms on their visit intention by advertising.
Hypothesis 3: There would be a significant effect of tourists' controls on their visit intention by advertising.
Hypothesis 4: There would be a significant effect of tourists' attitudes on their visit intention by public relations.
Hypothesis 5: There would be a significant effect of tourists' social norms on their visit intention by public relations.
Hypothesis 6: There would be a significant effect of tourists' controls on their visit intention by public relations.

METHOD

Study Sample

A survey for a random sample of 100 tourist representatives of the research population (in-bound tourists in Vietnam) was conducted in mid-June 2016 to elicit readily accessible behavioral outcomes, normative referents, and control factors. Although the participants can be assembled in groups, the elicitation is done individually in a free response format from the Theory of Planned Behavior (Ajzen, 2008)

Questionnaires

Instructions: Please take a few minutes to tell us what you think about the possibility of visiting Da Nang for at least once a year. There are no right or wrong responses; we are merely interested in your personal opinions. In response to the questions below, please list the thoughts that come immediately to mind. Write each thought on a separate line. (Five or six lines are provided for each question.)

Behavioral Outcomes

1. What do you see as the advantages of your intention of visiting Da Nang at least once per year?
2. What do you see as the disadvantages of your intention of visiting Da Nang at least once per year?
3. What else comes to mind when you think about intention of visiting Da Nang?

Normative Referents

When it comes to your intention of visiting Da Nang at least once a year, there might be individuals or groups who would think you should or should not have intention.

1. Please list the individuals or groups who would approve or think you should have intention of visiting Da Nang at least once a year.
2. Please list the individuals or groups who would disapprove or think you should not have intention of visiting Da Nang at least once a year.

3. Sometimes, when we are not sure what to do, we look to see what others are doing. Please list the individuals or groups who, after visiting Da Nang, are most likely to come back to Da Nang at least once a year.
4. Please list the individuals or groups who, after visiting Da Nang, are likely to visit Da Nang at least once a year.

Control Factors

1. Please list any factors or circumstances that would make it easy or enable you to visit Da Nang at least once a year.
2. Please list any factors or circumstances that would make it difficult or prevent you from visiting Da Nang at least once a year.

Results

The sample includes 40% of males and 60% of females. About 7% participants is under 18, 71% of participants in age of 18-30, 17% of participants in age of 30-50, and 5% of participants over 50 years old. The number of people participating in Northern Vietnam accounts for 3%, the number of people participating in Central Vietnam accounts for 86%, the number of people participating in Southern Vietnam accounts for 2%, and the number of foreigners participating accounts for 9%. The number of participants who earn less than VND 5 million accounts for 66%. The number of participants having income from VND 5 million to VND 10 million accounts for 25%. The number of people participating with income of over 10 million accounts for 9%.

Structure Equation Model was conducted to test 6 hypotheses. There are 6 models suggested as follows:

1. Model 1 (Figure 2) includes six independent variables (Advertising attitude, Public Relations attitude, Advertising control, Public Relations control, Advertising normative, and Public Relations normative) and one dependent variable (Visit Intention). The model was not well fitted with CMIN/DF: 13.1, RMSEA:.31, NFI:.48, CFI: .49 as follows:
    a. The six hypotheses were considered in Model 1. Three hypotheses 1, 3, and 5 that tourist attitude and control were stimulated by advertising and tourist normative was stimulated by public relations would be the key predictors for visit intention was confirmed (coefficients = .87. .13. & .13, respectively). The others were not significant.
2. Model 2 (Figure 3) includes three independent advertising variables (Advertising attitude, Advertising control, and Advertising normative) associated with other public relations variables and one dependent variable (Visit Intention). The model was not well fitted with CMIN/DF: 11.2, RMSEA:.32, NFI:.45, CFI: .46 as follows:
    a. Three hypotheses 1, 2, & 3 regarding advertising were considered in Model 2. Two hypotheses 1 and 3 that tourist attitude and control were stimulated by advertising would be the key factors for visit intention were confirmed (coefficient = .74 & .18, respectively). The other was not significant.
3. Model 3 (Figure 4) includes three independent public relations variables (Public relations attitude, Public relations control, and Public relations normative) associated with other advertising variables

Figure 2. Visit intention model by advertising and public relations

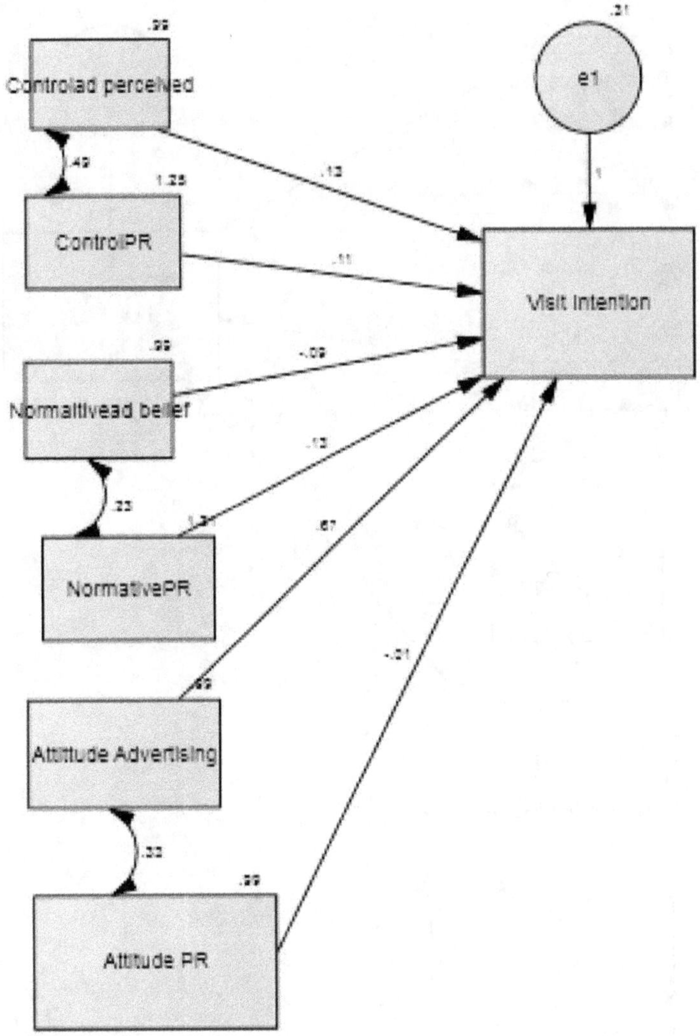

and one dependent variable (Visit Intention). The model was not well fitted with CMIN/DF:15.6, RMSEA:.35, NFI:.24, and CFI: .23 as follows:

a. Three hypotheses 4, 5 & 6 regarding public relations were considered in Model 3. Only tourist social norm was stimulated by public relations would be the key factor for visit intention. Hypothesis 5 were confirmed.

From the three above models, we selected the best model that was well fitted for visit intention including three independent variables (advertising attitude, advertising control, and public relations social norm) associated with other advertising and public relations variables and one dependent variable (Visit Intention) in model 4 (Figure 5). Model 4 was the best fitted with CMIN/DF: 2.4, RMSEA:.1, NFI:.87, CFI: .89 as follows.

In model 4, hypotheses 1, 3, and 5 were confirmed. That is, tourist attitude and control stimulated by advertising and tourist normative stimulated by public relations are key factors for visit intention.

Figure 3. Visit intention model by advertising

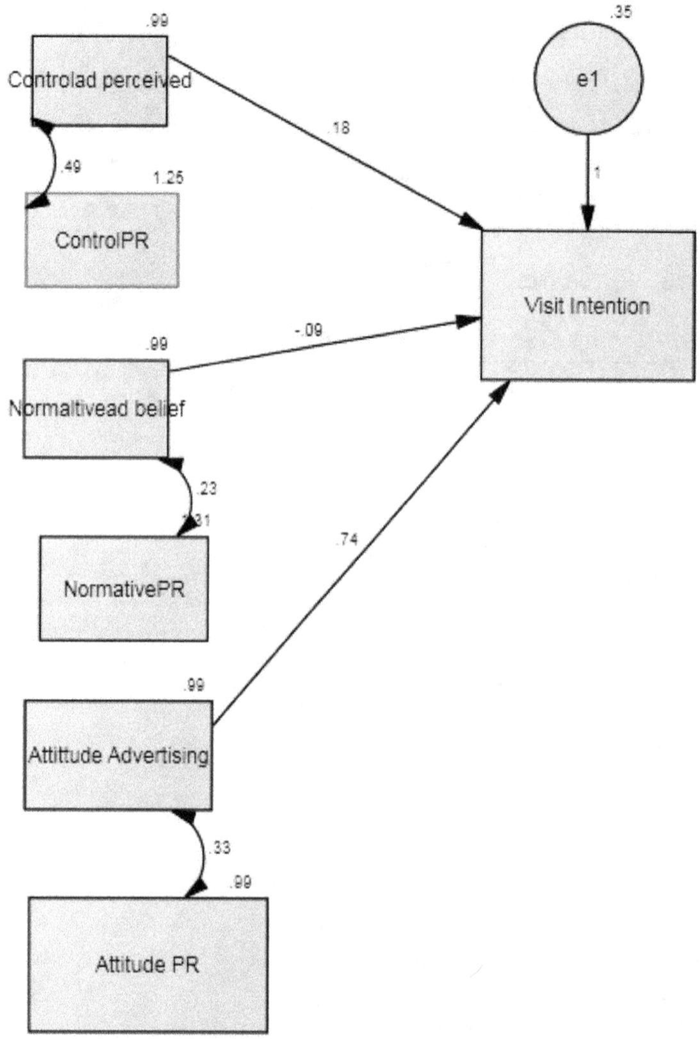

DISCUSSION

Advertising and public relations are important for tourist decision making. According to theory of planned behavior, tourist decision making based on their intention would be affected by their behavior (attitude), other people (normative), or circumstances (control). Study findings indicate that advertising attitude, advertising control, and public relations norm are only the three significant factors to predict consumer intention to visit. The present study in Da Nang tourist destination has shown that advertising would be more effective if it focuses on tourists' benefits of visiting Da Nang and it is distributed through reliable access such as TripAdvisor. In addition, public relations would be more productive if it provides benefits with other economic branches other than tourism such as industry, agriculture, environment, politics, etc.

From understanding the relationship between the influence of advertising, public relations and the number of tourists in Da Nang, it is clear that there is a positive impact on increase of the number of

Figure 4. Visit intention model by public relations

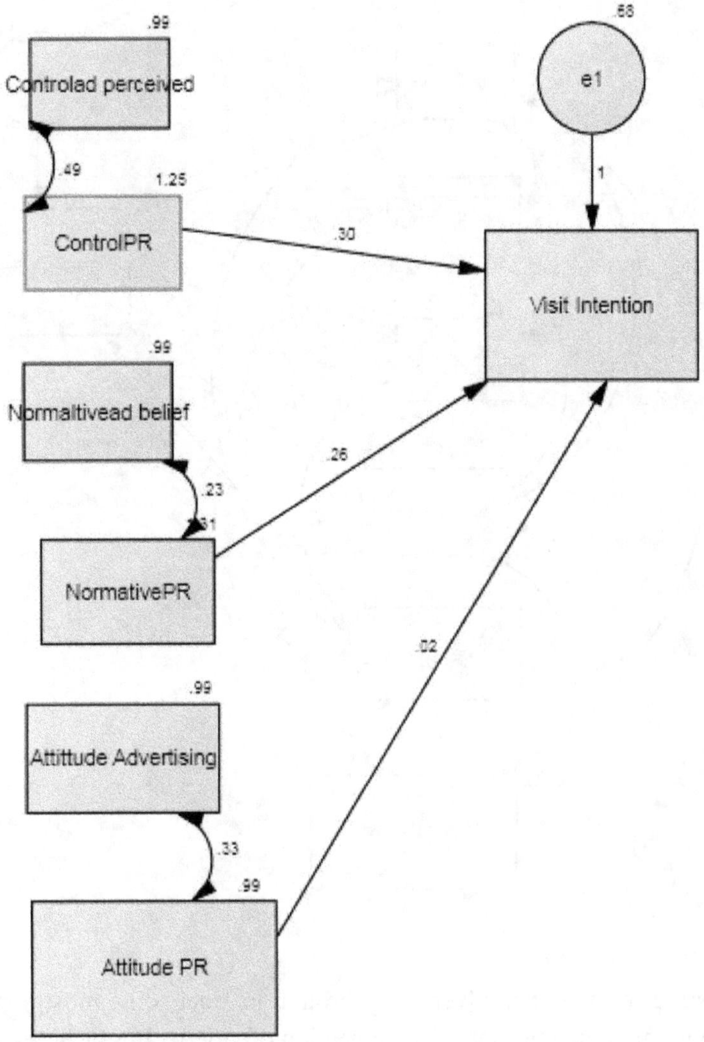

guests. Advertising InterContinental awards to tourists must be known to high-class tourists. Advertising Da Nang as the top Asia tourist destination have to be accessible through TripAdvisor or other trusted online travel agents. Public relations for the InterContinental awards and Da Nang as the top Asia tourist destination must be known not for tourism but for other economic branches other than tourism such as industry, agriculture, environment, politics, etc.

Because of this positive impact, which our team consider as the basis to give several recommendations improving the advertising process and advancing public relations activities to regain image of Da Nang tourism:

Solution 1:(Figure 6) Increase the frequency of watching advertising through advertising means.

Figure 5. Visit intention model of best fit by advertising and public relations

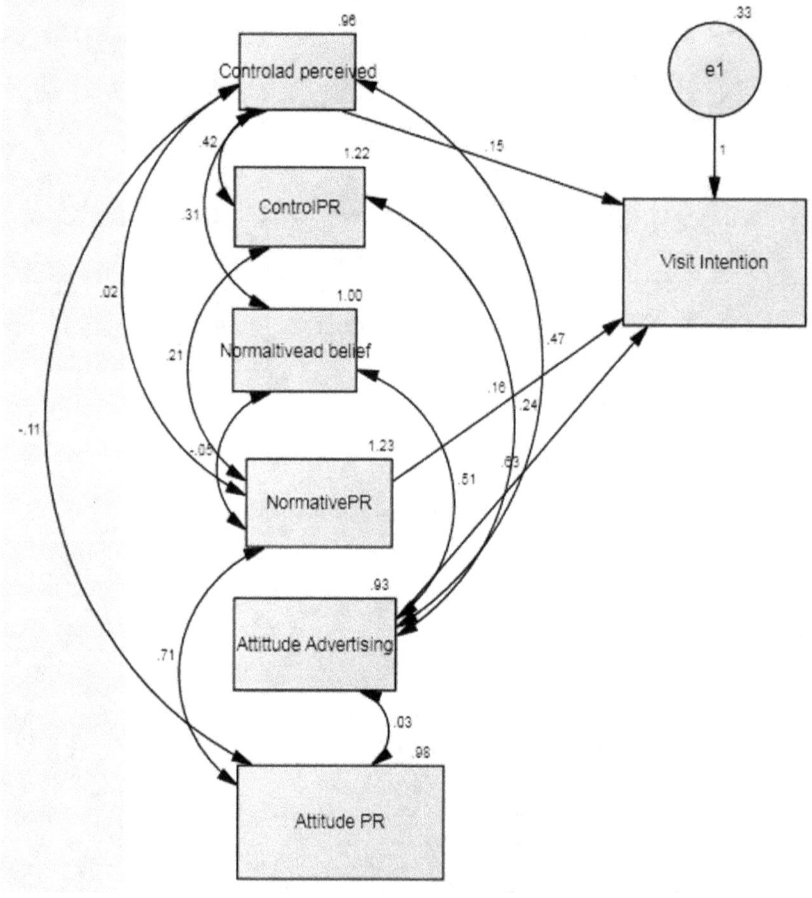

In Figure 6, we can determine that advertising through internet is the most popular. We need to increase advertising tourism in the internet. The connection of video, clips, articles, review, news, events should be controlled systematically. Furthermore, we also have to promote Da Nang tourism on television by cooperating with local radios and other areas in the country or overseas in order to expand the Da Nang tourism broadcast such as the tour exploring the vestiges of Da Nang, visiting some destinations for entertainment in Da Nang. Increasing advertising tourism in the internet and television are to help tourists determine destinations in Da Nang. Internet and television will be the two main channels that we should use to introduce tourists to Da Nang with everyone.

Solution 2: (Figure 7) Select the proper forms of advertising to increase extent of love for advertising.

In Figure 7, the uniqueness of advertising is the most interesting for audience. The chart above will clarify how to advertise efficiently. Based on the chart, it is clearly that the advertising promotion based on unique ideas will get more positive responses from tourists. Therefore, the emphasizing in advertising campaigns with creative, new and unique content will be the trend in the future. Advertisements should have a breakthrough in form and new content. It's required of qualified staffs in field of marketing.

Figure 6. The frequency of watching advertising through advertising means (unit: persons)

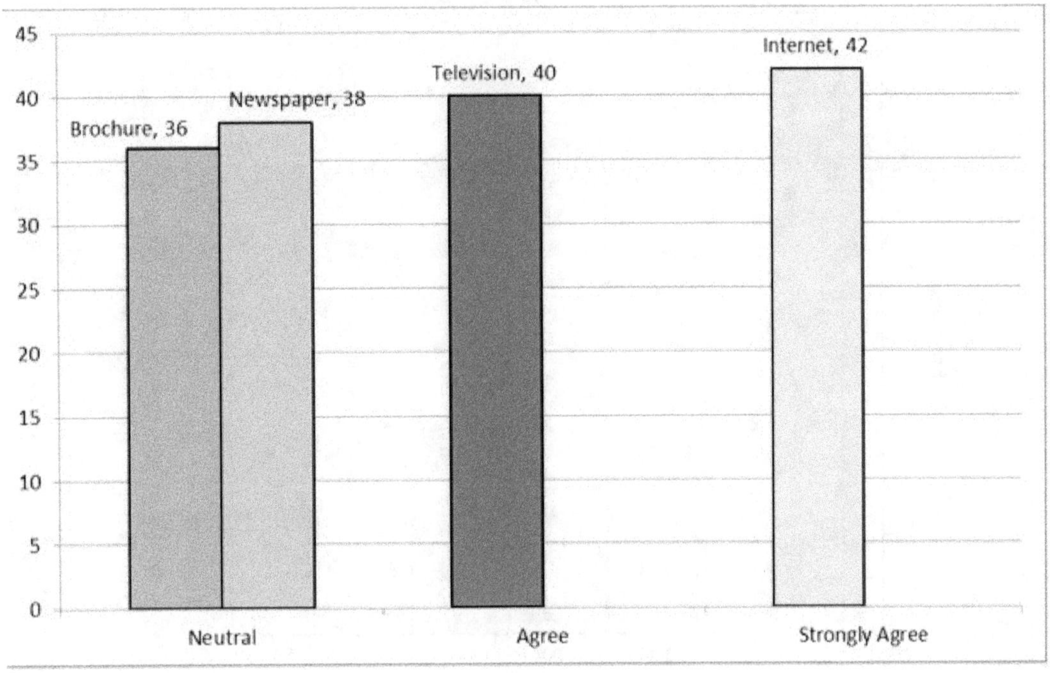

Figure 7. The extent of love for all forms of advertising (unit: persons)

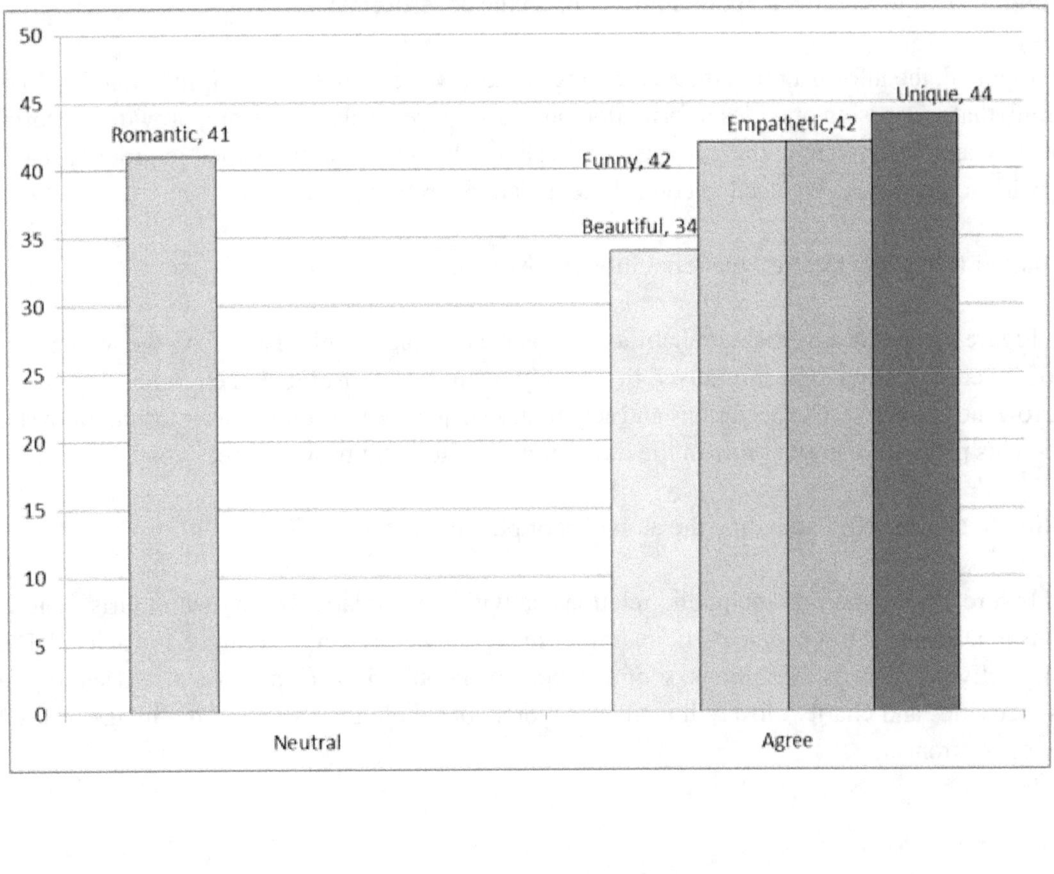

Figure 8. Information levels in advertising

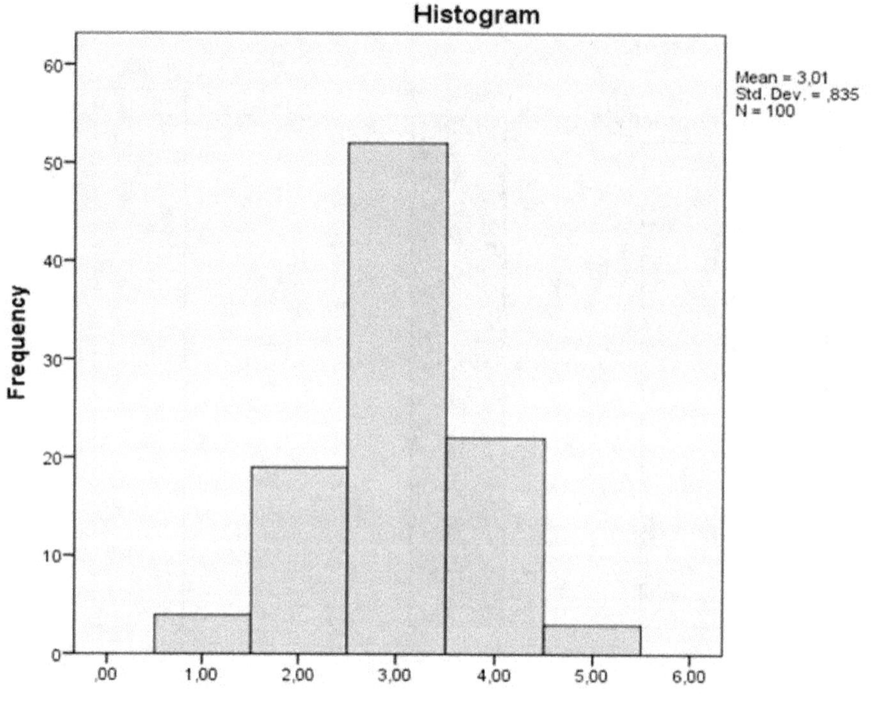

Solution 3: (Figure 8) Provide more information in the advertisements

In Figure 8, the information in the advertising content was evaluated not helpful enough. Most tourists think that advertising provides information only at average levels. Therefore, providing information adequately and objectively in the advertisements should be further strengthened in order to reach customers in an active way. We need to control the updating wrong information.

Solution 4: (Figure 9) Increase the reliability of advertising

In Figure 9, tourists advertising reliability is mostly at average levels. Therefore, the wrong information of advertising need to be minimized thoroughly in order to consolidate their belief. We have to try to narrow the gap between expectations and actual service quality and control the information systematically - This plays an important role in the development of tourism business' services.

Solution 5: (Figure 10) Expanding the activities of public relations

In Figure 10, we can find the public relations activities still relatively new with tourists and native persons in Da Nang. Most people participating in social activities such as volunteering at local. Besides making activities such as exhibitions, seminars become popular in Da Nang, we also need to promote social activities and charity closely linked ever more, contribute to improving the image of Da Nang cleaner and stronger.

Figure 9. Reliability level of advertising

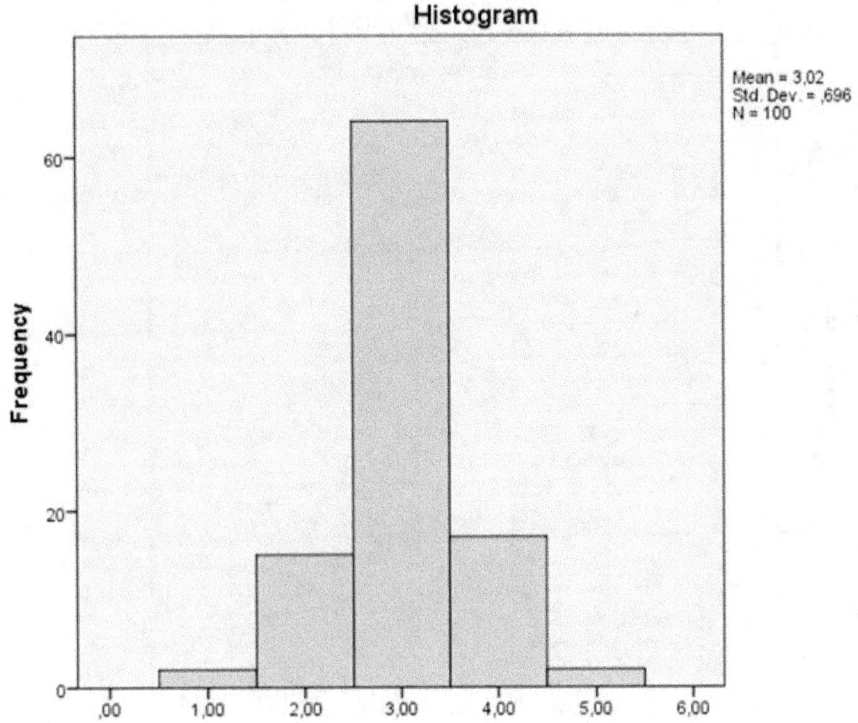

Figure 10. Frequency of participating in PR activities (Unit: Persons)

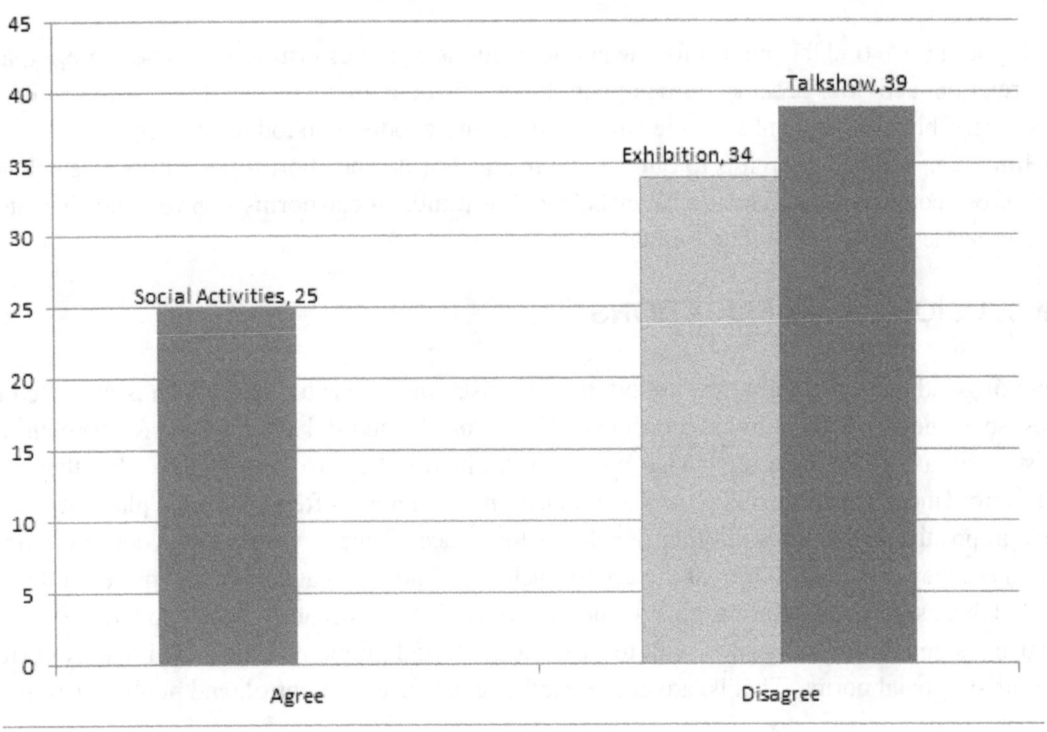

Figure 11. Public relations considerations for making decision to travel

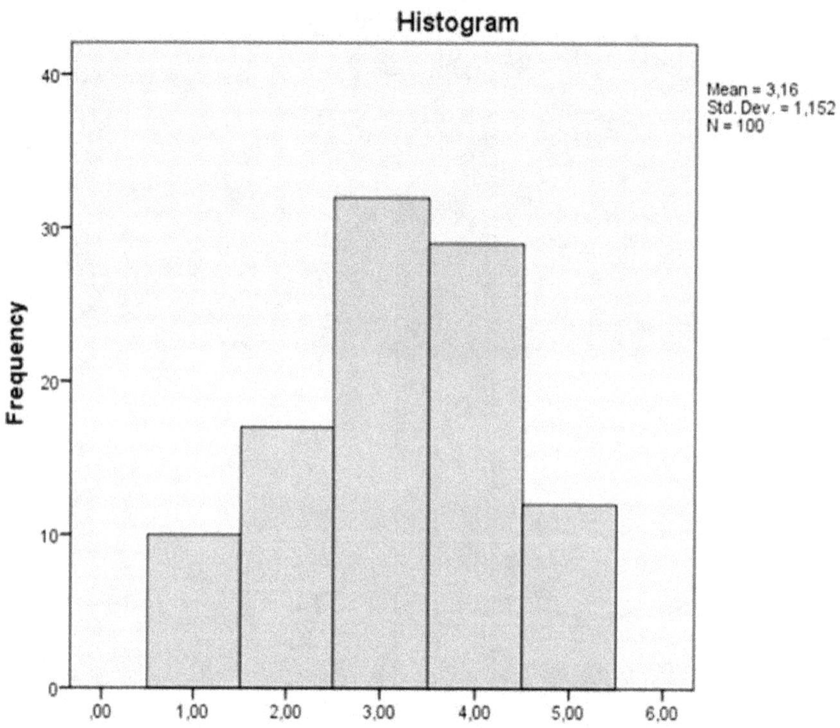

Solution 6: (Figure 11) Enhancing the tourism business units' interests in public relations activities.

In Figure 11, we find the interest for the public relations activities insufficient. Therefore, expanding public relations activities became more popular. It not only built up the image of the business in the eyes of customers, but also help enhance the value of truth and goodness in today's society.

A limitation of this research is to our sample in small-scale and short time. Future research should expand cross-country comparisons between behavioral attitude, social norms, controls and visit intention among other destinations in a longitudinal study.

CONCLUSION AND IMPLICATIONS

Advertising and public relations are important to tourists' intentions to visit, which is predicted by attitudes, social norms, and controls according to Theory of Planned Behavior (Ajzen & Fishbein, 1980). Tourists with a high attitude often visit a certain destination because they believe that they can get benefits from the destination visit. Tourists with a high social norm often visit some place because they believe in positive evaluations of other people for this place. Tourists with a high control often visit a place where they can control or trust the access such as online travel agents to that place. In this study, we found three significant relationships including advertising significantly related to tourists' attitudes, advertising significantly associated with tourists' controls and public relations significantly correlated with tourists' social norms. That is, advertising attitude, advertising control, and public relations norm are only the three significant factors to predict consumer intention to visit. The present study in Da Nang tourist destination has shown that advertising would be more effective if it focuses on tourists' benefits of visiting Da Nang and it is distributed through reliable access such as TripAdvisor. In addition, public relations would be more productive if it provides benefits with other economic branches other than tourism such as industry, agriculture, environment, politics, etc.

The fact that the InterContinental resort in Da Nang has been awarded as the top resort in South East Asia in consecutive years 2013, 2014, and 2015 and Trip Advisor as well as New York Times selected Da Nang as the top Asia tourist destination in 2015 has increased the attention of tourists worldwide. Advertising InterContinental awards to tourists must be known to high-class tourists. Advertising Da Nang as the top Asia tourist destination have to be accessible through TripAdvisor or other online travel agents. Public relations for the InterContinental awards and Da Nang as the top Asia tourist destination must be popular for any other people different from tourists.

The implication of the study is that companies should use different strategies and tactics in order to allocate advertising budgets. Advertising will be spent for reliable online travel agents such as Trip Advisor. In addition, free gifts, benefits and bonus points are only given for the tourists who already spent their own money for their visits. Public relations for tourist destinations are available for general audience in other economic branches other than tourism such as industry, agriculture, environment, politics, etc., in order to develop better image for tourists who intend to visit. The findings have contributed to destination brand development through attitude and control advertising and social norm public relations.

REFERENCES

Ajzen, I. (2008). Consumer attitudes and behaviour. In Handbook of consumer psychology. New York: Lawrence Erlbaum Associates.

Ajzen, I., & Fishbein, M. (1980). *Understanding attitudes and predicting social behavior*. Englewood Cliffs, NJ: Prentice-Hall.

Balakrishnan, M. S. (2009). Strategic branding of destinations: A framework. *European Journal of Marketing*, *43*(5/6), 611–629. doi:10.1108/03090560910946954

Ballman, G., Burke, J., Blank, U., & Korte, D. (1984). Toward higher quality conversion studies: Refining the numbers game. *Journal of Travel Research*, 22, 28–33.

Ekinci, Y., Sirakaya-Turk, E., & Preciado, S. (2013). Symbolic consumption of tourism destination brands. *Journal of Business Research*, *66*(6), 711–718. doi:10.1016/j.jbusres.2011.09.008

Gretzel, U., Fesenmaier, D., Formica, S., & OLeary, J. (2006). Searching for the future: Challenges faced by destination marketing organizations. *Journal of Travel Research*, *45*(2), 116–126. doi:10.1177/0047287506291598

Gretzel, U., Yuan, Y.-L., & Fesenmaier, D. R. (2000). Preparing for the new economy: Advertising strategies and change in destination marketing organizations. *Journal of Travel Research*, *39*(2), 146–156. doi:10.1177/004728750003900204

Kim, D.-Y., Hwang, Y.-H., & Fesenmaier, D. R. (2005). Modeling tourism advertising effectiveness. *Journal of Travel Research*, *44*(1), 42–49. doi:10.1177/0047287505276590

Kotler, P., & Armstrong, G. (2005). *Principles of Marketing*. Available online on June 18, 2016 at http://docslide.us/documents/advertising-and-public-relations-chapter-15-priciples-of-marketing-by-philip-kotler-and-gary-armstrong-pearson.html

Mok, H. (1990). A quasi-experimental measure of the effectiveness of destinational advertising: Some evidence from Hawaii. *Journal of Travel Research*, *29*(1), 30–34. doi:10.1177/004728759002900107

Pike, S., & Page, S. J. (2014). Destination Marketing Organizations and destination marketing: A narrative analysis of the literature. *Tourism Management*, *41*, 202–227. doi:10.1016/j.tourman.2013.09.009

Pitegoff, B., & Smith, G. (2003). Measuring the return on investment of destination welcome centres: The case of Florida. *Tourism Economics*, *9*(3), 307–323. doi:10.5367/000000003101298411

Pratt, S., McCabe, S., Cortes-Jimenez, I., & Blake, A. (2010). Measuring the effective- ness of destination marketing campaigns: Comparative analysis of conversion studies. *Journal of Travel Research*, *49*(2), 179–190. doi:10.1177/0047287509336471

Shields, P. O. (2006). State-funded tourism marketing: The effectiveness of state travel guides for the college market. *Journal of Travel & Tourism Marketing*, *20*(2), 31–49. doi:10.1300/J073v20n02_03

Thieke, D. (2007). *Talk to me: Making public relations meaningful to business executives, Public Relations Strategist, Spring 2007*. Available online on June 15 at https://www.prsa.org/Intelligence/BusinessCase/MeasurementResources/MeasuringValueofPublicRelations/#.V2XWMpCg9aU

Tidball, K. (1988). Creating a Culture Adds to Your Bottom Line. *The Cornell Hotel and Restaurant Administration Quarterly*, *29*(1), 1–96. doi:10.1177/001088048802900118

Tyrrell, T., & Johnston, R. (2003). Assessing expenditure changes related to welcome center visits. *Journal of Travel Research*, *42*(1), 100–106. doi:10.1177/0047287503253907

USTA. (2011). *The power of travel promotion*. Washington, DC: U. S. Travel Association.

Wober, K., & Fesenmaier, D. R. (2004). A multi-criteria approach to destination benchmarking: A case study of state tourism advertising programs in the United States. *Journal of Travel & Tourism Marketing*, *16*(2/3), 1–18. doi:10.1300/J073v16n02_01

Woodside, A., & Motes, W. (1980). Image versus direct-response advertising. *Journal of Advertising Research*, *20*, 31–37.

Woodside, A., & Reid, D. (1974). Tourism profiles versus audience profiles: Are upscale magazines really upscale? *Journal of Travel Research*, *12*(4), 17–23. doi:10.1177/004728757401200404

Woodside, A. G., & Dubelaar, C. (2002). A general theory of tourism consumption systems: A conceptual framework and an empirical exploration. *Journal of Travel Research*, *41*(2), 120–132. doi:10.1177/004728702237412

Woodside, A. G., & King, R. I. (2001). An updated model of travel and tourism purchase-consumption systems. *Journal of Travel & Tourism Marketing*, *10*(1), 3–27. doi:10.1300/J073v10n01_02

WTO. (2009). *Handbook on Tourism Destination Branding*. Madrid: Europe-World Tourism Organization.

Chapter 2
Environmental protection and Tourism:
Tourism in the Protected Area in Mongolia

Navchaa Tugjamba
University of the Humanities, Mongolia

Amarbayasgalan Gantumur
University of the Humanities, Mongolia

ABSTRACT

Mongolia is a unique and relatively unexplored tourism and leisure travel destination. In the world tourism market, the tourism sector offers a great combination of wild natural features, a wide variety of untouched landscapes, historical heritage reserves, and nomadic life style and culture. The Protected Area Network of Mongolia cover over 14.5 percent of the country's territory and has become major destinations for rapidly growing tourism and recreational activities for its natural beauty, rare species of wildlife and historical and cultural heritage sites. Orkhon valley National Park (OVNP) is one of Mongolian main tourism destinations regarding to natural beautiful landscape and including numerous cultural and historical remains and sites. Thus, promoting sustainable tourism development to improve local livelihoods based on the nomadic lifestyle and protection of land with natural wilderness, watersheds, important biodiversity, historical and cultural heritage and rare remains is challenging in the national park.

INTRODUCTION

The chapter aimed to define the appropriate approaches to promote sustainable tourism development in the protected area based on the assessment of ecosystem service, tourism carrying capacity.

Environment is a key component of tourism. Especially, the physical environment is often referred as the key element of tourism (Theobald, 1998, p20). Tourism has the power to enhance the environment, to provide funds for conservation, to preserve culture and history, to set sustainable usage limits, and to protect natural attractions (Goeldner & Ritchie, 2012). Tourism assets, which are important for

DOI: 10.4018/978-1-5225-2078-8.ch002

the sustainable growth of tourism in Mongolia, should be safeguarded from encroachment and damage by inappropriate development. These assets include special landscapes, important views, good water quality, the setting of historical resources, and biodiversity and access points to the mountains and vast steppe area.

The attractions and activities for tourists in Mongolia relate to the natural environment, historic feature and cultural heritage. Mongolia has diverse and distinctive vegetation and fauna, including some rare species such as the Argali Sheep, Przhevalsky Horse, Asiatic wild ass, wild Bacterian camels, snow leopard and ibex. The remains of dinosaurs have been found in the Gobi desert.

The historic heritage of Mongolia is mainly related to Chinggis Khaan. The traditional nomadic way of life, based on livestock raising and living in traditional gers, is of great interest to overseas tourists. As ecotourism has rapidly developed around the world, the demand for it in Mongolia has been steadily increasing due to our geographical location and ecotourism resources.

Despite the traditional cultural, historical and religious tours for which the Central region is famous for, it has a number of the most visited spots as sanatoriums and hot springs. In the western region, the eco- tours: bird and snow peak watching, animal and plant research, trophy hunting and photo safaris, cultural and historical tours are the main tourist products. Also, this mountainous region is a great attraction for foreign tourists who are interested in climbing, mountaineering, hiking, trekking, and jeep and bike riding.

Historical tourism is widespread in the Eastern region, including a monument for the Mongolian Great Khaan- Chinggis Khaan erected in his enthroned place-Khuduu Aral. The northern region has mainly developed mountain climbing, water sports and fly fishing. Rafting and kayaking are unique ways to explore the 45.000 kilometers long rivers of Mongolia and the Lake of Khuvsugul.

The Gobi desert is offering a wide variety tourist attractions including trips for search of dinosaur fossil, visit to famous monasteries and picturesque journey among the wildest animals like ibex, snow leopard, lynx, wild ass, gazelles, saiga, govi bear, fox, wolf and steppe fox.

The chapter covered the issues of tourism development in the protected area in Mongolia from environmental perspectives. Background section gives brief information of the Mongolian natural environment and tourism. The protected areas are main tourism destinations in Mongolia. A general model of ecosystem service assessment based tourism planning described in the case of the Orkhon Valley National Park. Estimating the tourism carrying capacity is a core part of the tourism development in the protected areas. As the result of the analysis, the tourism management goals and objectives were defined and the solutions and recommendations of the tourism policy were illustrated in the OVNP

Methodology of the Study

The papers, documents and guidelines related with tourism development at the protected areas were collected and revised to define the basic model of the research study. The following methods were used in the research study:

- Ecosystem services assessment
- Estimation of the Tourism carrying capacity analysis in the OVNP
- SWOT analysis.

BACKGROUND

Mongolia's competitive advantage in tourism lies in the vast unspoiled landscapes and enduring nomadic lifestyle, which are difficult to find anywhere else in the world (Bank, 2011). Some scholars refer that the natural environment is undeveloped resources, may be found both in urban and wilderness environments, but the degree to which they are recognized as such is person dependent as well as situation dependent (Fennel, 2008). Tourism, therefore, requires and uses a geographical component (Table 1). This space has a physical substrate, the natural environment, consisting of physical and biological elements (its climate, geology, topography, flora and fauna, etc.); and also has elements created by human activities (Martı´n, 2005).

Table 1. Natural resources in Mongolia

Resource Type	Characteristics	In Mongolia
Geographic location	The place where a particular point or object exists and is usually considered more precise than "place."	Mongolia is the East Asian land locked country and bordered Russia by 3485 km in the north and China with 4673 km in the south. The total territory is 1566 million square kms. 18th largest country in the world.
Climate and weather	Climate (sun hours, temperature, snow, wind, etc.) is often the main resource upon which a whole series of activities designed to satisfy tourist demand depend (Martı´n, 2005).	Mongolian weather has four distinct seasons and a temperature which ranges *from -40°C* in winter *to +40°C* in summer. Precipitation is highest in the north, which averages 200 to 350 millimeters per year, and lowest in the south, which receives 100 to 200 millimeters.
Topography and landforms	The general shape of the surface of the earth and the surface structures that make some geographical areas unique (landforms).	The terrain is one of mountains and rolling plateaus, with a high degree of relief. The land slopes from the high Altay Mountains of the west and the north to plains and depressions in the east and the south. Average altitude is 1580 m above the sea level. The highest point is Huiten Mountan, 4374 m above the sea level.
Surface materials	The earth's surface creating materials, such as rocks, sand, fossils, minerals, soil, sand etc.	Mongolia's soil distribution changes from north to south by a longitudinal zonal schema. The zones include a mountain taiga zone, a mountain forest-steppe zone, a dry-steppe zone with Kastanozems, a semidesert zone, and a desert zone. Typical forest-steppe and steppe soil is a chestnut soil, Kastanozem (Kenji Tamura, Maki Asano, Undarmaa Jamsran, 2012). Calcisols are distributed in the Gobi region. Mongolia has fossil fuel deposits which include oil and coal. There is a large number of metal resources such as copper, molybdenum, gold, silver, iron, tin, nickel and zinc.
Water	Tourism is directly and indirectly dependent on water availability and quality (Stefan Gössling, C. Michael Hall, Daniel Scott, 2015).	Water resources of Mongolia are limited and unevenly distributed within the country and there are three main hydrological Basins: Arctic Ocean basin, Pacific Ocean basin and Central Asia Internal Drainage basin (Batnasan.N, 2003). The total water resource of Mongolia is estimated to be 599 km3 /year, and is composed mainly from water stored in lakes (83.5%), glaciers (10.5%) and rivers (5.8%) (Dolgorsuren.G, Gerelchuluun.J, Puntsagsuren.Ch, Baldandorj.Ts, Jan Bron, Wim van der Linden, 2013).
Vegetation	Tourism and outdoor recreation are highly dependent on plant life.	Mongolia is located in a vegetation transition zone between the Siberian taiga, forest steppes, steppes, desert steppes, and the Central Asian desert region where the vegetation changes from the northern forest to the central steppe and the southern desert. Grassland and shrubland covers 55 percent of the country, forest covers only 6 percent in the steppe zone, 36 percent is covered by desert vegetation.
Fauna	Animals have an important role in tourism and outdoor recreation from consumptive and non-consumptive perspectives (Fennel, 2008).	Fauna reported in the wild consists of 139 mammal species, 448 species of birds (including 331 migratory and 119 resident birds), 76 species of fish, 22 reptile species, and six species of amphibians in Mongolia.

Atmospheric elements, independent of whether they are basic or complementary tourism resources, are somewhat different in character from other natural resources and these differences need to be considered when exploiting them. Especially, the landlocked temperate countries like Mongolia, tourism industry is highly dependent on climate resources. Mongolian highly continental dominated climate with warm summers and long, dry and very cold winters makes comparatively short seasonal tourism flow in Mongolia.

Many travel agencies and travel sites recommend the following situations visit in Mongolia, due to climate and weather condition. The average daily temperature of the spring is – 3 to + 12 ^{0}C during daytime and -10 to +2 ^{OC} at night. Sign of winter can be seen until mid of March in some years.

Most pleasant time to visit in Mongolia might be between1, May – 31, August. From 15 May to 20 June, the weather will be pleasant for those who don't like hot weather. The average daily temperature during this period is +14 to +25 ^{0}C, but may drop +3 to +9 ^{0}C at night. However, the May is possible to surprise with occasional snowfalls and may feel the spring chill until 20 May. End of June and the beginning of August is considered the warmest. You will feel hotter and drier in the Gobi. Average day temperature is +25 to +38^{0}C and night temperature is +7 to +18^{0}C.

Between 15 July and 10 August is considered the rainy season, but not as rainy as some rainy countries. It could be a temporary shower or drizzle rain. In the summer, between 11 and 13 July, Mongolian the most important holiday Naadam (Box.1) is celebrated through the country. The National Geographic included seeing the in Ulaanbaatar, a capital of Mongolia in the list of top 20 tourist attractions in 2011 and hopefully this colorful festival continue to attract more people.

In addition, Traveler Magazine included travelling Mongolia among in the world .

Water consumption in tourism has been growing year by year. The most prominent focus of water studies in tourism has been direct and indirect consumption of freshwater in destinations and hotels, usually from an applied management perspective, i.e. to measure, understand and more effectively use freshwater (Stefan Gössling, C. Michael Hall, Daniel Scott, 2015).

Box. 1

Where to go in 2016: Top 16 up-and-coming destinations (Shah, 2016)

Mongolia

Sandwiched between Russia and China, the land that birthed Genghis Khan, the Silk Road and the giant sand dunes of the magical Gobi Desert is one of the most sparsely populated nations in the world.

Mongolia's mystique lies in its primal lifestyle.Nomadic herders move to the beat of the seasons, raising yaks and camels and pitching up in gers across endless green steppe.

What's new?

The government plans to pave roads connecting all provinces to capital Ulaanbaatar by 2020.The city is a modern paradox. Designer suits brush shoulders with sandal-clad shepherds."Travel feels authentic, gritty and real for true isolation."

When to go: May to September. Naadam, the national festival of "three games of men" -- wrestling, horse-racing and archery -- takes place in mid-July.

Source: http://edition.cnn.com/2015/12/22/travel/emerging-destinations-2016/

TOURISM IN THE PROTECTED AREA

Protected areas are established primarily to preserve some type of biophysical process or condition such as a wildlife population, habitat, natural landscape, or cultural heritage such as a community's cultural tradition. Tourism can in fact be a major tool for the conservation of such areas and for raising the environmental awareness of residents and visitors (Eagles, McCool, & Haynes, 2002).

Mongolia has one of the world's oldest traditions of the protected area legislation. In 1778, the introduction of a formal ban on logging and hunting in Bogd Khan Mountain, south of Ulaanbaatar, created one of the world's oldest continuously protected areas. Similar bans were imposed for other essential mountain areas in Mongolia. In 1911, the Mongolian government established Bogd Khan Protected Mountain Administration. During the Socialist Era, the national constitution stated that all land, forests, water, and wealth was the property of the state and people. This nationalization of land helped continue the practice of land protection under state ownership. In 1972, The Decree on the Rational Utilization of Natural Resources and the Protection of the Natural Environment was passed by the government. The first legislation specifically on the protected areas was enacted in Mongolia when the Procedure on Strictly Protected Areas was approved in 1975.

Today, the Protected Area Network of Mongolia covers over 14.5 percent of the country's territory (Box 2) and has become major destinations for rapidly growing tourism and recreation; activities for its natural beauty, rare species of wildlife and historical and cultural heritage site. Over 80 percent of the protected area is occupied by tourism and related activities which impose such adverse impacts as environmental pollution, land degradation, loss and damage of historic and cultural heritage sites in Mongolia (Tugjamba & Sereeter, 2013).

In Mongolia, tourism is the third important economic sector after mining and agricultural industry. International tourists' flow has grown steadily over the past twenty years.

Box 2.

The protected areas network in Mongolia

Until 1990, Mongolia used the category of Strictly Protected area and Reserved area for hunting. Since the 1990s, the area of Mongolia designated as protected area (Law of Mongolia on Special Protected Area, 1994)has been expanded significantly, from less than 10 to the current total of 65 protected areas, which now cover a total of over 22 million hectares, or approximately 14% of the country's surface. Of Mongolia's 65 protected areas, there are:

- (1) 12 Strictly Protected Areas (IUCN categories Ia and Ib) covering an area of 10,494,283 ha
- (2) 23 National Parks (IUCN category II) covering an area of 9,481,622 ha
- (3) 21 Nature Reserves (IUCN category III) covering an area of 2,373,359 ha
- (4) 9 National Monuments (IUCN category III) covering an area of 109,545 ha.

As part of its commitment to the Convention on Biodiversity, the Government of Mongolia made a legislative commitment to conserve 30% of the country (46.9 million ha) in protected areas by 2030.

Most of the international tourists visit in the protected areas in Mongolia and over 20 percent of them travel along the Orkhon Valley National Park (Gansukh.D, Navchaa.T, Erdenetuul.S, 2012). Orkhon Valley National Park (OVNP) is one of Mongolian main tourism destinations regarding to natural, beautiful landscape and including numerous cultural and historical remains and sites. Based on its natural, beautiful landscape and historical importance for Mongolia, Orkhon Valley was registered as a National Park in 1996 (Tugjamba & Sereeter, 2013).

The National park is situated in the central part of Mongolia and from Ulaanbaatar approximately 360 km to the southeast (Figure 1). Territory of the OVNP covers territories of 6 Soums of 2 Aimags, namely: Kharkhorin, Khujirt, Uyanga and Bat-Ulzii Soums, Uvurkhangai Aimag and Khotont and Khashaat Soums of Arkhangai Aimag. Total area is 364538 hectares; of which 353036 hectares are included in the territory of the national park and 10600 hectares are included in the territory with historical and cultural monuments (Galragchaa, 2010).

The 121,967 hectare area of the national park was recognized by the UNESCO World Heritage as a cultural landscape in 2004.

As defined in the UNESCO World Heritage list, Orkhon Valley Cultural Landscape encompasses an extensive area of pastureland on both banks of the Orkhon River and includes numerous archaeological remains dating back to the 6th century. (UNESCO, 2004). As a home for centuries to major political, trade, cultural and religious activities of successive nomadic empires, the Orkhon Valley had been serving as a crossroads of civilizations, linking East and West across the vast Eurasian landmass.

The main monuments and tourism attractions of the Orkhon Valley are as follows (Navchaa.T, Amarbayasgalan.G, Erdenetuul.S, 2015):

- Early 8th-century Turkish memorials to Bilge Khan and Kul Tigin with their Orkhon inscriptions are admittedly the most impressive monuments from the nomadic Turkish people. They were excavated and deciphered by Russian archaeologists in 1889-93.
- Ruins of Khar Balgas, an 8th-century capital of the Uyghur Empire, which cover 50 square km and contain evidence of the palace, shops, temples, monasteries, etc.
- Ruins of Chingis Khaan's capital Karakorum, which could have included the famed Xanadu palace.
- The Erdene Zuu monastery is the first Buddhist monastery established in Mongolia. It was partly destroyed by Communist authorities in 1937-40.
- Tuvkhun Hermitage is another spectacular monastery, overlooking a hill at 2,600 m. above sea level. Likewise, it was almost totally destroyed by the Communists.
- The remains of the 13th and 14th century Mongol palace at Doit Hill.

The result of the tourism development analysis at the national park shows that international tourists' average annum growth is 4.0 percent and 80 percent of them visit in Kharkhorin, 3-5 percent of the tourists visit in Ulaan tsutgalan waterfall; 2-5 percent in Khuisiin Naiman nuur and 1-3 percent of the international tourists travel to Tuvkhun temple, respectively. The annual growth of the domestic visitors is approximately 10 percent. Intensive growth is registered in Tubkhun temple and Kharkhorin. Most of the tourists spend 1-7 days in the park and it is a transit route for them (Annex 1). The study explores that the walking trip and horse trip are included in the main trip itinerary of 25 tour operations (Gansukh, Navchaa, & Erdenetuul, 2012).

Figure 1. Protected area network of Mongolia and OVNP

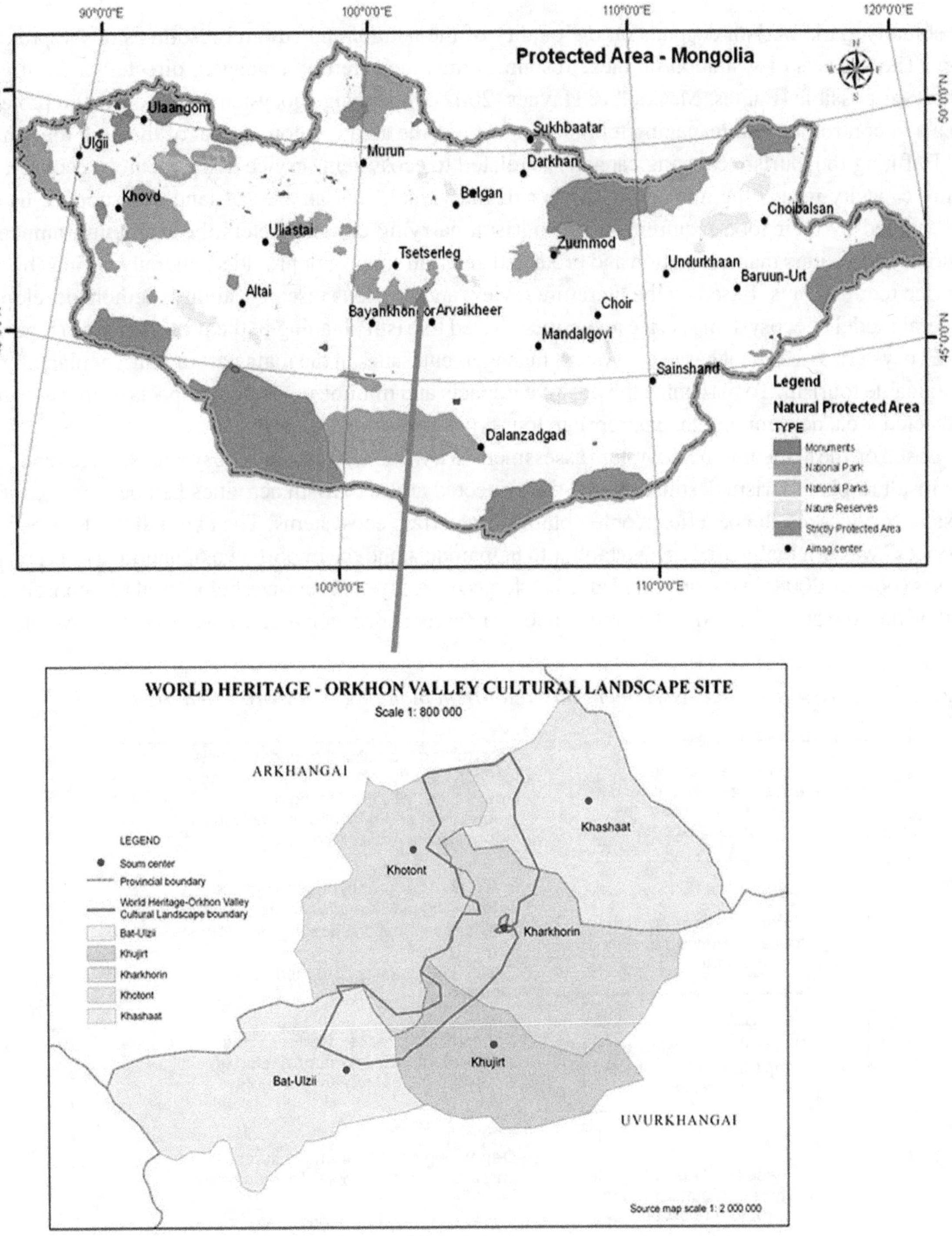

ECOSYSTEM SERVICES IN THE PROTECTED AREA AND TOURISM

Absolutely, park tourism depends on the quality of the natural and cultural resources of the protected area. The impacts of visitation on these resources must be carefully managed, directed and mitigated wherever possible (Eagles, McCool, & Haynes, 2002). Assessing ecosystem services of the protected area and controlling and managing tourism impacts on the area is a core aspect of the park tourism.

Defining the tourism carrying capacity is related to ecosystem service assessment. In ecology, carrying capacity means the maximum number of individuals that an area of land can support, usually determined by their food requirement. In tourism, carrying capacity refers the maximum number of tourists and visitors that destination and protected area can support or provide, generally defined by their service requirements. Based on the literature review and previous research studies, authors developed a general model of ecosystem service assessment based tourism planning in the protected area (Figure 2).

Ecosystem assessment based ecosystem management issues in the main part of tourism planning and sustainable tourism. To maximize the positive impacts and minimize negative impacts of tourism in the protected area, determining the appropriate tour types is essential.

Based on the Millennium Ecosystem assessment (MA, 2005), assessing ecosystem services and using the result to plan tourism destination and the protected area's tourism activities had been started. Ecosystem services are the benefits people obtain from certain ecosystems. The expression of "ecosystem services" was originally used as a metaphor to help understand the importance of natural assets and processes (Forum, 2008) in the protected areas. A focus on ecosystem services helps local and conservation authorities to make informed and planning and management decision regarding to tourism development.

Figure 2. Ecosystem service assessment based tourism planning in the protected area

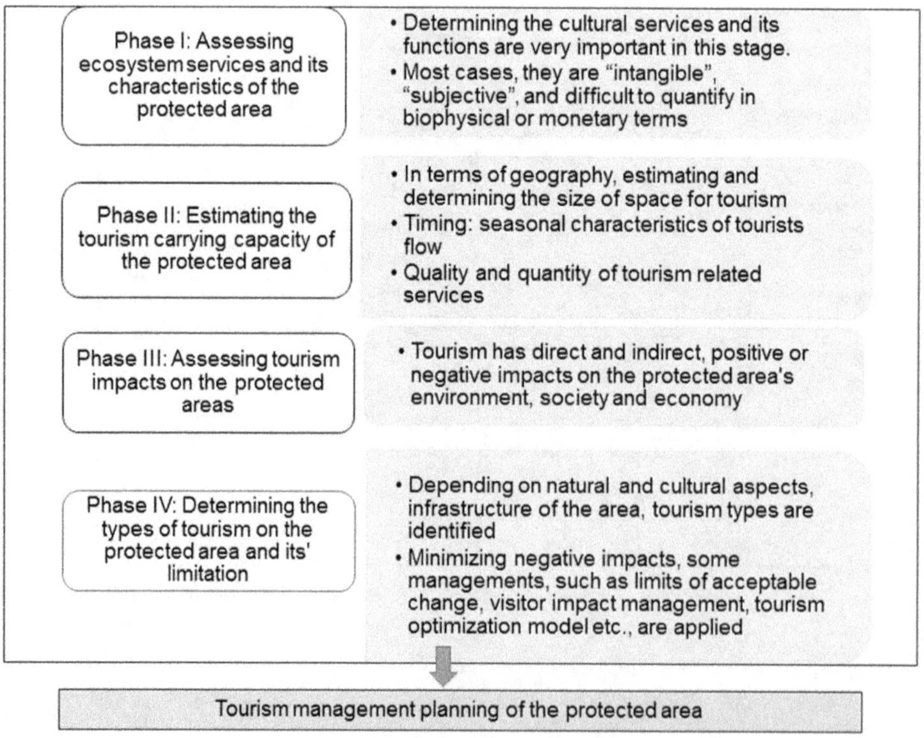

Tourism represents a major opportunity and a nexus for managing the interaction between ecosystems and people, including the development of a constituency that appreciates and supports protection of ecosystems (Daniel, 2012). Tourism activities in the protected areas give an opportunity for tourists and visitors to experience the benefits of ecosystem services directly.

Cultural services, one of the main benefits, what people obtain from ecosystems is more related in tourism and recreational activities. As defined in MA (MA, 2005, p. 40), ecosystem cultural service is "*nonmaterial benefits people obtain from ecosystem*". It includes "cultural diversity, spiritual and religious values, knowledge systems, educational values, inspiration, aesthetic values, social relations, sense of place, cultural heritage values, recreation and ecotourism". The importance of cultural services has consistently been recognized, but in the rare instances in which there is any further consideration, they are often characterized as being "intangible", "subjective", and difficult to quantify in biophysical or monetary terms.

For instance, many people value the "sense of place" that is associated with recognized features of their environment, including aspects of the ecosystem. Kharhorum, which was located in the Orkhon valley, the 13th-14th century capital of Chingis Khaan's vast Empire. Collectively the remains on the site reflect the symbiotic links between nomadic, pastoral societies and their administrative and religious centers, and the importance of the Orkhon Valley in the history of Central Asia (UNESCO, 2004).

Figure 3. Ecosystem services of the Orkhon Valley

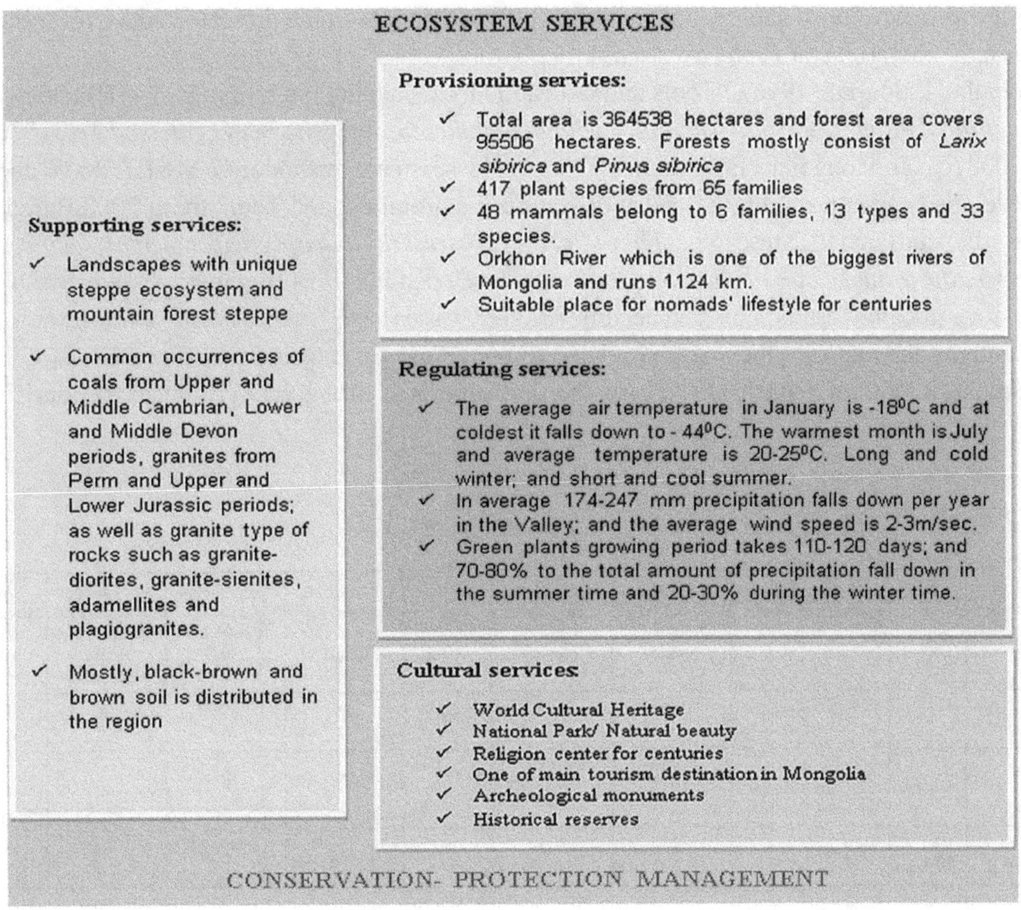

Another main aspect of ecosystem services is cultural heritage values. Many societies place high value in the maintenance of either historically important landscapes ("cultural landscapes") or culturally significant species. OVNP' cultural heritage value is well known due to historical footprints and reserved resources (Figure 3).

To define ecosystem services of the OVNP, required information and data were generated from the park management plan. Assessing ecosystem services of the protected areas are very important to develop the sustainable tourism and improve the conservation management through tourism development. In terms of sustainable development, tourism needs to make a positive contribution to the natural and cultural environment, generate benefits for the host communities, not put at risk the future livelihood of local people, and strive to anticipate and prevent economic, environment, social and cultural degradation. However, it might be hard to assess ecosystem services in the certain protected areas because the lack of information and methodology; any initiatives and considerations would be essential to improve the natural protection through tourism development.

Based on determining ecosystem services of the protected area, estimating the tourism carrying capacity is the next step. Evaluation of tourism carrying capacity (TCC) of OVNP was made in certain tourism destinations in the park (Table 2).

The next phase is assessing the tourism impacts on the protected area. Park tourism must be responsible and sustainable tourism. It aims to minimize the negative and maximize the positive social, economic and environmental impacts of tourism in destination communities and environments by promoting ethical consumption and production among all stakeholders (Saarinen, 2014). Various methods and methodologies were developed and applied to assess tourism impacts on the protected areas, for instance, in "*Tourism, Ecotourism and Protected Areas*"

(Ceballos-Lascurain, 1996), "Tools and indicators for managing tourism in parks" (Buckley, 1998), *"An Integrated Framework for developing ecological indicators of visit use of Protected Areas"* (Castley et al., 2008) etc. In Mongolia, "Environmental impacts assessment methodoly" (MNET, 2008) document was developed and approved by Ministry of Nature, Environment and Tourism, in 2008.Based on the comparative study and field research, "*The indicators to assess the tourism environmental, socioeconomic impacts on the protected areas, in Mongolia*" was developed in 2011 (Tugjamba & Sereeter, 2013).

Previous research results show that accumulation of waste issues is more negative impacts on OVNP. Main sources and cause of the waste is related to poor waste management and awareness of tourists. Assessment of tourism impacts OVNP was the first attempt in Mongolia to evaluate the tourism envi-

Table 2. Tourism carrying capacity in some destinations of OVNP[1]

Name of the Destination	Area	Accommodations and Number of Beds	Domestic Tourists / Summer Months	International Tourists / Summer Months	Number of Tourists per Day	Density of the Visitors (Person /ha/ Time)	Recreational Capacity (Person /ha/ Time)	Recreational Average Capacity per Day (Persons/ha)	Annual Recreational Capacity (Persons/ha)
Ulaantsutgalan waterfall	2 hectares	Guest house -12 192 beds/night	14200	10000	740	7,5	22,5	540	65880
Tuvkhun temple	50 hectares	265 beds -tour camp 100 beds-gust houses	1500	200	925	7,7	23,1	554	67635
Khuisiin Naiman Nuur	100 hectares	8 eco ger-35 beds	220	540	370	1,5	4,5	108	13176

ronmental, socioeconomic impacts on the Protected Areas. Methodological framework was described in the (Tugjamba & Sereeter, 2013) paper.

SWOT Analyze of OVNP Tourism Development

Our research results show that mixed tourism types have been developed in OVNP. And mixed tours of leisure and cultural tourism is assessed with quite high score. SWOT analysis of OVNP' (Table 3) tourism development shows that resources, visitors' patterns and stakeholder responses enable a summary of strengths, weaknesses, opportunities and threats to be made (Gansukh, Navchaa, Erdenetuul, 2012).

However, large, high wilderness plateau and plenty of historical and cultural resources are main strength and advantage for the OVNP, long distance between the destinations in the park area is one of weakness to develop intensive tourism in the area. On the other hand, there are high possibilities to develop eco tourism, cultural, adventure and religious tourism due to resource availability. Definitely, tourists demand high quality leisure opportunities and the services that support them. So, tourism complex services with high quality are requested in the main destinations of the national park. Tourists visit there to understand and appreciate the values for which the area was established and to gain personal benefits. Thus, how to show and express the value of the park without any damage and erosion of the historical and cultural sites is priority to tackle.

Table 3. SWOT analyze of OVNP tourism development

STRENGTHS	WEAKNESSES
• Large, high wilderness plateau and plenty of historical and cultural resources • Recognized as a cultural and historical landscape of ancient Mongolia • Recognized by the UNESCO World Heritage as a cultural landscape in 2004 • Relatively close to Ulaanbaatar • Quite well developed infrastructure • Cross junction of the vertical and horizontal tourism routes of Mongolia • Employers and local people are a bit experienced and involved in tourism business	• Lack of information sharing for tourists • Overcrowd of tourism accommodation in the certain place • Poor quality of the accommodations • Not active tourism sector • Lack of tourism marketing and promotion policy • No integrated information and data collections about international and domestic visitors • Lack of local level tourism policy
OPPORTUNITIES	**THREATS**
• High possibilities to develop eco tourism, cultural, adventure and religious tourism • Possible extension of the Park administration activities to cooperate with other Park administrations • Attract Asian tourists through cultural and religious tourism • Increase number of tourists while improve the quality of the tourism services • Receive mass tourists through developing the tourism programs for foreigners who work in the mining sectors • National level Program, such as Tourism National Complex would be built in OVNP	• Damage and erosion of the historical and cultural sites due to natural and human impacts • Lose the tourists to other promoting tourism regions • Environmental pollutions • Negative impacts due to unorganized domestic visitors

SOLUTIONS AND RECOMMENDATIONS

Generally, tourism mission in the protected areas is to help and strength the conservation measures and local development of the area. Thus, the main tourism development goal of OVNP is becoming the tourism destination for fostering tourism sector to conserve, enhance and gain value from the natural environment and heritage through the improved local residents' and every visitors' consideration for nature wilderness and nomadic cultural heritage. Commonly, people express concern about social injustices and environmental problems. They are increasingly aware of the need for low impact tourism, which does no harm.

Protected areas are very attractive settings for the growing demand for outdoor, appreciative activities in natural environments. Tourists visit these protected areas to understand and appreciate the values for which the area was established and to gain personal benefit (Paul F.J.Eagles, Stephen F.McCool, Christopher D.Haynes, 2002).

To protect the natural wilderness, historical sites and cultural heritages through tourism development, creating social awareness and increasing knowledge of the PAs amongst all those involved in tourism is main priorities (Figure 4). Based on the creative understanding and awareness of tourism stakeholders (park managers, tour operators, travel agencies, tourists and visitors, local citizens, administrative bodies, etc.) the planning and implementing the protection and development activities would be more realistic.

Stakeholder involvement is very important to develop the park tourism. All decision marks, policy makers, planners and managers, both in the public and private sector, should understand stakeholders'

Figure 4. OVNP tourism management: Protecting natural and cultural heritages

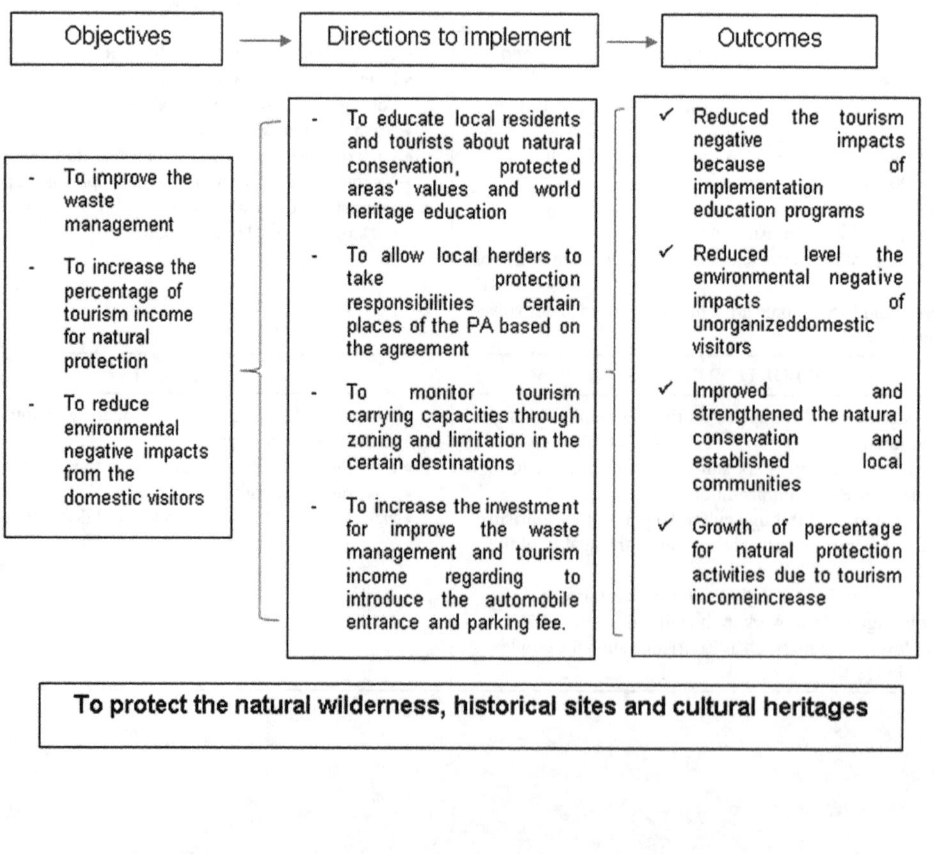

Table 4. Tourism zoning of the destinations in the OVNP

Destinations	"A" Zone	"B" Zone	"C" Zone	Explanation
Tuvkhun temple	Cycle zone with 2 km radius from the point of Tubkhun temple locates: Visitors number limitations during the peak periods are recommended by 3 hours	Outside cycle of "A" zone with 2-5 k m radius: Sites of the taking rest during the peak	Outside cycle of "B" zone with 5-10 km radius: Allowed parking and camping. To build the entrance complex	Allow to develop the hiking and horse riding in "A" and "B"zones and prohibit any type of automobile In the "C"zone, few camping sites are allowed
Ulaantsutgalan waterfall	Cycle zone with 1 km radius from the point of waterfall. Any types of actives, except of hiking and horse riding would be prohibited	Outside cycle of "A" zone with 1 km radius: Only Tourism information center is located	Outside cycle of "B" zone with 1-3 km radius: Guest houses and tour camps are located and parking and camping point build would be created	Allow to develop the hiking and horse riding in "A" and "B"zones and prohibit any types of automobile

Source: Adopted from "Orkhon Valley National Park: Tourism management plan (2012-2015)". (Gansukh.D, Navchaa.T, Erdenetuul.S, 2012)

attitudes towards the area. Educated stakeholders' involvement and awareness is base to implicate the mechanical and technical solutions to develop.

Tourism infrastructure is quite poor in the OVNP. However, there is direct transportation road is from Ulaanbaatar, the capital of Mongolia to the park, local road and its network development is issued. Thus, developing an environmental and local friendly tourism infrastructure is one of the main objectives of the park management plan. Reducing the tourism negative impact on the environment, our team recommended to establish a zoning mechanism in the main tourism destinations (Table 4) and introducing the entrance services at the national park.

As the result of the tourism current situation in the destinations', the tourism zoning policy is recommended in the OVNP.

It is spatial zoning with varying levels of intensity of human activity. The zoning mechanism of destinations in the OVNP would help managers, operators, visitors and local communities to understand what park values are located where.

The advantage of tourism destinations in the OVNP is appropriate to develop and offer "soft" adventure and ecotourism or nature-tourism types or trips.

FUTURE RESEARCH DIRECTIONS

Development considerations of some destinations, such as Tubkhun temple, Ulaantsutgalan waterfall and Khuisiin Naiman Nuur are described based on the research study (Table 5).

While some protected areas are rarely visited, others accommodate large numbers, far exceeding the size of the local population. For instance, Ulaantsutgalan waterfall, there are a huge number of domestic visitors around to visit in the water fall, during the summer holiday "Naadam" festival, every year. Thus, reducing the negative impacts of travel and visit of the short term crowds, need to introduce the inner zonning system. The main problem of the destination is over crowd of accommodation and poor waste management. Environmental friendly accomodation with good design is required.

Table 5. Tourism development possibilities in the certain destinations

Recommended Tourism Types	Main Customers	Issues	Possibilities to Tackle	Relation to Sustainable Development Approach
In the OVNP				
Nature-based tourism	International and domestic tourists	-Environmental negative impacts of domestic visitors - Non sustainable growth of tourism income -Low satisfaction of tourists	-Tourism zoning - Diversity of the tourism products - Improve the quality of the accommodations - Development of marketing	Needs to solve the arising issues
Ecotourism				
Hiking				
In the Area of Tubkhun Temple				
Religious tourism	Domestic visitors, European tourists	-Poor quality of the service entrance -Bad infrastructure -Lack of signing and information on the roads - Poor marketing -Soil degradation of the pressure of transportation -Overcrowd of the tourists	-Improve the conditions for entrance - Maintenance the road to reach the attractions - More road signing - Marketing policy - Limitations of automobiles during the peak period - Introduce the fee for the automobiles and parking	Supporting to tourism sustainable development
Eco tourism	International tourists			
Hiking				
Horse riding tour				
Ulaantsutgalan Water Fall				
Hiking	International and domestic tourists	-Overcrowd of accommodations and locate too close to the attractions - No attractiveness when the waterfall is not fallen - Lack of information - Poor waste management	-Inner zoning, - Diversity of the tourism products - Information Centre -Good waste management	Supporting to tourism sustainable development
Horse riding				
Eco tourism				
Khuisiin Naiman Nuur				
Hiking	International and domestic tourists	-Environmental negative impacts of domestic visitors - Poor waste management - No entrance service - Lack of information and road sign - Negative impacts of transportation	-Good waste management - Identify the camping points - Improve the information sharing and directional signing - Number limitations of automobiles due to TCC - Improve the conditions for entrance	Supporting to tourism sustainable development
Horse riding				
Eco tourism				
Fishing tour	Domestic visitors			

Another issue is a cultural heritage interpretation of the park for public and tourists. The heritage is still owned by a living culture and cultural presentation often involves careful analysis of the cultural conflicts involved in the presented themes (Eagles, McCool, & Haynes, 2002). The advantage of OVNP, there are cultural conflicts to interpret the heritages is almost zero within the country. And some negotiable and debated issues related to history and its interpretation is needed to take care in terms of international understanding. Traditional nomadic way of life, based on livestock raising and living in traditional gers is definitely main part of the cultural heritage interpretation.

Thus, strengthening and developing the information sharing and knowledge gaining activities and advertisements on the park' values, nature, biodiversity and historical sites and nomadic lifestyle need to be designed and implemented.

CONCLUSION

Our research covers tourism issues in the protected area, in case of Orkhon Valley National Park (OVNP), Mongolia.

In conclusion, OVNP is one of the main tourism destinations in Mongolia. The park was established primarily to preserve some type of biophysical conditions such as a wildlife population, habitat, and natural and landscape as well as cultural heritage. As the result of the tourism development assessment of the OVNP, this area is evaluated as an attractive and pleasurable to develop tourism.

The initial ecosystem assessment of the protected area was made in the case of the Orkhon Valley National park, for tourism management planning purpose. Historical reserves and archeological sites are the main parts of cultural services in the park. Even though, Orkhon Valley has been named as the World cultural heritage and cultural landscape, since 2004, cultural heritage interpretation for the public and tourists is not well developed. To improve understanding and appreciation of the protected area and cultural landscape, need to take action on interpretation and education, very carefully and continuously.

The OVNP needs a plan what describes how tourism and associated development will be managed by sustainable approach. A general model of "ecosystem service assessment based tourism planning in the protected area" was developed and used for strength protection management through tourism planning in the OVNP.

A zoning mechanism in the main tourism destinations was recommended to apply in some tourism destinations of the park. For the future, the tourism carrying capacity detailed estimation in the OVNP is recommended for tourism management planning maintenance. It is very important to conduct detailed research studies on "Ecosystem services assessment" and its values to achieve sustainable tourism development at the National Park. To undertake research leading to a clear understanding of the relationship between tourism and the environment along the country is required.

REFERENCES

Batnasan, N. (2003). Freshwater issues in Mongolia.*Proceeding of the National Seminar on IRBM in Mongolia*, 53-61.

Buckley, R. (1998). Tools and indicators for managing tourism in parks. *Annals of Tourism Research*, 207–210.

Castley, G., Hill, W., & Pickering, C. (2008). *An Integrated Framework for developing ecological indicators of visit use of Protected Areas.* CRC.

Ceballos-Lascurain, H. (1996). *Touris, Ecotourism and Protected areas.* Gland: IUCN.

Charles, R., Goeldner, J. R., & Brent, R. (2012). Toursim: Principles, Practicies, Philosophies. Hoboken, NJ: John Wiley & Sons, Inc.

Daniel, T. C. A. M., Muhar, A., Arnberger, A., Aznar, O., Boyd, J. W., Chan, K. M. A., & von der Dunk, A. et al. (2012). Contributions of cultural services to the ecosystem services agenda. *Proceedings of the National Academy of Sciences of the United States of America, 109*(23), 8812–8819. doi:10.1073/pnas.1114773109 PMID:22615401

Dolgorsuren, G., Gerelchuluun, J., Puntsagsuren, C., Baldandorj, T., Bron, J., & van der Linden, W. (2013). *Intergrated water management plan of Mongolia.* Ulaanbaatar: Ministry of Environment and Green Development.

Eagles, P. F. J., McCool, S. F., & Haynes, C. D. (2002). *Sustainable Tourism in Protected Areas: Guidelines for Planning and Management.* Gland, Switzerland: IUCN. doi:10.1079/9780851995892.0000

Fennel, D. (2008). *Ecotourism.* New York: Routledge. doi:10.4324/9780203121108.ch31

Forum, T. (2008). *Conceptualising the value of protected areas.* Victoria University.

Galragchaa, P. (2010). *Management Plan for Orkhon Valley National Park (2011-2015).* Ulaanbaatar: GIZ 454.

Gansukh, D., Navchaa, T., & Erdenetuul, S. (2012). *Orkhon Valley National Park: Tourism Management Plan (2012-2015).* Ulaanbaatar: Ministry of Nature, Environment and Green Development.

Gössling, S., Hall, C. M., & Scott, D. (2015). Water for Life: A Global Overview. In *Tourism and Water* (pp. 1–30). Bristol: Channel View Publications.

Law of Mongolia on Special Protected Area. (1994). Retrieved from http://www.legalinfo.mn/law/details/479

MA. (2005). *Ecosystems and Human Well-being: Synthesis.* Washington, DC: Island Press.

Martın, M. B. (2005). Weather, climate and tourism: A Geographical perspective. *Annals of Tourism Research, 32*(3), 571–591. doi:10.1016/j.annals.2004.08.004

MNET. (2008). *Environmental impact indicators in Mongolia.* Ulaanbaatar: Ministry of Nature, Environment and Tourism.

Navchaa, T., Amarbayasgalan, G., & Erdenetuul, S. (2015). Sustainable tourism and heritage protection in the Orkhon Valley National Park, Mongolia. *Euro-Asia Economic Forum 2015* (p. 115). Xi'an: BIT Group Global Ltd.

Saarinen, J. (2014). Critical Sustainability: Setting the Limits to Growth and Responsibility in Tourism. *Sustainability, 6*(1), 1–17. doi:10.3390/su6010001

Shah, A. (2016). *Where to go in 2016: Top 16 up-and-coming destinations.* Retrieved from http://edition.cnn.com/2015/12/22/travel/emerging-destinations-2016/

Tamura, K., Asano, M., & Jamsran, U. (2012). Soil diversity in Mongolia. In N. F. Norio Yamamura (Ed.), The Mongolian Ecosystem Network: Environmental Issues Under Climate and Social Changes (pp. 99-103). Springer Japan.

Tugjamba, N., & Sereeter, E. (2013). A Research Study on the Development of the Indicators to Assess the Tourism Impacts on Protected Areas of Mongolia. *Tourism Research & Hospitality*, *2*, 3. doi:10.4172/2324-8807.1000124

UNESCO. (2004). *World Heritage list*. Retrieved from Orkhon Valley Cultural Landscape: http://whc.unesco.org/en/list/1081

View Mongolia. (2016). Retrieved from http://www.viewmongolia.com/when_travel.html

World Bank. (2011). *Mongolia - Tourism sector policy note: Strengthening management of natural and cultural heritage assets to scale up tourism and stimulate local economic opportunity*. Washington, DC: World Bank. Retrieved 01 07, 2016, from http://www-wds.worldbank.org/external/default/WDSContentServer/WDSP/IB/2012/05/21/000425970_20120521123542/Rendered/PDF/686400ESW0P12208 0201100ENG04297547.pdf

KEY TERMS AND DEFINITIONS

Ecosystem Services: The benefits people obtain from certain ecosystems.

Kharkhorin: 13th- 14th century's capital of Mongolian Empire.

Orkhon Valley National Park (OVNP): The National park is situated in the central part of Mongolia and was recognized by the UNESCO World Heritage as a cultural landscape in 2004.

Sustainable Tourism: Tourism that can be sustained over the long term because it results in a net benefit for the social, economic, natural and cultural environments of the area in which it takes place.

Tourism Carrying Capacity: The maximum number of people that may visit a tourist destination at the same time, without causing destruction of environment and an unacceptable decrease in the quality of visitors' satisfaction.

Tourism Impacts: Tourism involves many activities that can have adverse environmental, economical and social effects.

Tourism Planning for Conservation: Tourism can significantly contribute to environmental protection, conservation and restoration.

Tourism in the Protected Area: Tourism is one of main tool to protect and reserve natural environment and biodiversity.

ENDNOTE

1 Adopted from: Tugjamba N, Sereeter E. (2013). A Research Study on the Development of the Indicators to Assess the Tourism Impacts on Protected Areas of Mongolia. *Tourism Research & Hospitality*, 2:3. doi:10.4172/2324-8807.1000124.

Chapter 4
Implication of SASEC Tourism Initiatives on North Eastern States of India:
A Descriptive Analysis - SASEC Tourism

Supriya Dam
Govt. Degree College, India

ABSTRACT

India's North Eastern Region (NER) stretches from the foothills of the Himalayas in the eastern range and is surrounded by international borders with countries like Bangladesh, Bhutan, China (Tibet Autonomous Region), Nepal, and Myanmar. The landlocked region is constrained by a brief spell of insurgency, and dismal unemployment has affected the region's progress since 1947. The advent of the Look East Policy coupled with a number of South Asia sub-regional arrangements with neighboring countries opened a "Pandora's Box" for this region. The SASEC initiatives of ADB helped to improve the status of tourism and infrastructure, including roads, air connectivity, and also opened cross-border land routes and roads within the North East (NE). The present study takes stock of tourism development from a sustainability perspective and examines the implementation of the SASEC tourism project in eight NE States of India with a view to suggest priority areas for action for promotion of tourism in this region.

INTRODUCTION

As per WTTC reports (2013), tourism is a high impact industry, a major generator of jobs in the service sector compared to manufacturing and agriculture as demonstrated by its rate of growth and employment around the world. Its total contribution comprised 9 per cent global Gross Domestic Product (GDP) (i.e. US $ 6.6 trillion) and generated over 260 million jobs—1 in 11 of the world total jobs. According to World Economic Forum's Travel and Tourism Competitiveness Report 2013, India ranks 11th in the Asia-Pacific region and 65th globally out 140 economies ranked on the travel and tourism competitiveness index. The total tourists' visits to India have increased at a rate of 16.3 per cent per annum from 577

DOI: 10.4018/978-1-5225-2078-8.ch004

million tourists in 2008 to 1057 million in 2012. Government of India (2013) suggests that international tourists arrivals pegged at 7.5 million in 2013 expected to witness an annual growth rate of 6.2 per cent over the next decade.

Tourism routes are key driver of regional development and integration and the volume of growth of world tourism, over the years, suggests that the sector deserves a higher degree of attention than it receives in South Asia. Amongst the sub-regional economic initiatives, promotion of South Asian Association for Regional Cooperation (SAARC) region as a common tourist destination by enhancing the role of private sector, human resource development, promotion of South Asian identity through tourism and also development of niche segment can augur well for promotion of SASEC tourism in the region. The ADB promoted SASEC initiatives involves four countries, Bangladesh, Bhutan, India and Nepal geographically covering Eastern Himalayan- Bay of Bengal Sub-region of South Asia. In India, it covers West Bengal, Bihar, Jharkhand, Uttar Pradesh, Orissa and eight North Eastern States (NESs) namely, Arunachal Pradesh, Assam, Manipur, Meghalaya, Mizoram, Nagaland, Tripura and Sikkim.

The SASEC program of ADB (2010) was designed to improve the status of five participating countries, namely, India, Bangladesh, Bhutan and Srilanka which essentially covers the landlocked countries/states of this sub-region. The program fundamentally includes five key sectors i.e. transport and communication, energy and power, tourism, environment and trade, investment and private sector participation. The thrust area of the project was to improve connectivity and destination infrastructure for sub-regional tourism development. The aim of the project was to promote joint development of tourism infrastructure along select multi-country tourism circuits that combine the region as whole into a marketable sub-regional tourism products The entire SASEC program of ADB is divided into nine tourism sub-circuits as a part of its collaborative effort. A list of such programs is portrayed in Table 1.

Present study covers eight NESs of SASEC region on the premise of promoting tourism as an engine of economic growth for this landlocked region. Study does not essentially follow ADB promoted SASEC tourism for NESs alone, rather it takes into all such initiatives of cross border tourism promotion which traverse through NER of India.

Table 1. SASEC Tourism Sub-circuits of ADB

No of Projects	SASEC Sub-Circuits	Countries Involved
1	Footstep of Lord Buddha Sub-circuit	Bangladesh, India, Nepal
2	Nepal Ecotourism Road Sub-circuit	Nepal
3	North East Himalayan Sub-circuit	India
4	Bangladesh India Heritage Highway Sub-circuit	Bangladesh, India
5	Bhutan-India Sub-circuit	Bhutan, India
6	Brahmaputra River Cruise Sub-circuit	India
7	Great Himalayan Trail Sub-circuit	India, Nepal
8	Srilanka Cultural Triangle Sub-circuit	Srilanka
9	Srilanka Southern Ecotourism Triangle Sub-circuit	Srilanka

Source: ADB 2010.

OBJECTIVES AND METHODOLOGY

The basic objectives of the study are:

- To make an overview of growth of tourism in the NESs;
- To assess the sustainability issues pertaining to NER;
- To explore the prospect of tourism in the region in the light of SASEC initiatives; and
- To suggest priority areas for action for tourism promotion.

Methodology

The study necessitates collection of secondary data. The data on the pattern and volume of tourists influx have been collected from different sources i.e. articles, reports, books, newspapers, internet documents etc. Annual India tourism statistics published by Ministry of Tourism, Government of India forms the base for statistical analysis of the study. As the study is entirely based upon secondary data, collection of primary data of any sort has been kept out of consideration. The collected data are processed and analyzed by using suitable statistical tools as per the need of the study.

NORTH EAST INDIA

India's North Eastern Region (NER) stretches from the foothills of the Himalayas in the eastern range and is surrounded by international borders with countries like Bangladesh, Bhutan, China (Tibet Autonomous Region), Nepal and Myanmar. It is comprised of eight states, namely, Arunachal Pradesh, Assam, Manipur, Meghalaya, Mizoram, Nagaland, Sikkim and Tripura. Richly endowed with natural resources, the region is identified as one of the world's biodiversity hotspots, hosts rich tropical rainforest along with diverse flora and fauna and several crop species. The forest cover of the region accounts for 52 per cent of the total geographical area. The region is covered by the Brahmaputra–Barak rivers and their tributaries along with Teesta, Rangit, Manu river provide attractions for tourism. Two-third of the region is covered by hilly terrain, with the exception of Brahmaputra, Barak, Imphal Valleys and flat lands in between hills of Meghalaya and Tripura. The region also houses a number of biosphere reserves, wildlife sanctuaries, monasteries, temples, mosques, mountain passes, waterfalls, lakes, and eco parks essential for expansion of different types of tourism activity.

The geographical positioning (Figure 1) of the region has made it one of the backward regions in the country which badly affected its economic progress since independence. NE Vision 2020, GOI (2005) suggests that NER is connected to the rest of India through a narrow 27 kilometre-wide Siliguri corridor (i.e., West Bengal) making it a remote land with constraining access for movement of goods and people. The region is predominantly hilly terrain in all states with the exception of Assam. In the economic front, the standard of living of the people of NER, measured by per capita income on the basis of Gross State Domestic Product (GSDP), has lagged behind the rest of India. The per capita incomes of all the states in NER are lower than the all-India average with the exception of Mizoram, Nagaland and Sikkim. Assam, the second largest state (Table 2), behind Arunachal Pradesh, having highest population in the NER, has the lowest annual per capita income of Rs 15,661 in 2004-05 which is lower than all India

Figure 1. Map of northern eastern states of India

average by 40 per cent. Even in the three states with higher income level than the national average of 6.3%, most of the income generated from public administration.

This figure is as high as 17 per cent in the states of Arunachal Pradesh, Manipur and Sikkim. This underlines the overwhelming dependence of the population of NER on governments for generating income and lack of productive economic activities in the primary, secondary and tertiary sectors among the NESs'. In the midst of these developments, NESs of India has undertaken a series of measures to develop tourism industry for reviving the industrially starved economy on the one hand and generating employment opportunities in the field of tourism on the other.

Table 2. Geographical area and population of NESs

State	Area Sq Km	% Area of NE	% Area of India	Population in 2001
Arunachal Pradesh	84743	31.94	2.55	1097968
Assam	78438	29.92	2.39	26655528
Manipur	22327	08.52	0.67	2166788
Meghalaya	22429	08.55	0.68	231822
Mizoram	21087	08.42	0.67	888573
Nagaland	16579	06.32	0.50	1990036
Sikkim	7096	02.7	0.22	540851
Tripura	10492	04.0	0.29	3199203
NE	262179	100	8.00	
India	524370			

Source: Census of India 2001

Table 3. Domestic tourist arrivals in NER during 2005-14

Year	Arunachal Pradesh	Assam	Manipur	Meghalaya	Mizoram	Nagaland	Sikkim	Tripura
2005	50,560	2467656	94299	375911	45999	17470	241697	222200
2006	80137	3268657	116984	400287	50244	15850	292486	229621
2007	91100	3436484	101484	457685	44226	22085	331263	243527
2008	149292	3617306	112000	549954	56793	21000	460564	245745
2009	195147	3851000	124000	591398	57639	26953	547810	320931
2010	227857	4050924	114062	652756	57292	21094	700011	342273
2011	133227	4339485	134505	667504	62174	25391	552453	359515
2012	132243	4511407	134541	680254	64249	35915	558538	361786
2013	125461	4684527	140673	691269	63377	35638	576749	359586
2014	180964	4826702	115499	716469	68203	58413	562418	361247
Mean	136599	3905415	118805	578269	57020	27981	482426	304643

Source: India Tourism Statistics 2007, 2010, 2012, 2014.

The following Table 3 demonstrates the dominance of Assam in terms of drawing domestic tourists across the nation and also registering consistent increase in growth rate throughout the period of six years from 2005 to 2014. The State recorded more than 6.75 times of second best domestic visiting State in the NER exhibits its supremacy in this field during course of ten years. The States' of Meghalaya and Sikkim stood follows it in terms of drawing domestic tourists' in the region during 2005-14. . Tripura, Arunachal and Manipur ranked third, fourth and fifth respectively in terms domestic visitors visiting these States'; while Mizoram and Nagaland had drawn least number of domestic tourists' during the course of ten years.

The mean growth rate of domestic tourists visiting NER (Figure2) also follows the same sequence as in the case of total domestic tourists' influx for eight North Eastern States' during 2005-14. The state of Assam stands way ahead in mean growth rate of domestic tourist influx followed by Meghalaya, Sikkim, Tripura in descending order during the period. However, the state of Meghalaya registered marginally higher mean growth rate of domestic tourist influx than Sikkim as depicted by Figure 2.

Table 4 highlights the status of foreign tourists visiting NER during the period of 2005-14. The state of Sikkim holds the dominant share in foreign tourists visiting the region followed by Assam, Meghalaya, Tripura, Nagaland etc. in descending order during the course of six years.

Figure 3 further justifies Sikkim's position as one of the preferred destination for foreign tourists visiting the NE states' during the period under review. The rest of NESs', apart from Assam, Meghalaya and Tripura, represents miniscule share foreign tourists' arrivals during 2005-14.

Table 5 portrays employment in hotels and restaurants in NESs during till 1999. It shows that apart from Assam, none of the NESs registered even one per cent of the employment level in hotels and restaurants of all India total during the survey. Of the remaining states, Meghalaya placed second in terms of peoples absorption in hotels and restaurants followed by Tripura and Arunachal Pradesh etc. in descending order during the period.

Table 6. highlights the status of five approved hotels and rooms in six NESs during 2010. The statistics of approved hotels and rooms are reflective of the fact that state of Assam dominates eight NESs in

Figure 2. Average growth rate of domestic tourists visiting North East India during 2005-2014
Source: Same as Table 2

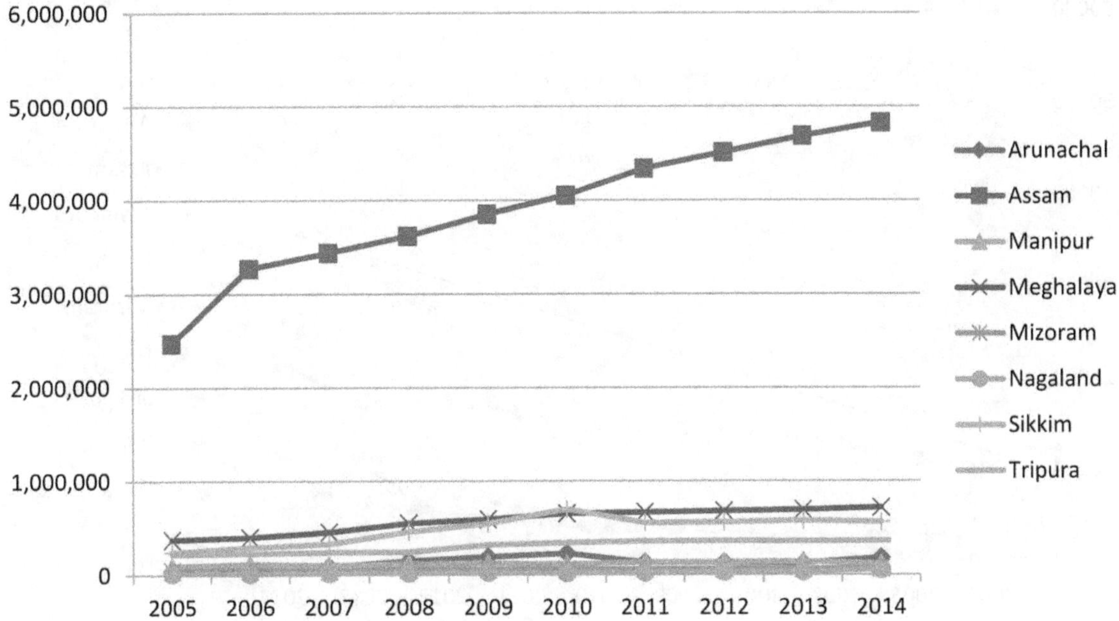

Table 4. Foreign tourist arrivals in NER during 2005-14

Year	Arunachal Pradesh	Assam	Manipur	Meghalaya	Mizoram	Nagaland	Sikkim	Tripura
2005	313	10782	316	5099	313	883	16837	2847
2006	706	11151	295	4259	542	426	18026	3091
2007	2212	13105	396	5267	735	936	17837	3177
2008	3020	14426	400	4919	842	1000	19154	4000
2009	3945	15000	300	4522	675	1423	17730	4000
2010	3395	15157	389	4177	731	1132	20757	5212
2011	4753	16400	578	4803	658	2080	23602	6046
2012	5135	17543	749	5313	744	2489	26489	7804
2013	10846	17638	1908	6773	800	3304	31698	11853
2014	5204	21537	2769	8664	836	3679	49175	26688
Mean	3953	15274	810	5380	688	1735	24131	7472

Source: India Tourism Statistics 2007, 2010, 2012, 2014

terms of hotels and rooms during the period. In fact, apart from Assam and Sikkim, the other NE states' represents a miniscule percentage of hotels and rooms during 2010.

The following table depicts number of telephone connections and tele-density of eight NE states' during 2004-05, an essential service for assessing tourism progress in NER. From the available data, it can be seen that apart from Assam (1.79%), no other state in the NESs are having even 1 per cent of

Figure 3. Growth of foreign tourists touring NER during 2005-2014
Source: Same as Table 3

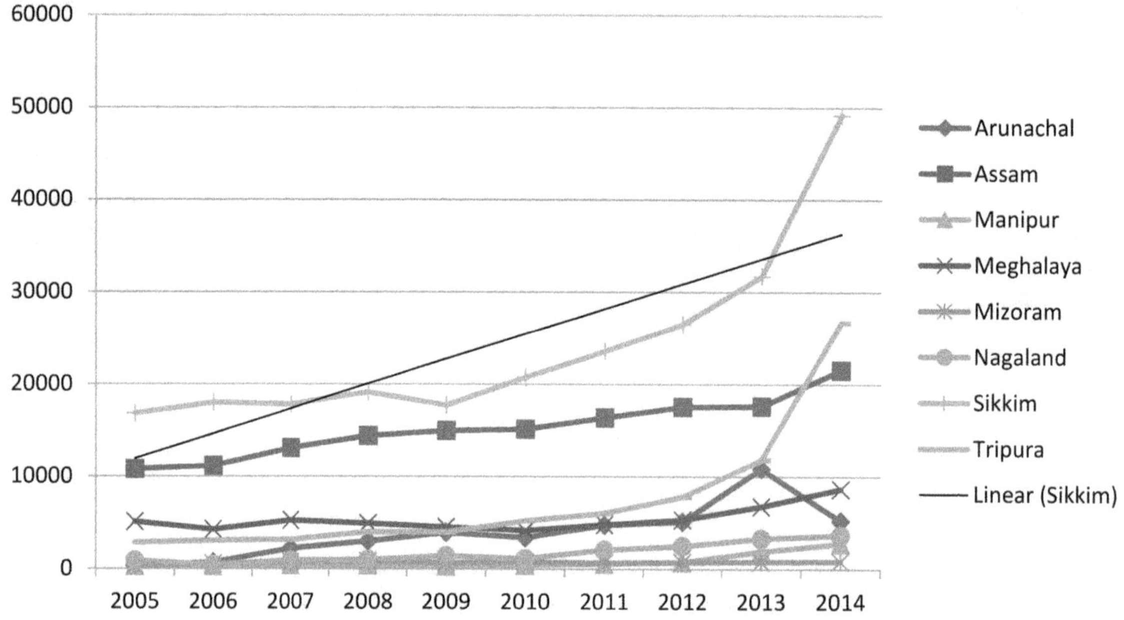

Table 5. Employment in hotels and restaurants in NER

NE States'	Own Account Enterprise	Establishment	Total	% India Share
Arunachal Pradesh	823	4740	5563	0.2
Assam	18186	56020	74206	2.68
Manipur	4400	3169	7569	0.27
Meghalaya	4430	11767	16197	0.59
Mizoram	1635	1706	3341	0.12
Nagaland	1301	4179	5480	0.20
Sikkim	593	1809	2402	0.09
Tripura	5172	3634	8806	0.32
India	1082749	1686576	2769325	

Source: Hotel and Restaurant Survey 1999, Tourism Statistics 1999, Department of Tourism, Govt. of India.

total number of connections in the country. But this information would be misleading unless we compare tele-density of NESs which measures number of telephones in terms of population of respective destinations. The tele-density of Sikkim is three times to national average and highest in the region followed by Mizoram, Arunachal Pradesh, and Nagaland etc. in that order. Assam, in spite of possessing highest number of connections, has the poorest tele-density in NER.

Apart from these, NESs possesses a number of nature made/ men made tourism resources which includes national parks, wildlife sanctuaries, biosphere reserves, butterfly park, mountain passes, hot springs, lakes, river islands, pilgrimage tourism sites and places of archeological and cultural importance

Table 6. Status of Approved Hotels and Rooms in NER during 2010

NE States		Different Grades of Hotels								Total	% NER Share
		Five Star Deluxe	Five Star	Four Star	Three Star	Two Star	One Star	Heritage	Silver and Gold B & B		
Assam	Hotels			2		8	1	20	2	32	61.54
	Rooms			148	720	225	13		6	1099	62.76
Manipur	Hotels				1					1	1.89
	Rooms				59					59	3.35
Meghalaya	Hotels			2						2	3.85
	Rooms			100						100	5.68
Nagaland	Hotels						1			1	1.89
	Rooms						19			19	1.08
Sikkim	Hotels	1	1		5	8		1		16	30.19
	Rooms	63	53		117	130		25		383	21.76
Tripura	Hotels				1					1	1.89
	Rooms				100					100	5.68

Source: India Tourism Statistics 2010, Ministry of Tourism, Govt. of India.

Table 7. Number of telephone connections and tele-density of NESs

NE States	No of Telephones	% of All India	Tele-Density
Arunachal Pradesh	126373	0.21	11.58
Assam	1075537	1.79	4.04
Manipur	110341	0.18	4.62
Meghalaya	122569	0.2	5.32
Mizoram	99229	0.16	11.14
Nagaland	148003	0.26	7.44
Sikkim	103014	0.17	19.06
Tripura	145737	0.24	4.57
NER	1930803	3.21	4.95
All India	60177380	100	6.04

Source: MoCIT, Govt. of India as mentioned in Annual Report 2005–06, Ministry for Development of NER.

etc. The cleanest village in Asia named as Mawlynnong is situated in the East Khasi Hill district of Meghalaya. Similarly, Neer Mahal of Tripura is the only water palace in the NER. A glimpse of national parks and wildlife sanctuaries are given in Table 8 and 9.

Amongst the national parks, the Kaziranga National Park in Assam is the oldest amongst NESs while the Khanchendzonga National Park in Sikkim and the Clouded Leopard National Park in Tripura are largest and smallest respectively in the NER. Amongst the wildlife sanctuaries (WLS) (Table 8), 28.57

Table 8. National parks of North East India

NESs	Name of National Parks	Year of Establishment	Area per Sq Km	Famous For
Arunachal Pradesh	Mouling NP	1986	483	
	Namdhapa NP	1974		
Assam	Kaziranga NP	1905	430	Indian Rhinocerous, World Heritage Centre UNESCO World Heritage Centre
	Manas NP	1928	500	
	Dibru-Saikhowa NP	1999	340	
	Nameri NP	1978	137.07	
	Orang NP	1999	78.81	
Manipur	Kaibul NP	1977	40	Only Floating Park in the World
	Sirohi NP	1982	41.36	
Meghalaya	Balphauran NP	2013	220	Wild Water, Buffalo, Red Panda UNESCO World Biosphere Reserve
	Nokrek NP	1986	47.48	
Mizoram	Murlem NP	1991	100	
	Phawngpui Blue Mountain NP	1992	50	
Nagaland	Ntanpui NP	1993	202.02	
Sikkim	Khangchendzonga NP	1977	1784	
Tripura	Bison (Rajbari) NP	2007	31.63	
	Clouded Leapard NP	2003	5.08	

Source: Compiled by author from different sources.

per cent are placed in Assam, 23 per cent of them are situated in Arunachal Pradesh and 14.28 per cent WLS of NESs spread throughout Sikkim.

Besides these, white water rafting, bungee jumping, trekking etc. are also promoted by NESs for growth of tourism in the region. Sikkim alone commands existence of 96 monasteries (some of which are more than 300 years old), gumpa's for Buddhist pilgrims, Solophok (Chardham) for Hindu pilgrims, a number of wildlife sanctuaries, national parks, biosphere reserves, butterfly parks, mountain passes, hot springs, and waterfalls attract a number of tourists from other parts of India and abroad. The famous Yuksam–Dzongri trekking trail draws attention of the good number of foreign tourists because of its clear visibility of the mount Khanchendzonga and surrounding scenic views. Similarly, rhododendron blooming season (especially in the months of April and May) draws nature loving tourists in the upper reaches of Sikkim. Likewise, white water rafting, mountain biking etc. are also popular amongst tourists visiting the state.

SUSTAINABILITY ISSUES OF NESs

Tourism Density Factor (TDF)

The TDF is measured in terms of annual tourists' turnover in relation to total population of destination area at certain point of time. Higher TDF purports to increased level of tourism activity on the one hand

Table 9. Wildlife sanctuaries of North East India

NE States'	Name of Wildlife Sanctuaries (WLS)	Year of Establishment	Area in Sq Km
Arunachal Pradesh	Pakhul Tiger Reserve	1977	861.95
	Dibang WLS	1991	41.49
	Kamlang WLS	1987	78.3
	Mehao WLS	1980	281.5
	Eaglenest WLS	1989	217
	D'ering Memorial WLS	1978	199
	Itanagar WLS	1978	140.3
	Sessa Orchid Sanctuaries	1989	100
	Kane WLS	1991	55
	Telly Valley		337
Assam	Kaziranga NP	1905	430
	Bor Nadi WLS	1988	26.22
	Dipor Bill	1989	40
	Garampani WLS		6.05
	Hoollongapar Gibbon Sanctuary	1997	2098.62
	Manas NP	1928	500
	Sonai Rupai WLS	1934	175
	Nameri NP	1985	137.07
	Orang NP	1985	72.6
	Lakhowa WLS	1979	70.14
	Pabha WLS		49
	Pobitra WLS	1987	38.83
Manipur	Yagoupokpi Lockchar	1989	184.8
Meghalaya	Nongkhyllen	1981	29
	Bhagmara		
	Ngengpui		
Mizoram	Dampa Tiger Reserve	1985	550
	Khewnglung	1991	41
	Ngengpui	1991	150
Nagaland	Fakim		
	Intanki	1988	202.02
	Pulebatza		
Sikkim	Barsey Rhododendron Sanctuary	1984	51.76
	Fambonglho WLS	1984	61
	Pangolakha WLS	1984	51
	Kyonhnosla Alpine Sanctuary	1977	
	Maenam WLS	1987	35.34
	Shingba Rhododendron Sanctuary	1984	32.5
Tripura	Charilan		
	Gomti WLS	1988	389.54
	Sipahijala WLS	1987	18.53
	Trishna WLS	1987	170.56

Source: same as Table 7.

Table 10. Tourist arrivals /population percentage of NESs during the Period of 2003–05

North East Rank	State/Union Territories (All India Rank)	Average Arrivals	Population#	Factor (%)
01	Sikkim (12)	235086	580000	40.53
02	Meghalaya (19)	401720	2488000	16.15
03	Assam (27)	2312366	28896000	08.00
04	Tripura (28)	247871	3432000	07.22
05	Mizoram (30)	39773	953000	04.17
06	Manipur (31)	93840	2325000	04.04
07	Nagaland (34)	11947	2135000	00.56
08	Arunachal Pradesh (35)	3540	1178000	00.30

Abbreviation: # population for 2006 estimated as per 2001 census, Average Arrivals: Average tourist arrivals in the years 2003, 2004,2005, Factor: Tourist arrivals as a percentage of population

Source: Lok Sabha Unstarred Question No 3306 dated 24/08/06 and Census of India

and deleterious impact on carrying capacity on the other. In the first phase (2003–05) Sikkim holds the highest TDF (Table 10) followed by Meghalaya, Assam, Tripura, Mizoram, Manipur, Nagaland and Arunachal Pradesh in that order. The TDF of Nagaland and Arunachal Pradesh is almost insignificant and possess the least rank among the States/Union Territories during the period.

In the second phase (2006–09) (Table 11), TDF of almost all NESs have shown improvements with the exception of Nagaland. During the period, TDF of Sikkim increased by 30.64% to 71.17%. Amongst remaining states', the TDF of Arunachal Pradesh gone up by 10.54% followed by Assam (3.93%), Meghalaya (3.57%), Mizoram (1.15%) in descending order. Nagaland is the only State in the NE having less than 1 per cent TDF in both the phases. However, higher level of TDF of Sikkim in both the phases indicates magnification of tourism activity which can cause irreparable damage to this ecologically fragile destination as evidenced by recent earthquakes in the state.

Table 11. Tourist arrivals /population percentage of NESs during the Period of 2006–09

NE Rank	State/Union Territories (All India Rank)	Average Arrivals	Population in 2009#	Factor (%)
01	Sikkim	425586	598000	71.17
02	Meghalaya	504931	2560000	19.72
03	Assam	3556684	29814000	11.93
04	Arunachal Pradesh	131390	1212000	10.84
05	Tripura	263167	3532000	7.45
06	Mizoram	52148	981000	5.32
07	Manipur	114058	2393000	4.77
08	Nagaland	21093	2197000	0.96

#Population in 2009 is calculated on the basis of Projected Population, Census of India, 2001

Source: India Tourism Statistics 2006,2007,2008,2009 & Projected Population of States and Union Territories, Census of India, 2001

Tourism Intensity Factor (TIF)

TIF is another technique of measuring the level of tourism activity in travel destinations. It is measured as tourist arrival per square kilometre of the host location and considered as another important tool for assessing the sustainability of the tourist destinations.

Table 12 depicts the TIF of eight tourism performing states' NER of India during 2003-09 in two phases. Data reveal that Sikkim enjoys the leading state status among the NESs in terms of TIF. The TIF of Sikkim is 33 persons per square kilometre area in 2003–05 which rose to 60 persons during the period of 2006–09. In case of Assam, TIF has increased from 30 persons per square kilometre area in 2003–05 to 45 persons in 2006-09. Similarly, Tripura, Meghalaya, have also registered an improved growth of TIF during two phases. For rest of the NESs, in spite of registering minor improvements, the growth of TIF for the states of Nagaland, Mizoram, and Arunachal Pradesh are negligible during the period.

Status of Tourism Infrastructure

Table 13 shows the basic amenities considered essential for growth of tourism in NER. These include per capita electricity consumption, road length per thousand square kilo metre, population under one post office, safe drinking water as well as socio-economic infrastructure index. During 1999–2000, per capita consumption of electricity of all NESs are less than national average. Against all India average of 354.7 kwh, Sikkim holds the highest per capita consumption of electricity of 192.4 kwh followed by Meghalaya, Mizoram, Assam, Tripura etc. in descending order.

During 2004–05, the same trend continued and per capita consumption of electricity in Sikkim, although doubled, 134 kwh adrift of national average. Meghalaya also followed the same suit as its per capita consumption of electricity increased during the period. Rest of the NESs has made reasonable progress during the course of five years with the exception of Assam in which per capita consumption of electricity has declined by 10.2 kwh during 2004–05. Road density of NER has shown a dismal picture

Table 12. TIF of North Eastern states during the period of 2003–2009

Sl No	States/UTs	Area in 2001	Average Tourist Arrival during 2003–05	TIF (Per Sq Km of Area)	TIF Ranking	Av. Tourist Arrival during 2006-09	TIF (Per Sq Km of Area)	TIF Ranking
01	Sikkim	7096	235086	33.13	1	425586	59.98	1
02	Assam	78438	2312366	29.48	2	3556684	45.34	2
03	Tripura	10486	247871	23.64	3	263167	25.10	3
04	Meghalaya	22429	401720	17.91	4	504931	22.51	4
05	Manipur	22327	93840	04.20	5	114058	5.11	5
06	Nagaland	16579	11947	00.72	6	21093	1.27	8
07	Mizoram	21087	39773	00.53	7	52148	2.47	6
08	Arunachal Pradesh	83743	5340	00.06	8	131390	1.57	7

Source: Indian Tourism Statistics 2003,04,05,06,07,08,09 and Census of India 2001

Table 13. Growth of tourism infrastructure among NESs

NESs	Infrastructure						
	Per Capita Consumption of Electricity 1999–2000 (in kwh)@	Per Capita Consumption of Electricity 2004–05 (in kwh)#	Road Length per 1000 sq km of area in 1996–97@	Road Length per 1000 sq km of area in 2002#	Population under one post office 1999–2000(2001 population)@	Access to safe drinking water in per cent of households in 1991@	Index of social and economic infrastructure 1999@
Arunachal Pradesh	68.6	144.8	168	219.3	3627	70.02	69.7
Assam	95.5	85.3	872	1140	6776	45.86	77.7
Manipur	69.5	70.05	190	512.1	3123	38.72	75.4
Meghalaya	160.3	352.2	278	426.5	4721	36.16	75.5
Mizoram	120.7	133.7	229	229.8	2221	16.21	82.1
Nagaland	84.7	87.2	1107	1268	6623	53.37	76.1
Sikkim	192.4	397.7	258	284.4	2647	73.19	109
Tripura	95.5	113.1	1405	1554	4464	37.18	74.9
India	354.7	411.1	749	755.4	6639	62.30	100

Source: @Planning Commission, Tenth Five Year Plan 2002-07, #Statistical Abstracts of India 2006

during 1996–97. With the exception of Tripura, Nagaland and Assam, the other NESs has poor road length per thousand square kilo metre area below the all India average of 749 square km during the period.

The coverage of population under post office also has shown a poor plight of NESs during the period 1999–2000. Assam is the only state in the NER which has more than 6639 persons under one post office during 1999–2000 followed by Nagaland, Meghalaya, Tripura etc. in that order. Mizoram has the lowest coverage of persons under one post office during the period.

Safe drinking water is another criterion in the supply side of tourism in which Sikkim has edge over other NESs as the 73.19% of the people of the state are accessible to it. Arunachal Pradesh is only other state among NESs which qualifies national average; while rest of the states lag behind with Mizoram has the poorest record during 1991. In social and economic infrastructure index, Sikkim is the only state in the NER to attain the national average and best equipped in socio-economic infrastructure for tourism development in the state.

Project Sanctioned

The following table shows the number of project sanctioned and amount sanctioned by Central Government during the period 2007–08 to 2009–10. The state of Sikkim leads in terms of number of projects sanctioned and amount sanctioned which represents 8.8 and 7.36 per cent of the national level. Arunachal Pradesh, Manipur, Nagaland, Assam, Mizoram etc follow it in terms of number of projects and amount sanctioned during the period. Significantly, the state of Meghalaya has attracted least number of projects and amount sanctioned during the course of three years.

Table 14. Tourism projects sanctioned during the period of 2007–08 to 2009–10 (Rs. In Lakh)

Sl No.	NE States	No. of Projects Approved	%age of all India	Amount Sanctioned	%age of all India	NE Rank
01	Arunachal Pradesh	37	4.86	10131.06	4.64	II
02	Assam	15	1.97	4455.39	2.04	V
03	Manipur	25	3.29	7344.17	3.36	III
04	Meghalaya	15	1.97	3386.32	1.55	VIII
05	Mizoram	16	2.10	4417.25	2.02	VI
06	Nagaland	47	6.18	7260.74	3.33	IV
07	Sikkim	67	8.80	16075.83	7.36	I
08	Tripura	30	3.94	3539.00	1.62	VII
	All India	761	100.00	218356.64	100.00	

Source: Outcome Budget 2010-11,Ministry of Tourism, Govt. of India

SASEC INITIATIVES AND NESs

Ryngnga's study (2011) emphasized the region's necessity to establish much needed corridor between India's North East (NE) as a bridge to South East Asia for economic cooperation and to make it a hub for trade and commerce as well as a popular destination. Both the Bay of Bengal Initiative for Multi-Sectoral Technical and Economic Cooperation (BIMSTEC) and Bangladesh, China, India, Myanmar (BCIM), being the sub-regional groupings, shares two common countries (i.e. Myanmar and Bangladesh) pass through predominantly three NESs, namely Tripura, Mizoram and Manipur. Sharma and Rathore (2015) concluded that tourism is one of the focus areas of BIMSTEC and BCIM and also for India represents another opportunity to extract mileage for its Look East Policy (LEP) though cooperation with Myanmar to develop NER as a tourist destination.

Sharma and Rathore (2015) reported that during 1997, Bay of Bengal Initiative for Multi-Sectoral Technical and Economic Cooperation (BIMSTEC) formed involving countries like Bangladesh, India, Myanmar, Srilanka, Thailand, Nepal, Bhutan, and in 1999, Bangladesh, China, India and Myanmar (BCIM) sub-regional groups opened up door for inter-regional trade and tourism facilitation for entire sub-region in general and NE in particular. CSIRD (2013) added that both the BIMSTEC and BCIM route directly share two common countries i.e. Bangladesh and Myanmar and three NESs namely Tripura, Mizoram and Manipur. Recently, Kolkata (West Bengal) to Kunming (China) (K2K) initiative was launched with sole aim to promote trade and tourism amongst landlocked sub-regions. The following Figure 4 depicts the route which essentially covers BIMSTEC, BCIM and K2K initiatives across the sub- region.

The Asian Development Bank (ADB) promoted South Asian Sub-regional Economic Cooperation (SASEC) initiatives involves four countries, Bangladesh, Bhutan, India and Nepal geographically covering Eastern Himalayan- Bay of Bengal Sub-region of South Asia. In India, it covers West Bengal, Bihar, Jharkhand, Uttar Pradesh, Orissa and eight NESs namely, Arunachal Pradesh, Assam, Manipur, Meghalaya, Mizoram, Nagaland, Tripura and Sikkim. SASEC's Tourism Development Plan (TDP) was released in 2002 with the approval of tourism working group comprising of members of National Tourism organizations (NTOs) of these four countries. The TDP focuses on development of tourism related infrastructure including roads, air connectivity, facilitating travel by minimizing border restrictions,

Figure 4. Kolkata to Kunming route via Bangladesh and Myanmar

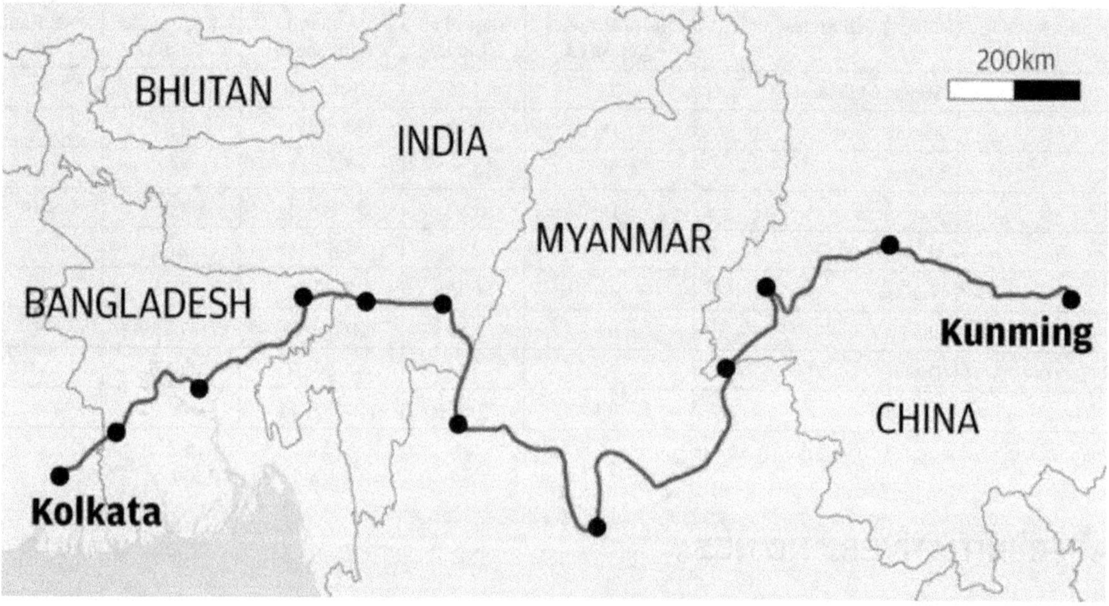

human resource development (i.e. training and resource building), branding and joint marketing and product development primarily for ecotourism and promotion of Buddhist circuits. The opening of cross border land routes and roads within North East (NE) was given top priority in the project.

Table 15 depicts foreign tourist arrivals of select SASEC countries during 2003-07. India registered highest foreign tourist arrivals (FTAs) during the period followed by Maldives, Srilanka, Nepal, Bangladesh and Bhutan in descending order. In terms of compound annual growth rate (CAGR), Bhutan tops the list largely due to wide fluctuations in inbound tourists to that country in successive years while Maldives tourism shows lack of dependence upon tourists from SASEC countries for its tourism development. CAGR of India is less than half of Bhutan during 2003-07 followed by Maldives, Nepal and Srilanka in that order.

Table 15. Foreign tourist arrival statistics of select SASEC countries during 2003-2007

South Asia	Year					Change2006/07(%)	CAGR2003-07(%)
	2003	2004	2005	2006	2007		
Bangladesh	244509	271270	207662				
Bhutan	6261	9249	13626	17342	21093	21.6	35.5
India	2726214	3457477	3918610	4447167	4977193	11.9	16.2
Nepal	275438	297335	277346	283819	360350	27.0	6.9
Srilanka	500642	566202	549308	559609	494008	-11.7	-0.3
Maldives	563593	616716	395320	601923	675889	12.3	4.6

Source: UN World Tourism Organization and Pacific Asia Travel Association Statistical Reports.

Table 16. Contribution of tourism industry in select South Asian sub-regional countries

Sub-Regional Countries	Percentage Contribution Tourism Industry	
	In Gross Domestic Product (GDP)	In Employment
Bangladesh	3.7	3.0
India	5.3	5.4
Nepal	8.2	6.4
Srilanka	9.6	7.9
World	10.3	8.7

Source: World Travel and Tourism Council (WTTC), Country Report in South Asian Yearbook of Trade and Development, 2006

From the table, it can be seen that apart from Srilanka, none of the South Asian Sub-regional Countries getting close to its percentage contribution either in world GDP or in tourism employment. However, India is the only country in the sub-region has registered higher percentage growth in tourism employment than its contribution to tourism GDP.

The SASEC tourism development plan (TDP) of 2004 spotted 23 cross border tourism projects to be developed within seven key areas, largely covering tourism segments like ecotourism, Buddhist circuits. Amongst the NESs, the said projects mainly cover three states', namely, Arunachal Pradesh, Sikkim and Tripura and also parts of countries like Bhutan, Nepal and Bangladesh; besides tourism transport connectivity throughout the SASEC region. Intra-regional travel amongst the member countries became the thrust area to adopt series of steps to promote highways, develop new airports and easing tension across the border. The thrust of the plan was given to community participation in tourism projects, a genuine commitment to achieve the desired end.

The Kathmandu declaration of BIMSTEC in August, 2006 on tourism cooperation and plan of action suggested promotion of joint action in the field of heritage, cultural, adventure and MICE tourism along with development of joint packages for member countries. It also incorporates setting up of information centre in India to disseminate tourism related information about BIMSTEC countries, setting up of tourism fund, annual meeting of members after a fixed interval as well as exploring synergies within SASEC. Regional measures of this kind led to regionalism amongst SASEC countries in general and NESs in particular.

Chang (1998) aptly defined regionalism is an integration process between locales, cities or countries to create a region creating mutually beneficial impact and synergistic growth. Chang (1998) further added that the relationship between regionalism as a whole and tourism is mutually beneficial because, 'while tourism provides an avenue for regionalization mission, simultaneously, regionalism also creates opportunities for sustaining the country's tourism growth. Timothy (2003) argued that alliances of member nations and vision from outside the region can travel virtually unhindered by international boundaries resulting in higher levels of domestic and intra-regional level travels. In fact, Timothy has provided a thematic perception of cooperation amongst regions which depicted in Table 17.

Of the five parameters listed by Timothy, transportation and infrastructure development was given its largest attention in the SASEC region since the adoption of TDP in 2002. For joint marketing and flow of people modalities were worked out to give it a complete shape while growth development of tourism was given due attention by independent National Tourism Organization (NTOs) as well as jointly as collective entity.

Table 17. Thematic issues for cooperation amongst regions

Parameters	Areas of Cooperation	Parameters	Areas of Cooperation
Environment Management	Balanced use of resources Natural and Environmental Quality Standardized conservation mechanism	Growth and Development of Tourism	Regional Destination Regional Origins Decreased barriers effect of borders
Marketing and Promotion	Shared promotional budgets Multination tour circuits Common accommodation standards	Flow of People	Tourists from within the alliance Tourists from outside the alliance Industry workers/ Human resources
Transportation and Infrastructure Development	Transportation agreements Facilities and infrastructure Enhanced accessibility		

Source: Timothy 2003.

DISCUSSION AND RECOMMENDATION

Of the above mentioned parameters, environmental management is not a big issue for majority of NESs because of low intensity tourism with the exception of Sikkim, which was subjected tourist concentration in select tourism pockets causing irreparable damage for the destination in the recent past. Manandhar and Rosul (2009) opined that here are evidences of dramatic increase in tourist flows in tourist destination of this sub-region where administrative and documentation processes are streamlined and destinations are opened upto a wider population. Further, standardized conservation mechanism can be worked out for NESs with appropriate emphasis on balanced use of resources amongst the NESs. Bhutanese model of tourism development with due emphasis on 'high value low impact' tourism can be of great help for the NESs like Sikkim to overcome the issues of sustainability.

Manandhar and Rosul (2009) further added that for tapping the true potential of the global tourism industry, there is still need for coordinated efforts among countries for South Asia to improve and optimal use of road, rail and air links along with other tourism infrastructure. In this regard, Robertson (2004) argued that government and donors across the world place little emphasis to regional tourism in tourism planning and instead giving more emphasis on international tourism. So, collaborative planning framework along with its implementation in specified time schedule is key for NESs.

Rehman's study (2014) reported that connectivity through Bangladesh and Myanmar hold the key for promotion of trade and tourism in the NER. In this regard, economic corridor via Bangladesh can be of great help for promotion of tourism in this peripheral region. Two important corridor between Bangladesh and North East India are Samdrup Jongkar (Bhutan)- Shillong (India) – Sylhet (Bangladesh) –Dhaka (Bangladesh) – Kolkata (India) and Agartala (India) – Akhura (Bangladesh) – Chittagong (Bangladesh). These economic corridor between Indian and Bangladesh should use a holistic approach for developing a cost effective transport system to move goods and people, while simultaneously promoting trade, investment, telecommunication, energy, infrastructure and tourism. In recent times, bus connectivity via Bangladesh was started connecting two states of the region, namely, Meghalaya and Tripura. In July 11, 2001, bus service was launched to connect Dhaka with Agartala to facilitate flow of commuters between these two destinations. Foreign nationals visiting Dhaka has the option of travelling to Tripura via Akhaura border post with appropriate visa. Subsequently, on 7th June, 2015 first direct bus between Kolkata and Agartala through *chicken neck* via Bangladesh flagged off by politician from both the parties. This step reduces the distance between two terminal points from 1650 km to 515 km pave the way for increased influx of tourists (both domestic and foreign) from a metro station to Tripura. Recently, metre gauge railway track in the state replaced with broad gauge track which can reduce the time required to visit the state, when fully operational. Efforts are on to extend this railway network to Bangladesh's Southeastern city of Akhaura, a fifteen km long track, linking it with Chittagong port, Sylhet and Dhaka through Indian initiative. An agreement to this effect was signed between Prime Minister, Dr. Manmohan Singh and his counterpart from Bangladesh, Sheik Hasina in January, 2010. In spite of these efforts, transport connectivity between these destinations is far from normal which is essential for not only NESs but also for Bangladesh.

The sub-regional initiatives has given emphasis on tourism infrastructure development, however, its progress in the sub-region is far from satisfactory. But increased investment in this sector, over the years, has improved the status of tourism infrastructure in the region which will pave the way for better prospect for tourism in the region.

Buhalis (2000) argued that cumbersome visa procedure is still a deterrent for some destinations and most of the destinations have taken effective measures to ease out the bottleneck. Relaxation of immigration regulations has also favored intra-regional tourism. Taking advantages of new technologies and internet enable destinations to enhance their competitiveness. In two NESs, the inner line permit (ILP) is still an issue which needs streamlining for tourism promotion without compromising security issues. Use of internet in North Eastern cities has improved a lot in the last ten years or so, however, this service is quite poor in rural areas of NER which needs immediate attention.

ADB initiated SASEC tourism project was a welcome development in the light of Act East Policy of government of India. But it failed to achieve its primary goal of involving community in each phase of tourism development. Engagement of private players in implementation of tourism project overlooked the welfare aspect of indigenous communities and their negligible participation which, in effect, has affected sustainability of tourism projects of the sub-region.

CONCLUSION

In spite of adversaries, the communities of the sub-region are gearing up to welcome tourist in their backyard. A conscious effort on the part of all the stakeholders can uplift the status of tourism in this peripheral region. The region is improving its track record in terms of its attitude towards tourism and also emergence of host community in Sikkim can augur well for overall tourism development of the sub-region.

REFERENCES

ADB. (2010). *Inception Report Improving Connectivity and Destination Management of Cultural and Natural Resources in the South Asia Sub-region*. package 4 India-Sikkim.

Buhalis, D. (2010). Marketing of Competitive Destinations of the Future. *Tourism Management*, *21*(1), 97–116. doi:10.1016/S0261-5177(99)00095-3

Centre for Studies in International Relations and Development (CSIRD). (2013). *9th K2K Forum-Strengthening Regional Economic Cooperation and Promoting Cultural Ties,* Report, in collaboration with Institute of Foreign Policy Studies, University of Calcutta. Retrieved on 7th March, 2016 from www.csird.org.in/rep/9th%20k2k%report.pdf

Chang, T. C. (1998). Regionalism and Tourism: Exploring Integral Links in Singapore. *Asia Pacific Viewpoint, 39*(1), 73–94. doi:10.1111/1467-8373.00054

Government of India. (2005). *North Eastern Region Vision 2020* (Vol. 2). Ministry of Development of North Eastern Region (MDoNER) & North Eastern Council (NEC).

Government of India. (2010). *India Tourism Statistics 2010*. New Delhi: Marketing Research Division, Ministry of Tourism.

Government of India. (2013). *Annual Report 2012-13*. Ministry of Tourism.

Rahman, M. M. (2014). Trade Potential and Economic Cooperation between Bangladesh and North East India. In Developing Economic Corridors in South Asia. ADB.

Rasul, G., & Manandhar, P. (2009). Tourism Potentials in Poverty Reduction in South Asia. *South Asia Economic Journal, 10*(1), 187–207. doi:10.1177/139156140901000108

Robertson, C. M. (2004). Regional Tourism in South Africa: A Case of Mass Tourism in the South. *GeoJournal, 60*(3), 229–237. doi:10.1023/B:GEJO.0000034730.05992.18

Ryngnga, P. K. (2011). Tourism: A Trade link between India's North East and South East Asia. *South Asian Journal of Tourism and Heritage, 4*(1), 84–89.

Sharma, A., & Rathore, C. K. (2015). *BIMSTEC and BCIM Initiatives and their importance for India.* Discussion Paper. Cuts International.

Timothy, D. J. (2003). Supranationalist Alliances and Tourism: Insights from ASEAN and SAARC. *Current Issues in Tourism, 6*(3), 250–266. doi:10.1080/13683500308667956

WTTC. (2013). Foreword. In *Travel and Tourism Economic Impact 2013* (p. i). WTTC.

ADDITIONAL READING

ADB. (2004). *South Asia Sub-regional Economic Cooperation, Tourism Development Plan, December*. Retrieved from http//www.adb.org/Document/Reports?SASEC/Tourism Development/default.asp?p=/sasec. On 29th April, 2016.

DAS, D. (2012). Tourism as a Long Run Economic Growth with Special Reference to North Eastern Region of India. *IOSR Journal of Humanities and Social Science* 2(2): 47–50.

GANGTE, M. (2011). Sustainable Community Development Alternative: Unlocking the Lock (Case of North East region of India). *Journal of Sustainable Development, 4*(2), 61–71.

Chapter 5
Mastering Sustainable Tourism and Rural Tourism in the Global Economy

Kijpokin Kasemsap
Suan Sunandha Rajabhat University, Thailand

ABSTRACT

This chapter explains the overviews of tourism, sustainable development, sustainable tourism, and rural tourism; the perspectives on rural tourism destination; rural tourism and entrepreneurship; the importance of sustainable tourism in the global economy; and the importance of rural tourism in the global economy. The fulfillment of sustainable tourism and rural tourism is necessary for modern tourism organizations that seek to serve suppliers and customers, increase business performance, strengthen competitiveness, and achieve continuous success in the global economy. Therefore, it is essential for modern tourism organizations to promote their sustainable tourism and rural tourism and develop a strategic plan to regularly check their practical advancements toward satisfying customer requirement. The chapter argues that promoting sustainable tourism and rural tourism has the potential to enhance organizational performance and gain sustainable competitive advantage in the global economy.

INTRODUCTION

Tourism is one of the most growing economic activities across the globe, and the nature-based tourism is a major component of the tourism industry (Lange, 2015). Tourism depends on the environmental, physical, and cultural resources (Simão & Partidário, 2012). The importance of tourism as an economic activity having a great impact on economic growth and job creation is recognized (Blancas, Lozano-Oyola, & González, 2015). Career and job opportunities can be created due to the expansion of tourism and hospitality businesses toward business success and economic growth (Kasemsap, 2016a). Sustainable tourism is regularly linked with the preservation of ecosystems, the promotion of human welfare, and public participation in decision making (Bramwell, 2015). Sustainable tourism focuses on the balance

DOI: 10.4018/978-1-5225-2078-8.ch005

of the triple bottom line (TBL) among environmental, sociocultural, and economic perspectives (Long, Vogelaar, & Hale, 2014).

Rural tourism is a new form of activity that can bring economic and social benefits to the society (Ghasemi & Hamzah, 2014). Rural tourism is an important tool for rural revitalization (Jaafar, Rasoolimanesh, & Lonik, 2015). Rural tourism can be considered as the potentially good product in promoting the country as well as getting the community involved in the tourism industry (Amir, Ghapar, Jamal, & Ahmad, 2015). Rural tourism is an opportunity for promoting the natural framework, comfortable accommodation, and personalized tourism experiences (Gavrila-Paven, 2015). Rural tourism incorporates various aspects of sustainable development, environmental protection, and development of entrepreneurship in direct activities and those related to tourism traditions and rural life in rural areas (Balan & Burghelea, 2015).

This chapter aims to bridge the gap on the thorough literature consolidation of sustainable tourism and rural tourism. The extensive literatures of sustainable tourism and rural tourism provide a contribution to practitioners and researchers by indicating the advanced issues and implications of sustainable tourism and rural tourism in order to maximize the business impact of sustainable tourism and rural tourism in the global economy.

BACKGROUND

The concept of sustainability has been used to preserve the limited resources due to the rapid increase in population and tourism development (Samsudin & Maliki, 2015). Sustainability can be the policy goal for almost all kinds and scales of tourism activities and environments (Moscardo, 2008). Sustainability has become a practical concept that is beneficial to the progress of tourism development (Chen, 2015). Sustainability is a driver for tourism sector development (Simão & Partidário, 2012). The goal of sustainability-oriented tourism development requires a number of human resource development (HRD) strategies aimed at the tourism industry personnel, host community, and the tourists, and established by the concepts and practices of sustainability (Jithendran & Baum, 2000).

Sociocultural sustainability includes human capital (e.g., awareness, experience, knowledge, skills, and behavior), and incorporates basic human rights (Cottrell, Vaske, & Roemer, 2013). Socioeconomic growth and developments have led to human communities toward the creation of tourism opportunities, which are likely to be considered as ways of spending leisure and reducing the impacts of tensions resulting from a rigorous urban and industrial life (Erfani, Afrougheh, Ardakani, & Sadeghi, 2015). Emissions from tourism and their contribution to climate change significantly set a major challenge for the sustainability of international tourism (Hall, Scott, & Gössling, 2013). Performing the environmentally friendly operations allows a tourism entity to build its image as an operation that cares about the living environment of human beings (Chiu, Lee, & Chen, 2014).

The outlook of sustainable tourism has spread over the last thirty years (Liu, Horng, & Chou, 2015). Research on the aspects of tourism and sustainability is growing with a concern that sustainable tourism principles are difficult to implement in developing countries (Reddy, 2008). Tourism studies on sustainable issues have shifted to focus on tourists' views to understand sustainable tourist consumption behavior (Deng & Li, 2015). Pulido-Fernández et al. (2015) stated that sustainable tourism brings economic benefit to nations, and a marketing program is essential for economic success. Nature-based tourism can contribute to economic development and can create strong incentives for sustainable management and ecosystem conservation when it generates income and employment to the local economy (Lange, 2015).

Rural areas are recognized for their complex, multifunctional capacities with a range of different interest groups claiming their rights to, and use of, different rural spaces (McAreavey & McDonagh, 2011). Zhang et al. (2015) indicated that with the development of rural tourism, the cooperation of villages has become very important. Leader approach offers a new opportunity for the development of rural communities through the organization of the local action groups, which must consider the problems the territory concerns, to define strategy, prioritize objectives, and implement its rural tourism development programs (Gavrila-Paven, 2015). Nunkoo and Gursoy (2012) indicated that rural tourism benefits local communities in terms of economic growth, sociocultural development, the provision of essential and non-essential services, and rising standards of living.

Bramwell and Lane (1994) stated that rural tourism include the activities about farming, nature, adventure, sports, health, education, arts, and heritage. Tourism in rural areas is developed utilizing the essential characters and resources of a particular place which include natural environments, local culture, and traditional system of land use and farming (Falak, Chiun, & Wee, 2014). The benefits of rural tourism can contribute to the development of positive attitudes among local communities concerning rural tourism development (Jurowski, Uysal, & Williams, 1997). Rural tourism often favors the substantial local support, receiving direct financial assistance from both the public and private sectors (Fleischer & Pizam, 1997). The capacity for rural tourism activities in rural areas varies regarding local resources (Lane, 1994).

SUSTAINABLE TOURISM AND RURAL TOURISM IN THE GLOBAL ECONOMY

This section emphasizes the overviews of tourism, sustainable development, sustainable tourism, and rural tourism; the perspectives on rural tourism destination; rural tourism and entrepreneurship; the importance of sustainable tourism in the global economy; and the importance of rural tourism in the global economy.

Overview of Tourism

Tourism is one of the largest economic sectors (Klak, 2007). Tourism is an increasingly important source of income, employment, and wealth in many countries (Neto, 2003). Tourism is important for the economic development and poverty alleviation in developing countries (Scott, Gössling, & Hall, 2012). Tourism has the prospective to mark a positive economic influence (Prabhakaran, Nair, & Ramachandran, 2014). In order to survive in an increasingly competitive and global environment, tourism companies, especially the small ones, must differentiate from the competitors utilizing innovation tools (Cosma, Paun, Bota, & Fleseriu, 2014).

Tourism is expected to grow substantially and to account for an increasingly large share of global greenhouse gas emissions, particularly if other sectors manage to achieve absolute emission reductions (Gössling, Scott, & Hall, 2013). Tourism can be a challenging industry due to its volatile nature and susceptibility to a wide range of influences (Shakya, 2011). If tourism develops without any specific plan or strategy to navigate these challenges, environmental and societal problems can intervene to the point where the negative effects of tourism on the host community will exceed its benefits (Sheykhi, 2009).

Tourism has become a very important non-agricultural sector of economic growth, it is expected to continue its positive performance, and it is regarded as an important component of the promoted sectoral diversification of the national economy (UNWTO, 2014). Positive economic effects and an improvement in the return on investment (ROI) by direct and indirect revenues from tourism are expected to result in the tourism-related jobs and the increasing incomes (Tekken & Kropp, 2015). With wise guidance and strict supervision, tourism development undertaken by the private sector can be both economically viable and developed and operated in an environmentally sensitive manner (Hu & Wall, 2005).

Tourism marketing keeps up with the dynamic evolutions and the demands of tourism industry in relation to the diversity of tourism marketing in modern organizations (Kasemsap, 2015a). Regarding the increasing advances in technology, information technology and knowledge management effectively improve the strategic tools for providing the direct link between customers and tourism organizations, thus encouraging the communication channels in global tourism (Kasemsap, 2016b). Tourism development has the social, economic, and environmental impacts on tourist destinations (Li et al., 2004). Tourism development policy should take into account both tourists' and locals' life modes in order to progress toward sustainable rural tourism development (Hjalager, 2004).

Overview of Sustainable Development

Sustainable development is one of the most cited examples of actions that make a community more resilient (Edwards, 2009). Sustainable development is a major conceptual framework for community and social development, and it incorporates a long-term perspective on resource exploitation (Amir et al., 2015). The vulnerability of tourism-dependent communities, coastal tourism facilities, and beaches to climate change demands the application of measures that can urgently minimize vulnerability and in the long term achieve sustainable development (Mycoo, 2014). Issues of power and politics are central to the development of the tourism sector and its prospects for contributing to sustainable development (Scheyvens, 2011).

International tourism is portrayed by many agencies and governments as an important contributor to sustainable development strategies (Hall et al., 2013). Place, location, and locality are examined in the context of the development of tourism in a way that is consistent with the concept of sustainable development (Eligh, Welford, & Ytterhus, 2002). Management of tourism resources is restricted by limited coordination between industry and government, and especially by inadequate resource provision to local authorities and land management agencies (Priskin, 2003). Ecotourism offers sustainable development opportunities in under-developed countries (Doan, 2013). Almeyda et al. (2010) stated that ecotourism promotes responsible travel to natural areas, environmental conservation and the well-being of local communities.

Overview of Sustainable Tourism

Tourism has the potential to destroy the available common environmental resources through overuse and poor management practices, as limited information revelation and poor monitoring of actions encourage the perpetuation and extension of environmental problems (Karatzoglou & Spilanis, 2010). The notions of corporate social responsibility (CSR) and sustainable tourism development have become the major parts of corporate strategies for tourism businesses (Kasemsap, 2016c). In response to the movement toward conservation in relation to social justice concerns, tourism academics and practitioners have furnished a variety of propositions on the prevailing challenges to sustainable development and have paved a successful path for sustainability in tourism operations (Chen, 2015).

Sustainable tourism is a range of environment-based activities and it follows that the sustainability of resources utilized during the execution of touristic activities is of great importance (Ekinci, 2014). Sustainable tourism is based on the concept of sustainable development which raised the need for a respectful, equitable, responsible and preserving interaction of humans and the environment (Tekken & Kropp, 2015). Sustainable tourism research increasingly utilizes the social science-related ideas and concepts, including those developed in critical perspectives, such as political economy, post-structuralism, and post-colonialism (Bramwell & Lane, 2014).

Sustainable tourism includes the issues around the physical and natural environment so it can engage with concepts and ideas in scientific fields, such as climatology and oceanography (Miller & Twining-Ward, 2005). Strategic marketing management can play an important role in the development of sustainable tourism principles (Gilmore & Simmons, 2007). The success of sustainable tourism implementation depends on the government's ability to organize managerial tasks and the interests of stakeholders through suitable strategies (Farmaki, Altinay, Botterill, & Hilke, 2015). The development of adequate sustainability criteria and the regular monitoring of the implementation systematically need to be steered by public institutions (e.g., planning authorities) to ensure the sustainability compliance of tourism businesses (Bramwell, 2011).

However, in the last few decades, responsible tourism has emerged as a significant trend in the Western world, as wider consumer market trends toward lifestyle marketing and ethical consumption have spread to tourism (Goodwin & Francis, 2003). Tourism organizations realize that promoting their ethical perspectives can be the favorable issue toward enhancing a company's profits, management effectiveness, public image, and employee relations in an ethical manner (Hudson & Miller, 2005). Organizations and leaders can change and develop the existing organizational ethical culture by establishing ethical codes, providing training to recognize ethical dilemmas, and informing ethical behavior suitable for ethical organizations (Kasemsap, 2015b).

Overview of Rural Tourism

Rural tourism is a composite of agricultural products, eco-products, cultural resources, and spatial amenities, involving many functions, such as economic, social, educational, environmental, recreational, and therapeutic activities (Lee & Kim, 2010). Rural tourism is defined as the tourism perspective related to rural areas, small-scale enterprises, open space, and sustainability (Reichel, Lowengart, & Milman, 2000). Rural tourism has long been considered as the method of accelerating the economic and social development, and has become the development tool for rural areas (Keyim, Yang, & Zhang, 2005). Tourism experience is very important for rural areas, which need to develop the appealing and distinctive offerings for a demanding and heterogeneous tourism market (Loureiro, 2014). The quality of the tourism experience is the major endogenous factor that positively affects expenditures for rural tourism (Skuras, Petrou, & Clark, 2006). Kastenholz et al. (2012) indicated that the population and tourism suppliers also have an important influence in shaping the tourist experience.

In recent years, the growing rural tourism becomes a real competitor to resorts and hotels (Snieška, Barkauskiene, & Barkauskas, 2014). Dimitrovski et al. (2012) explained that rural tourism is the descriptor of cultural activities associated with rural communities. Rural tourism, as an important form of the consumption of rural space, allows practitioners to explore the concept of the rural tourism in the context of rurality (Bell, 2006). Rural tourism has the intrinsic qualities of a sense of space, peace, and tranquility (Sharpley & Sharpley, 1997). The pursuit of sustainable development in rural regions has revealed that tourism is the important area of policy action which complements the traditional and agriculture-oriented rural tourism policies (Fleischer & Felsenstein, 2000).

Rural tourism can be considered as a complex plurality of multifaceted tourism activities, contributing both to the growth of economic activities in rural areas and to the improvement of life quality for local inhabitants (Naghiu, Vázquez, & Georgiev, 2005). The active support of local residents will have an influence on the success of rural tourism development (Palmer, Koenig-Lewis, & Jones, 2013). Local community participation is expected to improve the local resource management and the distribution of the economic benefits of rural tourism. Once a local community becomes a tourist destination, the lives of residents in the local community are affected by the rural tourism activities (Kim, Uysal, & Sirgy, 2013).

Rural tourism-related small businesses in rural areas often lack the governmental supports, including financial services, training programs, and other incentives for local community support for tourism activities (Ateljevic, 2009). The implementation and completion of regional and municipal programs can support rural tourism as part of the comprehensive development of rural territories (Barlybaev, Akhmetov, & Nasyrov, 2009). Bel et al. (2015) stated that rural tourism is related to the domestic activities, which often require low spending. MacDonald and Jolliffe (2003) indicated that rural tourism has become the important issue of encouraging the declining traditional industries, thus contributing toward the conservation of cultural traditions while simultaneously contributing toward the development of the local rural economy.

In the context of rural tourism, the quality of service offered by rural tourism providers is an essential factor in attracting customers (Rozman et al., 2009). The rural tourism plans often give the importance to economic gains and tourist satisfaction and less emphasis is being placed on the participation of local communities (Liu, 2006). The local community is an important stakeholder in rural tourism (Falak et al., 2014). Active participation of local communities is significant for a successful rural tourism and a high level of community integration in tourism planning leads to the greater socioeconomic benefits (Mitchell & Reid, 2001). Residents' participation may play an important role in the decision making process of the tourism initiatives (Sdrali, Goussia-Rizou, & Kiourtidou, 2015).

Remote communities often lack educational opportunities for small business owners to understand the intricacies of business management, marketing, and the tourism industry, often lack the capital or other sources of finance with which to maintain a business during a downturn, and are more strongly affected by the seasonal nature of tourism (Ateljevic & Doorne, 2000). The deployment of information and communication technology (ICT) is essential for the competitiveness of rural tourism businesses (Peña & Jamilena, 2010). The use of ICT is considered as a competitive strategy for rural tourism enterprises toward improving the outcomes of business activity (Peña & Jamilena, 2011).

Perspectives on Rural Tourism Destination

Rural tourism destinations have to invest in facilities and services (e.g., accommodation and infrastructures) to complement the natural and cultural conveniences (Fleischer & Tchetchik, 2005) to meet the expectations of consumers, while the availability of tourism infrastructure does not automatically lead to the development of rural areas (Dissart, Aubert, & Truchet, 2009). Rural tourism destination images can be utilized to practically link the representations of rurality with rural tourism destination marketing

(Zhou, 2014). The distribution of tourist demand results from the heterogeneous nature of consumer preferences, which is a product of rural tourism destination competitiveness (Dwyer & Kim, 2003).

Rural tourism destination communities must learn to adapt to the seasonal nature of tourism, developing the different types of tourism production around each seasonal trend, and adjusting the level of public services (Flognfeldt, 2001). It is necessary for rural tourism destination communities to have alternative income sources during the off-season when tourist density is at its lowest level, and government service providers may need to reallocate services during these times (Jaafar et al., 2015). Rural stays may reflect the preference of tourists for the different types of the existing activities and facilities in a particular rural destination and their spending behaviors (Bel et al., 2015).

Rajaratnam et al. (2014) stated that the assessment of tourists' satisfaction of the rural tourism destinations can assist the rural tourism practitioners to have a better understanding of tourists' perceptions and to emphasize their efforts to enhance tourists' positive experiences in the rural tourism destinations. It becomes imperative to develop a destination management and destination marketing for rural tourism that will be responsible for promoting the existing tourism business (Wang & Fesenmaier, 2007). Both destination management organizations and destination marketing organizations complement each other (Adeyinka-Ojo, Khoo-Lattimore, & Nair, 2014).

Rural Tourism and Entrepreneurship

The tourism industry, especially rural tourism, is largely dominated by small and medium-sized enterprises (SMEs) (Cosma et al., 2014). Entrepreneurship emphasizes opportunities to operate businesses and organizations (Zhao, Ritchie, & Echtner, 2011). Entrepreneurship has a significant influence on the evolution of tourist destinations (Russell & Faulkner, 2004). Entrepreneurs are drawn to small businesses in the tourism sector by their desire to provide employment for their families, earn additional income, support their lifestyle, and fulfill their interests (Getz & Carlsen, 2000).

Entrepreneurship in rural tourism can be promoted by governments by allocating the resources to commercialize the new products (Schendel & Hitt, 2007). Governments can promote partnerships between small businesses and larger tourism organizations concerning marketing perspectives (Gaddefors, 2005). The seasonal nature of tourism, especially rural tourism, has been cited as a constraint on small businesses in tourism sector (Getz & Nilsson, 2004). Small businesses in the rural tourism sector significantly experience a number of operational obstacles, such as a lack of basic knowledge concerning business management and the tourism sector, financial difficulties, and the seasonal nature of tourism (Krannich & Petrzelka, 2003).

Importance of Sustainable Tourism in the Global Economy

Tourism is a major source of foreign exchange earnings, export income, and total economic output (Mshenga & Richardson, 2013). Travel and tourism are known as a cultural and economic activity in different societies (Bazneshin, Hosseini, & Azeri, 2015). The major attributes of the sustainable tourism include the environmental conservation, education, and distribution of income to local people based on strong partnership (Singh & Mishra, 2004). It is possible to utilize tourism as a way to balance natural resource conservation and economic development under the preconditions of making effective policies to encourage and help local people participate in tourism business and to gain the benefit from it (Li, Zhang, Liu, & Xue, 2006).

Understanding the contribution of sustainable tourism to the domestic economy, employment, the balance of payments is necessary to determine how much to invest in tourism and supporting activities (Lange, 2015). Failed sustainable tourism implementation derives from the dominance of an economic imperative directing tourism development (Dabhnet, Scott, & Ruhanen, 2012). Other inhibiting factors of sustainable tourism include political misdirection, volatility, and conflict (Ruhanen, 2013). Poverty reduction and economic development will depend on sustainable management of its natural capital, especially the coastal ecosystem (Ruitenbeek, Hewawasan, & Ngoile, 2005).

The social context in which policymaking takes place and institutional arrangements pertaining to tourism planning are influential in shaping tourism development (Farmaki et al., 2015). A growing body of literature has documented efforts made by tourism enterprises to reduce pollution and improve the sustainability of their businesses including the best practices of zero waste initiatives (Sealey & Smith, 2014). Partnerships and networks are the prerequisites for the acceptance of the sustainable tourism development of the communities (Bitsani & Kavoura, 2014).

The significance of involving stakeholders in sustainable tourism initiatives is increasingly acknowledged and recommended within both academic and practical perspectives (Waligo, Clarke, & Hawkins, 2015). This appreciation stems from the nature of tourism destinations as networks of interdependent stakeholders (Cooper, Scott, & Baggio, 2009) and emerging sustainable tourism practices that rely on stakeholder partnerships in the global economy (Gössling, Hall, & Weaver, 2009). There are studies of failures of sustainable tourism strategies associated with ineffective stakeholder involvement (Dodds & Butler, 2010) and studies of uncertainty in the capability of some stakeholders to contribute meaningfully to tourism processes (Hamilton & Alexander, 2013).

Importance of Rural Tourism in the Global Economy

The tourism industry affords significant economic development opportunities for rural areas with natural, historic and cultural attractions, and a people willing to host visitors (Ghanian, Ghoochani, & Crotts, 2014). Rural tourism has been widely recognized for its effectiveness in contributing to rural areas' development (Park, Lee, & Yoon, 2014). Rural tourism is one of the most important strategies for the community to achieve better living conditions (Amir et al., 2015). The main idea of rural tourism is for the community to create a project that presents a sustainable development and promote the relationship between local community and tourists (Amir et al., 2015).

The shift from a basic rural economy to a new economic specialization involves experimentation, learning processes, new capabilities, new policies, adjustment, and reconfigurations (Randelli, Romei, & Tortora, 2014). Rural tourism is the determining factor in rural development and the driving force in some cases for the development of a region (Haven-Tang & Jones, 2012). Rural tourism is regarded as the important economic strategy for improving rural social conditions (Liu, 2006). Rural tourism significantly offers the ideal market for small businesses, thus bringing economic benefits to local businesses and encouraging the development of rural tourism-related small businesses (Campbell, 1999). Rural tourism significantly benefits the rural and isolated areas by serving as the impetus for development, revitalizing traditional industries on the boundary of extinction (MacDonald & Jolliffe, 2003).

Rural tourism facilitates rediscovering the values of rural resources that have been disregarded in the modernization process of the global economy (Hwang & Lee, 2015). Rural tourism is one of the most motivational patterns of tourist circulation, and represents a form of tourism in rural areas (Gavrila-Paven, 2015). The growth of rural tourism practically mirrors both a general expansion of all types of tourism and a diversification of tourist experiences (Woods, 2005), closely associated both with the rise of a lifestyle-led and leisure-oriented society, and with the widespread mobilization of tourism as a strategy for rural development and regeneration (Walmsley, 2003). The level of diversification significantly determines rural tourism development (Hegarty & Przezborska, 2005).

Rural tourism stimulates local economic development, creating job opportunities, and bringing in both domestic and foreign revenue (Gurung & DeCoursey, 2000). Strengthening the links to the local economy can increase the proportion of tourist spending that goes to the poor and can reduce poverty (Mitchell & Ashley, 2010). Brown and Hall (2000) stated that remote and difficult to reach places are perceived by tourists as having certain idiosyncratic qualities by virtue of their isolation, such as natural beauty, quietness, and uniqueness. Guzman-Parra et al. (2015) stated that it is advisable to promote rural tourism as the beneficial approach to fostering regional development. Policy on poverty and rural tourism should be informed by an understanding of the rural households' existing livelihood portfolios and the strategic decisions which create them (Biddulph, 2015).

Rural tourism, especially in developing countries, provides the valuable source of employment and income for local community members, reduce poverty, and drives the environmental preservation efforts (Ryan, Gu, & Zhang, 2009). Rural tourism represents a significant source of income and employment for rural economies (Hummelbrunner & Miglbauer, 1994), revitalizing rural economies (Din, 1993). Hall (2004) indicated that rural tourism significantly benefits the local communities by providing the supplementary sources of income to local farming, craft, and service sectors; the opportunity to realize the economic value of high-quality local food products; and the opportunity to reevaluate the region's heritage, symbols, environment, and identity.

Rural tourism is the developing tourism industry in many parts of the world, but mainly in developed countries, and has expanded since the 1970s, both in terms of demand and of supply (Lane, 2009). On the supply side, rural tourism provides a number of potential benefits to rural areas (Roberts & Hall, 2001). The demand for tourist attractions in rural areas often serves to stimulate the creation of rural tourism-related small businesses (Irvine & Anderson, 2004). In spite of the positive effects that it may have in some cases, tourism is not a remedy to the problems facing rural areas, that not all rural spaces are suitable for the development of tourism and, similarly, that tourism development often fails to stimulate the expected socioeconomic revitalization (Silva, 2015).

The benefits of rural tourism result in economic growth with the new primary sources of income from business catering to the immediate requirements of tourists, secondary incomes through the sale of handicrafts and other region-specific products, income protection, and employment opportunities (Sharpley, 2000). Clarke (2000) indicated that there are the increasing opportunities for rural businesses in the perspectives of accommodation, catering, information, transport, facilities, and other services for rural tourism development. However, the growth of rural tourism may negatively affect the rural communities concerning the amount of trash, the loss of tranquility, and the rising crime (Park, Lee, Choi, & Yoon, 2012).

FUTURE RESEARCH DIRECTIONS

The classification of the extensive literature in the domains of sustainable tourism and rural tourism will provide the potential opportunities for future research. The big part of the money that tourists will spend during their stay in the Asian countries, will go to the hospitality and tourism businesses. Local and international tourists traveling in the Asian countries will bring a lot of beneficial opportunities for tourism-related jobs and incomes, especially gained from sustainable tourism and rural tourism. Many tourism attractions (e.g., natural environment, the tropical sea, the beaches, and the mountainous areas) are in the Asian countries without any investment. Habitations and the cultural habits are very attractive for local and international tourists. These tourist attractions are almost free of investments.

To stimulate the tourism in Asia, investments are needed in the infrastructure. Facilities are needed in the tourist ports where the arrivals of the tourists are. In the specific tourist locations in the Asian countries, the water and electricity supply should be sufficient. The accommodations in the places where the tourists want to stay, have to be adjusted to the requirements of different tourists. All these facilities should be developed in a sufficient way. Developing the tourism sector is easier than developing the industrial sector. Enormous investments are needed to attract the foreign companies and develop the basic infrastructure for sustainable tourism and rural tourism. Particular investments are needed to have good accessible ports, power stations, communication infrastructure, and industrial zones. Sustainable tourism and rural tourism need far less investments.

Medical tourism represents a transitional phase between the formerly closed health care systems of the last century and a future of a fully globalized medical system with remote robotic operations controlled from anywhere in the world (Kasemsap, 2015c). Through electronic commerce (e-commerce), organizations can easily calculate and evaluate sales effectiveness, customer effectiveness, marketing campaigns, product mix, and customer engagement in global marketplace (Kasemsap, 2016d). From the business point of view, e-commerce provides better connectivity for its potential customer as their respective website can be virtually accessed from anywhere through the Internet (Kasemsap, 2016e).

Social media marketing provides organizations with a way to connect with their customers (Kasemsap, 2016f) and improves effective communication, increases thought leadership, enhances sales, and provides better customer service (Kasemsap, 2016g). Future research direction should broaden the important aspects in the promotion of medical tourism, sustainable tourism, and rural tourism through e-commerce and social media marketing in the Asia-based hospitality and tourism organizations. It will be useful to bring the additional disciplines together (e.g., strategic management, marketing, finance, and human resources) to support the promotion of sustainable tourism and rural tourism in the Asian countries.

CONCLUSION

This chapter highlighted the overviews of tourism, sustainable development, sustainable tourism, and rural tourism; the perspectives on rural tourism destination; rural tourism and entrepreneurship; the importance of sustainable tourism in the global economy; and the importance of rural tourism in the global economy. Tourism is one of the world's fastest growing industries and is an important source of foreign exchange and employment for many developing countries. The integrated approach to tourism management is required to achieve sustainable tourism. Tourism has to be sustainable in all three areas (i.e., environmental, sociocultural, and economic perspectives) to be considered as sustainable tourism.

Regarding environmental sustainability, both the natural environment (e.g., beaches, forests, and waterways) and the built environment (e.g., historic buildings and ruins) must be preserved for an area to be environmentally sustainable. Sociocultural sustainability means minimizing the negative impacts (e.g., increased congestion, overcrowding, and increased crime) of tourists on the host community and focusing on more positive impacts, such as promoting cultural exchange and preserving local traditions. Economic sustainability means building linkages, reducing leakages, and keeping the money local.

The important principles of sustainable tourism development include: tourism should be initiated with the help of broad-based community-inputs and the community should maintain control of tourism development; tourism should provide quality employment to its community residents and a linkage between the local businesses and tourism should be established; guidelines for tourism operations, impact assessment, monitoring of cumulative impacts, and limits to acceptable change should be established; and education and training programs to manage natural resources should be established. Promoting sustainable tourism choices may depend on more than one policy tool regarding good consumer intentions combined with the labeling confusion and lack of awareness. Sustainable tourism examines a package of measures including communications campaigns and labeling, certification and verification of sustainable destinations and tours, fines for unsustainable activities, and subsidies for sustainable energy, wastewater and waste treatment as well as recyclable buildings in tourism settings.

Rural tourism is one of the leading alternative tourism types in the global economy. Rural tourism is a new strategy for strengthening economic structure in rural area and is an opportunity for tourists who want to take a vacation while learning about historical, cultural and natural beauties. As rural tourism is one of the major elements of rural development and therefore it takes place in the development policies of many countries, it is a crucial phenomenon in the global economy. The effects of rural tourism on local people's income, employment, and investments are essential for the development and renewal of rural areas. The effects of rural tourism on social structure and culture of rural areas are significant in the global economy. Concerning rural tourism, governments and local administrations should support the rural tourism programs and utilize every opportunity to encourage rural tourism in their regions toward achieving the business success and economic growth in the global economy.

The fulfillment of sustainable tourism and rural tourism is necessary for modern tourism organizations that seek to serve suppliers and customers, increase business performance, strengthen competitiveness, and achieve continuous success in the global economy. Therefore, it is essential for modern tourism organizations to promote their sustainable tourism and rural tourism and develop a strategic plan to regularly check their practical advancements toward satisfying customer requirement. Promoting sustainable tourism and rural tourism has the potential to enhance organizational performance and gain sustainable competitive advantage in the global economy.

REFERENCES

Adeyinka-Ojo, S. F., Khoo-Lattimore, C., & Nair, V. (2014). A framework for rural tourism destination management and marketing organisations. *Procedia: Social and Behavioral Sciences*, *144*, 151–163. doi:10.1016/j.sbspro.2014.07.284

Almeyda, A. M., Broadbent, E. N., Wyman, M. S., & Durham, W. H. (2010). Ecotourism impacts in the Nicoya Peninsula, Costa Rica. *International Journal of Tourism Research*, *12*(6), 803–819. doi:10.1002/jtr.797

Amir, A. F., Ghapar, A. A., Jamal, S. A., & Ahmad, K. N. (2015). Sustainable tourism development: A study on community resilience for rural tourism in Malaysia. *Procedia: Social and Behavioral Sciences*, *168*, 116–122. doi:10.1016/j.sbspro.2014.10.217

Ateljevic, I., & Doorne, S. (2000). "Staying within the fence": Lifestyle entrepreneurship in tourism. *Journal of Sustainable Tourism*, *8*(5), 378–392. doi:10.1080/09669580008667374

Ateljevic, J. (2009). Tourism entrepreneurship and regional development: Example from New Zealand. *International Journal of Entrepreneurial Behavior & Research*, *15*(3), 282–308. doi:10.1108/13552550910957355

Balan, M., & Burghelea, C. (2015). Rural tourism and its implication in the development of the Fundata village. *Procedia: Social and Behavioral Sciences*, *188*, 276–281. doi:10.1016/j.sbspro.2015.03.393

Barlybaev, A. A., Akhmetov, V. Y., & Nasyrov, G. M. (2009). Tourism as a factor of rural economy diversification. *Studies on Russian Economic Development*, *20*(6), 639–643. doi:10.1134/S1075700709060094

Bazneshin, S. D., Hosseini, S. B., & Azeri, A. R. K. (2015). The physical variables of tourist areas to increase the tourists' satisfaction regarding the sustainable tourism criteria: Case study of Rudsar villages, Sefidab in Rahim Abad. *Procedia: Social and Behavioral Sciences*, *201*, 128–135. doi:10.1016/j.sbspro.2015.08.141

Bel, F., Lacroix, A., Lyser, S., Rambonilaza, T., & Turpin, N. (2015). Domestic demand for tourism in rural areas: Insights from summer stays in three French regions. *Tourism Management*, *46*, 562–570. doi:10.1016/j.tourman.2014.07.020

Bell, D. (2006). Variations on the rural idyll. In P. Cloke, T. Marsden, & P. Mooney (Eds.), *Handbook of rural studies* (pp. 149–160). London, UK: Sage Publications. doi:10.4135/9781848608016.n10

Biddulph, R. (2015). Limits to mass tourism's effects in rural peripheries. *Annals of Tourism Research*, *50*(1), 98–112. doi:10.1016/j.annals.2014.11.011

Bitsani, E., & Kavoura, A. (2014). Host perceptions of rural tour marketing to sustainable tourism in Central Eastern Europe. The case study of Istria, Croatia. *Procedia: Social and Behavioral Sciences*, *148*, 362–369. doi:10.1016/j.sbspro.2014.07.054

Blancas, F. J., Lozano-Oyola, M., & González, M. (2015). A European sustainable tourism labels proposal using a composite indicator. *Environmental Impact Assessment Review*, *54*, 39–54. doi:10.1016/j.eiar.2015.05.001

Bramwell, B. (2011). Governance, the state and sustainable tourism: A political economy approach. *Journal of Sustainable Tourism*, *19*(4/5), 459–477. doi:10.1080/09669582.2011.576765

Bramwell, B. (2015). Theoretical activity in sustainable tourism research. *Annals of Tourism Research*, *54*, 204–218. doi:10.1016/j.annals.2015.07.005

Bramwell, B., & Lane, B. (1994). Rural tourism as a factor in rural community economic development for economies in transition. *Journal of Sustainable Tourism*, *2*(1/2), 51–60.

Bramwell, B., & Lane, B. (2014). The "critical turn" and its implications for sustainable tourism research. *Journal of Sustainable Tourism*, *22*(1), 1–8. doi:10.1080/09669582.2013.855223

Brown, F., & Hall, D. D. (2000). *Tourism in peripheral areas: Case studies*. Buffalo, NY: Channel View Publications.

Campbell, L. M. (1999). Ecotourism in rural developing communities. *Annals of Tourism Research, 26*(3), 534–553. doi:10.1016/S0160-7383(99)00005-5

Chen, J. S. (2015). Tourism stakeholders attitudes toward sustainable development: A case in the Arctic. *Journal of Retailing and Consumer Services, 22*(1), 225–230. doi:10.1016/j.jretconser.2014.08.003

Chiu, Y. T. H., Lee, W. I., & Chen, T. H. (2014). Environmentally responsible behavior in ecotourism: Antecedents and implications. *Tourism Management, 40*, 321–329. doi:10.1016/j.tourman.2013.06.013

Clarke, J. (2000). Tourism brands: An exploratory study of the brands box model. *Journal of Vacation Marketing, 6*(4), 329–345. doi:10.1177/135676670000600404

Cooper, C., Scott, N., & Baggio, R. (2009). Network position and perceptions of destination stakeholder importance. *Anatolia: An International Journal of Tourism and Hospitality Research, 20*(1), 33–45. doi:10.1080/13032917.2009.10518893

Cosma, S., Paun, D., Bota, M., & Fleseriu, C. (2014). Innovation: A useful tool in the rural tourism in Romania. *Procedia: Social and Behavioral Sciences, 148*, 507–515. doi:10.1016/j.sbspro.2014.07.073

Cottrell, S. P., Vaske, J. J., & Roemer, J. M. (2013). Resident satisfaction with sustainable tourism: The case of Frankenwald Nature Park, Germany. *Tourism Management Perspectives, 8*, 42–48. doi:10.1016/j.tmp.2013.05.005

Dabhnet, S., Scott, N., & Ruhanen, L. (2012). Applying diffusion theory to destination stakeholder understanding of sustainable tourism development: A case from Thailand. *Journal of Sustainable Tourism, 20*(8), 1107–1124. doi:10.1080/09669582.2012.673618

Deng, J., & Li, J. (2015). Self-identification of ecotourists. *Journal of Sustainable Tourism, 23*(2), 255–279. doi:10.1080/09669582.2014.934374

Dimitrovski, D. D., Todorović, A. T., & Valjarević, A. D. (2012). Rural tourism and regional development: Case study of development of rural tourism in the region of Gruţa, Serbia. *Procedia Environmental Sciences, 14*, 288–297. doi:10.1016/j.proenv.2012.03.028

Din, K. (1993). Dialogue with hosts: An educational strategy towards sustainable tourism. In V. Hitchcock & M. Parnwell (Eds.), *Tourism in South-East Asia* (pp. 327–336). London, UK: Routledge.

Dissart, J. C., Aubert, F., & Truchet, S. (2009). An estimation of tourism dependence in French rural areas. In A. Matias, P. Nijkamp, & M. Sarmento (Eds.), *Advances in tourism economics* (pp. 273–294). New York, NY: Physica–Verlag/Springer. doi:10.1007/978-3-7908-2124-6_17

Doan, T. M. (2013). Sustainable ecotourism in Amazonia: Evaluation of six sites in Southeastern Peru. *International Journal of Tourism Research, 15*(3), 261–271. doi:10.1002/jtr.1866

Dodds, R., & Butler, R. W. (2010). Barriers to implementing sustainable tourism policy in mass tourism destinations. *Tourismos: An International Multidisciplinary Journal of Tourism, 5*(1), 35–53.

Dwyer, L., & Kim, C. (2003). Destination competitiveness: Determinants and indicators. *Current Issues in Tourism, 6*(5), 369–414. doi:10.1080/13683500308667962

Edwards, C. (2009). *Resilient nation: How communities respond to systemic breakdown*. London, UK: Demos.

Ekinci, M. B. (2014). The Cittaslow philosophy in the context of sustainable tourism development: The case of Turkey. *Tourism Management*, *41*, 178–189. doi:10.1016/j.tourman.2013.08.013

Eligh, J., Welford, R., & Ytterhus, B. (2002). The production of sustainable tourism: Concepts and examples from Norway. *Sustainable Development*, *10*(4), 223–234. doi:10.1002/sd.195

Erfani, M., Afrougheh, S., Ardakani, T., & Sadeghi, A. (2015). Tourism positioning using decision support system (case study: Chahnime–Zabol, Iran). *Environmental Earth Sciences*, *74*(4), 3135–3144. doi:10.1007/s12665-015-4365-z

Falak, S., Chiun, L. M., & Wee, A. Y. (2014). A repositioning strategy for rural tourism in Malaysia: Community's perspective. *Procedia: Social and Behavioral Sciences*, *144*, 412–415. doi:10.1016/j.sbspro.2014.07.310

Farmaki, A., Altinay, L., Botterill, D., & Hilke, S. (2015). Politics and sustainable tourism: The case of Cyprus. *Tourism Management*, *47*, 178–190. doi:10.1016/j.tourman.2014.09.019

Fleischer, A., & Felsenstein, D. (2000). Support for small-scale rural tourism: Does it make a difference? *Annals of Tourism Research*, *27*(4), 1007–1024. doi:10.1016/S0160-7383(99)00126-7

Fleischer, A., & Pizam, A. (1997). Rural tourism in Israel. *Tourism Management*, *18*(6), 367–372. doi:10.1016/S0261-5177(97)00034-4

Fleischer, A., & Tchetchik, A. (2005). Does rural tourism benefit from agriculture? *Tourism Management*, *26*(4), 493–501. doi:10.1016/j.tourman.2003.10.003

Flognfeldt, T. (2001). Long-term positive adjustments to seasonality: Consequences of summer tourism in the Jotunheimen area, Norway. In T. Baum & S. Lundtorp (Eds.), *Seasonality in tourism* (pp. 109–117). New York, NY: Taylor & Francis Group. doi:10.1016/B978-0-08-043674-6.50010-6

Gaddefors, J. (2005). Creating context entrepreneurial opportunities in a consumer market setting. *Journal of Enterprising Culture*, *13*(3), 199–224. doi:10.1142/S0218495805000148

Gavrila-Paven, I. (2015). Tourism opportunities for valorising the authentic traditional rural space-study case: Ampoi and Mures Valleys microregion, Alba County, Romania. *Procedia: Social and Behavioral Sciences*, *188*, 111–115. doi:10.1016/j.sbspro.2015.03.345

Getz, D., & Carlsen, J. (2000). Characteristics and goals of family and owner-operated businesses in the rural tourism and hospitality sectors. *Tourism Management*, *21*(6), 547–560. doi:10.1016/S0261-5177(00)00004-2

Getz, D., & Nilsson, P. A. (2004). Responses of family businesses to extreme seasonality in demand: The case of Bornholm, Denmark. *Tourism Management*, *25*(1), 17–30. doi:10.1016/S0261-5177(03)00067-0

Ghanian, M., Ghoochani, O. M., & Crotts, J. C. (2014). An application of European Performance Satisfaction Index towards rural tourism: The case of western Iran. *Tourism Management Perspectives*, *11*, 77–82. doi:10.1016/j.tmp.2014.04.005

Ghasemi, M., & Hamzah, A. (2014). An investigation of the appropriateness of tourism development paradigms in rural areas from main tourism stakeholder's point of view. *Procedia: Social and Behavioral Sciences, 144*, 15–24. doi:10.1016/j.sbspro.2014.07.269

Gilmore, A., & Simmons, G. (2007). Integrating sustainable tourism and marketing management: Can National Parks provide the framework for strategic change? *Strategic Change, 16*(5), 191–200. doi:10.1002/jsc.798

Goodwin, H., & Francis, J. (2003). Ethical and responsible tourism: Consumer trends in the UK. *Journal of Vacation Marketing, 9*(3), 271–282. doi:10.1177/135676670300900306

Gössling, S., Hall, C. M., & Weaver, D. B. (2009). *Sustainable tourism futures: Perspective on systems, restructuring and innovations*. Abingdon, UK: Routledge.

Gössling, S., Scott, D., & Hall, C. M. (2013). Challenges of tourism in a low-carbon economy. *Wiley Interdisciplinary Reviews: Climate Change, 4*(6), 525–538. doi:10.1002/wcc.243

Gurung, C. P., & DeCoursey, M. A. (2000). Too much too fast: Lessons from Nepal's lost Kingdom of Mustang. In P. Godde, M. Price, & F. Zimmermann (Eds.), *Tourism and development in mountain regions* (pp. 239–253). Wallingford, UK: CABI Publishing.

Guzman-Parra, V. F., Quintana-García, C., Benavides-Velasco, C. A., & Vila-Oblitas, J. B. (2015). Trends and seasonal variation of tourist demand in Spain: The role of rural tourism. *Tourism Management Perspectives, 16*, 123–128. doi:10.1016/j.tmp.2015.07.014

Hall, C. M., Scott, D., & Gössling, S. (2013). The primacy of climate change for sustainable international tourism. *Sustainable Development, 21*(2), 112–121. doi:10.1002/sd.1562

Hall, D. (2004). Rural tourism development in southeastern Europe: Transition and the search for sustainability. *International Journal of Tourism Research, 6*(3), 165–176. doi:10.1002/jtr.482

Hamilton, K., & Alexander, M. (2013). Organic community tourism: A cocreated approach. *Annals of Tourism Research, 42*, 169–190. doi:10.1016/j.annals.2013.01.015

Haven-Tang, C., & Jones, E. (2012). Local leadership for rural tourism development: A case study of Adventa, Monmouthshire, UK. *Tourism Management Perspectives, 4*, 28–35. doi:10.1016/j.tmp.2012.04.006

Hegarty, C., & Przezborska, L. (2005). Rural and agri-tourism as a tool for reorganising rural areas in old and new member states: A comparison study of Ireland and Poland. *International Journal of Tourism Research, 7*(2), 63–77. doi:10.1002/jtr.513

Hjalager, A. M. (2004). Sustainable leisure life modes and rural welfare economy. The case of the Randers Fjord area, Denmark. *International Journal of Tourism Research, 6*(3), 177–188. doi:10.1002/jtr.483

Hu, W., & Wall, G. (2005). Economic and environmental symbiosis in a tourism attraction: An example from Hainan, China. *International Journal of Tourism Research, 7*(4/5), 295–310. doi:10.1002/jtr.533

Hudson, S., & Miller, G. (2005). The responsible marketing of tourism: The case of Canadian mountain holidays. *Tourism Management, 26*(2), 133–142. doi:10.1016/j.tourman.2003.06.005

Hummelbrunner, R., & Miglbauer, E. (1994). Tourism promotion and potential in peripheral areas: The Austrian case. *Journal of Sustainable Tourism*, *2*(1/2), 41–50. doi:10.1080/09669589409510682

Hwang, J., & Lee, S. (2015). The effect of the rural tourism policy on non-farm income in South Korea. *Tourism Management*, *46*, 501–513. doi:10.1016/j.tourman.2014.07.018

Irvine, W., & Anderson, A. R. (2004). Small tourist firms in rural areas: Agility, vulnerability and survival in the face of crisis. *International Journal of Entrepreneurial Behavior & Research*, *10*(4), 229–246. doi:10.1108/13552550410544204

Jaafar, M., Rasoolimanesh, S. M., & Lonik, K. A. T. (2015). Tourism growth and entrepreneurship: Empirical analysis of development of rural highlands. *Tourism Management Perspectives*, *14*, 17–24. doi:10.1016/j.tmp.2015.02.001

Jithendran, K. J., & Baum, T. (2000). Human resources development and sustainability: The case of Indian tourism. *International Journal of Tourism Research*, *2*(6), 403–421. doi:10.1002/1522-1970(200011/12)2:6<403::AID-JTR239>3.0.CO;2-3

Jurowski, C., Uysal, M., & Williams, D. R. (1997). A theoretical analysis of host community resident reactions to tourism. *Journal of Travel Research*, *36*(2), 3–11.

Karatzoglou, B., & Spilanis, I. (2010). Sustainable tourism in Greek islands: The integration of activity-based environmental management with a destination environmental scorecard based on the adaptive resource management paradigm. *Business Strategy and the Environment*, *19*(1), 26–38. doi:10.1002/bse.627

Kasemsap, K. (2015a). The role of marketing strategies in the tourism industry. In N. Ray (Ed.), *Emerging innovative marketing strategies in the tourism industry* (pp. 174–194). Hershey, PA: IGI Global. doi:10.4018/978-1-4666-8699-1.ch010

Kasemsap, K. (2015b). The role of ethical leadership in ethical organizations: A literature review. In C. Anyansi-Archibong (Ed.), *Contemporary issues surrounding ethical research methods and practice* (pp. 135–168). Hershey, PA: IGI Global. doi:10.4018/978-1-4666-8562-8.ch006

Kasemsap, K. (2015c). The role of medical tourism in emerging markets. In M. Cooper, K. Vafadari, & M. Hieda (Eds.), *Current issues and emerging trends in medical tourism* (pp. 89–109). Hershey, PA: IGI Global. doi:10.4018/978-1-4666-8574-1.ch007

Kasemsap, K. (2016a). Facilitating hospitality and tourism management in global business. In N. Pappas & I. Bregoli (Eds.), *Global dynamics in travel, tourism, and hospitality* (pp. 283–305). Hershey, PA: IGI Global. doi:10.4018/978-1-5225-0201-2.ch016

Kasemsap, K. (2016b). The roles of information technology and knowledge management in global tourism. In A. Nedelea, M. Korstanje, & B. George (Eds.), *Strategic tools and methods for promoting hospitality and tourism services* (pp. 109–138). Hershey, PA: IGI Global. doi:10.4018/978-1-4666-9761-4.ch006

Kasemsap, K. (2016c). Encouraging corporate social responsibility and sustainable tourism development in global tourism. In L. Guliani & S. Rizwan (Eds.), *Corporate social responsibility in the hospitality and tourism industry* (pp. 197–224). Hershey, PA: IGI Global. doi:10.4018/978-1-4666-9902-1.ch016

Kasemsap, K. (2016d). Implementing electronic commerce in global marketing. In I. Lee (Ed.), *Encyclopedia of e-commerce development, implementation, and management* (pp. 591–602). Hershey, PA: IGI Global. doi:10.4018/978-1-4666-9787-4.ch043

Kasemsap, K. (2016e). Advocating electronic business and electronic commerce in the global marketplace. In S. Dixit & A. Sinha (Eds.), *E-retailing challenges and opportunities in the global marketplace* (pp. 1–24). Hershey, PA: IGI Global. doi:10.4018/978-1-4666-9921-2.ch001

Kasemsap, K. (2016f). The roles of social media marketing and brand management in global marketing. In W. Ozuem & G. Bowen (Eds.), *Competitive social media marketing strategies* (pp. 173–200). Hershey, PA: IGI Global. doi:10.4018/978-1-4666-9776-8.ch009

Kasemsap, K. (2016g). Utilizing social media in modern business. In I. Lee (Ed.), *Encyclopedia of e-commerce development, implementation, and management* (pp. 2171–2182). Hershey, PA: IGI Global. doi:10.4018/978-1-4666-9787-4.ch156

Kastenholz, E., Carneiro, M. J., Marques, C. P., & Lima, J. (2012). Understanding and managing the rural tourism experience: The case of a historical village in Portugal. *Tourism Management Perspectives*, *4*, 207–214. doi:10.1016/j.tmp.2012.08.009

Keyim, P., Yang, D. G., & Zhang, X. L. (2005). Study of rural tourism in turpan, China. *Chinese Geographical Science*, *15*(4), 377–382. doi:10.1007/s11769-005-0028-4

Kim, K., Uysal, M., & Sirgy, M. J. (2013). How does tourism in a community impact the quality of life of community residents? *Tourism Management*, *36*(5), 527–540. doi:10.1016/j.tourman.2012.09.005

Klak, T. (2007). Sustainable ecotourism development in Central America and the Caribbean: Review of debates and conceptual reformulation. *Geography Compass*, *1*(5), 1037–1057. doi:10.1111/j.1749-8198.2007.00055.x

Krannich, R., & Petrzelka, P. (2003). Tourism and natural amenity development: Real opportunities. In D. Brown & L. Swanson (Eds.), *Challenges for rural America in the twenty-first century* (pp. 190–199). University Park, PA: Penn State University Press.

Lane, B. (1994). What is rural tourism? *Journal of Sustainable Tourism*, *2*(1/2), 7–21. doi:10.1080/09669589409510680

Lane, B. (2009). Rural tourism: An overview. In T. Jamal & M. Robinson (Eds.), *The Sage handbook of tourism studies* (pp. 354–371). London, UK: Sage Publications. doi:10.4135/9780857021076.n20

Lange, G. M. (2015). Tourism in Zanzibar: Incentives for sustainable management of the coastal environment. *Ecosystem Services*, *11*, 5–11. doi:10.1016/j.ecoser.2014.11.009

Lee, S. W., & Kim, H. J. (2010). Agricultural transition and rural tourism in Korea: Experiences of the last forty years. In G. Thapa, P. Viswanathan, J. Routray, & M. Ahmad (Eds.), *Agricultural transition in Asia* (pp. 37–64). Bangkok, Thailand: Asian Institute of Technology.

Li, W., Lin, L., Shi-rong, T., Song, L., Zhao, Y., Yong, W., & Dong-dong, L. (2004). Residents' attitudes to tourism development in ancient village resorts. *Chinese Geographical Science*, *14*(2), 170–178. doi:10.1007/s11769-004-0027-x

Li, W., Zhang, Q., Liu, C., & Xue, Q. (2006). Tourism's impacts on natural resources: A positive case from China. *Environmental Management*, *38*(4), 572–579. doi:10.1007/s00267-004-0299-z PMID:16933085

Liu, A. (2006). Tourism in rural areas: Kedah, Malaysia. *Tourism Management*, *27*(5), 878–889. doi:10.1016/j.tourman.2005.05.007

Liu, C. H. S., Horng, J. S., & Chou, S. F. (2015). A critical evaluation of sustainable tourism from the integrated perspective: Conducting moderated-mediation analysis. *Tourism Management Perspectives*, *16*, 43–50. doi:10.1016/j.tmp.2015.05.008

Long, J., Vogelaar, A., & Hale, B. W. (2014). Toward sustainable educational travel. *Journal of Sustainable Tourism*, *22*(3), 421–439. doi:10.1080/09669582.2013.819877

Loureiro, S. M. C. (2014). The role of the rural tourism experience economy in place attachment and behavioral intentions. *International Journal of Hospitality Management*, *40*, 1–9. doi:10.1016/j.ijhm.2014.02.010

MacDonald, R., & Jolliffe, L. (2003). Cultural rural tourism: Evidence from Canada. *Annals of Tourism Research*, *30*(2), 307–322. doi:10.1016/S0160-7383(02)00061-0

McAreavey, R., & McDonagh, J. (2011). Sustainable rural tourism: Lessons for rural development. *Sociologia Ruralis*, *51*(2), 175–194. doi:10.1111/j.1467-9523.2010.00529.x

Miller, G., & Twining-Ward, L. (2005). *Monitoring for a sustainable tourism transition: The challenge of developing and using indicators*. Wallingford, UK: CABI Publishing. doi:10.1079/9780851990514.0000

Mitchell, J., & Ashley, C. (2010). *Tourism and poverty reduction: Pathways to prosperity*. London, UK: Earthscan Publications.

Mitchell, R. E., & Reid, D. G. (2001). Community integration: Island tourism in Peru. *Annals of Tourism Research*, *28*(1), 113–139. doi:10.1016/S0160-7383(00)00013-X

Moscardo, G. (2008). Sustainable tourism innovation: Challenging basic assumptions. *Tourism and Hospitality Research*, *8*(1), 4–13. doi:10.1057/thr.2008.7

Mshenga, P. M., & Richardson, R. B. (2013). Micro and small enterprise participation in tourism in coastal Kenya. *Small Business Economics*, *41*(3), 667–681. doi:10.1007/s11187-012-9449-5

Mycoo, M. (2014). Sustainable tourism, climate change and sea level rise adaptation policies in Barbados. *Natural Resources Forum*, *38*(1), 47–57. doi:10.1111/1477-8947.12033

Naghiu, A., Vázquez, J. L., & Georgiev, I. (2005). Rural development strategies through rural tourism activities in Romania: Chance for an internal demand? *International Review on Public and Nonprofit Marketing*, *2*(1), 85–95. doi:10.1007/BF02893253

Neto, F. (2003). A new approach to sustainable tourism development: Moving beyond environmental protection. *Natural Resources Forum*, *27*(3), 212–222. doi:10.1111/1477-8947.00056

Nunkoo, R., & Gursoy, D. (2012). Residents support for tourism: An identity perspective. *Annals of Tourism Research*, *39*(1), 243–268. doi:10.1016/j.annals.2011.05.006

Palmer, A., Koenig-Lewis, N., & Jones, L. (2013). The effects of residents' social identity and involvement on their advocacy of incoming tourism. *Tourism Management*, *38*, 142–151. doi:10.1016/j.tourman.2013.02.019

Park, D. B., Lee, H. J., & Yoon, Y. S. (2014). Understanding the benefit sought by rural tourists and accommodation preferences: A South Korea case. *International Journal of Tourism Research*, *16*(3), 291–302. doi:10.1002/jtr.1929

Park, D. B., Lee, K. W., Choi, H. S., & Yoon, Y. (2012). Factors influencing social capital in rural tourism communities in South Korea. *Tourism Management*, *33*(6), 1511–1520. doi:10.1016/j.tourman.2012.02.005

Peña, A. I. P., & Jamilena, D. M. F. (2010). The relationship between business characteristics and ICT deployment in the rural tourism sector. The case of Spain. *International Journal of Tourism Research*, *12*(1), 34–48.

Peña, A. I. P., & Jamilena, D. M. F. (2011). Market orientation adoption in rural tourism: Impact on business outcomes and the perceived value. *International Review on Public and Nonprofit Marketing*, *8*(2), 195–197. doi:10.1007/s12208-011-0068-7

Prabhakaran, S., Nair, V., & Ramachandran, S. (2014). Community participation in rural tourism: Towards a conceptual framework. *Procedia: Social and Behavioral Sciences*, *144*, 290–295. doi:10.1016/j.sbspro.2014.07.298

Priskin, J. (2003). Issues and opportunities in planning and managing nature-based tourism in the Central Coast Region of Western Australia. *Australian Geographical Studies*, *41*(3), 270–286. doi:10.1046/j.1467-8470.2003.00234.x

Pulido-Fernández, J. I., Andrades-Caldito, L., & Sánchez-Rivero, M. (2015). Is sustainable tourism an obstacle to the economic performance of the tourism industry? Evidence from an international empirical study. *Journal of Sustainable Tourism*, *23*(1), 47–64. doi:10.1080/09669582.2014.909447

Rajaratnam, S. D., Munikrishnan, U. T., Sharif, S. P., & Nair, V. (2014). Service quality and previous experience as a moderator in determining tourists' satisfaction with rural tourism destinations in Malaysia: A partial least squares approach. *Procedia: Social and Behavioral Sciences*, *144*, 203–211. doi:10.1016/j.sbspro.2014.07.288

Randelli, F., Romei, P., & Tortora, M. (2014). An evolutionary approach to the study of rural tourism: The case of Tuscany. *Land Use Policy*, *38*, 276–281. doi:10.1016/j.landusepol.2013.11.009

Reddy, M. V. (2008). Sustainable tourism rapid indicators for less-developed islands: An economic perspective. *International Journal of Tourism Research*, *10*(6), 557–576. doi:10.1002/jtr.700

Reichel, A., Lowengart, O., & Milman, A. (2000). Rural tourism in Israel: Service quality and orientation. *Tourism Management*, *21*(5), 451–459. doi:10.1016/S0261-5177(99)00099-0

Roberts, L., & Hall, D. (2001). *Rural tourism and recreation: Principles to practice*. Wallingford, UK: CABI Publishing. doi:10.1079/9780851995403.0000

Rozman, C., Potocnik, M., Pazek, K., Borec, A., Majkovic, D., & Bohanec, M. (2009). A multi-criteria assessment of tourist farm service quality. *Tourism Management*, *30*(5), 629–637. doi:10.1016/j.tourman.2008.11.008

Ruhanen, L. (2013). Local government: Facilitator or inhibitor of sustainable tourism development? *Journal of Sustainable Tourism*, *21*(1), 80–98. doi:10.1080/09669582.2012.680463

Ruitenbeek, J., Hewawasan, I., & Ngoile, M. (2005). *Blueprint 2050: Sustaining the marine environment in Mainland Tanzania and Zanzibar*. Washington, DC: The World Bank. doi:10.1596/0-8213-6123-6

Russell, R., & Faulkner, B. (2004). Entrepreneurship, chaos and the tourism area lifecycle. *Annals of Tourism Research*, *31*(3), 556–579. doi:10.1016/j.annals.2004.01.008

Ryan, C., Gu, H., & Zhang, W. (2009). The context of Chinese tourism: An overview and implications for research. In C. Ryan & H. Gu (Eds.), *Tourism in China: Destination, cultures and communities* (pp. 327–336). New York, NY: Routledge.

Samsudin, P. Y., & Maliki, N. Z. (2015). Preserving cultural landscape in homestay programme towards sustainable tourism: Brief critical review concept. *Procedia: Social and Behavioral Sciences*, *170*, 433–441. doi:10.1016/j.sbspro.2015.01.004

Schendel, D., & Hitt, M. A. (2007). Introduction to volume 1. *Strategic Entrepreneurship Journal*, *1*(1/2), 1–6. doi:10.1002/sej.16

Scheyvens, R. (2011). The challenge of sustainable tourism development in the Maldives: Understanding the social and political dimensions of sustainability. *Asia Pacific Viewpoint*, *52*(2), 148–164. doi:10.1111/j.1467-8373.2011.01447.x

Scott, D., Gössling, S., & Hall, C. M. (2012). International tourism and climate change. *Wiley Interdisciplinary Reviews: Climate Change*, *3*(3), 213–232. doi:10.1002/wcc.165

Sdrali, D., Goussia-Rizou, M., & Kiourtidou, P. (2015). Residents' perception of tourism development as a vital step for participatory tourism plan: A research in a Greek protected area. *Environment, Development and Sustainability*, *17*(4), 923–939. doi:10.1007/s10668-014-9573-2

Sealey, K. S., & Smith, J. (2014). Recycling for small island tourism developments: Food waste composting at Sandals Emerald Bay, Exuma, Bahamas. *Resources, Conservation and Recycling*, *92*, 25–37. doi:10.1016/j.resconrec.2014.08.008

Shakya, M. (2011). Local perceptions of risk and tourism: A case study from rural Nepal. *Recreation and Society in Africa, Asia and Latin America*, *1*(2), 31–64.

Sharpley, R. (2000). Tourism and sustainable development: Exploring the theoretical divide. *Journal of Sustainable Tourism*, *8*(1), 1–19. doi:10.1080/09669580008667346

Sharpley, R., & Sharpley, J. (1997). *Rural tourism: An introduction*. London, UK: International Thomson Business Press.

Sheykhi, M. (2009). Domestic tourism in Iran. *Tourismos: An International Multidisciplinary Journal of Tourism*, *4*(1), 109–123.

Silva, L. (2015). How ecotourism works at the community-level: The case of whale-watching in the Azores. *Current Issues in Tourism*, *18*(3), 196–211. doi:10.1080/13683500.2013.786027

Silva, L., & Leal, J. (2015). Rural tourism and national identity building in contemporary Europe: Evidence from Portugal. *Journal of Rural Studies*, *38*, 109–119. doi:10.1016/j.jrurstud.2015.02.005

Simão, J. N., & Partidário, M. D. R. (2012). How does tourism planning contribute to sustainable development? *Sustainable Development*, *20*(6), 372–385. doi:10.1002/sd.495

Singh, R. B., & Mishra, D. K. (2004). Green tourism in mountain regions-reducing vulnerability and promoting people and place centric development in the Himalayas. *Journal of Mountain Science*, *1*(1), 57–64. doi:10.1007/BF02919360

Skuras, D., Petrou, A., & Clark, G. (2006). Demand for rural tourism: The effects of quality and information. *Agricultural Economics*, *35*(2), 183–192. doi:10.1111/j.1574-0862.2006.00151.x

Snieška, V., Barkauskiene, K., & Barkauskas, V. (2014). The impact of economic factors on the development of rural tourism: Lithuanian case. *Procedia: Social and Behavioral Sciences*, *156*, 280–285. doi:10.1016/j.sbspro.2014.11.189

Tekken, V., & Kropp, J. P. (2015). Sustainable water management: Perspectives for tourism development in north-eastern Morocco. *Tourism Management Perspectives*, *16*, 325–334. doi:10.1016/j.tmp.2015.09.001

UNWTO. (2014). *Tourism highlights 2014 edition*. Madrid, Spain: United Nations World Tourism Organization.

Waligo, V. M., Clarke, J., & Hawkins, R. (2015). Embedding stakeholders in sustainable tourism strategies. *Annals of Tourism Research*, *55*, 90–93. doi:10.1016/j.annals.2015.09.002

Walmsley, D. (2003). Rural tourism: A case of lifestyle-led opportunities. *The Australian Geographer*, *34*(1), 61–72. doi:10.1080/00049180320000066155

Wang, Y., & Fesenmaier, D. R. (2007). Collaborative destination marketing: A case study of Elkhart county, Indiana. *Tourism Management*, *28*(3), 863–875. doi:10.1016/j.tourman.2006.02.007

Woods, M. (2005). *Rural geography: Processes, responses and experiences in rural restructuring*. London, UK: Sage Publications.

Zhang, R. Y., Xi, J. C., Wang, S. K., Wang, X. G., & Ge, Q. S. (2015). Village network centrality in rural tourism destination: A case from Yesanpo tourism area, China. *Journal of Mountain Science*, *12*(3), 759–768. doi:10.1007/s11629-014-3129-7

Zhao, W., Ritchie, J. R., & Echtner, C. M. (2011). Social capital and tourism entrepreneurship. *Annals of Tourism Research*, *38*(4), 1570–1593. doi:10.1016/j.annals.2011.02.006

Zhou, L. (2014). Online rural destination images: Tourism and rurality. *Journal of Destination Marketing & Management*, *3*(4), 227–240. doi:10.1016/j.jdmm.2014.03.002

ADDITIONAL READING

Bhat, M. G., Bhatta, R., & Shumais, M. (2014). Sustainable funding policies for environmental protection: The case of Maldivian atolls. *Environmental Economics and Policy Studies*, *16*(1), 45–67. doi:10.1007/s10018-013-0070-x

Brouder, P., & Ioannides, D. (2014). Urban tourism and evolutionary economic geography: Complexity and co-evolution in contested spaces. *Urban Forum*, *25*(4), 419–430.doi:10.1007/s12132-014-9239-z

Chuang, S. T. (2013). Residents' attitudes toward rural tourism in Taiwan: A comparative viewpoint. *International Journal of Tourism Research*, *15*(2), 152–170. doi:10.1002/jtr.1861

Cole, S. (2014). Tourism and water: From stakeholders to rights holders, and what tourism businesses need to do. *Journal of Sustainable Tourism*, *22*(1), 89–106. doi:10.1080/09669582.2013.776062

Fatimah, T. (2015). The impacts of rural tourism initiatives on cultural landscape sustainability in Borobudur area. *Procedia Environmental Sciences*, *28*, 567–577. doi:10.1016/j.proenv.2015.07.067

Ingelmo, I. A. (2013). Design and development of a sustainable tourism indicator based on human activities analysis in Inle Lake, Myanmar. *Procedia: Social and Behavioral Sciences*, *103*, 262–272. doi:10.1016/j.sbspro.2013.10.334

Jamal, T., & Camargo, B. (2014). Sustainable tourism, justice and an ethic of care: Toward the just destination. *Journal of Sustainable Tourism*, *22*(1), 11–30. doi:10.1080/09669582.2013.786084

Juvan, E., & Dolnicar, S. (2014). The attitude-behaviour gap in sustainable tourism. *Annals of Tourism Research*, *48*, 76–95. doi:10.1016/j.annals.2014.05.012

Kinyondo, A., & Pelizzo, R. (2015). Tourism, development and inequality: The case of Tanzania. *Poverty & Public Policy*, *7*(1), 64–79. doi:10.1002/pop4.92

Komppula, R. (2014). The role of individual entrepreneurs in the development of competitiveness for a rural tourism destination: A case study. *Tourism Management*, *40*, 361–371. doi:10.1016/j.tourman.2013.07.007

Lo, M. C., Mohamad, A. A., Songan, P., & Yeo, A. W. (2012). Positioning rural tourism: Perspectives from the local communities. *International Journal of Trade, Economics and Finance*, *3*(1), 59–65. doi:10.7763/IJTEF.2012.V3.173

Lozano-Oyola, M., Blancas, F. J., González, M., & Caballero, R. (2012). Sustainable tourism indicators as planning tools in cultural destinations. *Ecological Indicators*, *18*, 659–675. doi:10.1016/j.ecolind.2012.01.014

Minoli, D. M., Goode, M. K. H., & Smith, M. T. (2015). Are eco labels profitably employed in sustainable tourism? A case study on Audubon Certified Golf Resorts. *Tourism Management Perspectives*, *16*, 207–216. doi:10.1016/j.tmp.2015.07.011

Njoroge, J. M. (2014). An enhanced framework for regional tourism sustainable adaptation to climate change. *Tourism Management Perspectives*, *12*, 23–30. doi:10.1016/j.tmp.2014.06.002

Nogueira, S., & Pinho, J. C. (2015). Stakeholder network integrated analysis: The specific case of rural tourism in the Portuguese Peneda-Gerês National Park. *International Journal of Tourism Research*, *17*(4), 325–336. doi:10.1002/jtr.1989

Ohe, Y., & Kurihara, S. (2013). Evaluating the complementary relationship between local brand farm products and rural tourism: Evidence from Japan. *Tourism Management*, *35*, 278–283. doi:10.1016/j.tourman.2012.07.003

Panyik, E., Costa, C., & Rátz, T. (2011). Implementing integrated rural tourism: An event-based approach. *Tourism Management*, *32*(6), 1352–1363. doi:10.1016/j.tourman.2011.01.009

Pesonen, J. A. (2012). Segmentation of rural tourists: Combining push and pull motivations. *Tourism and Hospitality Management*, *18*(1), 69–82.

Piso, A. (2016). Migrant labour in rural tourism: Continuity and change. *International Journal of Tourism Research*, *18*(1), 10–18. doi:10.1002/jtr.2020

Rid, W., Ezeuduji, I. O., & Probstl-Haider, U. (2014). Segmentation by motivation for rural tourism activities in the Gambia. *Tourism Management*, *40*(1), 102–116. doi:10.1016/j.tourman.2013.05.006

Ruhanen, L., Weiler, B., Moyle, B., & McLennan, C. (2015). Trends and patterns in sustainable tourism research: A 25-year bibliometric analysis. *Journal of Sustainable Tourism*, *23*(4), 517–535. doi:10.1080/09669582.2014.978790

Saxena, G. (2014). Rural tourism partnerships and actor mobility. *International Journal of Tourism Research*, *16*(5), 488–495. doi:10.1002/jtr.1942

Tanguay, G. A., Rajaonson, J., & Therrien, M. C. (2013). Sustainable tourism indicators: Selection criteria for policy implementation and scientific recognition. *Journal of Sustainable Tourism*, *21*(6), 862–879. doi:10.1080/09669582.2012.742531

Torres-Delgado, A., & Palomeque, F. L. (2014). Measuring sustainable tourism at the municipal level. *Annals of Tourism Research*, *49*, 122–137. doi:10.1016/j.annals.2014.09.003

Wijesinghe, G. (2014). Reimagining the application of sustainability to the hospitality industry through a virtue ethics framework. *Journal of Sustainable Tourism*, *22*(1), 31–49. doi:10.1080/09669582.2013.819875

Williams, A. (2013). Mobilities and sustainable tourism: Path-creating or path-dependent relationships? *Journal of Sustainable Tourism*, *21*(4), 511–531. doi:10.1080/09669582.2013.768252

Xi, J., Wang, X., Kong, Q., & Zhang, N. (2015). Spatial morphology evolution of rural settlements induced by tourism. *Journal of Geographical Sciences*, *25*(4), 497–511. doi:10.1007/s11442-015-1182-y

Zou, T., Huang, S., & Ding, P. (2014). Toward a community-driven development model of rural tourism: The Chinese experience. *International Journal of Tourism Research*, *16*(3), 261–271. doi:10.1002/jtr.1925

KEY TERMS AND DEFINITIONS

Ecotourism: The low ecological-impact tourism that emphasizes the specific features other than entertainment, gaming, luxury, and shopping.

Rural Tourism: The type of tourism taking place in rural areas or settlements, providing employment and income to local population, and offering individualized holiday products to tourists.

Stakeholder: The individual that has the specific interest in an organization.

Sustainability: The continued development without the deterioration of the environment and the depletion of natural resources.

Sustainable Development: The economic development characterized by the low growth rate, the absence of pollution, and the diminished environment impact.

Sustainable Tourism: The concept of visiting a place as a tourist and trying to make a positive impact on the environment, society, and economy.

Tourism: The marketing of the enjoyable features of the travel destination and the provision of both facilities and services for tourists.

Tourist: The individual who visits a place for pleasure and interest, usually while on holiday.

Chapter 6
Sustainable Tourism Development in Asia:
Evaluation of the Potential and Challenges:

Gamini Herath
Monash University, Malaysia

ABSTRACT

Sustainable Tourism as a concept respects both local people, the traveler, cultural heritage and the environment. It should meet the needs of and opportunity for the future. But operationalizing sustainable tourism is problematic due to analytical weaknesses, conceptual criticisms and the need to redefine better perspectives. Asia faces many challenges in promoting sustainable tourism including political leadership, poor participation by all stakeholders, adverse environmental and social impacts. Another challenge is to ensure social sustainability and creating opportunities to transfer income to the poorer. The empirical study of island tourism in Malaysia shows that Marine Parks regulations are not adequately enforced and Malaysian coral reefs can suffer from increasing degradation. Water pollution, overfishing, beach erosion, coral bleaching and damage, fishing, snorkeling and poor recycling and sewage disposal all are still significant challenges to the Marine Park in in Tioman Island in Malaysia.

INTRODUCTION

Tourism is one of the world's fastest growing industries with a wide spectrum of employment opportunities and income for many countries in Asia. Tourism contributes 9 percent of the world's GDP, 8 percent of employment and 5 percent of GHGs emissions (UNEP 2002). Table 1 shows international tourism arrivals from many countries including Europe and Asia for the period 2000-2014. The table shows that tourist arrivals have increased continuously over the 2000-1014 period. Tourism can have serious impacts on the environment, society, cultural heritage and natural ecosystems. The environmental impacts of tourism began to be noticed early and several tourism concepts focusing on nature such as ecotourism, nature tourism etc emerged. These impacts later led to the emergence of sustainable tourism defined as

DOI: 10.4018/978-1-5225-2078-8.ch006

"tourism that respects both local people and the traveler, cultural heritage and the environment" (Buckley 2012; World Tourism Organization 2001a, 2001b; Cater 1993).

Sustainable tourism, focuses on the balance between the environmental, economic and socio-cultural aspects of tourism development. Sustainable tourism emphasizes economic, social and environmental dimensions in an integrated manner to minimize the impact on the environment and local culture so that it will be available for future generations, while contributing to income, employment, and the conservation of local ecosystems (Hall et al. 2003; Hall et al 1991). By doing so, sustainable tourism provides crucial economic incentives for habitat and biodiversity protection. Revenues from visitor spending are often channeled back into nature conservation or capacity building programs for local communities and poverty reduction and the achievement of common goals towards sustainable development (Driml & Common 1995).

Sustainable tourism is important in achieving Millennium Sustainable Development Goals (MSDGs) adopted in 2015. Sustainable tourism will raise pertinent issues in Asia including poverty, environmental degradation and biodiversity extinction. In Indonesia for example, tourism generates, foreign earnings, combat poverty, and support development of many remote areas. Sustainable tourism has promoted biodiversity conservation using conservation areas for tourism education and experience with new nature-based destinations, guidelines for visiting pristine areas and strict environmental standards for tourism.

Despite the rhetoric, the success of sustainable tourism remains mixed. Many factors have intervened on the success of sustainable tourism enterprises including financial and political conflicts and climate change. Private sector marketing approaches to promote sustainable tourism and ecocertification and corporate social responsibility largely failed (Black & Crabtree 2007, Buckley 2002). Thus insightful evaluation of sustainable tourism is timely.

The purpose of this chapter is to (a) review existing literature to ascertain the success and problems in implementing sustainable tourism in Asia (b) identify the challenges and opportunities of sustainable tourism in Asia (c) present the findings of a case study of sustainable island tourism in Malaysia and

Table 1. International tourist arrivals by country 2000-2014

Country	2000	2005	2008	2009	2010	2011	2012	2014
France	77,190,000	74,988,000	79,218,000	76,764,000	76,647,000	80,499,000	81,980,000	83,767,000
Unites States	51,238,000	49,206,000	58,007,000	55,103,000	60,010,000	62,821,000	66,657,000	75,011,000
China	31,229,000	46,809,000	53,049,000	50,875,000	55,664,000	57,581,000	57,725,000	55,622,000
Turkey	9,586,000	20,273,000	29,792,000	30,187,000	31,364,000	34,654,000	35,698,000	39,811,000
United Kingdom	23,212,000	28,039,000	30,142,000	28,199,000	28,295,000	29,306,000	29,282,000	32,613,000
Mexico	20,641,000	21,915,000	22,931,000	22,346,000	23,290,000	23,403,000	23,403,000	29,346,000
Hong Kong SAR, China	8,814,000	14,773,000	17,319,000	16,926,000	20,085,000	22,316,000	23,770,000	27,770,000
Malaysia	10,222,000	16,431,000	22,052,000	23,646,000	24,577,000	24,714,000	25,033,000	27,437,000
Thailand	9,579,000	11,567,000	14,584,000	14,150,000	15,936,000	19,23,000	22,354,000	24,810,000
Korea	5,322,000	6,023,000	6,891,000	7,818,000	8,798,000	9,795,000	11,140,000	14,202,000
Japan	4,757,000	6,728,000	8,351,000	6,790,000	8,611,000	6,219,000	8,358,000	13,413,000
Singapore	6,062,000	7,079,000	7,778,000	7,488,000	9,161,000	10,390,000	11,098,000	11,864,000

Source: World Data Atlas Tourism, Knoema.com 2015

(d) identify policy implications to improve sustainable tourism in Asia. The chapter is organized as follows. After the introduction, section 2 discusses the sustainable tourism concept. Section 3 examines the diversity of definitions and the challenges and opportunities for sustainable tourism especially in Asia. Section 4 presents the case of island tourism in Malaysia and section 5 presents the concluding remarks

SUSTAINABLE TOURISM

In the last few decades sustainable tourism has emerged as unifying theme providing new direction for a broader social, economic and environmental vision for future generations. There have been a number of institutional initiatives to foster sustainable tourism and the most recent being the adoption of 2017 as the International Year of Sustainable Tourism for Development by the United Nations (UN). Tourism is included as targets under three of the SDGs - SDG 8: *Pr*omote sustained, inclusive and sustainable economic growth, full and productive employment and decent work for all; *SDG 12:* Sustainable Consumption and Production *and SDG 14: c*conserve and sustainably use the oceans, seas and marine resources for sustainable development.

The Emergence of Sustainable Tourism

Prior to the mid-20th century, tourism was available only to limited number of tourists. Since the development in transport and communications from the mid-20th century, the travel industry began to expand even to the average citizen. The term "ecotourism" was introduced in 1965 when ecological aspects were integrated to tourism. Countries as diverse as Australia, Mexico, Malaysia and Fiji have developed ecotourism strategies broadly to include nature conservation, ecological integrity, community development and cultural preservation (Herath, 2002; Blamey, 1995; Buckley, 1994, 2012).

Soft Tourism" was introduced in German-speaking countries in 1980, to reduce adverse consequences of tourism through restrictive measures within spatial planning and regional policies. It is a structural alternative tourism with special focus on environmentally and socially acceptable holiday planning

Later several other tourism concepts emerged recognizing the importance of nature in the touristic experiences. These concepts are not completely mutually exclusive to ecotourism and the most common are 'nature tourism', 'environmental tourism', 'green tourism', 'adventure travel', 'cultural tourism', 'ecological tourism' and 'sustainable tourism'. These concepts embraced conservation, cultural and community development and were used synonymously with 'ecotourism' and even sustainable tourism (Figgis, 1993; Steele, 1993; Cater, 1993; Wight, 1993; Herath, 1996a, 1996b; Buckley, 2008, 2009a, 2009b, 2009c). These emerging concepts were not synonymous with Sustainable Tourism, but they were an important step towards sustainable tourism.

The importance of sustainable tourism came from the UN World Commission on Environment and Development which adopted the idea of sustainability in the "Brundtland report" in 1987 and defined "sustainable development as "development that meets the needs of the present without compromising the ability of future generations to meet their own needs."(UNEP 2002). The concept provided binding guidelines for general ecological, social and economic development for 179 countries within the Agenda 21. The Australian case exemplifies the development of the ecotourism phenomenon. In the late 1980s, ecotourism was an unknown entity that was just beginning to emerge in the popular lexicon. Its growth was spurred by the ongoing debate over tourism and the environment and as a direct result of the enthusiasm for ecologically sustainable development.

The emergence of ecotourism led to a lively debate among academics and industry leaders about the merits to the community. The Ecotourism Association of Australia, the Commonwealth Government (Allcock et al. 1994), state governments and regional associations produced a variety of ecotourism policies for the further development of the industry. The period was characterized by the expansion of specialist tour wholesalers and retailers to market a variety of ecotourism products in Australia.

Role of Sustainable Tourism in Asia

The rapid development of tourism with increasing numbers of visitors was a predisposing factors for adverse impacts on the environment (Othman et al., 2010; Camhi, 1995). In many developing countries, tourism destinations were overdeveloped (Neto 2003). Some of the environmental damages are not reversible and tourism numbers have declined, especially the nature-based segment. A small fishing village a Kerala, India was a good tourists attraction for some time but tourism collapsed due to poor disposal of solid waste. Environmental pollution and urban sprawl has already undermined sustainable tourism in countries such as Thailand and Malaysia (Neto, 2003).

In the last few decades, island tourism has had serious impacts on the environment (Alcock, 1995; Brodie, 1995; Kokasoy, 1995). Since the 1980s, Malaysia has declared many Marine Parks as a means of mitigating adverse impacts. Marine Parks are protected areas which allow only limited activities to avoid destruction of marine ecosystems. However the regulations are not adequately enforced and Malaysian coral reefs have suffered increasing degradation (Othman, 2010;mHerath et al 2014).

Many islands, particularly their coral reefs, have been severely degraded over the past 30 years as a result of tourism development (eg Malaysia, Indonesia, Thailand, Sri Lanka etc). Rubbish originating on the islands themselves and from the mainland, sediment pollution due to catchment clearing and construction activities, overfishing, beach erosion, coral bleaching and coral damage from boating, fishing, snorkeling and diving have caused massive destruction to coral reefs and have thus become significant and endemic challenges to island tourism and its sustainability (Herath et al 2014). In Indonesia, sustainable tourism is designed to increase earnings, to contribute to environmental conservation, to promote environmental education, and to empower local people in adjacent forests, remote areas and protected areas.

Definitions of Sustainable Tourism

There are many definitions of sustainable tourism, but there is no consensus on a broadly accepted definition and the use of the term has created a great deal of disagreement (Buckley 2012).

The World Tourism Organization WTO (2001b) defines sustainable tourism as "tourism that meets the needs of present tourists and host regions while protecting and enhancing opportunity for the future. It is an ethos that underpins all tourism activities. The objective of sustainable tourism is to retain the economic and social advantages of tourism development while reducing or mitigating any undesirable impacts on the natural, historic, cultural or social environment. Sustainable tourism is an industry committed to making a low impact on the environment and local culture, while helping to generate future employment for local people. The aim of sustainable tourism is to ensure that development is a positive experience for local people; tourism companies; and tourists themselves".

The ILO's (2010) definition of sustainable tourism is, that it is "composed of three pillars: social justice, economic development, and environmental integrity. It is committed to the enhancement of local prosperity by maximizing the contribution of tourism to the destination's economic prosperity, including the amount of visitor spending that is retained locally. It should generate income and decent employment for workers without affecting the environment and culture of the tourists' destination and ensures the viability and competitiveness of destinations and enterprises to enable them to continue to prosper and deliver benefits in the long term" (see Figure 1) (ILO 2010).

The German Forum on Environment and Development presented the following definition for "Sustainable Tourism" in 1999 at a UN Conference in New York. Sustainable tourism has to meet social, cultural, ecological and economic requirements. Sustainable tourism holds a long-term view, for present and future generations, ethically and socially just and culturally adapted, ecologically viable and economically sensible and productive." (German Forum on Environment and Development 1999).

Wikipedia defines sustainable tourism as "level of tourism activity that can be maintained over the long term because it results in a net benefit for the social, economic, natural and cultural environments of the area in which it takes place" (Wikipedia, 2007).

The Visit Scotland's definition of sustainable tourism is "tourism committed to generating a low impact on the surrounding environment and community by acting responsibly while generating income and employment for the local economy and aiding social cohesion. Sustainable tourism aims to ensure

Figure 1. Components of sustainable tourism 2010
Source: ILO 2010

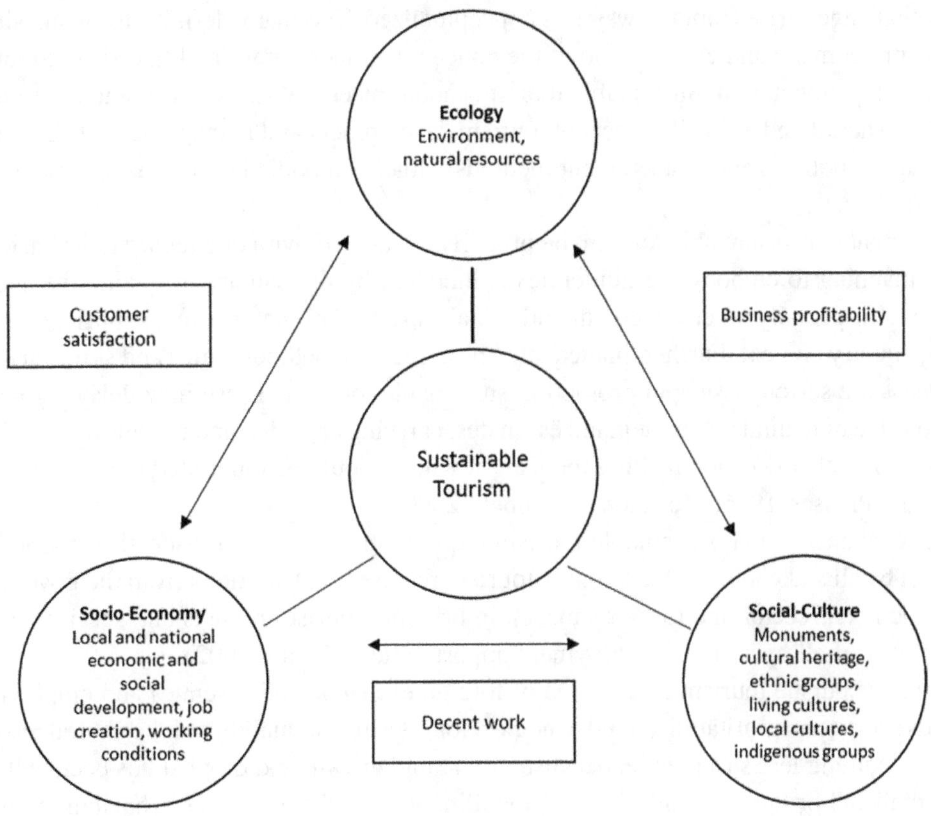

that economic development as a result of tourism is a positive experience for everyone involved; local community, tourism businesses and visitors. Because it safeguards the very assets on which Scottish tourism depends, taking a sustainable approach to tourism growth is the only way to ensure long-term tourism growth in Scotland. Ignoring the environmental or social impacts of tourism development will ultimately undermine the success of tourism in this country. Becoming a sustainable tourism destination will give Scottish tourism businesses a competitive edge by generating greater community support for tourism, achieving cost savings and creating new marketing opportunities".

The multitude of definitions imply that there is no unanimity on the concept. While this may be so, there is a high degree of commonality in all definitions. For example, they all embody economic, social and environmental sustainability and future generations. Some discrepancies may be still valid because the tourism environment is dynamic and new issues emerge all the time. New theories are developed and competition is fierce over time. Even international political issues such as the sharing the South China Sea and sharing the resource for tourism will become intensely political. Hence flexibility of the definition must be viewed in a positive light.

CHALLENGES AND OPPORTUNITIES FOR SUSTAINABLE TOURISM

The Major Challenges

The tourism industry faces a multitude of significant sustainability-related challenges. Planning and practices of sustainable tourism development in Asia need improved destination performance as a central issue. The challenges arise from the way it is conceptualized. Too many definitions of sustainable tourism may be problematic and clarification of the concept is important to facilitate clear communication and effective implementation. Sustainable tourism should meet the needs of present and future tourists and this ethos should underpin all aspects of tourism development and management. It should subscribe to the principles, policies and management methods' largely embodied in the sustainable development concept (WCE).

It is important that sustainable tourism be properly conducted, with due regard to its basic principle, but proper planning to embody the guidelines is hindered by the paucity of qualitative and quantitative information specially on environment and social aspects. This can prove a significant challenge in developing country context. Further, inadequate knowledge on methodologies and skills, and education and awareness are serious issues in promoting sustainable tourism. These may delay rigorous assessment of the value of natural assets, demand estimates, carrying capacity, and models of preservation and management and other decision making tools all of which should be integrated in a systematic manner (Herath, 2002; Prosser, 1986; Morrison & Bennett, 2000).

A major challenge is that sustainable tourism requires strong political leadership, to facilitate wide participation by all stakeholders. Sustainable tourism requires contributions from the government, tour operators, the hotels sector and tour organizers, in bringing tourist products and services to ensure financial viability of all operations, employment opportunities (Herath, 2002).

Governments pursue tourism as a source of foreign exchange and revenues and employment. This bias towards short-term profitability, tend to neglect long-term sustainability of the natural resource base. Tourism is becoming less sustainable, because of its rapid growth and of what has been called "veneer environmentalism" or "greenwash", *i.e.* the unwillingness to change travel behaviour (tourists) or to engage in operational and business behavioural changes that are more fundamental, *i.e.* going beyond measures that are profitable because of resource savings, branding benefits or improved customer relations (private and public components of tourism industry) (Herath, 2002).

The private tourism industry maximizes profit and return on equity and these groups often have very different levels of political power and influence with governments in decision-making (Schianetz et al., 2007; Tisdell, 1995; Watson & Herath, 1999). This may thwart the achievement of issues like poverty alleviation and social equity. Thus robust institutional framework with good governance principles are imperative for assessment of the environmental and social impacts of sustainable tourism investment projects.

Governments introduce laws, policies and incentives which can either reduce or increase pollution, environmental protection and social equity. But government institutions may promote individual choice (Wagner, 2011). In the tourism sector, Nelson (2010), and Yasarata, Altinay, Burns, and Okumus (2010), show that entrepreneurs in industry may abuse sustainability phenomena to create legitimacy.

Poor managerial skills, governance and lack of adequate resources and education lead to bad planning causing severe damage to cultural heritage which if planned well can encourage conservation. Cultural heritage is a valuable yet vulnerable and non-renewable resource .

Climate change may be a serious challenge. As the International Panel on Climate Change (IPCC) argues, global warming can affect the employment and livelihoods of stakeholder involved in nature tourism (Parry et al 2007). The tourism industry must adapt to climate change to minimize its impact on the environment. Over the next 30-50 years, GHG emissions from the tourism sector are projected to grow substantially and tourism is expected to account for a large share of emissions unless a major change in the emission trajectories is achieved (Peeters et al. 2010). Challenges that need to be resolved are reduced energy and GHG emissions; water consumption; waste management; loss of biological diversity; effective management of cultural heritage and poverty alleviation (Njoroge, 2015). More than 90% of tourism spending is thought to leak away from communities near most nature tourism sites (Lindberg, 1991).

Many assessments of the local employment benefits of ecotourism (Lindberg, Enriquez & Sproule, 1996; Powell & Chalmers, 1995) show that they vary widely. The employment impact of tourism depends on the quality of the attraction, access, and so on. Much of the expenditure leaks out of the local area. Estimates show that 70% of the tourist expenditure in Nepal and 60% in Thailand leaks out of the local area. Small-scale nature tourism uses more local goods than does large-scale traditional tourism but leakages may be higher due to lower diversity of goods is produced in small economies. Such leakages should be reduced where possible, but this may depend the nature of the sustainable tourism initiative and the nature of the remote communities where sustainable tourism is practiced.

A serious challenge is to strengthen the relationship between the local community and sustainable tourism especially for the social welfare of indigenous peoples, dignity and diversity of their cultures. Participation amongst the poor in the community and all groups enjoying tourism, ccontinuous monitoring of impacts, and corrective measures to minimize damage to touristic resources is essential (Herath, 2008) while maintaining a high level of tourist satisfaction and raising awareness about sustainability issues. New business models are needed as current models depend on energy intensive transportation and hence less sustainable.

Many public natural area systems face severe financial difficulties and the number of national parks and other areas have grown while funding has remained stable or declined (Eagles, 1995). How managers and environmentalists can turn to sustainable tourism as a source of revenue, to fund tourism related costs is a challenge. There have been numerous studies of user fees in the ecotourism context (Lindberg,

Enriquez & Sproule, 1996; Mak & Moncur, 1995). Appropriate fee systems to generate revenue need to be developed. In the case of developed country visitors to developing country public natural areas, it is particularly inappropriate for relatively poor local non-users to subsidize the visits of relatively wealthy users (Lindberg, 1991).

Most studies show that current fee levels could be increased with little or no impact on the number of visitors. In cases where fee increases would reduce the number of visitors, such increases may remain appropriate as a means to maximize total revenue and/or reduce negative environmental, experiential, or social impacts.

Sustainable tourism related jobs jobs can provide direct alternatives to practices, such as poaching of forest products, that threaten natural area conservation. As ecotourism jobs increase, it is likely that support for the natural areas providing the jobs will increase (Lindberg, Enriquez and Sproule 1996).

Opportunities for Sustainable Tourism

This section evaluates the opportunities for sustainable tourism in Asia. The focus is on how adverse development challenges in the economy, the environment and society in general can be transformed into opportunities for innovative sustainable tourism initiatives.

In many countries, coastal tourism development significantly altered the tourism experience due to poor waste management, wastewater collection and treatments and increased pollution of coastal seawaters (Anctil & Blanc, 2016). Pollution has caused loss of local marine biodiversity, declines in local fish stocks and seawater quality, affecting the attractiveness of coastal destinations for the avid tourist. Examples of such impacts abound in many countries such as in Turkey (Tosun, 2001), the Tioman and Langkawi Islands in Malaysia, Java in Indonesia and Hikkaduwa in Sri Lanka.

The declaration of marine parks by many countries in Asia helped boost sustainable coastal tourism, the Pemuteran Coral Reef Protection in Bali, Indonesia supported by Karang Lestari (Sustainable Reef) Foundation is a case in point. In1990 the redevelopment involved the local community, local dive shops and hotels, etc. to increase the resident awareness that tourism and reef conservation are critical to improve the local economy. This coral reef restoration project in a small fishing village in Northwest of Bali had only 1,800 residents 80% of whom are fishermen and village law predominates. Bali culture, temple festivals of Pura Pulaki, wellness, yoga and meditation are novel ideas of the project.

Coral bleaching and decline in fisheries led to drop in tourist numbers but the bottom-up community-run program enforced under village law, using local funding, and local leadership was successful. The corals came back and fish thrived. Twelve years later, tourism industry was vibrant and increasing number of visitors from Europe 45%, USA (environmentalists, spiritual tourism) 25%, and Japan were recorded.

Rural tourism with proper safeguards is a sustainable development strategy (Kim & Jamal, 2015; Hall, Roberts & Mitchell, 2003; Lane, 1994; Sharply & Roberts, 2004). Trade liberalization since the 1980s, reduced the viability of rural agriculture dominated by small farmers (Allen, 2004; Almas & Lawrence, 2002; Wright & Middendorf, 2008). New strategies to counteract such adverse effects in rural areas by promoting rural tourism emerged in the 1980s.Rural tourism promotes the synergy between rural markets and rural tourism to ensure sustainable livelihoods and community well-being.

Many countries in Asia such as Korea, Japan and China adopted rural tourism as a rural development strategy (Gao, Huang, & Huang, 2009; Hall et al., 2003; Lee & Nam, 2005; Thompson, 2004). Rural tourism invariably has links to rural food tasting and cookery demonstrations, wine tourism etc. and organic farming (Everett & Aitchison, 2008; Sims, 2009; Choo & Jamal, 2009).

The agro-industrial approach of the 1960s dominated agriculture and rural industry with emphasis on (Wilson, 2001; Marsden, 2003) the provision of goods and services to urban consumer (Marsden, 2003, p.11). We can transform agro-industrial models into agro-ecological model to offer holistic, people-based tourism development to resuscitate declining rural areas.

Environmentally friendly agricultural and organic farming methods that use less chemical fertilizers and pesticides and integrated pest management[1] was introduced in Japan (Aoki 2016). These new forms were environmentally sustainable and proved most attractive to tourists and provided supplementary incomes to rural populations. According to census data for 2010, the proportion of farmhouses that have introduced soil management and reduced the use of chemical pesticides or synthetic fertilizers accounts for 48%. The Japanese Government supported environmentally friendly farming, with certification as 'eco-farmers' and as crops produced in environmentally friendly ways.

The increased rural-to-urban migration in Japan left the countryside reliant on an aging population in Japan's rural areas. Mountainous regions, with paddy terraces of rice fields were abandoned (40%). The beginning of this change had its roots in the 1960s when rice production exceeded demand forcing farmers to abandon terraced paddy fields. The terraced paddy fields were used for tourists and other visitors who gained some experience about rice farming.

The Japanese Government also promoted biodiversity conservation in crop production and the introduction of biodiversity-friendly rice production in Shiga prefecture and '*konotori*-rice' cultivation, which helps to protect storks in paddy fields in Hyogo prefecture. The total area of terraced paddy fields in Ishikawa Prefecture is roughly about 2,500 ha grew Noto Tanada Rice and by 2013 chemical inputs have been reduced to 50 percent. Noto Tanada Rice branding will also contribute to the conservation of terraced paddy fields in the future. This biodiversity-friendly approach is spreading (Arahi, 1998; Aoki, 2016).

Home gardens are found in both rural and urban areas in most countries in Asia. They are subsistence production systems in small garden plots providing food and income for the family popular in Sri Lanka, Java, Malaysia etc. Home gardens can be agroforestry or food production systems, or a combination of both (Puri & Nair, 2004). There is also a substantial interest for home gardens in South and South-East Asia (Soemarwoto & Conway, 1991).

The benefits of home gardens are food and nutritional security, incomes for the poor, improved livelihoods, rural development, environmental conservation and social cohesion (Jacob & Alles, 1987). Studies from Nepal, Cambodia, and Papua New Guinea report that the income generated from the sale of home garden fruits, vegetables, education, and other services are significant. Families in mountain areas of Vietnam were able to generate more than 22% of their cash income through home-gardening activities. These gardens are a major resource for the development of sustainable tourism. We cite the case of Sri Lanka where some of the Kandyan home gardens were developed into sustainable tourism opportunities. Since the 1980s, after liberalization of the economy, tourism increased and garden tourism became a major feature. The small garden owners made minor changes to these gardens to make them suitable for access to tourists. They were easily accessible and located along the major highways. Most of the trees and plants were labeled with their botanical and local names and provided a calm, exhilarating educational experience for the environmentally conscious tourist.

CASE STUDY OF ISLAND TOURISM IN MALAYSIA

Problems of Island Tourism in Malaysia

This case study is based on a survey of samples of tourists and residents in Tioman Island, carried out in November 2013. The aim of this study was to survey the attitudes and perceptions of residents and tourists on Tioman Island on the impact of reef management, waste disposal and tourism on marine ecosystems, as well as to investigate their knowledge about coral reefs. Details of this study are found in Herath et al (2014).The study found that most tourists visiting the island originated from Europe comprising 49.0%. They were from France, Italy, and the UK. Malaysians comprised the second largest group accounting for 34.7% and 10.2% came from Singapore.

Majority of visitors spent less than 3 days. Nearly 12.8%, 12.8% and 19.1% spent 1, 2 or 3 days in the island respectively (ie nearly 44.7% spent 3 days or less). Few tourists stayed for longer periods as long as 6 months and they were involved in other activities such as social work.

The level of satisfaction among tourists was high. Nearly 51.1% of the tourists were very satisfied and 46.8% were satisfied. The main reasons for a high level of satisfaction were 'peaceful and calm atmosphere, nice people and diversity of the range of activities in the island'. The main reasons for dissatisfaction were (a) hygiene issues arising from poor water quality, dirty tap water, sand flies, expensive food and poor customer service (Herath et al 2014).

Evaluating Tourists Perceptions of the Negative Impacts of Tourism on the Island

Increases in island tourism have been implicated for deterioration of reef environment especially due to diving and snorkeling (Hawkins and Roberts, 1992). This damage is due to tourists stepping on the corals while snorkeling, diving, and equipment and fins used in diving near the corals.

Damage Due to Tourism Activities

Tourists were involved in snorkeling and scuba diving but these activities were generally perceived as not very harmful to the reef (Table 2). Nearly 75% considered both snorkeling and scuba diving to have either no impact or small impact on the coral reef system. Around 19.2% felt that tourism can have a large or very large impact on the reef. However, garbage disposal to the waters, sewage disposal, touching corals, standing on top of corals and anchoring on top of coral reefs were considered to have serious impacts reported by 71.2%, 59.6%.,56.9%, 61.5% and 64.7% of visitors.

Waste Disposal

Table 3 shows the pattern of waste disposal by tourists. For recyclable materials such as paper, glass, plastic and aluminium cans, the general bin was used by 68.8%, 56.5%, 59.6% and 51.1% of tourists respectively. For paper, glass, plastic and aluminium cans, the recycling bin was used by 25.0%, 39.1%, 31.9% and 46.7% of the visitors respectively. Disposal on mainland or dropping anywhere is not widely practiced. Nearly 96.8% of the tourists deposited their food waste into the general bin and ad hoc forms of disposal such as dropping anywhere is not widely reported.

Table 2. Perceptions of impact of activities on Tioman tourists (percent)

Activity	No Impact	Small Impact	Large Impact	Very large Impact	Not Sure
Snorkelling	19.2	55.8	15.4	3.8	5.8
Scuba diving	19.2	55.8	15.4	3.8	5.8
Boating	11.8	39.2	35.3	7.8	5.9
Swimming	61.5	34.6	.0	1.9	1.9
Sea Kayaking	56.9	33.3	2.0	.0	7.8
Recreational fishing	11.8	52.9	17.6	9.8	7.8
Commercial fishing	1.9	9.6	30.8	50.0	7.7
Garbage disposal (in the water)	3.8	3.8	13.5	71.2	7.7
Sewage disposal (in the water)	3.8	9.6	19.2	59.6	7.7
Feeding fish	25.5	27.5	25.5	11.8	9.8
Touching marine animals	9.6	26.9	25.0	30.8	7.7
Touching coral	2.0	11.8	23.5	56.9	5.9
Standing on top of coral reefs	1.9	9.6	15.4	61.5	11.5
Anchoring on top of coral reefs	5.9	.0	15.7	64.7	13.7

Source: Herath et al 2014

Table 3. Methods of waste disposal by tourists (percent)

Type of Material	General Bin	Recycling Bin	Disposal on Mainland	Drop Anywhere
a. paper	68.8	25.0	2.1	4.2
b. glass	56.5	39.1	2.2	2.2
c. plastic	59.6	31.9	2.1	6.4
d. Food waste	96.8	3.2	.0	.0
e. Aluminium cans	51.1	46.7	.0	2.2
f. Batteries	60.0	27.5	5.0	7.5
g. Nappies	78.9	13.2	2.6	5.3
h. Cigarettes	79.1	9.3	2.3	9.3
i. Polystyrene	72.1	20.9	2.3	4.7

Source: Herath et al 2014

Role of Recycling in the Island (Tourists Perceptions)

Recycling is important for resource management and is especially important for small islands such as Tioman. Nearly 52.8% believe that recycling occurs in the island and 30.2% were not aware. But 70.0% agree that recycling should be introduced and 30.8% do not know whether recycling should be introduced or not. Clearly there is scope for improvement of people's perceptions and knowledge on recycling and also examine the extent to which it can be adopted as a conservation strategy.

Table 4. Attitudes to recycling by tourists (percent)

Recycling Issue	Strongly Agree	Agree	Neutral	Disagree	Strongly Disagree
Recycling is Important	90.2	4.9	2.4	.0	2.4
Each consumer can contribute to the solution of the problem of waste	65.9	29.3	2.4	.0	2.4
Recycling helps with natural resource conservation	72.5	22.5	.0	.0	5.0
Useless to recycle	14.3	8.6	11.4	48.6	17.1

Source: Herath et al 2014

Table 4 s hows that more than 90% of the respondents strongly agree that recycling is important and nearly 72.5% agree that recycling will help in natural resource conservation (Table 4). Nearly 66.0% strongly agree that each consumer can contribute to solve the waste disposal problem .This is a good attitude as most tourists accept that they have an individual role to play in waste management on the island.

It is argued that consumers who hold higher individualistic and materialistic values are less likely to be involved in recycling behavior on Tioman. The study found that all types of recycling materials; paper, aluminum cans (metal), plastic bottles and glass are rather low (Latif and Omar 2008).

Snorkeling, scuba diving, boating, swimming and recreational fishing are the most visible forms of recreation on Tioman. Despite suspicions, all three activities were judged in a favorable light by the tourists. Nearly 78.4%, 71.7% and 92.0% of the tourists considered snorkeling, scuba diving and recreational fishing to have either no impact or small impact. Garbage disposal (in the water, sewage disposal, touching corals, standing on top of corals and anchoring on top of corals were perceived to be causing large or very large damage to the reef environment reported by 88.7%, 69.4%, 62.0%, 90.6%, 98.9% of the respondents respectively (Herath et al 2014).

Table 5 identifies tourist's attitudes towards reef management. An important feature is that most of the tourists (63.5%) agree that providing more educational opportunities to tourists would enhance the coral reef environment. Further they are more educated and hence do not need any special education to enable them to appreciate the importance of conservation of the environment. A majority of the tourists comprising 76.9% disagree that enforcing bans on fishing in the marine park is a good management approach. Similar ideas were expressed regarding recreation fishing inside the marine park amounting to 48.1%. .Nearly 53.0% disagreed that restricting the number of boats is a good management strategy. Nearly 56.9% of tourists disagreed that provision of additional moorings for boats would help in reef management. Only 3.9% and 2.0% strongly agree that we should limit the number of snorkelers or fishing boats per day. Around 64.7% either strongly disagree or disagree that increasing marine park staff would help.

Despite lack of confidence on the marine park management there is 100% support for the further strengthening of protected areas excluding tourism and fishing from threatened areas for reef protection. It is significant that many of the respondents knew that climate change can affect reef health reported by 98.1%. More than 90.0% of the respondents had the correct knowledge about reef biology and corals. Only 15.1% believe that dive and snorkeling activities do not affect the reef environment. This is heartening because such knowledge is very useful in enhancing the effectiveness of reef protection policy.

Table 5. Tourists responses to management policies of Tioman Island (percent)

Strategy	Strongly Agree	Agree	Neutral	Disagree	Strongly Disagree
Improve opportunities for tourists to learn about coral reef ecosystems	1.9	1.9	9.6	23.1	63.5
Increase presence of park staff	2.0	5.9	27.5	31.4	33.3
Restrict access to coral reefs showing signs of degradation	4.0	10.0	20.0	26.0	40.0
Provide additional mooring buoys for boats	3.9	5.9	33.3	29.4	27.5
Manage the number of snorkelers allowed to visit the coral reefs per day	3.9	11.8	45.1	23.5	15.7
Manage the number of boats allowed to visit the coral reefs per day	2.0	11.8	33.3	27.5	25.5
Enforce prohibition of commercial fishing inside marine park boundaries	7.7	1.9	7.7	5.8	76.9
Enforce prohibition of recreational fishing inside marine park boundaries	1.9	5.8	21.2	23.1	48.1

Source: Herath et al 2014

Evaluation of Local Community Perceptions of Tourism Impacts on the Island

Resident Sample Characteristics

A majority of the residents interviewed are males comprising 71.7% and the females constituted only 28.3% . The age distribution of the sample of respondents shows that the 15-25 and the 25-40 year age groups comprised 24.2% and 40.7% respectively. Clearly the 25-40 year age group is the dominant group here. Thus local residents comprise predominantly the younger age cohorts which can have important policy implications for future development of tourism on Tioman Island. This group may be an important target in future development activities in the island. The education level of the respondents is low compared to the tourists.. The predominant group is the group with secondary education accounting for 71% of the sample. Nearly 20.0% had only primary education. Only 8.6% reported university level education.

Tioman Island has changed towards a vibrant tourism destination. Nearly 75.0% of the respondents reported employment in the tourism industry. They work as tour operators, running food stalls and handicraft shops. The main sources of income of residents are directly or indirectly related to the tourism industry and may be indirectly involved by running handicraft shops, food stalls, etc. For this reason residents place great importance on the development of tourism in the island. Fishing is not a major source of income. Again other studies support our findings. In terms of employment, the islands' communities have various employment options since the marine parks' gazettement. Since gazettement, tourism activities have been booming which has opened up many employment opportunities to the locals in the tourism industry. Before the marine parks' gazettement, most of the locals (90%) were fishermen (Herath et al 2014).

Table 6. Major Issues on the Island

Issue	Percent
Sewage disposal	22.2
over fishing	17.8
tourism damage	26.7
statutory controls	11.1
poor management	80.0
other: e.g. fishing boats	

Source: Herath et al 2014

Residents Perception of the Marine Park Management in Tioman Island

Many residents viewed the marine park to be a good concept but it is poorly managed. Only 37.5% of the residents reported the marine park to be good and 41.7% reported it to be bad. The residents understand the importance of the coral reefs to the island. As shows in Table 6 nearly 95.9% of the residents believe that corals are important for tourism because it is a major attraction in the island. Nearly 80.0% felt that corals are important for fisheries and 77.6% thought than corals are important for recreation.

The major issue on Tioman appears to be the poor management of the marine park. Nearly 80% of the residents reported that it is the most significant problem in the island. Around 27% reported tourism damage as a problem and 22% reported sewage issues as important (Table 7).

Table 7. Disposal of waste on Tioman Island

Type of Waste	General Bin	Recycling Bin	Disposal on Mainland	Others
paper	66.7	22.9	6.3	4.2
Glass	63.3	14.3	18.4	4.1
plastic	65.3	16.3	16.3	2.0
food waste	71.7	4.3	17.4	6.5
sewage	18.4	2.6	15.8	63.2
aluminium cans	44.7	51.1	4.3	0
batteries	55.3	27.7	12.8	4.3
nappies	84.4	4.4	8.9	2.2
cigarettes	77.8	2.2	4.4	15.6
polystyrene	80.0	2.2	8.9	8.9
fishing nets	42.9	14.3	22.9	20.0
services oil	43.2	5.4	18.9	32.4
hard rubbish (e.g. old furniture, construction waste, electronics)	57.1	9.5	14.3	19.0

Source: Herath et. al. 2014

Waste Disposal and Recycling

The pattern of waste disposal by residents is given in Table 7 shows that a majority of the residents still deposit their recyclable waste such as paper and glass into the general bin although recycling bins are provided.

Several features are obvious from Table 7. Most of the materials that can be recycled are deposited in the general bin. Nearly 66.7%, 63.3% 65.35 and 44.75 deposited paper, glass, plastic and aluminium respectively in the general bin. The recycling bin was used only by 22.9%, 14.3%, 16.3% and 51.1% for paper, glass, plastic and aluminium cans respectively. Materials such as batteries, nappies, cigarettes, polystyrene were also predominantly deposited in the general bin. Aluminium cans appear to be the only waste disposed mostly to the recycling bin. A most noticeable feature is that 63.2% of the residents dispose of sewage using the adjoining forest. Some residents do not use toilets but use the adjoining forest areas for sewage disposal. This is an important issue for health in the island and also for tourism destination.

Nearly 62.2% of the respondents believe that recycling does not occur in the island but 37.8% believe that recycling does occur (Figure 1). But 100.0% of respondents agree that recycling should occur on Tioman. Nearly 85.4% believe that paper can be recycled and some 97.9% believe that plastic can be recycled. Around 77.6% believe that glass can be recycled.

Also there is general acceptance of recycling as a viable method of waste management. This study shows that 20.0% of the residents strongly agree that recycling is important and the rest (80.0%) agree that recycling is important. This perception is important because it helps introduction of any recycling much easier.

Residents' Perceptions of the Impact of Tourism on the Island

Table 8 shows the perceptions of the impact of tourism in the island. Dive-related tourism is the major industry and the coral reefs are main attraction. In reef tourism damage directly due to recreation could be high, chronic and concentrated. Substantial trampling damage to shallow water coral communities can occur by divers (Hawkins and Roberts 1992). Coral reefs are vulnerable to damage from recreational activities, as shown by a number of studies.

Table 8 shows that nearly 78.4%, 71.7% and 92.0% of the respondents considered snorkeling, scuba diving and recreational fishing to have either no impact or small impact. Boating, swimming, sea kayaking and recreational fishing appear to be the most innocuous activities reported by more than 90.0% of the respondents but these activities are not widespread compared to snorkeling and scuba diving. Garbage disposal (to the water, sewage disposal, touching corals, standing on top of corals and anchoring on top of corals were found to be causing large or very large damage to the reef environment reported by 88.7%, 69.4%, 62.0%, 90.6%, 98.9% of the respondents respectively.

The survey shows that diving is perceived as a less significant impact in the island but if areas are subjected to high levels of use in the future as tourism develops further, the damage to coral communities can be considerable. Fish feeding by divers is another impact on coral communities than direct contact (touching) or indirect contact (stirring up sediment). Fish feeding may attract predatory fish such as sharks into an area, which in turn damage the reef when seeking prey.

Table 9 shows respondents attitudes towards reef management. An important feature is that most of the respondents (43.4%) strongly support more moorings in the island. Nearly 38.5% strongly agree that commercial fishing should be prohibited. Nearly 92% of respondents either strongly agree or somewhat

Table 8. Impact of activities on Tioman coral reef ecosystems

Activity	No Impact	Small Impact	Large Impact	Very Large Impact	Not Sure
Snorkelling	35.3	43.1	9.8	5.9	5.9
Scuba diving	37.7	34.0	17.0	9.4	1.9
Boating	33.3	41.2	17.6	5.9	2.0
Swimming	72.5	23.5	2.0	2.0	.0
Sea Kayaking	64.2	28.3	5.7	.0	1.9
Recreational fishing	42.0	50.0	6.0	.0	2.0
Commercial fishing	13.7	29.4	15.7	37.3	3.9
Garbage disposal (in the water)	1.9	5.7	26.4	62.3	3.8
Sewage disposal (in the water)	12.2	14.3	20.4	49.0	4.1
Feeding fish	50.0	30.8	5.8	11.5	1.9
Touching marine animals	31.3	35.4	16.7	14.6	2.1
Touching coral	4.0	34.0	26.0	36.0	.0
Standing on top of coral reefs	3.8	3.8	18.9	71.7	1.9
Anchoring on top of coral reefs	5.6	1.9	14.8	74.1	3.7

Source: Herath et al 2014

agree for additional moorings. Thus this appears to be an issue needing attention. Around 69.3% either strongly agree or somewhat agree that commercial fishing should be prohibited. Only 7.8% and 7.7% strongly agree that we should limit the number of snorkelers or fishing boats per day. But this lower enthusiasm is obvious considering that these two activities are the lifeline for most residents. In fact 35.3% strongly or somewhat oppose any restrictions on snorkelling. Nearly 68.0% strongly agree or somewhat agree that park staff be increased.

Table 9. Reef management

Action	Strongly Oppose	Somewhat Oppose	Neutral	Somewhat Support	Strongly Support
Improve opportunities for tourists to learn about coral reef ecosystems	3.8	9.4	58.5	0	28.3
Increase presence of park staff	1.9	7.5	22.6	47.2	20.8
Restrict access to coral reefs showing signs of degradation	4.1	12.2	20.4	42.9	20.4
Provide additional mooring buoys for boats		3.8	3.8	49.1	43.4
Manage the number of snorkelers allowed to visit the coral reefs per day	11.8	23.5	11.8	45.1	7.8
Manage the number of boats allowed to visit the coral reefs per day	17.3	19.2	21.2	34.6	7.7
ibit commercial fishing inside marine park boundaries	7.7	11.5	11.5	30.8	38.5
Prohibit recreational fishing inside marine park boundaries	15.4	17.3	17.3	30.8	19.2

Source: Herath et al 2014.

Table 10. Responses on fishing restrictions (percent)

Response	Are Fishermen Restricted to Where and What They Can Fish?	Should They be Restricted?	Does Everybody Obey the Laws?
Yes	64.3	59.1	17.5
No	35.7	40.9	82.5
Valid respondents	28	44	40
Response rate	50.0	78.6	71.4

Source: Herath et al 2014.

Residents Knowledge Level

Table 10 shows that 64.3% of respondents are aware that fishing is restricted to certain areas and 35.7% were not aware that fishing is restricted in a marine park. Nearly 59.1% believe that fishing should be restricted and 40.1% believe that it should not be. Nearly 80.0% believe that stakeholders do not obey the law, again implicating the marine park authorities for poor management. Nearly 96% reported that there is no blast fishing and 97.8% reported that there is no cyanide fishing.

Local residents focus is mostly on fishing restrictions and control to minimize impacts. Obviously it is implicit in these answers that fishing somehow is still an issue that can cause adverse impacts. This is logical because it is something that they cannot control on their own as it is common property. There is some responsibility on the part of the Marine Park Authority here.

Knowledge of the reef system is high but there may be strategic bias in the responses which is difficult to detect. Despite lack of confidence on the marine park management there is 100% support for the further strengthening of protected areas excluding tourism and fishing from threatened areas for reef protection. It is significant that many of the respondents knew that climate change can affect reef health reposed by 90.6%.more than 90.0% of the respondents had the correct knowledge about reef biology and corals. This is heartening because such knowledge is very useful in in enhancing the effectiveness of reef protection policy.

CONCLUDING REMARKS

Sustainable tourism is a good concept but in terms of its applicability, many challenges exist. It is very complex and lack of local knowledge, poor planning skills, and poor regionally nuanced information thwart the ability to integrate the economic, social and environmental dimensions. Thus expansion of awareness, knowledge and planning skills is important. Political will is absent in some cases and it is important to encourage the political process to provide all incentives including financial support necessary for investment.

The case study of the Malaysian Tioman Island illustrate the potential of Marine Park Tourism. It has been largely successful and rapid increase in the number of tourists visiting the island has occurred.

Coral breakages kills the coral and reduces biodiversity of the reefs and thus can reduce the aesthetic appeal of the reefs to tourists, and degrade the reefs' ability to protect the islands from storms. Educating all snorkelers to avoid contact with corals and training them accordingly would have a multiplier effect in reducing damage. Some lodgings remain poorly managed, and causes of decline need to be identified by managers and government and preventive actions should be taken to avert unsustainable practices. Better lodging facilities may enhance the image of being one of the world's beautiful islands and enhance the tourists experience of the island's natural attractions. The island should provide for long -term sustainable development to ensure that stagnation does not occur.

The level of satisfaction among tourists is high being about 97.9% because of the peaceful and calm atmosphere, nice people and diversity of activities in the island. Divers are less satisfied with the provision of marine life education facilities, rental equipment, lodging, and the lack of other activities. The resort at the same time should ensure that the natural features of the island are sustainable, because they are the reasons for divers' visits. The conservation of the rich and beautiful natural environment seems to be the most important aspect of the development and management of Tioman, as perceived by the visitors.

It is recommended that (a) small local business community should be helped to maintain the sustainability of the Tioman Island tourism sector and (b) they should be supported by government grants and soft loans etc.The lack of educational facilities is a major factor accounting for low levels of education amongst residents in Tioman Island. Education can ensure responsible behaviors and a greater appreciation of the need to preserve the reef environment. Educational opportunities must be enhanced with better facilities to provide the labor force necessary for the tourism industry and will produce a population who will be more environmentally conscious.

Benign methods of sewage disposal must be found. Sewage disposal to the water is harmful to corals reported by 59.6% of tourists. In hotels which practice sewage treatment in-house, the treated effluent water still goes to the sea which may deposit pollutants and minerals damaging the corals. It is recommended that (a) sources of raw sewage be examined and that it should be contained by robust measures and (b) regular chemical testing of effluent at the outlet point be introduced as an important policy measure to avoid any long term damage to corals.

Recycling must be promoted. The recommendation here is to adopt measures to (a) improve peoples perceptions and knowledge on recycling (b) enhance awareness of the facilities already available for recycling in Tioman Island (c) encourage the use of the recyclable bins through greater persuasion and (d) provide other incentives such as environmental awards for using recycling bin. Moving towards green energy systems for electricity generation in Tioman is a step in the right direction.

Despite lack of confidence on the marine park management there is 100% support for further strengthening of protected areas and excluding tourism and fishing from threatened areas for reef protection. Since gazettement, of the Marine Park, tourism activities have been booming which has opened up many employment opportunities to the locals in the tourism industry. An important feature is that most of the tourists (63.5%) agree that providing more educational opportunities to to.0urists would enhance the coral reef environment.

Our results therefore suggest that there is a need for more management of diving activities if the island is to maintain its aesthetic appeal and biological characteristics. Such management might be directed either towards changing the behaviour of divers, such as better environmental education, banning access for users thought to cause most damage (e.g. novices and photographers), introducing charges/ transferable permits to reduce diver numbers at intensely dived or sensitive sites or resting some sites from all diving activity.

Regular consultation of Marine park staff, representatives of residents and tour operators to raise the level of awareness of the work of the marine park. With the gazettement, all activities that disrupt the stability of marine's eco-system are prohibited. The education element also needs to be addressed as there are still school dropouts among these islands' communities' children.

Climate change may be a serious factor for the Island in the long term and it is recommended that (a) adaptation measures be supported and (b) mitigations method must be introduced by the government.

Educational programs not only formal but also informal including reef related knowledge diffusion and awareness programs may be necessary for long term sustainable development of tourism on the island. Education can ensure responsible behaviors and a greater appreciation of the need to preserve the reef environment.

All in all, sustainable tourism is achievable provided that adequate attention is paid to the adverse impacts of tourism . This case study is limited and it is only through the cumulative studies of similar nature that the generality of the findings can be established.

REFERENCES

Alcock, A., Lane, S., & Grant, J. (1994). *National Ecotourism Strategy*. Canberra: Australian Government Publishing Service.

Alcock, D. (1995). Sustainable development of reef tourism. *Australian Science*, *16*, 26–27.

Allen, P. (2004). *Together at the table: Sustainability and sustenance in the American agrifood system*. Pennsylvania State University Press.

Almas, R., & Lawrence, G. (Eds.). (2002). *Globalization, localization and sustainable livelihoods*. Aldershot, UK: Ashgate.

Altieri, M. A. (1989). Agroecology: A new research and development paradigm for world agriculture. *Agriculture, Ecosystems & Environment*, *27*(1-4), 37–46. doi:10.1016/0167-8809(89)90070-4

Anctil, A., & Blanc, D. L. (2016). An educational simulation tool for integrated coastal tourism development in developing countries. *Journal of Sustainable Tourism*, *24*(5), 783–798. doi:10.1080/09669582.2015.1091463

Aoki, M. (2016). Does Mitigation and adaptation technologies in rice production affect product price? Evidence from Japan. In H. Ha (Ed.), *Climate Change Impacts in Urbanizing Asia*. London: Sage Publishers.

Arahi, Y. (1998). *Rural Tourism in Japan: The Regeneration of Rural Communities*. Food & Fertilizer Technology Center.

Black, R. S., & Crabtree, A. (Eds.). (2007). *Quality Assurance and Certification in Ecotourism*. Wallingford, UK: CABI Publishing. doi:10.1079/9781845932374.0000

Blamey, R. K. (1995). *The Nature of Ecotourism*. Occasional Paper No 21. Canberra: Bureau of Tourism Research.

Brodie, J. (1995). Terrestrial runoff and the Great Barrier Reef. *Australian Science*, *16*, 23–25.

Buckley, R. (2012). Sustainable tourism: Research and reality. *Annals of Tourism Research, 39*(2), 528–546. doi:10.1016/j.annals.2012.02.003

Buckley, R. C. (1994). A framework for ecotourism. *Annals of Tourism Research, 21*(3), 661–669. doi:10.1016/0160-7383(94)90126-0

Buckley, R. C. (2002). Tourism ecocertification in the international year of ecotourism. *Journal of Ecotourism, 1*(2-3), 197–203. doi:10.1080/14724040208668126

Buckley, R. C. (2008). Climate change: Tourism destination dynamics. *Tourism Recreation Research, 33*(3), 354–355. doi:10.1080/02508281.2008.11081559

Buckley, R. C. (2009a). *Ecotourism: principles and practices.* Wallingford, UK: CAB International.

Buckley, R. C. (2009b). Evaluating the net effects of ecotourism on the environment: A framework, first assessment and future research. *Journal of Sustainable Tourism, 17*(6), 643–672. doi:10.1080/09669580902999188

Buckley, R. C. (2009c). Parks and tourism. *PLoS Biology, 7*(6), e1000143. doi:10.1371/journal.pbio.1000143 PMID:19564895

Buckley, R. C. (2010). *Conservation tourism.* Wallingford, UK: CAB International. doi:10.1079/9781845936655.0000

Buckley, R. C. (2011). Reconciling air travel and climate change. *Annals of Tourism Research, 38*(3), 1178–1181. doi:10.1016/j.annals.2011.01.019

Camhi, M. (1995). Industrial fisheries threaten ecological integrity of the Galapagos Islands. *Conservation Biology, 9*(4), 715–724. doi:10.1046/j.1523-1739.1995.09040715.x

Cater, E. A. (1993). Ecotourism in the third world: Problems for sustainable development. *Tourism Management, 14*(2), 85–90. doi:10.1016/0261-5177(93)90040-R

Choo, H., & Jamal, T. (2009). Tourism on organic farms in South Korea: A new form of ecotourism? *Journal of Sustainable Tourism, 17*(4), 431–454. doi:10.1080/09669580802713440

Developments and Challenges in the Hospitality and Tourism Sector. (2010). Discussion Paper at the Global Dialogue Forum for the Hotels, Catering, Tourism Sector.

Driml, S., & Common, M. (1995). Economic and financial benefits of tourism in major protected areas. *Australasian Journal of Environmental Management, 2*(1), 19–29. doi:10.1080/14486563.1995.10648312

Eagles, P. F. (1995). *Key issues in ecotourism management.* Invited paper for State of Western Australia Annual Tourism Conference, Perth, Australia.

Emerson, R. M., Fretz, R. I., & Shaw, L. L. (2011). *Writing ethnographic field notes.* Chicago, IL: University of Chicago Press. doi:10.7208/chicago/9780226206868.001.0001

Everett, S., & Aitchison, C. (2008). The role of food tourism in sustaining regional identity: A case study of Cornwall, South West England. *Journal of Sustainable Tourism, 16*(2), 150–167. doi:10.2167/jost696.0

Figgis, P. (1993). Ecotourism: Special interest or major direction. *Habitat Australia, 21*, 8–11.

Gao, S., Huang, S., & Huang, Y. (2009). Rural tourism development in China. *International Journal of Tourism Research, 11*(5), 439–450. doi:10.1002/jtr.712

German Forum on Environment and Development. (1999). Definition of Sustainable Tourism. Author.

Hall, D. R., Roberts, L., & Mitchell, M. (2003). *New directions in rural tourism*. Aldershot, UK: Ashgate.

Hall, M., & Weiler, B. (Eds.). (1991). *Special Interest Tourism*. London: Belhaven.

Hawkins, J. P., & Roberts, C. M. (1993). Effects of recreational scuba diving on coral reef trampling on reef-flat communities. *Journal of Applied Ecology, 30*(1), 25–30. doi:10.2307/2404267

Hawkins, J. P., & Roberts, C. M. (1994). The growth of coastal tourism in the red sea: Present and future effects on coral reefs. *Ambio, 23*, 503–508.

Haywood, K. M. (1986). Can the tourist-area life cycle be made operational? *Tourism Management, 7*(3), 154–167. doi:10.1016/0261-5177(86)90002-6

Herath, G. (1995). Ecotourism development in Australia: Some relevant issues. *Annals of Tourism Research, 24*(2), 442–446. doi:10.1016/S0160-7383(97)80012-6

Herath, G. (1995). 'Ecotourism development in Australia: Some relevant issues. *Annals of Tourism Research, 24*(2), 442–446. doi:10.1016/S0160-7383(97)80012-6

Herath, G. (1996a). Ecotourism in Asia and the Pacific: potential, problems and an integrated planning model In *Proceedings of the Australian Tourism and Hospitality Research Conference. Coffs Habour: Southern Cross University.*

Herath, G. (1996b). *Ecotourism and nature conservation: the use of the Safe Minimum Standard (SMS)*. Paper presented at the 40th Annual Conference of the Australian Agricultural and Resource Economics Society.

Herath, G. (2000). Issues surrounding entrance fees as a suitable mechanism for enhancing natural areas in Australia. *International Journal of Wilderness, 6*, 35–39.

Herath, G. (2002). Research methodologies for planning ecotourism and nature conservation. *Tourism Economics, 8*(1), 77–101. doi:10.5367/000000002101298007

Herath, G., Yule, C., & Wilson, R. (2014). *Socio Economic features of Tioman Island Malaysia: Results of a Survey*. School of Business, Monash University.

Hong, S., Kim, S., & Kim, J. (2003). Implications of potential green tourism development. *Annals of Tourism Research, 30*(2), 323–341. doi:10.1016/S0160-7383(02)00060-9

ILO. (2010). *Development and Challenges in the tourism and hospitality sector*. Issues Paper for the Global Dialogue Forum for the Hotels, Catering & Tourism Sector. Available at http://www.ilo.org/public/english/dialogue/sectors/tourism.htm

Jacob, V. J., & Alles, W. S. (1987). The Kandyan gardens of Sri Lanka. *Agroforestry Systems, 5*(2), 123–127. doi:10.1007/BF00047517

Kim, S., & Jamal, T. (2015). The co-evolution of rural tourism and sustainable rural development in Hongdong, Korea: Complexity, conflict and local response. *Journal of Sustainable Tourism*, *23*(8-9), 1363–1385. doi:10.1080/09669582.2015.1022181

Kocasoy, G. (1995). Effects of tourist population pressure on pollution of coastal seas. *Environmental Management*, *19*(1), 75–79. doi:10.1007/BF02472005

Lane, B. (1994). What is rural tourism? *Journal of Sustainable Tourism*, *2*(1-2), 7–21. doi:10.1080/09669589409510680

Lane, B., & Kastenholz, E. (2015). Rural tourism: The evolution of practice and research approaches – towards a new generation concept? *Journal of Sustainable Tourism*, *23*(8-9), 1133–1156. doi:10.1080/09669582.2015.1083997

Lee, S., & Nam, S. (2005). Agro-tourism as a rural development strategy in Korea. *Journal of Rural Development*, *29*, 67–83.

Lindberg, K. (1991). *Policies for maximizing nature tourism's ecological and economic benefits*. Washington, DC: World Resources Institute.

Lindberg, K., Enriquez, J., & Sproule, K. (1996). Ecotourism questioned: Case studies from Belize. *Annals of Tourism Research*, *23*(3), 543–562. doi:10.1016/0160-7383(95)00074-7

Mac, J., & Moncuer, J. (1995). Sustainable tourism development: Managing Hawaiis unique touristic resources-Hanauma Bay. *Journal of Travel Research*, *33*(4), 51–57. doi:10.1177/004728759503300408

Marsden, T. (2003). *The condition of rural sustainability*. Assen: Van Gorcum.

Morrison, M., & Bennett, J. (2000). Choice modelling, non-use values and benefit transfer. *Economic Analysis and Policy*, *30*(1), 13–32. doi:10.1016/S0313-5926(00)50002-2

Nelson, F. (2010). *Community rights, conservation and contested land: The politics of natural resource governance in Africa*. London: Earthscan.

Neto, F. (2003). *A New Approach to Sustainable Tourism Development: Moving Beyond Environmental Protection*. DESA Discussion Paper 29. New York: The United Nations.

Njoroge, J. M. (2015). Climate change and tourism adaptation: Literature review. *Tourism & Hospitality Management*, *21*, 95–108.

Othman, P., & Rosli, M. M. (2010). The Impact of tourism on small business performance: Empirical evidence from Malaysian Islands. *International Journal of Business and Social Sciences*, *2*, 11–20.

Parry, M. L., Canziani, O. F., Palutikof, J. P., van der Linden, P. J., & Hanson, C. E. (Eds.). (2007). *Climate Change 2007: Impacts, Adaptation and Vulnerability. Contribution of Working Group II to the Fourth Assessment Report of the Intergovernmental Panel on Climate Change*. Cambridge, UK: Cambridge University Press.

Peeters, P., & Dubois, G. (2010). Tourism travel under climate change mitigation constraints. *Journal of Transport Geography*, *18*(3), 447–457. doi:10.1016/j.jtrangeo.2009.09.003

Powell, R., & Chalmers, L. (1995). *Regional Economic Impact, Gibraltar Range and Dorrigo National Parks*. Sydney: NSW National Parks and Wildlife Service.

Prosser, G. (1986). The limits of acceptable change. *Australian Parks and Recreation*, *22*, 5–10.

Puri, S., & Nair, P. K. R. (2004). Agroforestry research for development in India: 25 years of experiences of a national program. *Agroforestry Systems*, *61*(1-3), 437–452. doi:10.1023/B:AGFO.0000029014.66729.e0

Reopanichkul, P., Schlacher, T. A., Carter, R. W., & Worachananant, S. (2009). Sewage impacts coral reefs at multiple levels of ecological organization. *Marine Pollution Bulletin*, *58*(9), 1356–1362. doi:10.1016/j.marpolbul.2009.04.024 PMID:19515390

Schianetz, K., Kavanah, L., & Lockington, D. (2007). Concepts and tools for comprehensive sustainability assessments for tourism destinations: A comparative review. *Journal of Sustainable Tourism*, *15*(4), 369–389. doi:10.2167/jost659.0

Sharpley, R. (2000). Tourism and sustainable development: Exploring the theoretical divide. *Journal of Sustainable Tourism*, *8*(1), 1–19. doi:10.1080/09669580008667346

Sharpley, R., & Roberts, L. (2004). Rural tourism 10 years on. *International Journal of Tourism Research*, *6*(3), 119–124. doi:10.1002/jtr.478

Sharpley. (2009). *Tourism development and the environment: beyond sustainability?* London: Earthscan.

Sims, R. (2009). Food, place and authenticity: Local food and the sustainable tourism experience. *Journal of Sustainable Tourism*, *17*(3), 321–336. doi:10.1080/09669580802359293

Soemarwoto, O., & Conway, G. R. (1991). The Javanese homegarden. *Journal of Farming Systems Research Extension*, *2*, 95–118.

Steele, P. (1993). The economics of ecotourism. *Focus (San Francisco, Calif.)*, *9*, 4–6.

Thompson, C. S. (2004). Host produced rural tourism: Towas Tokyo antenna shop. *Annals of Tourism Research*, *31*(3), 580–600. doi:10.1016/j.annals.2003.11.004

Tisdell, C. (1995). Investment in ecotourism: Assessing its economics. *Tourism Economics*, *1*, 375–387.

Tosun, C. (2001). Challenges of sustainable tourism development in the developing world: The case of Turkey. *Tourism Management*, *22*(3), 289–303. doi:10.1016/S0261-5177(00)00060-1

UN. (1996). *Sustainable tourism development in small island developing states*. Report of the Secretary-General (document E/CN.17/1996/20/Add.3). New York: UN.

UN. (1999). *Tourism and sustainable development*. Report of the Secretary-General (Document No. E/CN.17/1999/5). New York: UN.

United Nations Environment Programme (UNEP). (2002). *Biological Diversity and Tourism: Development of Guidelines for Sustainable Tourism in Vulnerable Ecosystems, Secretariat of the Convention on Biological Diversity*. Montreal: UNEP/CBD.

Wagner, G. (2011). Going green but getting nowhere. *New York Times*, p. A29.

Wall, G. (1993). International collaboration in the search for sustainable tourism in Bali, Indonesia. *Journal of Sustainable Tourism*, *1*(1), 38–47. doi:10.1080/09669589309450699

Watson, A., & Herath, G. (1999). Research implications of the theme issues "recreation fees and pricing issues" in the public sector and societal responses to recreation fees on public lands'. *Journal of Leisure Research*, *31*, 325–334.

Wight, P. (1993). Sustainable tourism: Balancing economic, environmental and social goals within an ethical framework. *Journal of Tourism Studies*, *4*, 54–66.

Wilson, G. A. (2001). From productivism to postproductivism and back again? Exploring the (un) changed natural and mental landscapes of European agriculture. *Transactions of the Institute of British Geographers*, *26*(1), 77–102. doi:10.1111/1475-5661.00007

World Data Atlas. (2015). *Tourism*. Retrieved from https://knoema.com/atlas/topics/ /tourism-indicators / number-of-arrivals

Wright, W., & Middendorf, G. (Eds.). (2008). *The fight over food: Producers, consumers, and activists challenge the global food system*. Pennsylvania State University Press.

WTO, (2001a). *Actions in assisting developing countries to implement Agenda 21 undertaken by the World Tourism Organization since 1992*. (Document No. DESA/DSD/PC2/BP3). New York: UN.

WTO. (2001b). *The concept of sustainable tourism.* Retrieved from http://www.worldtourism.org/sustainable/ concepts.htm

Yasarata, M., Altinay, L., Burns, P., & Okumus, F. (2010). Politics and sustainable tourism development – can they co-exist? voices from North Cyprus. *Tourism Management*, *31*(3), 345–356. doi:10.1016/j.tourman.2009.03.016

ENDNOTE

1 According to FAO, the definition of Integrated Pest Management (IPM) is the careful consideration of all available pest control techniques; the subsequent integration of appropriate measures that discourage pest populations; keeping pesticides and other interventions to levels that are economically justified; and reducing or minimizing risks to human health and the environment. IPM emphasizes the growth of a healthy crop with the least possible disruption to agro-ecosystems and encourages natural pest control mechanisms.

Chapter 7
Prioritization of Eco-Tourism Forms at Sikkim, India

Ajeya Jha
Sikkim Manipal Institute of Technology, India

Somnath Mishra
Sikkim Manipal University, India

Sherap Shenga
Government of Sikkim, India

Manjushree Mishra
Sikkim Manipal University, India

ABSTRACT

Sikkim is the one of the smallest states in India. The state government is promoting eco-tourism as a primary sector of economy. Natural and cultural attributes make Sikkim an ideal destination for Cultural, wildlife, adventure and religious tourism. The objective of the paper is to prioritize these four identified forms of tourism with a view to measure their relative appropriateness in the context of Sikkim. The methodology is based on three tools based on continuous scale, Analytical Hierarchy process (AHP) and Quality Function Deployment (QFD) respectively. The data has been collected from 40 respondents (senior civil service officers) The paper concludes that that in terms of appropriateness cultural tourism emerges as best followed by religious, adventure and wildlife tourism in that order. Also the three tools appear valid as they arrive at matching conclusions. Our contribution is that prioritization of forms of tourism has been done for the first time and that too using a comprehensive methodology utilizing AHP, QFD and continuous scale.

INTRODUCTION

The study has been undertaken at Sikkim, a tiny Himalayan state of India and which offers exceptional opportunities for tourists from all over the world because of its diverse flora and fauna, cultural traditions, highly evolved religious philosophy and a terrain that provides possibilities of varied adventure activities. Government of Sikkim is keen to establish tourism as the mainstay of state economy and has evolved policies that cater to the broad concept of eco-tourism. The aim of the chapter is to prioritize four identified forms of tourism (Cultural, Wildlife, Adventure and Religious) with a view to identify their relative appropriateness in the context of Sikkim. The chapter begins by providing an overview of Sikkim, its evolution as a tourism destination, eco-tourism as a concept and in the context of Sikkim. It

DOI: 10.4018/978-1-5225-2078-8.ch007

provides the importance of planning and prioritizing in the context of tourism and then introduces a reader to the prioritizing techniques namely Analytical Hierarchy processing, Quality function deployment and Delphi. The third part of the study describes the methodology followed to undertake the study, followed by result and discussion and conclusion. Innovative features of the study are that this is for the first time prioritization of tourism forms has been undertaken using three established prioritizing techniques and has also validated these techniques by comparing the results obtained through them.

Sikkim

Sikkim, second smallest state in India is spread across an area of just 7,096 sq. km, this state has a varied terrain climate and altitude resulting in a wide range of bio-diversity. It is one of the most sought tourist destinations in India. It is completely a mountainous state. Altitudinal gradation ranges from 300 msl to over 8000 msl. It is therefore, we find, tropical, subtropical, temperate, sub-alpine and alpine region in this state, juxtaposed within a miniscule geographical region.

As a component of Eastern Himalayas it is one of the first recognized global biodiversity hotspot. 160 mammalian (Molur *et. Al* 1998b; Avasthe & Jha 1999; Agrawal 2000; Mandal 2003); over 500 bird species (Ali, 1989; Chettri, 2000; Chettri et al. 2001) Bhoj Kumar Acharya et al (2011) and Chhetri B (2011), 78 reptilian (Jha & Thapa, 2002), Chhetri B et al (2011), and 19 amphibian (Jha & Thapa, 2002); have been reported from Sikkim.

Sikkim has a matching cultural diversity too. It is a proverbial melting pot of cultures where the Lepchas (primordial people of Sikkim) reside with Bhutias and Nepalese – each having diverse, distinct and rich cultural traditions. Because of predominantly mountainous terrain Sikkim also provides ample scope for promoting adventure activities such as high altitude trekking, mountaineering, rock-climbing, river rafting, paragliding and Skiing. Himalayas have always been the spiritual abode for Hindu and Buddhist Philosophers. Even today People of Sikkim are deeply religious and spiritual. Buddhist philosophy is alive here. Many important ancient and modern religious places exist here which attract devotees from all over the world for religious and spiritual experiences.

These attributes make Sikkim an ideal destination for Cultural, wildlife, adventure and religious tourism.

Tourism in Sikkim

Karan (1989) in his research based study discusses the problems of environment and development in Sikkim Himalaya. Jacob (2000) focused upon Sikkim as a home to one of the richest varieties of flora and fauna on the globe. Jha and Jha (2001) defined tourism prospects in Sikkim in its entirety. Bora (2006) considers tourism in Sikkim as the engine of growth and affirms that the same can play a significant part in balanced sustainable development and generates benefits for the poor. Bora, Adhikary and Sikdar (2006) observe that the reopening of famed Silk Route Trade via Nathu la in Sikkim to Tibet Autonomous Region (TAR) of China on 6th July, 2006, is likely to have a wider scope in terms of tourism services. Bora and Adhikary (2006) aim in explored micro level the potentiality of 'Northeast Tourism' as a 'Gateway to Southeast Asia' linking across borders and multicultural nations. Bora, Adhikary and Sikdar (2007) believe that the integration of Northeast Tourism with ASEAN warrants a major highlight in terms of the highly acclaimed 'Look East Policy'. They further anticipate the tremendous potential of promoting Sikkim as a major tourism hub through integrating Trade and Tourism via Nathu la Route in East Sikkim. It is believed that a proper reconciliation of Nathula Trade with Tourism will certainly bring in an extra synergy in marketing cross border tourism opportunities in the state. Bora, Adhikary and Jha (2009) reveal that the encouragement of Tourism in Sikkim holds out an assured prosperity and the concerned stakeholders have catalytic role to play to deliver on its promise of making Sikkim a unique destination in the globe. Bora, Adhikary and Jha (2011) feel that development of a sustainable tourism infrastructure and a clear-cut roadmap is undoubtedly a pressing need of the hour for ensuring Sikkim's visibility in Global Tourism Map. Batabyal and Deyali (2013) specify that alpine State Sikkim is primarily known as an exotic, idyllic, multi-ethnic Indian hilly state since 1975 with its distinct bio-geographic and socio-cultural characteristics. Das and Batabyal (2014) claim that the types of tourists, types of tourism, trade and tourism promotion among stakeholders including local people, separate market and product development and analysis, aboriginal resource conservation and promotion, hidden natural attractions and adventures can be adequately utilized for a separate positioning and changing Unique Selling Proposition (USP) of Sikkim Himalaya. Saha and Debnath (2015) in their study make an attempt to examine the perceptions of tourists regarding present status of tourism in the state.

Eco-Tourism

Ecotourism is relatively a new approach in tourism. Ecotourism is a preserving travel to natural areas to appreciate the cultural and natural history of the environment, taking care not to disturb the integrity of the ecosystem, while creating economic opportunities that make conservation and protection of natural resources advantageous to the local people. Eco-tourism has been an attractive area of research for multitude of scholars (Fox J et al (2008), Lane M.B. 2010, Hall C.M. 2010, Cheia G. 2013, Aleksandrov K. 2014, Balmford A et al (2015)

Ecotourism in Sikkim

Government of Sikkim, considering the exceptional rich bio-cultural heritage of the state and its acute vulnerability advocate ecotourism and have formulated a policy in this respect Anonymous, (November 2002). It derives heavily from the concept of deep ecology Ghosh Manjulika (2011). Ecotourism in Sikkim is expected to be distinctive owing to visionary concept of the political leadership. This vision is like a revolution to free the human mind from negative thoughts and individualism which has led to differences among people causing human suffering and misery Shenga S, Jha A. (2014). It is important to review the policy and its implementation to ensure that lofty ideals of the policy may be achieved for better future of the state.

Planning and Prioritization

Policies important for success of tourism projects? Developing and enhancing tourism without a guiding framework and pre-determined strategies for achieving development goals and in ad hoc manner is impossible (Hall, C et al, 1998). Lack of proper planning has been identified as one of the major reasons of failure in the context of tourism (Ankomah et al, 1990). Tourism has been found to be multidimensional having physical, social, cultural geographic, climatic and other dimensions (Mathieson et al, 1992). Such dimensions are often conflicting and hence optimization without applying complex techniques becomes impossible. Prioritization of different forms of tourism and destinations therefore is an essential feature of future policy and planning formulations.

Ramin Asadi et al (2011) found that prioritization helps government associates in having a sustainable development as also in understanding the importance of tourism industry in Iran. Ryangnga P K, (2008), has also advocated use of GIS for prioritizing tourism destinations.

Prioritization Approaches

There are several techniques available for prioritization. This study uses Analytical Hierarchy process, Quality Function Development and Delphi.

Analytical Hierarchy Process (AHP) is a well-defined procedure for simplifying and analyzing complex situations and arriving at meaningful decisions. The approach is to first break-down their decision situation into a hierarchy of simple components, each of which can be understood and explained independently. The components of the hierarchy relate to various aspects of the decision situation and may be —tangible or intangible; meticulously measured or roughly estimated; well-understood or poorly-understood. After the hierarchical structure has been formed, the researcher methodically estimates each component by comparing each one to the other, one at a time to determine relative impact of a component in the hierarchy. In our case this has been based on the mean of the belief held by policy-makers and administrators of tourism in the state of Sikkim (Same individuals whose belief was measured by the first tool). A numerical weight is arrived through AHP for each component of the hierarchy. Hereafter, numerical priorities are determined for each of the decision alternatives through one-to-one. These numbers represent the alternatives' relative ability to reach the optimum levels. Literature is replete with various techniques for prioritization. Analytical Hierachy Process (AHP) has been a popular technique for prioritization Mishra, M. Jha, A. 2014) Hani Abu Qdais etal (2016), Rana Pratap Singh et al (2016) Pecchia L *et al* (2013), Taghipour H *et al* (2014), Cancela J *et al* (2015), Broekhuizen H *et al* (2015), Ishwar Dhami *et al* (2016), Chung-Ling Chen *et al* (2016), Ruggero Sainaghi *et al* (2016), Joyanta Pal *et al* (2016), K. Majumdar *et al* (2016), Tsung Hung Lee *et al* (2016), Erbas, Emre (2016). The present work is perhaps the first that applies AHP for prioritizing tourism forms.

Quality Function Deployment (QFD) is defined as *a method to transform qualitative user demands into quantitative parameters, to deploy the functions forming quality*. It facilitates in transforming customer-needs (the voice of the customer) into service/product feature/design characteristics. This makes it possible to come up with operational definitions of the requirements that may have been ambiguous when first conceptualized. The technique prioritizes identified product or service characteristic to make comparisons possible between various alternatives or decisions. Quality Function Deployment has been extremely popular (Claudia Grünewald et al, 2016), Kuo, T.C. Et al (2009), Ding, J.F. Et al (2009) Chen, L.H et al (2009), Andronikidis, A et al (2009), Raharjo, H et al (2010), Buyukozkan, G. Et al (2011), Ho, W et al (2011), Buyukozkan, G. et al (2013), Prasad, K.G.D et al (2013), Vinayak, K et al (2013) Gremyr, I. et al (2013), Iqbal, Z et al 2014), John, R et al (2014), Masamitsu Kiuchi et al (2016)

Delphi is a structured communication technique or method, originally developed as a systematic, interactive forecasting method which relies on a panel of experts (Dalkey et al (1963); Bernice B Brown I1968), Sackman H. ((1974); Harold A. et al (1975). Later its applications have been extended to other predictions also. The experts in the field respond to questionnaires in two or more rounds. Subsequent to each round, a facilitator (*MilbreyW. McLaughlin (1990)),* provides a summary (without naming the expert) of the experts' forecasts from the previous round as well as the reasons they provided for their judgments. Experts, thus, are encouraged to amend their earlier responses in the light of the replies of other member experts of their panel. It is believed with this process the range of the answers narrow down and the group comes together to "optimum" answer. Finally, the process is stopped after a predefined stop criterion (e.g. number of rounds, achievement of consensus, stability of results) and the mean or median scores of the final rounds determine the results (Rowe et al (1999)). Briedenhann J., Butts S. (2006), Kaynak E., Marandu E.E. (2006), Liu J.C. (1988), Rio D., Nunes L.M. (2012) relied upon Delphi for decision making with respect to tourism sector.

METHODOLOGY

To ensure the right perspective it is essential to identify the appropriateness of the eco-tourism forms in the context of the state. This will help in focusing efforts in the direction that maximizes the dividends. Keeping this in mind the study has been undertaken and the aim of the study is to prioritize four identified forms of tourism (Cultural, Wildlife, Adventure and Religious) with a view to identify their relative appropriateness in the context of Sikkim. Methodology is empirical and is based on three tools developed to measure the appropriateness of identified forms of ecotourism, for ecotourism initiatives in Sikkim. The tools are:

Ten-Point Continuous Scale

A tool measuring the belief held by the state-officers involved in planning, monitoring and promoting tourism in Sikkim on a continuous scale of ten points (with 1 being lowest and 10 as highest). The scale measures four eco-tourism sub-sectors (namely Cultural, Wildlife, Adventure and Religious) for their appropriateness in the context of the State on six criteria namely Tourist Volume, Climatic Flexibility, Infrastructural Simplicity, Eco-gentleness, Income Retention and Low investment. As no literature exists for this kind of a study the criteria were arrived at after consultation with experts monitoring eco-tourism in Sikkim. The data was collected from 40 respondents of which two were found to be invalid. The final sample size therefore is 38.

Tool Based on Analytical Hierarchy Process (AHP)

For our purpose a tool was designed with six major criteria developed for the first tool (Tourist Volume, Climatic Flexibility, Infrastructural Simplicity, Eco-gentleness, Income Retention and Low investment). Initially the relative importance of these criteria is determined and thereafter, six more matrices were designed to compare how the four eco-tourism sectors relatively measure on these criteria. The date was collected from the same 40 respondents of which six questionnaires were found to be invalid. The final sample size therefore is 34. In all cases consistency ratio is found to be well below 10 and hence results are acceptable.

Tool is Based on Quality Function Deployment (QFD)

In this study the researcher has continued with the criteria determined earlier (Tourist Volume, Climatic Flexibility, Infrastructural Simplicity, Eco-gentleness, Income Retention and Low investment). Further we also identified four customer needs (voice of customers) namely sustainability, Revenue potential, ease of setting-up and operational ease. Thereafter, we developed a correlation index of the criteria and customer voice using Delphi technique. The correlation scale ranges from 1 to 9 and 1 signifying no relationship and 9 signifying extremely strong relationship. For the delphi we identified three senior government-officers involved in state tourism policy formulation. It took three interactions to arrive at the final correlation matrix. Delphi was also used to determine the priority also. Priority scale ranges from 1 to 5 with 1 indicating lowest possible importance and 5 indicating highest possible importance.

Final weight- age has been calculated using the following formula:

Weight=Σpriority X corelation index

Final scores for the subsectors have been calculated using the formula:

Score=Σweight X normalised point

Normalized points has been obtained normalizing the values obtained for the eco-tourism sub-sectors using the first tool (based on continuous scale) as described earlier.

RESULT AND DISCUSSION

Continuous Scale-Based Tool

The result has been shown in Table 1. From the table we find that Cultural Tourism scores highest in criteria Tourist Volume, Climatic Flexibility, Eco-gentleness and Income retention with scores of 269, 280, 292 and 249 respectively. Religious tourism scores highest in criteria Infrastructural Simplicity and Low investment with scores of 277 and 254 respectively. Overall Cultural tourism with 1611 points is found to be most appropriate and is followed by Religious Tourism (1560), Adventure (1456) and Wildlife (1377) points. It may therefore, be concluded that Cultural Tourism is most appropriate in the state of Sikkim as a component of overall eco-tourism being promoted in here and may be accorded due primacy.

Table 1. Comparison of four eco-tourism sectors

	Tourist Volume	Climatic Flexibility	Infrastructural Simplicity	Eco-gentleness	Income Reten.	Low Investment	Total
Cultural	269	280	242	292	279	249	**1611**
Adventure	205	217	284	284	239	227	**1456**
Wildlife	207	225	218	268	236	223	**1377**
Religious	234	260	217	267	268	254	**1500**

Analytical Hierarchy Process

Comparison Matrix for Criteria

Table 2 provides the summary of comparative matrix for the criteria formulated for this study. The highest normalized Eigen vector is found with Climatic-flexibility (0.2388), followed by Eco-gentleness (0.2339), Income retention (0.2388), tourist volume (0.2111), infrastructural simplicity (0.0585) and low investment (0.0392) in that order. The experts, therefore, appear to lay emphasis on relatively uniform distribution of tourist season which otherwise in the context of Sikkim is highly narrow (October-November and then April-June). Emphasis is also upon tourism being eco-gentle and favour that most income retained through tourism should remain within the state. Emphasis is lower on volume of tourists and initial investments and infrastructure. Eco-tourism, therefore, is viewed primarily as a socio-environmental sector and is considered less on immediate economic concerns. This view is consistent with the scope of eco-tourism.

Tourist Volume

Volume of tourist visiting Sikkim are directly linked to the economic success of tourism sector in Sikkim. Comparison of the four subsectors eco-tourism in terms of tourist volume has been shown in Table 3. It may be noted that cultural tourism (0.476) attracts maximum number of tourists followed by religious tourism (0.306), wildlife tourism (0.142) and adventure tourism (0.076). This is logical as adventure and wildlife tourism will attract narrow array of tourists because of age and interest level constraints. Even religious tourism is somewhat narrower than the cultural tourism because of general interest of people in diverse music, dances, and festivals. Sikkim has a rich ethnic and cultural diversity and hence it attracts high number of tourists.

Climatic Flexibility

Tourism calendar as has already been stated has a constrained calendar. Tourists avoid visiting Sikkim from June to September because of heavy rains and then again from December to February because of severe winter. This leaves just two reduced windows – March-May and October-November. To attract

Table 2. Comparison matrix for criteria

	Tourist Vol	Climatic Flexibil	Infrastructu. simplicity	Eco-gentleness	Income retention	Low Investment	Normalised Eigen vector for ranking
Tourist Volume	1.000	1.336	3.539	0.906	0.784	4.235	0.2111
Climatic Flexibility	0.748	1.000	4.147	1.287	1.451	5.324	0.2388
Infrastructural simplicity	0.283	0.241	1.000	0.231	0.234	1.912	0.0585
Eco-gentleness	1.104	0.777	4.321	1.000	1.347	5.912	0.2339
Income retention	1.275	0.689	4.277	0.742	1.000	6.500	0.2185
Low Investment	0.236	0.188	0.523	0.169	0.154	1.000	0.0392

Table 3. Comparison matrix for various alternatives on 'tourist volume'

	Cultural Tourism	Adventure Tourism	Wildlife Tourism	Religious Tourism	Normalised Eigen Vector for Ranking
Cultural Tourism	1.000	5.290	3.550	1.800	0.476
Adventure Tourism	0.189	1.000	0.435	0.250	0.076
Wildlife Tourism	0.282	2.299	1.000	0.400	0.142
Religious Tourism	0.556	4.167	2.500	1.000	0.306

more tourists it is essential to encourage tourism during so called "non-tourism" time-frame. Table 4 depicts the comparative analysis of eco-tourism sub-sectors on climatic flexibility parameter. Once again we find cultural tourism (0.4662) scores higher than religious tourism (0.322), wildlife tourism (0.1278) and adventure tourism (0.0843) in that order. This stands to reason as adverse climate confines people to their homes without much work in an agricultural economy and hence most festivals and social get-togethers take place during such time across the various ethnic cultures. Hence tourists may find Sikkim an attractive proposition during adverse seasons because of the magnificent display of culture and religion during this time of the year. Further such activities take place in a social context and are very well within reach in terms of roads and other civil infrastructures. Adventure and wildlife tourism score low as they are impossible during adverse climate and generally require trekking to remote places with low infrastructure.

Infrastructural Simplicity

It may be argued that heavy infrastructural requirement may be a deterrent for any economic activity. Table 5 depicts the analysis of eco-tourism sub-sectors on infrastructural simplicity. Simpler and consequently economical infrastructure, by this argument, may therefore favour heavier inflow of tourists anywhere. Our results in this respect suggest that Adventure tourism (0.3737) scores the best followed by Cultural tourism (0.2504), wildlife tourism (0.1975) and religious tourism (0.1783) in that order. Perhaps the logic is that trekking, rock climbing, mountaineering and rafting do not require heavy infrastructure as mountains, rivers and forests are a natural resource requiring little infrastructural investment. Rather good infrastructure may make them less attractive to the tourists. Cultural tourism too scores high in here as it does not require additional infrastructure as cultural activities are an inherent component of socio-cultural setup.

Table 4. Comparison matrix for various alternatives on 'climatic flexibility'

	Cultural Tourism	Adventure Tourism	Wildlife Tourism	Religious Tourism	Normalised Eigen Vector for Ranking
Cultural Tourism	1	5.65	3.9	1.33	0.4662
Adventure Tourism	0.1770	1	0.66	0.268	0.0843
Wildlife Tourism	0.2564	1.5152	1	0.423	0.1278
Religious Tourism	0.7519	3.7313	2.3641	1	0.3218

Table 5. Comparison matrix for various alternatives on 'infrastructural simplicity'

	Cultural Tourism	Adventure Tourism	Wildlife	Religious Tourism	Normalised Eigen Vector for Ranking
Cultural Tourism	1	1.23	0.808	1.16	0.2504
Adventure Tourism	0.8130	1	4.24	1.75	0.3737
Wildlife Tourism	1.2376	0.2358	1	1.3	0.1975
Religious Tourism	0.8621	0.5714	0.7692	1	0.1783

Eco-Gentleness

For eco-tourism the eco-gentleness of an activity is crucial and rightly has been found to be most important in this study also. See Table 6. We find Cultural tourism (0.5151) to considerably higher that other sub-sectors in this respect. Adventure tourism (0.2624), wildlife tourism (0.1356) and religious tourism (0.868) in that order, score lower. This may be explained by arguing that cultural activities are confined to human habitations where awareness and mechanisms to conserve environment exist. As such the cultural activities in Sikkim are environmentally gentle because of the strong Buddhist influence. Religious tourism may have been relegated to lower position on account of the heavy investment in the state recently made to develop religious shrines. Also as our study is based on mere beliefs perhaps more scientific tools need to be applied to confirm such a conclusion. In a long term perspective perhaps religious tourism may be more eco-gentle than other sub-sectors, particularly adventure and wildlife tourism.

Income Retention

Retention of income (earned from tourism) within Sikkim in general and within specific locations is an important measure of tourism success as inclusive and geographically balanced growth are central components of eco-tourism. Table 7 clearly brings out appropriateness of eco-tourism sub-sectors under the study on this criterion. Once again we find cultural tourism (0.5567) performs better than Religious tourism (0.1923), Adventure tourism (0.1403) and Wildlife Tourism (0.1107). In case of cultural tourism as cuisine is distinctly local and tourists are accommodated at homestays owned by the local populace, practically, entire income is retained. In case of Wildlife and adventure tourism the equipment and facilities needed are not produced locally and even the food provided mostly comprises of ingredients brought from outside the state. This results in a lot of income not being retained in the state.

Table 6. Comparison matrix for various alternatives on 'eco-gentleness'

	Cultural Tourism	Adventure Tourism	Wildlife Tourism	Religious Tourism	Normalised Eigen Vector for Ranking
Cultural Tourism	1	2.675	3.64	4.87	0.5151
Adventure Tourism	0.3738	1	2.855	2.81	0.2624
Wildlife Tourism	0.2747	0.3503	1	2.024	0.1356
Religious Tourism	0.2053	0.3559	0.4941	1	0.0868

Table 7. Comparison matrix for various alternatives on 'income-retention

	Cultural Tourism	Adventure Tourism	Wildlife Tourism	Religious Tourism	Normalised Eigen Vector for Ranking
Cultural Tourism	1	3.97	4.13	3.6	0.5567
Adventure Tourism	0.2519	1	1.33	0.712	0.1403
Wildlife Tourism	0.2421	0.7519	1	0.483	0.1107
Religious Tourism	0.2778	1.4045	2.0704	1	0.1923

Table 8. Comparison matrix for various alternatives on 'low-investment'

	Cultural Tourism	Adventure Tourism	Wildlife Tourism	Religious Tourism	Normalised Eigen Vector for Ranking
Cultural Tourism	1	3.93	4.61	1.98	0.4788
Adventure Tourism	0.25445	1	1.66	0.25	0.1154
Wildlife Tourism	0.2169297	0.6024	1	0.304	0.0884
Religious Tourism	0.5051	4	3.2895	1	0.3174

Low-Investment

As tourism depends upon the participation of large number of small entrepreneurs, investment assume significance as high investments deter potential entrepreneurs, particularly in a region which economically has just begun to evolve. The details of comparisons of chosen sub-sectors on this scale have been provided in table-8. We find that cultural tourism still fares the best with Normalised Eigen vector of 0.4788 and is followed by religious tourism (0.3174), adventure tourism (0.1154) and wildlife tourism (0.0884). This perhaps can be explained on the basis of sophistication and caution required for adventure tourism and wildlife tourism which are carried out in far-flung areas (under relatively difficult circumstances) and carry physical risk for the tourists.

Overall Priority Vector

Overall priority vector (as shown in Table 9) has been calculated by summation of product of criterion Eigen vector value and vector values determined for subsector on a particular criterion. For example in case of cultural tourism overall priority vector is calculated as:

(0.2111*0.4761)+(0.2388*0.4660)+(0.0585*0.2504)+(0.2339*0.5151)+0.2185*005567+0.0392*0.4873).

In the overall priority vector, therefore, we find that highest score is for cultural tourism with a value of 0.4873). Religious tourism is a distant second with a score of (0.2267) followed by adventure tourism (0.1544) and wild-life tourism (0.1315). It may therefore be concluded that there is a merit in promoting cultural tourism in the state and the policy makers may provide necessary focus in this respect.

Table 9. Overall priority vector

	0.2111	0.2388	0.0585	0.2339	0.2185	0.0392		
Tourism	**TV**	**CF**	**IS**	**EG**	**IR**	**LI**	**Overall Priority Vector**	**Rank**
Cultural	0.4761	0.4660	0.2504	0.5151	0.5567	0.4788	0.4873	1
Adventure	0.0756	0.0840	0.3737	0.2624	0.1403	0.1154	0.1544	3
Wildlife	0.1422	0.1280	0.1975	0.1356	0.1107	0.0884	0.1315	4
Religious	0.3062	0.3220	0.1783	0.0868	0.1923	0.3174	0.2267	2

Quality Function Deployment

Correlation and Priority Matrix

Correlation and Priority matrix obtained using Delphi technique has been shown in table-10. From the table we note that Sustainability is strongly related to Eco-gentleness followed by climatic flexibility and income retention and is least related to tourist volume infrastructural simplicity and low investment. Similarly Revenue potential is strongly related to tourist volume and has low relationship with eco-gentleness. Ease of setting up is strongly related to infrastructural simplicity and has low relationship with tourist volume. Operational ease strongly relates to income generation and has lower relationship with infrastructural simplicity and low investment.

Further we find that hghest priority has been accorded to Sustainability (5), followed by revenue potential (4), operational ease (3) and ease of setting up (2). The weights obtained for the various criteria have been shown in the bottom row. Income retention (92) is found to have highest weightage and is followed by climatic flexibility (84), tourist volume (71), eco-gentleness (68), low investment (64) and infrastructural simplicity (62).

Final QFD Scores and Rank

Final scores as already stated have been calculated by summation of product of weightage obtained and normalized points of continuous scale values. Results have been shown in Table 11. We find that cultural tourism emerges as the most appropriate option with rank 1 and a summated score of 338.1343, followed

Table 10. QFD correlation and priority matrix

	TV	CF	IS	EG	IR	LI	Priority
Sustainability	3	7	3	9	7	3	5
Revenue potential	9	5	5	1	6	6	4
Ease of setting up	1	4	9	2	3	8	2
Operational Ease	6	7	3	5	9	3	3
Weights	71	84	62	68	92	64	

Table 11. Final QFD scores and rank

	TV	CF	IS	EG	IR	LI	Score	Rank
Cultural	1	1	0.3731	1	1	0.8387	338.1343	1
Adventure	0	0	1	0.68	0.0682	0.1290	114.5127	3
Wildlife	0.0313	0.1270	0.0149	0.0588	0	0	17.8108	4
Religious	0.4531	0.6825	0	0	0.7273	1	156.4143	2

by Religious tourism (with rank 2 and summated scores of 156.4143), Adventure Tourism (Rank 3 and score of 114.5127 and Wildlife tourism (Rank 4 and summated score of 17.8108).

Comparison of Results Obtained from the Three Tools

With the tool built on a continuous scale we found that the preferred eco-tourism sub-sector is cultural followed by religious, adventure and wildlife. Interestingly, with AHP and QFD also we arrive at the same conclusion. In an over-all context therefore the tools stand validated against each other. It will, however, be interesting to make a detailed comparison on the six criteria on which the comparisons have been made. Table 12 provides the details of comparison of ranking by continuous and AHP based tools. In the last row the respective correlation has also been provided.

We find that in cases of Climatic Flexibility, Infrastructural Simplicity, eco-gentleness and Income Retention the rankings are identical and hence we obtain rank correlations of 1. With Tourist Volume and low-investment we obtain rank correlations of 0.8. This because in both cases. The mean correlation is calculated as 0.9333. Therefore both the tools arrive at almost identical results. Minor differences could be because AHP, is relatively a complex tool involving paired-comparison.

Table 13 provides the details of comparison of ranking by continuous and QFD based tools. In the last row the respective correlation has also been provided.

We find that in cases of Tourist Volume, Climatic Flexibility, Infrastructural Simplicity, and Income Retention the rankings are identical and hence we obtain rank correlations of 1. With Tourist Volume we obtain rank correlations of 0.4, which is rather on the lower side. With low investment we find a

Table. 12 Result comparison continuous scale Vs AHP

Tourist Volume		Climatic Flexibility		Infrastructural Simplicity		Eco-Gentleness		Income Retention		Low Investment	
Conti	AHP	Conti	AHP	Conti	AHP	Conti	AHP	Conti	AHP	Conti	AHP
1	1	1	1	2	2	1	1	1	1	2	2
4	3	4	4	1	1	2	2	3	3	4	3
3	4	3	3	3	3	3	3	4	4	3	4
2	2	2	2	4	4	4	4	2	2	1	1
Correlation		Correlation		Correlation		Correlation		Correlation		Correlation	
0.8		1		1		1		1		0.8	

Table 13. Result comparison continuous scale Vs QFD

Tourist Volume		Climatic Flexibility		Infrastructural Simplicity		Eco-Gentleness		Income Retention		Low Investment	
Conti	QFD	Conti	QFD	Conti	QFD	Conti	QFD	Conti	QFD	Conti	QFD
1	1	1	1	2	2	1	1	1	1	2	2
4	4	4	4	1	1	2	3	3	3	4	3
3	3	3	3	3	3	3	4	4	4	3	4
2	2	2	2	4	4	4	2	2	2	1	1
Correlation		Correlation		Correlation		Correlation		Correlation		Correlation	
1		1		1		0.4		1		0.8	

Table 14. Result comparison AHP Vs QFD

Tourist Volume		Climatic Flexibility		Infrastructural Simplicity		Eco-Gentleness		Income Retention		Low Investment	
AHP	QFD	AHP	QFD	AHP	QFD	AHP	QFD	AHP	QFD	AHP	QFD
1	1	1	1	2	2	1	1	1	1	2	2
3	4	4	4	1	1	2	3	3	3	3	3
4	3	3	3	3	3	3	4	4	4	4	4
2	2	2	2	4	4	4	2	2	2	1	1
Correlation		Correlation		Correlation		Correlation		Correlation		Correlation	
0.8		1		1		0.4		1		1	

rank correlation of 0.8. The mean correlation is calculated as 0.867. Therefore both the tools arrive at almost identical results.

Table 14 provides the details of comparison of ranking by AHP and QFD based tools. In the last row the respective correlation has also been provided.

We find that in cases of Climatic Flexibility, Infrastructural Simplicity, Income Retention and Low investment the rankings are identical and hence we obtain rank correlations of 1. With Tourist Volume and low-investment we obtain rank correlations of 0.8 and 0.4 respectively. This because in both cases. The mean correlation is calculated as 0.867. Therefore both the tools arrive at almost identical results.

It therefore appears that the tools developed for the study are valid.

CONCLUSION

This study was undertaken to prioritize the ecotourism forms (namely cultural, adventure, wildlife and religious) in the state of Sikkim. From the result and discussion we find that in terms of appropriateness cultural tourism emerges as best followed by religious, adventure and wildlife tourism in that order. While developing eco-tourism in the state, therefore, priority may be accorded correspondingly. Such an approach will make implementation of eco-tourism in the state more meaningful and rewarding. We also find that the three techniques used for prioritizing, that is, continuous scale, Analytical Hierarchy process and Quality Function Deployment, all reach near-identical conclusion and this makes our results more reliable as also validate our tools in comparison to each other. The limitation of the study is that it is based on the beliefs expressed by the experts and not on more objective metrics. Future researchers may consider this for enhancing objectivity of their work.

The study provides important inputs to the policy makers and practicing managers. Policy-makers must make awesome cultural diversity which is unique to a great extent, central to the eco-tourism policy. Today tourists are looking for fresh cultural experiences set in their natural ambience. Cultural songs and dances performed during traditional festivities and observance provide powerful imagery not found with their manifestations when performed on artificial theaters. This will require visitors to move over to the remote villages which still remain the custodians of their cultural nuances and this will result in an evenly distributed tourism all over the state – an avowed aspect of eco-tourism. The practicing managers must capture this fundamental need of the modern tourists and come up with offers in this respect. They must ensure that cultural significance of such performances are not diluted due to their resulting commercialization. This may undo the charm that captivates the tourists.

The Government of Sikkim must consider placing greater emphasis on religious tourism also. Sikkim has a rich religious philosophy which attracts many a spiritual minds to visit the state as a tourist. A concrete understanding of this in the eco-tourism policies drafted for the state will facilitate providing memorable interpretative experiences to visitors as also have minimum impact on the fragile ecology of the state as Buddhism, the central religion of the state is known for its ecological sensitivity. Such an approach may bring up entirely a new dimension to the whole concept of eco-tourism. The policies in this respect may also embrace inclusion of people of the state who have been known for their spiritual dispensation and are ecologically and culturally highly refined. They may emerge as perfect hosts for religious tourists. For the eco-tourism managers this implies that they must develop mechanisms to comprehend the latent spiritual needs of their tourists in this respect and develop facilities and ambience that are consistent with religious tourism.

Though no threshold value could be developed during this study, yet it appears logical to recommend that wildlife tourism should not be pursued as of now despite the exceptional faunal richness in the state.

REFERENCES

Acharya & Chettri. (2011). Effect Of Climate Change On Birds, Herpetofauna And Butterflies In Sikkim Himalaya: A Preliminary Investigation Biodiversity of Sikkim. In Exploring and Conserving a Global Hotspot. IFS.

Agrawal, V. C. (2000). *Taxonomic studies on Indian Muridae and Hystricidae (Mammalia: Rodentia).* Records of the Zoological Survey of India, Occasional Paper No. 180.

Ajeya & Sangeeta. (2001). *Information Technology and Creativity to Develop Enterprises: A Case Study to Tourism in Sikkim.* National Seminar on Creativity and Innovation for Entrepreneurial Development, Raipur.

Aleksandrov, K. (2014). The Role of DMO for Sustainable Development of a Tourist Destination: Bulgaria Case Study. *Proceedings of 4th International Conference on Tourism & Hospitality Management,* 208-217. Retrieved May 19, 2015, from: http://jotr.eu/index.php/tourism-management/100-aleksandrov

Andronikidis, A., Georgiou, A. C., Gotzamani, K., & Kamvysi, K. (2009). The application of quality function deployment in service quality management. *TQM J.*, *21*(4), 319–333. doi:10.1108/17542730910965047

Ankomah, P. K., & Crompton, J. L. (1990). Unrealized tourism potential: The case of Sub-saharan Africa. *Tourism Management, 11*(3), 11-27.

Anonymous. (2002). *Final Report on 20 years Perspective Plan for Sustainable Tourism Development in the State of Sikkim*. Govt. of India, Ministry of Tourism & Culture, Department of Tourism, Market Research Division, Horizon Industrial Consultancy Services, New Delhi.

Asadi, R., & Daryaei, M. (2011). Prioritization of Forms of Tourism in Iran to Formulate National Strategies. *European Journal of Scientific Research, 65*(1), 144-152.

Avasthe, R.K., & Jha, A. (1999). *Mammals of Sikkim*. WWF-India.

Balmford, A., Green, J. M. H., Anderson, M., Beresford, J., Huang, C., Naidoo, R., & Manica, A. et al. (2015). Walk on the Wild Side: Estimating the Global Magnitude of Visits to Protected Areas. *PLoS Biology*, *13*(2), e1002074. doi:10.1371/journal.pbio.1002074 PMID:25710450

Bora, B., & Adhikary, A. (2006). Northeast Tourism as a Gateway to Southeast Asia-Connecting Across Borders & Cultures. *International Conference on Strategic Thought in the New Age Management*. University of Jammu.

Bora, B., Adhikary, A., & Ajeya, J. (2009). *Strategic Development of Tourism in Sikkim Himalaya -An Impetuous towards Sustainable Economy*. National Seminar on Science, Technology and Development in the Himalayas, North Bengal.

Bora, B., Adhikary, A., & Ajeya, J. (2011). *Marketing of Service Sector: An Infrastructural Road Map for Sikkim Tourism*. International Conference International Conference on Infrastructure Finance, (ICIF 2010), VGSOM, IIT Kharagpur.

Bora, B., Adhikary, A., & Sikdar, S. (2006). *Northeast Tourism-The Market Beyond Border*. Kurukshetra, No.9. Ministry of Rural Development Publication.

Bora, B., Adhikary, A., & Sikdar, S. (2007). Northeast Tourism and ASEAN-Gaining Momentum in terms of Sustainable Development, Focus. *The International Journal of Management Digest, 3*(2), 7-20.

Briedenhann, J., & Butts, S. (2006). The application of the Delphi technique to rural tourism project evaluation. *Current Issues in Tourism*, *9*(2), 171–190. doi:10.1080/13683500608668246

Broekhuizen, H., Groothuis-Oudshoorn, C. G. M., van Til, J. A., Hummel, J. M., & Ijzerman, M. J. (2015). A review and classification of approaches for dealing with uncertainty in multi-criteria decision analysis for healthcare decisions. *PharmacoEconomics*, *33*(5), 445–455. doi:10.1007/s40273-014-0251-x PMID:25630758

Brown. (1968). Delphi Process: A Methodology Used for the Elicitation of Opinions of Experts. RAND. (Document No: P-3925)

Buyukozkan, G., & Berkol, C. (2011). Designing a sustainable supply chain using an integrated analytic network process and goal programming approach in quality function deployment. *Expert Systems with Applications*, *38*, 13731–13748.

Buyukozkan, G., & Cifci, G. (2013). An integrated QFD framework with multiple formatted and incomplete preferences: A sustainable supply chain application Gülc. *Applied Soft Computing*, *13*(9), 3931–3941. doi:10.1016/j.asoc.2013.03.014

Cancela, J., Fico, G., & Arredondo Waldmeyer, M. T. (2015). Using the Analytic Hierarchy Process (AHP) to understand the most important factors to design and evaluate a telehealth system for Parkinsons disease. *BMC Medical Informatics and Decision Making*, *15*(S3), S7. doi:10.1186/1472-6947-15-S3-S7 PMID:26391847

Cheia, G. (2013). Ecotourism: Definition and concepts. *Revista de turism, North America, 15*, 56-60. Retrieved October 4, 2015, from: http://www.revistadeturism.ro/rdt/article/view/44

Chen, C.-L., & Bau, Y.-P. (2016). Establishing a multi-criteria evaluation structure for tourist beaches in Taiwan: A foundation for sustainable beach tourism. *Ocean and Coastal Management*, *121*, 88–96. doi:10.1016/j.ocecoaman.2015.12.013

Chen, L.-H., & Ko, W.-C. (2009). Fuzzy approaches to quality function deployment for new product design. *Fuzzy Sets and Systems*, *160*(18), 2620–2639. doi:10.1016/j.fss.2008.12.003

Chettri & Bhupathy. (2009). Occurrence of *Dinodon gammiei* (Blanford, 1878) in Sikkim, Eastern Himalaya, India. *Journal of Threatened Taxa, 1*(1).

Chettri, B., Acharya, B. K., & Bhupathy, S. (2011). An Overview of the Herpetofauna of Sikkim with Emphasis on Elevational Distribution Pattern and Threats and Conservation Issues: A Preliminary Investigation Biodiversity of Sikkim. In Exploring and Conserving a Global Hotspot. IFS.

Chettri, N. (2000). *Impact of habitat Disturbances on Bird and Butterfly Communities Along the Yuksom-Dzongri Trail in Khangchendzonga Biosphere Reserve* (Ph.D. dissertation). North Bengal University, India.

Chettri, N., Sharma, E., & Deb, D. C. (2001). Bird community structure along a trekking corridor of Sikkim Himalaya: A conservation perspective. *Biological Conservation*, *102*(1), 1–16. doi:10.1016/S0006-3207(01)00092-1

Chris, R. (2003). Recreational Tourism-Demand and Impacts (2nd ed.). Clevedon, UK: Channel View Publications.

Dalkey, N., & Helmer, O. (1963). An Experimental Application of the Delphi Method to the use of experts. *Management Science*, *9*(3), 458–467. doi:10.1287/mnsc.9.3.458

Debasish & Dilip. (2014). Assessing Impacts Through Community Perception: An Empirical Study for Sikkim. *Periodic Research, 3*(1), 118-122.

Debasish & Vivek. (2013). Purpose of Visit and Its Implication in Tourism Sector of Sikkim. *SIT Journal of Management, 3*(2), 157-172.

Dhami, Parks, Strager, & Conley. (2016). Suitability-sensitivity. *Journal of Ecotourismanalysis of Nature-Based Tourism Using Geographic Information Systems and Analytic Hierarchy Process.*

Ding, J.-F. (2009). Applying fuzzy quality function deployment (QFD) to identify solutions of service delivery system for port of Kaohsiung. *Quality & Quantity*, *43*(4), 553–570. doi:10.1007/s11135-007-9138-7

Erbas, E. (2016). Competitive Determinance–performance Analysis. *An Illustration on Turkish Winter Tourism Destinations Tourism Analysis*, *21*(1), 93–106.

Fox, J., Bushley, B. R., Miles, W. B., & Shimona, A. (2008). Connecting Communities and Conservation: Collaborative Management of Protected Areas in Bangladesh. Nishorgo Support Project, Bangladesh Forest Department.

Gremyr, I., & Raharjo, H. (2013). Quality function deployment in healthcare: A literature review and case study. *International Journal of Health Care Quality Assurance*, *26*(2), 135–146. doi:10.1108/09526861311297343 PMID:23534149

Grünewald, C., Schleuning, M., & Böhning-Gaese, K. (2016). Biodiversity, scenery and infrastructure: Factors driving wildlife tourism in an African savannah national park. *Biological Conservation*, *201*(September), 60–68. doi:10.1016/j.biocon.2016.05.036

Hall, C. M. (1998). *Tourism Development, Dimensions and Issues*. Melbourne: Academic Press.

Hall, C. M. (2010). Changing paradigms and global change: From sustainable to steady-state tourism. *Tourism Recreation Research*, *35*(2), 131–145. doi:10.1080/02508281.2010.11081629

Ho, W., Dey, P.K., & Lockstrom, M. (n.d.). Strategic sourcing: a combined QFD and AHP approach in manufacturing. Supply Chain Manag., 16(6), 446–461.

Hsieh, T. H. L. H.-P. (2016). Indicators of sustainable tourism: A case study from a Taiwan's wetland. *Ecological Indicators*, *67*(August), 779–787.

Iqbal, Z., Grigg, N. P., Govinderaju, K., & Campbell-Allen, N. (2014). Statistical comparison of final weight scores in quality function deployment (QFD) studies. *International Journal of Quality & Reliability Management*, *31*(2), 184–204. doi:10.1108/IJQRM-06-2013-0092

Jacob, M. M. (2000). *Speech*. GOPIO Convention–2000, Zurich, Switzerland.

Jha, A., & Thapa, K. (2002). *Reptiles and Amphibians of Sikkim*. Gangtok, India: WWF.

John, R., Smith, A., Chotipanich, S., & Pitt, M. (2014). Awareness and effectiveness of quality function deployment (QFD) in design and build projects in Nigeria. *J Facil. Manag.*, *12*(1), 72–88. doi:10.1108/JFM-07-2013-0039

Karan Pradyumna, P. (1989). Environment and Development in Sikkim Himalaya: A review. *Human Ecology, 17*(2), 257-271.

Kaynak, E., & Marandu, E. E. (2006). Tourism market potential analysis in Botswana: A Delphi study. *Journal of Travel Research*, *45*(2), 227–237. doi:10.1177/0047287506291595

Kuo, T.-C., Wu, H.-H., & Shieh, J.-I. (2009). Integration of environmental considerations in quality function deployment by using fuzzy logic. *Expert Systems with Applications*, *36*(3), 7148–7156. doi:10.1016/j.eswa.2008.08.029

Lalib, A. W., & Williams, G. B. (1998). An intelligent maintenance model (system): An application of analytical hierarchy process and a fuzzy logic rule-based controller. *The Journal of the Operational Research Society*, *49*(S7), 745–757. doi:10.1057/palgrave.jors.2600542

Lane, M. B. (2010). Affirming New Directions in Planning Theory: Co-management of Protected Areas. *Society & Natural Resources*, *14*(8), 657–667. doi:10.1080/08941920118212

Linstone & Turoff. (1975). The Delphi Method: Techniques and Applications. Reading, MA: Addison-Wesley.

Maharana, R. S. C., & Sharma, E. (2000). Valuing Ecotourism In a Sacred Lake of the Sikkim Himalaya. *Journal of G.B. Pant Institute of Himalayan Environment and Development*.

Majumdar, K., & Datta, S. (2014). *Study on Mitigation Measures of Gumti Hydro Power Plant Using Analytic Hierarchy Process and Concordance Analysis Techniques*. Dubai, UAE: Academic Press.

Manjulika, G. (2011). Buddhism and Deep Ecology, Buddhist Himalaya: Studies. In *Religion, History and Culture*. Namgyal Institute of Tibetology-Sikkim.

McLaughlin, M. W. (1990). *The Rand Change Agent Study Revisited: Macro Perspectives and micro Realities*. Stanford, CA: Stanford University.

Mishra, M., & Jha, A. (2014). Prioritizing Sectors for Economic Development in Sikkim, India. *International Journal of Asian Business and Information Management*, *5*(2).

Molur, S., & Walker, S. (1998b). *Conservation Assessment and Management Plan for Reptiles of India. Report submitted to WWF-India/BCPP*. Coimbatore, India: Zoo Outreach Organization.

Mondal, A. K. (2003). *A Checklist of Mammals of Sikkim*. Kolkata: Zoological Survey of India.

Nagai & Nakashima. (2016). A Study on the Effects of Client Company Information on the On-Site Logistics and Processes in a Supply Chain: A New Design Approach using Quality Function Deployment. *Expert Journal of Business and Management*, *4*(1), 56–62.

Okello, M. M., Wishitemi, B. E. L., & Lagat, B. (2005). Tourism Potential and Achievement of Protected areas in Kenya: Criteria and Prioritization. *Tourism Analysis, 10*(2), 151-164.

Pal, J., Pal, M., Roy, & Mazumdar. (2016). A Study on Mitigation Measures for the Development of Neermahal Palace and Surrounding Rudrasagar Lake Area in Tripura, India using Analytic Hierarchy Process. *International Journal of Applied Engineering Research, 11*(4), 2615-2619.

Passah, P. M. (2007). *Tourism as an Industry in North-Eastern Region in Ahmed Jaynal Uddin*. New Delhi: Mittal Publication.

Pecchia, L., Martin, J. L., Ragozzino, A., Vanzanella, C., Scognamiglio, A., Mirarchi, L., & Morgan, S. P. (2013). User needs elicitation via analytic hierarchy process (AHP). A case study on a Computed Tomography (CT) scanner. *BMC Medical Informatics and Decision Making, 13*(1), 2. doi:10.1186/1472-6947-13-2 PMID:23289426

Prasad, K. G. D., Subbaiah, K. V., & Rao, K. N. (2013). Supply chain design through QFD based optimization. *Journal of Manufacturing Technology Management, 25*(5), 712–733. doi:10.1108/JMTM-03-2012-0030

Pretty, J., Adams, B., & Berkes, F. et al.. (2009). The Intersections of Biological Diversity and Cultural Diversity: Towards Integration. *Conservation & Society, 7*(2), 100–112. doi:10.4103/0972-4923.58642

Qdais & Alshraideh. (2016). Selection of management option for solid waste from olive oil industry using the analytical hierarchy process. *Journal of Material Cycles and Waste Management, 18*(1), 177–185.

Raharjo, H., Chai, K. H., Xie, M., & Bramoacher, A. C. (2010). Dynamic benchmarking methodology for quality function deployment. *Benchmarking, 17*(1), 27–43. doi:10.1108/14635771011022307

Rio, D., & Nunes, L. M. (2012). Monitoring and evaluation tool for tourism destinations. *Tourism Management Perspectives, 4*, 64–66. doi:10.1016/j.tmp.2012.04.002

Rowe and Wright. (1999, October). The Delphi technique as a forecasting tool: Issues and analysis. *International Journal of Forecasting, 15*(4).

Ryangnga, P.K. (2008). Ecotourism Prioritization: A GIS approach. *South Asian Journal of Tourism and Heritage, 1*(1).

Sackman, H. (1974). *Delphi Assessment: Expert Opinion.* Forecasting and Group Process. R-1283-PR.

Sainaghi, R., Phillips, P., & Zavarrone, E. (2016). Performance measurement in tourism firms: A content analytical meta-approach. *Tourism Management, 59*, 36–56. doi:10.1016/j.tourman.2016.07.002

Salo, A. A., & Hamalainen, R. P. (1995). Preference programming through approximate ratio comparisons. *European Journal of Operational Research, 82*(3), 458–475. doi:10.1016/0377-2217(93)E0224-L

Shenga, S., & Jha, A. (2014). The Sikkim Ecotourism Policy - A Review. *Research Link - 121, 13*(2), 33-36.

Singh, R. P., & Nachtnebel, H. P. (2016). Analytical hierarchy process (AHP) application for reinforcement of hydropower strategy in Nepal. *Renewable & Sustainable Energy Reviews, 55*(March), 43–58. doi:10.1016/j.rser.2015.10.138

Swarup & Gopal. (2015). Present Pattern of Tourism – A Case Study Of Sikkim. *International Journal of Informative & Futuristic Research, 2*(11), 4128-4137.

Taghipour, H., Mohammadyarei, T., Asghari Jafarabadi, M., & Asl, H. A. (2014). *On-site or off-site treatment of medical waste: a challenge.* J Environ Health Sci Eng.

Vinayak, K., & Kodali, R. (2013). Benchmarking the quality function deployment models. *Benchmarking, 20*(6), 825–854. doi:10.1108/BIJ-07-2011-0052

Chapter 8

Can Educational Tourism Spur Economic Growth in Malaysia?

Evidence from Neoclassical Growth Model

Hylmee Matahir
Universiti Teknologi MARA Cawangan Sabah, Malaysia

Chor Foon Tang
Universiti Sains Malaysia, Malaysia

ABSTRACT

This paper employs the neoclassical growth model to investigate empirically the role of educational tourism in Malaysia's economic growth during the period of 2002:Q1 to 2014:Q4. The present study finds that all determinants including educational tourism have a significant positive impact on economic growth in Malaysia, especially in the long-run. In terms of Granger causality, our results show that educational tourism and economic growth are Granger-cause each other in both the short- and long-run. In light of this, educational tourism can be an effective stimulator of Malaysia's economic growth. Moreover, the generalised variance decomposition analysis also affirms that educational tourism explained most of the long-run variation in economic growth compared to other determinants. Therefore, educational tourism is found to be a new and reliable source for Malaysia's economic growth. For the sake of brevity, any macroeconomic policies that heading toward promoting inbound educational tourism will probably spur the growth of the Malaysian economy, especially in the long-run.

1. INTRODUCTION

Globalisation has brought significant changes in the process of economic development from growth-oriented industrial to a knowledge-based economy. In this regard, the role of education has been emphasised with aspects of life-long learning and has been highlighted in the government's policies in many countries. According to the report of the International Consultants for Education and Fairs Monitor (ICEF Moni-

DOI: 10.4018/978-1-5225-2078-8.ch008

tor), international students' mobility across the globe has raised significantly from 2.1 million in 2000 to nearly 5 million in 2014 (Anonymous, 2014). The rapid grow of mobility of international students across countries will significantly contribute to the educational tourism segment that either direct or indirectly promote the tourism market in the host country as a whole (Hsu & Sung, 1997; Huang, 2008; Rodríguez, Martínez-Roget & Pawlowska, 2012). Despite the changes in the tourism industry together with the expansion of education sector, there is little research devoted to the impact of educational tourism towards the economy of the host country as noted in Ritchie (2003) that the potential size of educational tourism is still unrecognised.

Among the Southeast Asian economies, Malaysia is eager to further develop the education tourism segment. Currently, Malaysia has been ranked at the 12th in terms of favoured destination among international students. The education tourism segment could be one of the important segment to the tourism industry with several initiatives have been taken by the government. Under the 10th Malaysia Plan, the government aims to increase about 200,000 international students' enrolment by the year 2020. This is in line with the documentation of the National Higher Education Strategic Plan (NHESP) with the aim to transform and internationalise the Malaysian Higher Education Institutions (HEIs) so that this can enhance the role of Malaysia as a hub of excellence centre (see Tham, Mahmod, & Alavi, 2013). In 2015, the government launched the *Malaysian 101 Edutourism Packages* under the collaboration of the Ministry of Higher Education (MOHE) and the Ministry of Tourism and Culture (MOTAC) to provide opportunities for the international students undertaking their tourism activities and experience that mostly offered by the respective local higher education institutions.

Despite continuing to promote her higher education institutions to the global market, negative problems arise from some of the international students should be a concern to the policymakers and the stakeholders. The positive influence of educational tourism on economic growth is further dampened by social problems committed by the international students. For example, according to the Sidang Dewan Negara (2014) reports, there are thousands of cases were reported involving the international students for violating the immigration laws such as violating their visa and extended stays in the country without permission from the Malaysian government. Other than that, they were also cases involving the international students in several criminal activities, for instance, drug trafficking, fraud and murder, thus leads to additional economic costs to the government in handling the issues. The negative implication of educational tourism has challenged the policymakers as well as the stakeholders to seek for a greater understanding of the actual impact of educational tourism on economic growth in order to use it as a channel to promote economic growth, especially in the long-run. Therefore, we examine the role of educational tourism in Malaysia's economic growth rigorously. To make our study more reliable and theoretically sound, the Feder's (1983) growth model will be used as a theoretical framework to explain and examine the impact of educational tourism on economic growth in Malaysia. Furthermore, advanced time series econometric methods such as unit root, cointegration, Granger causality, and the generalised variance decomposition methods will be utilised to achieve the objective of this study.

The balance of this paper is organised as follows. Section 2 presents the data and methodology used in this study. Empirical results and discussion will be presented in Section 3. Finally, the conclusion and policy implications will be discussed in Section 4.

2. DATA AND METHODOLOGY

2.1 Empirical Model and Data

This study follows the work done by Tang and Tan (2015a) to extend the neoclassical Feder's growth model by accommodating the element of tourism into the model. The growth model used in this study can be written as follow:

$$\ln\mathrm{GDP}_t = a_0 + a_1\ln\mathrm{CAP}_t + a_2 \ln\mathrm{XG}_t + a_3 \ln\mathrm{ETOUR}_t + e_t \tag{1}$$

where $\ln\mathrm{GDP}_t$ is the log of per capita real gross domestic products (GDP), $\ln\mathrm{CAP}_t$ is the log of per capita real capital stock, $\ln\mathrm{XG}_t$ is the log of per capita real exports of goods, and $\ln\mathrm{ETOUR}_t$ is the log of per capita educational tourism.

This study uses quarterly data from 2002:Q1 to 2014:Q4 provided by Bank Negara Malaysia (BNM) and the Ministry of Higher Education (MOHE) Malaysia. The GDP deflator is used to calculate the real term. It is essential to note here that a total number of international students at the higher education institutions in Malaysia is used as a proxy for educational tourism. However, quarterly data for educational tourism is unavailable. Therefore, we interpolate the quarterly data of educational tourism based on the proportion of international tourist arrivals for each quarter to the annual international tourist arrivals. Since educational tourism is part of international tourism (Katircioğlu, Fetih, and Caner, 2014), interpolation based on international tourist arrivals could be the best choice. Additionally, a Monte Carlo study done by Zhou (2001) discovered that increase data frequency will enhance statistical power and reduce size distortion.

2.2 Econometric Techniques

In this section, we discuss the major econometric approaches used in this study to investigate the long-run and the causal relationships between economic growth, educational tourism and other determinants in Malaysia.

2.2.1 Unit Root Analysis

A pre-requisite step in dealing with time series data is to determine the stationarity properties of the variables as Nelson and Plosser (1982) argued that most macroeconomic variables contain a unit root. This is because if the variables are found to be non-stationary, regression with such non-stationary variables is likely to provide spurious results which may lead to wrong policy implication. Therefore, testing for the order of integration of each series is extremely important. For this purpose, we conduct the non-breaks test for a unit root, namely Augmented Dickey-Fuller (ADF) and also the structural break unit root tests proposed by Clemente, Montañés and Reyes (1998). One of the advantages of using Clemente, Montañés and Reyes (1998) test for unit root is that it allows the two unknown breakpoints to be determined endogenously within two forms of models, i.e. additive outlier (AO) model, which captures an instantaneous change in the mean of the series or innovational outlier (IO) model, allowing for a gradual shift in the mean of the series.

2.2.2 Cointegration Analysis

In this study, the bounds testing approach to cointegration developed by Pesaran, Shin and Smith (2001) is employed to examine the presence of a long-run relationship between economic growth, educational tourism, exports of goods and capital in Malaysia. This technique is widely known for its advantages over other cointegration methods because it can be carried out irrespective of the order of integration of the variables, that is either $I(0)$ or $I(1)$. Moreover, the bounds testing approach to cointegration is also suitable and well perform in the study with a small sample (Narayan & Narayan, 2006; Tang & Tan, 2013). The following autoregressive distributed lag (ARDL) model is estimated using the ordinary least square (OLS) procedure in order to test the presence of cointegrating relationship between the variables of interest:

$$\Delta \ln GDP_t = \beta_0 + \beta_1 \ln GDP_{t-1} + \beta_2 \ln ETOUR_{t-1} + \beta_3 \ln XG_{t-1} + \beta_4 \ln CAP_{t-1} + \sum_{t=1}^{p} \delta_{1i} \Delta \ln GDP_{t-i} + \sum_{t=0}^{q} \delta_{2i} \Delta \ln ETOUR_{t-i} + \sum_{t=0}^{r} \delta_{3i} \Delta \ln XG_{t-i} + \sum_{t=0}^{s} \delta_{4i} \Delta \ln CAP_{t-i} + \varepsilon_t \quad (2)$$

where Δ is the first difference operator and the ε_t is the error term that follows the IID conditions. Notations p, q, r, and s are the appropriate lag order determined by Akaike Information Criterion (AIC). To check for the presence of long-run relationship, Pesaran, Shin and Smith (2001) suggested to carry out joint F-test to impose a restriction on the lagged level variables (i.e. $\ln GDP_{t-1}$, $\ln ETOUR_{t-1}$, $\ln XG_{t-1}$ and $\ln CAP_{t-1}$) in equation (2). More specifically, the joint significance F-test will be performed on the null hypothesis $\beta_1 = \beta_2 = \beta_3 = \beta_4 = 0$ against the alternative hypothesis $\beta_1 \neq \beta_2 \neq \beta_3 \neq \beta_4 \neq 0$.

It is essential to note that the computed F-statistic for bounds testing approach to cointegration does not follow the standard distribution of F-statistic. Thus, Pesaran, Shin and Smith (2001) provided two sets of critical values, i.e. lower bound, $I(0)$ and upper bound, $I(1)$. If the computed F-statistic is less than the lower bound critical value, then the null hypothesis cannot be rejected, and this indicates that long-run relationship cannot be found between the variables. On the other hand, if the computed F-statistic exceeds the upper bound critical value, the null hypothesis will be rejected, indicating there is a long-run relationship between the variables under investigation. Finally, if the computed F-statistic lies between the lower bound and the upper bound critical values, it is inconclusive and other cointegration approaches should be applied. According to Narayan (2005), the critical values tabulated in Pesaran, Shin and Smith (2001) are based on large sample sizes and thus it may not suitable for small sample study. In light of this, Narayan (2005) specifically computed the new sets of critical values with the range of sample sizes from 30 to 80 observations. Given the sample size of our study is relatively small ($T = 40$), the computed F-statistic will then be compared with the critical values simulated by Narayan (2005).

2.2.3 Granger Causality Analysis

If the variables are found to be cointegrated, the next step is to implement the Granger causality test in error-correction model (ECM). The Granger causality test in the framework of ECM allows one to examine both the short- and the long-run causalities. To carry out the Granger causality analysis, we estimate the following ECM equations:

$$\begin{aligned}\Delta \mathrm{lnGDP}_t = {} & c_1 + \sum_{i=1}^{p} \varpi_{1i} \Delta \mathrm{lnGDP}_{t-i} + \sum_{i=0}^{q} \varphi_{1i} \Delta \mathrm{lnETOUR}_{t-i} + \sum_{i=0}^{r} \psi_{1i} \Delta \mathrm{lnXG}_{t-i} + \sum_{i=0}^{s} \kappa_{1i} \Delta \mathrm{lnCAP}_{t-i} \\ & + \vartheta_1 \mathrm{ECT}_{t-1} + \xi_{1t}\end{aligned} \quad (3)$$

$$\begin{aligned}\Delta \mathrm{lnCAP}_t = {} & c_2 + \sum_{i=1}^{p} \kappa_{2i} \Delta \mathrm{lnCAP}_{t-i} + \sum_{i=0}^{q} \varpi_{2i} \Delta \mathrm{lnGDP}_{t-i} + \sum_{i=0}^{r} \varphi_{2i} \Delta \mathrm{lnETOUR}_{t-i} + \sum_{i=0}^{s} \psi_{2i} \Delta \mathrm{lnXG}_{t-i} \\ & + \vartheta_2 \mathrm{ECT}_{t-1} + \xi_{2t}\end{aligned} \quad (4)$$

$$\begin{aligned}\Delta \mathrm{lnETOUR}_t = {} & c_3 + \sum_{i=1}^{p} \varphi_{3i} \Delta \mathrm{lnETOUR}_{t-i} + \sum_{i=0}^{q} \varpi_{3i} \Delta \mathrm{lnGDP}_{t-i} + \sum_{i=0}^{r} \psi_{3i} \Delta \mathrm{lnXG}_{t-i} + \sum_{i=0}^{s} \kappa_{3i} \Delta \mathrm{lnCAP}_{t-i} \\ & + \vartheta_3 \mathrm{ECT}_{t-1} + \xi_{3t}\end{aligned} \quad (5)$$

$$\begin{aligned}\Delta \mathrm{lnXG}_t = {} & c_4 + \sum_{i=1}^{p} \psi_{4i} \Delta \mathrm{lnXG}_{t-i} + \sum_{i=0}^{q} \varpi_{4i} \Delta \mathrm{lnGDP}_{t-i} + \sum_{i=0}^{r} \varphi_{4i} \Delta \mathrm{lnETOUR}_{t-i} + \sum_{i=0}^{s} \kappa_{4i} \Delta \mathrm{lnCAP}_{t-i} \\ & + \vartheta_4 \mathrm{ECT}_{t-1} + \xi_{4t}\end{aligned} \quad (6)$$

where Δ is the first difference operator while p, q, r, and s, are the appropriate lag order of the short-run dynamic of the independent variables determined by AIC. The notation ξ_{it} are the error terms with the white noise properties. ECT_{t-1} is the one period lagged error-correction terms derived from the long-run equation. The long-run causality is captured by the t-significance of ϑ_{it}. However, the short-run causalities are the joint significant F-test of the first difference explanatory variables.

3. EMPIRICAL RESULTS AND DISCUSSIONS

We begin the analysis by identifying the order of integration of each series using the standard ADF unit root test. With respect to the results of ADF test, we notice that at the 5 per cent significance level all the variables contain a unit root at the level but the variables are stationary after first differencing. Therefore, the ADF unit root test suggests that lnGDP_t, $\mathrm{lnETOUR}_t$, lnXG_t and lnCAP_t are integrated of order one $I(1)$ process.[1] Knowing that the standard ADF unit root test may be low power, especially when the series suffered from structural break, we perform the single- and double-break unit

Table 1. The results of unit root tests with structural break(s)

Variables	Single-Break Unit Root Test				Double-Break Unit Root Test			
	AO Model		IO Model		AO Model		IO Model	
	t-statistics	*TB*1	t-statistics	*TB*1	t-statistics	*TB*1 *TB*2	t-statistics	*TB*1 *TB*2
$\ln GDP_t$	–0.274 (3)	2010:Q4	–0.149 (4)	2009:Q1	–0.683 (4)	2005:Q4 2010:Q3	–0.111 (4)	2005:Q1 2010:Q1
$\ln ETOUR_t$	–0.536 (0)**	2007:Q2	–0.325 (2)	2007:Q3	–0.625 (1)	2002:Q4 2007:Q2	–0.405 (2)	2003:Q1 2007:Q3
$\ln XG_t$	–0.463 (4)	2007:Q4	–0.814 (1)**	2008:Q2	–0.603 (4)	2005:Q3 2007:Q4	–1.126 (4)**	2006:Q1 2008:Q2
$\ln CAP_t$	–0.274 (4)	2010:Q3	–0.133 (4)	2009:Q4	–0.873 (4)	2005:Q3 2011:Q3	–0.311 (4)	2004:Q4 2011:Q2

root tests proposed by Clemente, Montañés and Reyes (1998) to re-confirm the order of integration of each variable.

Table 1 reports the results of single- and double-break unit root tests based on the additive outlier (AO) and the innovation outlier (IO) models. Based on the results, both the AO and the IO models do not reject the null hypothesis of a unit root at the level for most variables, except for educational tourism and export of goods. As a result, the order of integration of the explanatory variables are mixed and seem to be either $I(0)$ or $I(1)$ process.

With the results of mix order of integration among the explanatory variables, the bounds testing approach to cointegration is very appropriate in the context of this study. The cointegration results and the diagnostic tests are reported in Panel A of Table 2. In general, we find that our model passes a battery of diagnostic tests.[2] The computed F-statistic for cointegration is 9.558, which is greater than the upper bound critical value at the 1 per cent significance level. Therefore, we have sufficient evident to reject the null hypothesis of no cointegrating relationship between economic growth, educational tourism, export of goods and capital stock in Malaysia. It other words, Malaysia's economic growth and its determinants are cointegrated and there must be a meaningful long-run relationship between them.

Since the bounds testing approach to cointegration suggest that variables are cointegrated and the interest of this study is to assess the impact of educational tourism and other determinants on economic growth in Malaysia, estimation of long-run coefficients are necessary. For comparison and robustness, we estimate the long-run coefficients with two long-run estimators, namely ordinary least square (OLS) estimator and also the fully modified OLS (FM-OLS) estimator proposed by Phillips and Hansen (1990). As shown in Panel B of Table 2, both the estimated results of OLS and FM-OLS show that all the explanatory variables are significantly positive in explaining Malaysia's economic growth at the 1 per cent significance level. On average, we find that the impact of educational tourism toward economic growth is approximately 0.08, which means GDP will grow around 0.8 per cent for every 10 per cent increase in educational tourism. However, these values are slightly lower than the impact of export of goods and capital on economic growth in Malaysia. A 10 per cent increase in export of goods and capital, GDP will increase about 2 per cent and 4 per cent, respectively. Our empirical findings are consistent with Tang and Tan (2015b), who have also found that economic growth and its determinants are cointegrated and economic growth is also positively responded to tourism, exports and capital.

Table 2. Results of cointegration analysis

Panel A: Bounds Testing Approach to Cointegration	F-Statistic	
$\ln\text{GDP}_t = f\left(\ln\text{ETOUR}_t, \ln\text{XG}_t, \ln\text{CAP}_t\right)$	9.558***	
Narayan (2005) critical values		
Significance level	Lower bounds	Upper bounds
1 per cent	4.865	6.360
5 per cent	3.500	4.700
10 per cent	2.873	3.973
Diagnostic check	Statistics (*p*-values)	
χ^2_{NORMAL}	[2]: 1.031 (0.5970)	
χ^2_{SERIAL}	[1]: 1.291 (0.2558); [2]: 1.379 (0.5017)	
χ^2_{ARCH}	[1]: 0.045 (0.8304); [2]: 0.253 (0.8812)	
χ^2_{RESET}	[1]: 2.782 (0.0953)	
CUSUM	Stable at the 5 per cent level	
CUSUMSQ	Stable at the 5 per cent level	
Panel B: The estimate of long-run coefficients (*p*-values)		
Variables	Ordinary Least Squares (OLS)	Fully Modified OLS (FM-OLS)
Constant	4.7844*** (0.0000)	4.8579*** (0.0000)
$\ln\text{ETOUR}_t$	0.0820*** (0.0000)	0.0778*** (0.0000)
$\ln\text{XG}_t$	0.2077*** (0.0019)	0.1872*** (0.0039)
$\ln\text{CAP}_t$	0.4075*** (0.0000)	0.4183*** (0.0000)

Note: *** indicates statistically significant at the 1 per cent level. [.] indicates the order of diagnostic tests.

Given the variables are cointegrated, we perform the Granger causality analysis within the ECM to verify the direction of causality among the variables under review. The Granger causality results are shown in Table 3. In the short-run, the null hypothesis of non-causality, either from $\ln\text{ETOUR}_t$ to $\ln\text{GDP}_t$ or reciprocally, are rejected at the 1 per cent significance level. This implies that educational tourism and economic growth is inter-dependent in the short-run. Apart from that, the short-run Granger causality results also suggest that there is one-way causality running from $\ln\text{ETOUR}_t$ to $\ln\text{CAP}_t$

Table 3. Results of Granger causality analysis

Variables	$\Delta \ln GDP_t$	$\Delta \ln ETOUR_t$	$\Delta \ln XG_t$	$\Delta \ln CAP_t$
Likelihood Ratio Statistics (*p*-values)				
$\sum \Delta \ln GDP_{t-i}$	–	11.9910*** (0.0074)	34.1958*** (0.0000)	30.8999*** (0.0000)
$\sum \Delta \ln ETOUR_{t-i}$	13.6734*** (0.0034)	–	7.6108 (0.0548)	12.4291** (0.0144)
$\sum \Delta \ln XG_{t-i}$	41.1326*** (0.0000)	11.4555*** (0.0033)	–	1.5157 (0.2183)
$\sum \Delta \ln CAP_{t-i}$	20.7958*** (0.0001)	2.1247 (0.1449)	12.0259** (0.0172)	–
ECT_{t-1}	−0.2234** (0.0449)	−0.2603*** (0.0041)	−0.1567 (0.1637)	−0.3176*** (0.0028)
Diagnostic Analysis				
χ^2_{NORMAL}	[2]: 3.643	[2]: 1.353	[2]: 0.453	[2]: 3.281
χ^2_{SERIAL}	[1]: 0.9561 [2]: 1.3761	[1]: 0.923 [2]: 0.929	[1]: 3.142 [2]: 3.421	[1]: 0.109 [2]: 0.153
χ^2_{ARCH}	[1]: 0.188 [2]: 0.432	[1]: 1.566 [2]: 5.398	[1]: 0.002 [2]: 1.391	[1]: 0.162 [2]: 0.126
χ^2_{RESET}	[1]: 4.666** [2]: 4.670	[1]: 2.465 [2]: 2.969	[1]: 1.494 [2]: 1.744	[1]: 2.936 [2]: 3.494

Note: *** and ** indicate statistically significant at the 1 and 5 per cent level, respectively. [.] indicates the order of diagnostic tests.

and from $\ln XG_t$ to $\ln ETOUR_t$. With respect to the long-run causality, we find that the coefficients of one period lagged error-correction term (ECT_{t-1}) are statistically significant only when the dependent variables are GDP, educational tourism and capital. Our causality results suggest that there are two-way causality among $\ln ETOUR_t$, $\ln GDP_t$ and $\ln CAP_t$ in Malaysia. However, only one-way causality is found running from $\ln ETOUR_t$, $\ln GDP_t$ and $\ln CAP_t$ to $\ln XG_t$ in the long-run. In summary, we can conclude that educational tourism is an effective engine of growth for the Malaysian economy in both the short- and long-run.

The findings of cointegration and the Granger causality analyses discussed earlier provide us some insight about the long-run and the causal relationships among the variables under review. However, the empirical evidence would be more persuasive to examine the relative strength of educational tourism, export of goods and capital in explaining Malaysia's economic growth using the generalised variance decomposition analysis. A major advantage of using generalised version of variance decomposition is that this method is insensitive to the order of the variables in the system (Wang, 2003; Tang, Cheam and Ong, 2015). The results are reported in Table 4. In short-run (i.e. 8-quarters), about 47.98 per cent

Table 4. Results of generalised variance decomposition – lnGDP

Horizon	GDP	Educational tourism	Export of goods	Capital
1	50.16	0.12	38.82	10.89
2	49.12	0.36	37.63	12.90
3	46.82	3.46	35.86	13.86
4	47.93	9.16	30.50	12.41
8	47.98	13.68	22.97	15.37
16	49.11	16.40	17.82	16.67
17	49.84	16.64	17.37	16.15
18	50.07	17.02	17.05	15.86
19	49.33	17.44	17.08	16.15
20	49.73	17.93	16.50	15.84

Note: The variance is re-scaled to 100.

forecast error variance in economic growth is attributed to its own variations. While shock in educational tourism, capital and export of goods explain approximately 13.68 per cent, 15.37 per cent and 22.97 per cent variations respectively of the variation in economic growth. In the long-run (i.e. 20-quarters), we notice that educational tourism is relatively more important than other determinants (i.e. capital and export of goods) of economic growth in Malaysia. More formally, a shock in educational tourism explains about 17.93 per cent of the fluctuation in economic growth. However, a shock in the export of goods and capital only explain about 16.50 per cent and 15.84 per cent respectively of the variation in economic growth. In summary, our empirical evidence again signifies the importance of educational tourism to Malaysia's economic growth, especially in the long-run. Therefore, educational tourism can be a potential contributor towards Malaysia's economic growth in the long-run.

4. CONCLUSION AND POLICY IMPLICATIONS

Many studies have investigated the role of tourism on economic growth, but empirical work that focuses on the possibility of promoting economic growth through the channel of educational tourism, particularly in Malaysia remains unknown. In light of this, it is essential to investigate the role of educational tourism in Malaysia's economic growth using time series analysis. To doing so, we employ the neoclassical growth model as a theoretical framework to allow us to reasonably examine the impact of educational tourism on economic growth in Malaysia. Our empirical results show that educational tourism, economic growth, export of goods and capital in Malaysia are cointegrated. Therefore, we utilise the ECM-based Granger causality test to find the causal link among the variables under review. One of the key findings derived from the Granger causality results is that educational tourism and economic growth in Malaysia are inter-dependent in both short- and the long-run. Additionally, we find that export of goods and capital are Granger-cause economic growth in Malaysia. Finally, our results of variance decomposition suggest that educational tourism is relatively an important determinant of growth for the Malaysian economy, especially in the long-run. Therefore, our study concludes that it is possible to promote long-term economic growth in Malaysia through the channel of educational tourism.

Apart from the concluding remarks, it is also important to draw some policy recommendations from the findings of this study. As our findings suggest that educational tourism is a reliable determinant of economic growth in Malaysia, policymakers should head toward promoting educational tourism in Malaysia. To promote educational tourism in Malaysia, MOHE and MOTAC should collaborate to design new educational tourism marketing programme or further enhance the existing educational tourism programme such as the *Malaysia 101 Edutourism Packages* to cover both public and private HEIs. Apart from that, MOHE and MOTAC should also utilise the information and communication technologies (ICTs) in promoting educational tourism as it is an important tool in disseminating information. According to Eder, Smith, and Pitts (2010), more than 90 per cent of international students have used the internet to obtain information prior to deciding their study destination. Thus, it is vital to design more attractive and informative website by the HEIs and the respective ministries (i.e. MOHE and MOTAC) so it can cater information as much as possible about the educational tourism products in Malaysia. Additionally, in line with the point raised by Tang and Abosedra (2014, 2016), policymakers should encourage the HEIs to conduct more educational exchange programme in order to attract greater numbers of international students coming to enrol their short-term courses in Malaysia. Moreover, the HEIs should organise international conferences more frequent in Malaysia as it is a good channel to increase the inflows of international researchers. Given their time attending the conferences, the organisers can exploit their presence by arranging tours to some attractive places nearby, allowing cross-cultural interaction between the local people, and learn about the local arts and cultures so that it can create a valuable tourism experience while they are in Malaysia. Through these experiences, they, either under the student exchange programme or travel for attending conferences, will indirectly become an agent in transferring information about Malaysia to their family and friends when returning to their home country. This eventually helps to promote educational tourism in Malaysia. As a result, economic growth in Malaysia can be sustained via educational tourism and the aim to be an educational hub in the region can also be achieved.

ACKNOWLEDGMENT

We would like to thanks the two anonymous reviewers for their valuable comments and suggestions on the earlier draft of this research paper. Additionally, research funding provided by the Fundamental Research Grant Scheme (203/CDASAR/6711528) from the Ministry of Higher Education in Malaysia is gratefully acknowledge.

REFERENCES

Anonymous. (2014). *Summing up international student mobility in 2014*. Retrieved from http://monitor.icef.com/2014/02/summing-up-international-student-mobility-in-2014/

Clemente, J., Montañés, A., & Reyes, M. (1998). Testing for a unit root in variables with a double change in the mean. *Economics Letters*, *59*(2), 175–182. doi:10.1016/S0165-1765(98)00052-4

Eder, J., Smith, W. W., & Pitts, R. E. (2010). Exploring factors influencing student study abroad destination choice. *Journal of Teaching in Travel & Tourism*, *10*(3), 232–250. doi:10.1080/15313220.2010.503534

Feder, G. (1983). On exports and economic growth. *Journal of Development Economics*, *12*(1-2), 59–73. doi:10.1016/0304-3878(83)90031-7

Hsu, C. H., & Sung, S. (1997). Travel behaviors of international students at a Midwestern university. *Journal of Travel Research*, *36*(1), 59–65. doi:10.1177/004728759703600109

Huang, R. (2008). Mapping educational tourists experience in the UK: Understanding international students. *Third World Quarterly*, *29*(5), 1003–1020. doi:10.1080/01436590802106247

Katircioğlu, S., Fethi, S., & Caner, H. (2014). Testing the higher education-led growth hypothesis in a small island: An empirical investigation from a new version of the Solow growth model. *Quality & Quantity*, *48*(2), 729–744. doi:10.1007/s11135-012-9798-9

Narayan, P. K. (2005). The saving and investment nexus for China: Evidence from cointegration tests. *Applied Economics*, *37*(17), 1979–1990. doi:10.1080/00036840500278103

Narayan, P. K., & Narayan, S. (2006). Saving behaviour in Fiji: An empirical assessment using the ARDL approach to cointegration. *International Journal of Social Economics*, *33*(7), 468–480. doi:10.1108/03068290610673243

Nelson, C. R., & Plosser, C. R. (1982). Trends and random walks in macroeconomic time series: Some evidence and implications. *Journal of Monetary Economics*, *10*(2), 139–162. doi:10.1016/0304-3932(82)90012-5

Pesaran, M. H., Shin, Y., & Smith, R. J. (2001). Bounds testing approaches to the analysis of level relationships. *Journal of Applied Econometrics*, *16*(3), 289–326. doi:10.1002/jae.616

Phillips, P. C. B., & Hansen, B. E. (1990). Statistical inference in instrumental variables regression with I(1) processes. *The Review of Economic Studies*, *57*(1), 99–125. doi:10.2307/2297545

Ritchie, B. W. (2003). *Managing educational tourism* (Vol. 10). Channel View Publications.

Rodríguez, X. A., Martínez-Roget, F., & Pawlowska, E. (2012). Academic tourism demand in Galicia, Spain. *Tourism Management*, *33*(6), 1583–1590. doi:10.1016/j.tourman.2012.01.010

Sidang Dewang Negara. (2014). *Parlimen Ketiga Belas Penggal Kedua Mesyuarat Kedua*. Retrieved from https://www.cljlaw.com/files/hansard/DR/pdf/DR-09062014.pdf

Tang, C. F., & Abosedra, S. (2014). Small sample evidence on the tourism-led growth hypothesis in Lebanon. *Current Issues in Tourism*, *17*(3), 234–246. doi:10.1080/13683500.2012.732044

Tang, C. F., & Abosedra, S. (2016). Tourism and growth in Lebanon: New evidence from bootstrap simulation and rolling causality approaches. *Empirical Economics*, *50*(2), 679–696. doi:10.1007/s00181-015-0944-9

Tang, C. F., Cheam, C. L., & Ong, S. C. (2015). Comparing the contributions of tourism and non-tourism exports to economic growth in Malaysia. *Current Issues in Tourism*, 1–14. doi:10.1080/13683500.2015.1057108

Tang, C. F., & Tan, E. C. (2013). How stable is the tourism-led growth hypothesis in Malaysia? Evidence from disaggregated tourism markets. *Tourism Management*, *37*, 52–57. doi:10.1016/j.tourman.2012.12.014

Tang, C. F., & Tan, E. C. (2015a). Tourism-led growth hypothesis in Malaysia: Evidence based upon regime shift cointegration and time-varying Granger causality techniques. *Asia Pacific Journal of Tourism Research*, *20*(S1), 1430–1450. doi:10.1080/10941665.2014.998247

Tang, C. F., & Tan, E. C. (2015b). Does tourism effectively stimulate Malaysias economic growth? *Tourism Management*, *46*, 158–163. doi:10.1016/j.tourman.2014.06.020

Tham, S. Y., Mahmod, N. K., & Alavi, R. (2013). Assessing policies for attracting international students: Case of Malaysia. *Asia Pacific Journal of Education*, *33*(1), 112–126. doi:10.1080/02188791.2012.759536

Wang, P. (2003). *Financial Econometrics*. London: Routledge.

Zhou, S. (2001). The power of cointegration tests versus data frequency and time spans. *Southern Economic Journal*, *67*(4), 906–921. doi:10.2307/1061577

ENDNOTES

1. To conserve space, the full results of ADF unit root test are not report here, but it is available upon request from the authors
2. Based upon the computed diagnostic tests, the Jarque-Bera test for normality, the Breusch-Godfrey test for serial correlation and the Lagrange Multiplier (LM) test for autoregressive conditional heteroscedasticity (ARCH) show that the residuals are white noise. Additionally, the Ramsey RESET test suggest no mis-specification error at the 5 per cent significance level. Finally, both CUSUM and CUSUMSQ tests indicate that the estimated parameters are stable at the 5 per cent significance level.

Chapter 9
Changing Behavioural of Patterns of Travelers to Urban Ecotourism Sites of Kuala Lumpur

Sudipta Kiran Sarkar
Berjaya University College of Hospitality, Malaysia

ABSTRACT

This underlying motivation behind this chapter is to examine and understand the changing patterns of travel behaviour of travellers to urban nature attractions of 2010 and 2015 (5 year gap period) in the context of Kuala Lumpur. Kuala Lumpur, the capital of Malaysia offers a major potential for the growth and development of urban ecotourism given the natural hotspots in both inside and on the peripheries of the city. The results emanating from the descriptive statistics employed in this study demonstrate that changes have occurred in terms of benefits of urban ecotourism, ecotourism activity, source of ecotourism knowledge and in terms of more female ecotourists than male. These results put forth a range of implications from the perspectives of understanding the evolving tourist behaviour in urban spaces and significance of urban eco-travel in Malaysia. In light of challenges and prospects faced in terms of survival of nature-based areas in and around Kuala Lumpur, the findings of the study have been discussed.

INTRODUCTION

Cities across the world have always been the point of confluence of diverse communities, cultures and individuals. Cities being confluence points have initiated the exchange and co-production of new ideas, develop epistemic values and bring innovation that has paved the path towards progress for humanity (Mitra, 2016). More interestingly, cities which enable vast travel opportunities for many due to the facilities it provides; lodging, entertainment and other utilities, have been instrumental in the construction of global citizenship through social exchanges in diverse cultural spaces it abounds (Mitra, 2016). It is in cities that ideas of ecological conservation and environmental awareness emerge and this helps in

DOI: 10.4018/978-1-5225-2078-8.ch009

educating eco-travellers before they venture into wilderness spots for nature-based recreation (Kastelein, 2004). Nature spots in urban areas often become the means through which environmental learning and appreciation takes place that makes urban ecotourism a growing phenomenon in many cities across the world where an increasing number individuals seeking nature-based experiences (Okech, 2009; Weaver & Lawton, 2007). Urban Ecotourism is a concept that promotes environmental responsibility, local economic vitality, cultural diversity and experiential richness in urban tourism settings (Gibson, Dodds, Joppe & Jamieson, 2003). Global urban destinations like Singapore, Hong Kong, Taiwan and Toronto have focused on urban ecotourism as a part of their promotion of urban tourism experiences to international tourists (Wu, Wang & Ho, 2010).

The cities of Kuala Lumpur and Penang in Malaysia also hold a lot of potential for urban ecotourism given the natural hotspots both cities abound. Ecotourism in Malaysia is considered an area of major emphasis and is a part of broader growth and development of tourism in the country (Bhuiyan, Siwar, Ismail & Islam, 2011). Malaysia also won the Best Ecotourism Destination Award at The Travel Weekly (Asia) Industry Award in 2007 and 2008 (Tourism Malaysia, 2008). Malaysia is also among the twelve mega-biologically diverse countries with its tropical rainforests covering upto 60 percent of its landmass abounding diverse species of flora and fauna (Tourism Malaysia, 2008). Ecotourism in Malaysia by 2002 was growing at a rate of 35 percent annually and constituting 10 percent of its tourism (Marker, Blanco, Lokanathan & Verma, 2008). Given this significance of ecotourism in Malaysia, urban ecotourism can be posited as a recreational activity able to provide satisfying urban nature-based experiences to tourists and visitors and motivating them to re-visit urban nature-based attractions is imperative. Moreover, development of smart cities based on development of sustainable natural environments and information technology has been the call of the day across the world. Urban ecotourism development in the cities of Kuala Lumpur and Penang can foster and set examples of best practice smart destinations in Malaysia.

Visitors and tourists to urban ecotourism attractions have been found to give priority to ecological and environmental aspects (experiential value), experiential knowledge and seek alternative tourism activity in urban areas that are related to nature and authentic nature-based experience (Okech, 2009; Weaver & Lawton, 2007). Moreover, socialization between visitors and tourists while visiting urban ecotourism sites is an important aspect that renders them satisfactory ecotourism experiences and influences their behavioural intentions (Chan & Baum, 2007; Eubanks Jr, Stoll, & Ditton, 2004). Besides, opportunities for environmental education as well as environmental resilience experienced by urban ecotourism attractions provide enhanced opportunities for visitors and tourists to engage in nature-based recreation in such attractions (Kastelein, 2004). Accessibility in terms of developed transport systems and technological connectivity in terms of Wi-Fi availability, internet zones and social media sharing in urban areas can benefit visitors and tourists to derive satisfaction and intention to re-visit urban ecotourism attractions. Unique nature spots in and around cities and urban areas can be used sustainably by local tourism authorities through the promotion of urban ecotourism to all sections of the urban population in order to educate them and make them aware about the value of natural environments to human societies (Okech, 2009).

Tourists engaged in urban eco-travel or eco-tourists in urban settings are driven by the factors of self-fulfillment, thrill and excitement in experiencing ecotourism activities. Eco-tourists visiting urban ecotourism destinations give priority to ecological and environmental aspects (experiential value) and seek alternative tourism activity in urban areas that are related to nature and authentic nature-based experience (Gibson et al., 2003). Moreover, eco-tourists tend to have higher levels of education and as a result seek to acquire knowledge through learning on key aspects of urban ecotourism attractions particularly environmental values and ecotourism activities (Okech, 2009). Experiential knowledge of ecotourism sites and learning and interpretation of environmental aspects in those sites are critical for eco-tourists' intention to engage in their visitation behaviour (Gibson et al., 2003; Lu & Stepchenkova, 2012; Weaver & Lawton, 2007). Social aspects are also important for eco-tourists due to the social relationships established between eco-tourists in sharing the fun, thrill and enjoyment in experiencing ecotourism activities (Chan & Baum, 2007; Harlow & Pomfret, 2007).

Given this significance of eco-tourist travel intentions and attitudes with the proliferating importance of eco-travel in modified urban spaces, this study attempts to examine and understand the changing patterns of travel behaviour of eco-travellers to urban nature attractions in Kuala Lumpur attractions. The study looks at 2010 and 2015 (5 year gap period in terms of the changing travel behavioural patterns of eco-travellers to the different nature-based attractions in Kuala Lumpur. Due to increased awareness and emphasis on sustainability issues and greening of urban spaces, it is imperative to understand how an urban eco-travel destination is perceived over a period of time by travellers.

URBAN ECOTOURISM

Urban ecotourism was a concept first coined in 1996 and is considered as one sustainable means of experiencing tourism in urban areas. Urban destinations like Singapore, Hong Kong, Taipei and Kuala Lumpur have focused on urban ecotourism as a part of their promotion of urban tourism experiences to international tourists (Wu et al., 2010).

Urban Ecotourism or Urban Green Tourism is a concept that promotes environmental responsibility, local economic vitality, cultural diversity and experiential richness (Dodds & Joppe, 2001; Gibson et.al, 2003). Urban Ecotourism involves visiting natural areas in and around urban areas for enriching experiences of tourists on nature and ecology, adventure, society and culture which contributes to sustainable development and alternative recreational opportunities within an urban tourism destination (Gibson et al., 2003). Planeta.com an award winning website on ecotourism in a conference dedicated to urban ecotourism in 2004 described it as "simply nature travel and conservation in a city environment" (Kastelein, 2004). The Toronto Green Tourism Association (2006) defined urban ecotourism as "travel and exploration in and around a city that provides visitors and residents with a greater appreciation of the cities' natural resources and cultural resources".

URBAN ECOTOURISM GROWTH POTENTIAL

Urban ecotourism is growing in many urban tourism destinations across the world and individuals seeking nature-based experiences in urban settings are increasing in the recent times (Okech, 2009). In addition to the rationalities of urban ecotourism mentioned earlier as posited by Weaver & Lawton (2007), it is imperative to mention that cities are more conducive for the development of urban ecotourism as cities play an important part in educating tourists about natural environment and biodiversity (Kastelein, 2004). Moreover, it is through these cities that majority of the global tourist movements take place as they act as gateways and urban ecotourism would provide a perfect opportunity to the tourists for experiencing unique ecological experiences in and around the cities in turn leading tourism revenues for the cities (Kastelein, 2004). Urban ecotourism that also takes place in modified spaces with altered natural state can be a resilient in terms of the volume and capacity of ecotourism activities it can permit areas (Weaver & Lawton, 2001). Urban ecotourism settings in modified natural spaces could be urban parks, cemeteries, Zoos and botanical gardens 'naturalized' golf courses, stormwater control ponds and landfill sites (Weaver & Lawton, 2007). Ecotourism in modified spaces of urban areas can harness the improved urban transportation systems making it an egalitarian affair in terms of being less costly and more efficient as compared to ecotourism attractions in non-rural areas (Weaver & Lawton, 2001). In the context of ecotourism in China or locally called as 'shengtai luyou', natural destinations can also be inclusive of cultural aspects like arts and architecture as well also modern structures that is believed to enhance the aesthetic appeal of the natural setting (Buckley, Cater, Lingshen & Chen, 2008). This Chinese view falls in line with rationale behind urban ecotourism that grows in urban settings involving modern, cultural structures and modified landscapes.

KEY ASPECTS OF URBAN ECOTOURISM

Being an offshoot of traditional ecotourism, urban ecotourism consists of some of the main features of it which are: biodiversity conservation, education and interpretation of nature-based attractions and contribution to environmental values rather than economic (Wu et al., 2010). As mentioned earlier, some of the pertinent components of urban ecotourism are environmental responsibility, local economic vitality, cultural diversity and experiential richness. Environmental responsibility refers to conservation and enrichment of the natural environment for its long –term sustainability and ecological balance (Dodds & Joppe, 2001). According to the Urban Ecotourism Declaration (2006) urban ecotourism has the following objectives:

- Conserving natural landscape, biodiversity and cultural heritage
- Maximizing local benefits and engaging the local community as owners, investors, hosts and guides
- Educating visitors and residents on environmental matters, heritage resources, sustainability
- Reducing ecological footprint

URBAN ECOTOURISM ACTIVITIES AROUND THE GLOBE

Examples of urban ecotourism operations can be found at different parts of the world. The Dolphin watch tours in Hong Kong, caving, canopy walk and hiking at Batu Caves, Bukit Nanas and Forest Research Institute of Management (FRIM) in and around Kuala Lumpur as well as the cities of Singapore, Tehran, Pune or ecotourism at Yangmingshan National Park near Taipei are some of the examples of urban ecotourism destinations and attractions in Asia (Liaghati, Khoshbakht, Mahmodi, Koucakzade, & Omidvar, 2010; Wu et al., 2010). In other parts of the world the Detours in New Zealand, pedestrian 'alternative guided tours' in European cities, as well as the parks in central Belgrade, urban green tourism in Toronto or the areas close to Babitonga Bay in Brazil and Edinburgh in Scotland, are some of the examples of urban ecotourism worldwide (Anastasijevic, Anastasijevic, Bobic, Stojanovic, Mesicek, 2009; Dodds & Joppe, 2001; Higham & Luck, 2002; Tsipidis, 2004).

KUALA LUMPUR AS AN URBAN ECOTOURISM DESTINATION

Ecotourism is one of the main sub-areas of Malaysia's tourism industry. The nation promotes ecotourism as one of its principal tourism products to inbound tourists. Malaysia is among the twelve mega-biologically diverse countries with its tropical rainforests covering upto 60 percent of its landmass abounding diverse species of flora and fauna (Tourism Malaysia, 2008). Ecotourism by 2002 was growing at a rate of 35 percent annually and constituting 10 percent of its tourism (Marker, Blanco, Lokanathan & Verma, 2008).

Kuala Lumpur, the capital of Malaysia and one of the most prosperous urban centres in South East Asia is noted for its modern and old urban architectures, nightlife, gastronomic hotspots, shopping and entertainment. It is also known as the most important business and commercial centre of the country making it one of the most congested and busy urban settings of the country. But despite being a heavily urbanized area it holds a distinction of abounding ample spaces of nature and wilderness both within it and along its peripheries. Considerable tracts of natural areas provide bounteous opportunities for eco-tourism development in the forest reserves at Bukit Nanas (11 hectares), Bukit Sungai Putih (7.41 hectares) and Bukit Sungai Besi (42.11 hectares), ridges at Bukit Gasing and Bukit Dinding together with other undeveloped hilly areas of Kampong Sungai Penchala (Dewan Bandaraya Kuala Lumpur [DBKL], 2012). These forest reserves that extend well beyond the city limits and its suburbs have rendered a perfect setting for nature-based recreational activities and abundant nature spots to thrive for the appreciation and consumption of eco-travelers.

Kuala Lumpur is a city where the concept of 'urban forest' (informality and naturalness characteristic) is perfectly adaptable to its informal character and layout of its natural regenerating ecology (Justice, 1986). This provides ample opportunities for ecotourism in Kuala Lumpur and an opportunity to tourists to reach a nature trail within a very short time. Eco-tourism is increasingly being promoted in Kuala Lumpur as a means of protecting the natural environment that might otherwise be under the threat of development (Tourism Malaysia, 2008). The 2nd World Ecotourism Conference in 2010 held in Kuala Lumpur addressed the potential and scope of urban ecotourism development in Kuala Lumpur significantly for the first time (World Ecotourism Conference, 2010).

Ecotourism opportunities in Kuala Lumpur consist of the Taman Tasik Perdana or the lake gardens, the Forest Research Institute of Management (FRIM), Bukit Nanas Forest Reserve, the Dark Caves which is a part of the geological formations in Batu Caves, a major Hindu pilgrimage site in Kuala Lumpur. Besides, there are many recreational forests on the periphery of the city that abound abundant rainforests and waterbodies in the form of lakes and waterfalls. The Taman Tasik Perdana or the lake gardens is an urban park stretching over an area of 92ha. (227 acres) parkland (Kuala Lumpur Tourism Association [KLTA], 2012). It includes the famous Kuala Lumpur Bird Park, the butterfly park, deer park and the orchid garden. The Kuala Lumpur is one of the largest bird parks in South East Asia and houses about 5,000 birds from about 160 species belonging to different parts of South-East Asia (Kuala Lumpur Tourism Association [KLTA], 2012). It covers an area of 20.9 hectares and is popularly known as the "World's Largest Free-flight Walk-in Aviary". The Orchid garden houses about 3000 species from around the world and 800 species from Malaysia (Kuala Lumpur Tourism Association [KLTA], 2012).

The Bukit Nanas Forest Reserve is a unique small stretch of original rainforest lying in the heart of Kuala Lumpur city covering an area of 11 hectares. The forest was gazette as a Forest Reserve in 1906 and was subsequently as a Wildlife Reserve and Bird Sanctuary in 1934 and in 1950 (Kuala Lumpur Tourism Association [KLTA], 2012). About 5 hectares of the pristine section of the forest was gazetted as a Virgin Jungle Reserve. It was also established as a recreational forest on July 29, 1970(Kuala Lumpur Tourism Association [KLTA], 2012). The Forest Reserve offers two main nature trails, Merbau Trail (361 m long and the Jelutong Trail (300 m long) and houses an educational forestry information centre (Kuala Lumpur Tourism Association [KLTA], 2012).

The Forest Research institute of Malaysia (FRIM) is a well-managed forest science park in Kuala Lumpur located within the Bukit Lagong Forest Reserve (Ramlan, Radam, Yacob & Yahya, 2011). It covers an area of 600 hectares and offers unique ecotourism related recreational activities like the canopy walkway approximately 300 meters above sea level and one of the oldest canopy walkways in Malaysia (Ramlan et al, 2011). It also offers opportunities for bird-watching, trekking through forest trails and nature photography. It abounds water-bodies like lakes and waterfalls that abounds many aquatic and avian fauna species.

The Dark cave is one of the attractions at Batu Caves hill, a major Hindu pilgrimage site in Kuala Lumpur that offers educational, research and tourist recreational opportunities. It offers opportunities for rock climbing and caving opportunities organized by the Malaysian Nature Society. It consists of geological formations of stalactite, stalagmite, flowstone, cave pearls, cave curtains, column and pools and abound 100 million years old fauna species like the Trapdoor spider, the rarest spider in the world, rousettus fruit bats and cave racer snakes (darkcavesmalaysia.com, 2012).

The expanse of nature delights found within close proximity of the city include the nature-based recreational hot spots of Kanching recreational forest that features the Kanching falls, Templer Park featuring the multi-tiered Templer Park waterfalls, Sungai Chilling waterfalls and Fish Sanctuary and the Ampang Recreational Forest. The Kanching Recreational Forest is about 24 kms from Kuala Lumpur city and provides recreational opportunities of picnicking, photography and bathing in the Kanching waterfalls and some moderate adventure activities like hiking along the path of the waterfalls as well as jungle walking along the dipterocarp hill forest it abounds. The Templar Park also located 25kms north of Kuala Lumpur is known for nature-based recreational activities and is known for a number of mammals and bird species. Sungai Chilling is a nature reserve consisting of the picturesque Chilling waterfalls and the Sungai Chilling Fish sanctuary, a project under the Selangor State Fisheries Department. Sungai Chilling is located at a distance of 75kms from Kuala Lumpur and involves about an hour and half drive. It is one of the main eco-travel spots closest to the busy urban spaces of Kuala Lumpur. Visitation of the Chilling waterfalls involve a 4 hour trek with a fast flowing hill stream to be crossed 5 times before one can reach the pool at the base of the Chilling waterfalls. At the entrance of the Sungai Chilling Fish Sanctuary, there are camping sites for overnight camping activities.

METHODOLOGY

Kuala Lumpur demonstrates an example of a modified ecotourism space in urban settings. It offers abundant scope for urban eco - travel activities in non-traditional settings. The significance of Kuala Lumpur as an eco-travel destination in modified urban spaces received a further impetus in the World Ecotourism Conference 2010. Moreover, the eco-travel activities in Kuala Lumpur form a part of Malaysian ecotourism which is expected to grow by 4.3% by 2017 as the Malaysian government regards ecotourism a special area of importance in the overall tourism growth in the country (Bhuiyan, Siwar, Ismail & Islam, 2011). Given that urban modified spaces have the capability to attract a wide range of eco –travellers with varying motivations and needs (Wight, 2001), Kuala Lumpur is expected to attract a major part of travellers passing through this city to different parts of the country and also those visiting the city itself.

In terms of the sample size, 600 respondents were reached both in the cases of 2010 and 2015 as it was considered appropriate and likely to provide more reliable results. Data for the study was collected at 4 nature-based attractions in and around Kuala Lumpur; KL Bird Park, Forest Research Institute of Malaysia(FRIM) in Kepong, at Dark Caves in Batu Caves and Bukit Nanas. Based on descriptive statistics covering aspects of eco-tourists profile, activities and demographic details, the data was analysed. The aspects covered were purpose of travel to Kuala Lumpur, ecotourism activities to participate, benefits of ecotourism, source of ecotourism information and knowledge, and demographic aspects like age, gender, education levels and countries of origin.

DISCUSSIONS

Benefits from Urban Eco Travel

The results unfolding reflect some really interesting change between 2010 and 2015. One of the most observable changes has been in the benefits from urban eco-travel. The findings from the 2010 demonstrate eco-travellers derived significant levels of environmental learning benefits from urban eco-travel to nature-based sites in Kuala Lumpur. Seeking learning experiences has been one of most important motivations of eco-tourists that distinguish them from other types of tourists when it comes to experiencing ecotourism (Chan & Baum, 2007; Beaumont, 2011). In 2015, the findings reveal that this has been replaced by socialisation as the most important benefit derived from eco-travel to the nature spots of Kuala Lumpur. Socialisation among urban eco-travellers entails meeting likeminded individuals during the process of ecotourism experience and engaging in intense interaction with them. Such a process of social interaction with peer-eco travellers plays an important factor in enhancing the quality of their nature-based experiences and bringing satisfaction to eco travellers in their ecotourism experiences (Lu & Stepchenkova, 2012).Moreover, socialisation that occurs between eco-tourists during their participation in ecotourism activities influences their quality of ecotourism experience (Harlow & Pomfret, 2007). Socialisation is an important aspect for eco-tourists that influences their behavioural intentions by means of sharing their experiences in an affective way (emotions and feelings) (Chan & Baum, 2007; Eubanks Jr, Stoll, & Ditton, 2004).

A wide number of previous studies based on different nature-based recreational contexts have emphasized on socialisation as a key activity eco-tourists engage in. It has been instrumental in inten-

Table 1. Benefits from urban eco-travel

	2010	2015
Environment Learning	65%	55%
Socialisation	45%	70%
Experiential & Recreational Value	60%	60%

Note: The frequency does not sum up to 100% because of multiple responses.

sifying and invigorating the wilderness experiences of eco-tourists. Socialisation is brought about by social influences emanating from travelling with friends, or the relationships among eco-tourist group members initiated by communities, like voluntary environmental organizations or birding communities (Eubanks Jr, Stoll, & Ditton, 2004; Harlow & Pomfret, 2007). This leads to the development of a deep social bondage brought about by firstly, hedonic means (sharing of moments of thrill, fun and enjoyment while engaging with nature, wildlife and nature-based activities together) and secondly, epistemic means (interactions involving knowledge and experience sharing on wildlife, ecology and environmental awareness) of socialisation (Chan & Baum, 2007; Eubanks Jr, Stoll, & Ditton, 2004; Harlow & Pomfret, 2007). This process of social bondage through socialisation builds collective virtues in an eco-tourists' group and their collective commitment towards the living environment, resulting in a profound collective consciousness (Harlow & Pomfret, 2007). This has been manifested in the studies of Ryan, Hughes and Chirgwin (2000), Weaver (2002), Holden and Sparrowhawk (2002), Lee, Graefa and Li (2007), Kuentzel and Heberlein (2006).

Weaver (2002) found that the social element in terms of meeting likeminded individuals is reasonably high for ecotourists during their ecotourism experiences. Holden and Sparrowhawk (2002) observed among trekkers' to Annapurna, Nepal demonstrating a significant need to socialise with each other and deeply appreciating the camaraderie of fellow-trekkers in the trekking tour groups. Chan and Baum (2007) and Lu and Stepchenkova (2012) found socialisation factors to play a considerable role in making ecotourists' select and visit ecolodges and in providing them satisfying ecolodge experiences. Chan and Baum (2007) observed socialising with peer eco-tourists was a vital social-psychological push factors that motivated them to visit ecolodges in Sukau, East Malaysia. Similarly, Lu and Stepchenkova (2012) while studying eco-tourists' experiences shared online in the context of ecolodges in Costa Rica found that the eco-tourists derived gratification only from socialising with fellow eco-tourists in the ecolodge with similar interests as it enriched the quality of their experience.

More specialised eco-tourists have been found to consider socialisation with peer eco-tourists a highly critical factor in their engagement with nature and nature-based recreational activities. Eco-tourists engaging with specialised nature-based activity like birding tend to consider socialisation with friends and individuals of the same birding community or with family members significant in their specialisation process as it initiates knowledge gathering and participation in birding activities (McFarlane, 1996). Socialisation among eco-tourists' engaging in specialized nature-based recreational activities leads to the creation of strongly knit communities as it involves sharing "similar attitudes, beliefs, and ideologies, engage in similar behaviour, and have a sense of group identification" (MacFarlane, 1996, p. 37). This leads to the creation of strong specialist communal values and principles, which in turn, necessitates the community members to continuously communicate with each other to keep the said communal values and principles intact (McFarlane, 1996). Similar findings were reflected in the study of Lee, Graefa and Li (2007), where it was observed that social aspects are critical in recreational paddling. The paddling groups, which involved a considerable level of socialisation, were most common since they involved group members who were friends, confirming that specialised recreational individuals required significant levels of interaction with likeminded individuals with similar values and views (Lee et al., 2007). Similar observations were made by Moore, Scott and Moore (2008) and Kuentzel and Heberlein (2006), where socialisation, relationships and cooperative interactions formed a critical part of specialised nature-based recreationalists' experiences. For many eco-tourists, being participants in specialised nature-based recreational activities like bird-watching and water-based recreational experiences like paddling and boating, the social aspects in terms of socialisation between peer eco-tourists are reasonably imperative (Eubanks Jr, Stoll, & Ditton, 2004).

Eco-tourists's satisfaction with a particular ecotourism activity has also been found to be based on opportunities for socialisation among them in the form of sharing of information and knowledge through interactions with peer eco-tourists which were equally educational (Ryan, Hughes and Chirgwin, 2000). This facilitates desires of personal development among eco-tourists that drives them into attaining spiritual cognizance, understanding of the value of ecology and its conservation (Harlow & Pomfret, 2007). Socialisation hence facilitates a process of social awareness by being the means to build collective intelligence among eco-tourists about the environment, ecology and nature-based recreation (Harlow & Pomfret, 2007; Galley & Clifton, 2004).

Socialisation have been found to strongly enrich the ecotourism experiences of softer eco-tourists who seek opportunities of intense social interactions with peer eco-tourists as a part of intensely stimulating and recreational nature trips that they seek (Cini, Leone & Passafaro, 2010). In contexts like cave tours, softer eco-tourists tend to take a lot of pleasure in socialising with their friends, peer eco-tourists and relatives (Kim, Kim, Park & Guo (2008)

Socialisation becomes an integral part of the activities of softer eco-tourists in their experiences of nature-based attractions as travelling with bigger groups and seeking of intense recreational and affective moments with them are what they primarily look for (Laarmen & Durst, 1987; Weaver & Lawton, 2007). Though seeking nature still remains a basis of their travel, softer eco-tourists seek more gratifying social experiences and less challenging engagements with the environment. This opens up the opportunities of mass involvement of soft eco-tourists in ecotourism taking place in less geographically challenging yet ecologically rich areas.

Eco-Tourists' Participation in Activities

Moreover, photography which was the most practised activity in 2010 have changed to nature-viewing and jungle trekking as the most practised activities in 2015. This reflects the observations of Tao, Eagles and Smith (2004) and Zografos and Allcroft (2007) where self-defined eco-tourists or soft eco-tourists as in the case of this study were found to engage in hiking/walking as a popular activity far more than photography as an activity. Environmental values driven by pro-environmental behaviour among eco-tourists has been identified as one of their main intentions of participating in ecotourism activities.

Higham and Luck (2002) identified 3 cases of urban ecotourism in New Zealand where the potential of natural environment restoration in urban areas was being met through eco-tourists' pro-environmental activities as in all the 3 cases populations of floral and faunal species were allowed to regenerate. Harlow and Pompfret (2007) found that one of the main driving forces for eco-tourists to visit nature-based

Table 2. Eco-tourists' participation in activities

	2010	2015
Photography	60%	50%
Nature Viewing	45%	60%
Jungle Trekking/Hiking	45%	65%

Note: The frequency does not sum up to 100% because of multiple responses.

areas were for their keen interest in experiencing environment as well as their willingness to contribute towards conservation of natural elements like flora and fauna through nature-viewing and nature-based activities like hiking. Zografos and Allcroft (2007) identified environmental values as one of the main concern among a wide group of eco-tourists. Most eco-tourists irrespective of their demographic and trip characteristics considered 'biodiversity preservation' as the most critical element of nature seeking activities in their ecotourism experience. Tao, Eagle & Smith (2004) found strong pro-environmental attitudes among self-defined eco-tourists and general eco-tourists visiting ecotourism sites in terms of their nature-seeking motivations. Cini, Leone & Pacafaro (2010) found holiday motivations of eco-tourists were driven by ecocentric viewpoints which reflected profound commitment for the intrinsic value of environment and the importance of human-nature interactions. Chan & Baum (2007) identified viewing wildlife in wilderness settings and preservation of such settings as one of the main aspects of ecotourism experiences of eco-tourist visiting Sabah in Malaysia. Nature-viewing experiences in clean and undisturbed ecological state of Sabah and the affective experience of it were one of the main aspects eco-tourists seek.

Eco-Tourists' Purpose of Travel

The results emanating from the data of the descriptive statistics employed in this study demonstrate that majority of eco-travellers to Kuala Lumpur travelled with the purpose of culture and leisure in mind instead of nature and ecotourism in 2010 and that has remained the same as in 2015. This is clearly indicative of the presence of soft eco-travellers who consider urban nature travel as one of the aspects of their overall trip to the city. Eco travellers visiting ecotourism hot spots in urban settings tend to be more on the 'soft' side as they seek recreational, social with certain levels of physically challenging-based activities in natural settings. This is in contrary to hard eco- tourists who seek risky, challenging and longer interactions with nature (Weaver & Lawton, 2007). Soft eco-travellers tend to travel more for the recreational and socialisation benefits they derive with moderate motivations for deep ecological experiences. Henceforth, the primary purpose of visit has remained as culture and leisure instead of nature and ecotourism over the period of time from 2010 till 2015.

Eco-Tourists' Source of Information and Knowledge

Finally and also quite interestingly, social media which was the most important source of urban eco-travel related information and knowledge in 2010, has been replaced by websites of ecotourism attractions as the top source of information and knowledge in 2015. This is a vital change since social media platforms

Table 3. Eco-tourists' purpose of travel

	2010	2015
Culture & Leisure	60%	62%
Entertainment & Shopping	50%	50%
VFR	40%	40%
Nature-based recreation	25%	27%

Note: The frequency does not sum up to 100% because of multiple responses.

Table 4. Eco-tourists' source of information and knowledge

	2010	2015
Social Media	65%	60%
Ecotourism websites	54%	65%
Print Media (Travel books/brochures)	35%	30%
Word of mouth	25%	25%

Note: The frequency does not sum up to 100% because of multiple responses.

have been traditionally found to be the best sources of electronic word of mouth information (Nusair, Erdem, Okumus & Bilgihan, 2012).

The development of wireless technologies like Worldwide Interoperability for Microwave Access (WiMAX), and mobile technologies have enabled internet to reach destination of low digital access as well as users of digital gadgets like smartphones, tablets to have access to internet from any remote natural location (Buhalis & Law, 2008). This increased access to internet is cost-saving and in turn provides access to internet for effective destination management information and planning (Buhalis & Law, 2008; Sigala & Marinidis, 2010). Social media platforms connected to destination websites can be accessed with the use of much handy devices will therefore enable eco-tourists an improved network for dialogue among them in nature-based settings.

In terms of the range of age of eco-travellers, the average is between 26-45 that remains unchanged between 2010 and 2015. Past literature on eco-tourists' demographic profiles have found that eco-tourists were relatively younger and also relatively with higher educational levels (Lu & Stepchenkova, 2012; Wight, 2001). In terms of nationalities, majority of eco-travellers were from Europe and Western countries and they were younger individuals instead of belonging to the baby boomer generation. In both 2010 and 2015, close to 70% of eco-travellers to urban ecotourism sites in Kuala Lumpur were from UK, USA and Australia. Marker, Blanco, Lokanathan and Verma (2008) observed that demand for ecotourism in Malaysia were driven by higher income developed countries of Western Europe and North America.

However, what has interestingly changed is the number of female and married eco-travellers. In 2010, there were more male travellers and in 2015, female travellers seem to travel more as per the results of the study. This seems to indicate a surge in women travellers in the context of urban nature-based tourism. Solo women travel has increased over the past 5-10 years due to change in type of lifestyle choices and pleasure in travelling alone (Miller, 2010).

The development of 'smart cities' throughout the world have focused on the embedding green spaces and green lifestyles as one of its hallmarks. Conserving natural spaces in mega-urban areas and utilizing them for recreational, educational and ecological purposes for the well-being of urban communities is a striking feature of smart cities. Connecting these urban natural spaces with the help of soft mobility means like mass rapid transit systems involving metro/subway trains, trams and fuel efficient vehicles is believed to be the way forward towards sustainable and smart cities. With 74.5% of the Malaysia's population living in urban areas particularly Kuala Lumpur and an estimated 90% of the population to live in urban spaces by 2050 (Fong, 2016), the significance of its urban eco-travel spots will be growing. The vitality and resilience factors existent in urban nature spots of Kuala Lumpur will have the potential to meet the nature-based recreational and educational needs of this increasing urban population. In terms of international travellers seeking to experience nature-based in Kuala Lumpur, the city is being branded and promoted in a way in which ecotourism (alongwith food tourism, health tourism and educational tourism) is prioritized as one of the main tourism clusters to allure 12 million tourists with an estimated revenue of RM62 billion (Lim, 2016).

The expanse of wilderness spots in and around of urban areas necessitates the qualitative development of urban eco-travel as an alternative path to protecting the natural environment that might otherwise be under the threat of real estate development (Gibson et al., 2003). Kuala Lumpur having that kind of a setting requires sustained development of urban ecotourism. Even though, the Klang valley which represents Kuala Lumpur alongwith adjoining suburbs have experienced high levels of pollution and deforestation due to urban expansion and industrialisation threatening the urban forest cover to disappear, deforestation has been reported to have slowed down in the last 20 years (Miyamoto, Parid, Aini & Michinaka, 2014). This opens opportunities for urban eco-travel activities to grow in the future with different patterns of urban eco-travel activities and travellers. However, developmental projects continue to threaten the ecology, flora and fauna of the forest cover in and around Kuala Lumpur as it was alleged in the case of Kanching Forest Reserve and the Ampang Forest Reserve (Cheng & Foo, 2012; Reduan, 2016). Many of these developments in turn, also threaten ecotourism. The Ampang Forest Park, which is claimed to be one of the closest nature escapades from the centre of Kuala Lumpur city abounding a mountain stream offering multiple nature-based activities to eco-travellers, is facing challenges from the construction of East Klang Valley Expressway (EKVE) (Reduan, 2016). While eco-activist organisations and individuals are debating on this issue with the parties responsible for building the expressway, the park's future and its ecological sustainability remains at stake (Mustafa, 2016). As per latest observations posted in some eco-travellers' blogs, the Ampang Recreational Forest often frequented by joggers, cyclists and foreign backpackers, appears to be closed for public use. Given the increasing importance on the development of smart cities across the world which emphasizes on reducing private automobile consumption and automobile transportation to prevent impending environmental consequences, the expansion plans of expressways and highways in Kuala Lumpur seem to be in complete discordance with the shared global vision of a sustainable future (Mustafa, 2016). However, on other hand, there has been an extensive expansion of the light rail transit (LRT), a light metro transit operated by Rapid KL since the mid-90s. It will be connecting a number of adjoining urban areas like Subang Jaya, Petaling Jaya, Shah Alam, Puchong and Ampang with Kuala Lumpur covering a distance of 18.6 Kms (Smith, 2016). Another 36 kms LRT link connecting the adjoining urban areas of Shah Alam and Petaling Jaya with Kuala Lumpur is targeted to be completed by 2020 (Smith, 2016). Besides, the Mass Rapid Transit (MRT) project consisting of 2 lines, Line 1 (51 kms), and Line 2 (52.2 kms), are some of the smart mobility projects already underway and expected to be completed within the next 5-6 years (Mansoor & Ching, 2016). The MRT Line 1 which will be connecting the suburban town of Kajang with Kuala Lumpur is expected to be completed and operational by 2017 (Mansoor & Ching, 2016). These smart mobility initiatives are expected to significantly reduce dependence on road/automobile transportation, enhance social inclusion and foster sustainable development (Mansoor & Ching, 2016; Smith, 2016). Urban ecotourism which benefits from improved urban mass transit systems due to the ease in accessibility and less carbon footprint travel the latter offers, can experience sustainable and resounding development in Kuala Lumpur. Hence, popularisation and enhanced development of urban ecotourism is necessary that can potentially enforce the imperativeness of the ecological vitality of these nature spots in turn, making urban environments sustainable, well protected and financially lucrative due to the revenues ecotourism has been known to bring (Gibson et al., 2003; Okech, 2009).

A striking aspect observed in urban natural environments is its resilience. It has been observed in a number of instances that abandoned urban projects close to natural areas have been reclaimed and transformed by nature and its ecology. Văcărești, now a wild wetland In Bucharest, Romania was an under-construction water project under the erstwhile Communist regime, abandoned in 1989. Covering an area 183 hectare, Văcărești transformed into a wild wetland organically and now abounds 96 species of birds, mammals like weasels and otters as well as turtles and snakes (Tribillion, 2016). Based on the efforts of a few environmental activists, this nature spot was declared a protected area and is one of largest urban nature parks in Europe (Tribillion, 2016). This place stands testimony to the resilient power of nature in urban settings that can turn ambitious human projects into pieces of pristine wilderness with no human involvement but offer humanity a piece of green escapade (Bird, 2014). Given the challenges faced from urban infrastructural projects taking place in Kuala Lumpur, this resilience power of nature can revive natural escapades and inspire nature-seekers and nature-based voluntary and activist organisations to explore newer as well as regenerated places of wilderness for nature-based recreation, education and environmental protection. This would in turn, shape the behavioural patterns of eco-tourists to urban eco-travel destinations in Kuala Lumpur. Moreover, changes emanating from environmental conditions of urban nature spots, availability of urban natural spaces for recreational use and development of efficient and smarter public transport in Kuala Lumpur in the future, will bring new behavioural and attitudinal patterns of eco-tourists.

In terms of management perspectives, the implications emanating from this study provide useful insights that are supportive in terms of Kuala Lumpur Tourism Master Plan (2015-2025) prepared by the Kuala Lumpur City Hall(Kuala Lumpur Tourism Master Plan 2015-2025, 2015). This Plan emphasizes on nature and adventure as one of the main focus areas. The changing behavioural patterns of eco-tourists in 2010 and 2015, in terms of benefits from ecotourism - changing from environmental learning to socialisation, and in terms of ecotourism activities, the shift from photography being the most important activity to nature-viewing and jungle trekking, supports the initiatives of building clusters and offerings in nature-based recreation and adventure under the Kuala Lumpur Tourism Master Plan 2015-2025 (Kuala Lumpur Tourism Master Plan 2015-2025, 2015). The initiatives to offer products like nature trails, canopy walk and bird-watching as well as hosting of trekking events as stated in the above Plan are clearly supported by these changes observed in this study. Moreover, in terms of the changes with respect to more relative usage of websites of nature-based sites to social media sites and emergence of more female travellers, this study can enable organisations like the Kuala Lumpur Tourism Bureau, a unit of the Kuala Lumpur City Hall as well as national tourism bodies like Tourism Malaysia, in understanding the changing communication platforms, demography and target markets.

CONCLUSION

This study observed the changes of eco - tourists visiting Kuala Lumpur's rare nature spots over a span of 5 years and found some key changes in the areas of benefits from eco-travel, eco-tourists participation in nature-based activities and source of information and knowledge. Socialisation have turned out to be a major travel benefit and will get more impetus with the enhanced use of social media technologies through the use of modern digital gadgets like smartphones and due to the increased availability of Wi-Fi and data connectivity in different urban spaces including nature-based settings. Nature seeking activities like nature-viewing and hiking have become more popular due to the predominance of younger travellers to eco-travel spots in Kuala Lumpur. Younger traveller's especially younger soft eco - tourists tend to explore more in soft adventure like moderate hiking and nature-viewing as offered by urban nature spots. In terms of source of information and knowledge to urban eco – tourists, attraction websites have turned out to be more effective than social media sites. This is indeed a surprising finding and requires to be explored more since social media has emerged as the most dominant platform for information and knowledge exchange in almost all spheres of consumer activity. Furthermore, the role of smartphones in general and mobile learning of ecological aspects in urban natural areas in particular, with the assistance of high bandwidth Wi-Fi access in determining eco - tourists behavioural patterns at urban nature spots is a prospective area of investigation. Besides, the rise of single women travellers in the domain of eco-travel and emergence of travellers from Western countries having no alliance to the baby-boomer generation seems to have substantially increased. This generational change in an area so traditionally dominated by baby boomers is phenomenal and hence need to be examined more deeply in future studies.

REFERENCES

Anastasijevic, N., Anastasijevic, V., Bobic, A., Stojanovic, N., & Mesicek, M. (2009). Ecological and tourist potential of central Belgrade. *Turizam*, *13*(2), 75–83.

Bhuiyan, M. A. H., Siwar, C., Ismail, S. M., & Islam, R. (2011). The role of government for ecotourism development: Focusing on East Coast economic region. *Journal of Social Sciences*, *7*(4), 557–564. doi:10.3844/jssp.2011.557.564

Bird, M. (2014). *The hole in Bucharest that's become a nature reserve.* Retrieved from http://www.citymetric.com/skylines/hole-bucharest-s-become-nature-reserve-398

Buckley, R., Cater, C., Linsheng, Z., & Chen, T. (2008). Shentai Luyou: Cross-Cultural Comparison in Ecotourism. *Annals of Tourism Research*, *35*(4), 945–968. doi:10.1016/j.annals.2008.07.002

Buhalis, D., & Law, R. (2008). Progress in information technology and tourism management: 20 years on and 10 years after the internet – the state of etourism research. *Tourism Management*, *29*(4), 609–623. doi:10.1016/j.tourman.2008.01.005

Chan, J. K. L., & Baum, T. (2007). Ecotourists perception of ecotourism experience in Lower Kinabatangan, Sabah, Malaysia. *Journal of Sustainable Tourism*, *15*(5), 574–590. doi:10.2167/jost679.0

Cheng, N., & Foo, N. (2012). *Templer Park under threat.* Retrieved from http://www.thestar.com.my/news/nation/2012/11/20/templer-park-under-threat/

Cini, F., Leone, L., & Passafaro, P. (2010). Promoting ecotourism among young people: A segmentation strategy. *Environment and Behavior*, *44*(1), 87–106. doi:10.1177/0013916510389313

Dodds, R., & Joppe, M. (2001). Promoting urban green tourism; the development of the other map of Toronto. *Journal of Vacation Marketing*, *7*(3), 261–167. doi:10.1177/135676670100700306

Eubanks, T. L. Jr, Stoll, J. R., & Ditton, R. B. (2004). Understanding the diversity of eight-birder subpopulations: Socio-demographic characteristics, motivations, expenditures and net benefits. *Journal of Ecotourism*, *3*(3), 151–172. doi:10.1080/14664200508668430

Fong, V. (2016). *Smart Cities Today: Chapter Four – The Tale of Malaysia Pt. 1.* Retrieved from http://www.smartcitiesasia.com/smart-cities-malaysia/

Galley, G., & Clifton, J. (2004). The motivational and demographic characteristics about research ecotourists: Operation Wallacea volunteers in Southeast Sulawesi, Indonesia. *Journal of Ecotourism*, *3*(1), 69–82. doi:10.1080/14724040408668150

Gibson, A., Dodds, R., Joppe, M., & Jamieson, B. (2003). Ecotourism in the city? Torontos green tourism. *International Journal of Contemporary Hospitality Management*, *15*(6), 324–327. doi:10.1108/09596110310488168

Harlow, S., & Pomfret, G. (2007). Evolving environmental tourism experiences in Zambia. *Journal of Ecotourism*, *6*(3), 184–209. doi:10.2167/joe182.0

Higham, J., & Luck, M. (2002). Urban ecotourism: A contradiction in terms? *Journal of Ecotourism*, *1*(1), 36–51. doi:10.1080/14724040208668111

Holden, A., & Sparrowhawk, J. (2002). Understanding the motivations of ecotourists: The case of trekkers in Annapurna, Nepal. *International Journal of Tourism Research*, *4*(6), 435–446. doi:10.1002/jtr.402

Justice, L. C. (1986). The Concept of the Urban Forest as Applied to Kuala Lumpur, Malaysia. *Journal of Arboriculture*, *12*(7), 178–181.

Kastelein, B. (2004). Urban ecotourism: impossible conundrum? Mexican cities must clean up their acts to keep tourists. *Business Mexico*, 36-42.

Kim, S. S., Kim, M., Park, J., & Guo, Y. (2008). Cave tourism: Tourists characteristics, motivations to visit, and the segmentation of their behavior. *Asia Pacific Journal of Tourism Research*, *13*(3), 299–318. doi:10.1080/10941660802280448

Kuala Lumpur Tourism Association (KLTA). (2012). Retrieved on 25th December, 2013 from http://www.klta.org.my/content.cfm

Kuala Lumpur Tourism Master Plan 2015-2025. (2015). *Tourism Unit.* Kuala Lumpur City Hall, Kuala Lumpur, Malaysia.

Kuentzel, W., & Heberlein, T. A. (2006). From novice to expert? a panel study of specialization progression and change. *Journal of Leisure Research*, *38*, 496–512.

Laarman, J. G., & Durst, P. B. (1987). *Nature travel and tropical forests (FPEI working series).* Raleigh, NC: South Eastern Center for Forest Economics Research, North Carolina State University.

Lee, S., Graefe, A., & Li, C. (2007). The effects of specialization and gender on motivations and preferences for site attributes in paddling. *Leisure Sciences*, *29*(4), 355–375. doi:10.1080/01490400701394873

Liaghati, H., Khoshbakht, K., Mahmodi, H., Koucakzade, M., & Omidvar, P. (2010). Exploring Characteristics and Profile of Urban Ecotourism (A Case Study from Tehran). *Journal of Environmental Studis*, *36*(55), 7–11.

Lim, J. (2016). *City Hall to aggressively promote KL as a destination.* Retrieved from http://www.thestar.com.my/metro/community/2016/02/20/city-hall-to-aggressively-promote-kl-as-a-destination/

Lu, W., & Stepchenkova, S. (2012). Ecotourism experiences reported online, classification of satisfaction attributes. *Tourism Management*, *33*(3), 702–712. doi:10.1016/j.tourman.2011.08.003

MacFarlane, B. L. (1996). Socialization influences of specialization among birdwatchers. *Human Dimensions of Wildlife*, *1*(1), 35–50. doi:10.1080/10871209609359050

Mansoor, L., & Ching, O. T. (2016). *MRT project on track and well within budget.* Retrieved from http://www.nst.com.my/news/2016/02/128832/mrt-project-track-and-well-within-budget

Marker, M. A., Blanco, A., Lokanathan, S., & Verma, A. (2008). *Ecotourism in Malaysia. Project for PP5279: Cluster and National Competitiveness*. Lee Kuan Yew School of Public Policy.

Miller, L. (2010). *Solo women's travel surges in popularity*. Retrieved from http://gadling.com/2010/08/16/solo-womens-travel-surges-in-popularity/

Mitra, K. (2016). *Cities, like dreams, are made of…* Retrieved from http://kindlemag.in/cities-like-dreams-made/

Miyamoto, M., Parid, M. M., Aini, Z. K., & Michinaka, T. (2014). Proximate and underlying causes of forest cover change in Peninsular Malaysia. *Forest Policy and Economics*, *44*, 18–25. doi:10.1016/j.forpol.2014.05.007

Moore, R. L., Scott, D., & Moore, A. (2008). Gender-based differences in birdwatchers participation and commitment. *Human Dimensions of Wildlife*, *13*(2), 89–101. doi:10.1080/10871200701882525

Mustafa, M. (2016). *Farewell to Taman Rimba Ampang as it makes way for controversial new highways.* Retrieved from http://malaysiandigest.com/features/619173-farewell-to-taman-rimba-ampang-as-it-makes-way-for-controversial-new-highways.html

Nussair, K., Erdem, M., Okumus, F., & Biligan, A. (2012). Users attitudes toward online social networks in travel. In M. Sigala, A. Christou, & U. Gretzel (Eds.), *Social Media in Travel, Tourism and Hospitality: theory, practice and cases. Ashgate Publication.*

Okech, R. N. (2009). Developing urban ecotourism in Kenyan cities: A sustainable approach. *Journal of Ecology and Natural Environment*, *1*(1), 1–6.

Ramlan, M. A. B., Radam, A., Yacob, M. R., & Yahya, N. A. (2011). Willingness to pay towards the sustainability of Forest Research Institute Malaysia's (FRIM's) canopy walkway. *International Journal of Business, Management and Social. The Sciences*, *2*(3), 85–92.

Reduan, H. (2016). *Three environmental NGOs get go-ahead to challenge Taman Rimba Ampang closure.* Retrieved from http://www.nst.com.my/news/2016/05/147533/three-environmental-ngos-get-go-ahead-challenge-taman-rimba-ampang-closure

Ryan, C., Hughes, K., & Chirgwin, S. (2000). The gaze, spectacle and ecotourism. *Annals of Tourism Research*, *27*(1), 148–163. doi:10.1016/S0160-7383(99)00061-4

Sigala, M., & Marindis, D. (2010). DMOs, e-Democracy and collaborative destination management: an implementation framework. In U. Gretzel, R. Law, & M. Fuchs (Eds.), *Information and Communication Technologies in Tourism 2010* (pp. 235–246). New York: Springer Wien. doi:10.1007/978-3-211-99407-8_20

Smith, K. (2016). *Kuala Lumpur's ambitious urban rail plan starts to deliver results.* Retrieved from http://www.railjournal.com/index.php/asia/ambitious-expansion-plan-starting-to-deliver-results.html

Tao, C. H., Eagles, E. F. J., & Smith, S. L. J. (2004). Profiling Taiwanese ecotourists using a self-definition approach. *Journal of Sustainable Tourism*, *12*(2), 149–168. doi:10.1080/09669580408667230

Tribillion, J. (2016). *How nature turned a failed communist plan into Bucharest's unique urban park.* Retrieved from https://www.theguardian.com/cities/2016/jun/14/nature-europe-urban-protected-area-vacaresti-nature-park-romania?CMP=fb_gu

Tsipidis, V. (2004). *Assessing the urban ecotourism potential of a local nature reserve: The case of Corstorphine Hill, Edinburgh, Scotland.* Ecoclub.com E-paper series, Nr.10.

Weaver, D. B. (2002). Hard-core eco-tourists in Lamington National Park, Australia. *Journal of Ecotourism*, *1*(1), 19–35. doi:10.1080/14724040208668110

Weaver, D. B., & Lawton, L. J. (2007). Twenty years on: The state of contemporary ecotourism research. *Tourism Management*, *28*(5), 1168–1179. doi:10.1016/j.tourman.2007.03.004

Wight, P. A. (2001). Eco-tourists: not a homogeneous market segment. In K. F. Backman, E. Cater, P. F. J. Eagles, & B. McKercher (Eds.), *The Encyclopedia of Ecotourism* (pp. 565–579). CAB International.

Wu, Y. Y., Wang, H. L., & Ho, Y. F. (2010). Urban ecotourism: Defining and assessing dimensions using fuzzy number construction. *Tourism Management*, *31*(6), 739–743. doi:10.1016/j.tourman.2009.07.014

Zografos, C., & Allcroft, D. (2007). The environmental values of potential eco-tourists: A segmentation study. *Journal of Sustainable Tourism*, *15*(1), 44–66. doi:10.2167/jost572.0

Chapter 10
Critical Review of Tourism in India

Neeta Baporikar
Namibia University of Science and Technology, Namibia & University of Pune, India

ABSTRACT

Tourism plays a pivotal role in socio-economic development. It fosters international understanding, trust among people and brings many social benefits. According to United Nations World Tourism Organization, travel and tourism can be part of the solution to world problems of poverty employment and sustainability. Today, tourism has grown to become a major social and economic force and it is a well-known fact. Hence, it certainly is an activity of global importance and significance. With abundant nature's gift, one of the oldest culture and civilization India as tourist destination is in an envious position to locus itself as one of the best global destination by adopting innovative and holistic tourism policies. Through exploratory and descriptive examination and in depth literature review of policy documents and reports, the aim of this chapter is review critically the tourism policies and intends to suggest new avenues and innovations in tourism.

INTRODUCTION

India's glorious traditions and rich cultural heritage are closely related with the development of tourism. Its magnificent monuments attract a large number of tourists from all over the world. The natural surroundings, the architectural masterpieces, the music, dance, paintings, customs and languages all these go to make India as tourist paradise (Ratti, 2007). In ancient India, there were no travel formalities and the famous Chinese pilgrim Fa Hien travelled between A.D. 401 and 410 without a passport. But in the 3rd century B.C. a passport or mudra was essential, according to Kautilya's Arthashastra, for all travelers. During the Vedic period, the tourists were accommodated at 'dhams' or holy places. The new sea route discovered by Vasco - de - Gama resulted further in a remarkable increase of the travelers to India, When Alexander the Great reached in India, he found well maintained roads lined with trees and wells, and rest houses. Along with the royal highway which is 1920 kilometers long and 19 meters wide, men travelled in chariots, palanquins, bullock - carts, etc.

DOI: 10.4018/978-1-5225-2078-8.ch010

India is also storehouse of art, paintings and handicrafts. Crafts appeared on pots found in the Indus valley civilization as early as the 3rd century B.C. The cave paintings of Ajanta and Ellora date back to the 1st to 5th century A.D (Khan, 2005). India, a land of geographical diversity, blessed with a long history of rich civilization and culture is a potential tourism paradise with a wide variety of attractions. Indian cuisine is as fine, rich, and diverse as its culture. In Sanskrit literature the three famous words "Aththi Devo Bhava" means "Guest is God" which is a dictum of hospitality in India. So, with one of the world's richest natural heritage, thousands of species of fauna and flora and hundreds national parks and 441 sanctuaries including some of the largest wildlife sanctuaries in Asia viz. Kanha National Park –Madhya Pradesh (Tiger project), Jim Corbett National Park (Utter Pradesh) Gir (Gujarat) (Lion), Ranthambor (Rajasthan) (Peacock), Kaziranga (Assam) (Rihnosours), Bandipore (Karnataka) etc. India is able to attract large number of tourists. Through in-depth literature review and grounded approach this chapter aims to contribute to the understanding of tourism development in India and the approaches adopted to tourism policy.

LITERATURE REVIEW

Tourism policy is an important area for study because of its practical and theoretical importance. Tourism is of practical significance as international travel requires government cooperation in, for example, bilateral airline negotiations, decisions about provision of facilities and services, interactions with other sectors, use of publicly 'owned' resources such as national parks as attractions, the issuing of tourist visas and in the funding of marketing of particular destinations (Ahmed & Krohn, 1990). However, study of tourism policy is a herculean task for many reasons. A first reason is that tourism policy, explicitly or implicitly involves beliefs and values, about what is good and bad. Policy concerns goals and allocation of resources in situations, and to social problems, sometimes called 'wicked' problems (Rittel & Weber, 1973), where there is no clear answer. Policy is seen as complex (McDonald, 2009) requires system and complexity thinking (Farrell & Twining-Ward, 2005), and is best dealt with as a complex adaptive system. In many policy-related studies there is a 'tourism as industry' perspective that may, for example, examine how destinations can secure a competitive edge in increasingly global consumer markets (Ritchie & Crouch, 2000). According to Bramwell and Lane (2006), "as distinctly positivist and empirical in outlook; it leaves the impression that it is dealing with objective, value-free or neutral knowledge" (p. 1). The alternative is to consider tourism policy as a domain for examination of concepts such as trust, collaboration, social identity, the exercise of power, and so on; and best viewed through a variety of disciplinary and ideological 'lenses', that are becoming increasingly diverse, especially as researchers work at, and sometimes cut across, different levels (macro, meso, micro) of analysis (Jenkins, 2001). Studies of tourism public policies provide useful insights into who gets what, when, and why in the tourism policy process, and might also make a contribution to better informed government decision-making and policy-making (Hall & Jenkins, 2004).

Tourism policy making is seen by Hall (2008b) as first and foremost a political activity, influenced by the economic, social and cultural characteristics of a particular society, and by the formal structures of government and other features of the local political system. Policy involves consideration of the 'political debate about what the agenda is, what the issues are, who is involved or affected, and the alternative courses of action to address the problems' (Dredge & Jenkins, 2007, p. 10). This debate may extend beyond government and include policymaking tourist organizations (national tourist organizations, information offices, consumer associations) and the tourist industry (hotels, restaurants, tour operators, travel agencies); even pressure groups might have a say in the policy making processes (Van Doorn, 1982). Many of the issues that affect tourism transcend borders. Globalization is a factor that has influenced the development of multi-country policy (Hannam, 2002; Hjalager, 2007; MacLeod, 2001; Sugiyarto, Blake, & Sinclair, 2003), as it emphasises coordination across national boundaries. The development of the General Agreement on Trade in Services (GATS) is an example of how transnational policy and processes are affecting tourism (Edgell, 1995). Multi-country policy is also becoming more important (Church, Ball, Bull, & Tyler, 2000). Pearlman (1990) for example discusses macro-policy conflicts between social tourism subsidised by the state for domestic tourists and international tourism as well as difficulties with central planning of the economy. Richter (2003) notes, that there is a lack of coordinated policy making in the area of health and tourism across countries. Pearce (1998) discusses the development of tourism in Paris as significantly related to urban planning and policy. Tourism policy is often driven by a broad policy agenda and action in other spheres rather than particularly targeted at tourism (Church, et al., 2000). Tourism policy also may in turn affect other policy domains with Expo events policy affecting housing (Olds, 1998). It is also used to rationalise other interests, such as a desire amongst enthusiasts to see trams in Christchurch, New Zealand (Pearce, 2001).

Hall (2002) suggests that a five stage pattern of policy attention to emergent issues will be followed: pre-problem stage, alarmed discovery and euphoric enthusiasm, realisation of the cost of significant progress, gradual decline of intense public interest and the post-problem stage. However this can only be a first approach as it does not recognise the complexity of policy development. Instead policy making is a complex process of identification and attention. Weed (2006, p. 238) describes it as a "continuing iterative process" in which .....factors are interpreted and reinterpreted, thus further influencing the perceptions of policy makers. According to (Wray, 2009), 'Policy formulation is better conceptualised as a process of issue identification and management where multiple issues are being simultaneously identified, framed, prioritised and de-prioritised' (p. 675). Issues can be further influenced by events, personalities, pressures groups and institutional failure, as well as scale and time (Lawrence & Dredge, 2007). McCoy (1982, p. 277) considers 'public policy formulation is a process of conflict and compromise; a matter of mediating between competing factions with "private interests" and defining the "public interest" or the "national interest" which Bramwell & Cox (2009) considers path dependent. It is essentially a social process, involving communication and negotiation between people in the context of wider change (Stevenson, Airey, & Miller, 2008). Thus there is general agreement that policy making is complex and more of an art that a science, involving communication, negotiation, interests and issue framing. The issues considered in policy may be 'national' interests and be considered important by all the population. Ritchie (1988), argues for consensus policy formulation in tourism through surveys of resident attitudes. However policy development is often considered as controlled by elites (Yasarata, Altinay, Burns, & Okumus, 2009) or power blocs; with a dominance of dominance of close business-government ties (Craik, 1990; Hall, 1999).

This review is arranged in four main sections. After introduction, background and the genesis of tourism policy in India to provide the reader with an orientation to the chapter, it will discuss issues related to the field of policy making and development including the need to study tourism policy. After these two sections, the chapter will review the tourism polices till dated, followed by solutions and recommendations, a discussion of areas for further research with some conclusions are given at the end.

GENESIS OF TOURISM POLICY

The tourist organization of India had its beginning from the year 1945. A committee was appointed in 1945 under the Chairmanship of Sir John Sargent, Educational Advisor, and Government of India. The Sargent Committee submitted their interim report in October 1946, but implication of the suggestions given by this committee was implemented after independence. As per the report of Sargent Committee, Tourist Traffic Committee was appointed in 1948. On the recommendation a Tourist Traffic Branch was setup in 1949 with regional offices at Kolkata and Chennai. On March 1, 1958, a separate Department of Tourism was created in place of a Tourist Traffic Branch under the Ministry of Transport and Communication which provides services such as accommodation, food facility, hospitality, etc. One committee was appointed in March, 1963 under the Chairmanship of L. K. Jha. This Committee made several recommendations to improve tourist flow in India, especially in regards to facilitation; three new corporations were setup in 1965, viz. Hotel Corporation, Indian Tourism and India Tourist Traffic Corporation but they did not work well and therefore merged to make a single unit as India Tourism Development Corporation (ITDC) on October, 1966. ITDC is the main agency of the Ministry of Tourism and Civil Aviation, which promoted tourism in India. Yet, tourism development was a largely unplanned exercise. This held true for different states to different degrees. In Kerala, Jammu and Kashmir, Goa and Himachal Pradesh tourism was much more consistently incorporated into state (five year) plans than in other states, even relatively early on - in the 1970s. At that time, these states already attracted a relatively large share of India's international tourists and were to become India's main tourist states and 'models for tourism development' (Singh, 2001, p. 143). Still, even in these states, tourism was largely left to the private sector and to a comparatively unrestricted market. While there have been slight modifications in policy, this basic condition has not changed much until the present day.

Policy Studies: Need and Significance

'Policy' is derived from the word 'polis', denoting a city-state of ancient Greece, from which the terms 'politics', 'polity' and 'police' are also derived (Colebatch, 2009). One way of defining policy is as a 'handle on the way we are governed, a concept which we use to make sense of what we do' (Colebatch, 2009) or 'whatever governments choose to do or not to do' (Dye, 1992, p. 2). In this sense policy is a name to describe the general actions and outcomes of government. However, as governments are complex and produce many outcomes, such a definition may be considered summative only (Dubin, 1976), useful as an introduction to a complex phenomenon but which requires further elaboration. Hall (2008a) provides three reasons to study policy: to understand the shaping of policy decisions and their impacts (the policy cycle approach); to provide information about solutions to practical problems and to then feed this information into the policy process (scientific approach); and to understand the interests and values involved in policy and planning processes (associated with the social approach). But these are general reasons for the study of policy and may not justify the study of policy related to tourism in particular. According to (Elliot, 1997), it is only governments which have the power to provide the political stability, security and the legal and financial framework which tourism requires. They provide essential services and basic infrastructure. It is only national governments which can negotiate and make agreements with other governments on issues such as immigration procedures or flying over and landing on national territory. Governments have control of factors such as the amount of paid holidays and the application of currency restrictions (Wanhill, 1987), international affairs, border security, social and community development. The government involvement is pervasive and can be at national, provincial and local levels with some authors considering that 'good' policy requires involvement of all three (Kerr, 2003). Reasons for government involvement and policy formulation include market failure (Smeral, 1998), governments seeking to understand and mitigate the cultural, social and environmental effects of tourism, use by tourism of public goods, and the spatial nature of tourism that requires land use planning (Kerr, 2003).

Policy Implementation

There has been increasing examination of the effectiveness of tourism policies in achieving their stated aim (Andriotis, 2001). Policy implementation can be considered part of the policy process, and requires the development of skills and competences (Henry & Jackson, 1996), and may involve vested interests (Thomas & Thomas, 1998). Ioannides (1995) found that to avoid a failure of sustainable policy implementation, it is important to maintain effective dialogue between communities and policy makers, and that one way to achieve this is through community visioning workshops whereby different interest groups in the host locality express their fears and aspirations. Tourism policy involves collective action and how collective choices are made, implemented and enforced in and for a society (Buhrs, 2000). Hence, the ideology of a government is important, for it can determine whether tourism development will be supported. Normally the ideology reflects the national political culture and political parties (Elliott, 1997). Thus policy and the policy process will change over time, and what is 'good' policy must be determined by argument not scientific information although science has an important role to play in policy development.

Policy has also been seen as a social process that involves and is influenced by the institutional context, issue drivers such as macro-environment factors, actors, agencies and networks, policy dialogues, and events, as well as space and time (Lawrence & Dredge, 2007). An increasingly important view associated is that policy communities or networks of interested stakeholders play an important part in the development of issues and policy formulation processes. Thus some authors stress that policy making is a 'soft' human process rather than a rational scientific process. Stevenson et al., (2008) indicates 'tourism policy is essentially about communication'. An ambiguous strategy effectively meant that policy outcomes would depend largely on policy implementation - especially at lower levels in the policy chain (Greenwood, Williams, & Shaw, 1990, p. 55). The policy implementation process may also require a number of other steps such as administrative coordination and policy coordination (Hall, 1999) as well as support from effective legislation. Policy implementers require the power to 'make and enforce decisions which are binding upon their members', they have responsibilities which are interpreted by ideologies in shaping objectives (Elliott, 1997). Swain (1999) suggests that the study of policy and power in tourism 'includes a broad range of concepts from ideology to exchange rates and visa control'. Thus policy involves the exercise of power (Marzano & Scott, 2009).

Policy also involves actions, decision, politics, values and ideological beliefs, social processes involving communication, outcome such as legislation and implementation. Tourism is a complex domain (Grant, 2004) that touches upon a wide ranges of 'problem areas' such as aboriginal rights, aviation, biodiversity, disability and access, domestic tourism, events, health, innovation, knowledge and learning, development/land use, national parks, place identity, political legitimacy, regional development, rural tourism, safety/crisis management, training and human resources, recreation, urban development. Each of these numerous related domains is the subject of a specific literature and various policy prescriptions leading to a view of policy as 'an outcome' rather than 'a process' (Colebatch, 2009). Mathews (1975) discusses politics and hence policies as influenced by ideological arguments about tourism, especially in developing countries, while Whitford (2009) writes that it is important to understand the ideological basis for policy development in order to obtain insight into workings of government. Different ideologies form the basis of developing policy. O'Neil (2007) discusses the characteristics of four different types of political economic systems; liberalism, social democracy, communism and mercantilism.

GOVERNMENT AND TOURISM POLICY

Governments are increasingly recognising tourism as a resilient activity with the capacity to stimulate economies and help to achieve many national economic objectives. In recent years, tourism has consistently demonstrated the ability to create employment, stimulate capital markets, attract foreign investment, earn foreign currency, and add value nationally, regionally and locally (Haxton, 2015). Governments are also interested in tourism due to the magnitude of its economic, social and environmental impacts. Perhaps tourism policy would not be so important if these economic benefits were only available for particular countries or tourism was a closed system. However, the existence of formally stated and publicly accessible national tourism policies is by no means universal (Baum, 1994). Government tourism policy may also be indirect, whereby government actions influence tourism as a by-product of an interest in some related area; or direct whereby governments actively seek to influence tourism or some aspect of tourism in pursuit of a policy objective (Airey, 1983). The purpose hereto is to provide a *strategic* review of the academic tourism policy literature such as that provided by Ambrosie (2010) which arranged policy research along a social versus rational continuum. Its purpose is to provide integrative frameworks with which to organize a 'diverse and fragmented literature' (Coles, Hall, & Duval, 2006, p. 296) about which there is 'little agreement about how [it] should be studied and the reasons underpinning such studies' (Hall & Jenkins, 1995, p. 2). An alternative to this strategic approach is to provide a discussion of the literature on tourism policy and its sub-topics, theories and evolution, an approach that would require a substantial book, and indeed a number of discussions of this type are available in books. An example is the focused review of Connelly (2007), which arranged the literature as a series of subject areas relevant to his topic area (urban tourism competitiveness policy), such as tourism governance and state intervention, public/private partnerships, and regimes of accumulation and modes of regulation. On the other hand, studying public policy is a difficult task that comprises analysis of numerous decisions made by numerous individuals and organisations that have often been shaped by earlier policies and may be linked closely with other seemingly unrelated decisions (Wray, 2009). Another alternative would be to focus on current issues or particular streams of theory or methodology which, while perhaps more complete within its boundaries, would have excluded a recognition of the complex interplay of theory and practice, evolving ideas and action, that the tourism policy literature represents. Nevertheless, the nature of the policy-making process in any nation-state varies over space and time, and varies among policy sectors or policy communities. Attempts to analyse policy are made complex not only by decisions, actions, and events, but by the knowledge that there is no coherent or universally accepted theory of public policy processes, and no single means of explaining events (Hall & Jenkins, 2004).

TOURISM POLICY DEVELOPMENT IN INDIA

The Ministry of tourism headed by the 'Union Minister for Tourism' is the nodal agency for the formation of national policies and programs related to tourism. It also coordinates all the activities of the central government agencies, state government undertakings and the private sector for the development and promotion of tourism. The administrative head of the ministry is the secretary (tourism) who also acts as the Directorate General (DG) tourism. Directorate General of tourism has 20 offices within India and 13 offices overseas. The work of the ministry is divided into 10 divisions which are headed by either a Director or Deputy Secretary level officer. These include administration, public sector undertakings (PSU) planning & coordination, division, publicity, international cooperation and IT & Events divisions, market research division, overseas marketing division, hotels and restaurants division, travel & trade division, integrated finance, e-governance division, official language division, human resource development and domestic tourism division and parliament vigilance, administration & public grievances divisions. The first conscious and organized efforts to promote tourism in India were made in 1945 when government set up a committee under the chairmanship of Sir John Sargent, the then educational advisor to the Government of India (Singh, 2001). Thereafter, the development of tourism was taken up in a planned manner in 1956 coinciding with the second five year plan. The approach has evolved from isolated planning of single unit facilities in the second and third five year plan. The sixth plan marked the beginning of a new era when tourism began to be considered as a major instrument for social integration and economic development. But it was only after the 80s that tourism activity gained momentum. In the preceding pages these are discussed.

Milestones in Tourism Policy Development in India

- 1946: Sir John Sarjant Committee on Tourism
- 1947: Report of Sir John Committee
- 1949: Sir John Committee Recommendations
- 1949-50: Started Tourism Branches in Delhi, Calcutta, Bombay and Madras
- 1951-55: First Five Year Plan, No allotment for tourism development
- 1956-60: Allotment for tourism under the name of Transportation Division
- 1957: Establishment of Department of Tourism
- 1958: Establishment of Tourism Department Council
- 1960: Establishment of Indian Tourism Development Corporation (ITDC)
- 1966: Establishment of Department of Aviation
- 1966: Establishment of Department of Aviation and Tourism
- 1967: Establishment of Ministry of Tourism and civil Aviation
- 1982: Declared First time Tourism Policy
- 1986: Establishment of National Committee on Tourism
- 1986: Separate Department of Tourism
- 1986: Tourism as an industry declared by Government
- 1986: Separate department with cabinet minister
- 1988: Establishment of Ministry of Civil Aviation Tourism
- 1991: Tourism as a Source of Foreign Investment
- 1992: Nation Action Plan

- 1992: Tourism Year
- 1995: Establishment of Tourism Cell
- 1988-99: Tourism with Export Businesses
- 1999-2000: Visit India Year
- 2002: Launch of agricultural and rural tourism concepts along with 'Incredible India' campaign
- 2009: Campaign titled as 'Atithi Devo Bhava' introduced
- 2010: Convergence for Integrated development of Tourism Destinations
- 2012: International Campaign 'Find What You Seek', launched at "World Travel Market 2012"
- 2012: Domestic Campaign 'Go Beyond', launched at "World Travel Market 2012"
- 2013: India Joined Global Leaders for Tourism Campaign
- 2014: Electronic Tourist Visa Scheme Launched

Tourism Policy (1982)

The first significant policy initiatives were forged in the early 1980s. With the prospect of hosting the Asian Games of 1982, the Indian Government had to start thinking about accommodating, transporting and entertaining the large number of visitors attracted by the event. This awakened a serious public interest in tourism, which was enhanced by the fact that tourism was India's largest net earner of foreign currency. The public interest was translated into the Tourism Policy of 1982 which provided an action plan based on the development of so-called tourism circuits (Singh, 2001). A tourist circuit consists of a number of tourist sights which are geographically and/or thematically grouped together with the idea that the value of their sum is more than an adding up of the values of the parts. Rather than being the result of an in-depth analysis and marketing study, the circuit idea was born out of the feeling that 'the Golden Triangle' destinations of Delhi-Jaipur-Agra and the Bombay-Goa shopping-and-beach circuit were grossly oversold. In order to lure away the tourists from these overcrowded 'circuits', into the myriad of other potentially popular destinations in India, the concept of alternative *circuits* - rather than alternative *places* that could be grouped together by tourists themselves - was somehow thought imperative (Gantzer & Gantzer, 1983).

Tourism Development (1990s)

In the 1980s, the growing public interest in tourism resulted in the recognition of tourism as an export industry (including the implied tax exemptions) and the creation of a special public tourism finance corporation (1987). These initiatives were thought to openly and explicitly invite private investors and entrepreneurs to participate in tourism development. In 1997 the department of tourism published a (new) National Tourism Action Plan. Apart from identifying a few areas for 'integrated tourism development', along the lines of the aforementioned (thematic) tourism circuits, the aim of the plan was to achieve an overall growth and improvement of the tourism sector in India, by stepping up marketing, infrastructure building and human resource development. According to some, the plan didn't present anything new. It just was phrased in a more fashionable development sector jargon (Singh, 2001). Others maintained that the plan was over-ambitious and unrealistic. In fact, from independence onwards the budget outlays for tourism have always been very small (less than 0.2%). This goes for India's share in worldwide international tourism too. During the first fifty years of independent India, the portion of international tourists visiting India has not been more than 0.4%. It is claimed to have risen to some 0.45% in 2004

(GOI 2004). Given the rise of international tourists in the world, this implies that there has been a steady increase in tourist arrivals which accelerated in 2004. Indeed, according to the Indian Tour Operators Promotion Council (ITOPC), over the period 2001-2006, the number of foreign tourists in India has nearly doubled (to some 4.4 million). The opening of its markets in the early 1990s and the recent years of high economic growth have profoundly changed its surface. With the opening up of the Indian market, a lively competition between the states emerged in attracting investors in industry and other sectors. Along similar lines, states started competing for their share of international and domestic tourists. Particularly in the traditional tourist states there was an urge to develop tourism to its full potential (Singh, 2008). Varied packages including nature, local tradition and culture, heritage and relaxation were developed by a rapidly increasing number of entrepreneurs (Sreekumar & Parayil, 2010).

National Action Plan (1992)

In 1992, a National Action Plan was announced. It was regarded as an emerging action plan to set things right in some key areas, and to provide directions to achieve quick results. The objectives set out rightly stroked at the perceived inadequacies of the system and incorporate all those areas which have been identified as the weakness of India's tourism development policy. The strategies outlined in the Action Plan for achieving these objectives included: improvement of tourism infrastructure, developing areas on a selective basis for integrated growth along with marketing of destinations to ensure optimal use of existing infrastructure, restructuring and strengthening of the institutions for development of human resources and evolving a suitable policy for increasing foreign tourist arrivals and foreign exchange earnings.

Tourism Policy (2002)

In 2002, the action plan was finally translated into a tourism policy. Tourism policy officially became a joint central-state government concern. The new policy itself, however, was designed by the central government. It holds the kind of goals and expectations exemplary for the first policy. To start with, the policy document attempts to establish tourism's great contribution to national development and its role as an *engine of growth*. It suggests that tourism not only generates government revenue, foreign currency, but also provides an optimal use of India's scarce resources, sustainable development, high quality employment (especially to youngsters, women and disabled people), and finally, peace, understanding, national unity and stability (GOI, 2002). The policy starts from the idea that tourism can be used as a development tool. In more practical terms, the policy aims at increasing the number of domestic and international tourists and to do this, the government proposes to diversify the Indian tourism product and substantially improve the quality of (tourism) infrastructure, marketing, visa arrangements and air-travel. The aforementioned *tourism-as-a-development-tool* largely concerns *domestic tourism*, which in this capacity is conceptually linked to 'sustainable' *rural* development. As far as *international tourism* is concerned the Government mainly wants to target the *'high-yielding variety'* of tourists (GOI, 2002).

These major policy aims are derived from three main sources. The idea of tourism-as-a-development-tool leading to sustainable rural development is rooted in traditional socialist-style Indian Government thinking. An equally important source however, is the ideology of the international development community, represented by organizations such as the UNDP. The idea to specifically target the long haul, high yielding variety of international tourists, on the other hand, is part and parcel of the worldview of lobby organizations representing international airline and hotel companies. The WTTC in particular has played an important role in shaping the Indian tourism policy. Its predictions and suggestions form an integral part of the policy. While it is understandable that organizations such as the WTTC and the UNDP have influenced the Indian Tourism Policy, it is surprising to see how apparently easily and without much adaptation their recommendations have become official policy. This implies that the policy is founded upon rather contrasting ideas. The policy does *not* include a clear strategy, linking means and ends, assigning responsibilities and roles across government and private agencies, and setting realistic targets according to a list of prioritized goals. Rather, it seems an expression of intent to improve on everything. The policy document itself reads like a tourist brochure, piling up a great variety of tourist activities and sights that could and should be developed (it includes a 4 page list of all forms of tourism) one can possibly think of (GOI, 2002).

The same goes for the 'world class infrastructure' (including 'integrated' tourist circuits) through which such activities and sights are to be connected to the rest of the world. But there is nothing like the kind of systematic approach one would normally associate with government plan and policy. An obvious complication in the Indian context, particularly with respect to the division of roles and responsibilities, is the federal system of government. While the central government is not powerless and does in fact determine policy and control most of the funds, for the implementation of its policy it is largely dependent on state governments, whose plans, policies and projects are often determined by concerns other than those formulated in national plans. However, to address inequality and improve the resilience of economies, it is necessary to adopt and mainstream a holistic approach to policy making, in which economic growth is recognised as a means but not as an end (OECD 2014). A key aspect of increased interconnectedness and complexity relates to the relationship between growth, environment and social outcomes. Unless more significant policy action on environmental challenges is taken now, continued environmental degradation will pose risks to the economy and to human well-being. A good understanding of the relationship between environmental policies and economic growth is vital for policy-makers aiming to achieve greener growth (Haxton, 2015). On the whole, policy responses to date have tended to be inadequate, perhaps due in part to the consequences of policy actions not being fully anticipated, especially in terms of spill-overs across policy areas or countries, but also over time (OECD 2014).

The new national policy starts from the largely implicit assumption that domestic and international tourism concern different market segments, with distinct products (destinations and tourist services) catering to distinct sets of demand. In many countries, an industrial policy approach has been used to address tourism development. The main aim of industrial policy is to secure a framework of conditions that favour competitiveness, thereby enhancing the productivity and performance of businesses within and across that industry sector (Warwick, 2013). The advantage of tourism being framed as an industry is that industry productivity and competitiveness are fundamental planks in many national economies and, as a result, tourism has received high exposure in a sea of competing policy issues (Baporikar, 2016a). In most jurisdictions, tourism policy development is characterised by a complex set of roles and responsibilities distributed across different levels of government, different agencies within the same level of government, and shared between public, private and non-government organisations (Dredge and Jenkins, 2007).

Current trends suggest that tourism will continue to be an important driver of economic, social and personal growth (Baporikar, 2016b). People are living longer, disposable incomes are higher, people are more mobile and leisure and tourism experiences are rapidly integrating into daily life. These changes suggest that there will be increased demand for tourism products, services and experiences and that the lines between tourism, recreation and leisure will become increasingly blurred (Williams & Shaw,

2009). Under these circumstances, tourism will continue to grow but the type; style, scale and nature of this development will be shaped by innovations that are presently unknown (Baporikar, 2014a; 2014b). By taking a proactive long-term approach significant opportunities exist to reduce the negative consequences of crises and disasters on human lives and economic activity associated with tourism (Becken & Hughey, 2013).

National Tourism Policy 2015: Formulation of New Tourism Policy

The Ministry of Tourism is currently in the process of formulating a National Tourism Policy 2015 with the aim of positioning India as a "Must Experience" and "Must Revisit" destination for Global Travellers, encouraging Indians to explore their own country and realising the potential of tourism as a major engine for economic growth, employment generation and poverty alleviation in a responsible framework (GOI, 2015). This new policy has been welcomed by the stake holders as the move by Ministry of Tourism is to make the new National Tourism Policy, 2015 to be based on fixed timeframes. They said that the 'S's used in previous policy i.e., Swagat (welcome), Soochna (Information), Suvidha (Facilitation), Suraksha (Security), Sahyog (Cooperation), Samrachana (Infrastructure Development) and Safai (Cleanliness) are relevant even today. So the new policy intends to aim at value addition over the previous one and will also give a serious thought to the causes of non-implementation of various schemes under 2002 policy. The new policy also gives direct access to the Prime Minister's Office (PMO) in deciding the course of the crucial sector that is expected to contribute highly to the country's GDP. The policy aims to cash in the tourist wanderlust to increase India's share in world tourist arrivals.

SOLUTIONS AND RECOMMENDATIONS

Based on the studies of Collier (1989); Baporikar & Sokhalingam (2010, 2011 and 2012); Baporikar (2011) and Briedenhann & Wickens(2004), the key characteristics of tourism include: it being a commercial activity, involves consumption of experiences, is an entertainment, has positive and negative impact apart from being demand driven activity. The OECD's *Towards Green Growth* (2011a) argues that the world faces the twin challenges of needing to expand economic opportunities for a growing global population, whilst addressing environmental pressures that, if left unaddressed, could undermine our ability to seize these opportunities. Tourism is not immune; for example, based on a business-as-usual scenario, which considers projected growth in international arrivals, changes in travel frequency, length of stay, travel distance, and technological efficiency gains, greenhouse gas (GHG) emissions from tourism could grow considerably in the coming 25 years and become an important source (OECD 2011b). Despite the impact of the global economic, financial and social crisis and other external shocks, the tourism industry has demonstrated its resilience by sustaining moderate growth levels in recent years. As a result, governments are increasingly recognising tourism as a resilient activity with the capacity to stimulate economies and help achieve many national economic objectives (Haxton, 2015). However, it is well documented that, in general, policy makers and economists failed to recognise growing tensions in the global economy. A fact not helped by many prevailing economic models and analytical methods favouring a silo approach to policy development; and thus preventing a comprehensive understanding of the true complexity of the global economy and the interconnectedness between and within economies (OECD 2014a). These need to be borne in mind as this section discusses some solutions and recommendations to make the tourism sector more competitive and place India in its rightful position on the global tourism map, through holistic and well integrated tourism policy.

1. **Recommendation**: Positioning for long-term growth by stimulating consumer demand and securing jobs (Baporikar, 2014c). The government has the opportunity to team up with the banks and help finance and underwrite smaller and locally driven tourism projects, which will have a less destructive impact on our environment and will also spread the benefits of tourism to all parts of the country thus giving rise to a local supply and demand chain, a vital ingredient for job creation which will help to achieve the goal of nationalization in the real sense (Sokhalingam & Baporikar, 2011).

   Action: Broaden and strengthen Indian tourism capacity and functions to incorporate industry development and online distribution (Baporikar, 2015b), while retaining its primary focus on international marketing and enhancing its strategic domestic marketing role.
2. **Recommendation**: Leadership - strategic and coordinated leadership that will drive the national tourism agenda as the nature of tourism development requires both public and private sectors active participation. Additionally, if long-term tourism policy is to be successful, there is a need to re think. A more strategic approach for tourism development which is inclusive is required (Sokhalingam & Baporikar, 2012).

   Actions: Reinvigorate the Ministry of Tourism to enable stronger participation from state and territory governments and industry to:
   a. Oversee implementation of national tourism priorities.
   b. Maintain whole-of-government links through committee meetings periodically to identify and progress strategy-related impediments and monitor strategy implementation.
   c. Broaden and include in National Tourism Advisory Committee, the top government officials including ministers' for aviation, infrastructure, transport, regional development and local government and tourism-related transport operators.
3. **Recommendation**: Information to industry and government - a research and development agenda that will provide information to industry and government (Baporikar, 2016b).

   Actions: Establish a new governance structure for:
   a. Research and development to drive a national tourism research agenda, and advance high quality research that informs industry and policy development.
   b. Producing an annual state of the industry report, providing a quantitative and qualitative assessment of current industry performance, challenges and trends. The future research agenda will incorporate work on issues affecting tourism including investment, productivity, labour and skills, and taxation.
   c. For leading industry communications, including an annual industry outlook conference and disseminate research and development information.
4. **Recommendation**: Facilitating investment and regulatory reform – ensure investment that will make Indian tourism products remains competitive in a global marketplace.

   Action: Establish or appoint an investment and regulatory reform working group, including industry, and state and territory stakeholders, to implement and progress the tourism regulatory reform priorities.

5. **Recommendation**: Labour and skills - development that will support tourism industry needs. Today, travel and tourism has become part of the people's regular activity, for the economies worldwide the sector generates not only revenues but is also a great provider of employment (Baporikar, 2011).
   Action: To work with universities, institutions and industries to implement the Tourism and Hospitality Workforce Development Strategy.
6. **Recommendation**: Develop competencies for responding to challenges by tourism businesses that will adapt to the impact of change, climate change and other external shocks (Baporikar, 2016c; 2015c).
   Action: Work for continuing to deliver the actions of the climate change and global warming issues to improve industry understanding of the impact of climate change, and to prepare the Indian tourism industry for a clean green future.
7. **Recommendation**: Excellence in product and service delivery that will ensure India is a high-value destination.
   Action: Ministry of Tourism including State level organizations to endorse and implement mechanisms to accredit brand and recognise Indian tourism products and services.
8. **Recommendation** 8: Strengthening our competitiveness with industry and product development through effective destination management and tourism product that will make the most of our unique attribute. Moreover, entrepreneurial opportunities which the tourism sector provides as successful tourism can change external perceptions of a country, improve intercultural understanding, and create a positive internal frame of reference for a country (Baporikar, 2011).
   Action: Encourage continued advancement of the innovation and tourism development programmes to:
   a. Investigate use of the initiative as a model for further collaboration between government and industry in destination development.
   b. Review capacity of current indigenous development programs to develop indigenous tourism products like rural tourism, handicrafts tourism, academic tourism etc.
9. **Recommendation**: Performance measurement through performance indicators that will track progress and support strategic priorities. Profitability can be assisted through the introduction of greater efficiencies – for example co-operative marketing, or through ensuring that increases in volume sales are not achieved on low price competition strategies (Baporikar, 2015a).
   Actions: Establish and support Research and Development Advisory Board focused on research to inform policy, marketing, and industry development. Balanced research regarding supply and demand; objective and behavioural, triple bottom line - economic, social, and environmental, etc. need to be undertaken. Metrics ought to include tourism volume, value, and satisfaction indicators at the national and regional levels.
10. **Recommendation**: Holistic and Integrated Approach to Tourism Development. The focus on short-term industry interests and the lack of attention to longer-term consequences and synergies with other policy sectors, such as land use planning, environmental management and infrastructure policy have compromised destination competitiveness over the long-term (Ivars Baidal, 2004).
    Action: Forums and e-platforms to be created (Baporikar, 2014d; 2015d), for inputs from different stakeholders to facilitate a holistic and integrated tourism policy.

FUTURE RESEARCH DIRECTIONS

As discussed above, the tourism policy field is broad and fragmented and one first area for research is the writing of comparative studies. In particular cross-country comparisons using examples of Western policy development may be useful. Certainly there is a need for monitoring and evaluation of policy after implementation (Bramwell & Lane, 2006). Policy evaluation studies are a possible short cut to information about the effects and efficiency of various specific interventions (Hjalager, 2010). Policy research thus, remains a critical area for further research. Areas for further research also include tourism laws – depending on the sensitivity and security aspects especially for countries like Egypt, India, and Nepal etc. Tourism policy networks, governance of tourism, tourism destinations as a commons (Ostrom, 1990, 1998, 2005) and especially the design principles for robust management of common pool resources (Connelly, 2007; Haase, et al., 2009) would also provide scope for further research. Hall and Jenkins (2004) suggest a need examination of the linkage between power, ideology, values, and institutions.

CONCLUSION

Interestingly, Bandyopadhyay and Morais (2005), discourse on the dissonance between the representation of India as a tourist destination by the Indian Government, on the one side, and its depiction by the American media (representing 'the Western tourist'). Based on a thorough scrutiny of brochures and other publications (1998-2003), they argue that the greatest discrepancy in the respective pictures of tourist-India concerns a theme euphemistically labelled 'cultural diversity', the essence of which is captured by the idea of bewildering chaos and uncertainty... at least by the American media. These media also appeared keen on feeding descriptions of poverty and confusion to Western tourists.

However, the Indian Government's picture of tourist-India is completely devoid of such descriptions. In contrast to this, it emphasizes luxury, modernity and even 'royal treatment'. Highlighting some of the most inconsistencies on tourism by the policy makers in India, an attempt is made to provide recommendations and actions required to some major policy questions. Businesses can develop strategies to become good corporate citizens within their host community such as sponsoring local events, schools, and developing educational and training programs to address specific issues that are important to the local community (Nunkoo, Gursoy & Ramkissoon 2013). Tourism businesses can engage in corporate social responsibility programs aiming at community improvement, environmental enhancement, and improving the general welfare of residents (Xu & Gursoy, 2014).

Thus the new tourism policy of India, intends to give something to everyone - from catering to weary souls looking for spirituality, India will market spirituality circuits based on Hinduism, Buddhism, Jainism, Sikhism to ancient India's contribution now discovered world over through yoga. It will also offer products based on medical and rural tourism, Ayurveda and heritage. The policy also lists beaches, rivers, backwaters, cruises, adventure, wildlife, festivals, shopping destinations, cuisine trails showing the diversity of food, cinematic tourism, emerging concepts like heritage walks, and lesser-known wedding destinations. If Hollywood is coming to India to get married in opulent palaces of Rajasthan in colourful and elaborate rituals, then Honeymoon Tourism will be a part of it. The new policy says it all. "India is over-blessed with an array of offerings, each able to create a compelling invitation for travellers. This, however, risks causing confusion for travellers as to what to experience. It also risks overwhelm when travellers try to do too much on one trip," says the policy, explaining the reason for careful preparation of these tourism products to help the discerning tourist decide on their itinerary. Keeping in view the technological changes, different mobile applications for various sectors of tourism in order to disseminate information to the interested tourists are also likely to be launched. The setting up of 'Digital Museum' is also proposed in order to promote the rich and unique local cultures and their heritage. Long standing demand for establishing a 'Hospitality University' is also likely to be considered. Moreover, India possesses all the main elements of ethos which attract tourist include: pleasant climate, scenic beauty, historical and cultural attraction, accessibility, and wide variety for shopping, adventure facilities, delicious cuisines, accommodation, and health - care services projects (Ghosh, 1999).

On a final note, issues discussed and the policy reviewed brings to light the vast potential for tourism development in India. No doubt, in the near future, the greater opportunities will rise in the domestic sector (Baporikar, 2016c). From a research and policy perspective, the present roles of the Tourism Development Corporations in the states, identifying and developing new destinations, merits much greater attention. Some serious thinking on purposeful guidance for such development strategies seems in place by policy makers!

REFERENCES

Ahmed, Z. U., & Krohn, F. B. (1990). Reversing the United States declining competitiveness in the marketing of international tourism: A perspective on future policy. *Journal of Travel Research*, *29*(2), 23–29. doi:10.1177/004728759002900204

Airey, D. (1983). European government approaches to tourism. *Tourism Management*, *4*(4), 234–244. doi:10.1016/0261-5177(83)90001-8

Akehurst, G., Bland, N., & Nevin, M. (1993). Tourism policies in the European community member states. *International Journal of Hospitality Management*, *12*(1), 33–66. doi:10.1016/0278-4319(93)90040-G

Bandyopadhyay, R., & Morais, D. (2005). Representative dissonance, Indias self and western image. *Annals of Tourism Research*, *32*(4), 1006–1021. doi:10.1016/j.annals.2005.02.002

Baporikar, N. (2016a). Infrastructure Development as a Catalyst for Social-Economic Advancement. [IJSDA]. *International Journal of System Dynamics Applications*, *5*(4), 101–113.

Baporikar, N. (2016b). Strategic Approach to Tourism Development in Namibia.[IJSEM]. *International Journal of Sustainable Economies Management*, *5*(3), 1–12.

Baporikar, N. (2016c). Entrepreneurship Culture of SMEs in India's Tourism Sector.[IJSITA]. *International Journal of Strategic Information Technology and Applications*, *7*(2), 14–27.

Baporikar, N. (2015a). Effect of National Culture on Development of International Business in the Sultanate of Oman. In B. Christiansen (Ed.), Handbook of Research on Global Business Opportunities. Hershey, PA: Business Science Reference.

Baporikar, N. (2015b). Role of Entrepreneurship in Networked Indian Economy. In P. Ordóñez de Pablos (Ed.), *Technological Solutions for Sustainable Business Practice in Asia* (pp. 36–59). Hershey, PA: Business Science Reference.

Baporikar, N. (2015c). Motivating Tourism: A Case of Club Mahindra Holidays.[IJABIM]. *International Journal of Asian Business and Information Management, 6*(2), 1–15.

Baporikar, N. (2015d). Holistic Framework for Evolving Effective Information Systems Strategy.[IJSITA]. *International Journal of Strategic Information Technology and Applications, 6*(4), 30–43.

Baporikar, N. (2014a). Innovation Strategies in SME: Global Perspective. In C. Machado & P. Melo (Eds.), *Effective Human Resources Management in Small and Medium Enterprises: Global Perspectives* (pp. 315–341). Hershey, PA: Business Science Reference.

Baporikar, N. (2014b). Innovation in the 21st Century Organization. In B. Christiansen, S. Yildiz, & E. Yildiz (Eds.), *Transcultural Marketing for Incremental and Radical Innovation* (pp. 339–365). Hershey, PA.

Baporikar, N. (2014c). Youth Entrepreneurship in Indian Scenario.[IJABIM]. *International Journal of Asian Business and Information Management, 5*(2), 74–84.

Baporikar, N. (2014d). Information Strategy as Enabler of Competitive Advantage.[IJSITA]. *International Journal of Strategic Information Technology and Applications, 5*(1), 30–41.

Baporikar, N., & Sokhalingam, C. P. (2012). Holistic Approach to Tourism Entrepreneurship: A Case of Tamil Nadu. *International Journal of Tourism and Travel, 5*, 57–66.

Baporikar, N. (2011). Emerging Trends in Tourism Industry in Oman. In Global Hospitality and Tourism management Technologies. IGI Global.

Baporikar, N., & Sokhalingam, C. P. (2010). *Strategic Management of Tourism – A Case of Oman* (1st ed.). VDM Verlag.

Baum, T. (1994). The development and implementation of national tourism policies. *Tourism Management, 15*(3), 185–192. doi:10.1016/0261-5177(94)90103-1

Becken, S., & Hughey, K. F. D. (2013). Linking tourism into emergency management structures to enhance disaster risk reduction. *Tourism Management, 36*, 77–85. doi:10.1016/j.tourman.2012.11.006

Bramwell, B., & Cox, V. (2009). Stage and path dependence approaches to the evolution of a national park tourism partnership. *Journal of Sustainable Tourism, 17*(2), 191–206. doi:10.1080/09669580802495782

Bramwell, B., & Lane, B. (2006). Editorial: Policy Relevance and Sustainable Tourism Research: Liberal, Radical and Post-structuralist Perspectives. *Journal of Sustainable Tourism, 14*(1), 1–5. doi:10.1080/09669580608668587

Briedenhann, J., & Wickens, E. (2004). Tourism routes as a tool for the economic development of rural areas – vibrant hope or impossible dream? *Tourism Management, 25*(1), 71–79. doi:10.1016/S0261-5177(03)00063-3

Buhrs, T. (2000). The environment and the role of the state in New Zealand. In P. A. Memon & H. Perkins (Eds.), *Environmental Planning and Management in New Zealand* (pp. 27–35). Palmerston North: Dunmore Press.

Church, A. (2004). Local and regional tourism: policy and power. In A. Lew, C. M. Hall, & A. Williams (Eds.), *A companion to tourism* (pp. 555–568). Oxford, UK: Blackwell. doi:10.1002/9780470752272.ch44

Church, A., Ball, R., Bull, C., & Tyler, D. (2000). Public policy engagement with British tourism: The national, local and the European Union. *Tourism Geographies*, *2*(3), 312–336. doi:10.1080/14616680050082544

Collier, A. (1989). Principles of Tourism Pitman. Academic Press.

Cooper, C. (1999), Tourism Principles and Practices. Addison Wesley Longman Publishing.

Colebatch, H. (2009). *Policy*. Maidenhead, UK: McGraw-Hill.

Coles, T., Hall, C. M., & Duval, D. T. (2006). Tourism and Post-Disciplinary Enquiry. *Current Issues in Tourism*, *9*(4/5), 293–319. doi:10.2167/cit327.0

Connelly, G. (2007). *Testing Governance - A Research Agenda for Exploring Urban Tourism Competitiveness*. Academic Press.

Craik, J. (1990). A classic case of clientelism: The Industries Assistance Commission inquiry into travel and tourism. *Culture and Policy*, *2*(1), 29–45.

Dredge, D., & Jenkins, J. (2007). *Tourism Planning and Policy*. Brisbane: Wiley and Sons.

Dredge, D., & Jenkins, J. (2007). *Tourism Planning and Policy*. Brisbane: John Wiley and Sons.

Dubin, R. (1976). *Theory Building in Applied Areas*. Chicago: Rand McNally.

Dye, T. (1992). Understanding Public Policy (7th ed.). Englewood Cliffs, NJ: Prentice Hall.

Edgell, D. Sr. (1995). A barrier-free future for tourism? *Tourism Management*, *16*(2), 107–110. doi:10.1016/0261-5177(94)00020-B

Elliott, J. (1997). *Tourism, Politics and Public Sector Management*. London: Routledge.

Farrell, B., & Twining-Ward, L. (2005). Seven steps towards sustainability: Tourism in the context of new knowledge. *Journal of Sustainable Tourism*, *13*(2), 109–122. doi:10.1080/09669580508668481

Grant, M. (2004). Innovation in Tourism Planning Processes: Action Learning to Support a Coalition of Stakeholders for Sustainability. *Tourism and Hospitality Planning & Development*, *1*(3), 219–237. doi:10.1080/1479053042000306493

Gantzer, H., & Gantzer, C. (1983, June). Managing Tourists and Politicians in India. Tourism Management, 118-125. doi:10.1016/0261-5177(83)90029-8

GOI. (2004). India Tourism Statistics 2004. Ministry of Tourism, Market Research Division New Delhi: GOI.

Government of India (GOI). (2002). *National Tourism Policy 2002*. New Delhi: GOI.

Government of India (GOI). (2015). *GOI - Press Release, July, 2015*. GOI.

Ghosh, P. (1999). *Name it, India has got it, except tourists; The Rediff Business Special/Tourism in doldrums*. Retrieved from http://www.rediff.com/business/1999

Greenwood, J., Williams, A. M., & Shaw, G. (1990). Policy implementation and tourism in the UK. Implications from recent tourism research in Cornwall. *Tourism Management, 11*(1), 53–62. doi:10.1016/0261-5177(90)90008-W

Hall, C. M. (1999). Rethinking Collaboration and Partnership: A Public Policy Perspective. *Journal of Sustainable Tourism, 7*(3/4), 274–289. doi:10.1080/09669589908667340

Hall, C. M. (2002). Travel safety, terrorism and the media: The significance of the issue-attention cycle. *Current Issues in Tourism, 5*(5), 458–466. doi:10.1080/13683500208667935

Hall, C. M. (2008a). *Tourism Planning: Policies, Processes and Relationships* (2nd ed.). Harlow, UK: Pearson Education.

Hall, C. M. (2008b). *Tourism Planning: Policies, processes, relationships* (2nd ed.). London: Prentice Hall.

Hall, C. M., & Jenkins, J. (2004). Tourism and Public Policy. In A. Lew, C. M. Hall, & A. Williams (Eds.), *A companion to tourism* (pp. 425–540). Oxford, UK: Blackwell. doi:10.1002/9780470752272.ch42

Hall, C. M., & Jenkins, J. M. (1995). *Tourism and Public Policy*. Routledge.

Hannam, K. (2002). Tourism and development: Globalisation and power. *Progress in Development Studies, 2*(3), 227–234. doi:10.1191/1464993402ps039pr

Henry, I. P., & Jackson, G. A. M. (1996). Sustainability of Management Processes and Tourism Products and Contexts. *Journal of Sustainable Tourism, 4*(1), 17–28. doi:10.1080/09669589608667256

Hjalager, A. M. (2007). Stages in the economic globalization of tourism. *Annals of Tourism Research, 34*(2), 437–457. doi:10.1016/j.annals.2006.10.006

Hjalager, A. M. (2010). A review of innovation research in tourism. *Tourism Management, 31*(1), 1–12. doi:10.1016/j.tourman.2009.08.012

Ioannides, D. (1995). A flawed implementation of sustainable tourism: The experience of Akamas, Cyprus. *Tourism Management, 16*(8), 583–592. doi:10.1016/0261-5177(95)00081-X

Haxton, P. (2015). *A Review of Effective Policies for Tourism Growth, OECD Tourism Papers*. Paris: OECD Publishing. doi:10.1787/23071672

Ivars Baidal, J. A. (2004). Tourism Planning in Spain. *Annals of Tourism Research, 31*(2), 313–333. doi:10.1016/j.annals.2003.12.001

Jenkins, J. (2001). Editorial. *Current Issues in Tourism, 4*(2), 69–77. doi:10.1080/13683500108667882

Kerr, W. (2003). *Tourism Public Policy, and the strategic Management of Failure*. New York: Pergamon.

Khan, M. A. (2005). *Introduction to Tourism*. Anmol Publication Pvt. Ltd.

Lawrence, M., & Dredge, D. (2007). Tourism planning and policy processes. In D. Dredge & J. A. Jenkins (Eds.), *Tourism planning and policy* (pp. 191–224). John Wiley & Sons.

MacLeod, G. (2001). New regionalism reconsidered: Globalization and the remaking of political economic space. *International Journal of Urban and Regional Research, 25*(4), 804–829. doi:10.1111/1468-2427.00345

Marzano, G., & Scott, N. (2009). Power in destination branding. *Annals of Tourism Research, 36*(2), 247–267. doi:10.1016/j.annals.2009.01.004

Mathews, H. G. (1975). International Tourism and Political Science Research. *Annals of Tourism Research, 2*(4), 195–203. doi:10.1016/0160-7383(75)90032-8

MacIntosh, R. W. (1995). *Tourism: Principles, Practices, Philosophies.* John Wiley and Sons, Inc.

McCoy, P. (1982). The new national tourism policy act the state role in implementation. *Annals of Tourism Research, 9*(2), 276–279. doi:10.1016/0160-7383(82)90056-1

McDonald, J. R. (2009). Complexity science: An alternative world view for understanding sustainable tourism development. *Journal of Sustainable Tourism, 17*(4), 455–471. doi:10.1080/09669580802495709

Nunkoo, R., Gursoy, D., & Ramkissoon, H. (2013). Developments in hospitality marketing and management: Social network analysis and research themes. *Journal of Hospitality Marketing & Management, 22*(3), 269–288. doi:10.1080/19368623.2013.753814

OECD. (2014a). *New Approaches to Economic Challenges Synthesis Paper.* Available on Olis at [C (2014)41].

OECD. (2011a). *Towards Green Growth, Green Growth Strategy Synthesis report.* Paris: OECD.

OECD/UNEP. (2011b). *Climate Change and Tourism Policy in OECD Countries, OECD Studies on Tourism.* OECD Publishing.

O'Neil, P. (2007). *Essentials of Comparative Politics* (2nd ed.). Norton.

Olds, K. (1998). Urban mega-events, evictions and housing rights: The Canadian case. *Current Issues in Tourism, 1*(1), 2–46. doi:10.1080/13683509808667831

Ostrom, E. (1990). *Governing the commons: The evolution of institutions for collective action.* Cambridge University Press. doi:10.1017/CBO9780511807763

Ostrom, E. (1998). A Behavioral Approach to the Rational Choice Theory of Collective Action. *The American Political Science Review, 92*(1), 1–22. doi:10.2307/2585925

Ostrom, E. (2005). *Understanding institutional diversity.* Princeton, NJ: Princeton Univ Pr.

Pearce, D. G. (1998). Tourism development in Paris: Public intervention. *Annals of Tourism Research, 25*(2), 457–476. doi:10.1016/S0160-7383(97)00096-0

Pearce, D. G. (2001). Tourism, trams and local government policy-making in Christchurch, New Zealand. *Current Issues in Tourism, 4*(2-4), 331–354. doi:10.1080/13683500108667892

Pearlman, M. V. (1990). Conflicts and constraints in Bulgarias tourism sector. *Annals of Tourism Research, 17*(1), 103–122. doi:10.1016/0160-7383(90)90117-A

Manish. (2007). *Tourism Planning and Development.* Rajat Publication.

Ritchie, J. R. B. (1988). Consensus policy formulation in tourism. Measuring resident views via survey research. *Tourism Management, 9*(3), 199–212. doi:10.1016/0261-5177(88)90037-4

Ritchie, J. R. B., & Crouch, G. I. (2000). The competitive destination: A sustainability perspective. *Tourism Management*, *21*(1), 1–7.

Rittel, H., & Weber, M. (1973). Dilemmas in a general theory of planning. *Policy Sciences*, *4*(2), 155–169. doi:10.1007/BF01405730

Robinson, G. (1993). Tourism and tourism policy in the European community: An overview. *International Journal of Hospitality Management*, *12*(1), 7–20. doi:10.1016/0278-4319(93)90038-B

Sharma, P. (2015). *New Tourism Policy to Make India Incredible*. Available at: http://www.newindianexpress.com/thesundaystandard/New-Tourism-Policy-to-Make-India-Incredible/2015/05/03/article2794202.ece

Singh, S. (2001). Indian Tourism: Policy, Performance and Pitfalls. In D. Harrison (Ed.), *Tourism and the Less Developed World, Issues and Case Studies*. Oxon, UK: Cabi.

Singh, S. (2008). Destination Development Dilemma - case of Manali in Himachal Himalaya. *Tourism Management*, *29*(6), 1152–1156. doi:10.1016/j.tourman.2008.02.018

Smeral, E. (1998). The impact of globalization on small and medium enterprises: New challenges for tourism policies in European countries. *Tourism Management*, *19*(4), 371–380. doi:10.1016/S0261-5177(98)00036-3

Sokhalingam, C. P., & Baporikar, N. (2011). Tourism Entrepreneurship in Tamil Nadu – A Case of Inclusive Approach, *Matrix. Business Review (Federal Reserve Bank of Philadelphia)*, *1*(2), 16–26.

Sreekumar, T. T., & Parayil, G. (2010). Contentions and contradictions of tourism as development option: The case of Kerala, India. *Third World Quarterly*, *23*(3), 529–548. doi:10.1080/01436590220138411

Stevenson, N., Airey, D., & Miller, G. (2008). Tourism Policy Making: The Policymakers Perspectives. *Annals of Tourism Research*, *35*(3), 732–750. doi:10.1016/j.annals.2008.05.002

Sugiyarto, G., Blake, A., & Sinclair, M. T. (2003). Tourism and globalization: Economic Impact in Indonesia. *Annals of Tourism Research*, *30*(3), 683–701. doi:10.1016/S0160-7383(03)00048-3

Swain, M., Brent, M., & Long, V. (1999). Annals and Tourism Evolving: Indexing 25 years of publication. *Annals of Tourism Research*, *25*, 991–1014.

Thomas, H., & Thomas, R. (1998). The implications for tourism of shifts in British local governance. *Progress in Tourism and Hospitality Research*, *4*(4), 295–306. doi:10.1002/(SICI)1099-1603(199812)4:4<295::AID-PTH115>3.0.CO;2-0

Van Doorn, J. W. M. (1982). Can Futures Research Contribute to Tourism Policy. *Tourism Management*, *3*(3), 149–166. doi:10.1016/0261-5177(82)90064-4

Wanhill, S. R. C. (1987). UK: Politics and tourism. *Tourism Management*, *8*(1), 54–58. doi:10.1016/0261-5177(87)90040-9

Weed, M. (2006). The Influence of Policy Makers Perceptions on Sport Tourism Policy Development. *Tourism Review International*, *10*(4), 227–240. doi:10.3727/154427206779367091

Warwick, K. (2013). *Beyond Industrial Policy: Emerging issues and new trends. OECD Science, Technology and Industry Policy Papers, No. 2*. OECD Publishing. doi:10.1787/23074957

Whitford, M. (2009). A framework for the development of event public policy: Facilitating regional development. *Tourism Management*, *30*(5), 674–682. doi:10.1016/j.tourman.2008.10.018

Williams, A. M., & Shaw, G. (2009). Future Play: Tourism, recreation and land use. *Land Use Policy*, *265*, 5326–5335.

Wray, M. (2009). Policy communities, networks and issue cycles in tourism destination systems. *Journal of Sustainable Tourism*, *17*(6), 673–690. doi:10.1080/09669580903071979

Xu, X. & Gursoy, D. (2014). A Conceptual Framework of Sustainable Hospitality Supply Chain Management. *Journal of Hospitality Marketing & Management*. DOI: 10.1080/19368623.2014.909691

Yasarata, M., Altinay, L., Burns, P., & Okumus, F. (2009). Politics and sustainable tourism development - Can they co-exist? Voices from North Cyprus. *Tourism Management*, *31*(3), 345–356. doi:10.1016/j.tourman.2009.03.016

KEY TERMS AND DEFINITIONS

Community Based Approaches: The involvement and empowerment of the destination community in the planning and management of tourism in their community.

Non-Governmental Organisations (NGOs): Organisations that are not affiliated or connected with the government.

Policy Cycle: A conceptual tool used to identify and trace the development of a piece of policy. It assists in the understanding of the shaping of policy decisions and their impacts.

Policy Implementation: The practical realisation of policy through legislation, planning and the involvement of non-state actors.

Policy Instruments: The regulatory and economic tools used to measure policy.

Policy: A plan of action by an individual, group, company or government that guides decisions.

Public/Private Partnerships: Public-private partnerships refer to a government service or private venture that is a partnership (funded and operated) between a government and a company in the private sector.

Stakeholders: Individuals, groups, companies or individuals that have a direct or indirect stake in a particular organisation. Stakeholders can include owners, investors, employees, the community and unions.

Tourism Development: An increase in material prosperity due to tourism. This usually refers to some country or region.

Tourism Policy: Policy involves actions, decision, politics, values and ideological beliefs, social processes involving communication, outcome such as legislation and implementation carried out under the coordination of public administrations related to the processes of analysis, attraction, reception and evaluation of the impacts of tourism flows in a tourism system or destination.

Chapter 11
The Life Cycles of Destination Life Cycle Models:
A Critical Comparison and Synthesis in the Context of Destinations in Asia

Sudipta Kiran Sarkar
Berjaya University College of Hospitality, Malaysia

Babu P. George
Fort Hays State University, USA

ABSTRACT

Product Life Cycle (PLC) has always been a hot topic in the tourism literature. Butler's Tourism Area Lifecycle model and Plog's destination life cycle model have both been applied and analysed extensively in tourism destination development and lifecycle studies. This study attempts to offer a critical conversation on the similarities and differences as well as the strengths and weaknesses of these two widely referred generic models of destination life cycle. It also identifies some recent socio-political, economic, and technological developments that have changed the nature of tourism destination development in many parts of the world and in particular to Asia and the implications of these developments upon life cycles. Based on more recent research, the present authors suggest that the reality of destination development lies somewhere in between, as a resultant of interaction with the processes laid out by Plog and Butler.

INTRODUCTION

In marketing, *product lifecycle management* refers to the process of managing an enterprise's products from inception to demise and possible resurrection (Stark, 2015). In tourism, tourism destination is an important class of products to be managed. Tourist destination life cycle has been an area of extensive research since the last 40 -50 years (Alemeida & Correia,2010; George, Henthorne, & Williams, 2013). Studies on tourism destination lifecycle have taken various approaches and have been done from various perspectives. Many studies have taken sociological, economic as well as business and marketing

DOI: 10.4018/978-1-5225-2078-8.ch011

approaches to destination life cycle (Butler, 2009, 2011; McKercher, 1995; Plog, 2001; Prideaux, 2000). Various studies from all these perspectives have used and tested different models on different life cycles developed by researchers and academics in the past (George & George, 2004). Many of such models used have been commended theoretically but have also been found to be empirically challenging (McKercher, 2005a, 2005b; Prideaux, 2000). Yet such models are continued to be used in present research in spite of being debatable in terms of its practical application.

Destination Management Organisationshave looked into destination life cycle aspects and used models for marketing, demand forecasting as well as for other strategic purposes(Agrusa et al., 2011; Edward & George, 2008). Many researchers who developed destination life cycle models have considered tourism destinations as products and brands (Butler, 2011; Plog, 2001; McKercher, 2005a, 2005b). As a result, destinations life cycles have been compared with product life cycles and similarities between the two have been drawn (Butler,2011;Mckercher,2005b).

The most widely used models on destination life cycle in tourism research have been the Plog's life cycle which was developed more than 3 decades ago and the Butlers life cycle model also developed a little over 3 decades ago (Butler, 2009 ; McKercher, 2005 ; Plog, 1974). Both of these models consider tourism destinations as products (Butler, 2011;McKercher, 1995;Plog, 2001). Both models have been suggestive of a destination life cycle which starts from a stage of low tourist activity then moving to a stage of high tourist activity and ending at a stage of decreasing tourist activity resulting from negative environmental and cultural impacts of high volume tourist activity (Butler,2011 ; Plog, 2001). Between the two models, based on literary evidence, Butler's model appears to be more relevant and acceptable than Plog's model. However, this does not mean that the models are at loggerheads. As evidenced in the recent research by George, Henthorne, & Williams (2013), a synthesis of these two generic models might help to substantially increase our understanding of the dynamics of destination life cycle.

BUTLER'S TOURISM AREA LIFE CYCLE (TALC) MODEL

Butler's model of tourism destination lifecycle also known as Tourism Area Life Cycle (TALC) is one of the most widely used models in several studies as well as one of the most highly cited (Diedrich& Garcia-Buades, 2009; McKercher, 2005b; Prideaux, 2000). The Tourism Area Lifecycle was first introduced in a paper written in 1980 at an Australian CAUTHE Conference (McKercher, 2005b). The model was significantly based on the theory of product life cycle (McKercher, 2005b).

Model Specifics

Considering destinations as products, the model suggested that destinations or tourism areas evolve through different stages which are "exploration", "involvement", "development","consolidation", "stagnation" (Alameda& Correia,2010 ; Butler,2009 ; Butler,2011 ; McKercher, 2005b). These stages are quite identical to the stages through which products advance in the product life cycle which are– "introduction", "growth", "maturity" and "decline" (Butler,2009; Butler, 2011;McKercher,2005b). Followed by the stagnation period are 5 alternatives which are rejuvenation, reduced growth, stabilisation as well as decline and immediate decline. See Figure 1.

Figure 1. Butler's TALC curve

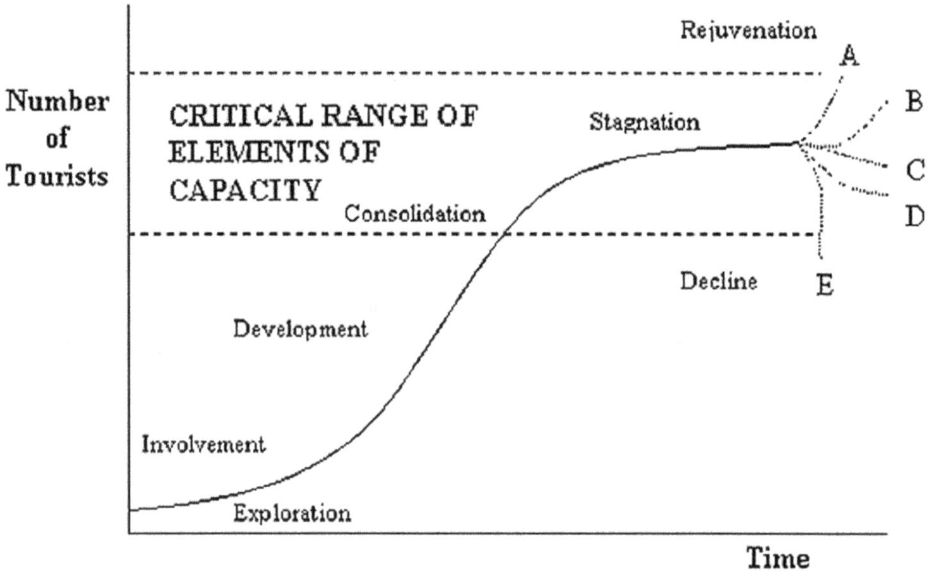

The decline aspect refers to the notion that "tourism destroys tourism". McKercher(2005b) have argued that the phase after stagnation does not indicate the end of tourism at the destination but is a single cycle in the overall progression of the destination.

Criticism

A central issue with the Butler model is that it superimposes product maturity with user demand. It is not impossible that certain products become very mature in their technologies at a very early age and stage and then live a longer life without much changes (Jian, Cai, & Chen, 2017). The resort development spectrum of Prideaux (2004) challenged decline aspect by referring to a similar viewpoint as McKercher(2005b) that resorts pass through many life cycles starting from catering to local, regional, national and finally international markets. According to original Butler's life cycle model in 1980 another issue that is associated with decline option is carrying capacity and limits to growth(Butler, 2009 ; Butler, 2011; McKercher, 2005b). Exceeding the limits of carrying capacity will result in the demise of the destination. This viewpoint has been found debatable by other researchers as determining carrying capacity is challenging. Cooper & Jackson (1989) argued that there are considerable challenges in measuring carrying capacity since the elements within it may differ from each other and the issues of seasonality as well as tourist movement patterns are not taken into consideration. Moreover, the decline of a destination due to fall in tourists arrivals as claimed in Butler's model according to some studies is due to exhaustion of markets and not carrying capacity being exceeded (Ma & Hassink, 2013).

Deficiencies

A major deficiency of the Butler's life cycle model is its inability to play a role as a predictive tool. Prideaux (2000) commented that decline that occurs as one of the options after stagnation as suggested in the Butler's model is unpredictable. In other words, the model mentions about decline but is unable to indicate exactly when it is likely to occur. Douglas (1997) in their study on Melanesia found weaknesses in the model when it came to its application in destinations with colonial and post-colonial societies. Their study found that Butler's life cycle model was unable to predict at which point or in what circumstances can a destination move from one stage to the other (Douglas, 1997). According to their study, certain destinations like Papua New Guinea, Solomon Islands and Vanuatu remained in the earlier stages for a considerable period of time after which certain factors political, economic or social caused the destination to reach "modified decline" stage (Douglas, 1997). Almeida & Correia (2010) in their study on Madeira observed that the maturity stage of a destination can continue indefinitely. The study found Madeira's positive image and time span within each of the life cycle stages challenged the traditional life cycle model (Almeida & Correia, 2010).

Cooper and Jackson (1989) in their study on the case of Isle of Man, found that Butler's life cycle model was not effective in forecasting as well as identifying stages in destination's life cycle. This is due to the reason that such progression along the stages is dependent upon the actions of destination managers and events (Cooper & Jackson, 1989). McKercher (2005b) while raising the issue of treating destinations as products by the Butler's lifecycle model argued that destinations are not a single product but a combination of many products. Having made these arguments on the challenges that Butler's life cycle face in terms of it being empirically inapplicable, it must be mentioned that the model was not intended neither to be predictive in nature nor "designed to be proven" (McKercher, 2005b, p. 101). When the life cycle model was designed first time, markets and tourism were identical in nature and as a result destination life cycles were predictable (Butler, 2009). But in the present times, tourism destinations have become complex due socio-economic developments. As a result, Butler's model in the context of some studies is found to be lacking the ability to predict the patterns and dynamics of destination growth and cycles (Butler, 2009).

Papatheodorou (2006) and Coles (2006) were critical on the absence of the aspects of competitiveness and price in the model which significantly plays a role in destination development in a complex tourism environment of the present times. However, there are quite a number of aspects found in many studies that could be counterarguments against these criticisms. One of the most important aspects with regards to this is Butler's suggestion of 'tourism changes tourism' as against his 'tourism destroys tourism' notion (McKercher, 2005b, pp. 98-99). Butler (2011) argues that the process in which destinations are managed influences a lot as to whether a destination reaches its demise or not. This was the basic argument of the original model (Butler, 2011). A well - managed destination that is inclusive of strategic planning and innovation is likely to be successful to avert its decline (Butler, 2011). This may involve transformation of its image that was earlier nature-based or ethnic to the one based on built-attractions (McKercher, 2005b). Technology-related aspects found in Casino destinations and theme parks like Las Vegas or Macao provide alternative means of survival for a destination (Butler, 2011).

The Evolutionary Principle in the Butler's Model

The concept of evolution in Butler's destination life cycle model has been challenged in the arguments of researchers like Ravenscroft & Hadjihambi (2006). The arguments were that destinations are not living entities and therefore using the word 'evolution' in the original study is not apt since the term 'evolution' in terms of Darwin applies to living organisms (Butler,2011 ; McKercher, 2005b). The evolution process of living organism involves radical changes of the organism in the passage of time in terms of form and appeal. Some aspects of the organism existing at the earlier stage may remain; some disappear while some other aspects may alter (McKercher, 2005b). This aspect of evolution links it with what Butler described as 'tourism changes tourism' where destinations radically transform into something new compared to its initial image based on the actions of destination managers. Destination development progression is evolutionary in nature as it is a process and largely involves alterations for its very own survival in a dynamic environment (Butler, 2011; Ritchie & Crouche, 2003). Therefore looking at the nature of similarity what evolution means and how tourism destinations progress, it could be said that using the evolution word is justified.

Carrying Capacity

With regards to the concept of carrying capacity, the viewpoint of Butler that exceeding of the carrying capacity in terms of visitor numbers could lead to the destination to decline was challenged in some studies (McKercher, 2005b). These arguments were addressed by Butler (2011, p.6) that suitable modifications "would be the key to ensuring that the various carrying capacities (economic, social-cultural and environmental) of the resort were not exceeded, or where possible, were increased to meet growing pressures". The aspect of suitable modification which Butler (2011, p.6) mentions as "appropriate interventions" was part of the original model's fundamental argument and more so the subtitle of the paper that talked about the model was titled "Implication for Management of Resources"(Butler,2011, p.5). The same applies to the arguments made against the model from the perspective of competitiveness (Coles, 2006; Papatheodorou, 2006) that there is no mention of competition/price at different scales, its influences on the destination development as well as the role of individual actions.

Integrating Perspectives

Butler's model in spite of its weaknesses as highlighted by many researchers is flexible and have undergone changes. The discussions revealed that the model following the evolutionary patterns of that of living organism is valid as it suggests the similar changes and transformations in destinations as evident in the evolution of living organism. This is particularly relevant in the current scenario of tourism. Secondly, the original model's fundamental aspect was appropriate interventions will help in the survival of destinations. "Appropriate interventions" can address the issue of competition by means of addition of the dimension of competition between destinations into the original model (Butler, 2011, p.5). It could be further said the element of price/competition is inherent if not openly implied in the life cycle model that explains why destinations decline at different scales (Butler, 2011). Moreover, the model also suggests rejuvenation as an option for a destination to re-establish itself by looking at new market segments (Butler, 2011). The aspect of "appropriate interventions" also answers for the arguments made against the validity of the model from the perspective of carrying capacity and limits to growth. Appropriate intervention that may prevent a destination's decline as suggested by the model is implicit of the aspects of competition, price and modification of carrying capacity (Butler, 2011). Moreover, the various studies that show its validity in terms of applications in a dynamic tourism environment, adaptation of the model and most importantly its ability as a predictive tool, justifies its relevance in current and future research.

Even after a number of papers that have been strongly critical of the model, it has been increasingly adopted and extensively by researchers only making it survives long into the future (Prosser, 1995). The number of applications of the model in various studies clearly reveals its relevance in a complex and dynamic modern tourism industry of the present times. The studies of Cole (2009), Dodds and McElroy (2008), Kapczyski and Szromac (2008), Xie and Lane (2006), Putra and Hitchcock (2006), Tomljenovic and Getz (2009), Moss, Ryan and Wagoner (2003), Diedrich and Garcia-Buades (2009), Manate and Pechlaner (2006) and Berry (2006) affirm the relevance of the model from different perspectives. The value that a product has for a customer, by the fact of its current stage in the product lifecycle, is different for different customer segments. The lifecycle cost and how it factors into customer willingness to pay have become topics for research recently (Lapašinskaitė & Boguslauskas, 2015).

Cole (2009), Dodds and McElroy (2008), Kapczyski and Szromac (2008) focussed on the relevance of the model in vibrant and fast changing tourism industry. Xie and Lane (2006), Putra and Hitchcock (2006), Tomljenovic and Getz (2009), Moss et al. (2003) have adapted the model in probing the life cycles of specific events and cases in tourism. Tomljenovic and Getz (2009) and Whitfield (2008) were able to apply the models in their respective studies of wine tourism in Croatia and conference tourism in U.K. (Butler, 2011). Most significantly, Manate and Pechlaner (2006) and Berry (2006) were able to use the model as a predictive tool. These studies provide an answer to a number of those studies that strongly criticised the inability of the model to be used as a predictive tool. Manate and Pechlaner (2006) used the model to offer an early warning of decline and Berry (2006) used the model to detect the point at which a destination moved from one stage to the other. With regards to the aspects of carrying capacity, limits to growth and sustainability, Diedrich and Garcia-Buades (2009) found in their study that the model was useful in detecting a decline of a destination based on local perceptions of tourism impacts in Belize. The study affirmed the relevance of carrying capacity was instrumental in the decline of a destination (Diedrich & Garcia-Buades, 2009). The study found that considering local population perceptions of tourism impacts as a yardstick to measure destination decline is important since it can be an important element in taking suitable intervention measures to prevent decline (Diedrich & Garcia-Buades, 2009). Besides, most studies have affirmed the importance of the model as a descriptive tool (McKercher,2005b; Cooper & Jackson,1989; Douglas, 1997; Alemeida & Correia, 2010).

PLOG'S DESTINATION LIFE CYCLE MODEL

Stanley C. Plog developed one of the oldest destination life cycle models in 1974 (McKercher, 2005a). This model is centered on the concept of progression of a destination based on the type of tourists visiting it from the beginning till the end of a continuum.

Model Specifics

This continuum consists of two main types of tourists at its two ends, one being allo-centric which is at the beginning of the continuum and psycho-centric which is at the end of the continuum (Plog, 1974, 2001) (See Figure 2). The other points in the continuum are Near- allocentrics that fall after allo-centrics followed by mid – centrics and then Near Psychocentric that falls before psychocentric (Plog,1974,2001). Plog (1974) explains a destination moves on a consistent basis, from appealing first to Allo - centrics and last to Psycho-centrics. Plog(1974) described Allo - centrics as "persons with varied interests" as the word "allo" means "varied". Psycho-centrics on the other hand, are self-conscious people as the word "psyche" means "self" (Plog, 1974). In another paper by Plog in 2001, new terms like "venturer" (allo-centric), "near-venturer" (near-allocentric), "Near- dependable"(Near-psychocentric), and "depend-

Figure 2. Plog's traveller personality typology across a life cycle

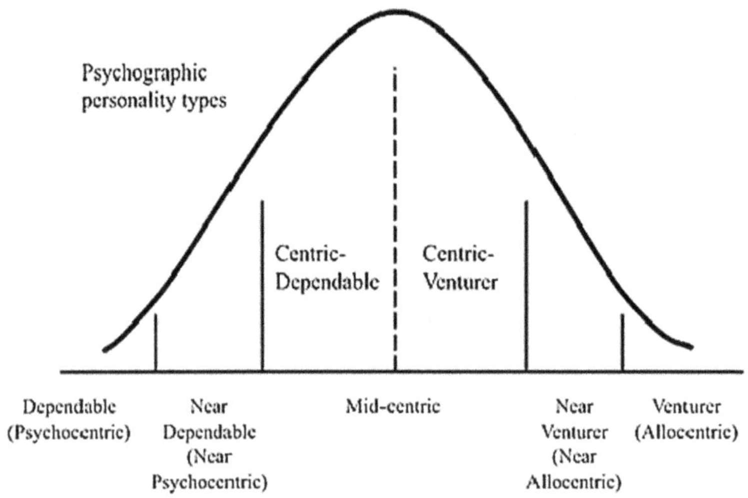

able" (psychocentric) were introduced. Besides, two types of tourists, "centric-venturer" and "centric dependable" were introduced on either sides of the mid-point in the continuum.

Criticism

The progression of the destination based on the type of visitors from one end of a continuum to another in the form of a bell-shaped curve is based on a single market standpoint (McKercher, 1995, 2005a). This reveals the first weakness of this model as it fails to realise the viewpoint of different markets instead of one market about the destination. The single market-centric standpoint of Plog and the failure to realise the existence of varied and complex nature of markets is a major deficiency it has. McKercher (2005a, p.51) also argued that destinations may grow with some markets and in the perspective of other markets it might be on the decline mode since they are not inert in nature but are "constantly evolving in manner akin to a complex living ecosystem".

The greatest weakness or limitation of Plog's model as one for destination life cycle is the inevitability of decline and the absence of corrective and intervening actions that will prevent decline or rejuvenate a destination. This is in contrast to Butler's model which considers decline as possible eventuality but its "inevitability is far less determined" (Butler, 2011; McKercher, 2005a). Plog (2001) suggests that the pattern of progression most destinations follow results in the ultimate decline of it since the causes of the decline are found to occur at the early stages (Plog, 2001). The justification in considering the inevitable decline as a weakness in the model lies in the many examples of destinations that have rejuvenated themselves by responding to the demands of many new market segments (McKercher, 2005a). Besides, the causes of decline may not be necessarily the shift from one end of the continuum to other but certain external factors that are significantly instrumental in a destination's decline (Mckercher, 2005a).

However, Plug (2001) also suggested that by means of appropriate understanding of the model, management of destinations can monitor the pattern of development to prevent decline. Though Plog is inclined towards destinations primarily having an appeal for venturers or Allo-centrics, he suggests that based on the curve of the model, destination planners can place visitors from market at any point of the continuum (Plog, 2001). Venturers/ Allo-centrics from certain markets might find established destination interesting as long as it offers them something new (Plog, 2001). This is followed by the usual pattern of progression as suggested in the Plog model where the progression of the destination reaches the Dependable/ psycho-centric end of the continuum. Here again lies another aspect of the weakness of the model. The assumption that certain markets will progress through the continuum from venturers to dependable is debatable.

The effects of distance decay and cultural decay are not seen to be considered to play a role in the progression through the continuum (McKercher, 2005a). Distance factors like geographical proximity, travelling time and cost play a major role in tourist movement (McKercher, 2005a). Similarly cultural distance factors like cultural familiarity or strangeness, cultural links, also play a major role (McKercher, 2005a). These factors can determine whether the markets will move along the continuum or not. From the North American perspective, a destination like Sydney is most likely to be always for Allo-centrics/ venturers while for Australians, Bali and Fiji were always for tourists ranging from mid-centric or psycho-centric/dependable (McKercher, 2005a). This weakness can also be attributed to the single geographic market approach of the model where its inability to measure the viewpoint of different markets about a destination is clearly evident (McKercher, 2005a).

Integrating Perspectives

However, Plog's life cycle model seems to explain market behaviour to a destination than describing or analysing the destination life cycle itself. According to McKercher (2005a, p. 54), Plog's model has the "ability to understand the diversity of tourists that exist within a destination or experience that different segments prefer". Moreover, the model is also capable of analysing the varied behaviour of different tourists. Therefore in order to study the nature and behaviour of different markets or tourists from different markets to a destination, such model would be very useful especially for Destination Management Organisations. Liu, Siguaw, and Enz (2008) in their study used the Plog's psychographic destination life cycle model to analyse Costa Rica's status as a destination in a life cycle based on consumer preferences and patterns. The study's analysis found most tourists visiting Costa Rica were in the middle of psychographic distribution and destination management bodies based on these findings should streamline future patterns of development (Liu, Siguaw, & Enz, 2008). Many other studies have used Plog's model to study the patterns, behaviour and movements of different tourists to a destination (Plog, 2002).

Plog's model though appears similar to Butler's model in terms of the stages of destination development, has certain significant shortcomings as revealed from the discussion. Firstly, it is more inclined towards explaining the nature and behaviour of a market along a continuum than describing the life cycle itself. Secondly, the single geographic market the model has in its original form makes it unable to gauge the behaviour of different geographic markets as evident in tourism in the present times. Thirdly, it considers decline as inevitable for destinations as well as it does not offer any scope for revival after a decline. Finally, the model tends to suggest that markets always move from the Allo-centric end of the continuum to the psycho-centric end. This is challenged by the unavoidable factors of distance decay and cultural which can be instrumental in preventing a market to move along the continuum. Therefore, based on this analysis, it could be suggested that Butler's tourist Area life cycle (TALC) offers more progressive perspective than the relatively more static Plog's life cycle model.

However, Plog's model used widely in different studies that focus on travel preferences, tourist behaviour from certain markets as well as in niche cases like ecotourism destinations or ones based on nature makes it significant in tourism research. Moreover, as researchers, models can be criticised but more importantly should be applauded for their theoretical contribution (Litvin, 2006). In this case, though Plog's model has been found less acceptable, its relevance as a theoretical model is much appreciated nevertheless.

CHANGING ENVIRONMENTAL: BEHAVIOURAL DYNAMICS

It is imperative to notice that both these models evolved more than 3 decades ago when the socio-political structures of the times were in sharp contrast to the socio-political structures now. The collapse of Soviet Union and Communism on one hand, and the emergence of neo-liberalism driven globalisation on the other hand, since the 80s have brought about a significant overhaul in the dynamics of tourism (Butler, 2009). Tourism is a complex, fast changing phenomenon now and its growth in the present times is not limited to Western countries but has expanded to emerging economies like China and India primarily as well as many other nations (McKercher, 2005b). Many of these nations are either major contributors to international travel or are emerging new destinations themselves (Butler, 2009; McKercher, 2005b). Continued economic growth in these Asian countries has accelerated outbound tourism considerably over the last one decade resulting in increasing implications for tourism destination development patterns.

However, it is interesting to see the effects of the relatively recent developments like global financial crisis, considered the worst since the 1930s Great Depression, on tourism destination development models whether Butler or Plog. As in the case of Benidorm, Spain, which is at the maturity stage of its development cycle, the ongoing financial crisis that started in 2008 has had a significant effect on it (Baidal, Sanchez & Rebollo, 2013). Decrease in overnight stays, low levels of occupancy rates led to many hotels being closed down. It also resulted on very tight competitions that resulted in enormous reductions in levels of business profitability (Baidal et al., 2013).. As a result significant investments were made to revitalise tourist activities by adding new projects through collaboration between local authorities and tourism entrepreneurs (Baidal et al., 2013). But it is to be seen whether the impact and aftershocks of 2008 global economic crisis, will have has an effect on the destination revitalisation process referred as "appropriate interventions" by Butler. Moreover, in the light of massive austerity measures adopted by governments in the Western world, slower economic growth in both developing and developed countries both as an outcome of the 2008 economic crisis and the more recent development of Brexit, it is to be seen whether there will be a significant impact on the progression of destinations according to the life cycles stages suggested by both the models. This will also potentially have implications in terms of the predictability and applicability of the both the destination lifecycle models.

Asian Perspectives

Asians destinations like Malaysia provide new prospects for understanding the implications of Butler model. Malaysia is believed to be in the development stage and is yet to complete the full cycle as suggested by Butler (Hussin, 2014). Hence when it reaches the final stages of the cycle, the trajectory it takes will be significant in terms of understanding the evolutionary nature of the Butler's lifecycle model. Destinations like Macao and Singapore which have emerged as Casino tourism hubs of Asia, are going through their respective stages of development. The development of new forms of casino and enclave resorts driven by casino liberalisation and external demands in these destinations can lead them to revival and rejuvenation processes validating the evolutionary nature of Butler's lifecycle model (Henderson, 2015; McCartney, 2005). Factors like socio-political conditions, government administrative efficiencies and economic environment have profound impact on the process of destination development. Singapore's growth from a third world country to a first world during the period of 1965-2015 also transformed it into a leading tourism destination of the region. Stable government, effective economic policies and sustained economic growth were the factors instrumental in its economic success and in turn, had profound impact on its development as a popular global tourism destination (Henderson, 2015). The economic and social achievement it made has led Singapore to be a globally-oriented destination known for its multi-culturalism and international business hub. The future development of Singapore as a tourism destination will be shaped by future economic growth prospects in the region and socio-economic challenges it is likely to face internally (Henderson, 2015). Given this scenario, it would be interesting to examine how the evolutionary nature of Butler's model will take shape in the context of Singapore's progress in terms of tourism development.

One of the new areas of growth potential for global theme parks industry is Asia (IAAPA, 2015, Palmeri, 2015). Family-centric values and increasing affluence in the societies of many emerging Asian countries is bringing benefits to this industry (Liu, 2015; IAAPA, 2015). Some very apparent manifestations of this are the opening of Asia's first Legoland in Malaysia in 2012, the recent opening of the Shanghai Disneyland and Legoland Discovery in Shanghai in 2016 as well as the expected opening of Legoland Dubai later in 2016, Legoland Korea in 2017 and the opening of world's first 20th Century Fox World in Genting, Malaysia, expected to be also in 2017(Liu, 2015). The opening of these world class theme parks in Asia is potentially going enhance the tourist movement patterns and potentially impact the growth and development process of tourism destinations across the region. Infact, theme park attendance in Asia has grown to 42 percent by 2015 (Palmeri, 2015). The opening of Shanghai Disneyland attracted twice the number of visitors (137.9 million) compared to its closest rival, Merlin Entertainment (Trigau, 2016). Theme park spending in Asia is expected to grow by $19.7 billion by 2019 with the GDP in the region expected to rise to $11000 (Liu, 2015; IAAPA, 2015). Macao, a destination known for its cultural heritage, colonial Portuguese and Chinese, reached the beginning of the maturity stage a few years ago (Meng, Wai &Yu, 2011). However, with the introduction of the Casino industry since the early 2000s, which is now in the growth stage, the possibilities of decline for Macao as a whole have diminished (Lim & Crossley, 2014).

Though slowing economies in Asia may stand in the way of unhindered growth of high investment –oriented theme parks industry in the coming years, it is currently placed in the growth stage in the context of Asia and has a lot of ground to cover before it can consolidate and mature (Liu, 2015). In the period of the next 5-10 years the growth process of destinations impacted by the growth of the theme park industry can be examined and evaluated based on the destination life models and implications be drawn.

Other Perspectives

Democratically Managed and Grassroots Tourism Initiatives in Destinations

Another important development in regards to emerging destinations is the rise of indigenous community-driven tourism in certain parts of the world. Such grassroots–driven initiatives for tourism development are found to be independent from the involvement of traditionally power controlling elements in tourism like transnational tourism corporations, local private businesses as well as significant top-down state-led involvements. Such independent initiatives involve tourism that is democratically managed by indigenous communities in relation to key areas like socio-environmental management, knowledge management and equitable distribution of revenue from tourism among the community (Ruiz-Ballestros, 2011). The development of local grassroots community-driven tourism in Ecuador also referred to as "tourismo communitaro" has led to socio-ecological sustainability in Ecuador (Ruiz-Ballestros, 2011). Such grassroots democratic initiatives of community-based tourism have been a part of the increasing empowerment of communities that resulted from the indigenous social movements in Ecuador in the 90s.

The case of Agua Blanca is a successful example of "tourismo communitario" where local grassroots have almost total control on tourism that takes place there and has also attained buoyancy in facing unforeseeable and external challenges (Ruiz-Ballestros, 2011). The "tourismo communitario" movement have been instrumental in shaping an entirely distinct, democratic and truly local community-controlled tourism that is firmly underpinned in consensus-based participation, resonant native community control and collective indigenous decision-making systems in Ecuador (Ruiz-Ballesteros, 2011). Another example is the small scale community-based tourism development in Chiapas, Mexico, a place that is closely associated with the indigenous revolutionary movement called the "Zapatista movement". San Cristobal, the capital of Chiapas, is often frequented by non-mainstream tourists like backpackers whose primary interest is not leisure and holidays but for their 'revolutionary experiences' and commitment to understand the philosophy and self-deterministic virtues of the Zapatista indigenous movement (Florez, 2013). The recuperation and running of the Agua Clara Spa resort by the Zapatistas is claimed to be a true ecological tourism by independent of any capitalist investments and capitalist nature of development (Florez, 2013). The Zapatistas determine where there must be tourism and where it should not be. In other words, it is an example of local grassroots-indigenous controlled, self-deterministic tourism development without the interference and dictates of external elements (Florez, 2013).

The development of social tourism based on workers participation and local community organised initiatives in Venezuela has been a major feature of the country as a destination under the Bolivarian Socialist revolution (Pearson, 2012). These interesting unique and transformational models and patterns of tourism development that is emerging in Latin America is clearly different from neo-liberal growth development patterns of tourist destinations in most parts of the world which are often analysed using the Butler's 'organic' market –driven growth sequence led destination development model. The trajectory destinations in many parts of the world have taken up in its evolution (reflective of Butler's market driven growth sequences) is clearly an outcome of capitalist development models predominant in the world (Weaver, 2012). It therefore unfolds interesting implications for seeking insights into the applicability and compatibility of the Plog and particularly Butler's tourist area lifecycle model, with such transformative, revolutionary and non-capitalist patterns of tourism development in Latin America involving entirely indigenous management systems.

Digital Technologies and Destinations

However, the most striking development of the recent times has been the explosion of the internet technology and social media in particular. The internet has enabled easy available destination related information for tourists and a faster mode of communication between tourists (Buhalis& Law, 2008). Social media which is a two-way interactive medium for social interactions based on User-generated –content (UGC) has been effective in tourist decision-making on destination choices, destination visitation aspects like trip planning as well as visit intentions of tourists (Chung & Buhalis, 2008; Volo, 2010; Xiang & Gretzel, 2010). Information, experiences and recommendations shared through social media have had influences on destination visit intentions of tourists (Fakharyan et al., 2012; Volo, 2010). However the most radical feature of social media has been its ability to enable customers of business to co-create and democratically exchange information and knowledge. This has been possible through the Community-based co-creative approach that involves collaboration between individuals/customers independently of the business firm (Martini, Massa & Testa, 2012). Customer take control in terms of reviewing, critiquing, designing and innovating of products and services of business firms without the intervention and influence of the very business firms (Asmussen, Harridge-March, Occhiocupo & Farquhar, 2012). It can also be referred to a bottom-up approach where a contributing consumer in content co-creation uses the online space in exchange of self-esteem enhancement, better services and also for some hedonic reasons (Pellegrini, 2007).

This approach leads to a democratic activity and involvement of consumers in making business firms accountable and provide transparency in terms of the quality and efficiency of the products and services they offer to them. In the context of tourism, tourists through the use of social media co-produce by mutually sharing and creating tourism information and knowledge in the form of pictorial, textual and audio-visual content (Dwivedi, Shibu & Venkatesh 2007). This has empowered tourists to share experiences with others, spread awareness on the credibility of tourism products as well as raise issues, challenge and critique tourism destination management organisations and tourism service providers without being controlled (Dwivedi, Shibu &Venkatesh 2007).This phenomenal development of internet technology can have implications for tourism destination evolution and growth patterns as tourists have now more information and power to exercise their control on the quality and attractiveness of tourism products and services they consume.

PROBING FURTHER: TOWARDS A SYNTHESIS

In a recent paper published in Tourism Recreation Research, George, Henthorne, & Williams (2013) investigated internal structure of destination life cycle curve. What comes out of their analysis is a much refined and extensive model with five normal distributions each characterizing a tourist persona, within the larger normal distribution of tourist flows to a destination over time. An immediate application of these findings lies in the identification of normally distributed allocentric, near allocentric, midcentric, near psychocentric and psychocentric sub-segments within the overall visitation model (See Figure 3).

Among other things, identification of these sub-segments provides enhanced opportunities for marketers to cater to the unique needs of these sub-segments. One quite unexpected finding that emerged from the analysis of empirical data was that, while allocentrics largely preferred nascent destinations, destinations that are close to the end of their life cycles would become attractive to them once again (See Figure 4).

What this investigation implies is that Plog's and Butler's models are not necessarily in opposition. The reality of destination development lies somewhere in between, as a resultant of interaction with the processes laid out by Plog and Butler. This inference is utmost evident when we note that allo-centric tourists tend to re-patronize destinations that have lost out in popularity. Their newfound interest in such destinations and the new meanings they bring into these destinations might be a key reason why destinations bounce back and possibly begin their reincarnated journey along an extended lifecycle.

Figure 3. George-Henthorne-Williams model

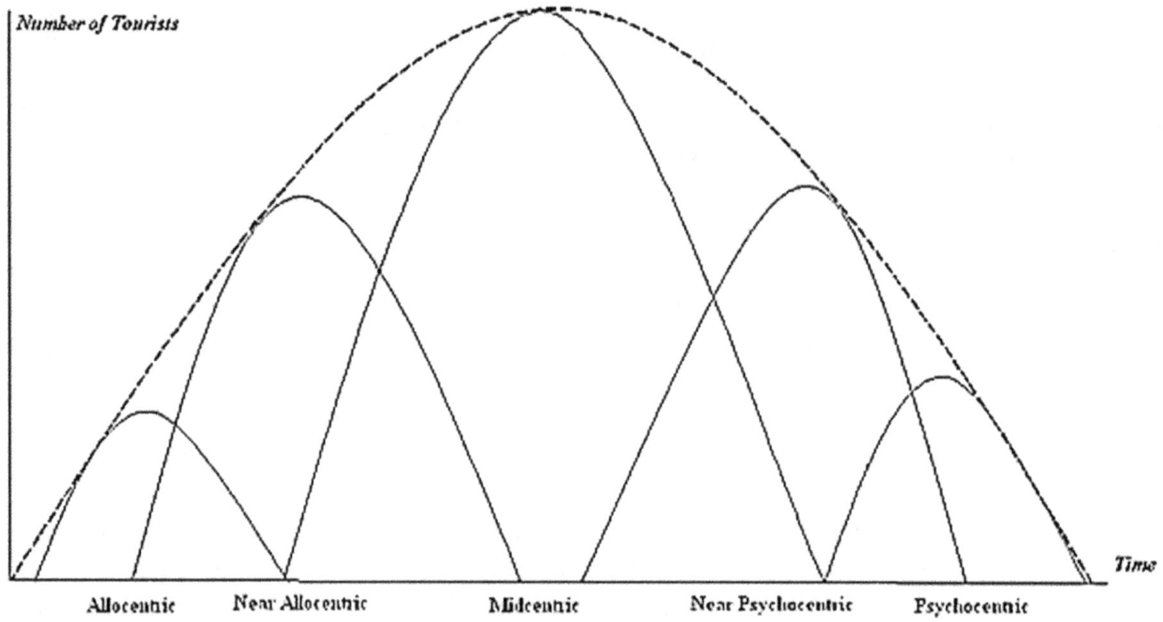

Figure 4. Psychographic segment distribution along destination area life cycle

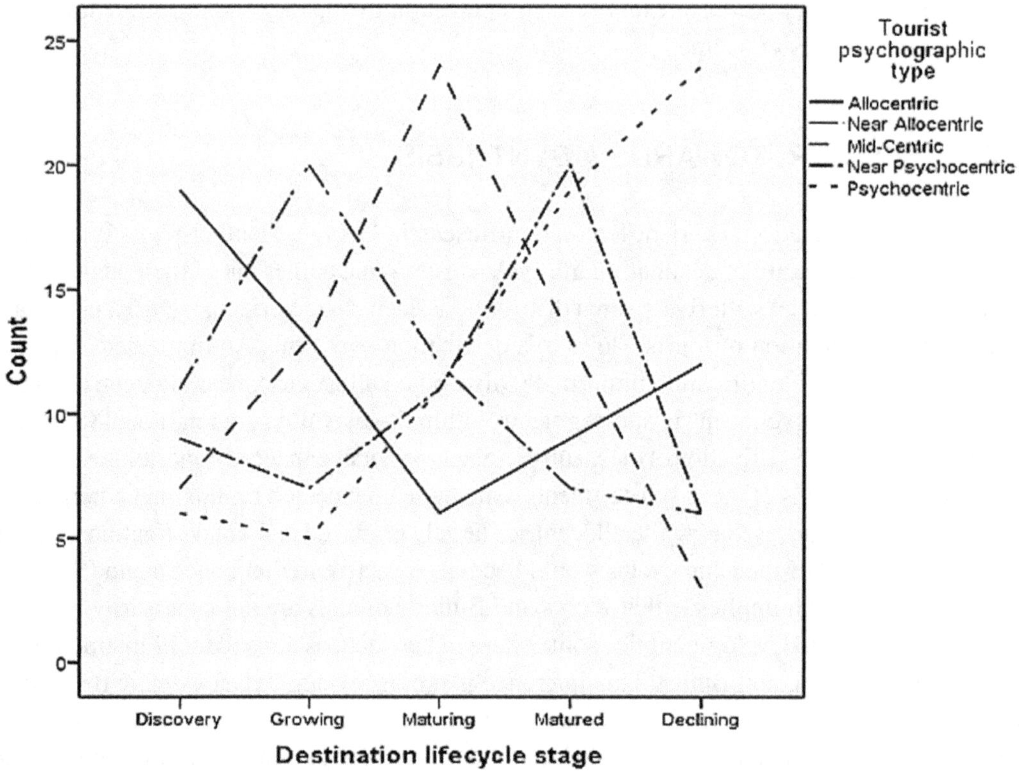

CONCLUSION

Based on the discussion made on the two generic models, it can be concluded that both are very simplistic and descriptive models and the notion of 'tourism changes tourism' is underlying belief of both. While Butler suggests that tourism destination development patterns lead to enhanced developments of tourism infrastructures and superstructures as destination revitalising efforts altering both the personality of the destination and visiting tourists, Plog suggests the evolution of the nature of tourists from 'hard' to 'soft' as the destination grows. Both models, though one from the supply-side demand changing perspective and other from demand - side changing supply perspective, suggests the strong possibilities of decline for a destination though Plog tends to be more absolute. Both models are not predictive as they were neither designed to be and are not also linear even though evolutions tend to be linear in nature (Singh, 2011). However, Butler's TALC model refers to destinations life cycles as evolutionary phases which destinations experience through revitalisation process or 'appropriate interventions'. This clearly reflects the 'business as usual' phenomenon evident in capitalistic models of development and hence the Butler TALC model is clearly more 'progressive' and compatible than the static Plog model.

However as mentioned earlier, recent developments in relation to global economy, grassroots socio-political developments as that of Latin America and technological developments may alter the traditional patterns of tourism destination development. This can question the applicability and validity of the Butler and Plog's tourist area lifecycle models as they were both developed during the 70s and applied in cases of tourism destination development of the times that are radically different from the potentially transforming and complex global situation of today. The most significant event is the current global economic crisis that is raising questions on the validity of the neo-liberal development and capitalist globalisation that started in the late 70s/early 80s, almost the same times the tourist area lifecycle models of Plog and Butler emerged. Besides, grassroots democratic social movements and the empowerment enabled by recent internet technologies to consumers/tourists have also radically changed the dynamics of tourism development across the world.

In the light of these new developments, it would be interesting to explore whether new and anticipative tourist area life cycle models emerge replacing the traditional ones like Plog and Butler as well as many other sophisticated ones of the later times, that can explain the future patterns of tourism destination lifecycle and developments based on the current complex and revolutionary events from a more comprehensive and contemporary perspective. The revised George, Henthorne, & Williams (2013) model proposed as a synthesis helps practitioners, especially destination management organizations, to better understand visitation dynamics. It refines and extends Plog's and Butler's original models, the result of which is a more robust model with substantially improved predictive power. As scholars and practitioners seek responsive marketing strategies in the tourism industry that has dramatically evolved in the recent past, it is important to rethink the extant models and their underlying theories. The re-examination of our ideas of destination life cycle is one important step in that direction.

REFERENCES

Agarwal, S. (2002). restructuring seaside tourism: The resort lifecycle. *Annals of Tourism Research*, *29*(1), 25–55. doi:10.1016/S0160-7383(01)00002-0

Agrusa, J., Lema, J., Tanner, J., Afo, A., Prideaux, B., & George, B. P. (2011). Destination image of Tahiti as perceived by international tourists: A study. *Asia Pacific World: The Journal of the International Association for Asia Pacific Studies*, *2*(2), 25–39. doi:10.3167/apw.2011020207

Alemeida, A., & Correia, A. (2010). Tourism development in Madeira; an analysis based onthe life cycle approach. *Tourism Economics*, *16*(2), 427–441. doi:10.5367/000000010791305644

Asmusen, B., Harridge-March, S., Occhiocupo, N., & Farquhar, J. (2012). The multi-layered nature of Internet democratization of brand management. *Journal of Business Research*, *66*(9), 1473–1483. doi:10.1016/j.jbusres.2012.09.010

Baidal, J. A. V. I., Sanchez, I. R., & Rebollo, J. F. B. (2013). The evolution of mass tourism destinations: New approaches beyond deterministic models in Benidorm (Spain). *Tourism Management*, *34*(1), 184–195. doi:10.1016/j.tourman.2012.04.009

Baum, T. (2006). Revisiting the TALC: is there an off-ramp? In R. W. Butler (Ed.), *Tourism Area Life Cycle; Conceptual and Theoretical Issues* (pp. 27–50). Clevedon, UK: Channelview Publications.

Berry, T. (2006). The predictive potential of the TALC model. In The Tourism Area Life Cycle, Conceptual and Theoretical Issues (pp. 167-175). Clevedon, UK: Channelview Publications.

Buhalis, D., & Law, R. (2008). Progress in information technology and tourism management: 20 years on and 10 years after the internet – the state of etourism research. *Tourism Management*, *29*(4), 609–623. doi:10.1016/j.tourman.2008.01.005

Butler, R. (2009). Tourism in the future: Cycles, waves or wheels? *Futures*, *41*(6), 346–352. doi:10.1016/j.futures.2008.11.002

Butler, R. W. (2011). Tourism Area Life Cycle. In C. Cooper (Ed.), *Contemporary TourismReviews* (pp. 1–33). Oxford, UK: GoodfellowPublishers Limited.

Chung, J. Y., & Buhalis, D. (2008). Information needs in online social networks. *Information Technology & Tourism*, *10*(4), 267–281. doi:10.3727/109830508788403123

Cole, S. (2009). A logistic tourism model – resort cycles, globalisation and chaos. *Annals of Tourism Research*, *36*(4), 689–714. doi:10.1016/j.annals.2009.07.004

Coles, T. (2006). Enigma variations? The TALC, marketing models and the descendants of the product life cycle. In R. W. Butler (Ed.), *The Tourism Area Cycle, Conceptual and Theoretical Issues* (pp. 49–66). Channelview Publications.

Cooper, S., & Jackson, S. (1989). Destination life cycle, the Isle of Man case study. *Annals of Tourism Research*, *16*(3), 377–398. doi:10.1016/0160-7383(89)90051-0

Diedrich, A., & Garcia-Buades, E. (2009). Local perceptions of tourism as indicators of destination decline. *Tourism Management*, *30*(4), 512–521. doi:10.1016/j.tourman.2008.10.009

Dodds, R., & McElroy, J. (2008). St Kitts at a crossroads. *ARA Journal of Travel Research*, *1*(2), 1–10.

Douglas, N. (1997). Applying the life cycle model to Melanesia. *Annals of Tourism Research*, *24*(1), 1–22. doi:10.1016/S0160-7383(96)00011-4

Dwivedi, M., Shibu, T. P., & Venkatesh, U. (2007). Social software on the Internet; implications for the hotel industry. *International Journal of Contemporary Hospitality Management*, *19*(5), 415–426. doi:10.1108/09596110710757570

Edward, M., & George, B. P. (2008). Tourism development in the State of Kerala, India: A study of destination attractiveness. *European Journal of Tourism Research*, *1*(1), 16–38.

Fakharyan, M., Jalilvand, M. R., Elyasi, M., & Mohammadi, M. (2012). The influence of online word of mouth communications of tourists attitudes toward Islamic destinations and travel intentions: Evidence from Iran. *African Journal of Business Management*, *6*(33), 9533–9542. doi:10.5897/AJBM12.628

Florez, K. C. (2013). *Tourism in Chiapas; a conversation with Hermann Bellinghausen*. Retrieved on 22nd May,2013 from http://upsidedownworld.org/main/mexico-archives-79/4208-tourism-in-chiapas-a-conversation-with-hermann-bellinghausen

George, B. P., & George, B. P. (2004). Past visits and the intention to revisit a destination: Place attachment as the mediator and novelty seeking as the moderator. *Journal of Tourism Studies*, *15*(2), 37–50.

George, H., Henthorne, T. L., & Williams, A. J. (2013). The bells within the bell curve: Destination cisitation model revisited. *Tourism Recreation Research*, *38*(3), 341–348. doi:10.1080/02508281.2013.11081758

Henderson, J. C. (2015). Destination development and transformation: 50 years of tourism after independence in Singapore. *International Journal of Tourism Cities*, *1*(4), 269–281. doi:10.1108/IJTC-05-2015-0011

Hussin, N. Z. (2014). Tracing the Malaysia Tourism Lifecycle and Strategy Assessment from the First Malaysia Plan to Ninth Malaysia Plan. *International Journal of Business and Social. Science*, *5*(3), 2014.

IAPPA. (2015). IAAPA Global Theme and Amusement Park Outlook.

Jian, X., Cai, S., & Chen, Q. (2017). A study on the evaluation of product maintainability based on the life cycle theory. *Journal of Cleaner Production*, *141*, 481–491. doi:10.1016/j.jclepro.2016.09.073

Kapczynski, A., & Szromek, A. R. (2008). Hypothesis concerning the development of Polish spas in the years 19492006. *Tourism Management*, *29*(5), 1035–1037. doi:10.1016/j.tourman.2007.10.001

Lam, C. S., & Crossley, J. (2014). Las Vegas Versus Macao as Diversified Travel Destinations. *Journal of Tourism Insights*, *5*(1), 1–26.

Lapašinskaitė, R., & Boguslauskas, V. (2015). The maintenance cost allocation in product life cycle. *The Engineering Economist*, *44*(4), 17–23.

Litvin, S. W. (2006). Revisiting Plogs model of allocentricity and psychocentricity…one more time. *The Cornell Hotel and Restaurant Administration Quarterly*, *47*(3), 245–253. doi:10.1177/0010880406289138

Liu, P. (2015). *Merry - go-round in Australia*. Retrieved from http://asiaweekly.com/merry-go-round-in-asia/

Liu, Z., Siguaw, J. A., & Enz, C. A. (2008). Using tourist travel habits and preferences to assess strategic destination positioning: The case of Costa Rica. *Cornell Hospitality Quarterly*, *49*(3), 258–281. doi:10.1177/1938965508322007

Ma, M., & Hassink, R. (2013). An evolutionary perspective on tourism area development. *Annals of Tourism Research*, *41*, 89–109. doi:10.1016/j.annals.2012.12.004

Manate, M., & Pechlaner, H. (2006). How to define, identify and monitor the decline of tourist destinations: towards an early warning system. In R. W. Butler (Ed.), *The Tourism Life Cycle, Conceptual and Theoretical Issues* (pp. 235–253). Clevedon, UK: Channelview Publications.

Martini, A., Massa, S., & Testa, S. (2012). The role of social software for customer co-creation; does it change the practice for innovation. *International Journal of Engineering Business Management*, *4*(40), 1–10.

McKercher, B. (1995). The destination-market matrix: A tourism market portfolio analysis model. *Journal of Travel & Tourism Marketing*, *4*(2), 23–40. doi:10.1300/J073v04n02_02

McKercher, B. (2005a). Are psychographics predictors of destination life cycles? *Journal of Travel & Tourism Marketing*, *19*(1), 49–55. doi:10.1300/J073v19n01_05

McKercher, B. (2005b). Destinations as products? A reflection on Butlers life cycle. *Tourism Recreation Research*, *30*(3), 97–102. doi:10.1080/02508281.2005.11081491

Meng, Z., Wei, Y., & Yu, Y. (2011). On Life Cycle of Cultural Heritage Engineering Tourism: A Case Study of Macau. *Engineering and Risk Management*, *1*, 351–357.

Moss, S. E., Ryan, C., & Wagoner, C. B. (2003). An empirical test of Butlers resort product life cycle: Forecasting casino winnings. *Journal of Travel Research*, *41*(4), 393–399. doi:10.1177/0047287503041004008

Palmeri, C. (2015). *Theme Park Growth Shifts to Asia in Business the U.S. Pioneered.* Retrieved from http://www.bloomberg.com/news/articles/2015-06-03/theme-park-growth-shifts-to-asia-in-business-the-u-s-pioneered

Papatheodorou, A. (2006). TALC and spatial implications of competition. In R. W. Butler (Ed.), *The Tourism Life Cycle: Conceptual and Theoretical Issues* (pp. 67–82). Clevedon, UK: Channelview Publications.

Pearson, T. (2012). *Beautiful Venezuela: tourism with a social conscience.* Retrieved on 22nd May, 2013 from http://venezuelanalysis.com/analysis/6996

Pellegrini, T. (2007). Co-production on the web: Social softwares as a means of collaborative value creation in web-based infrastructures. *International Review of Information Ethics*, *7*(09), 1–6.

Plog, S. (2001). Why destinations areas rise and fall in popularity, an update of a Cornell quarterly classic. *The Cornell Hotel and Restaurant Administration Quarterly*, *42*(3), 13–24. doi:10.1016/S0010-8804(01)81020-X

Plog, S. C. (1974). Why destinations areas rise and fall in popularity. *The Cornell Hotel and Restaurant Administration Quarterly*, *14*(4), 55–58. doi:10.1177/001088047401400409

Plog, S. C. (2002). The power of Psychographics and the concept of venturesomeness. *Journal of Travel Research, 40*(3), 244–251. doi:10.1177/004728750204000302

Prideaux, B. (2000). The resort development spectrum – a new approach to modelling resort development. *Tourism Management, 21*(3), 225–240. doi:10.1016/S0261-5177(99)00055-2

Prosser, G. (1995). *Tourism destination life cycles; progress, problems and prospects.* Paper to*National Tourism Research Conference*, Melbourne, Australia.

Putra, N. D., & Hitchcock, M. (2006). The Bali bombs and the tourism development cycle. *Progress in Development, 6*(2), 157–166. doi:10.1191/1464993406ps134oa

Ravenscroft, N., & Hadjihambi, I. (2006). The implications of Lamarckian theory for the TALC model. In R. W. Butler (Ed.), *Tourism Area Life Cycle: Conceptual and Theoretical Issues* (pp. 150–163). Cleveland, OH: Channelview Publications.

Ritchie, J. R. B., & Crouch, G. I. (2003). The Competitive Destination: A Sustainable Tourism Perspective. CABI.

Ruiz-Ballestros, E. (2011). Social-ecological resilience and community-based tourism; an approach from Agua Blanca, Ecuador. *Tourism Management, 32*(3), 655–666. doi:10.1016/j.tourman.2010.05.021

Singh, S. (2011). The tourism area life cycle: A clarification. *Annals of Tourism Research, 38*(3), 1178–1187. doi:10.1016/j.annals.2011.03.005

Stark, J. (2015). Product lifecycle management. In *Product Lifecycle Management* (pp. 1–29). Springer International Publishing. doi:10.1007/978-3-319-17440-2_1

Tomljenović, R., & Getz, D. (2009). Life cycle stages in wine tourism: A comparison of wine regions in Croatia. *Tourism Review International, 13*(1), 31–49. doi:10.3727/154427209789130666

Trigau, R. (2016). *In Game of Theme Parks, Orlando rules but Asia eyes the throne.* Retrieved on 15th August, 2015 from http://www.tampabay.com/news/business/corporate/in-game-of-theme-parks-orlando-rules-but-asia-eyes-the-throne/2279234

Volo, S. (2010). Bloggers reported tourist experiences: Their utility as a tourism data source and their effect on prospective tourists. *Journal of Vacation Marketing, 16*(4), 297–311. doi:10.1177/1356766710380884

Weaver, D. B. (2012). Organic, incremental and induced paths to sustainable mass tourism convergence. *Tourism Management, 33*(5), 1030–1037. doi:10.1016/j.tourman.2011.08.011

Whitfield, J. (2006). A temporal analysis of conference venue refurbishment within U.K. conference sector. *Journal of Convention & Event Tourism, 8*(3), 1–19. doi:10.1300/J452v08n03_01

Xiang, Z., & Gretzel, U. (2010). Role of social media in online travel information search. *Tourism Management, 31*(2), 179–188. doi:10.1016/j.tourman.2009.02.016

Xie, P. F., & Lane, B. (2006). A life cycle model for aboriginal arts performance in tourism: Perspective on authenticity. *Journal of Sustainable Tourism, 14*(6), 545–561. doi:10.2167/jost 601.0

Chapter 12
The Relevance of the Tourism-Led Growth Hypothesis to Malaysia:
A View Through Rolling-Samples and Disaggregated Tourism Markets

Chor Foon Tang
Universiti Sains Malaysia, Malaysia

Eu Chye Tan
University of Malaya, Malaysia

ABSTRACT

This paper explored whether the tourism-led growth (TLG) hypothesis is empirically relevant to Malaysia based upon both full sample and rolling sample analyses. Data from January 1995 to December 2010 have been utilised for the purpose. Instead of relying upon aggregated data of tourist arrivals, disaggregated data of arrivals from 12 major tourism markets are relied upon for more insightful and accurate findings. The empirical results suggest that there was cointegration between Malaysia's economic growth and tourist arrivals from these tourism markets. However, the results of the full sample Granger causality test indicate that only 2 out of 12 tourism markets contributed to economic growth in the short-run. The TLG hypothesis is only supported in the long run by tourist arrivals from 10 out of the 12 tourism markets. The rolling-based Granger causality test shows that it is also these 10 markets situated mostly in developed countries that could provide a stable support for the TLG hypothesis.

1. INTRODUCTION

Malaysia is one of the important fast growing countries for tourism in the Asia Pacific region. Based upon the 2015 Tourism Highlights presented by the United Nation World Tourism Organisation (UNWTO, 2015), Malaysia is the third most visited destination in Asia with 27.4 million international tourist arriv-

DOI: 10.4018/978-1-5225-2078-8.ch012

als in 2014, and fourth in the ranking in terms of international tourism receipts with the record of USD 21.8 billion in 2014. In light of the impressive performance in tourism attraction, research on tourism, especially the validity of the tourism-led growth (TLG) hypothesis in Malaysia has been given special attention by the scholars. According to our reading, studies on Malaysia can be summarised into five major strands based upon the methodology used.

The first strand of the literature (e.g. Lau, Oh and Hu, 2009; Mulok et al., 2012) analysed the validity of the TLG hypothesis in Malaysia within a bivariate framework, whereas the second strand (e.g. Loganathan, Ibrahim and Harun, 2008; Kadir, Nayan and Abdullah, 2010; Othman, Salleh and Sarmidi, 2012; Tang, 2013; Cheam et al., 2013; Lean, Chong and Hooy, 2014; Kumar et al., 2015; Tang and Tan, 2015a; Tang, Cheam and Ong, 2015) extended the analysis by employing a multivariate framework in order to avoid the omission of relevant variable(s) problem. However, the results of these two strands of past studies are mixed with regard to the validity of the TLG hypothesis. The third strand of the literature (e.g. Hassan and Jenggie, 2012; Mazumder, 2009; Salleh et al., 2012) presumed that tourism is the engine of growth, and they thus applied the Input-Output (I-O) approach to estimate the multiplier effects of tourism on the Malaysian economy. The fourth strand of the literature (e.g. Kadir & Karim, 2012; Tang, 2011) argued that the use of aggregated tourism data in examining the validity of the TLG hypothesis in Malaysia is prone to the aggregation bias problem. This may offer unclear guidance for policymakers when designing tourism marketing strategies and economic growth policies. To overcome these imperfections, this strand of studies have analysed tourist arrivals from different tourism markets. This could provide knowledge about which inbound tourism markets that are to be focused upon in policymaking. The fifth strand of the literature (e.g. Lean and Tang, 2010; Tang and Tan, 2013, 2015b) brought in the issue of stability of the TLG hypothesis. Their argument is that testing for the validity of the TLG hypothesis based upon full samples may be inappropriate as relationships between variables may vary over time due to changes in the global economic and political environments as well as policies. Therefore, studies in this strand would focus on the stability or the persistence of the TLG hypothesis in Malaysia using the time-varying Granger causality methods, especially the recursive- and the rolling-based causality tests.[1]

Based upon our review of the studies on the TLG hypothesis, especially for Malaysia, research at the disaggregated level remains limited and also imperfect in terms of the methodology used. We noticed that only Tang and Tan (2013) investigated the validity as well as the stability of the TLG hypothesis at the disaggregated level of inbound tourism markets in Malaysia using the recursive-based test for Granger causality in a bivariate framework. It is well noted in the econometrics literature that a bivariate framework may suffer from the omitted variable bias problem while the recursive-based tests would not able to differentiate between changes in a causal relationship and changes in statistical power due to a recursive increase in sample sizes. Motivated by these imperfections, this study applies the rolling regression-based test for Granger causality in a multivariate framework to re-assess both the validity and the stability of the TLG hypothesis in Malaysia over a sample period from January 1995 to December 2010. The rolling-based test is more appropriate and superior to a recursive-based test because the sample size for rolling-based test is fixed over the length of the available time series. In such a case, the change in the test statistics would mainly reflect the variation in the causal relationship rather than change in the sample size.

The rest of the paper is organised as follows. Section 2 presents the model, the econometric techniques and information about the data used in this study. Section 3 then discusses the empirical findings of the study. Finally, the conclusion and policy implications are presented in Section 4.

2. METHODOLOGY AND DATA

2.1 Empirical Model and Data

With regard to the TLG hypothesis, researchers have utilised a variety of model specifications to test the hypothesis. Among them, the model proposed by Balaguer and Cantavella-Jordá (2002) is one of the most popular models utilised for analysing the hypothesis. In fact, Balaguer and Cantavella-Jordá (2002) suggested that real exchange rate is an important variable that must be included because it influences both international tourism and economic growth. This was also affirmed by Katircioğlu (2009, 2011). Hence this study will examine the validity of the TLG hypothesis in Malaysia by using the following model:

$$\ln \mathrm{Y}_t = \beta_0 + \beta_1 \ln \mathrm{TOUR}_{j,t} + \beta_2 \ln \mathrm{RER}_t + \varepsilon_t \quad (1)$$

where ln denotes the natural logarithm, Y_t is the output level, $\mathrm{TOUR}_{j,t}$ is international tourist arrivals from the *j*th tourism markets, and RER_t is the real exchange rate. The residuals ε_t are assumed to be normally distributed and white noise.

Monthly data of the Industrial Production Index (IPI, 2000 = 100), the real effective exchange rate (RER, 2000 = 100) and of the various international tourism markets were extracted from International Financial Statistics (IFS) published by the International Monetary Fund (IMF) and the CEIC database. The various tourism markets covered in the present study include tourist arrivals from Australia, Brunei, China, Germany, Indonesia, Japan, South Korea, Singapore, Taiwan, Thailand, the United Kingdom (UK) and the United States (USA). All variables in the present study are transformed into the natural logarithm, so that they can be interpreted in growth terms after first difference.

2.2 Narayan and Popp (2010) Unit Root Test with Break

Narayan and Popp (2010) proposed two endogenous break models to investigate the null hypothesis of a unit root. Model M1 allows for two structural breaks in the intercept, while Model M2 allows for two structural breaks in both the intercept and the slope of the trend function. The models for testing the two structural breaks unit root are as follows:

$$\text{M1: } w_t = \alpha_1 + \delta_1 w_{t-1} + \beta t + \varphi_1 D\left(T_B\right)_{1,t} + \varphi_2 D\left(T_B\right)_{2,t} + \theta_1 DU_{1,t-1} + \theta_2 DU_{2,t-1} + \sum_{i=1}^{p} \lambda_j w_{t-j} + e_{1t} \quad (2)$$

$$\text{M2: } \begin{aligned} w_t &= \alpha_1 + \delta_1 w_{t-1} + \beta t + \varphi_1 D\left(T_B\right)_{1,t} + \varphi_2 D\left(T_B\right)_{2,t} + \theta_1 DU_{1,t-1} + \theta_2 DU_{2,t-1} \\ &+ \phi_1 DT_{1,t-1} + \phi_2 DT_{2,t-1} + \sum_{i=1}^{p} \lambda_j w_{t-j} + e_{2t} \end{aligned} \quad (3)$$

where, Δ is the first difference operator, *p* is the optimal lag length and the residuals e_{it} are assumed to be normally distributed and white noise. $DU_{i,t} = 1\left(t > T_{B,i}\right)$ and $DT_{i,t} = 1\left(t > T_{B,i}\right)\left(t - T_{B,i}\right)$, $i =$

1, 2, denote the dummy variables for breaks in the intercept, while the slope of the trend function occur at time T_{B1} and T_{B2}, respectively. The t-statistic of w_{t-1} can be used to examine the null hypothesis of a unit root against the alternative hypothesis of stationary. Finally, potential break dates $\left(T_{B1}, T_{B2}\right)$ can be chosen simultaneously using the grid search or the sequential procedure as is discussed in Narayan and Popp (2010).

2.3 Combined Tests for Cointegration

Perman (1991) documented that a model is well-specified if the variables in it are cointegrated. Therefore, testing for cointegration is essential not only to verify true causal relationships, but it is also required for determining the appropriateness of the model. The idea of cointegration and the residual-based testing procedure for cointegration originated from Engle and Granger (EG, 1987). Since then, a large number of studies have applied this procedure while others have developed alternative testing procedures for cointegration. Renowned tests for cointegration include the system-based test of Johansen (JOH, 1988), the ECM-based F-test of Boswijk (BO, 1994) and the ECM-based *t*-test of Banerjee, Dolado and Mestre (BDM, 1998). Nonetheless, cointegration test results are very sensitive to the choice of techniques because no one technique is perfect and completely robust in all applications (Elliott, Jansson & Pesavento, 2005; Gregory, Haug & Lomuto, 2004). To enhance the power of the cointegration test, the newly-designed cointegration technique as suggested by Bayer and Hanck (2013) will be used to investigate the presence of cointegration between tourism and economic growth in Malaysia. A uniqueness of this test is that it allows us to combine various individual cointegration test results in order to generate a more conclusive finding. With respect to this, Bayer and Hanck (2013) utilised the following Fisher's formulae to combine the *p*-values of different individual cointegration tests:

$$\text{EG-JOH} = -2\left[\ln\left(p_{EG}\right) + \ln\left(p_{JOH}\right)\right] \tag{4}$$

$$\text{EG-JOH-BO-BDM} = -2\left[\ln\left(p_{EG}\right) + \ln\left(p_{JOH}\right) + \ln\left(p_{BO}\right) + \ln\left(p_{BDM}\right)\right] \tag{5}$$

Here p_{EG}, p_{JOH}, p_{BO} and p_{BDM} are the *p*-values of Engle-Granger (EG), Johansen (JOH), Boswijk (BO), and Banerjee-Dolado-Mestre (BDM) cointegration tests, respectively.[2] If the calculated Fisher statistic exceeds the critical value tabulated in Bayer and Hanck (2013), the null hypothesis of no cointegration is rejected.

2.4 Granger Causality Analysis

The Granger causality test is used to determine the direction of causality between tourism and economic growth. If the variables are not cointegrated, one can establish their short-run causal relationship using the first difference vector autoregressive (VAR) framework. However, if the variables are cointegrated, the Granger causality test conducted within the first difference VAR framework would be inappropriate as it ignores the long-run information (Granger, 1988). In such circumstances, the Granger causality tests should be conducted using the Error-Correction Model (ECM) as outlined below:

$$\Delta \ln Y_t = a_0 + \pi_1 ECT_{t-1} + \sum_{k=1}^{p} a_{1k} \Delta \ln Y_{t-k} + \sum_{k=1}^{q} a_{2k} \Delta \ln TOUR_{j,t-k} + \sum_{k=1}^{r} a_{3k} \Delta \ln RER_{t-k} + \xi_{1t} \quad (6)$$

$$\Delta \ln TOUR_{j,t} = b_0 + \pi_2 ECT_{t-1} + \sum_{k=1}^{p} b_{1k} \Delta \ln TOUR_{j,t-k} + \sum_{k=1}^{q} b_{2k} \Delta \ln Y_{t-k} + \sum_{k=1}^{r} b_{3k} \Delta \ln RER_{t-k} + \xi_{2t} \quad (7)$$

where ln is the natural logarithm, Δ is the first difference operator, Y_t is the output level, $TOUR_{j,t}$ refers to international tourist arrivals from the *j*th tourism markets and RER_t is the real exchange rate. The residuals (ξ_{1t}, ξ_{2t}) are assumed to be white noise and normally distributed. ECT_{t-1} is a one period lagged error-correction term calculated from the long-run equation. If the variables are cointegrated, the causal relationships can be segregated into short- and long-run. For short-run Granger causality, it can be tested based upon the likelihood ratio (LR) test. For example, from equation (6), $a_{2k} \neq 0 \ \forall_k$ implies that causality runs from tourism to economic growth, while from equation (7), $b_{2k} \neq 0 \ \forall_k$ indicates that economic growth Granger-causes tourism. For the case of long-run Granger causality, this study will test the null hypothesis of $a_{2k} = \pi_1 = 0$ using the LR test. Rejection of this hypothesis would imply that there exists an overall long-run Granger causality running from tourism to economic growth. Similarly, if the null hypothesis of $b_{2k} = \pi_2 = 0$ was rejected, it would imply that there is an overall long-run Granger causality running from economic growth to tourism.

3. EMPIRICAL RESULTS

Before conducting the cointegration analysis, this study employs the Augmented Dickey-Fuller (ADF) unit root test to check the order of integration of each series. The results of the ADF test suggest that tourist arrivals from Taiwan follow the *I*(0) process while the other variables, namely tourist arrivals from other countries, output and real exchange rate adhere to the *I*(1) process.

The design of the ADF unit root test is principally based on the assumption that there is no structural break in the series. In light of this, the results of the ADF test may be biased if a series has a structural break. To circumvent this problem, this study performs the Narayan-Popp unit root test with two structural breaks to confirm the order of integration of each series. Table 1 presents the results of the Narayan-Popp unit root test. Unlike the results of the ADF test, at the 5 per cent significance level, none of the Narayan-Popp test statistics reject the null hypothesis of a unit root, including tourist arrivals from Taiwan. Therefore, it can be concluded that all variables are integrated of the order one, *I*(1). This result is consistent with the findings of Nelson and Plosser (1982) which noted that most macroeconomic variables are non-stationary at level and become stationary after taking first difference.

After performing the unit root tests to check the order of integration of each series, the next step involved examining the existence of a cointegration relationship. According to Engle and Granger (1987), two series are said to be cointegrated if the series are integrated at the same order and their linear combination is stationary. Since all variables are integrated of order one, *I*(1), the combined test for cointegration proposed by Bayer and Hanck (2013) is then applied to ascertain the existence of a long-run equilibrium

Table 1. Results of Narayan-Popp unit root tests with two structural breaks

Variables	Models for unit root test with two structural breaks					
	M1			M2		
	TB1	TB2	Test statistics	TB1	TB2	Test statistics
lnY_t	1998:M1	2007:M1	–2.461 (5)	1998:M1	2007:M1	–3.692 (5)
$lnRER_t$	1998:M4	1998:M8	–2.121 (7)	1998:M8	2005:M2	–1.821 (7)
Australia	1999:M12	2001:M10	–2.585 (11)	1998:M3	1999:M12	–1.954 (12)
Brunei	1999:M8	2003:M12	–1.980 (11)	1999:M8	2003:M12	–1.816 (11)
China	2003:M4	2003:M7	–3.718 (8)	2001:M10	2003:M4	–4.094 (8)
Germany	1997:M3	1998:M1	–1.410 (11)	1997:M3	1998:M2	–1.610 (11)
Indonesia	2000:M6	2003:M4	–2.140 (12)	1998:M12	2000:M7	–2.589 (12)
Japan	2003:M3	2003:M8	–3.104 (11)	1998:M7	2003:M3	–3.216 (12)
Singapore	1998:M8	2003:M3	–3.681 (11)	2001:M9	2003:M3	–2.910 (11)
South Korea	1997:M3	1998:M1	–2.556 (4)	1997:M3	1998:M1	–2.498 (4)
Taiwan	1998:M6	2003:M3	–4.165 (12)	1998:M6	2003:M3	–4.405 (12)
Thailand	1997:M3	1998:M1	–1.338 (11)	1997:M4	1998:M1	–1.393 (11)
UK	1997:M3	1998:M1	–1.944 (11)	1997:M3	1998:M2	–2.225 (10)
USA	1997:M3	1998:M1	–3.188 (12)	1997:M3	1998:M1	–3.183 (12)
Significance level		Critical values			Critical values	
1 per cent		–4.958			–5.576	
5 per cent		–4.316			–4.937	

Note: The optimal lag length for Narayan-Popp test is selected using the general-to-specific approach applied to the t-statistics. Figures in parentheses () denote the optimal lag length. The critical values are collected from Narayan and Popp (2010). GAUSS programming code has been used to perform the above unit root test.

relationship between tourism, economic growth and real exchange rate in Malaysia. Table 2 exhibits the results of the combined tests for cointegration statistics – EG-JOH and EG-JOH-BO-BDM.

There are two forms of combined tests for cointegration – EG-JOH and EG-JOH-BO-BDM obtained from the Fisher's statistics calculation. For the case of EG-JOH, the results show that the statistics were consistently greater than the 5 per cent critical values for all selected tourism markets. Therefore, the results of the EG-JOH combined cointegration test suggest that Malaysia's economic growth is cointegrated with tourist arrivals from the 12 major tourism markets. Alternatively, the EG-JOH-BO-BDM combined test for cointegration results reveal that tourist arrivals from Australia may not be cointegrated with Malaysian's economic growth at the 5 per cent significance level. Nonetheless, the EG-JOH-BO-BDM statistics rejected the null hypothesis of no cointegration at the 10 per cent level for all selected tourism markets. Therefore, it can be inferred that economic growth, tourism and real exchange rate in Malaysia are cointegrated regardless of tourism market, implying that a long-run relationship exists between Malaysia's economic growth, tourism and the real exchange rate. These results are consistent with the findings of Kumar et al. (2015), Lean, Chong and Hooy (2014), Tang (2013), and Tang and Tan (2013, 2015a).

Table 2. Results of the combined tests for cointegration

Tourism markets	Fisher statistics		
	EG-JOH	EG-JOH-BO-BDM	Conclusion
Australia	13.564**	19.409*	Cointegrated
Brunei	19.823***	45.574***	Cointegrated
China	24.742***	56.613***	Cointegrated
Germany	24.098***	51.651***	Cointegrated
Indonesia	18.663***	37.124***	Cointegrated
Japan	13.109**	27.615**	Cointegrated
Singapore	11.852**	28.616**	Cointegrated
South Korea	11.993**	25.571**	Cointegrated
Taiwan	28.653***	65.494***	Cointegrated
Thailand	12.343**	29.701**	Cointegrated
UK	19.790***	47.342***	Cointegrated
USA	13.330**	30.702**	Cointegrated
Significance level	Critical values		
1 per cent	16.720	32.601	
5 per cent	10.858	21.342	
10 per cent	8.451	16.507	

Note: ***, ** and * denote statistical significance at the 1, 5 and 10 per cent levels, respectively. EG-JOH is the combination of two cointegration tests developed by Engle and Granger (EG, 1987) and Johansen (JOH, 1988). EG-JOH-BO-BDM is the combination of four cointegration tests developed by Engle and Granger (EG, 1987), Johansen (JOH, 1988), Boswijk (BO, 1994) and Banerjee, Dolado and Mestre (BDM, 1998).

Given that the variables are cointegrated, there must be at least one direction of Granger causality to explain the existence of the long-run equilibrium relationship. Table 3 reports the short- and long-run Granger causality results within the ECM framework.[3] The results suggest that all the tourism markets under review support the economic growth-led tourism hypothesis in the long-run, while in the short-run only 5 tourism markets, namely, China, Germany, Japan, Thailand and the United Kingdom support this hypothesis at the 5 per cent significance level.

In terms of the TLG hypothesis, the results show that of the 12 tourism markets under investigation, only 2 international tourism markets, namely, Germany and Thailand Granger-cause economic growth in the short-run, while 10 out of the 12 international tourism markets such as Australia, Brunei, Germany, Japan, Singapore, South Korea, Taiwan, Thailand, the United Kingdom and the United States are found to Granger-cause economic growth in the long-run. In contrast, 2 out of the 12 international tourism markets, that is, China and Indonesia did not Granger-cause economic growth in both the short- and long-run.[4] Thus even though the findings generally show support for the TLG hypothesis in Malaysia, this particular finding implies that not all international tourism markets contribute to economic growth. This is because high rates of tourist arrivals are not necessarily associated with high rates of tourism earnings as not all arrivals are genuine tourists.

All of the above Granger causality analysis of the TLG hypothesis is based on the full sample. However, the causal relationship may vary over sub-sample periods due to changes in policy, economic and

Table 3. Results of Granger causality tests

Tourism Markets	Tourism-led growth hypothesis		Growth-led tourism hypothesis	
	Short-run causality	Long-run causality	Short-run Causality	Long-run causality
Australia	2.431	14.360***	3.704	16.444***
Brunei	0.280	9.830***	10.142	23.447***
China	0.998	4.185	20.359***	48.742***
Germany	7.035**	15.136***	39.965***	69.874***
Indonesia	0.639	4.009	0.027	23.288***
Japan	0.510	9.799***	38.259***	61.200***
Singapore	1.175	13.188***	0.045	16.605***
South Korea	0.207	8.727**	4.563	29.650***
Taiwan	1.050	10.677***	7.898	65.457***
Thailand	51.717***	60.472***	18.131***	33.420***
UK	3.458	12.976***	13.415***	39.112***
USA	2.693	11.269**	2.040	27.529***

Note: The asterisks *** and ** denote statistically significance at 1 and 5 per cent level, respectively. The optimal lag order is determined by using AIC.

political environments. Therefore, following Thoma (1994), Lean and Tang (2010), Tang (2013b), and Tang and Tan (2013, 2015b) the stability of the causal relationship is tested. As Malaysia's economic growth is cointegrated with tourist arrivals from all the selected tourism markets, the rolling regression-based Granger causality test is performed based upon equation (6) to ascertain the stability of the TLG hypothesis in Malaysia. Generally, the rolling Granger causality test is conducted by setting the initial rolling window size T and then moving forward by adding a new observation to the end of the sample period and delete the first observation at the beginning of the sample period. Therefore, the size of the sample for estimation is fixed over the sample period. For example, if the initial setting is 5 years, i.e., $T = 60$ observations, the first Granger causality test statistic is obtained by using a sub-sample period from 1995:M1 to 2000:M1 (i.e. $T = 60$ observations). Next, the second test statistic is obtained by using data from 1995:M2 to 2000:M2. This process will continue until the last observation is included. The null hypothesis that tourism does not Granger-causes economic growth is rejected if the LR test statistic for $\left(H_0 : a_{2k} = \pi_1 = 0\right)$ exceeds the 10 per cent critical value. This means that a large number of LR test statistics fluctuating above the cut-off line would be observable if the TLG hypothesis in Malaysia is valid and stable. Timmermann (2008) suggested a short rolling window because it provides better information compared to a long rolling window. However, the size of the short rolling window must be able to perform estimation and should not be subject to any size distortion problem. Considering the sample size of this study, we set the rolling window at 50 observations which is in line with Tang and Chua (2012).

The plots of the rolling Granger causality test statistics and a summary of rejection frequencies are presented in Figure 1 and Figure 2, respectively. The plots reveal that the stability of the TLG hypothesis varies among tourism markets. Specifically, this study finds that tourist arrivals from developed countries are more likely to support the TLG hypothesis over time. For example, a substantial portion

Figure 1. Plots of the rolling Granger causality tests
(rolling window = 50 observations)

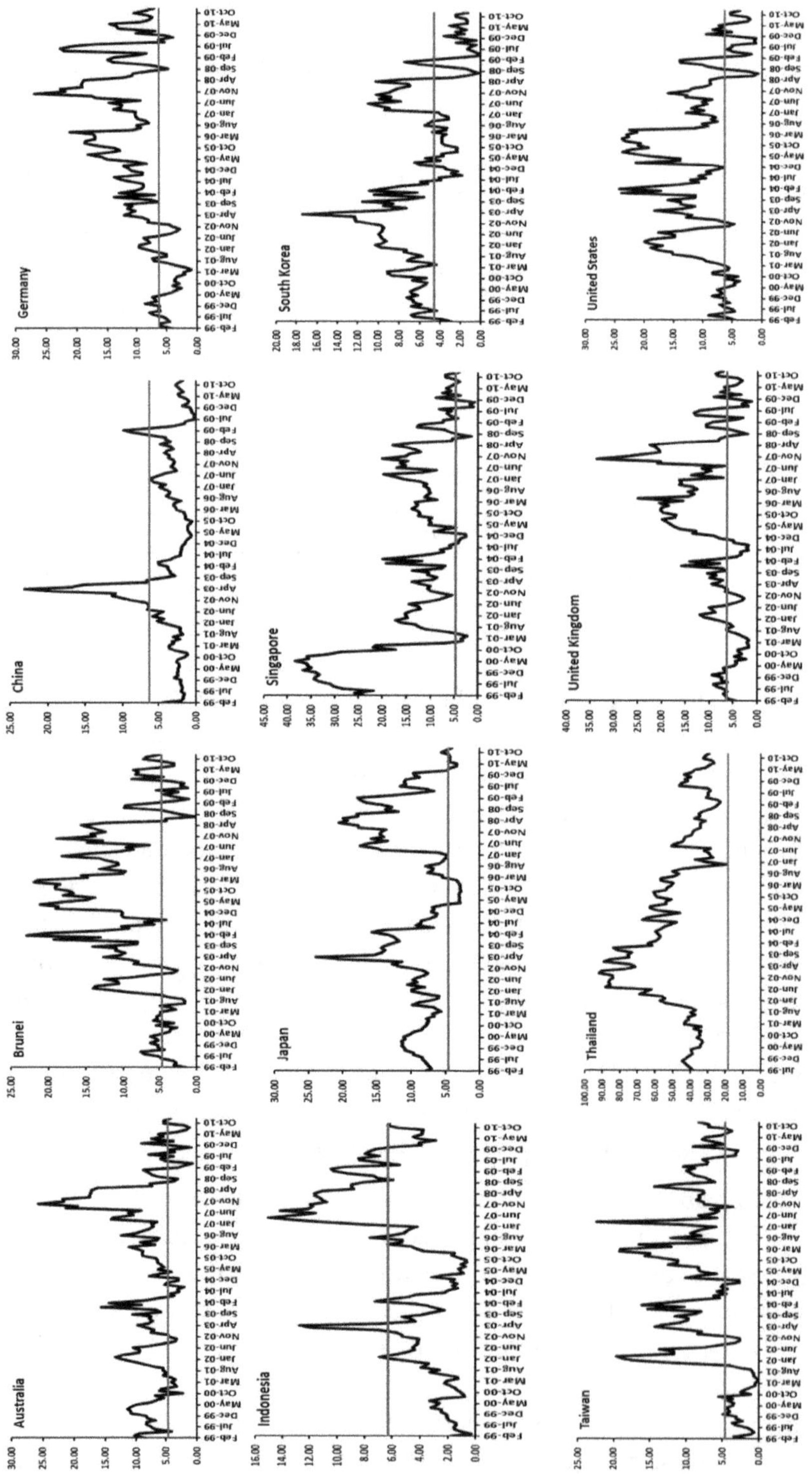

Figure 2. Summary of rejection frequencies of the rolling Granger causality tests

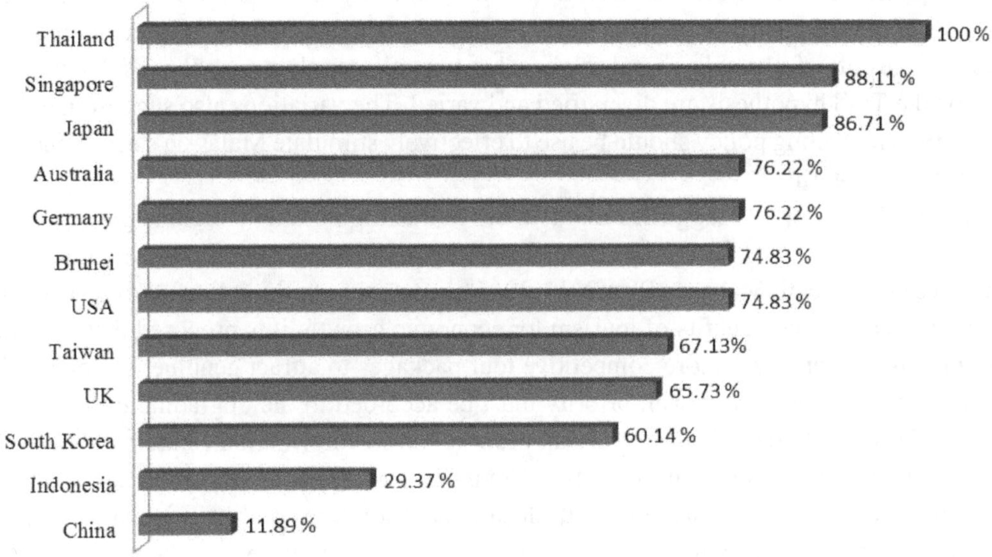

of the rolling LR statistics for Australia, Brunei, Germany, Japan, Singapore, South Korea, Taiwan, Thailand, the United Kingdom and the United States fluctuate above the 10 per cent cut-off line. Figure 2 illustrates that the lowest rejection frequency amongst these tourism markets is 60.14 per cent. The rejection frequencies for Thailand, Singapore and Japan are more than 85 per cent. This finding implies that international tourist arrivals from these developed economies are more likely to stimulate Malaysia's economic growth.

In contrast, Figure 1 shows that the support for the TLG hypothesis is relatively weak with respect to tourist arrivals from China and Indonesia because the rolling LR statistics related to these tourism markets tend to fluctuate more frequently below the 10 per cent cut-off line. The rejection frequencies for these tourism markets are only 11.89 and 29.37 per cent respectively, implying that the TLG hypothesis is weak and unstable as far as tourist arrivals from these markets are concerned. Based on the overall results, it can be concluded that tourism does function as an engine of growth though not all tourism markets contribute to the economic growth of Malaysia. Among the 12 tourism markets analysed, 10 support the TLG hypothesis.

4. CONCLUSION AND ITS IMPLICATION ON POLICY

This study investigated the relevance and the stability of the TLG hypothesis in Malaysia with respect to tourist arrivals from 12 major tourism markets over the sample period from January 1995 to December 2010. Our empirical results reveal that Malaysia's economic growth is cointegrated with tourist arrivals from these tourism markets. The results of full sample Granger causality test, however, showed that only 2 out of 12 tourism markets contributed to economic growth in the short-run whereas in the long-run, 10 out of 12 tourism markets supported the TLG hypothesis. In terms of stability, the results of the rolling-based Granger causality test illustrated that only 10 out of the 12 tourism markets provide stable support for the TLG hypothesis in Malaysia, and it is mostly dominated by tourist arrivals from the developed countries. Hence, not all tourist arrivals could significantly stimulate Malaysia's economic growth. Additionally, the results of unstable causal relationship may also explain why the results provided by past studies on the TLG hypothesis are diversified and varied. The variations also suggest that different degrees of tourism marketing policy should be use to effectively stimulate Malaysia's economic growth, especially for the long-term.

Based on these findings, it is suggested that tourism marketing policies should target those tourism markets that can firmly support Malaysia's economic growth. This could help in the attainment of one of the objectives of the Tenth Malaysia Plan 2011-2015, i.e. to enhance the role of tourism in economic growth. In order to enjoy the benefits of tourism for economic growth, it is proposed that the Ministry of Tourism in Malaysia provides more competitive tour packages to attract genuine international tourists from the target countries. Moreover, priority must be accorded to the upgrading of tourist-related infrastructures. This should include the setting up of more tourist information centres, providing better accommodation as well as a good transportation system because they are the key elements to facilitate the growth of the tourism sector. Apart from that, educational institutions such as universities in Malaysia should be encouraged to organise more educational programmes and international conferences as such activities could attract more international students and researchers which in turn could help promote tourism. This could also make Malaysia a hub for educational excellence in the Asia and Pacific region.

REFERENCES

Arslanturk, Y., Balcilar, M., & Ozdemir, Z. A. (2011). Time-varying linkages between tourism receipts and economic growth in a small open economy. *Economic Modelling*, *28*(1-2), 664–671. doi:10.1016/j.econmod.2010.06.003

Balaguer, J., & Cantavella-Jordá, M. (2002). Tourism as a long-run economic factor: The Spanish case. *Applied Economics*, *34*(7), 877–884. doi:10.1080/00036840110058923

Banerjee, A., Dolado, J. J., & Mestre, R. (1998). Error-correction mechanism tests for cointegration in a single-equation framework. *Journal of Time Series Analysis*, *19*(3), 267–283. doi:10.1111/1467-9892.00091

Bayer, C., & Hanck, C. (2013). Combining non-cointegration tests. *Journal of Time Series Analysis*, *34*(1), 83–95. doi:10.1111/j.1467-9892.2012.00814.x

Boswijk, H. P. (1994). Testing an unstable root in conditional and structural error correction models. *Journal of Econometrics*, *63*(1), 37–60. doi:10.1016/0304-4076(93)01560-9

Brahmasrene, T., & Lee, J. W. (2016). Assessing the dynamic impact of tourism, industrialization, urbanization, and globalization on growth and environment in Southeast Asia. *International Journal of Sustainable Development and World Ecology*, 1–10. doi:10.1080/13504509.2016.1238021

Cheam, C. L., Mahmood, R., Abdullah, H., & Ong, S. C. (2013). Economic growth, tourism and selected macroeconomic variables: A triangular causal relationship in Malaysia. *Margin: The Journal of Applied Economic Research*, *7*(2), 185–206.

Chiu, Y. B., & Yeh, L. T. (2016). The threshold effects of the tourism-led growth hypothesis: Evidence from a cross-sectional model. *Journal of Travel Research*. doi:10.1177/0047287516650938

Elliott, G., Jansson, M., & Pesavento, E. (2005). Optimal power for testing potential cointegrating vectors with known parameters for nonstationary. *Journal of Business & Economic Statistics*, *23*(1), 34–48. doi:10.1198/073500104000000307

Engle, R. F., & Granger, C. W. J. (1987). Co-integration and error-correction: Representation, estimation, and testing. *Econometrica*, *55*(2), 251–276. doi:10.2307/1913236

Granger, C. W. J. (1988). Some recent development in a concept of causality. *Journal of Econometrics*, *39*(1-2), 199–211. doi:10.1016/0304-4076(88)90045-0

Gregory, A. W., Haug, A. A., & Lomuto, N. (2004). Mixed signals among tests for cointegration. *Journal of Applied Econometrics*, *19*(1), 89–98. doi:10.1002/jae.733

Hassan, M. K. H., & Jenggie, S. T. (2012). The impact of tourist's expenditures on Malaysian economy: An input-output analysis. *BIMP-EAGA Journal for Sustainable Tourism Development*, *1*(1), 47–54.

Johansen, S. (1988). Statistical analysis of cointegration vectors. *Journal of Economic Dynamics & Control*, *12*(2-3), 231–254. doi:10.1016/0165-1889(88)90041-3

Kadir, N., & Karim, M. Z. A. (2012). Tourism and economic growth in Malaysia: Evidence from tourist arrivals from ASEAN-5 countries. *Economic Research Journal*, *25*(4), 1089–1100.

Kadir, N., Nayan, S., & Abdullah, M. S. (2010). The causal relationship between tourism and economic growth in Malaysia: Evidence from multivariate causality tests. *Tourism and Management Studies*, *6*, 16–24.

Kassim, A. (1997). Illegal alien labour in Malaysia: Its influx, utilization, and ramifications. *Indonesia and the Malay World*, *25*(71), 50–81. doi:10.1080/13639819708729889

Katircioğlu, S. T. (2009). Testing the tourism-led growth hypothesis: The case of Malta. *Acta Oeconomica*, *59*(3), 331–343. doi:10.1556/AOecon.59.2009.3.4

Katircioğlu, S. T. (2011). Tourism and growth in Singapore: New extension from bounds test to level relationships and conditional Granger causality tests. *The Singapore Economic Review*, *56*(3), 441–453. doi:10.1142/S0217590811004365

Kumar, R. R., Loganathan, N., Patel, A., & Kumar, R. D. (2015). Nexus between tourism earnings and economic growth: A study of Malaysia. *Quality & Quantity*, *49*(3), 1101–1120. doi:10.1007/s11135-014-0037-4

Lau, P. H., Oh, S. L., & Hu, S. S. (2009). Tourist arrivals and economic growth in Sarawak. *Sarawak Development Journal*, *9*, 36–45.

Lean, H. H., Chong, S. H., & Hooy, C. W. (2014). Tourism and economic growth: Comparing Malaysia and Singapore. *International Journal of Economics and Management*, *8*(1), 139–157.

Lean, H. H., & Tang, C. F. (2010). Is the tourism-led growth hypothesis stable for Malaysia? A note. *International Journal of Tourism Research*, *12*(4), 375–378. doi:10.1002/jtr.759

Loganathan, N., Ibrahim, Y., & Harun, M. (2008). Tourism development policy, strategic alliances and impact of consumer price index on tourist arrivals: The case of Malaysia. *TOURISMOS: An International Multidisciplinary Journal of Tourism*, *3*(1), 83–98.

Maddala, G., & Kim, I. (1998). *Unit Roots, Cointegration, and Structural Change*. Oxford, UK: Cambridge University Press.

Mazumder, M. N. H., Ahmed, E. M., & Al-Amin, A. Q. (2009). Does tourism contribute significantly to the Malaysian economy? Multiplier analysis using I-O technique. *International Journal of Business and Management*, *4*(7), 146–159. doi:10.5539/ijbm.v4n7p146

Mulok, D., Kogid, M., Asid, R., Lily, J., & Mansur, K. M. (2012). Tourism and economic growth linkages in Malaysia. *BIMP-EAGA Journal for Sustainable Tourism Development*, *1*(1), 3–10.

Narayan, P. K., & Popp, S. (2010). A new unit root test with two structural breaks in level and slope at unknown time. *Journal of Applied Statistics*, *37*(9), 1425–1438. doi:10.1080/02664760903039883

Nelson, C. R., & Plosser, C. R. (1982). Trends and random walks in macroeconomic time series: Some evidence and implications. *Journal of Monetary Economics*, *10*(2), 139–162. doi:10.1016/0304-3932(82)90012-5

Othman, R., Salleh, N. H. M., & Sarmidi, T. (2012). Analysis of causal relationship between tourism development, economic growth and foreign direct investment: An ARDL approach. *Journal of Applied Sciences*, *12*(12), 1245–1254. doi:10.3923/jas.2012.1245.1254

Paramati, S. R., Alam, M. S., & Chen, C. F. (2016). The effects of tourism on economic growth and CO2 emissions: A comparison between developed and developing economies. *Journal of Travel Research*. doi:10.1177/0047287516667848

Perman, R. (1991). Cointegration: An introduction to the literature. *Journal of Economic Studies (Glasgow, Scotland)*, *18*(3), 3–30. doi:10.1108/EUM0000000000151

Salifou, C. K., & Haq, I. (2016). Tourism, globalization and economic growth: A panel cointegration analysis for selected West African States. *Current Issues in Tourism*, 1–4. doi:10.1080/13683500.2016.1175421

Salleh, N. H. M., Othman, R., Hasim, M. S., & Jaafar, A. H. (2012). The pattern and the impact of Middle Eastern tourist spending on Malaysia's economy. *Jurnal Ekonomi Malaysia*, *46*(1), 53–63.

Samad, N. (2012). *We can't help but ask the pertinent questions*. Retrieved December 26, 2013, from http://www.nst.com.my/mobile/opinion/columnist/we-can-thelp-but-ask-the-pertinent-questions-1.65614

Tang, C. F. (2011). Is the tourism-led growth hypothesis valid for Malaysia? A view from disaggregated tourism markets. *International Journal of Tourism Research*, *13*(1), 97–101. doi:10.1002/jtr.807

Tang, C. F. (2013a). Temporal Granger causality and the dynamic relationship between real tourism receipts, real income and real exchange rates in Malaysia. *International Journal of Tourism Research*, *15*(3), 272–284. doi:10.1002/jtr.1869

Tang, C. F. (2013b). A revisitation of the export-led growth hypothesis in Malaysia using leveraged bootstrap simulation and rolling causality techniques. *Journal of Applied Statistics*, *40*(11), 2332–2340. doi:10.1080/02664763.2013.810195

Tang, C. F., & Abosedra, S. (2016a). Does tourism expansion effectively spur economic growth in Morocco and Tunisia? Evidence from time series and panel data. *Journal of Policy Research in Tourism. Leisure and Events*, *8*(2), 127–145. doi:10.1080/19407963.2015.1113980

Tang, C. F., & Abosedra, S. (2016b). Tourism and growth in Lebanon: New evidence from bootstrap simulation and rolling causality approaches. *Empirical Economics*, *50*(2), 679–696. doi:10.1007/s00181-015-0944-9

Tang, C. F., Cheam, C. L., & Ong, S. C. (2015). Comparing the contributions of tourism and non-tourism exports to economic growth in Malaysia. *Current Issues in Tourism*, 1–14. doi:10.1080/13683500.2015.1057108

Tang, C. F., & Chua, S. Y. (2012). The savings-growth nexus for the Malaysian economy: A view through rolling sub-samples. *Applied Economics*, *44*(32), 4173–4185. doi:10.1080/00036846.2011.587784

Tang, C. F., & Tan, E. C. (2013). How stable is the tourism-led growth hypothesis in Malaysia? A view from disaggregated tourism markets. *Tourism Management*, *37*, 52–57. doi:10.1016/j.tourman.2012.12.014

Tang, C. F., & Tan, E. C. (2015a). Does tourism effectively stimulate Malaysias economic growth? *Tourism Management*, *46*, 158–163. doi:10.1016/j.tourman.2014.06.020

Tang, C. F., & Tan, E. C. (2015b). Tourism-led growth hypothesis in Malaysia: Evidence based upon regime shift cointegration and time-varying Granger causality techniques. *Asia Pacific Journal of Tourism Research*, *20*(sup1S1), 1430–1450. doi:10.1080/10941665.2014.998247

Tang, C. F., Tiwari, A. K., & Shahbaz, M. (2016). Dynamic inter-relationships among tourism, economic growth and energy consumption in India. *Geosystem Engineering*, *19*(4), 158–169. doi:10.1080/12269328.2016.1162113

Thoma, M. A. (1994). Subsample instability and asymmetries in money-income causality. *Journal of Econometrics*, *64*(1-2), 279–306. doi:10.1016/0304-4076(94)90066-3

Timmermann, A. (2008). Elusive return predictability. *International Journal of Forecasting*, *24*(1), 1–18. doi:10.1016/j.ijforecast.2007.07.008

ENDNOTES

1 Apart from the Malaysian studies, studies on other countries have also considered the tourism-growth nexus (e.g. Brahmasrene and Lee, 2016; Chiu and Yeh, 2016; Paramati et al., 2016; Salifou and Haq, 2016; Tang and Abosedra, 2016a; Tang et al., 2016) and some of them have also looked into the issue of stability in causality as this will contribute to a more optimal utilisation of resources (e.g. Arslanturk, Balcilar and Ozdemir, 2011; Tang and Abosedra, 2016b).

2 To conserve space, we suggest that interested readers refer to Maddala and Kim (1998) for detailed testing procedures of the individual cointegration tests.

3 This study conducted several diagnostic tests on the ECM equations. The results show that the ECM equations are free from serial correlation and ARCH problems. In addition, the residuals are spherically distributed and the Ramsey RESET test indicates no misspecification error. Therefore, Granger causality tests based upon the VECM equations are valid and reliable. The diagnostic tests results are not reported here but available upon request.

4 This probably indicates that tourist arrivals from China and Indonesia are less likely to be genuine tourists as a point raised by Kassim (1997). Moreover, Lee (2013) reported that China and Indonesia are the contributors of illegal workers in Malaysia. Apart from that, Samad (2012) revealed that 3175 tourists from Indonesia and approximately 3000 tourists from China were denied entry to Malaysia because the custom officers suspect that they may have other intentions apart from visiting the country. Since tourist arrivals from China and Indonesia are more likely to be non-genuine, it is plausible to find that tourist arrivals from these countries do not Granger-cause Malaysia's economic growth.

Chapter 13

Tourism Development and Rural Tourism in Taiwan: A Literature Review

I-Ting Chen
Sheffield Hallam University, UK

Konstantin Karl Weicht
Vienna University of Economics and Business, Austria

ABSTRACT

Although tourism plays an increasingly important role in Taiwan's economy, and despite increasing government and academic interest in tourism development and rural tourism in Taiwan, the literature currently lacks of a concise review that brings together the various aspects of tourism development in Taiwan. The present chapter aims to contribute to closing this gap. It does so in six concise sections: a brief overview of Taiwan; the development of tourism in Taiwan; tourism and the economy in Taiwan; tourism and politics in Taiwan; rural tourism development; and small hotels in Taiwan. It is hoped that this account would serve as an important context specific prerequisite for future and more in-depth studies on tourism development and rural tourism in Taiwan.

INTRODUCTION AND RESEARCH CONTEXT

Despite political upheaval, economic uncertainty and natural disasters the travel and tourism industry continues to be one of the largest industries in the world (World Travel and Tourism Council, 2012). Chen, Lin, and Kuo, 2013, the World Travel and Tourism Council (WTTC, 2012), Chen (2011), C. L. Chen (2010), Wang (2010), Chen and Chiou-Wei (2009) or Lee and Chien (2008) point out the connection between the economy and tourism development and many countries have turned tourism into a vehicle for economic growth. As such the global tourism and hospitality industry is a key driver for socio-economic progress through the creation of jobs, enterprises, infrastructure development, and export revenues earned (Chen et al., 2013; Wang, 2010).

DOI: 10.4018/978-1-5225-2078-8.ch013

Taiwan, with its well-known high-tech and urban face, is a major economic player as one of the four "Asian Tigers", together with Singapore, South Korea, and Hong Kong. It lies within the Asia and the Pacific region, which is one of the fastest growing tourism destinations in the world [United Nations World Tourism Organization (UNWTO), 2010; WTTC, 2012]. Accordingly Taiwan's tourist economy is changing substantially and is also growing very rapidly (Chen et al., 2013; Taiwan Tourism Bureau, 2013a; Wang, 2010; Weng & Wang, 2004). The new importance given to tourism in the economic development of Taiwan has become evident in national development plans such as the "six flagship" plan of the Executive Yuan (Ministry of Economic Affairs, 2009). The six flagship plan funds tourism in Taiwan with 30 billion New Taiwanese Dollar and has an expected production value of 550 billion New Taiwan Dollar (NTD) and 410,000 additional tourism-related jobs within four years (Ministry of Economic Affairs, 2009; Wang, 2009). Other tourism promotion programs such as "Project Vanguard for Excellence in Tourism" (Taiwan Tourism Bureau, 2010a) and international marketing promotions contribute to rising numbers of inbound visitors to Taiwan. Changing regulations affecting international relations, such as the recent relaxations of travel restrictions between Taiwan and the People's Republic of China, brings an additional 3,000 tourists from Mainland China to Taiwan every day (Taiwan Tourism Bureau, 2010b). International arrivals have increased over the past decade (WTCC, 2012) from almost 3 million visitor arrivals in 2002 to 7,3 million visitor arrivals in 2012 (Taiwan Tourism Bureau, 2013c).

While international tourism development plans have taken effect and are reflected in the rising numbers of international arrivals in Taiwan, changes in regulations have also affected domestic tourism in Taiwan. Important indexes of Taiwanese travellers show an increase in Taiwanese domestic travel (Taiwan Tourism Bureau, 2013b) with 95% of the Taiwanese population taking domestic tourist travel, a total of 152,268,000 trips in 2011, an increase of 1.5% to 2010 (Taiwan Tourism Bureau, 2012). Rising household incomes continue to fuel increased leisure demand (WTTC, 2012).

However, to continue to upgrade and transform its industries and protect itself from economic crises it is important for Taiwan to understand its tourism industry (Su, 2011; Wang, 2010). Tourism has long been considered a vehicle for socio-economic development and regeneration, especially for those affected by the decline of traditional agrarian activities (Chen et al., 2013). For example, when Taiwan joined the Word Trade Organization in 2002, large volumes of agricultural goods were imported from foreign countries and this had a major impact on traditional agricultural businesses on the island. Local production and marketing became much more competitive and it was increasingly difficult for small independent agricultural businesses to survive (Council of Agriculture Executive Yuan of Taiwan, 2004). Authors, for example Chen et al. (2013), Robinson and O'Connor (2013), Su (2011), Urry (2002), or Oppermann (1995) suggest that these economic constraints can be alleviated when the land is used differently, for example through the transformation of traditional agricultural businesses into small hospitality businesses.

Development over the past decade in Taiwan has shown that more and more land that has previously been used for agricultural purposes is now being used for leisure, recreation and tourism purposes. Several nature-based establishments, such as tourism farms, rural hotels and rural festal activity centres have been created (Tourism Bureau, 2008) and these have altered the use of Taiwan's agricultural areas (Chen et al., 2013). Based on gross domestic product, tourism in Taiwan has overtaken the contribution of agriculture, a traditional strong point of the Taiwanese economy (Taiwan Tourism Bureau, 2013b; WTTC, 2012).

However, although tourism plays an increasingly important role in Taiwan's economy, and despite increasing government and academic interest in tourism development and rural tourism in Taiwan, the literature currently lacks of a concise review that brings together the various aspects of tourism development in Taiwan. The present chapter aims to contribute to closing this gap.

The chapter sets out with a brief overview of Taiwan with information on its inhabitants, geography and natural characteristics. The section on tourism development in Taiwan takes a look at international arrivals, travel from mainland China, and domestic tourism. The chapter then moves on to review the relationship between the economy and tourism. It discusses changes in Taiwan's economy and elaborates how the reciprocal relationship between tourism expansion and economic growth in Taiwan (Kim & Chen, 2006) acts as a vehicle for the island's development. Because of the increasing scholarly interest in the relationship between tourism and politics (for example Chen, Lee, & Yang, 2012; Ingram, Tabari, & Watthanakhomprathip, 2013; Mak, 2013) and the special political status of Taiwan (Bates & Bates, 2005; Central Intelligence Agency (CIA), 2013) a discussion of tourism and politics is added. Because rural hotels are usually located in the small business sector the chapter then focuses onto small hotels in Taiwan. The remainder of the chapter presents a section discussing solutions and recommendations, a section discussing future research directions, and closes with the conclusion.

A BRIEF OVERVIEW OF TAIWAN

Taiwan, or Formosa, is a leaf-shaped island in North-East Asia, southeast of mainland China, and on the western edge of the Pacific Ocean. To the north lies South Korea, in the north-east Japan, and to the south are the Philippines (C. L. Chen, 2010). During its long history prehistoric people, aborigines, European settlers from Denmark and Spain, Japanese, and Han Chinese have successively populated Taiwan. This has resulted in a varied culture that inherits different local customs from many different ethnic groups, recently also from the Americans (Taiwan Tourism Bureau, 2013a). Today officially known as the "Republic of China" it has a population of 23 million people and covers an area of 36,000 square kilometres (CIA, 2013). Accordingly Taiwan has a population density of 668 people per square kilometre (in comparison England has a population of 51 million people and an area of 130,395 square kilometres, with a density of 395 people per square kilometre) (CIA, 2013). Taiwan's tropical, subtropical and temperate climates provide clear differentiation between the different seasons (Taiwan Tourism Bureau, 2013a).

Taiwan may be said to have two faces: an industrial and a green one. Due to the dramatic changes in Taiwan's industry over the past 60 years Taiwan is often associated with attributes such as modern, high-tech and urban. Alongside with Singapore, South Korea and Hong Kong, Taiwan is one of the "Four Asian Tigers", or one of the four economic powers in the region. International attention is often focused on this industrial face of Taiwan (Taiwan Tourism Bureau, 2013a). However, Taiwan is not just crowded, clamorous and urban. It also has another and green face with more traditional and low-tech attributes (Liu, 2002).

Two thirds of Taiwan are covered by forested mountains and the remaining area consists of hilly country, platforms and highlands, coastal plains and basins (Taiwan Tourism Bureau, 2013a). Taiwan has a rich diversity of organic life and some variations are rarely found elsewhere in the world. There are about 18,400 species of wildlife on the island, 20 percent of which are rare or endangered (Taiwan Tourism Bureau, 2013a). Taiwan is also home to Northeast Asia's tallest mountain, Yushan (or Jade Mountain), with a height of 3,952 meters (Taiwan Tourism Bureau, 2013a). Yushan is part of a 270 kilometre long mountain range with 200 peaks running from north to south and forming Taiwan's most dominant topographical feature. This mountain range served as a natural barrier and helped to protect the eastern part of the island from industrial impacts (Taiwan Tourism Bureau, 2013a). The island's east coast is the most isolated and unspoiled region of Taiwan. For example Hualien County, which faces the Pacific Ocean to the east and leans against the grand central mountain range, is famous for its beautiful scenery and stunning marble canyon of Taroko Gorge. These areas are not only important nature reserves that protect the environment but they also provide great opportunities for recreational activities, environmental education and academic research (Taiwan Tourism Bureau, 2013a). These eastern, mostly rural, areas have progressed differently. Away from the industrialisation Eastern Taiwan has seen the development of rural tourism and the inception of the Taiwanese rural hotel (Tsai, 2007).

In line with the rural hotel development (for example Chen et al., 2013; Liu, 2010; Tsai, 2007) in Eastern Taiwan tourism in general is playing an increasingly important role in the economy of Taiwan (for example M. H. Chen, 2010; Taiwan Tourism Bureau, 2013c; WTTC, 2012). Moreover, with the democratisation progress in Taiwan environmental protection has become an increasingly important political topic (Bates & Bates, 2005; C. L. Chen, 2010). As of 2013 the government has established eight national parks, 13 national scenic areas and many forest recreation areas to preserve Taiwan's best natural ecological environment and cultural sites (Taiwan Tourism Bureau, 2013a).

DEVELOPMENT OF TOURISM IN TAIWAN

International Arrivals in Taiwan

When tourism started to grow in the 1960s and 1970s also the local accommodation industry in Taiwan changed. From the 1970's on the Taiwanese government provided incentives in the form of low-interest loans and tax breaks for new businesses, in particular for building international-class hotels and standard-class hotels (Taiwan Review, 2009). From the late 1970s onwards to the early 1990s tourism development slowed down due to changes in the diplomatic recognition of Taiwan and the difficult relationship with mainland China (Lee & Chien, 2008). To counteract these influences and to increase international arrivals in Taiwan the government lifted some of the self-imposed travel restrictions. For example in 1994 the government introduced a five-day visa free entry program for 15 countries (Lee & Chien, 2008; Weng & Wang, 2004). Thanks to further loosening of travel restrictions, a gradual opening to tourists from the mainland, the rapid economic growth of the Asia and the Pacific region and the economic growth of Taiwan the number of international arrivals to Taiwan has since been increasing.

International tourist arrivals have reached a new record high in 2012, with 7,311,470 visitors, an increase of 20 percent compared to 2011 (Taiwan Tourism Bureau, 2013c). A recent survey report from the Taiwan Tourism Bureau (2013c) with detailed information on international travel in Taiwan shows that by 2011 the number of inbound visitors had reached a total of 6,087,484 persons, an increase of 9.3 percent from 2010. The visitor expenditures in tourism in 2011 were 11,065 million US Dollar, equivalent to an annual growth rate of 27 percent. Inbound visitors spent on average 1,818 US Dollars during their stay, which was on average seven nights long. Table 1 gives an overview of visitor arrivals and annual growth rate in Taiwan for the period 2002 until 2012 (Taiwan Tourism Bureau, 2013c). The drop in visitor arrivals and annual growth rate in Taiwan of 25 percent in the period from 2002 until

Table 1. Visitor arrivals and annual growth rate in Taiwan

Year	Number of visitors	Growth rate (%)
2002	2,977,692	5.18
2003	2,248,117	-24.50
2004	2,950,342	31.24
2005	3,378,118	14.50
2006	3,519,827	4.19
2007	3,716,063	5.58
2008	3,845,187	3.47
2009	4,395,004	14.30
2010	5,567,277	26.67
2011	6,087,484	9.34
2012	7,311,470	20.11

(adapted from *Taiwan Tourism Bureau, 2013c*)

2003 can be explained by the outbreak of the Severe Acute Respiratory Syndrome (SARS) in Hong Kong and South China between November 2002 and July 2003 (World Health Organization (WHO), 2013).

Tourism Travel from Mainland China to Taiwan

Although political differences between the Republic of China and the People's Republic of China remain unresolved the two countries have close economic links (CIA, 2013; Chiang, 2012). Because of the geographical proximity, similar culture and language people from mainland China are also potential tourism customers for Taiwan. However, the tensions between the Republic of China and the People's Republic of China made travelling between the two countries cumbersome. In 1987 Taiwan introduced an opportunity for visiting relatives on the mainland through a third country (Chiang, 2012). This was the inception of travel activities between the two countries. In addition, the People's Republic of China's huge population and economic success makes people from mainland China important potential stimulants for Taiwan's tourism industry (Chiang, 2012). The People's Republic of China is the fastest growing tourism source market in the world and the first tourism source market globally in terms of spending (UNWTO, 2013). Changes in Taiwan's government have resulted in new bilateral agreements between Taiwan and the People's Republic of China. As of 2008 mainland Chinese visitors are allowed on Taiwan (Chiang, 2012). This created a new flow of tourists from China to Taiwan and creates a potential market in catering to tourists from mainland China (M. H. Chen, 2010). Of the 4.3 million international visitors in Taiwan in 2009 1.6 million were mainland Chinese, an increase of 84 percent compared to 2008 (Tourism Bureau, 2011b). Of the 7.3 million international arrivals in Taiwan in 2012 3.5 million were mainland Chinese, equivalent to 48 percent of the total arrivals (Taiwan Tourism Bureau, 2013c). However, until recently mainland Chinese still had to cope with additional limitations and regulations when travelling to Taiwan and this coincided with other aspects of tourism development in Taiwan. For example, travellers from mainland China were only allowed on pre-organised, travel agency booked group travels. Accordingly these tourist-groups from The People's Republic of China had no choice but stay in big hotels. This travel restriction coincided with the regulations of the Taiwanese rural hotels (Taiwan Tourism Bureau, 2013b), which have restrictions on the number of rooms they can have. Until recently this made travellers from the People's Republic of China less attractive for rural hotels.

Research into the dynamics of cross strait relations, for example Liu (2011), C. M. Chen (2010), or Guo, Kim, Timothy, & Wang (2006) suggests that, in principal, tourism may avert escalation of the conflict and normalise the political relations between the two states. However, contributors come to the conclusion that, as yet, tourism development between Taiwan and China is not stable (C. M. Chen, 2010; Chiang, 2012) and that any political disagreement between the two may negatively impact tourism growth in Taiwan (Chiang, 2012). Hence, tourism development in Taiwan is, to some extent, dependent on the political relationship between Taiwan and mainland China.

Domestic Tourism in Taiwan

The increase of international visitors in Taiwan also coincides with the overall development of domestic tourism and changes in leisure and holiday structures in Taiwan. The Taiwanese have increasingly more spare time which allows them to take holiday and go travelling. The Taiwanese used to work a minimum of 12 hours per day, seven days a week (Ministry of Transportation and Communication, 1999). It was not unusual to never leave home city or county. It was only in January 1998 that Taiwanese government agencies, for example the Council for Economic Planning and Development (CEPD) and the Central Personnel Administration (CPA), developed and put into effect the alternating two-day weekend policy, a policy whereby the second and fourth Saturdays of every month are days off (Ministry of Transportation and Communication, 1999).

Since then domestic tourism has been growing in Taiwan. A survey of domestic travel in Taiwan published by the Taiwan Tourism Bureau (2013c) shows that in 2011 95 percent of Taiwanese were taking domestic travel. The average number of trips per person in 2011 was 7.4 trips, equalling a total of 152,269,000 domestic trips for that year. On average domestic trips lasted 1.5 days and accounted for 1,359 NTD expenses per person day and trip. The total expenditure of domestic travels in 2011 was 310.3 billion NTD (Taiwan Tourism Bureau, 2013c). An overview of this information on domestic tourism in Taiwan in presented in table 2.

Table 2. Overview of domestic tourism in Taiwan in 2011

Proportion of people taking domestic tourist travel	95%
Average number of trips per person	7.4 trips
Total number of trips	152,268,000 trips
Average number of days per trip	1.5 days
Average expenses per person day on trip	1,359 NTD
Total expenditure of domestic travels	310.3 billion NTD

(adapted from *Taiwan Tourism Bureau, 2013c*)

TOURISM AND THE ECONOMY IN TAIWAN

Taiwan's Changing Economy

As part of the fast developing Asia and the Pacific region, Taiwan went through a rapid economic development over the past six decades (CIA, 2013). This development impacted traditional industries, such as the agriculture industry. Since the mid-1960s there was a constant decline in the number of workers engaged in agriculture (Council of Agriculture Executive Yuan (COA), 1999), mainly due to increasing use of machinery. Changes in agricultural production also saw greater utilisation of pesticides and fertilisers, which made farming more expensive. At the same time profits from agricultural production did not match increased costs, largely because the government controlled market prices so to ensure the stability of food supply. The average annual income of a farm household in 1998 was about 77 percent of that of non-farmers (COA, 1999). While in 1961 almost 50 percent of the population worked in agriculture in 1999 it was only 8.3 percent (COA, 1999). Those who stayed in agriculture suffered from low income generated by farming and the comparatively long working hours to other industries. The situation further worsened when Taiwan joined the World Trade Organization in 2002 (COA, 2004; Wang, 2010). Traditional domestic agricultural businesses on the island with local production and marketing were opened up to competitive pressures from abroad. Importantly agricultural globalisation became more intensive, more varieties and especially larger volumes of agricultural goods have been imported from foreign countries. It became increasingly difficult for small independent agricultural businesses to survive and traditional Taiwanese farmers were under severe pressure (COA, 2004). This created the need, especially for farmers, to look for new sources of income. At the turn of the century the challenge was to deal with the changing economy and with tourism as a new and potential vehicle for economic growth.

Tourism and Economic Growth in Taiwan

Authors (for example M. H. Chen, 2010; Chen, 2011; Chen & Chiou-Wei, 2009; Kim & Chen, 2006; Lee & Chien, 2008; Nissan, Galindo, & Méndez, 2011; Wang, 2010) stress the connection between the economy and tourism development. To promote tourism internationally the Taiwanese government introduced several development concepts to reinforce the economy, for example in 2002 with the 'Doubling Tourist Arrivals Plan', which was part of the national development plan 'Challenge 2008' (Kim & Chen, 2006; Lee & Chien, 2008). The importance of tourism in the economic development of Taiwan is also evident in the "six flagship" plan of the Executive Yuan (Ministry of Economic Affairs, 2009). This six flagship plan was implemented to promote the development of the six key emerging industries. Amongst tourism these are the green energy industry, biotech, health care, high-value-added agriculture, and cultural and creative industries (see table 3). Tourism was funded with 30 billion NTD. The production value was expected at 550 billion NTD as well as an additional 410,000 tourism-related jobs within four years (Ministry of Economic Affairs, 2009; Wang, 2009).

Kim and Chen (2006), in a study on tourism expansion and economic development in Taiwan, investigated the causal relationship between these two variables, i.e. if economic development was a driver for tourism or if it was the other way around. They (Kim & Chen, 2006) found a reciprocal relationship between the tourism expansion and economic development in Taiwan. This suggests that resources should be equally allotted to tourism and other major industries in Taiwan. In this respect the six flagship plan from the Ministry of Economic Affairs in Taiwan (Ministry of Economic Affairs, 2009) indicates that

Table 3. The six flagship plan

Item	Funding	Production value created	Industries that will benefit
"Green" energy industry	NT$20 billion over 5 years	NT$1 trillion	Mainly the solar cell and LED industries
Biotech industry	NT$60 billion in biotech venture capital funding	Doubling of production value to NT$260 billion within 4 years	Pharmaceuticals and biotech industries
Tourism	NT$30 billion tourism development fund	NT$550 billion within 4 years	Restaurant and hotel industries, etc.
Healthcare	NT$86.4 billion in investment over 4 years	NT$346.4 billion over 4 years	Medical electronics and medical devices industries
High-value-added agriculture	NT$24.2 billion over 4 years	NT$158.9 billion over 4 years	Orchid cultivation, agro-tourism, etc.
Cultural and creative industries	NT$20 billion to establish venture capital funds	NT$1 trillion within 4 years	TV, film, music, handicrafts, design and digital content industries

(*Ministry of Economic Affairs, 2009*)

Taiwan's overall economy and economy driven tourism development are heading in the right direction of reciprocal growth.

As part of a "domestic tourism development plan" (Taiwan Tourism Bureau, 2013b) in Taiwan the government introduced a number of incentives to boost domestic travelling. For example from 2003 onwards public servants had paid holidays. The "National Travel Card", a kind of credit card for public servants was introduced. Public servants are allowed a certain amount of money, as well as discounts, when they travel at certain times of the year (e.g. low-season), when they travel outside their own county, or when they stay more than one night (Executive Yuan, 2011). In 2011 approximately 600,000 National Travel Cards were issued and the compulsory vacation subsidies amounted to 7.8 billion NTD, 60 percent of which were used through the national travel card in the tourism industry (Taiwan Tourism Bureau, 2013b).

The economic development of the Asia and Pacific region and of Taiwan also means that the Taiwanese people have increasingly more time and money for travelling. The gross income per capita had grown by 80 percent in the period 1992 until 2005 to over 10,000 US Dollar (National Statistics Bureau, 2005). This increase in national income per capita and more leisure time combined creates a great potential for tourism activities. In 2011 tourism had a direct contribution to Taiwan's GDP of 239.3 billion NTD, an equivalent of 1.7 percent, and generated 212,500 jobs (WTTC, 2012).

TOURISM AND POLITICS IN TAIWAN

Taiwan and the UN

The Republic of China was a founding member of the United Nations (UN) in 1945 (United Nations, 2013) and of affiliate organisations such as the United Nations Educational, Scientific and Cultural Organization (UNESCO) in 1946 (United Nations Educational, Scientific and Cultural Organization, 2013). As a member of the UN the Republic of China played an important international role. For example it proofed to be a useful ally for the United States, especially during the Korean War (1950-1953) and the

Vietnam War (1955-1975) (Bates & Bates, 2005). However, due to international developments and a growing number of sovereign states that were increasingly in favour of the People's Republic of China (on the mainland) diplomatic recognition of the Republic of China (Taiwan) started to shift towards the People's Republic of China on the mainland. As a result, since October 1971, all of China's seats in the United Nations and membership in the United Nations Security Council, which were held by the Republic of China from 1945 until 1971, are now occupied by the People's Republic of China (UN, 2013). Chinese, one of the official UN languages, changed from the traditional form that is used on Taiwan to the simplified form that is used on the mainland (UN, 2013). Moreover, in 1972, the United States and the People's Republic of China signed the Shanghai Communiqué, acknowledging the One-China policy, stating that Taiwan is part of China and that the 'Taiwan question' was to be an internal problem of the People's Republic of China (UN, 2013). In 1978 the United States officially ended diplomatic relations with the Republic of China (Taiwan) and established relations with the People's Republic of China on the mainland (UN, 2013).

As a consequence the Republic of China has no representative ambassador at the United Nations or any of its affiliate organisations, such as the United Nations Educational, Scientific and Cultural Organization (UNESCO, 2013) or the UNWTO, which was founded in 1974 (UNWTO, 2013). Many attempts have since been made by the Taiwanese, either as the Republic of China on Taiwan, the Republic of China (Taiwan), or simply as Taiwan, in order to attain membership at the United Nations and to represent the 23 million Taiwanese people. However, all such efforts have been blocked by the veto of the People's Republic of China (UN, 2013).

It is argued that this has a negative impact on tourism development in Taiwan. The exclusion of the Republic of China from the United Nations (UN, 2013) and the non-acceptance of Taiwan as an independent and sovereign state prohibit that tourist attractions, such as the Chinese Imperial treasures in the National Palace Museum in Taipei, or natural wonders such as the Taroko Gorge in Hualien, can be declared as UNESCO World Heritage sites. This is of disadvantage to the Taiwan tourist economy as studies (for example Yang et al., 2010) show that natural and cultural resources are widely recognised as essential tourism assets for a country. In particular they are considered attractive when they are listed as UNESCO World Heritage Sites (Li, Wu, & Cai, 2008). Declared UNESCO world heritage sites are regarded as significant and rapidly growing factors in tourism and are considered as a major driving force for further growth in many developed countries (for example Herbert, 2001; McIntosh & Prentice, 1999). Moreover they can help to develop a national image and produce a national identity (Li et al., 2008), which is an important factor in tourism development (Gertner & Kotler, 2004; Johansson, 2005; Park, 2009; Popescu, Paun, Nicolescu, & Draghici, 2008).

Conflict With Mainland China

The People's Republic of China continuously threatens Taiwan with its military power. This is evident for example in the Taiwan Strait Crises. The latest, the Third Taiwan Strait Crisis, lasted from 1995 to 1996 (Bates & Bates, 2005). In 2005 the People's Republic of China passed an anti-secession law, threatening the use of non-peaceful means. Article 8 of the law states that:

In the event that the "Taiwan independence" secessionist forces should act under any name or by any means to cause the fact of Taiwan's secession from China, or that major incidents entailing Taiwan's secession from China should occur, or that possibilities for a peaceful reunification should be completely exhausted, the state shall employ non-peaceful means and other necessary measures to protect China's sovereignty and territorial integrity. (Anti-Secession Law, 2005: Article 8)

This anti-secession law forbids Taiwan to use the name 'Taiwan' (Anti-Secession Law, 2005). Taiwan has to refer to itself officially as the "Republic of China (Taiwan)" or "Chinese Taipei", for example at the Olympic Games. This may have negative connotations regarding tourism promotion and identification with the tourism product "Taiwan". Authors (for example Gertner & Kotler, 2004; Johansson, 2005; Park, 2009; Popescu et al., 2008; or Pritchard & Morgan, 2001) stress the important role tourism promotion plays in enhancing competitive advantage over other tourist destinations. It is not enough for a destination just to possess outstanding tourism resources. Countries should also have a clear, credible, appealing and distinctive image in a global marketplace (Chen et al., 2012). Travellers rank safety and security as key factors in planning a holiday (Ingram et al., 2013). A lack of safety and security at the destination negatively affects business and leisure travel (Edgell, Allen, Smith, & Swanson, 2007). If actual events cause, or potential events are considered to cause, political instability then a country becomes unattractive as a tourist destination (Ingram et al., 2013).

Apart from the promotional issues the ongoing conflict with the People's Republic of China causes, the conflict is also responsible for the constant presence of military on Taiwan. The military presence means that places that might be perceived by 'Westerners' as the best nature tourist spots and viewpoints are often military no-go areas. Although Taiwan is an island with beautiful beaches it is not regarded as a typical 'ocean' state (Yuan Control, 2004). This is due to a martial law that was imposed on Taiwan over four decades ago which led to a long term separation of the Taiwanese people and the sea (Yuan Control, 2004). This law highly restricted public access to coastal areas. Since the law was lifted in 1987 the restriction has been relieved and the government has started to take a more liberal and active attitude toward unlocking coastal and maritime resources in order to develop Taiwan into a genuine ocean state (C. L. Chen, 2010).

RURAL TOURISM IN TAIWAN

Tourism in rural areas has been an effective catalyst of rural socio-economic regeneration for over a century in the Western world (Jing-Ming, 2003). The correlation between overall economic development, international tourist arrivals and domestic tourism (for example Sharpley & Roberts, 2004) has also impacted rural tourism development in the Asia and the Pacific region (Wang et al., 2013). Especially over the past three decades rural tourism in Asia has undergone a rapid development and is seen as a catalyst that promotes industrial restructuring, agricultural development and upgrading of rural areas (Wang et al., 2013). There are now several accounts of rural tourism in China (for example Su, 2011; Wang et al., 2013) and Taiwan (for example Chen et al., 2013; Liu, 2010; Tsai, 2007).

In 1998 the China National Tourism Administration introduced the 'Urban and Rural Tourism Year', which was followed by the 'Eco-Tourism Year' in 1999, the 'Chinese Life Tourism Year' in 2004, and the 'China Rural Tourism Year' in 2006 (Su, 2011; Wang et al., 2013).

Also in Taiwan rural tourism has been growing (Chen et al., 2013; Huang, 2008; Liu, 2010; Tsai, 2007). Liu (2010) asserts that rural tourism emerged in Taiwan due to a culmination of factors such as urbanisation, an increasingly affluent population, shifts in consumer patterns, increase in leisure time, and improvement in traffic. The development of rural tourism in Taiwan is also often brought into relation with the decline of traditional agricultural businesses, when Taiwan joined the World Trade Organization in 2002 (for example Huang, 2008; Taiwan Tourism Bureau, 2008; Tsai, 2007;). To alleviate the negative consequences of joining the World Trade Organization in 2002 the Tourism Board of Taiwan developed several strategies to promote rural tourism in Taiwan (Taiwan Tourism Bureau, 2008). These development strategies include plans to develop tourism orchards, leisure farms and leisure agriculture, the one-township-one tourism-area development strategy, plans to combine rural tourism development and community development models, food, beverage services and DIY demonstrations, as well as the development of a hostel model (Tsai, 2007).

Development strategies for rural tourism in Taiwan encompass a wide range of activities, and so does the term "rural tourism". In comparison to Europe, tourism in rural areas in Taiwan is a relatively recent phenomenon. This is probably one of the reasons why different forms of tourism in rural areas in Taiwan cannot yet easily be differentiated amongst or categorised, for example into 'rural tourism', 'agriculture tourism', 'eco-tourism', or 'leisure farm tourism'. Liu (2000, in Liu, 2010:217) for example describes rural tourism in Taiwan as *any tourist activity in rural areas that is known to be a way of enjoying rural life, enjoying beautiful rural scenery and maintaining rural prosperity and environmental quality.* Tsai (2007) notes that rural tourism in Taiwan includes tourism in orchards, farms, and scenic areas, agricultural-activity based tourism, several culture based activities as well as nature-oriented activities. Liu (2010) describes rural tourism as a kind of lifestyle and a critical part of the rural leisure industry. Rural tourism in Taiwan is *the utilisation and integration of the unique quality and rich resources of the rural environment* (Liu, 2010:217). Rural tourism is a combination of agriculture activities, rural culture and recreation service, and serves economic, social, educational, environmental, recreational, therapeutic, and cultural purposes (Liu, 2002, 2010).

These descriptions of 'rural tourism' in Taiwan currently overlap with descriptions of agriculture tourism, leisure agriculture, leisure farm tourism, or eco-tourism (for example Chen, 2010; Ecotourism Society Taiwan, 2011; Taiwan Tourism Bureau, 2013b; Tsai, 2007). The Ecotourism Society in Taiwan (2011), an independent and government funded organisation across the whole of Taiwan, lists activities such as whale watching, bird watching, river tracking, climbing, and nature and culture study under eco-tourism, but these activities do equally fit Tsai (2007) and Liu's (2010) description of rural tourism.

Despite its potential for the development of rural areas, rural tourism in China and Taiwan faces problems of clear rural development policies, a lack of management norms, a lack of market analyses, and a lack of capital input (Tsai, 2007). In addition rural tourism is said to be monotonous, many rural areas are unattractive for tourists because they lack of natural beauty, and many old rural communities are unattractive in appearance (Tsai, 2007). The development of rural areas into rural tourism areas is dependent on the interplay between rural tourism development, environmental protection and industrial development (Liu, 2010; Tsai, 2007). It can be concluded that, despite increasing government and academic interest in rural tourism in mainland China and Taiwan, there remains little understanding about the core issues of rural tourism and there is no unified approach or authoritative conclusion to its connotations, principles, development models and future directions (Wang et al., 2013).

SMALL HOTELS IN TAIWAN

The existent literature on small hotels in Taiwan is relatively small. This makes it difficult to follow Thomas, Shaw, and Page's (2011) call for recognition of spatial and sectoral differences in small businesses in hospitality and tourism studies. None of the few academic contributions (for example Chen et al., 2013; Liu, 2010; Tsai, 2007; Wu & Yang, 2010) take a particular focus on the nature and characteristics of the Taiwanese rural hotel, although Hu, J. H. Wang, & R. Y. Wang, (2012) make an interesting contribution on Taiwanese homestays. Information provided by the Taiwanese Tourism Bureau is mostly bureaucratic or informational. This is surprising because Taiwan's tourist economy has been growing very rapidly (UNWTO, 2012; WTTC, 2012) and along with the development of the domestic tourism sector rural tourism has been growing. According to the Taiwanese Tourism Bureau (2013b) small hotels in rural areas have become a fast growing component of the hospitality and tourism industry in Taiwan.

To cope with the increase in rural hotels the Taiwanese Bureau for Hospitality and Tourism set out a regulation for rural hotels in Taiwan in December 2002. This new regulation had to effect that existing rural hotels were classified into either legal or illegal rural hotels. In February 2003 there were a total of 65 legal rural hotels in Taiwan. The number of hotels that did not meet the legal requirements was much greater, with 535 illegal rural hotels in February 2003 (Tourism Bureau, 2003). Since 2003 the number of rural hotels in Taiwan has been growing and many of the former illegal rural hotels now meet the regulations. By 2008 the number of rural hotels had grown to 2,582 (Taiwan Tourism Bureau, 2008) and 3407 rural hotels in 2012 (Taiwan Tourism Bureau, 2013b).

Rural hotels exist across the whole island and the majority of rural hotels are spread around the scenic areas of the three counties Hualien, Nantow, and Ilan (Taiwan Tourism Bureau, 2013b). Rural tourism in Taiwan is concentrated on those three counties, partly because of the natural beauty of these areas, and partly because respective farmer associations have promoted the development of the rural hotel product in those areas (Liu, 2010; or Tsai, 2007). Hualien had an increase of rural hotels from only four rural hotels in 2002, to 661 in 2008, and 805 in 2012. Accordingly Hualien is the county with the most rural hotels in Taiwan. This is followed by Ilan, which had 21 rural hotels in 2003, 299 rural hotels in 2008, and 593 rural hotels in 2012. Nantow, in central Taiwan, had 21 rural hotels in 2003, 421 in 2008, and 478 rural hotels in 2012 (Taiwan Tourism Bureau, 2013b). Table 4 provides an overview of this data.

The Taiwanese government responded to the growth in number of rural hotels through the introduction of a regulation in 2002 (Tourism Bureau, 2003). The regulation is mostly bureaucratic and regulates things such as application, licensing, and registration, and several health and safety issues. It includes a spatial regulation in that rural hotels shall be limited to scenic spots, tourist sites, national parks, aboriginal reservations, remote areas and offshore islands, recreational agriculture farms, nature villages and non-urban land (Tourism Bureau, 2003). The size of the establishment should, in principle, not exceed five guest rooms and a total floor area of 150 square meters. Rural hotels in certain areas, such

Table 4. Overview of B&Bs in top counties in Taiwan

Location / Year	02/2003	02/2008	02/2012
Hualien	4	661	805
Ilan	21	299	593
Nantow	21	421	478
Taiwan	65	2353	3407

(adapted from *Taiwan Tourism Bureau, 2013b*)

as aboriginal areas, may be exempt from this regulation and are allowed an operating scale of 15 guest rooms and a total floor area of up to 200 square meters. In regard of basic service criteria rural hotels shall have adequate ventilation and sufficient sunlight in each guest- and bath room. Hot and cold water and sanitation equipment shall be provided. The equipment and surroundings of the rural hotel should be clean and tidy and comply with pest control (Tourism Bureau, 2003).

Article 3 of the regulations (Tourism Bureau, 2003) describes a rural hotel as

a lodging facility run as a family sideline business, using the spare rooms of a self-used residence to provide tourists with a rural living experience. Such lodging facilities usually incorporate local culture, natural landscape, ecological environment, environmental resources, and agricultural, forestry, fishery, or livestock farming activities. (Tourism Bureau, 2003; Article 3)

However, the regulations do not go into any more detail in regard to customer service attributes. From a service perspective this is critical as the drastic increase in rural hotels is not accompanied by any guidance or standard of what services should be provided and at what quality level. Taking into consideration the role that rural tourism can play in the transformation of agriculture economies into tourist economies (Wang et al., 2013) this would be important. Many of the former agriculture workforces are now expected to be tourist service providers. Without a clear conceptualisation of the Taiwanese rural hotel and without guidance and support how to run a rural hotel it is questionable how these rural tourism entrepreneurs, who are often farmers with a low educational level or with another profession in accumulation (Loureiro & Gonzalez, 2008), can contribute to the development of rural tourism into a sustainable economic element in Taiwan.

SOLUTIONS AND RECOMMENDATIONS

Within the increase of global tourism the Asia and the Pacific region is one of the fastest growing tourism regions (UNWTO, 2012). This is also reflected in the statistics on tourism development in Taiwan, both internationally and domestically (Taiwan Tourism Bureau, 2013c; WTTC, 2012). Tourism growth in Taiwan may be explained through wider socio-economic factors. Murphy (1985) for example developed an explanatory model for the evolution of tourism using the three growth factors motivation, ability, and mobility. According to Murphy (1985) changes in those growth factors allow a population to move chronologically through four eras of development, from pre-industrial to industrial to consumer society to future. Murphy's growth factors (Murphy, 1985) can also be used to explain the evolution of tourism on Taiwan. Taiwan managed to evolve under colonial power from a pre-industrial society into an industrial society, with the building of schools and universities, income security and higher income, and ease of transport. The country now still seems to be adapting from an industrial society to a consumer society, for example through regulations for a shorter work week, the introduction of mass marketing and package tours, and more efficient and faster transport. The Taiwanese have more discretional income that may be used for travelling. The Taiwanese also become increasingly used to the mass consumption of tourism and increasingly perceive vacation as a right and necessity. This boosts domestic tourism on Taiwan as a new form of consumerism. With the increase of tourism on Taiwan also rural tourism and customer satisfaction, two important phenomena in hospitality and tourism research, become increasingly relevant.

Despite its potential, rural tourism in Taiwan (and also in China) faces several challenges that remain to be adequately addressed. While rural tourism is seen internationally as an instrument in the transformation of traditional agricultural economies into tourism economies (Chen et al., 2013; Wang et al., 2013) and as an important tool in broader rural development objectives (Su, 2011; Urry, 2002) and customer satisfaction is seen as a concept for creating a competitive advantage (Zehrer, Crotts, & Magnini, 2011; Ziegler, Dearden, & Rollins, 2012) and as a concept for business success (Ritchie, Mules, & Uzabeaga, 2008; Song, van der Veen, Li, & Chen, 2012) these issues are relatively new phenomena in Taiwan and remain little understood (Wang et al., 2013). There is a lack of a clear rural development policy, a lack of management norms, market analyses, and capital input (Tsai, 2007). National tourism development plans such as 'Challenge 2008' or the 'six flagship plan', which were introduced over the past century in order to boost tourism in Taiwan, remain to be adequately analysed. No research was conducted in order to investigate whether or not the promises of expected production value and the goal of creation tourism related jobs have been fulfilled. This would be important in order to assess the efficiency of past and current tourism development plans in Taiwan. It has been argued that rural tourism still carries with it a flavour of old rural communities that are unattractive in appearance (Tsai, 2007). Although more recent research (for example Hu et al., 2012; Wu and Yang, 2010) indicates that this perception is improving there is a lack of review that investigates if there is any reciprocal relationship between the government's rural tourism development plan and the new perceived improvement of rural areas. Anecdotal evidence suggests that not all development plans work out as intended, and the lack of an independent review of programs allows rooms for speculations if only a small and privileged group of people benefit from certain development projects while the overall usefulness and effectiveness of those development programs remain unclear.

Several contributors point out the important role of small businesses in economic restructuring, economic development and job creation (e.g. Blackburn, Hart, & Wainwright, 2013; Department for Business, Innovation and Skills, 2011; Thomas, Shaw, & Page, 2011) and suggest that wider conceptualisations, such as the development of rural tourism, can be achieved by understanding its inherent elements, such as the small businesses that operate within the sector. Because the discourses on SMEs on one hand and small hotels on the other hand are closely related (Thomas, 1998) Thomas et al. (2011) suggest that understanding small hospitality businesses, such as the rural hotel (in Taiwan), can provide a stepping stone in the wider conceptualisation of rural tourism (in Taiwan). Accordingly, critically appraising the small hotel in Taiwan may be seen as a prerequisite for synthesising the concept of rural tourism in Taiwan. However, as the review in this chapter shows, this is not a straight-forward task. There are several persistent issues in the conceptualisation of small businesses themselves, and small hotels therein. These concern semantic issues, such as definition of a small hotel by size, number of employees, or turnover. In the same line customer satisfaction in Taiwanese in B&Bs and rural hotels remains little understood. It has been argued that in recent years B&Bs in Taiwan, of which the Taiwanese rural hotel is a sub-group (i.e. B&Bs in rural areas), have transformed and that tourists now expect better quality of service and satisfaction from the environment and local features in these leisure facilities (Wu & Yang, 2010). However, from a customer service perspective it is unclear what sort of standard can be expected when visiting a rural hotel. There is a gap in the literature in regard to what kind of services and to what standard Taiwanese rural hotels provide for their guests. At current it is simply not known what services are provided and how satisfied customers of Taiwanese rural hotels are with those services, and where a potential for possible improvement might be present. Likewise, although some contributors have conducted studies in related fields, such as hot spring hotels in Taiwan (Deng, 2007; Hsieh, L.

H. Lin, & Y. Y. Lin, 2008), B&Bs in Taiwan (Wu & Yang, 2010) and homestays in Taiwan (Hu et al., 2012), little is known about the Taiwanese rural hotel customers' profile. As a result small businesses in tourism, although they are considered to play an important role in the tourism system, remain little understood (Thomas et al., 2011).

FUTURE RESEARCH DIRECTIONS

Following the above discussion of solutions and recommendations this section discusses potential areas for future research.

The present review shows that the increase in tourism in Taiwan came alongside national tourism development programs such as the 'six flagship plan' of the Executive Yuan (Ministry of Economic Affairs, 2009) or 'Project Vanguard for Excellence in Tourism' (Taiwan Tourism Bureau, 2010a). Future research projects could continue work from authors such as Kim and Chen (2006) and investigate the causal relationship between tourism growth and economic development to assess if economic development is a driver for tourism or if it is the other way around. Similarly it would be interesting to know if predictions for rural tourism growth in China (Wang, 2013), which were made for 2015, have been fulfilled.

The gradual lifting of travel restrictions for tourists coming from mainland China over the past decade resulted in a further increase in international arrivals in Taiwan. There is a lack of review that addresses this phenomenon. How does large group travel by mainland Chinese comply with efforts of developing rural and sustainable tourism concepts in Taiwan, for example in the Taroko National Park on the East Coast of Taiwan?

Given the special political situation of Taiwan and given that Taiwan is electing a new president in early 2016, it would be interesting to investigate the effect that a potential change of political colour in Taiwan might have on the cross-strait relationships. While a continuance of the Nationalist Kuomintang party is likely to further strengthen the relationship and tourist travel between mainland China and Taiwan, a change back to a ruling of the Green Party is considered by critics as potentially further complicating the relationship between the two countries. This could inhibit tourism travel from mainland China to Taiwan.

CONCLUSION

In the Asia and the Pacific region rural tourism has undergone a rapid development over the past three decades and is generally seen as a catalyst that promotes economic development, through industrial restructuring, agricultural development and upgrading of rural areas (Wang et al., 2013). Despite the increasing interest in rural tourism, by both government and academic institutions, the core issues of rural tourism in Taiwan, and also in its neighbouring mainland China, remain little understood. It seems not much has changed since Wang et al.'s (2013) notion that there was no unified approach or authoritative conclusion to tourism in Taiwan and its connotations, principles, development and future.

Here, the authors would like to point to two main areas of concern. First, there is a lack of assessment and review of tourism development plans that have been put into practice since the turn of the century. From an economic and sustainability point of view it would be interesting to find out what mistakes, if any, have been made. What were the areas that worked out particularly well? Where were expectations even exceeded? Second, given the recent development of rural tourism and the drastic growth of B&Bs

and Taiwanese rural hotels over the past decade it is surprising that the literature is devoid of tourism studies that take a particular and in-depth focus on them. At current it is not known what kind of services a customer can expect when visiting a Taiwanese rural hotel. Likewise very little is known about the Taiwanese rural hotel customer's profile and, importantly, customer satisfaction in Taiwanese rural hotels.

The present work discloses that, probably due to tourism still being a relatively new phenomenon in Taiwan, tourism and especially the Taiwanese rural hotel sector present a rather untapped area of research. The increasing economic importance of tourism in Taiwan and the still growing Taiwanese rural hotel product present an interesting research environment. What this chapter has aimed to accomplish is to provide an overview of what is known about tourism development and rural tourism in Taiwan. It highlights some of the conceptual problems tourism development in Taiwan is associated with within the wider rural tourism and general tourism paradigm. The authors hope that their work will serve as a stimulus and basis for future research on tourism and its economic impact in Taiwan.

REFERENCES

Anti-Secession Law. (2005). *10th National People's Congress and Chinese People's Political Consultative Conference.* Article 8. Adopted at the Third Session of the Tenth National People's Congress on March 14, 2005.

Bates, C., & Bates, L. L. (2008). *Culture Shock!* Taiwan: Marshall Cavendish International Asia Pte Ltd.

Blackburn, R. A., Hart, M., & Wainwright, T. (2013). Small business performance: Business, strategy and owner-manager characteristics. *Journal of Small Business and Enterprise Development, 20*(1), 8–27. doi:10.1108/14626001311298394

Chen, C. A., Lee, M. H., & Yang, Y. H. (2012). Branding Taiwan for tourism using Decision Making Trial and Evaluation Laboratory and Analytic Network Process methods. *Service Industries Journal, 32*(8), 1355–1373. doi:10.1080/02642069.2010.545881

Chen, C. L. (2010). Diversifying fisheries into tourism in Taiwan: Experiences and prospects. *Ocean and Coastal Management, 53*(8), 487–492. doi:10.1016/j.ocecoaman.2010.06.003

Chen, C. M. (2010). Role of tourism in connecting Taiwan and China: Assessing tourists perceptions of the Kinmen–Xiamen links. *Tourism Management, 31*(3), 421–424. doi:10.1016/j.tourman.2009.04.010

Chen, L., Lin, S., & Kuo, C. (2013). Rural tourism: Marketing strategies for the bed and breakfast industry in Taiwan. *International Journal of Hospitality Management, 32*, 278–286. doi:10.1016/j.ijhm.2012.07.005

Chen, M. H. (2010). The economy, tourism growth and corporate performance in the Taiwanese hotel industry. *Tourism Management, 31*(5), 665–675. doi:10.1016/j.tourman.2009.07.011

Chen, M. H. (2011). The response of hotel performance to international tourism development and crisis events. *International Journal of Hospitality Management, 30*(1), 200–212. doi:10.1016/j.ijhm.2010.06.005

Chi, C. G. Q., & Qu, H. (2009). Examining the relationship between tourists attribute satisfaction and overall satisfaction. *Journal of Hospitality Marketing & Management, 18*(1), 4–25. doi:10.1080/19368620801988891

Chiang, M. H. (2012). Tourism development across the Taiwan Strait. *East Asia, 29*(3), 235–253. doi:10.1007/s12140-012-9178-z

Council of Agriculture Executive Yuan. (1999). *Basic Agricultural Statistics*. Retrieved October 20, 2015, from http://bulletin.coa.gov.tw

Council of Agriculture Executive Yuan. (2004). *Basic Agricultural Statistics*. Retrieved October 20, 2015, from http://bulletin.coa.gov.tw

Deng, W. (2007). Using a revised importance–performance analysis approach: The case of Taiwanese hot springs tourism. *Tourism Management, 28*(5), 1274–1284. doi:10.1016/j.tourman.2006.07.010

Department for Business Innovation and Skills. (2011). *BIS Small Business Survey*. Sheffield, UK: Author.

Ecotourism Society Taiwan. (2011). Retrieved January 1, 2011, from www.ecotour.org.tw

Edgell, D., Allen, M., Smith, G., & Swanson, J. (2007). *Tourism Policy and Planning: Yesterday, Today and Tomorrow*. Burlington: Butterworth Heinemann.

Executive Yuan. (2011). Retrieved January 12, 2014, from http://www.ey.gov.tw

Gertner, D., & Kotler, P. (2004). How can a place correct a negative image? *Place Branding, 1*(1), 50-57.

Guo, Y., Kim, S. S., Timothy, D. J., & Wang, K. C. (2006). Tourism and reconciliation between Mainland China and Taiwan. *Tourism Management, 27*(5), 997–1005. doi:10.1016/j.tourman.2005.08.001

Headland, R. K. (1994). Historical development of Antarctic tourism. *Annals of Tourism Research, 21*(2), 269–280. doi:10.1016/0160-7383(94)90044-2

Herbert, D. (2001). Literary places, tourism and the heritage experience. *Annals of Tourism Research, 28*(2), 312–333. doi:10.1016/S0160-7383(00)00048-7

Hsieh, L. F., Lin, L. H., & Lin, Y. Y. (2008). A service quality measurement architecture for hot spring hotels in Taiwan. *Tourism Management, 29*(3), 429–438. doi:10.1016/j.tourman.2007.05.009

Hu, Y. C., Wang, J. H., & Wang, R. Y. (2012). Evaluating the performance of Taiwan homestay using analytic network process. *Mathematical Problems in Engineering*.

Huang, L. (2008). Bed and breakfast industry adopting e-commerce strategies in e-service. *Service Industries Journal, 28*(5), 633–648. doi:10.1080/02642060801988159

Ingram, H., Tabari, S., & Watthanakhomprathip, W. (2013). The impact of political instability on tourism: Case of Thailand. *Worldwide Hospitality and Tourism Themes, 5*(1), 92–103. doi:10.1108/17554211311292475

Jing-Ming, H. E. (2003). A Study on Rural Tourism Overseas. *Tourism Tribune, 1*, 16.

Johansson, J. K. (2005). The new Brand America. *Place Branding, 1*(2), 155–163. doi:10.1057/palgrave.pb.5990017

Kim, H. J., Chen, M. H., & Jang, S. C. S. (2006). Tourism expansion and economic development: The case of Taiwan. *Tourism Management, 27*(5), 925–933. doi:10.1016/j.tourman.2005.05.011

Lee, C. C., & Chien, M. S. (2008). Structural breaks, tourism development, and economic growth: Evidence from Taiwan. *Mathematics and Computers in Simulation*, *77*(4), 358–368. doi:10.1016/j.matcom.2007.03.004

Li, H., Ye, Q., & Law, R. (2013). Determinants of customer satisfaction in the hotel industry: An application of online review analysis. *Asia Pacific Journal of Tourism Research*, *18*(7), 784–802. doi:10.1080/10941665.2012.708351

Li, M., Wu, B., & Cai, L. (2008). Tourism development of World Heritage Sites in China: A geographic perspective. *Tourism Management*, *29*(2), 308–319. doi:10.1016/j.tourman.2007.03.013

Liu, C. Z. (2002). A Study on Leisure Agriculture and Rural Development. *The Journal of Rural Development Perspectives*, *3*, 19–33.

Liu, C. Z. (2010). Rural Development and Rural Tourism in Taiwan. *Asian Journal of Arts and Sciences*, *1*(2), 211–227.

Loureiro, S. M. C., & González, F. J. M. (2008). The importance of quality, satisfaction, trust, and image in relation to rural tourist loyalty. *Journal of Travel & Tourism Marketing*, *25*(2), 117–136. doi:10.1080/10548400802402321

Magnini, V. P., Crotts, J. C., & Zehrer, A. (2011). Understanding customer delight an application of travel blog analysis. *Journal of Travel Research*, *50*(5), 535–545. doi:10.1177/0047287510379162

Mak, B. (2013). The Influence of Political Ideology on the Outbound Tourism in China: 政政治思想对中国出境旅游的影响. *Journal of China Tourism Research*, *9*(1), 1–26. doi:10.1080/19388160.2013.756764

McIntosh, A. J., & Prentice, R. C. (1999). Affirming authenticity: Consuming cultural heritage. *Annals of Tourism Research*, *26*(3), 589–612. doi:10.1016/S0160-7383(99)00010-9

Ministry of Economic Affairs. (2009). *Reaction plans for accelerating economic recovery*. Taipei.

Ministry of Transportation and Communication. (1999). Study on the effects of fewer working days on domestic tourism activities. Taipei: Statistics Bureau, MOTC.

Murphy, P. E. (2013). *Tourism: A Community Approach (RLE Tourism)*. Routledge.

National Statistics Bureau. (2005). *Statistic of Social Development in R.O.C. Taipei*. Retrieved March 4, 2005, from http://www.stat.gov.tw

Nissan, E., Galindo, M. A., & Méndez, M. T. (2011). Relationship between tourism and economic growth. *Service Industries Journal*, *31*(10), 1567–1572. doi:10.1080/02642069.2010.485636

Oppermann, M. (1995). Holidays on the farm: A case study of German hosts and guests. *Journal of Travel Research*, *34*(1), 63–67. doi:10.1177/004728759503400108

Park, A. (2009). 'Sellinga small state to the world: Lithuanias struggle in building its national image. *Place Branding and Public Diplomacy*, *5*(1), 67–84. doi:10.1057/pb.2008.25

Popescu, I. A., Paun, C., Nicolescu, L., & Draghici, A. (2008). Romania trying to be a European brand. *Management & Marketing-Bucharest*, (1), 61-72.

Pritchard, A., & Morgan, N. J. (2001). Culture, identity and tourism representation: Marketing Cymru or Wales? *Tourism Management*, *22*(2), 167–179. doi:10.1016/S0261-5177(00)00047-9

Ritchie, B., Mules, T., & Uzabeaga, S. (2008). *Visitor attraction satisfaction benchmarking project*. Sustainable Tourism CRC.

Robinson, J., & OConnor, N. (2013). Ballyhoura - A Case Study of Cohesive Rural Tourism Planning in Ireland. *Tourism Planning & Development*, *10*(3), 307–318. doi:10.1080/21568316.2012.747988

Song, H., van der Veen, R., Li, G., & Chen, J. L. (2012). The Hong Kong tourist satisfaction index. *Annals of Tourism Research*, *39*(1), 459–479. doi:10.1016/j.annals.2011.06.001

Su, B. (2011). Rural tourism in China. *Tourism Management*, *32*(6), 1438–1441. doi:10.1016/j.tourman.2010.12.005

Su, C. S., & Sun, L. H. (2007). Taiwans Hotel Rating System A Service Quality Perspective. *The Cornell Hotel and Restaurant Administration Quarterly*, *48*(4), 392–401. doi:10.1177/0010880407305836

Taiwan Review. (2009, August 1). Welcoming the World. *Taiwan Review*.

Taiwan Tourism Bureau. (2010a). Taiwan Tourism Bureau, R.O.C. *2010 Annual Survey Report on Visitors Expenditure and Trends in Taiwan*. Retrieved January 1, 2013, from http://admin.taiwan.net.tw

Taiwan Tourism Bureau. (2010b). *Taiwan Tourism Bureau, R.O.C.* Retrieved September 12, 2013, from http://www.tbroc.gov.tw

Taiwan Tourism Bureau. (2011). *Regulations for the Management of Home Stay Facilities*. Taiwan Tourism Bureau.

Taiwan Tourism Bureau. (2012). *2011 Survey of Travel by R.O.C Citizens*. Retrieved January 21, 2014, from http://admin.taiwan.net.tw

Taiwan Tourism Bureau. (2013a). *Taiwan Tourism Bureau, R.O.C.* Retrieved May 20, 2013, from http://www.taiwan.net.tw

Taiwan Tourism Bureau. (2013b). *Taiwan Tourism Bureau, R.O.C.* Retrieved May 18, 2013, from http://admin.taiwan.net.tw/statistics

Thomas, R. (1998). *Management of small tourism and hospitality firms*. Cassell plc.

Thomas, R., Shaw, G., & Page, S. J. (2011). Understanding small firms in tourism: A perspective on research trends and challenges. *Tourism Management*, *32*(5), 963–976. doi:10.1016/j.tourman.2011.02.003

Tourism Bureau. (2003). *The 2002 annual report on tourism*. R.O.C.

Tourism Bureau. (2008). Welcome to Taiwan: Experience the true heart of Taiwan. *Travel in Taiwan, 28*.

Tsai, H. C. (2007). Agricultural Globalization and Rural Tourism Development in Taiwan. *Asia Journal of Management and Humanity Sciences*, *2*(1-4), 1–13.

United Nations. (2013). Retrieved May 27, 2013, from http://www.un.org/en/aboutun/history/index.shtml

United Nations Educational, Scientific, and Cultural Organization. (2013). Retrieved May 27, 2013, from http://www.unesco.org/new/en/unesco/about-us/who-we-are/history

Urry, J. (2002). *The Tourist Gaze* (2nd ed.). London: Sage.

Wang, J. C. (2009). An analysis on the development strategy of Taiwan's six new emerging industries. *Economic Outlook*, *127*, 35–38.

Wang, J. C. (2010). The strategies adopted by Taiwan in response to the global financial crisis, and Taiwans role in Asia-Pacific economic integration. *Japan and the World Economy*, *22*(4), 254–263. doi:10.1016/j.japwor.2010.06.006

Wang, L. E., Cheng, S. K., Zhong, L. S., Mu, S. L., Dhruba, B. G., & Ren, G. Z. (2013). Rural tourism development in China: Principles, models and the future. *Journal of Mountain Science*, *10*(1), 116–129. doi:10.1007/s11629-013-2501-3

Weng, C. C., & Wang, K. L. (2004). Scale and scope economies of international tourist hotels in Taiwan. *Tourism Management*, *25*(6), 761–769. doi:10.1016/j.tourman.2004.06.005

World Health Organization. (2013). *Summary of probable SARS cases with onset of illness from 1 November 2002 to 31 July 2003*. Retrieved May 20, 2013, from http://www.who.int/csr/sars/country/table2004_04_21/en/index.html

World Tourism Organization. (2010). *United Nations World Tourism Organization Tourism Highlights, 2010 Edition*. Retrieved January 14, 2016, from http://www.unwto.org/facts/eng/pdf/highlights/UN-WTO_Highlights10_en_HR.pdf

World Tourism Organization. (2012). *United Nations World Tourism Organization Tourism Highlights, 2012 Edition*. Retrieved January 14, 2016, from http://www.unwto.org/facts/eng/pdf/highlights/UN-WTO_Highlights10_en_HR.pdf

World Tourism Organization. (2013). *United Nations World Tourism Organization Annual Report 2013*. Retrieved January 14, 2016, from http://www2.unwto.org/publication/unwto-annual-report-2013

World Travel and Tourism Council. (2012). Travel and Tourism Economic Impact 2012 Taiwan. London, UK: Author.

Wu, W. C., & Yang, C. Y. (2010). An empirical study on the impact of differences in bed and breakfast service quality attributes on customers' revisiting desires. *The International Journal of Organizational Innovation*, *2*(2), 223–240.

Yang, C. C., Jou, Y. T., & Cheng, L. Y. (2011). Using integrated quality assessment for hotel service quality. *Quality & Quantity*, *45*(2), 349–364. doi:10.1007/s11135-009-9301-4

Yang, C. H., Lin, H. L., & Han, C. C. (2010). Analysis of international tourist arrivals in China: The role of World Heritage Sites. *Tourism Management*, *31*(6), 827–837. doi:10.1016/j.tourman.2009.08.008

Yuan Control. (2004). *The survey of issues related to Ocean and Taiwan*. Taipei: Author.

Zane, B. (1997). The B&B guest: A comprehensive view. *The Cornell Hotel and Restaurant Administration Quarterly*, *38*(4), 6–75. doi:10.1016/S0010-8804(97)84308-X

Zehrer, A., Crotts, J. C., & Magnini, V. P. (2011). The perceived usefulness of blog postings: An extension of the expectancy-disconfirmation paradigm. *Tourism Management*, *32*(1), 106–113. doi:10.1016/j.tourman.2010.06.013

Ziegler, J., Dearden, P., & Rollins, R. (2012). But are tourists satisfied? Importance-performance analysis of the whale shark tourism industry on Isla Holbox, Mexico. *Tourism Management*, *33*(3), 692–701. doi:10.1016/j.tourman.2011.08.004

Chapter 14
Tourism-Led Growth Hypothesis and Foreign Direct Investment in ASEAN

Praopan Pratoomchat
Bates College, USA

ABSTRACT

This study tests the relationships of visitor spending, foreign direct investment in the tourism sector, and the gross domestic product (GDP) per capita among members of the Association of Southeast Asian Nations (ASEAN) during the period of 1988 to 2011 to prove the tourism-led growth hypothesis. The results of panel regression show that tourism-led growth hypothesis is valid for the ASEAN countries. Factors determining the GDP per capita in these countries are visitor spending, foreign investment and government consumption in tourism sector, human capital and trade openness. The results from this study suggest that the governments of the ASEAN countries are able to have effective growth policies by encouraging foreign direct investment in the tourism sector and improving their human capital. Therefore, ASEAN Economic Community (AEC) which will strengthen and facilitate investment cooperation and human capital developments in the tourism sector among ASEAN countries will have a significant benefit to economic growth in the region.

INTRODUCTION

Tourism is one of the world's fastest growing industries. It is an agglomeration of many activities: transportation, accommodation, the restaurant industry, the entertainment industry, sports and recreation, and other activities that support the demand derived from tourists. Tourism requires strong support from financial facilities, telecommunication services, and other environmental factors to determine visitor demand. Players in the industry range from small-scale businesses to transnational corporations (TNCs).

In developing countries, the tourism industry has become a major source of foreign exchange revenues. It generates jobs and promotes economic diversification. It can generate spillover effects: further investments, jobs, and growth in other sectors of the economy. However, since the tourism sector

DOI: 10.4018/978-1-5225-2078-8.ch014

depends largely on the demand of foreign visitors, it is sensitive to external shocks, whether economic, environmental, or political. Wages in the tourism sector are considered relatively low, and jobs in this sector are considered labor intensive. The tourism sector is sometimes called a pro-poor industry. It can be associated with criminal activities such as sex tourism. With all the positive and negative effects, a country has to carefully consider the net benefits before making a decision to support the expansion of tourism. A fine balance needs to be maintained in order for developing countries to capture the benefits of this growing economic activity at minimum or sustainable costs (UNCTAD, 2007).

By 2015, Association of Southeast Asian Nations (ASEAN) aim to establish the ASEAN Economic Community (AEC), a security, economic and socio-cultural community of over 600 million people which will account for nearly 5% of world GDP (World Economic Forum, 2012). The Southeast Asian region endowment for tourism includes a wealth of cultural heritage and nature. It possesses a long tradition of tourism and locates in the heart of Asia. They have been joining forces to address travel and tourism–related issues, which greatly benefit from regional cooperation, such as promotion and marketing, connectivity, environment protection, visa policies and mobility, and sector liberalization. The ASEAN member have reached agreements on several aspects. If the AEC makes ASEAN members a stronger connection through market liberalization and factor of production flows, there are a significant opportunity for travel and tourism sector to grow from both inside and outside the region.

Because most countries in Southeast Asia are in the developing country group, there are some gap of investment and saving represented by problems of infrastructure and financial resources. Domestic capital is not sufficient to facilitate a growing sector such as tourism. Also there is little recent literature on FDI and tourism in developing countries, particularly from the empirical perspective (UNCTAD, 2007) and little evidence of either mapping of FDI in the tourism industry or the economic impact of FDI in the tourism industry. The impact of FDI varies according to the specific country and the historical context. UNCTAD (2007) finds that the impact depends upon the host country's level of economic and human development, including the extent to which it can leverage the presence of TNCs to foster domestic enterprise. This ability is related to host countries' absorptive and productive capacities. Another factor influencing the impact of FDI is the motivation and corporate strategy. The main questions in this study are whether FDI in the tourism sector strongly contributes to economic growth in the country, what are directions of causality among FDI in tourism sector, tourist spending, human capital index, exchange rate, trade openness, government consumption in tourism sector and economic growth in the country and is the tourism-led growth hypothesis valid in Southeast Asia.

This paper evaluates the causality and long-run relationship of international tourist spending, FDI in tourism industry, and economic growth in ASEAN countries using the panel co-integration approach and causality test then proves the tourism-led growth hypothesis using FDI as one of the main variables. The study estimates the relationship among expansion in the tourism sector (visitor spending), FDI in tourism industry, and the GDP per capita in the case of members of the Association of Southeast Asian Nations (ASEAN) during 1988-2011. The method used in the study is ordinary least square analysis. The results show that the FDI in the tourism industry has a significant role in the GDP per capita in the Southeast Asian region. Other factors determining the GDP per capita in these countries are human capital, trade openness, and government consumption per output. The results from this study confirm the tourism-led growth hypothesis and indicate that the governments of ASEAN countries are able to have an effective growth policy through the tourism sector using the promotion of tourism FDI.

DEFINITION OF TOURISM AND ITS ECONOMIC IMPACTS

The World Tourism Organization defines travel and tourism as follows:

Traveling to and staying in places outside their usual environment for not more than one consecutive year for leisure, business and other purposes. (World Tourism Organization, 1995, p.10).

The first tier of the tourism industry definition includes enterprises that are directly involved in the production and consumption of tourism services. The second tier is called "tourism economy." It involves people and firms that indirectly participate. Tourism industry does not appear as a formal industry in the national account systems. Therefore, it has been a difficult task to collect the data and quantify the size of the industry since some tourism-related activities fall into categories of other formal industries. For example, hotels and restaurants are counted in the construction industry. WTO-OECD-Eurostat Inter-secretariat Working Group has developed tourism satellite account (TSA). TSA was endorsed by the Statistical Commission of the United Nations in 2000 (UNCTAD, 2007). TSA adopts the basic system of concepts, classifications, definitions, tables, and aggregate systems of national accounts 2008 (NSA, 2008), the international standard for a systematic summary of national economic activity, from a functional perspective. There are 12 national account industries, all of which are in the service sector, with half related to transportation.

According to the World Travel & Tourism Council, this study categorizes the impact of the tourism sector on the economy as direct or indirect impacts. Direct impacts are from the industries that deal directly with tourists, including hotels, travel agents, airlines and other passenger transportation services, as well as the activities of restaurant and leisure industries that deal directly with tourists. Direct impact is equivalent to total internal travel and tourism spending within a country less the purchases made by those industries (including imports). Indirect and induced impacts include three factors: capital investment by all industries directly involved in travel and tourism, government collective spending in support of tourism activity, and supply-chain effects, which include purchases of domestic goods and services directly by different industries within travel and tourism as input to their final tourism output. The induced contribution to GDP is the boarder contribution to GDP and employment of spending by those who are directly or indirectly employed by the travel and tourism industry.

The World Travel & Tourism Council and World Tourism Organization emphasized three roles of tourism. Firstly, tourism benefits through the creation of sustainable enterprises and decent jobs, provides the necessary security for millions of people worldwide. Secondly, it is a major source of foreign exchange which is needed for developing countries' development. Finally, tourism is increasingly interconnected with environmental sustainability (Chheang, 2013). Environmentally responsible tourism is one of the new growth poles of the 'green economy', providing sustainable infrastructure, business opportunities and jobs and income (World Tourism Organization, 2012).

FACTS AND FIGURES OF TOURISM AND FDI IN SOUTHEAST ASIA

Tourism is a part of the service sector, which has an increasing share in the GDP component of the ASEAN countries. In 2012, the service sector accounted for the highest share of GDP in eight ASEAN member states, whereas in 2008, it was the main source of national income in only six ASEAN countries (ASEAN Secretariat, 2013). Therefore, the service sector has become the main driver of growth. Strong support of the tourism-led growth hypothesis can lead to effective growth policy implications. The ASEAN tourism industry has played a significant role in the economic growth of the region. Tourists are attracted to ASEAN countries because of the culture and history, the good weather, and the natural beauty of the region. It is interesting to speculate how much the tourism industry affects overall economic growth in this region. The Asia Pacific is one of the most dynamic regions which attract both domestic and international tourists from all over the world (Chheang, 2013). It is estimated by the World Tourism Organization that the Asia Pacific region will be the world's second-most important tourist destination after Europe in 2020.

Up until early 1980s, ASEAN relied largely on agriculture and the export of primary products as a foreign exchange receipts. The global economic recession after the oil crisis in 1970s forced the government in ASEAN to find a new source of foreign exchange. Tourism had become a key industry in the exports to earn foreign exchanges.

The World Economic Forum (2012) had measured the travel and tourism competitiveness index (TTCI) in collaboration with expert from the sector. Their framework aims to measure the factors and policies that make it attractive to develop the travel and tourism sector in different countries (World Economic Forum, 2012, pp.vii). They used three subindexes to measure including regulatory framework, business environment and infrastructure, and the human cultural and natural resources. Singapore has the highest rank, followed by Malaysia, Thailand, Brunei, Indonesia, Vietnam, the Philippines, and Cambodia. The government prioritization of travel and tourism is a significant strength shared by the most ASEAN countries. Also, the region's affordability is also considered a major reason why a lot of visitors decide to travel to ASEAN countries. On the other hand, the World Economic Forum's study revealed that major challenges for ASEAN countries for travel and tourism are inadequate infrastructure, poor public health situation and environmental stewardship. The governments experience the challenge of balancing the socio-economic interest of different stakeholders.

Economic Contribution of Tourism in Southeast Asia

With respect to tourism statistics in ASEAN, tourist per capita or tourist spending in ASEAN is presented in Table 1, calculated using total tourism receipts (Current $US) per number of tourist arrivals. In 2012, three countries with the highest tourist spending per capita among ASEAN countries were Singapore, Thailand, and Brunei. The countries with lowest tourist spending per capita were Laos, Cambodia, and Myanmar. The overall trend of tourist spending per capita fluctuated from 1995 to 2012. In Lao, Malaysia, Myanmar, Thailand, and Singapore, tourist spending per capita dropped in 2005 compared to 1995 figures and picked up again in 2012. In Brunei, the Philippines, and Vietnam, tourist spending per capita increased in the 17-year period. In Cambodia, the trend increased in 2005 and then slightly dropped in 2012.

For the number of international arrivals, ASEAN is expected to receive approximately 107 million international tourists in 2015. ASEAN tourism is strongly linked with Northeast Asian countries like China, Japan and South Korea which are very important market for Southeast Asia. Malaysia, Thailand, and Singapore had the highest number of visitors in 2012. The highest growth in number of international arrivals was in Lao in 2012 at 21.8.45% compared to the number in 2005. Cambodia's visitors in 2005 compared to 1995 increased by 546.36%. In 2012, the number of international arrivals in Cambodia increased 152.04% compared to the number in 1995. Vietnam is another country with high growth in the number of visitors. In 2005, there was a 157.36% increase compared with 1995 and a 96.95% increase in 2012 compared with 2005. Myanmar in 2012, compared with 2005, had a significant increase of 155.60%. Among other countries in ASEAN, the number of international visitors also has increased substantially during the 17 years.

From the outstanding performance of the tourism industry in ASEAN, we can see that it has been expanding for almost two decades. Since the tourism sector is becoming a great player in the GDP of ASEAN countries, research on the relationship between the performance of the tourism sector and GDP can provide crucial information for policy formulation and strategic planning by ASEAN governments, as well as tourism businesses. This study estimates the relationship between GDP per capita in nine countries that were members of ASEAN from 1995 to 2011 using dynamic panel data analysis.

Table 1. Tourist per capita in ASEAN for 1995, 2005, and 2012 (Current US Dollars)

	1995	2005	2012
Brunei	N/A	1515.87	1617.83
Cambodia	322.73	653.31	558.04
Indonesia	1209.30	1018.39	1176.40
Laos	866.67	212.80	215.42
Malaysia	675.3247	632.28	808.97
Myanmar	1444.44	357.76	749.36
The Philippines	648.30	1050.32	1146.74
Thailand	1331.56	1046.25	1688.29
Singapore	1253.87	877.10	1735.54
Vietnam	N/A	661.49	997.37

*Brunei data in the 2012 column are the tourists per capita in 2009 from the data availability limit.
**Myanmar data in the 2012 column are the tourists per capita in 2011 from the data availability limit.
Source: World Travel and Tourism Council (2015)

Table 2. Number of international tourist arrivals (Person)

	1995	2005	2012
Brunei	N/A	126,000	209,000
Cambodia	220,000	1,422,000	3,584,000
Indonesia	4,324,000	5,002,000	8,044,000
Laos	60,000	672,000	2,140,000
Malaysia	7,469,000	16,431,000	25,033,000
Myanmar	117,000	232,000	593,000
The Philippines	1,760,000	2,623,000	4,273,000
Thailand	6,952,000	11,567,000	22,354,000
Singapore	6,070,000	7,079,000	11,098,000
Vietnam	1,351,000	3,477,000	6,848,000

Source: World Travel and Tourism Council (2015)

The results confirm that the better performance of the tourism industry led to higher GDP per capita in these countries. Other significant factors determining GDP per capita in this model are human capital, government consumption share, and trade openness.

Visitors generate important service exports revenues for Southeast Asian countries. In 2014, visitor exports generated $112.0 billion or 7.1% of total exports. This is forecast to grow by 4.2% in 2015 and by 5.7% from 2015 to 2025.

The total GDP contribution of travel and tourism to GDP in Southeast Asian countries was $291 billion or 12% of GDP in 2014, which includes both direct and indirect contributions. The direct contribution of travel and tourism to GDP in Southeast Asian countries was 4.8% of GDP in 2014, and is forecast to rise by 5.0% in 2015 and by 5.4% from 2015 to 2025, to $209.4 billion in 2025 (WTTC, 2015). Of 12 regions in the world, Southeast Asia has the second fastest growth rate. The total contribution of travel and tourism to employment, including jobs indirectly supported by the industry, was 9.7% of total employment (29,358,000 jobs). This contribution is expected to rise by 2.9% in 2015 to 30,196,000 jobs and by 2.7% to 39,227,000 jobs in 2025 (11% of total).

Table 3. Role of travel and tourism in Southeast Asian economies

	Southeast Asia		World Average	
	2014	2015 (% Growth)	2014	2015 (% Growth)
Direct Contribution to GDP (USD Billion)	117.9	5.0	2,364	3.7
Total Contribution to GDP (USD Billion)	291.8	5.4	7,580.9	3.7
Visitor Exports (USD Billion)	112.0	4.2	1,383.8	2.8
Capital Investment (USD Billion)	49.0	5.8	814.4	4.8
Direct Contribution to Employment (1,000 jobs)	11,262	2.8	105,408	2.0
Total Contribution to Employment (1,000 jobs)	29,358	2.9	276,845	2.6

Source: Compiled from WTTC Travel & Tourism Economic Impact 2015, World Travel & Tourism Council (WTTC)

Figure 1. Total contribution of tourism industry to GDP
Source: WTCC (2015)

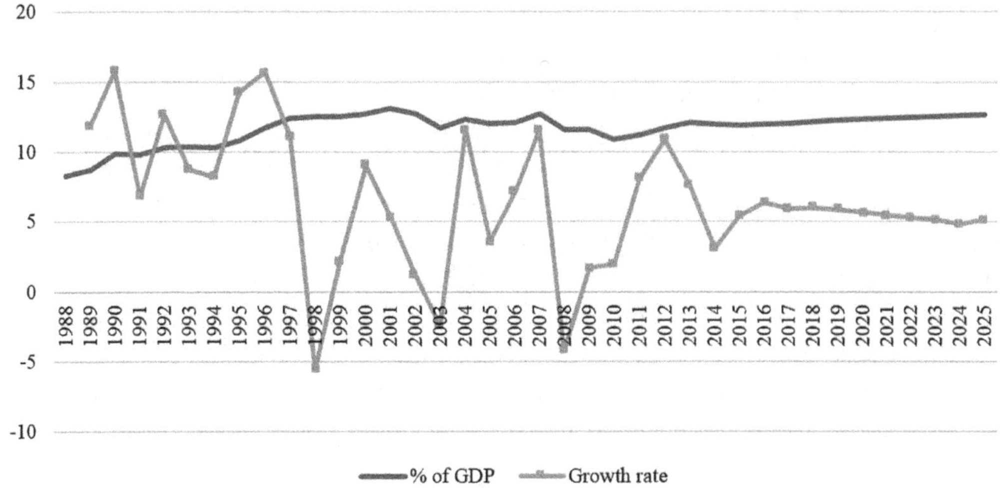

Figure 2. Total contribution to employment in tourism industry
Source: WTCC (2015)

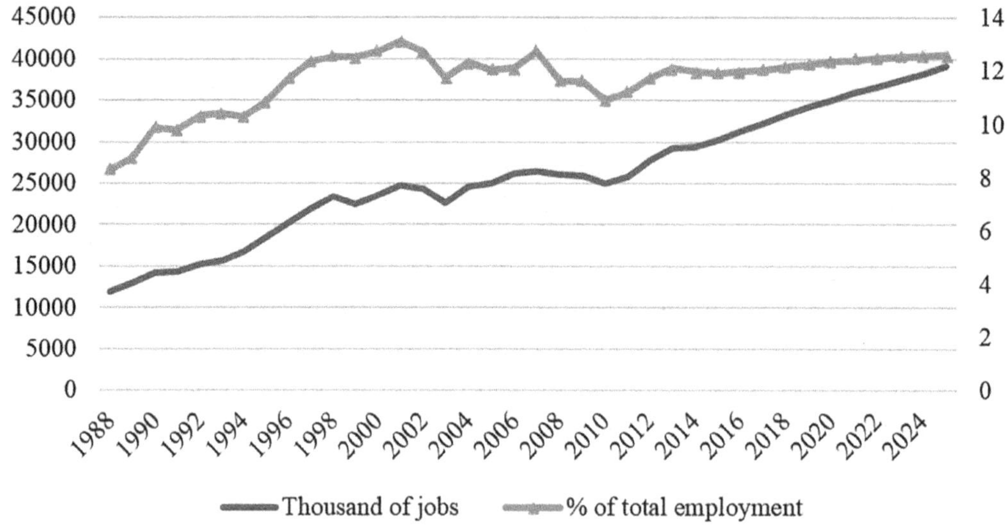

Tourism FDI in Southeast Asia

Strong macroeconomic fundamentals, improved policy environment and greater regional market prospects in ASEAN have increased foreign investors' confidence. In 2013, ASEAN attracted $122 billion, accounting for 8% of the global FDI (ASEAN and UNCTAD, 2014). ASEAN member states also increase their investment inside the region (17% of total FDI inflows).

According to Table 4 total net inflows of ASEAN in 2014 was $136,181.4 million. Singapore had the highest total net inflow share of 53% of all ASEAN countries, followed by Indonesia, Thailand and Malaysia. Most of net inflow to Singapore was from outside of ASEAN while Indonesia had the highest share of Intra-ASEAN inflows. Since Southeast Asian countries have diverse levels of development, the effects from FDI are different by country. Singapore is the only developed country in the region. Malaysia is in the upper-middle income group. Thailand, the Philippines, and Indonesia share middle-income status, but other countries in this region are in the lower-income group.

According to UNCTAD's World Investment Report (UNCTAD, 2012), FDI in service sector and primary sector rebounded in 2011 after falling sharply in 2009 and 2010, at the expense of manufacturing sector. Developing Asia remains the world's largest recipient region of FDI inflows (UNCTAD, 2014). Service has the largest share of announced green field project and mergers and acquisition (M&A) deals. However, FDI growth in ASEAN has been slowing down due to some economic situations. Indonesia got affected from financial turmoil in mid-2013. Malaysia's inflows has increased in 2014 by 22% as a result in rising FDI in services (UNCTAD, 2014). Thailand's political instability has discouraged a lot of FDI inflows especially from Japanese investors. ASEAN's low income economies inflows varied. Myanmar's inflows increased in 2014 by 17% (UNCTAD, 2014) while Cambodia, Vietnam and Lao's inflows are fairly constant.

The perception of the expanding tourism industry leads to misconceptions about the trend in tourism FDI. UNCTAD (2007) finds that FDI in tourism is still rather low in both developed and developing coun-

Table 4. Foreign direct investment net inflows, intra- and extra-ASEAN ($ million)

Country	2013[2/]			2014 p/			Share to total, 2014		
	Intra-ASEAN	Extra-ASEAN	Total net inflow	Intra-ASEAN	Extra-ASEAN	Total net inflow	Intra-ASEAN	Extra-ASEAN	Total net inflow
Brunei Darussalam	-58.0	783.5	725.5	141.2	427.0	568.2	0.6	0.4	0.4
Cambodia	298.8	976.1	1,274.9	372.5	1,354.0	1,726.5	1.5	1.2	1.3
Indonesia	8,721.1	9,722.7	18,443.8	13,458.8	8,817.5	22,276.3	55.2	7.9	16.4
Lao PDR	104.6	322.1	426.7	137.9	775.3	913.2	0.6	0.7	0.7
Malaysia	2,187.5	10,109.9	12,297.4	2,771.1	7,943.0	10,714.0	11.4	7.1	7.9
Myanmar	1,186.8	1,434.1	2,620.9	683.6	262.6	946.2	2.8	0.2	0.7
Philippines	(41.7)	3,901.5	3,859.8	78.6	6,121.9	6,200.5	0.3	5.5	4.6
Singapore	3,665.0	52,473.3	56,138.3	4,532.7	67,565.6	72,098.3	18.6	60.4	52.9
Thailand	1,256.8	11,743.0	12,999.8	653.9	10,884.0	11,537.9	2.7	9.7	8.5
Viet Nam	2,078.6	6,821.4	8,900.0	1,547.1	7,653.0	9,200.1	6.3	6.8	6.8
Total	**19,399.6**	**98,287.5**	**117,687.0**	**24,377.4**	**111,803.9**	**136,181.4**	**100.0**	**100.0**	**100.0**
ASEAN 6[1/]	15,730.7	88,733.8	104,464.5	21,636.3	101,759.0	123,395.3	88.8	91.0	90.6
CLMV[1/]	**3,668.9**	**9,553.6**	**13,222.5**	**2,741.1**	**10,045.0**	**12,786.1**	11.2	9.0	9.4

Note: p/ is preliminary figures. 1/ is ranked according to FDI inflows in 2014; covers countries on which data is available.
Source: ASEAN Foreign Direct Investment Statistics Database as of 26 May 2015 (Data is compiled from submission of ASEAN Central Banks and National Statistical Offices through the ASEAN Working Group on International Investment Statistics (WGIIS).

tries compared to FDI in other sectors. UNCTAD (2007) noted that this is partly because tourism-related FDI is concentrated in just a few of many related activities covered by the definition of tourism, mostly hotels and restaurants and car rentals. On the basis of the UNCTAD research, FDI and TNC presence is concentrated in a handful of 12 classified activities, including hotels, restaurants, second homes, travel agencies, cultural services, sports and recreational services, and all modes of passenger transportation services. Although the absolute value of FDI is low, it can be very important to the host economies.

Asia is a growing destination for tourism industry investors. Greenfield investments are the most common form of investment. Global data on green field investments in foreign hotels show that South, East, and Southeast Asia were the top regions in which the hotel TNCs planned to expand their investment during the period of 2006-2011 (UNCTAD, 2007). Travel and tourism investment in Southeast Asian countries in 2014 was $49.0 billion or 7.4% of total investment. It should rise by 5.8% in 2015 and by 6.4% over the next 10 years to $96.4 billion in 2025 or 8.1% of total investment.

FDI in Tourism of Southeast Asia is relatively low compared to other sectors. Numbers of foreign affiliates in hotels and restaurants compared to total number of foreign affiliates in 2012 of Southeast Asia are relatively low compare to electrical and electronic equipment sector as shown in Table 5.

The significant recipient industries in ASEAN were electronics and automotive and automotive parts (ASEAN and UNCTAD, 2014). According to ASEAN Secretariat and UNCTAD (2014), service and the manufacturing sector continued to dominate FDI flows in the region. Two sectors accounted for about 90% of FDI flows in ASEAN in 2012 and 2103. According to Table 6, there was an increasing trend of foreign value added in ASEAN exports. Service sector had 21.9% share of total foreign value added

Table 5. Share of foreign affiliates in ASEAN's hotels and restaurants and electric and electronic equipment in 2012

Country	Hotels and Restaurants		Electric and Electronic Equipment	
	Number of Foreign Affiliates	% of Total Foreign Affiliates	Number of Foreign Affiliates	% of Total Foreign Affiliates
Singapore	53	1.46	199	5.49
Malaysia	39	1.09	527	14.67
Thailand	38	3.07	373	30.15
Indonesia	65	1.89	382	11.10
Philippines	43	2.80	222	14.47
Brunei	1	1.45	1	1.45
Vietnam	11	0.89	185	14.98
Cambodia	2	2.70	2	2.70
Lao	3	12.50	N/A	5.49
Myanmar	2	4.65	N/A	14.67

Sources: Calculated from International Trade Center and World Development Indicators (2012)

in exports in 2011. However, when the author consider the categories of the service sector, hotels and restaurants shared only 17.9% of total service sector.

Shares of number of foreign affiliates in hotels and restaurant which are the main subsector in tourism industry are around 1% to 4% in 2012 in ASEAN countries except Lao which had higher share of foreign hotels and restaurants than electric and electronic equipment sector. According to UNCTAD (2007), hotels and restaurants are the subsector inside tourism sector which has the highest FDI flow.

Table 6. Share of foreign value added in ASEAN export, 1990 and 2011

Sector/Industry	1990	2011
All Industries	**34.1**	**37.0**
Primary total	7.5	37.0
Manufacturing total	44.4	45.8
Service total	18.6	21.9
Electricity, gas and water	10.9	21.8
Construction	24.9	31.3
Trade	14.9	14.9
Hotels and restaurants	12.4	17.9
Transport, storage and communications	27.7	30.8
Finance	10.6	14.3
Business activities	19.2	23.1
Health and social services	18.3	22.6

Note: Based on two-to three-digit level of ISIC
Source: UNCTAD-Eora GVC Database, ASEAN and UNCTAD (2014)

We can see that even it is the subsector with the highest FDI in tourism, it is still very low compared with other important sector in the Southeast Asian economies. According to the statistics of UNCTAD based on Bloomberg and companies' website (2014), among 50 largest ASEAN companies with regional presence only two companies on the list are in the tourism sector (Genting of Malaysia is in hotel and leisure and Singapore Airline is in airlines). Therefore, ASEAN countries have a lot of room for the investment from both developed countries and intra-ASEAN in tourism sector. The potential benefit that ASEAN countries can get from FDI are technological transfers in terms of physical capital and human capital, management skills for sustainable tourism, and sufficient tourism infrastructure that can support the expanding tourism sector. FDI in the tourism sector of the Southeast Asia hence becomes an important issue to study.

Despite of the increasing FDI in tourism, its share is relatively low compared to manufacturing sectors. Total contribution of travel and tourism in Southeast Asia is 12% of GDP in 2014 (WTCC, 2015). However, the investment was only 7.4% of total investment. UNCTAD's report on FDI in tourism (2007) noted that even though tourism is the largest industry in many countries, it appeared to be one of the least globalized. Moreover, tourism FDI is concentrated primary in developed countries. It appears that 85-90% of TNC hotels are located in developed countries with only small proportion in developing countries. For the investment trend, travel and tourism investment growth in Southeast Asia is 5.7%, slower than South Asia, Middle East and Northeast Asia (WTCC, 2015).

STUDIES OF TOURISM-LED GROWTH HYPOTHESIS

The field of research on the relationship between tourism and economic growth is still in development. Many studies have been conducted examining the impact of expansion of tourism sector. There are both

Figure 3. Capital Investment in Travel and Tourism Industry of ASEAN
Source: WTCC (2015)

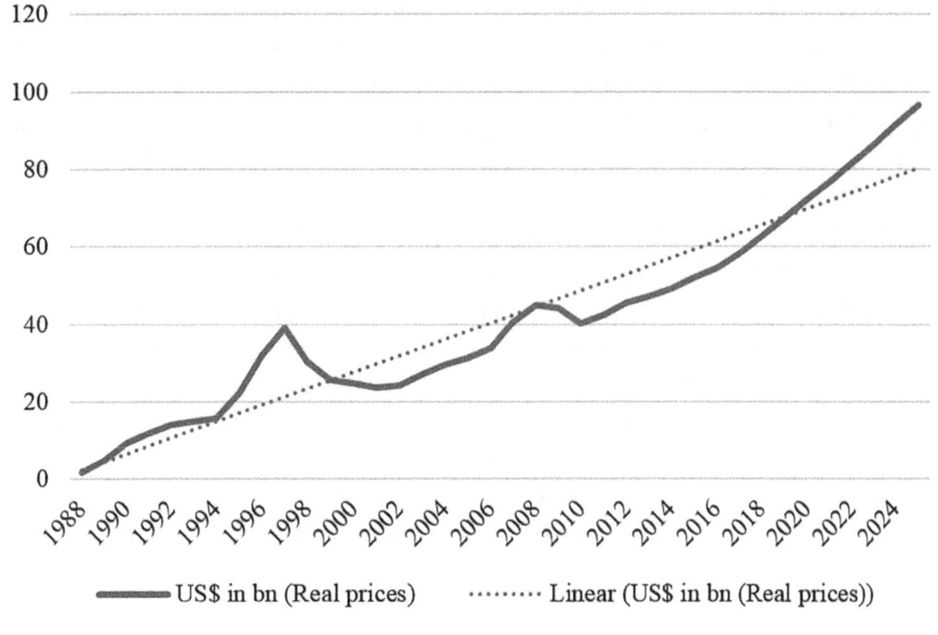

Table 7. Regional Ranking of Travel and Tourism Investment

Rank	Travel & Tourism Investment	2015% Growth
1	South Asia	9.2
2	Middle East	6.6
3	North East Asia	6.4
4	South East Asia	5.7
5	Latin America	5.1
6	North Africa	5.1
7	Sub Saharan Africa	4.8
8	North America	4.7
9	Caribbean	4.2
10	European Union	3.4
11	Oceania	1.1
12	Other Europe	-2.3

Source: WTCC (2015)

positive and negative economic impacts from tourism expansion. It leads to economic development in terms of job creation and poverty reduction. However, many side effects from tourism expansion without cautions can lead to environmental or cultural degradations such as sex tourism.

There are two generally accepted methodologies that can be applied to estimate the impact of tourism on GDP: the Tourism Satellite Account (TSA) and the Computable General Equilibrium (CGE) models (Cortes-Jimemez, Pulina, Prunera, & Artis, 2009). The Tourism Satellite Account (TSA) approach uses the contribution of tourism and traveling to different sectors of the economy. This method is commonly employed by international organizations and governments. There are two mainstream schools of thought stemming from the export-led growth hypothesis since tourism is one component of the service sector that can be exported. Nowak et al. (2007) argue that the growth is derived from the volume of production inputs, so-called Tourism Capital Imports to Growth (TKIG). Economic development in this proposition is achieved through imports of capital goods, which are mainly financed by tourism receipts (Sinclair & Bote Gomez, 1996). Another school of thought is the tourism-led growth hypothesis, which states that output growth can be generated by expanding international tourism as a non-traditional export. In contrast to the extensive literature on exports and growth, empirical studies that focus on the tourism-led growth hypothesis are still scarce.

The tourism-led growth hypothesis was first proposed by Ghali (1976) for the case of Hawaii. Ghali (1976) followed the method of Caves and Holton (1959), who studied the impact of exports on the Canadian economy. Ghali (1976) used the construction of an econometric model that captures as best as possible the essential features of the economy. Ghali's model became the starting point for the tourism-led growth hypothesis. In this study, the author uses the same basic model as Ghali (1976). Oh (2002) studied the contribution of tourism development to economic growth in the Korean economy using Engle and Granger's two-stage approach and a bivariate vector autoregression (VAR) model. He found that there is no long-run equilibrium relation between tourism growth and economic growth. Oh's test implies the one-way causal relationship of economy-driven tourism growth. He concluded that the tourism-led growth hypothesis does not hold for the Korean economy. However, Chen and Chiou-Wei's (2009) study of the causal relationship between tourism and economic growth in Korea and Taiwan found that the tourism-led growth hypothesis is supported for both countries. Chen and Chiou-Wei (2009) used a method different from that proposed by Oh. They used the EGARCH-M model with an uncertainty factor to capture the uncertainty in the economies. Balaguer and Cantavella-Jorda (2004) found indirect causality for tourism and economic growth. Later, Eugenio-Martin et al. (2004) studied the relationship between tourism and economic growth for Latin American countries from 1985 to 1998 using the panel data approach and the Arellana-Bond estimator for dynamic panels. They found that the tourism sector is adequate for the economic growth of medium- or low-income countries, though not necessarily for developed countries. They also estimated inverted causality to explain the tourism arrivals conditional on GDP and other covariates. Eugenio-Martin et al. (2004) used the generalized least square AR(1) panel data model to conduct the estimates and found that low-income countries seem to need adequate levels of infrastructures, education, and development to attract tourists. Medium-income countries need a high level of social development, such as health services, and high GDP per capita levels to attract tourists. They also found that the price of the destination is irrelevant for tourism growth.

Sequeira and Compos (2005) studied international tourism and economic growth using the panel data approach. They reported that tourism-specialized countries grow more than others, which is inconsistent with the endogenous growth theory since tourism is not high intensity in R&D or the large-scale sector. Sequeira and Compos (2005) added variables linked to the proportion of tourism in exports and GDP rather than using only arrivals of tourists per capita as a proxy for tourism intensity. They used the panel data method and concluded that tourism on its own cannot explain the higher growth rates. Lee and Chang (2007) applied the new heterogeneous panel cointegration technique to reinvestigate the long-run comovements and casual relationship between tourism development and economic growth for OECD and non-OECD countries for the 1990-2002 period. On a global scale, Lee and Chang (2007) found a substantial relationship between GDP and tourism development. Tourism development has a greater impact on GDP in non-OECD than in OECD countries. The greatest impact is in Africa. In the long run, Lee and Chang (2007) found that there is a unidirectional causality relationship for tourism development and economic growth in OECD and bidirectional relationships in non-OECD countries, but only weak relationships in Asia.

Cortes-Jinenez et al. (2009) studied tourism and exports as a means of growth by considering both exports and tourism as potential influencing factors for economic growth. They used data from Italy from 1954 to 2000 and Spain from 1964 to 2000. They used standard cointegration and Granger causality techniques to prove the hypothesis and found that both exports and tourism have a significant effect on long-term growth in both countries. Kartircioglu (2009) used the bound test for cointegration and Granger causality tests to investigate level relationships and the direction of causality between international tourism and economic growth in the case of Malta. His results revealed that a long-run equilibrium relationship exists between international tourism and economic growth in Malta. On the other hand, Granger causality test results suggest that both the tourism-led growth hypothesis and the output-driven tourism hypothesis can be confirmed. In Pakistan's case, Khalil et al. (2007) attempted to determine whether there is a unidirectional or bidirectional causal relationship between tourism and economic growth using the cointegration test. They found that tourism growth influences increases in the economy in the short run, that the combination of results points to two-way causality for economic growth and tourism growth, and that economic expansion is necessary for the development of tourism in Pakistan. They found a significant impact of tourism on Pakistan's economy, which justifies the necessity of public intervention aimed at promoting the demand for tourism and providing the development of the supply side of tourism industry. Lean and Tang (2010) extended the Gunduz and Hatemi-JA (2005) study on the tourism-led growth hypothesis with Malaysian data and found that the causality is valid and stable over the sample period, January 1989 to February 2009.

Brida et al (2014) conducted a literature review on the tourism-led growth hypothesis. They provided an in-depth analysis of the tourism-led growth hypothesis based on a revision of approximately 100 published empirical papers together with the theoretical papers. Brida et al (2014) found that the tourism-led growth hypothesis is confirmed for the studied countries with few exceptions. The validity of tourism-led growth hypothesis is consistent with the fact that the government can promote economic growth through tourism industry. However, they found that the results should not be generalized to all countries since the number of studied countries is still limited and unbalanced.

Tourism needs support from global market access, capital, and infrastructure. The availability of financial resources is critical for achieving further tourism development and economic growth (Samimi, A.J., Sadeghi, S. and Sadeghi, S., 2013). Capital inflow can facilitate the financial resource factor for the tourism industry. Hence, foreign direct investment (FDI) is important for steady and sustainable growth in the tourism sector. Transnational corporations (TNCs) are key players in the flow of international capital. Green field investment generates technological transfer and a spillover effect. FDI is seen as an important element in the solution to the problem of scarce local capital and overall low productivity in many developing economies (De Mello, 1999; Eller et al., 2005).

The literature reviews on the tourism-led growth hypothesis demonstrates the different methods were used to conduct the study. The most frequently used method is Granger causality tests to consider the direction of the relationship between tourism growth and output growth. Another important method is dynamic panel analysis to estimate the relationship between growth and tourism development. However, panel data analysis using ordinary least square is chosen to conduct the estimation in this study because of the limit of time-series data to conduct dynamic model. The use of panel data not only allows an increase in degree of freedom and better estimation of large sample properties but also reduces the endogeneity problem from a specific country effect that can be correlated with the repressor (fixed effects) or random effects (Sequeira & Compos, 2005). In this study, the author also adds FDI in the tourism sector as an important factor to stimulate the economic growth and benefits other variables in the model specification.

DATA AND METHODOLOGY

This study tests tourism-led growth hypothesis using econometric technique. Before running the regression, the author conducts nonstationary test using the Im, Pesaran, and Shin (2003) method which allow the heterogeneity of autoregressive root under the alternative hypothesis. Being unable to reject the null hypothesis of this test implies that the variables have a unit root.

After nonstationary test, the paper presents tests for the long-run relationship among variables using the method based on Engle and Granger (1987) co-integration test. To test the co-integration, if the variables are co-integrated or have a long-run relationship, the residuals of the regression will be the integration of order zero, I(0), or stationary. Co-integration implies that there are relationships between the variables but does not tell the direction of the causal relationship. To adapt the co-integration test using panel data, Pedroni (1999, 2004) extended the Engle and Granger's test (1987) to allow heterogeneous intercepts and trend coefficients across cross-sections.. Kao's (1999) Augmented Dickey-Fuller (ADF) test and Pedroni's (1999) test are employed in this study to test the long-run equilibrium relation between the dependent variables and all independent variables as a group. Kao's (1999) test is based on the ADF test with a null hypothesis of no co-integration with a *t*-distribution. Kao's test provides an alternative hypothesis of four statistics: *v*-statistics, *rho*-statistics, PP-statistics, and ADF-statistics. For Pedroni's (1999) test, the null hypothesis is also no co-integration in panel against two alternatives. Pedroni's test allows for an individual-specific fixed effect and time trend. The second alternative hypothesis is tested using group *rho*-statistics, group PP-statistics, and group ADF-statistics. Pedroni (1999, 2004) showed that the panel ADF-statistics and group ADF-statistics have better sample properties than other co-integration tests.

After the long-run relationship test, the study uses the pairwise Granger causality test to test the causality between variables. Each of the null hypotheses states that one variable does not cause another variable using F-statistics. To test for Granger causality in the time domain, the minimum mean square prediction error is used as the criterion to evaluate incremental predictive power. In the bivariate case, the presence of Granger causality is tested by evaluating the predictive power of one time series for another. The linear-reduced form vector autoregression (VAR) follows:

$$X_t = A(L)X_t + B(L)Y_t + U_{x,t} \quad (1)$$

$$Y_t = C(L)X_t + D(L)Y_t + U_{Y,t} \quad (2)$$

where A(L), B(L), C(L), and D(L) are one-sided lag polynomials of orders a, b, c, and d in the lag operator L with roots outside the unit circle and no roots in common. The regression errors, $\{U_{X,t}\}$ and $\{U_{Y,t}\}$, are assumed to be mutually independent and individually i.i.d. with zero mean and constant variance. To test for strict Granger causality from Y to X in this linear framework, a standard joint test (F or chi-square test) of exclusion restrictions is used to determine whether the lagged Y has significant linear predictive power for current X. Bidirectional causality exists if Granger causality runs in both directions, in which case, the coefficients on the elements in both B(L) and C(L) are jointly different from zero.

The last step in the methodology in this study is to conduct the ordinary least square estimation of the relationship between real GDP and variables determining the income. The hypothesis of this study is that real GDP is determined by foreign direct investment in tourism industry, visitor spending, human capital, degree of trade openness, government spending, and exchange rates (local currency to $US). The study adopts the ordinary least square technique to eliminate the biased estimator from the presence of outlying observation.

Theoretical Framework

In the Neoclassical growth model developed by Solow-Cass-Koopman, GDP growth depends on the initial level of income. Barrow and Sala-i-Martin (1992) and Mankiw, Romer, and Weil (1992) proposed the concept of conditional convergence, allowing the differences among countries in the model. Letting y_{it} denote log per capita of income or output, the growth rate can be written as:

$$y_{it} - y_{it-1} = a + \beta y_{it-1} + u_{it} \tag{3}$$

where a is the steady state, $-1 < \beta < 0$, if there is convergence between countries, and u_{it} is the error term.

If the steady state among countries is different, the structural model can be extended to:

$$y_{it} - y_{it-1} = a + \beta y_{it-1} + \varphi X_{it-1} + u_{it} \tag{4}$$

where X_i is the vector of determinants of the steady state per capita income. The determinants can be in terms of population growth, government policies, political stability, physical and human capital, openness, and other growth-related variables.

Model and Variables

The augmented Solow-Swan model from (4) can be taken as the baseline empirical growth model. There are four important determinations of growth: initial income, rate of physical accumulation, human capital accumulation, and population growth. This study constructs the augmented Solow-Swan model as the core and then adds more specific variables including visitor spending and foreign direct investment in the tourism sector, as well as trade openness, human capital, government consumption, and exchange rate into the model specification. The model specification used in this study's estimation is:

$$\begin{aligned}\log\left(PERCAPITA_{it}\right) = c + \varphi_1 \log\left(\frac{VS}{POP}\right)_{it} + \varphi_2 \log(HC)_{it} + \varphi_3 \log(EXR_{it}) + \\ \varphi_4 \log\left(OP_{it}\right) + \varphi_5 log\left(\frac{FDIT}{POP}\right)_{it} + \varphi_6 \log(GOVC / POP)_{it} + \alpha_i + n_t + u_{it}\end{aligned} \tag{5}$$

with $t = 1,\ldots,24\left(1988 - 2011\right); i = 1,\ldots,9$ and $u_{it} \sim N\left(0, \sigma_i^2\right)$

To test the relationship between tourism and economic growth, this study uses the flows variables, which are standard in the endogenous growth literature (Barro, 1991; Barro & Sala-i-Martin, 1995). The variables in the equation (5) are defined:

- Visitor spending per capita (*VS/POP*) is used to represent tourism activity in the country. Visitor spending data is obtained from WTCC (2015) measured by money spent from foreign visitors to a country. This variable is a key component of direct contribution of tourism and travels to the economy. Positive sign is expected;
- Index of Human Capital (*HC*) is used as a proxy for human capital. The data is obtained through the Penn World Table 8 (Feenstra et al., 2-15) and a positive sign is expected;
- EXR is the exchange rate in local currency to $US;
- Openness is measured by exports plus imports to output ratio (*OP*). It represents the impact of trade openness on economic growth. Data is obtained from World Economic Indicator (World Bank, 2015). A positive sign is expected;

- Government spending per capita (*GOVC/POP*) is amount of government spending on tourism industry per number of population. It is used to measure long-run crowding-out and the overall negative effect of government spending in long-run growth or the effect of government purchase in tourism sector to GDP per capita. There is no expectation on the sign since it depends on which side's magnitude is bigger;
- Foreign direct investment in tourism industry per capita (*FDIT/POP*) represents the capital investment spending by all industries directly involved in the travel and tourism industry. *FDI/POP* also constitutes investment spending by other industries on specific tourism assets such as new visitor accommodations and passenger transport equipment, as well as restaurants and leisure facilities for specific tourism use, which is consistent with total tourism gross fixed capital formation in Table 8 of the TSA: RMF 2008. Positive sign is expected.

The study uses E-views 8.0 software to obtain the result of all test and estimations. The dataset used in this study are obtained from the Penn World Table 8 (Feenstra et al., 2-15), the World Development Indicators (World Bank, 2015) and United Nations Conference on Trade and Development (UNCTAD, 2007), and the World Travel & Tourism Council (WTTC, 2015). The panel data consist of a 24-year period from 1988 to 2011 in nine countries in ASEAN: Brunei, Cambodia, Indonesia, Lao, Malaysia, the Philippines, Singapore, Thailand, and Vietnam.

RESULTS

Unit Root Test

Table 8 gives the Im, Pesaran and Shin W-test on a unit root for the variables under consideration. The null hypothesis is that there is a unit root (assumes individual unit root process). The results show that every variable except population (pop) is integrated order 1 or I(1).

After testing the unit root, although the variables are not stationary at their levels, they are stationary at their first-differenced series. Therefore, the panel data of these variables can be used in the study at least for long-run relationship.

Table 8. Im, Pesaran and Shin W-tests for a Unit Root

Variables	Level (with intercept)	1st differenced	P-value
realgdp	Unit root	Stationary	0.0050
VS	Unit root	Stationary	0.0000
HC.	Unit root	Stationary	0.0103
OP	Unit root	Stationary	0.0000
FDIT	Unit root	Stationary	0.0000
POP	Stationary		0.0255
EXR	Unit root	Stationary	0.0001
GOVC	Unit root	Stationary	0.0000

Table 9. Kao and Pedroni Panel Co-integration Test

Kao test ADF-stat	Pedroni test						
	Panel				Group		
	v-stat	*rho*-stat	PP-stat	ADF-stat	*rho*-stat	PP-stat	ADF-stat
-1.5559*	13.0027**	2.1854	-4.6170**	-6.7989**	3.5921	-8.3765**	-4.9477**

**Indicates statistical significance at 5% level. *Indicates statistical significance at 10%. Individual fixed effect and individual trend are allowed in the Pedroni test.

Panel Co-integration Test

The next step is testing the long-run relationships between these variables. This study uses Kao's and Pedroni's panel co-integration test.

From the Kao test, the ADF-statistics show that the null hypothesis of no co-integration can be rejected at the 10% level of significance. This is supported by the Pedroni test in which v-statistics, PP-statistics, and ADF-statistics show the rejection of the null hypothesis. For the group test, PP-statistics and ADF-statistics also demonstrate co-integration among the variables.

Causality Test

The co-integration test is able to show long-run relationships between variables. However, it does not show the direction of the relationships or the causality. The technique to show the directions of relationships is the pairwise Dumitrescu Hurlin panel causality test, which allows an individual coefficient for each country. The results are shown in Table 10.

From the results of Pairwise Dumitrescu Hurlin panel causality test, this study found the following:

- GDP Per capita in Southeast Asia is determined by government consumption in tourism per capita (GOVCPOP) and human capital (HC)
- Foreign Direct investment inflows in the tourism industry per capita (FDITPOP) are caused by trade openness (OP) and visitor spending per capita (VSPOP).
- The human capital index (HC) is caused by GDP Per capita (PERCAPITA), trade openness (OP) and visitor spending per capita (VSPOP)
- Government consumption in tourism per capita (GOVCPOP) is caused by human capital (HC).
- Trade openness (OP) is caused by GDP Per capita (PERCAPITA), government consumption in tourism industry per capita (GOVCPOP), and human capital (HC),
- Visitor spending per capita (VSPOP) is caused by GDP per capita (PERCAPITA) and human capital (HC).
- The exchange rate (EXR), in term of local currency to US dollar, is caused by GDP per capita (PERCAPITA), foreign direct investment in tourism industry per capita (FDITPOP), human capital (HC), trade openness (OP), and government spending in tourism sector per capita (GOVCPOP)

The focus of this study is the relationships among FDI in the tourism industry, GDP Per capita, and visitor spending. From the causality test, the author found that FDI in the tourism industry and visitor

Table 10. Pairwise Dumitrescu Hurlin Panel Causality Tests (Lag 2)

Null Hypothesis:	Prob.
GOVCPOP does not homogeneously cause FDITPOP	0.0146
FDITPOP does not homogeneously cause GOVCPOP	0.4113
HC does not homogeneously cause FDITPOP	0.0937
FDITPOP does not homogeneously cause HC	0.2169
PERCAPITA does not homogeneously cause FDITPOP	4.E-05
FDITPOP does not homogeneously cause PERCAPITA	0.1336
OP does not homogeneously cause FDITPOP	0.0947
FDITPOP does not homogeneously cause OP	0.8275
EXR does not homogeneously cause FDITPOP	0.1976
FDITPOP does not homogeneously cause EXR	0.0044
VSPOP does not homogeneously cause FDITPOP	4.E-09
FDITPOP does not homogeneously cause VSPOP	0.9364
HC does not homogeneously cause GOVCPOP	0.0003
GOVCPOP does not homogeneously cause HC	0.2107
PERCAPITA does not homogeneously cause GOVCPOP	0.8806
GOVCPOP does not homogeneously cause PERCAPITA	0.0001
OP does not homogeneously cause GOVCPOP	0.6240
GOVCPOP does not homogeneously cause OP	0.0001
EXR does not homogeneously cause GOVCPOP	0.1181
GOVCPOP does not homogeneously cause EXR	2.E-07
VSPOP does not homogeneously cause GOVCPOP	0.2485
GOVCPOP does not homogeneously cause VSPOP	0.3283
PERCAPITA does not homogeneously cause HC	0.0786
HC does not homogeneously cause PERCAPITA	0.0003
OP does not homogeneously cause HC	4.E-16
HC does not homogeneously cause OP	1.E-06
EXR does not homogeneously cause HC	0.4878
HC does not homogeneously cause EXR	2.E-09
VSPOP does not homogeneously cause HC	0.0018
HC does not homogeneously cause VSPOP	1.E-08
OP does not homogeneously cause PERCAPITA	0.1243
PERCAPITA does not homogeneously cause OP	0.0022
EXR does not homogeneously cause PERCAPITA	0.1937
PERCAPITA does not homogeneously cause EXR	0.0679
VSPOP does not homogeneously cause PERCAPITA	0.1688
PERCAPITA does not homogeneously cause VSPOP	0.0512
EXR does not homogeneously cause OP	0.8214
OP does not homogeneously cause EXR	0.0026

continued on following page

Table 10. Continued

Null Hypothesis:	Prob.
VSPOP does not homogeneously cause OP	0.0001
OP does not homogeneously cause VSPOP	0.2390
VSPOP does not homogeneously cause EXR	0.7126
EXR does not homogeneously cause VSPOP	0.1724

**Indicates statistical significance at 5% level. *Indicates statistical significance at 10%.

spending does not have direct effects to GDP per capita. However, the effects from the visitor spending and FDI in tourism sector can possibly have indirect effect through other variables. The effect of each variables will be estimated using ordinary least square estimation.

Tourism-Led Growth Hypothesis Estimation Results

The focus of this study is to test tourism-led growth hypothesis using visitor spending and FDI in tourism sector as representatives of tourism sector. The contribution of hypothesized variables to real GDP per capita in Southeast Asia is presented in Table 11.

Table 11 gives the estimation result for the panel least square estimation. The results show that visitor spending per capita (VS/POP), FDI in the tourism industry per capita (FDIT/POP), human capital (HC),

Table 11. Tourism-Led Growth Hypothesis Estimation Dependent variable: log(PERCAPITA)

Variable	Coefficient	Std. Error	t-Statistic	Prob.
C	3.394200	0.199679	16.99827	0.0000
LOG(VS/POP)	0.075579	0.013229	5.713275	0.0000
LOG(FDIT/POP)	0.094711	0.009832	9.633192	0.0000
LOG(HC)	2.770748	0.130604	21.21484	0.0000
LOG(OP)	-0.141603	0.040719	-3.477535	0.0006
LOG(EXR)	0.023516	0.014573	1.613606	0.1083
LOG(GOVC/POP)	0.093318	0.031700	2.943772	0.0036
	Effects Specification			
Cross-section fixed (dummy variables)				
R-squared	0.997985	Mean dependent var		7.689407
Adjusted R-squared	0.997837	S.D. dependent var		1.547638
S.E. of regression	0.071976	Akaike info criterion		-2.354935
Sum squared resid	0.989489	Schwarz criterion		-2.112614
Log likelihood	257.5583	Hannan-Quinn criter.		-2.256932
F-statistic	6756.327	Durbin-Watson stat		0.454124
Prob(F-statistic)	0.000000			

trade openness (OP) and government consumption in tourism sector per capita (GOVC/POP) have statistically significant effects to determine real GDP per capita. Trade openness has negative coefficients. Exchange rate does not have statistically significant in GDP per capita change.

From the result, we can confirm that the tourism-led growth hypothesis is valid for ASEAN countries from the positive significant coefficient of visitor spending per capita (VS/POP). When the visitor spending per capita increases by 1%, the GDP per capita will increase by 0.08%. In addition of foreign investment in the tourism sector per capita into the model, the result shows that it significantly has a positive effect to the GDP per capita. When the foreign investment in the tourism sector increases by 1%, GDP per capita will increase by 0.01%.

In terms of relationship between human capital and GDP per capita, if human capital index increases by 1%, GDP per capita will increase by 2.77%. If the trade openness increase by 1%, GDP per capita tend to decrease by 0.14%. The trade openness coefficient has unexpected sign which will be needed to study further. The government consumption in the tourism industry also has a statistically significant effect to the GDP per capita. If the government consumption in the tourism sector increases by 1%, GDP per capita increases by 0.09%.

From the causality analysis, the result showed that FDI and visitor spending do not homogeneously cause GDP per capita to change while the panel least square estimation result shows that there are some significant effects. The author's hypothesis is that there are some indirect effect of FDI of tourism industry and visitor spending through other variables that can pass the contribution to economic growth or the relationship is not in the linear form.

Panel least square estimation also allow the cross-sectional effects to identify the differences among ASEAN countries. The magnitude of cross-sectional effects is shown in table 12. Singapore and Brunei have highest intercepts since they are in high-income country group. Malaysia, Thailand, Indonesia are in the middle income country group therefore the intercept is positive. The lowest intercept is in Lao, Cambodia, Vietnam

Table 12. Cross-sectional effects

Country	Cross-Sectional Effects
Brunei	1.283616
Cambodia	-0.901738
Indonesia	0.006223
Lao	-1.114873
Malaysia	0.185871
Philippines	-0.791436
Singapore	1.649491
Thailand	0.144499
Vietnam	-0.767364

CONCLUSION AND DISCUSSION

With the best tourism assets in terms of culture, heritage, natural sites and wildlife, Southeast Asian countries attract a steady flows of international visitors. The tourism industry has a growing share in the GDP of this region. This study tests the relationships between real GDP per capita and tourism sector in terms of visitor spending and FDI in this sector and other related variables. The study empirically estimates the contribution of the tourism FDI and visitor spending to GDP per capita in nine ASEAN countries-- Brunei, Cambodia, Lao, Malaysia, the Philippines, Singapore, Thailand, and Vietnam--from 1988 to 2011. The result of panel least square from this study is consistent with the tourism-led growth hypothesis, which states that the tourism industry can bring sustainable economic growth in the long run.

The methods used in this study are panel co-integration using Kao's and Pedroni's tests, causality test and panel data analysis using Ordinary Least Square (OLS).The variables hypothesized to influence the GDP per capita are visitor spending per capita, FDI in tourism industry per capita, government consumption in tourism per capita, trade openness, human capital, and exchange rate. The study tests the presence of a unit root and panel co-integration before conducting the causality test and regression. The results of panel cointegration test show that there are long-run relationships among variables. For the direction of causality, the study uses pairwise Dumitrescu Hurlin panel causality test which allows an individual coefficient for each country and found that human capital and the government consumption in the tourism industry per capita can cause the real GDP to change. For other causalities, it can be summarized by figure 4.

The empirical findings have implications in providing policy makers directions for achieving a path of growth through tourism industry. The evaluation of tourism-led growth hypothesis in ASEAN countries benefit the governments that are willing to stimulate the economy using travel and tourism sector. The increasing number of international arrivals stimulates the demand for other goods and services. The extended linkages of the tourism sector to other downstream sectors are key to success if governments use tourism as a focused sector of their growth policy. The tourism sector is closely related to the food

Figure 4. Causality of Real GDP, FDI in Tourism sectors, Visitor Spending and Other Relating Variables

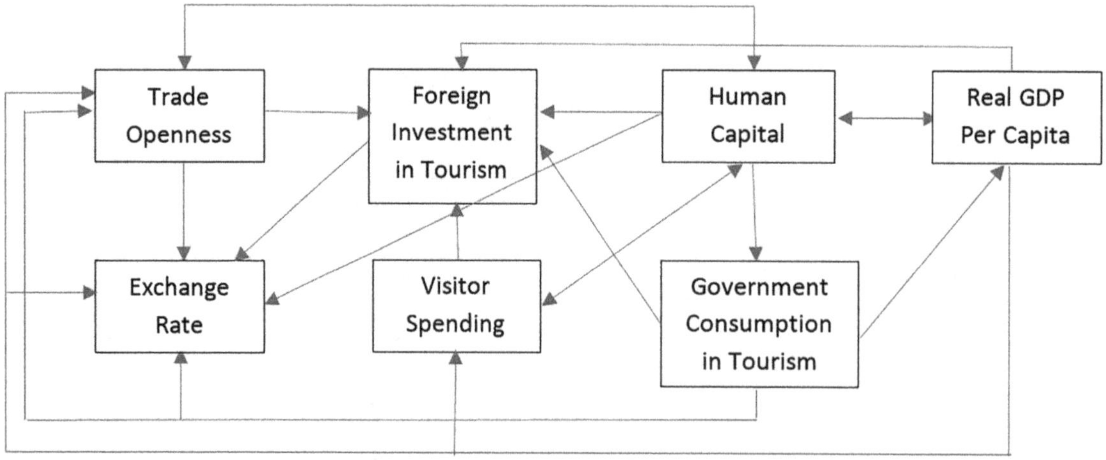

and restaurant industries, hotel and accommodation services, healthcare industries, the transportation industry, and other related goods industries. In addition, tourism provides greater foreign exchange, which leads to appreciation of the local currency and alleviates a gap in foreign exchange and finance imports of capital goods.

However, governments should also aware of the disadvantages of tourism development, the potentially negative influences on communities and their residents. Moreover, when the domestic demand is stimulated, the possible result can be rising domestic prices or inflation. The expenditures by foreign tourists may also alter domestic consumption patterns via the so-called demonstration effect, and this can, in fact, be inflationary (Lee & Chang, 2008). According to Sinclair (1998), another possible cost of the expansion of tourism industry is the expenditure for the provision and maintenance of infrastructure in the form of water, roads, airports, sanitation, and energy. Gursoy and Rutherford (2004) studied the host attitudes toward tourism and concluded that tourism imposes other costs on the host country such as increased pollution, congestion, or despoliation of fragile environments. In short, countries should be aware of the adverse economic, socio-cultural, and environmental impacts that result from the expansion of tourism.

The estimation results also reveal that trade openness and human capital are effective channels to promote growth in ASEAN. Trade openness can spur expansion in exports, which will lead to higher productivity and more efficient resource allocation in ASEAN countries. Human capital contributes to economic growth through the supply side. Human capital allows the production function of the aggregate economy to shift upward without experiencing the diminishing return on capital. This finding is satisfactory and also consistent with Keynesian economic theory and the literature on trade and human capital.

POLICY RECOMMENDATIONS

Tourism-related policies should be consistent with the wider economic policy framework. In order to obtain the maximum benefits and minimize the cost of expanding travel and tourism sector, the host country has to be prepared to absorb the negative impacts. Since tourism industry involves in many economic sectors and activities, the number and range of policies that need attention are large and diverse. They include town planning, environmental regulations, labor standards, tourism educational policies, transportation safety standards, a wide range of financial regulations and telecommunication laws and regulations.

1. From the result of the study, human capital can be increased by FDI in the tourism sector and has a large role in promoting GDP per capita. Spillover effects can be a major source of human capital increase. The government can encourage more FDI in term of green field investment which there are on-the-job trainings. In other direction, the government can allocate the budget to promote the tourism educations to provide some skills in the tourism industry in order to prepare local communities for the foreign investment in their areas.
2. Degree of openness is another important factor to attract the FDI in the tourism industry in ASEAN. Government can provide some incentives to attract FDI such as grants or loans at discount interest rates, tax holidays, or facilitate the TNC by providing some infrastructure.
3. ASEAN has an advantage of regional integration which has been accelerated in recent years. At the ASEAN Economic Ministers Meeting in August 2011, member states agreed to accelerate the

implementation of programs towards the ASEAN Economic Community (AEC) in 2015, focusing on initiatives that would enhance investment promotion. This can be an opportunity to enhance competitiveness in attracting FDI in tourism sector and TNC activities.

4. The development of infrastructure alongside the tourism can assist the process of industrialization and modernization (Hitchcock et al., 1993). When the infrastructure is ready, FDI in tourism will increase and that will stimulate the GDP per capita according to the result of this study.

REFERENCES

Arellano, M., & Bond, S. (1991). Some tests of specification for panel data: Monte Carlo evidence and an application to employment equations. *The Review of Economic Studies*, *58*(2), 277–297. doi:10.2307/2297968

ASEAN Secretariat. (2015). *ASEAN Statistics*. Available: http://www.asean.org/news/item/tourism-statistics

ASEAN Secretariat and United Nation Committee of Trade and Development (UNCTAD). (2015). *ASEAN Investment Report 2013-2014: FDI Development and Regional Value Chains*. Available: http://investasean.asean.org/files/upload/AIR%202013-2014%20FINAL.pdf

Balaguer, J., & Cantavella-Jorda, M. (2004). Structural change in exports and economic growth: Cointegration and casuality. Analysis for Spain (19612000). *Applied Economics*, *36*(5), 437–477. doi:10.1080/00036840410001682179

Barro, R. J. (1991). Economic growth in a cross section of countries. *The Quarterly Journal of Economics*, *106*(2), 407–443. doi:10.2307/2937943

Barro, R. J., & Sala-i-Martin, X. (1992). Convergence. *Journal of Political Economy*, *100*(2), 223–251. doi:10.1086/261816

Barro, R. J., & Sala-i-Martin, X. (1995). *Economic growth*. New York, NY: McGraw Hill.

Benhabib, J., & Spiegel, M. (2000). The Role of Financial Development in Growth and Investment. *Journal of Economic Growth*, *5*(4), 341–360. doi:10.1023/A:1026599402490

Brida, J. G., Coretes-Jimenez, I., & Pulina, M. (2014). Has the tourism-led growth hypothesis been validated? A Literature review. *Current Issues in Tourism*.

Caselli, F., Esquivel, G., & Lefort, L. (1996). Reopening the Convergence Debate: A New Look at Cross-Country Growth Empirics. *Journal of Economic Growth*, *1*(3), 363–360. doi:10.1007/BF00141044

Caves, R. E., & Holton, R. H. (1959). *The Canadian Economy: Prospect and Retrospect*. Cambridge, MA: Harvard University Press. doi:10.4159/harvard.9780674493704

Chen, C. F., & Chiou-Wei, S. Z. (2009). Tourism expansion, tourism uncertainty and economic growth: New evidence from Taiwan and Korea. *Tourism Management*, *30*(6), 812–818. doi:10.1016/j.tourman.2008.12.013

Chheang, V. (2013). *Tourism and Regional Integration in Southeast Asia. V.R.F. Series No. 481, Institution of Developing Economies*. Japan External Trade Organization.

Cortes-Jimemez, I., Pulina, M., Prunera, C. R., & Artis, M. (2009). *Tourism and Exports as a Means of Growth. Working Paper 2009/10*. Research Institute of Applied Economics.

De Mello, L. R. (1999). Foreign Direct Investment-Led Growth: Evidence from Time-Series and Panel Data. *Oxford Economic Papers*, *51*(1), 133–151. doi:10.1093/oep/51.1.133

Eller, M., Haiss, P., & Steiner, K. (2005). *Financial Direct Investment in the Financial Sector: The Engine of Growth for Central and Eastern Europe?* Europalnstitut Working paper No.69. Vienna University of Economics and Business Administration.

Engle, R. F., & Granger, C. W. J. (1987). Cointegration and error correction: Representation, estimation, and testing. *Econometrica*, *2*(2), 251–276. doi:10.2307/1913236

Eugenio-Martin, J.L., Morales, N., & Scarpa, R. (2004). Tourism and Economic Growth in Latin American Countries: A Panel Data Approach. *Nota di lavora, 26.*

European Commission, International Monetary Fund, OECD, United Nations and World Bank. (2009). *System of National Accounts 2008*. Available: https://unstats.un.org/unsd/nationalaccount/docs/SNA2008.pdf

Feenstra, R. C., Inklaar, R., & Marcel, P. (2015). The Next Generation of the Penn World Table. *American Economic Review*. Available at www.ggdc.net/pwt

Ghali, M. A. (1976). Tourism and economic growth: An empirical study. *Economic Development and Cultural Change*, *24*(3), 527–538. doi:10.1086/450895

Gunduz, L., & Hatemi-J, A. (2005). Is the tourism-led growth hypothesis valid for Turkey? *Applied Economics Letters*, *12*(8), 499–504. doi:10.1080/13504850500109865

Gursoy, D., & Rutherford, D. G. (2004). Host attitudes toward tourism: An improved structural model. *Annals of Tourism Research*, *31*(3), 495–516. doi:10.1016/j.annals.2003.08.008

Heston, A., Summers, R., & Aten, B. (2012). *Penn World Table Version 7.1*. Center for International Comparisons of Production, Income and Prices at the University of Pennsylvania.

Im, K.S., Pesaran, M.H., & Shin, Y. (2003). Testing for Unit Roots in Heterogeneous Panels. *Journal of Econometrics, 115*, 53-74.

Kao, C. (1999). Spurious Regression and Residual Based Tests for Cointegration in Panel Data. *Journal of Econometrics*, *90*(1), 1–44. doi:10.1016/S0304-4076(98)00023-2

Katircioglu, S. T. (2009). Testing the tourism-led growth hypothesis: The case of Malta. *Acta Oeconomica*, *59*(3), 331–343. doi:10.1556/AOecon.59.2009.3.4

Khalil, S., Kakar, M. K., & Waliullah, A. (2004). Role of tourism in economic growth: Empirical evidence from Pakistan economy. *Pakistan Development Review*, *46*(4), 985–995.

Lean, H. H., & Tang, C. F. (2010). Is the tourism-led growth hypothesis stable for Malaysia? A note. *International Journal of Tourism Research*, *12*(4), 375–378. doi:10.1002/jtr.759

Lee, C. C., & Chang, C. P. (2008). Tourism development and economic growth: A closer look at the panels. *Tourism Management*, *29*(1), 180–192. doi:10.1016/j.tourman.2007.02.013

Mankiw, N. G., Romer, D., & Weil, D. N. (1992). A contribution to the empirics of economic growth. *The Quarterly Journal of Economics*, *107*(2), 407–437. doi:10.2307/2118477

Nowak, J. J., Sahli, M., & Cortes-Jimenez, I. (2007). Tourism, capital good imports and economic growth: Theory and evidence for Spain. *Tourism Economics*, *13*(4), 515–536. doi:10.5367/000000007782696113

Oh, C. O. (2005). The contribution of tourism development to economic growth in the Korean economy. *Tourism Management*, *26*(1), 39–44. doi:10.1016/j.tourman.2003.09.014

Pedroni, P. (1999). Critical Values for Cointegration Tests in Heterogeneous Panels with Multiple Regressions. *Oxford Bulletin of Economics and Statistics*, *61*(s1), 653–670. doi:10.1111/1468-0084.61.s1.14

Pedroni, P. (2004). Panel Cointegration; Asymptotic and Finite Sample Properties of Pooled Time Series Tests, With an Application to the PPP Hypothesis. *Econometric Theory*, *20*(03), 597–625. doi:10.1017/S0266466604203073

Phakdisoth, L., & Kim, D. (2007). The determinants of inbound tourism in Laos. *ASEAN Economic Bulletin*, *24*(2), 225–237. doi:10.1355/AE24-2C

Sequeira, T. N., & Compos, C. (2005). *International tourism and economic growth: A panel data approach*. FEEM Working Paper 141.05. Fondazione Eni Enrico Mattei.

Sinclair, M. T., & Bote Gomez, V. (1996). Tourism, the Spanish economy and the balance of payments. In M. Barke et al. (Eds.), *Tourism in Spain: Critical perspectives*. Wallingford: C.A.B. International.

United Nation World Tourism Organization (UNWTO). (2008). *Statistics and Tourism Satellite Account*. Available: http://statistics.unwto.org/content/tsarmf-2008

United Nations Commission for Trade and Development (UNCTAD). (2007). *FDI in Tourism: The Development Dimension*. Available: http://unctad.org/en/Docs/iteiia20075_en.pdf

United Nations Commission for Trade and Development (UNCTAD). (2012). *World Investment Report*. Available: http://unctad.org/en/PublicationsLibrary/wir2011_en.pdf

United Nations Commission for Trade and Development (UNCTAD). (2014). *World Investment Report*. Available: http://unctad.org/en/PublicationsLibrary/wir2014_en.pdf

United Nations International Trade Statistics. (2008). *Trade Statistics Knowledgebase*. Available: http://unstats.un.org/unsd/tradekb/Knowledgebase/TSA-RMF-2008

World Bank. (2015). *World Development Indicators*. Available: http://databank.worldbank.org/data/home.aspx

World Economic Forum. (2015). *The ASEAN Travel & Tourism Competitiveness Report 2012: Fostering Prosperity and Regional Integration Through Travel and Tourism*. Available: http://www3.weforum.org/docs/WEF_TTCR_ASEAN_Report_2012.pdf

World Tourism Organization. (2012a). *Open Letter to Heads of Government*. Available: http://www2.unwto.org/sites/all/files/pdf/final_golden_book_open_letter_text_0/pdf

World Tourism Organization. (2012b). *Myanmar set to rejoin UNWTO*. Available: http://media.unwto.org/en/press-release/2012-05-11/myanmar-set-rejoin-unwto

World Travel and Tourism Council. (2015). *WTTC Data Gateway*. Available: http://www.wttc.org/datagateway/

KEY TERMS AND DEFINITIONS

ASEAN: Association of Southeast Asian Nations.
AEC: ASEAN Economic Community.
FDI: Foreign Direct Investment.
TNCS: Transnational Corporations.
GVCs: Global Value Chains.
ISIC: International Standard Industrial Classification.
UNCTAD: United Nation Committee on Trade and Development.
WGIIS: Working Group on International Investment Statistics.

Chapter 15 UNESCO World Heritage Designation: An Opportunity or a Threat to Hoi An Ancient Town (Vietnam)?

Huong T. Bui
Ritsumeikan Asia Pacific University, Japan

Tuan-Anh Le
Southern Cross University, Australia

Chung H. Nguyen
Vietnam National University, Vietnam

ABSTRACT

The chapter analyzes the impacts of World Heritage List designation on the local economy, residents, and environment in the Vietnamese site of Hoi An Ancient Town. Findings from the study raise concerns about managing heritage tourism in developing countries. While Hoi An successfully attracts a large number of tourists and enjoys economic success from tourism, social and environmental sustainability are in question. This case study demonstrates that management of tourism at World Heritage-listed sites is facing challenges of land speculation, inflation, commodification of local culture, and environmental degradation.

INTRODUCTION

In 1986, Vietnam embarked on a process of economic reform under the *doi moi* renovation program, and during the thirty years of implementation of a socialist market economy, tourism has been one of Vietnam's most rapidly growing economic sectors. Within the tourism economy, the ancient city of Hoi An, a UNESCO World Heritage Site, is the most important tourist destination in the centrally located Quang Nam Province. Hoi An has taken advantage of the increased international profile that accompanies UNESCO World Heritage Lists inscription by capturing external expertise and mobilizing local

DOI: 10.4018/978-1-5225-2078-8.ch015

community support to build a well-defined image of a historic city (Brooks, 2008). While the majority of studies present a supportive and positive view of tourism development in Hoi An (Hoi An Center for Monuments Management and Conservation, 2008; Di Giovine, 2009a,b), there are warnings that the town may be moving off the track of sustainable development (Avieli, 2015).

This chapter offers a critical view of the impact of World Heritage Site designation on economic, social, and environmental sustainability of the Hoi An Ancient Town. The chapter starts with a literature review of heritage tourism and UNESCO World Heritage Lists, and then provides background of the ancient town along the timeline of its development. The review encompasses a series of studies conducted by UNESCO, NGOs, scholars, and various stakeholders at the site. A comprehensive analysis of impact of tourism on the living cultural heritage of Hoi An is followed by a discussion of the influence of World Heritage designation on tourism development and town planning of the historic city.

BACKGROUND

Heritage, Heritage Tourism, and UNESCO World Heritage Designation

Recent literature on heritage study focuses on heritage connection to both the present and the future (Graham, Ashworth, & Tunbridge, 2000). Importantly, the modern-day use of heritage involves "a contemporary commodity purposefully created to satisfy contemporary consumption" (Ashworth, 1994, p. 16). Preservation of heritage links the past to the present and the future (Orbasli, 2000) by preserving not only the structure of buildings but also culture (Nyaupane, 2009). Heritage—in both its tangible and intangible aspects—is a critical resource for international tourism (Graham, 2002), particularly for developing countries (Garrod & Fyall, 2000).

Heritage tourism emerges as the most important economic activity in Vietnam (Lask & Herold, 2004). Two cities in central Vietnam—Hue and Hoi An—are examples of cities that have enjoyed both public relations and economic benefits from inscription on the UNESCO World Heritage List (Bui & Lee, 2015). However, designation as a World Heritage Site might also present dilemmas to some destinations, as UNESCO emphasizes preservation—essentially "freezing" the heritage in time—dominance of a colonial vision of history, placing universal over local values, and issues of personnel (Avieli, 2015). Capacity to manage the site after designation is also critical, as a top-down approach may centering on tangible aspects while ignoring human aspects and culture. Tourism may introduce major social change, commodify culture, and impose unwarranted modernity (Harrison, 2004).

This chapter highlights the touristic use of cultural heritage as reflected in the experiences of Hoi An Ancient Town. In transitioning from a centrally planned to a market-based economy, the government of Vietnam sees heritage tourism as a powerful economic and diplomatic tool. Consequently, heritage preservation has received a great deal of attention relative to other cultural endeavors (Saltiel, 2014). However, the politicization of heritage property, driven by enormous economic gain from tourism development, often ignores the dark side of designation as a heritage site. Using the UNESCO World Heritage Site of Hoi An as a case study, this chapter evaluates the impacts of World Heritage List designation on economic, social, and environmental aspect of the historic town.

METHODOLOGY

This research utilized intrinsic case study method (Stake, 1995; Yin, 2009) to investigate the impacts of UNESCO World Heritage Site designation on economic, social, and environmental sustainability of the Hoi An Ancient Town. The case study approach is used extensively in tourism research (Beeton, 2004; Xiao & Smith, 2006; Kibichio 2008; Le, Weaver, & Lawton, 2015). According to Yin (2009), the case study is an empirical inquiry that investigates a contemporary phenomenon in depth and within its real-life context, especially when the boundaries between phenomenon and context are not clearly evident. While impact study is not new in tourism research, little research associates UNESCO World Heritage designation to tourism impact assessment. Adopting the intrinsic case study method, the authors take a story-telling approach focusing on the case itself within the context of contemporary Vietnam and describe the phenomenon without much concern of established theories.

Hoi An Ancient Town

Hoi An Ancient Town is located in Vietnam's central coastal region of Quang Nam Province, approximately 30 km from Da Nang City and 812 km from Ha Noi to the north and 845 km from Ho Chi Minh City to the south. The history of Hoi An can be traced to the late Sa Huynh period (200 BC to 200 AD). During the Cham period (200–1500 AD), Hoi An became an important commercial port, which attracted many Arabian, Persian, and Chinese merchants trading goods such as silk, pearls, tortoise shell, gold, agar wood, and drinking water. The Cham were followed by the Dai Viet (Vietnamese), who ruled from the 15th to the early 19th century. Hoi An grew to be an important trading center both in the region and within the country, with a significant influx of Chinese and Japanese traders, and became a melting pot of migrants. In the same period, Dutch and other European traders established trading ports and Hoi An developed into one of the gateways for Christianity. By the late 18th century, Hoi An's importance as a trading port had diminished owing to political changes in the country and the region, combined with changes in Hoi An's harbor caused by siltation.

From the late 19th century, under French colonialization (1859) to the end of World War II in 1945, the return of the French to Indochina (1946–1954), the division of Vietnam into North and South Vietnam (1959–1975), and the reunification of Vietnam in 1975, Hoi An remained a quiet, rural town. However, in the 1990s it began to receive significant numbers of tourists, which brought changes in its economy and population. In 1999, Hoi An Ancient Town was added to the UNESCO World Cultural Heritage List under two criteria: as "an outstanding material manifestation of the fusion of cultures over time in an international commercial port" and as "an exceptionally well preserved example of a traditional Asian trading port" (Hoi An Center for Monuments Management and Conservation, 2008). Today, Hoi An is one of the "must-see" destinations for trans-Vietnam tours and within the triangle of Hoi An–My Son–Hue, three World Heritage Sites endorsed by UNESCO (Parnwell, 2016).

TOURISM DEVELOPMENT IN HOI AN

Tourism development in Hoi An experienced two major turning points: in 1991 and 2000. Before the 1990s, Hoi An was a small, quiet town, and young Hoianese had to move to Ho Chi Minh City (formerly

Saigon) to find jobs. The town became smaller, quieter, and virtually lifeless, as only the old stayed to care for the houses inherited from their ancestors, who were traders in the more prosperous days (Phan Nhu Ngoc Han, 2004). After the first descriptions of Hoi An appeared in the 1991 budget tourist guidebook *Lonely Planet*, backpackers began to arrive in such numbers that the Ministry of Culture and Information almost immediately established a program of tourism service (Di Giovine, 2009a). In 1991, the number of international and domestic tourists was about 3,400. By 1999, tourists numbered 158,315 (Nguyen Thi Thu Ha, 2008). In 2000, Hoi An was designated a World Heritage Site, and the number of visitors began to increase, with the number of domestic visitors doubling between 2000 and 2001 and the number of international visitors increasing by half in the same period. Figure 1 shows tourist arrivals to Hoi An from 1991–2007.

The number of both domestic and international visitors began to grow more rapidly, and in 2007, Hoi An saw a huge influx of international tourists—almost 1.5 times more than domestic tourists (608,477 vs. 424,320)—arguably resulting from the designation of Hoi An as a UNESCO World Heritage Site. This marked increase in international visitors began to place unusual demands on Hoi An for tourism amenities. As domestic tourists usually stop by Hoi An for a day or less in their trans-Vietnam tour, during the early years of growth the majority of domestic tourists were day trippers, who do not stay overnight in the town (Phan Nhu Ngoc Han, 2004). The shift to international tourism status created the need for a vastly different tourism infrastructure.

As Hoi An is well-branded with the World Heritage label, provincial government plans placed a heavy emphasis on rapid economic growth to be achieved through structural elements such as public infrastructure, private investment, and land development, with particular emphasis on resort and hotel development (Hoi An Center for Monuments Management and Conservation, 2008). Most projects are concentrated along the Da Nang–Hoi An corridor (Parnwell, 2016). It is clear that such large-scale,

Figure 1. Tourist arrivals to Hoi An (1991 – 2007)

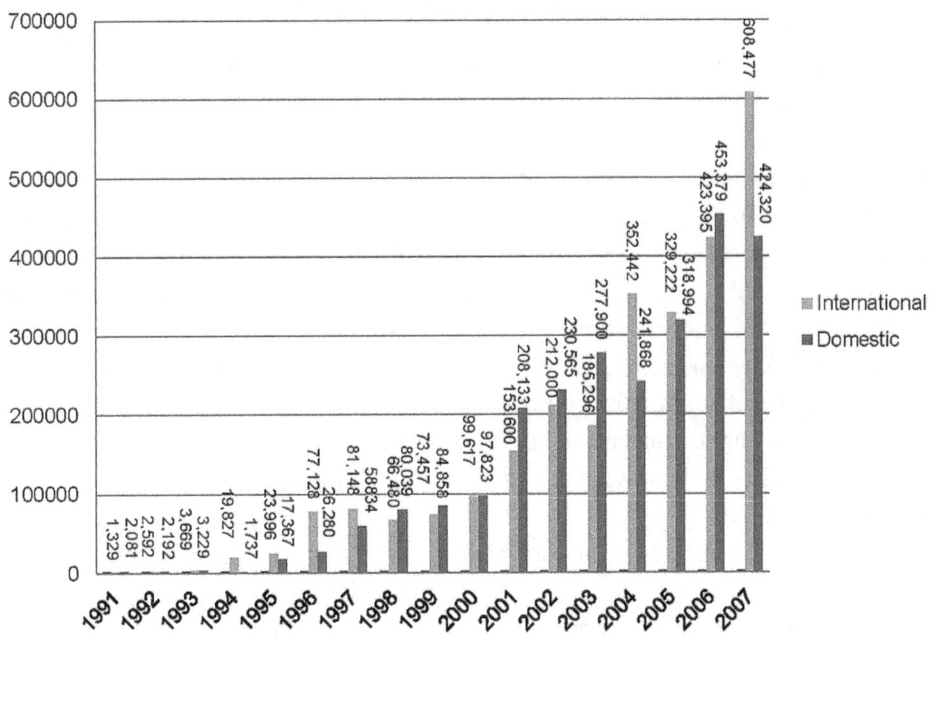

rapid development, with a heavy emphasis on building infrastructure, is likely to have a pronounced social, economic, and environmental impacts on Hoi An and the surrounding areas (Hoi An Center for Monuments Management and Conservation, 2008).

From being a backpacking, off the beaten track destination in the early 1990s, Hoi An has now transformed into a highly institutionalized mass tourist destination. However, while the physical remnants of this historic port town are evidently a factor in its inclusion on the north–south routes that most Western tourists follow in Vietnam, truly meaningful tourist engagement with the various elements of tangible heritage appears to be extremely limited (Parnwell, 2016). Most tourists seem to be more intent on purchasing tailor-made clothes, eating, drinking, partying, and spending time on the beach.

Tourism has affected the old quarter of Hoi An in several ways (Avieli, 2015). First, the traditional lifestyle, religion, and customs that had previously been attractive to tourists came under unprecedented pressures and virtually collapsed. Second, young, independent and adventurous tourists noticed that the town was becoming exceedingly touristy, grew critical of this process, increasingly expressed disappointment and left. For example, a tourist commented on Trip Advisor (2016) that "this small and cozy city is overcrowded by tourists. It is too loud and looks like decoration of a very poor theater." Thus, in becoming a mass tourism destination, Hoi An has moved away from its original identity as a uniquely cultural destination. In a further investigation of irreversible changes to the Ancient Town, the following section scrutinizes impacts resulting from increasing visitation to the site.

Heritage Conservation

The preservation of the old house, an element of tangible heritage, has fruitful results in that it brings profits from tourism to the people. Local people generally have a strong motivation to preserve their houses out of respect for the past and their ancestors (Phan Nhu Ngoc Han, 2004), and in Hoi An an entrance ticket system introduced in 1995 generates income to assist local residents in restoring their homes by supporting from 80% to 100% of the total cost of restoration. As a result, numerous homes within the historic center of Hoi An have been restored in accordance with international standards of preservation (Di Giovine, 2009a). However, while the exterior and the structure of buildings are well preserved, the functions of buildings and the living environments have changed radically, and very few traditional shops catering to the residents remain in the old quarter (Hoi An Center for Monuments Management and Conservation, 2008).

Structural preservation efforts have been accompanied by revival of intangible elements of culture for tourist consumption. To attract more tourists and lengthen their stay, Hoi An has revitalized or recreated numerous traditions, such as the Lantern Festival, an "invented tradition" designed to portray an idealized vision of Hoi An's past by bringing back "a night of the old days" (Di Giovine, 2009b, p. 224). The Lantern Festival, held each lunar month, has strongly affected the economics of Hoi An, for example through the making and selling of silk lanterns for tourist consumption and export. The festival also contributes to a sense of community constructed on the unique experience of living within the city's cultural bubble. Along with the reinvention of the Lantern Festival, other cultural initiatives seem to be successful in luring tourists to the town, such as a program banning motorcycles within the city center (Phan Nhu Ngoc Han, 2004).

Government policies also influence the economic status of Hoi An. While government policy toward the hotel sector is arguably successful in economic terms, it does not appear to favor local residents. In 2000, the local authorities decided to support only what they viewed as "quality tourism," shifting the promotional emphasis from backpacker or individual tourism to package tourism with average per-person spending of US$200 a day. The main decision regarding development was that new hotels would be allowed only if the investment involved exceeded US$1 million. In practical terms, this decision meant that only outside investors would build most new hotels, as very few people in Hoi An had the required capital (Avieli, 2015). As a result, the lifeblood of Hoi An has been replaced owing to an increasing number of investors often from Da Nang, Ho Chi Minh City and Ha Noi, who have bought properties and land for construction. This change has been accompanied by an in-migration of poor and low income people from the nearby rural areas who are looking for work. Without proper management, this rural migration could lead to social problems and unsightly slums in Hoi An (Phan Nhu Ngoc Han, 2004).

Demographic change in the local population presents authorities with a great challenge to maintain the Hoianese identity, which has been perceived as a factor driving tourists to the town. Since 2001, to ease congestion in the old quarters, the authorities have encouraged people to move by selling them land at the outskirts of the town at subsidized prices with infrastructure provided by the government (Phan Nhu Ngoc Han, 2004). Consequently, the local residents have largely moved out of their houses in the Ancient Town, taking with them the identity and the authentic traditions of Hoi An. As a result, preservation of tangible and intangible aspects of Hoi An heritage, while perceived positively by tourists, is also criticized as "museumification" (Di Giovine, 2009a, p. 261) or "the empty shell syndrome" (Avieli, 2015, p. 47). That is, the old quarter of the town is becoming a museum display, with the activities that were once part of locals' daily life now presented as if in a theater and therefore having little meaning or community function. Social life and traditions, either original or revived, have been dramatized for tourist consumption.

Village Life of Locals

The radical economic changes in Hoi An resulting from tourism are reflected in the economies of villages nearby. Agriculture, fishing, and handicraft production, which once were the backbone of Hoi An's economy, have been integrated into the tourism product supply chain. Fishing villages that once lived on catching and processing seafood products for both domestic consumption and the export market are now major suppliers for local restaurants and hotels. Handicraft industries such as tailoring, carpentry, and pottery now cater to tourists. The Hoi An municipal government actively supports traditional craft villages surrounding Hoi An, such as Kim Bong (carpentry and wood work), Thanh Ha (pottery) and Tra Que (horticulture), as well as traditional fishing villages, and the municipal authorities have included the villages on tourist maps and promote tours and shopping trips to the villages, thus helping to sustain the local economy and maintain traditional skills and other elements of intangible cultural heritage in these villages (Hoi An Center for Monuments Management and Conservation, 2008).

The contribution of the tourism–trade–service sector to the town's GDP increased noticeably from 59.19% in 2005 to 61.47% in 2006 and 63.27% in 2007 (Hoi An People's Committee, 2007 cited in Nguyen Thi Thu Ha, 2008), while the proportion of other industries in Hoi An's GDP, such as construction (22.18%) and agriculture, forestry, and aquaculture (18.63%) in 2005, has declined over the years. The accommodation sector has been the most prosperous sector in Hoi An, in terms of both numbers and revenue generation. While in 1991 the town had only one state-owned hotel (the Hoi An hotel), which provided nine rooms, in 2001, there were 30 hotels supplying 872 rooms (Nguyen Thi Thu Ha, 2008). In 2007, Hoi An had 79 enterprises offering tourist accommodation services, of which 19 were three- to five-star hotels providing 1,684 rooms and accounting for 56% of total hotel rooms available. In addition, 26 one- and two-star hotels provided 28% of total rooms, and numerous guest houses provided 10% of the total rooms (Hoi An Center for Monuments Management and Conservation, 2008). Further developments reflecting tourism growth include the decision to widen the 7-km long road connecting Hoi An and Cua Dai beach and the opening of An Bang beach nearby. These actions, together with investment along the costal corridor of Da Nang–Hoi An, have transformed the Ancient Town from a strictly historic cultural destination into a beach holiday destination as well (Parnwell, 2016).

A tourism-based economy offers opportunities to develop new livelihoods and has created jobs and income for 5,000 direct laborers and 12,500 indirect laborers (Hoi An Center for Monuments Management and Conservation, 2008). Through diverse tourism products such as home stay, ecotourism services, and visits to craft villages, the job-creation effect extends into the countryside to the communities of Tan Hiep, Cam Thanh, and Cam Kim, and many younger people who had left to seek jobs outside of their villages have come back (Nguyen Thi Thu Ha, 2008). However, some critical issues related to the tourism economy have caught the authorities' attention. First was the need to spread the income derived from tourism into other sections of the historic town. Second was the need to develop long-term sustainable mechanisms to enhance the livelihood of local people while conserving and presenting the unique and multi-layered cultural heritage to the outside world (Brooks, 2007; Le, Bui, & Weaver, 2012).

Some criticism of the tourism-based economy concerns revenue leakage after the decision to promote "quality tourism" in 2000. Even though the new hotels employed local people and paid them steadily higher wages, the senior management was foreign—mainly European, Australian, or Japanese—while the middle managers were from Hanoi and Ho Chi Minh City. Graduates of the much better schools and universities in those cities had stronger qualifications than local people, especially English-language qualifications. Hoianese therefore found work mainly as cleaners, maids, gardeners, guards, kitchen hands and the like, receiving the lowest pay for work in the lowliest positions (Avieli, 2015). As a result, most of the profit from "quality tourism" is siphoned out of the town and out of the country.

In addition, rapid tourism development poses pressure on local population. Annual in-migration to the town is high owing to the growth of tourism industry. Except for a decline of 10% the population between ten years after the unification from 68, 153 people in 1976 to 61,834 in 1986, Hoi An has experienced steady increase in pollution since 1990s. The population reached 83,000 people in 2006 (Hoi An Department of Statistics cited in Hoi An Hoi An Center for Monuments Management and Conservation, 2008). In the same year, 2006, international and domestic visitors to Hoi An was 876,000 (See Figure 1), which was ten folds of the local population. Locals and tourists pack in small area of the historic town, making it the most population density area in Vietnam (Tien Phong, 2009). The high density, consequently results on quality of life of the locals in the town.

Further, while a higher living standard of the locals and lower poverty rates are positive outcomes of a tourism-based economy, local residents are experiencing significant increases in their cost of living as a result of increased tourism. Demand for commodities has increased owing to the greater number of tourists, who are willing to pay more for the same goods or services as locals, driving up prices. Gradually, the higher price becomes the norm, even for local residents of Hoi An. A tourist commented on Trip Advisor (2016) that "everything in this town is 2-3 times as expensive as in other parts of Vietnam." The poorest and most vulnerable residents are especially affected by the increase in prices (Hoi An Center for Monuments Management and Conservation, 2008).

Response from the Environment

As the preceding discussion makes clear, the character of Hoi An changed dramatically after its designation as a World Heritage Site. The designation has been accompanied by a large expansion of built-up areas, a tremendous increase in retailing, and a huge growth in tourism-related accommodation and services (Parnwell, 2016). The tranquil small-town atmosphere is being lost as large tour buses and other vehicles jam the narrow streets and create noise and air pollution. In addition, tour boats and over a hundred smaller local boats ply the local rivers, transporting people and goods and causing significant noise pollution and river bank erosion. Currently, Hoi An has no effective wastewater treatment and disposal system, so raw sewage and other wastewater from guesthouses, restaurants, and laundries flow into rivers and other waterways. In the surrounding villages, waste is burned or dumped into the ocean and rivers. Such pollution has adverse impacts on local wildlife and is causing irreparable damage to the natural beauty of Hoi An (Hoi An Center for Monuments Management and Conservation, 2008).

An additional factor is a change in the frequency of natural events, particularly increasing storm surges. The World Heritage Site of Hoi An comprises many ancient wooden houses, which are subject to regular floods. Between 1979 and 2010, more than a hundred flood events were recorded in Quang Nam, and the frequency of these events is accelerating: 1980–1989 recorded 21 typhoons and 22 floods, 1990–1999 recorded 17 typhoons and 26 floods, and 2000–2009 recorded 26 typhoons and 49 floods along with a significant increase in natural disasters (Asian Development Bank, 2014). The ancient buildings were designed for a specific climate, and are less isolated from the ground than newer buildings that employ geomembranes and other technologies to limit exposure to water and soil processes. Changes in water levels or salinity may accelerate the deterioration of ancient structures' foundations, and changes in wet and dry cycles can induce crystallization and dissolution of salts and affect other heritage assets (UNESCO, 2007). Further effects of flooding are evident in the surrounding roads. According to the Hoi An People's Committee, flooding in 2007 caused damage to roads estimated at VND 2,842 billion (approximately US $136 million).

While beaches have become a major tourist attraction, they are being strongly affected by erosion brought about by tourism development and rising sea levels. Among the major causes of erosion is construction of tourist resorts and protection structures on the beach (Asian Development Bank, 2014). Additionally, during the last 50 years, Vietnam's sea level along the coastline has risen by approximately 20 cm (Asian Development Bank, 2014). Along the coastline of the Cua Dai area, between 10 and 20 meters of land on the shoreline are eroded every year, resulting in coastal erosion of 150 meters in 8 years. In addition, the rising sea level has intensified the severity of floods, particularly as large areas of the city around the Thu Bon and De Vong Rivers are two meters below sea level and therefore especially sensitive to flooding effects.

SOLUTIONS AND RECOMMENDATIONS

Both opportunities and threats follow the placement of Hoi An on the World Heritage List. On the one hand, the report of the Hoi An Center for Monuments Management and Conservation (2008) shows generally positive outcomes of the inscription to heritage conservation with respect to the local economy, the environment, and society—a viewpoint shared by Vietnamese government officers (Phan Nhu Ngoc

Han, 2004; Nguyen Thi Thu Ha, 2008; Le, Bui & Weaver, 2012). An official narrative often promoted by the governmental sector casts Hoi An as a successful case of tourism development at living heritage sites in Vietnam. On the other hand, an opposite opinion expresses strong concern about the sustainability of Hoi An's tourism-based model. For instance, Avieli (2015) critically concludes that inclusion on the World Heritage List may prove to be a "death sentence" (p. 37) for a site, both culturally and materially.

Heritage tourism has been implemented as a powerful economic device to boost the regional development of Hoi An as well as contribute successfully to the restructuring of the local economy. In fact, the revenue gained from tourism contributes significantly to the conservation of both tangible and intangible heritage. However, while the conservation of the restricted core zone inside the Ancient Town has been at least superficially successful, the rapid commodification of the intangible heritage underscores the urgent need to strengthen the governance of the heritage property. In particular, the creation of a buffer zone in harmony with the identity of the destination is suggested to policy makers (Avieli, 2015).

A similar scenario occurs with respect to managing the environmental impacts of tourism. Solutions to mitigate the effects of climate change have not yet been effectively implemented at the national and provincial levels owing to lack of coordination between different divisions, limited capability, and a highly centralized decision-making process (UN Habitat, 2012). Hoi An suffers from weak environmental planning and a poor waste and wastewater treatment infrastructure, and sprawling resort developments have brought economic growth without due consideration of environmental sustainability. These circumstances could also threaten the development of the region (UNIDO, 2012). However, the Hoi An People's Committee has shown its determination to develop Hoi An to become an Eco-City by 2030. The Eco-City concept aims to apply best environmental practices in service delivery to cities' residents and businesses, especially focusing on opportunities for green industries to deliver services that improve environmental amenities and on the potential for the greening of existing businesses, especially in the key economic sectors of accommodation and crafts (UNIDO, 2012).

FUTURE RESEARCH DIRECTIONS

This chapter analyzes multiple impacts of tourism development on Hoi An Ancient Town in light of World Heritage Site designation. On the one hand, the designation is an opportunity for economic development and, to a lesser extent, the conservation of the heritage. On the other hand, the designation threatens the authenticity and cultural identity of the heritage. Weakness of local stakeholders in managing impacts on local lives is, in fact, a threat to the sustainability of tourism development. As this examination relies on secondary data, future work might include surveys of tourists or interviews with stakeholders to identify further constraints and problems concerning mass tourism to uncover effective solutions that mitigate impacts of massive development on the fragile nature of the ancient town.

REFERENCES

Ashworth, G. (1994). From history to heritage: From heritage to identity: In search of concepts and models. In G. J. Ashworth & P. J. Larkham (Eds.), *Building a new heritage: tourism, culture and identity in the new Europe* (pp. 13–30). London, UK: Routledge.

Asian Development Bank. (2014). *VIE: Urban environment and climate change adaptation project (Hoi An City, Quang Nam Province)*. Hanoi, Vietnam: Asian Development Bank.

Avieli, N. (2015). The rise and fall (?) of Hoi An, a UNESCO World Heritage Site in Vietnam. *SOJOURN: Journal of Social Issues in Southeast Asia, 30*(1), 35–71. doi:10.1355/sj30-1b

Beeton, S. (2004). The case study in tourism research: A multi-method case study approach. In B. W. Ritchie, P. Burns, & C. Palmer (Eds.), *Tourism research methods: Integrating theory with practice* (pp. 37–61). Cambridge, MA: CAB International.

Brooks, G. (2008). Exploiting the benefit of World Heritage Listing: Evora, Portugal and Hoi An, Vietnam. In B. Hayllar, B., T. Griffin, T., & D. Edwards (Eds.), City spaces–tourist places (pp. 341-356). Amsterdam: Elsevier.

Bui, H. T., & Lee, T. J. (2015). Commodification and politicization of heritage: Implications for heritage tourism at the Imperial Citadel of Thang Long, Hanoi (Vietnam). *Austrian Journal of South-East Asian Studies, 8*(2), 187–202.

Di Giovine, M. A. (2009a). *The heritage-scape: UNESCO, World Heritage and tourism*. Plymouth, MA: Lexington Books.

Di Giovine, M. A. (2009b). Revitalization and counter-revitalization: Tourism, heritage, and the Lantern Festival as catalysts for regeneration in Hoi An, Vietnam. *Journal of Policy Research in Tourism. Leisure and Events, 1*(3), 208–230. doi:10.1080/19407960903204364

Garrod, B., & Fyall, A. (2000). Managing heritage tourism. *Annals of Tourism Research, 27*(3), 682–708. doi:10.1016/S0160-7383(99)00094-8

Graham, B. (2002). Heritage as knowledge: Capital or culture? *Urban Studies (Edinburgh, Scotland), 39*(5-6), 1003–1017. doi:10.1080/00420980220128426

Graham, B., Ashworth, G. J., & Tunbridge, J. E. (2000). *A geography of heritage*. London, UK: Arnold.

Harrison, D. (2004). Contested narratives in the domain of world heritage. *Current Issues in Tourism, 7*(4/5), 281–290. doi:10.1080/13683500408667985

Hoi An Center for Monuments Management and Conservation. (2008). *Cultural tourism and heritage management in the World Heritage Site of Ancient Town of Hoi An, Vietnam*. Bangkok: United Nations Educational, Scientific and Cultural Organization.

Kibicho, W. (2008). Community-based tourism: A factor- cluster segmentation approach. *Journal of Sustainable Tourism, 16*(2), 211–231. doi:10.2167/jost623.0

Lask, T., & Herold, S. (2004). An observation station for culture and tourism in Vietnam: A forum for World Heritage and public participation. *Current Issues in Tourism, 7*(4-5), 399–411. doi:10.1080/13683500408667993

Le, T. A., Bui, T. H., & Weaver, D. (2012). Community-based tourism and economic sustainability: A case study at Kim Bong wood carpentry village in Vietnam. *Proceedings of the 4th Asia-Euro Conference 2012 in Tourism, Hospitality and Gastronomy*. Subang Jaya, Malaysia: Taylor University.

Le, T. A., Weaver, D., & Lawton, L. (2015). Community-based tourism and development in the periphery/ semi-periphery interface: A case study approach. In S. McCool & K. Bosak (Eds.), *Reframing Sustainable Tourism* (pp. 161–181). Springer.

Nguyen Thi Thu Ha. (2007). *Tourism development and the sustainable management of cultural heritage – A case study of Hoi An Ancient Town in Vietnam* (Master thesis). KDI School of Public Policy and Management.

Orbasli, A. (2000). *Tourists in historic towns*. New York: Taylor & Francis. doi:10.4324/9780203479001

Parnwell, M. (2016). Heritage management and tourism development in Hoi An, Vietnam. In V. King (Ed.), *UNESCO in Southeast Asia: World Heritage Sites in comparative context*. Copenhagen: NIAS Press.

Phan Nhu Ngoc Han. (2004). *Tourism management in Vietnam: Hoi An – A case study* (Master thesis). National University of Singapore.

Saltiel, L. (2014). Cultural governance and development in Vietnam. *University of Pennsylvania Journal of International Law*, *35*(3), 893–915.

Stake, R. E. (1995). *The art of case study research*. Thousand Oaks, CA: Sage Publications.

Tien Phong. (2009). *Mat do dan so tai Hoi An cao nhat the gioi?* Retrieved from http://www.tienphong.vn/xa-hoi/mat-do-dan-so-tai-hoi-an-cao-nhat-the-gioi-171691.tpo

Tripadvisor. (2016). *Hoi An Ancient Town*. Retrieved from https://www.tripadvisor.com.au/Attraction_ Review-g298082-d4507121-Reviews-Hoi_An_Ancient_Town-Hoi_An_Quang_Nam_ Province.html#REVIEWS

UN Habitat, . (2014). *Hoi An – Vietnam: Climate change vulnerability assessment*. Nairobi: United Nations Human Settlements Programme.

UNESCO. (2007). *Climate change and World Heritage*. Paris: United Nations Educational, Scientific and Cultural Organization. Available at: http://whc.unesco.org/en/activities/474

UNIDO. (2012). *Towards green growth through green industry development in Vietnam*. Vienna: United Nations Industrial Development Organisation.

Xiao, H., & Smith, S. L. J. (2006). Case studies in tourism research: A state-of-the-art analysis. *Tourism Management*, *27*(5), 738–749. doi:10.1016/j.tourman.2005.11.002

Yin, R. K. (2009). *Case study research: Design and methods*. Thousand Oaks, CA: Sage Publications.

Chapter 16
Actor Network Theory in Tourism

Xuan Tran
University of West Florida, USA

ABSTRACT

The purpose of this study is to use actor network theory to explore the short-term and long-term relationships between two Asian countries: Malaysia and China, the two most visited countries in Asia in 2012. The Actor Network theory explains the roles of two actors China and Malaysia in tourism as mobility and performativity, respectively. The tourism in China is composed of culture differences whereas the tourism in Malaysia focuses on business concentration. Vector Auto Regressive, Vector Error Correction, and Granger analysis were conducted to explore the time series data of tourism receipts. Findings indicate that both Malaysia and China do not have short-term influence of tourism development. Interestingly, the long-term tourism of Malaysia will depend on the disequilibrium of tourism receipts between China and Malaysia but not vice versa. The findings have contributed to supporting the Actor Network Theory in developing tourism of China and Malaysia.

INTRODUCTION

China and Malaysia are the two most visited countries in Asia in 2012. Tourist receipts of China and Malaysia have been constantly changing in the Asia market share. During the 3-year period (2010, 2011, and 2012), the market share of China has been decreasing 17%, 16%, and 15% respectively, whereas the market share of Malaysia has been also decreasing 7%, 6%, and 5% (UNWTO, 2013). The question is whether or not there is a bilateral relationship of tourism receipts between two countries in the long term. Can the Actor Network theory explain the relationship between Malaysia and China? What are these networks composed of? What do they generate? What resistances do they face, and how do they protect themselves from the resistance? These questions are the main focus of this study.

In order to find the answers for the above questions, this study has conducted the vector auto regressive (VAR), vector error correction (VEC), and the Granger analysis. The VAR model is a general framework used to describe the dynamic interrelationship among stationary variables to estimate the short-term and

DOI: 10.4018/978-1-5225-2078-8.ch016

long-term relationship between two time series variables. If the estimation of the relationship among series is co-integrating, the VAR will become the vector error correction (VEC) model that can be used to identify predictors for long-term impacts. In this study, we will use both VEC and VAR for the case of tourism development in China and Malaysia. In addition, we use Granger analysis to forecast the predictor of the long-term relationship between Malaysia and China.

Malaysia and China both offer history, culture, heritage, and art for tourists to explore. Over the last quarter century, beginning off a low base, Malaysia has developed a major travel and tourist industry. In 1980 Malaysia attracted a modest 2.3 million international tourist arrivals, but by 2005 this figure had increased to 16.4 million, making Malaysia the second most visited country in Asia after China. The direct and indirect effect of travel and tourism in Malaysia in 2006 accounts for 14.6 per cent of GDP and makes tourism Malaysia's second largest foreign exchange earner after the manufacturing sector.

To increase tourist numbers from China, Tourism Malaysia has established offices in Beijing, Chengdu, Guangzhou, Shanghai and Kunming and invested in a number of initiatives to make Malaysia more attractive to Chinese tourists. From 2001 to 2005 this program attracted 7,308 participants; of which the main markets were China (24 per cent), Bangladesh (15 per cent), United Kingdom (8 per cent) and Singapore (6 per cent) (Government Malaysia, 2006).

In the long-term period, the visions of different countries might affect tourism development in reality. China Tourism Organization (2013) ranks Tourism development in their economic development as follows: "Tourism and leisure as our starting point and ultimate goal in line with the overall requirements for completing the building of an initially prosperous society in China." The Malaysian government regards tourism as an important vehicle to diversify its economic structure. To accelerate private investment in tourism two funds were launched in 2001; namely, the Tourism Infrastructure Fund with an initial allocation of RM700 million and a Special Fund for Tourism and Infrastructure with an initial allocation of RM400 million. In 2005 the allocation to both funds was increased to RM1.2 billion (Government Malaysia, 2006). Under the Ninth Malaysian Plan (2006-2010), altogether the Malaysian government will spend RM1.8 billion (US$486.5 million) to upgrade tourist destinations and on tourist infrastructure as well as on marketing campaigns in major source markets (Government Malaysia, 2006). Tourism is set to increase in importance as a source of growth.

Thus, the purpose of this research is to explore the short-term and long-term relationships of tourism development between China and Malaysia. In the literature, we will discuss contemporary research about tourism concept in terms of mobilities, performativity and the actor network theory for the relationships between China and Malaysia related to tourism development. In methodology, we will provide an overview of Vector Auto Regressive, Vector Auto Correction, and Granger analyses. Finally, in discussion, we will analyze implications of these findings.

LITERATURE

Tourism is constantly developing and changing over time. Today, tourism has developed into two areas described by the Actor Network Theory: Mobilities and Performativity (Cohen & Cohen, 2012). First, tourism has been developed into Mobilties. The Mobilities in tourism are the binary distinctions between 'home' and 'away', 'work' and 'leisure', 'ordinary life' and 'extraordinary holidays', 'reality' and 'fantasy', 'hosts' and 'guests', 'domestic' and 'international'. Based on Urry (2000), mobilities indicate that tourism has transformed 'social as society' to 'social as mobility'. Tourists have brought their original beliefs or cultures to a society to make it changes and moves. Local people love new things and tourists also learn different ones from the society. The two actors "local people" and "tourists" have created the binary distinctions "family" and "friend", "rules" and "no rules", "normal" and "exciting". That is the first stage of tourism development. Tourism in China has been exemplified for the concept of mobilities in tourism when China and Tourism Organization (2013) confirms "Tourism and Leisure as our starting point." Second, tourism has been changed into Performativity. It implies de-differentiation, integration, penetration, or blurring of the border between the above binary concepts to bring virtuality to reality. Performativity has shifted from 'authenticity' to 'fun and enjoyment', from 'Western' to 'Non-Western', from 'original' to 'post-modern', from 'romantic' to 'collective', from 'control and surveillance' to 'power and authority', from 'synchronic' to 'diachronic', from ''being' to 'doing', from 'permanence' to 'flux', from 'structure' to 'agency', and from 'sediment' to 'emergent'. Hannam et al. (2006) indicates the performativity characteristics for tourist destinations as "places are not fixed but rather implicated complex networks by which hosts, guests, buildings, objects, and machines are continually brought together to perform certain performances" (p. 13). This concept applies to countries that have made long-term efforts in tourism development, such as Malaysia and other western countries. Tourism becomes a network to combine people and non-human entities together in order to perform tourism services. Local people and tourists learn each other to become a unity. The two actors have integrated the binary differences into a new trend; from "strangers" to "one family", from "conservatives" to "one opening", from "individuals" to "one brand", and from "multiples" to "one trust." Tourism in Malaysia is an example for the performativity concept. In the Actor Network theory, tourism is a durable network that will be utilized differently by different countries. When China and Malaysia become parts of this network, they have played different roles. China mainly generates cultural tourism whereas Malaysia mainly provides business tourism. Over the past six decades, this network continued expansion and diversification. Many new Asia countries have emerged apart from the traditional favorites of Europe and America. China and Malaysia have two parts of actor-networks among them. Is China the resistance of Malaysia or Malaysia the resistance of China? In the short term there is no resistance between two countries. In the long term, Malaysia will be the resistance of China but not vice versa. China protects itself from Malaysia by providing varieties of traditional cultures while Malaysia protects itself from China by providing varieties of business network stations. In the long term, thus, Malaysia will continue to develop its business networks with China so that it keeps relying on the disequillibrum of tourism between two countries. China, on the other hand, exploits the past historical cultures that are not related to Malaysia so that China will be independent to the disequillibrum of tourism between China and Malaysia. Actor Network theory states that all domains of tourism including hosts, guests, properties, objects, motivations, efforts, good wills, etc. are required to be connected to perform tourism services. Latour (2005) indicates that in the complex contemporary world, the processes by which the ''social characteristic'' is actually produced should become the principal task of sociological inquiry. He argues that social characteristic is not the glue but is what is glued. The implication "what is glued" is assumed in this study that China's tourism is in Mobilities and Malaysia's tourism is in Performativity. In addition to viewing tourism in the conceptual development, this study examines tourism as a three-stage process: coexistence, exploitation, and imaginative reconstruction. While the tourism industry impacts local society in China, its consequences can be managed and engineered by promotion authorities. Many researchers have recommended cultural preservation must be invested to match with commercial interests (Chang 1997a, 1997b; Garrod & Fyall 2000; Teo & Yeoh 1997; van der Borg, Costa & Gotti 1996). Newby defines conceptual relationships between heritage and tourism (1994:208–215), as a continuum along three principal spotlines: coexistence, exploitation, and imaginative reconstruction. Tourism and heritage coexist when the former does not dominate the local economy—it is the case of China. China is the most powerful tourism country in Asia today since it started its opening door policy. The relationship becomes exploitative when cultural heritage becomes the basis for generating a cash flow—it is the case of Malaysia. Malaysia is considered a Western country in Asia since its tourism has been developed for a long time. Although Malaysia has developed its tourism for a long time, this country still maintains its unique culture. The reason for this is the government can control the imaginative reconstruction that allows preservation without being swallowed by commercialism. This balanced and desired strategy ensures that the heritage remains "alive", but the separation among coexistence, exploitation, and creative redevelopment is still arguable. Malaysia's tourism will continue to be considered Performativity and in the exploitation process while China's tourism is considered Mobilities and in the coexistence process. In order to support the above assumption, this study aims to forecast the long-term trend of tourism development between China and Malaysia using the data of tourism receipts during the 16-year period (1995-2011).

The three null hypotheses for this study are as follows:

- **Null Hypothesis 1:** There is no integrated equation in which tourism developments of both countries would be independent.
- **Null Hypothesis 2:** There is no integrated equation in which tourism development of Malaysia would predict the one of China but not vice versa.
- **Null Hypothesis 3:** There is no integrated equation in which tourism developments of China would predict the one of Malaysia but not vice versa.

METHODOLOGY

In order to identify the predictor of the two time-series variables tourism development and economic growth, Granger approach focuses on integration between them; that is, if x is a predictor of y, x is able to increase the accuracy of the prediction of y considering only past values of y. "Assuming to have an information set Ω_t with the form $(x_t, \ldots x_{t-j,}\ y_t, \ldots y_{t-i})$, we say that x_t is Granger causal for y_t within Ω_t if the variance of the optimal linear predictor of y_{t+h}, based on Ω_t has smaller variance than the optimal linear predictor of y_{t+h} based only on lagged values of y_t, for any h. Thus, x causes y if and only if $\sigma^2(y_t: y_{t-j}, x_{t-i}) < \sigma^2(y_t: y_{t-j})$ with j and i = 1, 2, 3, ...n and σ^2 representing the variance of the forecast error." (Granger, 1969).

Thus, the two variables Tourism Development (Tourism Receipts, TR) of China and Japan are written into the following vector equations:

$$(\Delta TRChina)_t = \alpha + \Sigma^m{}_i \beta_i (\Delta TRChina)_{t-i} + \Sigma^n{}_j\ \tau_j (\Delta TRMalaysia)_{t-j} + \mu_t \quad (1)$$

$$(\Delta TRMalaysia)_t = \theta + \Sigma^p{}_i \Phi_i \Delta\ (\Delta TRMalaysia)_{t-i} + \Sigma^q{}_j \Psi_j \Delta\ (\Delta TRChina)_{t-j} + \eta_t \quad (2)$$

where:

$(\Delta TRChina)_t$ changes in economic growth at time t; which is measured by the growth rate of TRChina.

α: Constant

$\Sigma^m{}_i\beta_i$: Total short-run coefficients from i=0 to i=m lags of TRChina for equation 1
$\Sigma^n{}_j\tau_{j:}$ Total short-run coefficients from j=0 to t=n lags of TRMalaysia for equation 1
$\mu_{t:}$ Residuals at time t in the equation 1

$(\Delta LnTRMalaysia)_t$: changes in tourism development at time t, which is measured by the rate of growth of tourism receipts.

θ: Constant
$\Sigma^p{}_i\Phi_i$: Total short-run coefficients from i=0 to i=p lags of TRMalaysia for equation 2
$\Sigma^q{}_j\Psi_{j:}$ Total short-run coefficients from j=0 to t=n lags of TRChina for equation 2
$\eta_{t:}$ Residuals at time t in the equation 2

In order to be selected in the Granger test, the two variables tourism development for two countries (tourism receipts, TRChina and TRMalaysia) must be stationary after first differencing. Augmented Dickey Fuller (ADF) test was conducted to check the unit root of the two variables as follows:

$$\Delta_{yt} = \gamma_0 + \gamma_1 t + (\beta - 1)y_{t-1} + \delta_1\Delta_{t-1} + e_t \quad (3)$$

Δ_{yt}: Difference operator
$\gamma_0 + \gamma_1 t$: Trend including constant γ_0 and trend $\gamma_1 t$
$(\beta - 1)y_{t-1}$: Trend and intercept
$\delta_1\Delta_{t-1}$: Intercept

The null hypothesis for ADF test is the variable is not stationary.

Data Analysis

The study data of Tourism receipts of China and Malaysia are taken from the United Nations Database (2013). In this paper, the time series are given from 1995 to the end of 2011. The two series of Tourism Receipts of China and Malaysia, obtained in real values of the growth ratios and converted into natural logarithm to avoid heteroscedasticity and we can use coefficients as elasticity.

Empirical Analysis and Results

Both tourism receipts of China and Malaysia are not stationary in levels as follows in Figure 1.

Then, the differences of China tourism receipts as well as Malaysia tourism receipts seem, however, stationary in Figure 2.

We used the ADF tests for the stationary of China and Malaysia in Tables 1 and 2 as follows.

There are no significant relationships so the null hypothesis for ADF test for China that the variable is not stationary is accepted. The variable is stationary and qualified for Granger test.

There are no significant relationships so the null hypothesis for ADF test for Malaysia that the variable is not stationary is accepted. The variable is stationary and qualified for Granger test.

The insignificant coefficients of Malaysia and China in tables 1 & 2 also indicate that in the short-term Malaysia and China have no significant relationships for tourism development.

Figure 1. Tourism receipts (in Ln) between China and Malaysia (1995 – 2011)

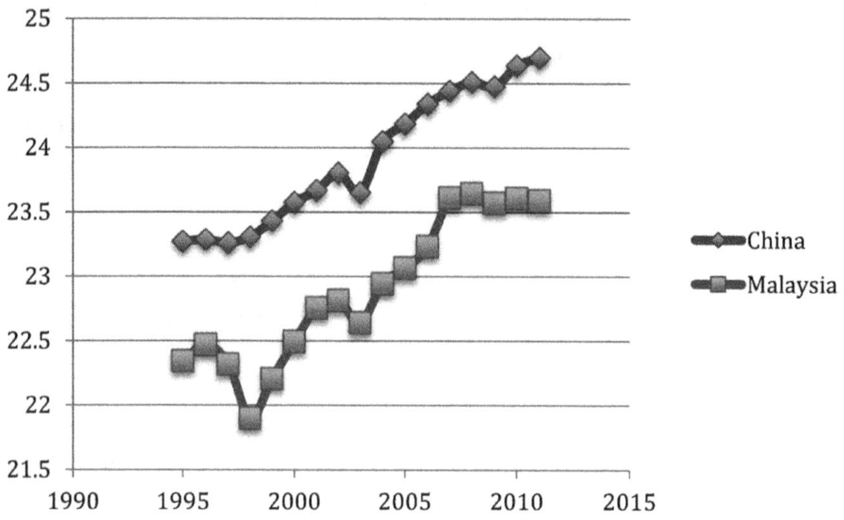

Figure 2. Differences of China tourism receipts and Malaysia tourism receipts

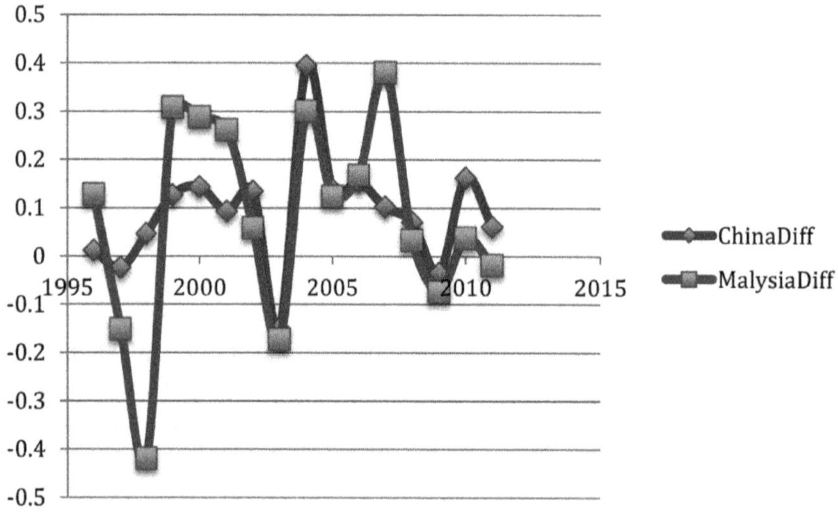

Table 1. Regression analysis between China tourism receipts difference and the lags of China and Malaysia tourism receipts

ChinaDiff	*Coefficients*	*Standard Error*	*t Stat*	*P-value*
Intercept	0.154864	0.061538	2.516556	0.036001
ChinaDiff1	-0.48272	0.396988	-1.21595	0.258664
ChinaDiff2	0.255033	0.389968	0.653983	0.531468
MalaysiaDiff1	0.055892	0.203463	0.274703	0.790505
MalaysiaDiff2	-0.29987	0.184804	-1.62263	0.143325

Table 2. Regression analysis between Malaysia tourism receipts difference and the lags of China and Malaysia tourism receipts

MalaysiaDiff	*Coefficients*	*Standard Error*	*t Stat*	*P-value*
Intercept	0.114159	0.09022	1.265347	0.241356
ChinaDiff1	0.022892	0.582017	0.039333	0.969589
ChinaDiff2	0.70167	0.571725	1.227285	0.254603
MalaysiaDiff1	-0.08363	0.298293	-0.28035	0.786319
MalaysiaDiff2	-0.50331	0.270938	-1.85767	0.100289

Next, Granger's regression analysis was conducted for tourism receipts of China and Malaysia. We saved the residual of to for the Engle-Granger test of cointegration.

The residuals saved from the regression between two tourism receipts were regressed with its lag in Table 3 as follows:

The t-ratio is 2.45. The 5% critical value for the model with no intercept is 2.76. The t-ratio falls within the rejection region and the null hypothesis of no cointegration is rejected and we conclude that the two real tourism receipts are cointegrated. The null hypothesis 1 was rejected; there was an integrated vector between TRMalaysia and TRChina. That is, TRChina and TRMalaysia have long run associations.

To get the VEC model results for Tourism Receipts of Malaysia, we estimated the following regression of the difference of Malaysia tourism receipts on the saved residuals in Table 4 as follows:

The significant coefficient on lag e indicates that the Malaysia Tourism Receipts responds to disequilibrium between the China and Malaysia. The null hypothesis 2 was rejected.

To get the VEC model results for Tourism Receipts of China, we estimated the following regression of the difference of China tourism receipts on the saved residuals in Table 5 as follows:

China does not appear to respond to the disequilibrium between the two tourism receipts of China and Malaysia. The null hypothesis 3 was not rejected. These findings support the idea that the tourism conditions in Malaysia depend on those in the China but not vice verse. In this simple model of two tourism industries, China acts as a large closed tourism economy and Malaysia as a small open tourism economy.

Table 3. Regression analysis between the residual of Tourism Receipts of two countries and its lag (1)

ChinaMalaysiaCointegration	*Coefficients*	*Standard Error*	*t Stat*	*P-value*
Intercept	0	#N/A	#N/A	#N/A
X Variable 1	-0.570423388	0.232816881	-2.450094623	0.027036344

Table 4. Regression analysis between Malaysia tourism receipts difference and the residual of the two countries' tourism receipts

MalaysiaChi	*Coefficients*	*Standard Error*	*t Stat*	*P-value*
Intercept	0.079087523	0.044625534	1.77224822	0.098105335
X Variable 1	0.743839985	0.272521154	2.729476131	0.016287989

Table 5. Regression analysis between China tourism receipts difference and the residual of the two countries' tourism receipts

ChiMalaysia	Coefficients	Standard Error	t Stat	P-value
Intercept	0.089595706	0.028939222	3.095995652	0.007894934
X Variable 1	0.206977435	0.176727302	1.171168419	0.261079229

In addition, when running regression analyses from SPSS for the model with tourism as the dependent variable and gross domestic product per capita and higher education as independent variables for both countries, the results indicate that the associations between tourism and economy or higher education were not significant for China ($p>.05$), but significant for Malaysia ($p<.05$). This finding supports the theory of Actor Network theory for Malaysia as performativity and China as mobility when the difference between tourism development of China and Malaysia is the integration.

DISCUSSION

The purpose of tourism is to stimulate culture exchange. This study has examined the change in two directions: concepts and time. In term of concepts, Malaysia's tourism has been considered Performativity while China's tourism is considered Mobilities. In terms of time, China is in the exploitation process whereas Malaysia is in the coexistence process. Using the data of time series tourism receipts, the hypotheses are supported. In the short term, there is no relationship of tourism development between two countries, Malaysia and China. In the long term, Malaysia will depend on the tourism development of China. China develops its tourism in accordance with social mobility whereas Malaysia develops its tourism in a network with actors and non-human entities in the same project. Implications of this study have shown that the Actor Network theory in tourism has been explained in China and Malaysia. Tourism in China is in the mobilities stage, while the tourism in Malaysia is in the performativity stage. The results of this study have indicated that in the short term there are no mutual influence between the two countries, but in the long term, Malaysia will continue to rely on the disequilibrium of tourism between China and Malaysia due to its 'agency'. The study is important for researchers and practitioners to understand the trend of tourism operating under the Actor Network theory.

CONCLUSION

The Actor Network theory explains the roles of two actors China and Malaysia in tourism as mobility and performativity, respectively. The tourism in China is composed of culture differences whereas the tourism in Malaysia focuses on business concentration. The correlation between tourism and education or economy is not significant whereas the differences of tourism stages in Malaysia are integrated with education and economy. In addition, the Malaysia tourism relies on China tourism since its role (Malaysia) as second stage in the Actor Network theory depending on the first stage (China). The process of resistance between two countries has located the positioning for both countries in the tourism competition in Asia. In PATAa (2015), Malaysia has launched Edutourism packages whereas China hosts the "New Dimensions of Heritage and Culture Tourism" (PATAb, 2015).

REFERENCES

Chang, T. (1997a). From Instant Asia to Multi-Faceted Jewel: Urban Imaging Strategies and Tourism Development in Singapore. *Urban Geography*, *18*(6), 542–562. doi:10.2747/0272-3638.18.6.542

Chang, T. (1997b). Heritage as a Tourism Commodity: Traversing the Tourist–Local Divide. *Singapore Journal of Tropical Geography*, *18*(1), 46–68. doi:10.1111/1467-9493.00004

China. (2013). Available online May 13, 2013, http://jameskennell.files.wordpress.com/2013/04/china-tourism-policy-2013-2020.pdf

Cohen, E., & Cohen, S. (2012). Current sociological theories and issues in tourism. *Annals of Tourism Research*, *39*(4), 2177–2202. doi:10.1016/j.annals.2012.07.009

Garrod, B., & Fyall, A. (2000). Managing Heritage Tourism. *Annals of Tourism Research*, *27*(3), 682–708. doi:10.1016/S0160-7383(99)00094-8

Government Malaysia. (2006). *Ninth Malaysia Plan 2006-2010, Economics Planning Unit*. Prime Minister's Department.

Granger, C. J. (1969). Investigating Causal Relationships by Econometrics Models and Cross Spectral Methods. *Econometrica*, *37*(3), 425–435. doi:10.2307/1912791

Hannam, K., Sheller, M., & Urry, J. (2006). Editorial: Mobilities, immobilities, moorings. *Mobilities*, *1*(1), 1–22. doi:10.1080/17450100500489189

Latour, B. (2005). *Resembling the social*. Oxford, UK: Oxford University Press.

Newby, P. (1994). Tourism: Support or Threat to Heritage? In G. Ashworth & P. Larkham (Eds.), *Building a New Heritage: Tourism, Culture and Identity in the New Europe* (pp. 206–228). London: Routledge.

PATA. (2015a). *Ministry of Higher Education and Tourism Malaysia Launches the Malaysia 101 Edutourism Packages to Promote Malaysian Culture*. Available online from "https://www.pata.org/ministry-of-higher-education-and-tourism-malaysia-launches-the-malaysia-101-edutourism-packages-to-promote-malaysian-culture/"

PATA. (2015b). *All posts tagged New Dimensions of Heritage and Culture Tourism*. Available online from https://www.pata.org/tag/new-dimensions-of-heritage-and-culture-tourism/

Teo, P., & Yeoh, B. (1997). Remaking Local Heritage for Tourism. *Annals of Tourism Research*, *24*(1), 192–213. doi:10.1016/S0160-7383(96)00054-0

The United Nations Database. (2013). Available online May 13, 2013, http://unctadstat.unctad.org

The World Travel & Tourism Council. (2011). *Travel & Tourism Economic Impact 2011*. Author.

UNWTO. (2013). *Annual reports, progress and priorities*. The World Travel and Tourism Council.

Urry, J. (2000). Mobile sociology. *The British Journal of Sociology*, *51*(1), 185–203. doi:10.1080/000713100358499 PMID:20092503

van der Borg, J., Costa, P., & Gotti, G. (1996). Tourism in European Heritage Cities. *Annals of Tourism Research*, *23*(2), 306–321. doi:10.1016/0160-7383(95)00065-8

Chapter 17
Adequacy of Government Policy on Ecotourism:
A Case Study of Sikkim

Ajeya Jha
Sikkim Manipal Institute of Technology, India

Somnath Mishra
Sikkim Manipal University, India

Sherap Shenga
Government of Sikkim, India

Manjushree Mishra
Sikkim Manipal University, India

ABSTRACT

Sikkim is known as a natural and ideal destination for the tourists looking for exotic and varied experiences. The study explores the adequacy of the policy in the context of eco-tourism principles espoused by eco-tourism society (TES) which are - minimize physical, social and psychological impact, Build environmental and cultural awareness, Provide positive experiences for both visitors and hosts, Produce direct financial benefits for conservation, and Recognize the rights and spiritual beliefs of the Indigenous People. Methodology used is case study for based on a structured questionnaire with 55 statements (on Likert scale) responded by the civil officers of the state government involved with eco-tourism policy and its implementation. To make it more meaningful one sample t-test has been conducted to test hypotheses. It concludes that the policy document has areas with distinct adequacies and inadequacies. The purpose of the study is to identify inadequacies that need to be addressed to make the policy document holistic and help in facilitating its proper implementation.

INTRODUCTION

The present case-study was undertaken at Sikkim, a small Indian state located between Nepal and Bhutan. It provides distinct and diverse opportunities for the eco-tourists and sensing this opportunity the Government of Sikkim has come up with an eco-tourism policy document with a view to harvest benefits of this economic sector while ensuring that negative effects are contained sufficiently, if not eliminated completely. This chapter investigates the adequacy of the policy in the context of internationally accepted

DOI: 10.4018/978-1-5225-2078-8.ch017

eco-tourism principles advocated by eco-tourism society (TES) and are - minimize physical, social and psychological impact, Build environmental and cultural awareness, Provide positive experiences for both visitors and hosts, Produce direct financial benefits for conservation, Generate financial benefits for both local people, Deliver memorable interpretative experiences to visitors, Design, construct and operate low-impact facilities and Recognize the rights and spiritual beliefs of the Indigenous People. The chapter begins by providing an insight into the Sikkim as a tourism destination, followed by emergence of eco-tourism and then succinctly introducing the principles of eco-tourism mentioned earlier. The chapter thereafter focuses on describing the methodology adopted to undertake the study, followed by result and discussion and conclusion. Innovative features of the study are that eco-tourism policy of Sikkim has been explored for the first-time. Also no studies (exploratory or otherwise) measuring eco-tourism on its proposed principles exists so far. Use of one-sample t-test in a case study also is sufficiently innovative.

Sikkim

Sikkim is a tiny Himalayan Indian state with an area of 7096 km^2 and a population of 6, 07,000 (2011 Census). Physically, it is an enclosed basin, nearly 60 km wide, between two deeply dissected north-south transverse ridges, each of them about 128 km long (Karan, 1969). The state is blessed with exquisite natural beauty, salubrious climate, rich biodiversity and a friendly host population. In addition to this the state's unique cultural traits adds to its attraction (Sattar, 2011). Despite its remarkable potential, tourism is rather new to Sikkim (Jha A, 2001) but has quickly emerged as a major economic sector in the state.

Tourism

Despite its immense economic benefits and contribution tourism till recently has been associated with socio-environmental and developmental problems. Batra and Kaur (1996) clearly bring out conflict involving tourism and environment by using environment-audit. They concluded that two dissimilar kinds of relationships exist between tourism and environment - coexistence and contradictory. Coexistence results in a well-balanced relationship between tourism and environment. conflicting relationship between the two, however lead to the problems of pollution and other ecological issues. They further opine that social costs in tourism are far higher than caused by other types of industries Unfortunately these costs largely have remained unacknowledged. Brohman (1996) underlines issues concerning increasing crime, overcrowding, overloaded infrastructure, pollution and environmental degradation particularly in the context of tourism in the third world countries. Once again he highlights that these issues are ignored as tourism results in fast economic growth in the third world countries. Noronha (1999) reports that tourism in Goa has caused uncontrolled increase in land prices, enhanced consumption, rapid and unplanned development, drug abuse and prostitution. He further found that inhabitants of Goa feel threatened and degraded by inappropriate values and behaviour of the tourists. Madan and Rawat (2000) in their study focussed upon the impact of tourism on the environment of Mussoorie. They brought out that random and scattered development of tourism infrastructure because of high demand for lodges, hotels and other basic amenities lead to pollution and environment degradation, Singh (2002) found positive-correlation between ecological degradation and perceived erosion of cultural values in Garhwal.

Emergence of Eco-Tourism

Eco-tourism has emerged as a global phenomenon in recent times (Rogerson, 2015). It has been propelled by the demand for nature-based tourism (Eshun and Tonto, 2014). The problems found to coexist with tourism led the social scientists to mitigate them without negating the positive aspects of tourism including the economic ones. It then appeared that tourism does not necessarily results in socio-environmental issues there are certain notable exceptions. Gupta (1999), for example, found pilgrimage in Indian Himalayas since a long time hardly resulted in any negative environmental, cultural and social impacts. Such exceptions gave insight in to the tourism as a whole and certain principles appeared to ensure that tourism may remain economically beneficial without corresponding socio-cultural and environmental fallouts. These principles gave rise to the concept of eco-tourism.

By eco tourism we mean preserving travel to natural areas to appreciate the cultural and natural history of the environment, taking care, not to disturb the integrity of the ecosystem, while creating economic opportunities that make conservation and protection of natural resources advantageous to the local people. In simple, ecotourism can be categorized as tourism programme that is - "Nature based, ecologically sustainable, where education and interpretation is a major constituent and where local people are benefited." All this together can be called ecotourism. If a travel does not satisfy any one of these constituents, then it is not appropriate to be called an ecotourism venture.

Fundamentally, ecotourism implies making as little environmental impact as possible and at the same time helping to sustain the indigenous populace, thereby encouraging the preservation of wildlife and habitats when visiting a place. This is responsible form of tourism and tourism development, which encourages going back to natural products in every aspect of life. It is also the key to sustainable ecological development. Biju (2003) states that *eco-tourism is both nature based and ecologically sustainable. It entails minimum impact on environment because as required less infrastructure facilities and services when compared with conventional tourism.* Eco-tourism attracted many a researchers to explore this multidimensional phenomenon (Fox et al, 2008; Lane, 2010; Hall, 2010: Aleksandrov, 2014; Balmford et al, 2015). This is because eco-tourism is a complex maze of nature, culture economics and technology and has no easy answers (Ostrom (2007))

Principles of Eco-Tourism

Eco-tourism principles have been formalized by TES as Appropriate planning, minimizing physical, social and psychological impact, Building environmental and cultural awareness, Providing positive experiences for both visitors and hosts, Producing direct financial benefits for conservation, Generating financial benefits for both local people, Delivering memorable interpretative experiences to visitors, Designing, constructing and operating low-impact facilities and Recognizing the rights and spiritual beliefs of the Indigenous People.

Appropriate Planning

Brohman (1996) while studying tourism in third world countries concluded that the third world countries must adopt proper tourism planning. Caprihan and Shivakumar (2004) Authors viewed that India had vast potential of ecotourism but lacked proper planning for protecting natural resources fundamental to it. Elnokaly, (2013) and Wilson and John (2001) identified support of local government and strategic planning, as essential for rural tourism development in particular. The authors viewed that rural tourism provided income and employment opportunities to local people in rural areas having unutilized huge natural resources. Singh (2002) reported that tourism policies in India were neither detailed nor properly implemented. George (2003) also identified master planning as one of the key functions associated with successful tourism projects. Others emphasizing importance of planning vis-à-vis eco-tourism are Bahuguna (2004). It, therefore, emerges that tourism in genera and ecotourism in particular require careful and elaborate plans to be successful. This is understandable as eco-tourism is a blend of conflicting issues and needs to be implemented in a holistic manner and hence it is strongly a function of appropriate planning.

Build Environmental and Cultural Awareness, and Respect

Eco-friendly attitude and behaviour of both – the visitors and the hosts, understandably is essential for any and every eco-tourism project. This calls for intense and continual awareness and educational efforts. Seema et al (2006) concluded that in eco-tourism in Indian context has significant implications conservation education along with for nature and culture conservation and rural livelihood. Existing documents on ecotourism policy are briefly reviewed in this paper to draw insights for the Indian context. They proposed approaches to link indicators of impacts and incentives in this respect. Earlier Tejvir Singh et al (1995) also considered conservation education as important component of nature tourism. Education is expected to result in attitudinal and behavioural changes and hence it is expected that the tourists are transformed into greater eco-friendly entities thus making conservation a cultural norm.

Provide Positive Experiences for Both Visitors and Hosts

Experiences such as clean air, natural and cultural values opportunities for walking, climbing, watching views influence people to come and visit the area (Mete Sezgin 2016). Eco-tourism cannot succeed if the experiences of a visitor and hosts get diluted due to any confines enforced onto it. Siva Shankaran, (2007) and Tejvir Singh et al (1995) opine that eco-tourism rather than diluting has the potential to enhance the experience of the tourists as well as the hosts. In order to be sustainable eco-tourism need to be attractive to new and repeat visitors. Sanjay Gubbi (2008), Eshun et al, (2014) and Eshun et al, 2015)) holds similar views.

Produce Direct Financial Benefits for Conservation

It may be argued that nature-tourism preys upon the very base on which it stands upon thus becoming highly sustainable. Caprihan and Shivakumar (2004) brought out conservation (along with supportiveness, improved livelihood opportunities to local people) as the pillars of eco-tourism. The negative impact of eco-tourism on natural resources need to be countered with equally effective conservation efforts. To sustain such conservation efforts part of eco-tourism revenue needs to be utilized on continual basis.

Generate Financial Benefits for Local People

Financial benefits naturally are the most important motivation for the hosts to accept eco-tourism projects. Indeed financial sustainability is entirely dependent on this. Tourism is believed to be the leading global voluntary transfer of wealth from rich people to poor people (Mitchell and Ashley, 2010). Eco-tourism is important as it perhaps is the distinct sector that provides favorable balance of trade to the developing world (Brunet et. al, 2009) Brohman (1996) advocated that revenue generated from tourism should be used for the benefit of local community. Similar views have been expressed by Noronha (1999), Wilson and John (2001), Kolas (2004), V.P. Raghavan, (2005). Economic benefits of Sikkim has been reported by Shenga S et al (2015)

Deliver Memorable Interpretative Experiences to Visitors that Help Raise Sensitivity to Host Countries' Political, Environmental, and Social Climates

Eco-tourism will be self-defeating if the political, environmental, and social climate of the host populace is adversely affected. Indeed it is socio-cultural diversity that propels eco-tourism and negative effects invariably will result in promoting dominant cultures of the tourists leading to mono-cultures. Few studies have been designed to explore this aspect of eco-tourism (Jaafar and Maideen, 2012).

Design, Construct, and Operate Low-Impact Facilities

Tourism often results in massive and negative impact. Batra and Kaur (1996), Brohman (1996), Noronha (1999), Usha Bande, (2002) and Singh (2002) could find strong linkages between tourism and socio-environmental degradation. This, because, to accommodate influx of tourists the infrastructure that is erected invariably results in substantial and irreversible negative impact. Hence a cautious and a deliberate effort to design, construct and operate low-impact facilities are vital to keep eco-tourism projects sustainable.

Recognize the Rights and Spiritual Beliefs of the Indigenous People and Work in Partnership with Them to Create Empowerment

Eco-tourism often involves the indigenous people. Lack of recognition of their rights and spiritual belief will not only be unethical but may result in unnecessary conflicts and which may destroy the sustainability of eco-tourism. Rather the effort must be to devise ways and means to enhance their participation as equal partners. It does not always happen. Suntikul, Wantanee, Dorji, Ugyen (2016), empirically measured the impact of tourism on religious festivals of Bhutan and concluded that increase in tourism may endanger the integrity and value of the festivals as per the belief held by host population. Kapil Dev, Walter, Pierre (2016). Also suggest that rather than following "modernist" eco-tourism, emphasis on locally owned, participatory form of community-based tourism will be more beneficial for Nepal and other developing countries. Nakata et al. (2012) in the context of developmental activities in general advocated moving away from colonized thinking.

METHODOLOGY

An empirical approach has been applied to the research work utilizing descriptive statistics based on the data on the belief expressed by the State government officers involved in formulating and implementing tourism policy. The study explores the adequacy of the policy in the context of eco-tourism principles espoused by eco-tourism society (TES) which are - minimize physical, social and psychological impact, Build environmental and cultural awareness, Provide positive experiences for both visitors and hosts, Produce direct financial benefits for conservation, Generate financial benefits for both local people, Deliver memorable interpretative experiences to visitors, Design, construct and operate low-impact facilities and Recognize the rights and spiritual beliefs of the Indigenous People. The research-design for the research work is conclusive. To arrive at conclusions descriptive approach has been used.

Objectives of the Study

Objective of the study is to ascertain whether the Government ecotourism policies adequately cater to the fundamental principles of eco-tourism or not. The subsidiary objectives of the study include the following:

- To determine if Appropriate eco-tourism Planning exists for Sikkim
- To determine if policies cater to contain negative impacts that can damage or destroy the character of the natural, social and psycho-emotional environment
- To find if policy adequately focuses on building environmental and cultural awareness, and respect
- To find if policy adequately focuses to provide positive experiences for both visitors and hosts
- To find if policy adequately focuses in producing direct financial benefits for conservation
- To find if policy adequately focuses Generate financial benefits for local people
- To find if policy adequately focuses in deliver memorable interpretative experiences to visitors that help raise sensitivity to host countries' political, environmental, and social climates
- To find if policy adequately focuses in design, construct and operate low-impact facilities
- To find if policy adequately focuses in recognizing the rights and spiritual beliefs of the Indigenous People and work in partnership with them to create empowerment

Hypothesis: *The corresponding Null Hypothesis therefore is that ecotourism policies of Sikkim do not adequately cater to the fundamental principles of eco-tourism.*

The subsidiary Hypotheses are as follows:

- There is no significantly appropriate eco-tourism Planning in Sikkim
- Policies do not cater to contain negative impacts that can damage or destroy the character of the natural, social and psycho-emotional environment
- The policies do not adequately focuses on building environmental and cultural awareness, and respect
- The policies do not adequately focuses to provide positive experiences for both visitors and hosts
- The policies do not adequately focuses in producing direct financial benefits for conservation
- The policies do not adequately focuses Generate financial benefits for local people

- The policies do not adequately focuses in deliver memorable interpretative experiences to visitors that help raise sensitivity to host countries' political, environmental, and social climates
- The policies do not adequately focuses in design, construct and operate low-impact facilities
- The policies do not adequately focuses in recognizing the rights and spiritual beliefs of the Indigenous People and work in partnership with them to create empowerment

Sample and Sample Size

The study has been based on a specific group of civil officers of the state government involved with eco-tourism policy and its implementation. Details collected from 38 such officers. Sample size is adequate as it is based on expert view and also as it is an exploratory study. Random sampling methods were used for the research. For the purpose list of all the civil officers was obtained and from which individuals were selected on random basis.

The tool is developed using Likert scale in a range of 1 to 5 with 1, 2, 3, 4 and 5 corresponding to Strongly Disagree, Disagree, Neither agree Nor Disagree, Agree and Strongly Agree respectively. In all it contained statements to be answered on a Likert scale. There no refusals. The respondents were contacted personally by the researcher and after general introduction the tool was handed over to them. The confidentiality of the information obtained from the respondents was guaranteed. The filled questionnaires were collected the same day and on a few occasions after few days.

Reliability Analysis

Reliability analysis was done by calculating the Cronbach's Alpha and its details are being provided in Table 1.

Table 1. Reliability analysis of data

Dimension	No. of Indicator Variables	Cronbach's Alpha
1. Eco-tourism Planning	5	0.83
2. Containing negative impacts that can damage or destroy the character of the natural, social and psycho-emotional environment	5	0.78
3. Building environmental and cultural awareness, and respect	6	0.74
4. Producing direct financial benefits for conservation	4	0.85
5. Generating financial benefits for local people	9	0.88
6. Delivering memorable interpretative experiences to visitors that help raise sensitivity to host countries' political, environmental, and social climates	6	0.92
7. Designing, constructing and operating low-impact facilities	6	0.79
8. Recognizing the rights and spiritual beliefs of the Indigenous People and work in partnership with them to create empowerment	9	0.87

Data Analysis

All analyses were conducted using Statistical Software (SPSS) 16.0 version. t - test were used to determine the significance of beliefs. For the hypothesis testing the confidence limit is set at 95%. Null Hypothesis is accepted if mean value is below 3 and if Z value is within ± 1.96.

H_0: (1.96 >Z< - 1.96)

OrIf Z is within ± 1.96 null hypothesis is accepted else rejected

To ascertain long term plans of the state government for the development of eco- tourism in the state

RESULT AND DISCUSSION

The pertinent details of the study have been provided under following 9 sub-sections, each one corresponding to an internationally recognized eco-tourism principle.

Appropriate Planning

In all 5 questions were asked to measure the robustness of eco-tourism plans. The result has been provided in Table 2.

We find that as per the expressed belief policies are drawn on long term, are clearly formulated, are adequately detailed, specific and flexible as in all cases the calculated t-value is higher than the tabulated one. Weakest link appears to be insufficient detailing as the mean stands at just 3.29 barely above 3 – the chance mean. Minor modifications may also be made in the policies to enhance their clarity, detailing specificity and flexibility. The hypothesis that there is no significantly appropriate eco-tourism planning in Sikkim stands rejected.

Minimize Physical, Social, Behavioral, and Psychological Impacts

In all 5 questions were asked to measure the impact. The findings have been provided in Table 3.

As per the expressed belief we find that policies appear to be appropriate in terms of the mountainous (and fragile) physical geography of the state as well as its phenomenal biodiversity and high earth-quake

Table 2. Results

Variable	Mean	S.D.	t-value	Sign
1. The government has drawn long term policies for eco-tourism in the state of Sikkim	4.23	0.76	17.52	0.00
2. The policies are clearly formulated	3.81	1.14	8.70	0.00
3. The policies are detailed to the required degree	3.29	0.95	3.37	0.00
4. The policies are specific to the requisite extent	3.46	0.96	5.28	0.00
5. The policies have due flexibility inbuilt into it	3.53	1.14	5.06	0.00

Table 3. Impact findings

Variable	Mean	S.D.	t-value	Sign
6. The policies are appropriate in the context of this mountainous state	4.01	0.90	12.26	0.00
7. The policies take into account the phenomenal biodiversity of Sikkim	3.94	0.85	12.12	0.00
8. Policies include earth-quake resistant infrastructure	3.61	0.92	7.15	0.00
9. Policies ensure that social fabric of Sikkim remains unaffected	3.68	0.94	7.19	0.00
10. Policies ensure that psycho-emotional vibrancy of people in Sikkim remains unaffected	3.55	0.89	7.12	0.00

prone disposition. We also find that policies ensure that social fabric of Sikkim and that psycho-emotional vibrancy of people in Sikkim remains unaffected. Since in all instance we find that the mean is above 3 we accept the hypothesis that policies cater to contain negative impacts that can damage or destroy the character of the natural, social and psycho-emotional environment. Yet as most mean values lie below 4, it is felt that improvements need to be incorporated in the policy in this respect. Our hypothesis that policies do not cater to contain negative impacts that can damage or destroy the character of the natural, social and psycho-emotional environment, stands rejected.

Build Environmental and Cultural Awareness, and Respect

In all 6 questions were asked to measure the adequacy of building environmental and cultural respect. The result has been provided in Table 4.

Eco-tourism has been envisioned for its educative potential too and accordingly an important principle defining it is that it should build environmental and cultural awareness and respect. How do the contemporary policies on eco-tourism in Sikkim measure on this aspect needed to be explored. We find that it is being believed that Policies are based on explicit assumption that Sikkim has to play a leadership role in promoting environmentalism, world peace, non-violence and diversity. This conclusion is

Table 4. Adequacy of building environmental and cultural respect

Variable	Mean	S.D.	t-value	Sign
11. Policies are based on explicit assumption that Sikkim has to play a leadership role in promoting environmentalism	3.35	0.97	3.97	0.00
12. Policies are based on explicit assumption that Sikkim has to play a leadership role in promoting world peace	3.61	0.92	7.15	0.00
13. Policies are based on explicit assumption that Sikkim has to play a leadership role in promoting universal brotherhood	2.74	1.28	2.22	0.03
14. Policies are based on explicit assumption that Sikkim has to play a leadership role in promoting Non-violence	3.76	0.88	9.48	0.00
15. Policies are based on explicit assumption that Sikkim has to play a leadership role in promoting eco-tourism	3.23	1.15	2.14	0.03
16. The policies promote diversity	3.58	0.96	6.55	0.00

arrived at as mean value in all these variables is calculated to be over 3 and the t-value is also above 1.96, the tabulated value. As mean-values are below 4 for all the variables we may also conclude that definite improvements are needed in the policies in this respect and this message needs to percolate down to lowest rung tour operators as well as the people of Sikkim. We find that mean-value for the statement *policies are based on explicit assumption that Sikkim has to play a leadership role in promoting universal brotherhood* is below 3 and hence the conclusion is promoting universal brother-hood needs to be incorporated strongly within the policies of the state. Our hypothesis that policies do not adequately focuses on building environmental and cultural awareness, and respect, stands rejected

Provide Positive Experiences for Both Visitors and Hosts

In all 6 questions were asked to measure the adequacy in providing positive experience for both visitors and hosts. The result has been shown in Table 5.

Tourism needs to be a rewarding experience for visitors as well as the hosts. This is possible when creativity and innovation lead the tourism landscape. Sikkim has much to offer tourists in terms of positive experience but has it been incorporated in tourism policies needed to be investigated. We find that policies are silent on introduction of traditional knowledge in school curriculum, familiarizing hosts with biodiversity, cultural songs and dances, significance of festivals, history and cultural philosophy of the state. If people of Sikkim themselves are not aware of the same they in no way will share with visitors and consequently enriching experiences will be denied to the visiting tourists and simultaneously the hosts will also fail to derive the happiness and pride of sharing bio-cultural diversity of the state. This needs to be incorporated urgently in the existing policies. Our hypothesis that policies do not adequately focuses to provide positive experiences for both visitors and hosts is accepted as in all cases the mean values are below 3.

Table 5. Adequacy in providing positive experience for both visitors and hosts

Variable	Mean	S.D.	t-value	Sign
17. The policies include introduction of traditional knowledge in school curriculum	1.55	0.97	20.97	0.00
18. The policies include familiarizing hosts with biodiversity of the state	2.76	1.24	2.22	0.03
19. The policies include familiarizing hosts with cultural songs and dances of the state	2.97	1.12	0.40	0.69
20. The policies include familiarizing hosts with significance of festivals of the state	3.04	1.09	0.42	0.68
21. The policies include familiarizing hosts with significance of cultural philosophy of the state	1.58	0.95	21	0.00
22. The policies include familiarizing hosts with significance history of the state	2.68	1.12	3.12	0.00

Table 6. Results of the adequacy in producing financial benefits for conservation

Variable	Mean	S.D.	t-value	Sign
23. Policies include directing funds for conservation of natural water-falls	3.50	1.10	4.98	0.00
24. Policies include directing funds for conservation of bio-diversity	3.96	0.87	12.05	0.00
25. Policies include directing funds for conservation of natural forests	3.76	0.88	9.48	0.00
26. Policies include positive afforestation in areas affected by tourism activities	3.23	1.15	2.14	0.03

Produce Direct Financial Benefits for Conservation

In all 4 questions were asked to measure the adequacy in producing financial benefits for conservation. The result has been shown in Table 6.

Tourism must not prey upon the very base that attracts tourists a long term sustainability is an avowed economic and ecological principle that fosters eco-tourism. Do the eco-tourism policies formulated at Sikkim consider this aspect diligently? We find that the policies do cater to directing profits of ecotourism for conserving natural water-falls, natural forests and state bio-diversity as also provide funds for afforestation in areas affected by tourism activities. Our hypothesis that policies do not adequately focus in producing direct financial benefits for conservation, therefore, stands rejected.

Generate Financial Benefits for Both Local People and Private Industry

In all 9 questions were asked to measure the adequacy in generating financial benefits for local people. The findings have been given in Table 7.

Table 7. The results of the adequacy in generating financial benefits for local people

Variable	Mean	S.D.	t-value	Sign
27. Policies identify preferred tourist-segments	2.74	1.28	2.22	0.03
28. Policies provide clear-guidelines to encourage revisits by tourists	3.23	1.15	2.14	0.03
29. Mechanisms exist to measure the value of a tourist	2.74	1.28	2.22	0.03
30. Policies provide guidelines to identify and wean out unsustainable tourists	2.72	1.27	2.22	0.03
The policies provides guidelines for strengthening village level institutions to the appropriate extent	3.20	1.12	2.14	0.03
The policies provide adequate measures for coordination amongst various stake-holders	3.74	1.92	8.02	0.00
The policies define institutional arrangements at District level.	3.58	0.96	6.55	0.00
The policies have inbuilt guidelines for partnerships with village level Institutions	2.67	1.14	3.13	0.00
Policies provide clear-guidelines to use local resources	3.23	1.15	2.14	0.03

A fundamental principle of eco-tourism is that it must facilitate in generating financial benefits for local people. How do eco-tourism policies as laid down by the government of Sikkim fare in this respect? Our findings provide answer to this question more or less in affirmative. We find that as per the expressed belief by the experts Policies provide clear-guidelines to encourage revisits by tourists, provides guidelines for strengthening village level institutions to the appropriate extent, provide adequate measures for coordination amongst various stake-holders, provide clear-guidelines to use local resources. Yet the corresponding low mean values (just above 3) do reveal that possibilities exist to strengthen the policies in this respect. We also find that there is a need to refine policies that identify preferred tourist-segments, of establishing mechanisms to measure the value of a tourist, weaning out unsustainable tourists and strengthening guidelines for instituting robust and resilient partnerships with village level Institutions. High standard deviations indicate differences in opinion expressed by the experts. Our hypothesis that The policies do not adequately focuses Generate financial benefits for local people stands rejected.

Deliver Memorable Interpretative Experiences to Visitors that Help Raise Sensitivity to Host Countries' Political, Environmental, and Social Climates

In all 6 questions were asked to measure the adequacy in terms of delivering memorable interpretative experiences to visitors that help raise sensitivity to the state's political, environmental and social climate. The results have been given in Table 8.

Four out of six variables point to the belief that policies are inadequate for delivering memorable interpretative experiences to visitors that help raise sensitivity to host countries' political, environmental, and social climates. This reflects violation of an essential precept of eco-tourism. Though it is encouraging to find that the state policies have succeeded in building strong partnership with local community and include appropriate training mechanisms for the people of the state in this respect yet we find that polices fall short on familiarizing hosts with biodiversity, cultural songs and dances and significance of festivals of the state. This gap needs to be addressed urgently as it is memorable experiences of tourists which alone can keep the flow of tourists to the state steady and uninterrupted. Including traditional-

Table 8. The results of the adequacy in terms of delivering memorable interpretative experiences to visitors that help raise sensitivity to the state's political, environmental and social climate

Variable	Mean	S.D.	t-value	Sign
36. The policies have succeeded in building strong partnership with local community	3.50	1.10	4.98	0.00
37. The plan includes appropriate training to people involved in providing tourist-services	3.61	0.92	7.15	0.00
38. The policies include familiarizing hosts with biodiversity of the state	2.76	1.24	2.22	0.03
39. The policies include familiarizing hosts with cultural songs and dances of the state	2.97	1.12	0.4	0.69
40. The policies include familiarizing hosts with significance of festivals of the state	3.04	1.09	0.42	0.68
41. The policies include familiarizing hosts with significance of cultural philosophy of the state	1.58	0.95	21	0

cultural knowledge in school-curriculum may help the state to achieve this objective. From the findings we may conclude that our hypothesis that the eco-tourism policies do not adequately focuses on delivering memorable interpretative experiences to visitors that help raise sensitivity to host countries' political, environmental, and social climates stands accepted.

Design, Construct, and Operate Low-Impact Facilities

In all 6 questions were asked to measure the adequacy in terms of designing, constructing and operating low-impact facilities. The findings have been given in Table 9.

Our findings indicate that designing, constructing and operating low-impact facilities, which is a fundamental tenet of eco-tourism is believed, to have been largely ignored within the policy framework. High values of corresponding standard variations indicate that views in these respects are more or less polarized. It emerges that policies do not include expansion plans for low impact roads, satellite townships and sewerage. Even though the policies are believed to have clearly defined norms for low-impact upkeep and maintenance of infrastructure include expansion plans for low-impact power infrastructure it is only marginally so as is evident from the corresponding mean-values which are marginally above 3 (3.46 and 3.29 respectively), implying that even on this score there is definite room for improvement. Our hypothesis that the policies do not adequately focuses on designing, constructing and operating low-impact facilities stands accepted. This gets further validated from the corresponding p-values.

Recognize the Rights and Spiritual Beliefs of the Indigenous People and Work in Partnership with Them to Create Empowerment

In all 8 questions were asked to measure the adequacy in terms of recognizing rights and spiritual beliefs of the local people and empowering them as partners. The findings have been given in Table 10.

From the results it is apparent that rights and spiritual beliefs of the Indigenous People are being given due credence in eco-tourism policies of the state. Yet it emerges that the policies do not include measures to protect cultural heritage of Sikkim from technological onslaught. The impression could be because of the opposition to the Hydro-electric power projects that have been proposed in the northern areas of the state and which people believe may affect the cultural sites that also are ecologically vital for the well

Table 9. The adequacy in terms of designing, constructing and operating low-impact facilities

Variable	Mean	S.D.	t-value	Sign
42. The policies have clearly defined norms for the sustainability of infrastructure created for ecotourism	3.96	0.87	12.05	0.00
43. The policies have clearly defined norms for low-impact upkeep and maintenance of infrastructure	3.46	0.88	4.48	0.00
44. The policies include expansion plans for low impact roads.	2.74	1.28	2.22	0.03
45. The policies include expansion plans for low-impact satellite townships	1.44	0.76	21.52	0.00
46. The policies include expansion plans for low-impact sewerage	2.96	1.14	0.40	0.69
47. The policies include expansion plans for low-impact power infrastructure	3.29	0.95	3.37	0.00

Table 10. The adequacy in terms of recognizing rights and spiritual beliefs of the local people and empowering them as partners

Variable	Mean	S.D.	t-value	Sign
48. The policies are consistent with prevailing socio-cultural beliefs	3.77	1.07	8.33	0.00
49. The policies are consistent with religious beliefs of the Sikkimese people	3.71	1.06	8.02	0.00
50. The policies include measures to protect cultural heritage of Sikkim from social changes	3.46	0.96	5.28	0.00
51. The policies include measures to protect cultural heritage of Sikkim from market forces	4.01	0.90	12.26	0.00
52. The policies include measures to protect cultural heritage of Sikkim from technological onslaught	2.94	0.85	0.52	0.00
53. The policies include measures to protect cultural heritage of Sikkim from globalized culture	3.77	1.07	8.33	0.00
54. The policies provide for an integrated approach to preserve, protect and document tangible heritage (monument, historical places, antiquities, art treasures, public and private records) of cultural and artistic importance	1.53	0.64	19.06	0.00
55. Policies are silent on promoting traditional types of houses	3.65	0.82	8.62	0.00

being of the state. The policies also are believed to fail to provide for an integrated approach to preserve, protect and document tangible heritage (monument, historical places, antiquities, art treasures, public and private records) of cultural and artistic importance. If these concerns are found to be valid immediate efforts need to be made to include them within the policy-framework. As in six (out of eight) cases the mean-value is found to be above 3 and the corresponding t-value is above 1.96 we may conclude that the null hypothesis policies do not adequately focuses in recognizing the rights and spiritual beliefs of the Indigenous People and work in partnership with them to create empowerment stands rejected. This is further confirmed by the respective p-values which remain substantially below 0.05.

CONCLUSION

The present study was undertaken to measure the adequacy of the eco-tourism policy in the Himalayan state of Sikkim in terms of the eco-tourism principles arrived at internationally in view the very people who have been responsible for formulating and implementing it. We find that planning appears to be adequate, elaborate and flexible. Indeed, the policy-makers have made the best use of world-wide experience and understanding of eco-tourism. This however, neen not make us complacent as eco-tourism is a dynamic phenomenon and very sensitive to the factors affecting it and hence the local and global experiences must be carefully recorded to keep on making required modification in the policies on regular basis. In terms of adequacy of containing physical, social and psychological impact we again conclude that policy addresses this issue in a fair manner though improvements in this respect are still possible. Adequacy of policies in building environmental and cultural awareness also appear to have been taken into consideration. Though it may still be argued that People of Sikkim are in a position to provide leadership in this respect as their religious and philosophical beliefs as also their embrace of modern environmental principles all converge well to exploit this potential. The policy-makers may consider pondering over this possibility and filling the gaps in their existing eco-tourism policy. The findings are unambiguous about the policy inadequacies in terms of providing positive experiences for both – the visitors and the hosts. They are grossly inadequate in exploiting the rich bio-cultural diversity of the state to weave experiences that may be truly unique. For achieving this capacity building of the people perhaps need to be revamped in holistic manner. Introducing traditional knowledge bio-cultural diversity at school level may pay high dividends. Policies appear to be adequate in terms of directing financial benefits for conservation, though a more elaborate study may be needed to confirm this issue. A lot appears to have been done to ensure financial benefits for the local people, yet gaping holes in this respect need to be addressed. The policy makers may consider to refine policies that identify preferred tourist-segments, of establishing mechanisms to measure the value of a tourist, weaning out unsustainable tourists and strengthening guidelines for instituting robust and resilient partnerships with village level Institutions. Polices need consolidation in terms of on familiarizing hosts with biodiversity, cultural songs and dances and significance of festivals of the state. This gap needs to be addressed urgently as it is memorable experiences of tourists which alone can keep the flow of tourists to the state steady and uninterrupted. Similarly though due consideration has been provided to construct and operate low-impact facilities, yet vital issues still need to addressed appropriately to make policies adequate in this respect. Policies perhaps because have been formulated by indigenous people do recognize the rights and spiritual beliefs of the Indigenous People yet they will o well to provide for an integrated approach to preserve, protect and document tangible heritage of the state.

REFERENCES

Aleksandrov, K. (2014). The Role of DMO for Sustainable Development of a Tourist Destination: Bulgaria Case Study. *Proceedings of 4th International Conference on Tourism & Hospitality Management*. Retrieved May 19, 2015, from: http://jotr.eu/index.php/tourism-management/100-aleksandrov

Bahuguna, A. (2004). Tourism in India: Development Perspective. *The Indian Economic Journal*, *52*(1-2), 137–141.

Balmford, A., Green, J. M. H., Anderson, M., Beresford, J., Huang, C., Naidoo, R., & Manica, A. et al. (2015). Walk on the Wild Side: Estimating the Global Magnitude of Visits to Protected Areas. *PLoS Biology*, *13*(2), e1002074. doi:10.1371/journal.pbio.1002074 PMID:25710450

Batra, A. (2003). Indian Tourist Sites-In the Footprints of the Buddha. *ABAC Journal*, *23*(2), 46–57.

Batra, G. S., & Kaur, N. (1996). New Vistas in Reducing the Conflicts Between Tourism and the Environment: An Environmental Audit Approach. *Management Auditing Journal*, *11*(4), 3–10. doi:10.1108/02686909610119985

Biju, M. R. (2003). Eco-Tourism: Tourism of the New Millennium. *South Asian Journal of Social Political Sciences*, *4*(1), 89–95.

Brohman, J. (1996). New Directions in Tourism for Third World Development. *Annals of Tourism Research*, *23*(1), 48–70. doi:10.1016/0160-7383(95)00043-7

Caprihan, V., & Shivakumar, K. (2004, December). Eco-Tourism in India. *South Asian Journal of Social Political Sciences*, *4*(2), 80–85.

Elnokaly, A., & Elseragy, A. (2013). Sustainable Heritage Development: Learning from Urban Conservation of Heritage Projects in Non Western Contexts. *European Journal of Sustainable Development, 2*, 31-54.

Eshun, G., & Tagoe-Darko, E. (2015). Ecotourism Development in Ghana: A Postcolonial Analysis. *Development Southern Africa*, *32*(3), 392–406. doi:10.1080/0376835X.2015.1020218

Eshun, G., & Tonto, J. N. P. (2014). Community-based ecotourism: Its socio-economic impacts at Boabeng-Fiema Monkey Sanctuary, Ghana. Bulletin of Geography, 26, 67–81 doi:10.2478/bog-2014-0045

Fox, J., Bushley, B. R., Miles, W. B., & Shimona, A. (2003, December). *Connecting Communities and Conservation: Collaborative Management of Protected Areas in Bangladesh*. Nishorgo Support Project, Bangladesh Forest Department. East-West Center.

George, P. O. (2003). Strategic Management in Tourism. *South Asian Journal of Social Political Sciences*, *4*(1), 86–88.

Gupta, V. (1999). Sustainable Tourism: Learning from Indian Religious Tradition. *International Journal of Contemporary Hospitality Management*, *11*(2/3), 91–95. doi:10.1108/09596119910250751

Hall, C. M. (2010). Changing paradigms and global change: From sustainable to steady-state tourism. *Tourism Recreation Research*, *35*(2), 131–145. doi:10.1080/02508281.2010.11081629

Jaafar, M., & Maideen, S. A. (2012). Ecotourism Related Products and Activities and the economic sustainability of small and medium island chalets. *Tourism Management*, *33*(3), 683–691. doi:10.1016/j.tourman.2011.07.011

Jha, A. (2001). Information Technology and Creativity to Develop Enterprise, a Case Study of Tourism in Sikkim. *Proceedings of National Seminar supported by AICTE*.RaipurInstitute of Technology.

Dev, K., & Walter, P. (2016). Modernisation theory, ecotourism policy, and sustainable development for poor countries of the global South: Perspectives from Nepal. *International Journal of Sustainable Development and World Ecology*.

Karan, P. P. (1969). The kingdom of Sikkim, Annals Map Supplement Number 10. *Annals of the Association of American Geographers*, *59*, 211–213. doi:10.1111/j.1467-8306.1969.tb00665.x

Kolas, A. (2004). Tourism and the Making of Place in Shangri-La. *Tourism Geographies*, *6*(3), 262–278. doi:10.1080/1461668042000249610

Lane, M. B. (2010). Affirming New Directions in Planning Theory: Co-management of Protected Areas. *Society & Natural Resources*, *14*(8), 657–667. doi:10.1080/08941920118212

Madan, S., & Rawat, L. (2000). The Impact of Tourism on the Environment of Mussoorie, Garhwal Himalaya, India. *The Environmentalist*, *20*(3), 249–255. doi:10.1023/A:1006760015997

Sezgin & Gumus. (2016). The Evaluation of Beysehir Lake National Park (Konya-Turkey) in the Framework Ecotourism. *Journal of Advanced Management Science, 4*(4).

Mitchell, J., & Ashley, C. (2010). Tourism and Poverty Reduction. London, UK: Earthscan Publishing.

Nakata, N. M., Nakata, V., Keech, S., & Bolt, R. (2012). Decolonial goals and pedagogies for Indigenous studies. *Decolon Indig Educ Soc*, *1*, 120–140.

Noronha, F. (1999). Ten Year later, Goa Still Uneasy Over the Impact of Tourism. *International Journal of Contemporary Hospitality Management*, *11*(2/3), 100–106. doi:10.1108/09596119910250977

Ostrom, E. (2007). A diagnostic approach for going beyond panaceas. *Proceedings of the National Academy of Sciences of the United States of America*, *104*(39), 15181–15187. doi:10.1073/pnas.0702288104 PMID:17881578

Rogerson, C. M. (2015). Tourism and Regional Development: The case of South Africa depressed areas. *Development Southern Africa*, *3*(3), 277–291. doi:10.1080/0376835X.2015.1010713

Gubbi, S. (2008). Wildlife Tourism: The Great Indian Green Trick. Sanctuary Asia, 28(5), 40-44.

Sattar, S. (2011). *Tourism and Development in Sikkim, Tourism and Development in Sikkim*. IIPS Mumbai.

Seema, P., Jojo, T. D., Freeda, M. S., Santosh, B., Sheetal, P., Gladwin, J., . . . Sidharth, K. (2006). *White Paper on Eco-Tourism Policy*. Center for Conservation Governance and Policy, Ashoka Trust for Research in Ecology and the Environment (ATREE).

Shenga, S. S. N., Mishra, S. N., Sharma, N., & Jha, A. (2015). Economic Benefits of Eco-tourism in Sikkim. *Southern Economist, 54*(6).

Singh, M. (2004). *Management of State Tourism Development Corporations*. Deep and Deep Publications Private Ltd.

Singh, R. K., & Mishra, D. K. (2004). Green Tourism in Mountain Regions- Reducing Vulnerability and Promoting People and Place Centric Development in the Himalayas. *Journal of Mountain Science*, *1*(1), 57–64. doi:10.1007/BF02919360

Shankaran. (2007). Rural tourism and Handicrafts. *Yojana*, *51*(20), 29-31.

Singh, Valene, Fish, & Ricter. (1995). *Tourism Environment- Nature, Culture and Economy*. Inter-India Publications.

Suntikul, W., & Dorji, U. (2016). Local Perspectives on the Impact of Tourism on Religious Festivals in Bhutan. *Asia Pacific Journal of Tourism Research*, *21*(7), 741–762. doi:10.1080/10941665.2015.1069365

Usha Bande. (2002). Eco-Tourism and Mountains. Yojana, 24(15), 20-24.

TIES. (2015). *The International Eco Tourism Society*. Retrieved from TIES: http://www.ecotourism.org /what-is-ecotourism

Raghavan, V. P. (2005). Economy of Eco-Tourism in Kerala. Kerala Calling, 15(2), 40-41.

Wilson, H., & Venes, J. (2001). Factors for Success in Rural Tourism Development. *Journal of Travel Research*, *40*, 132-138.

Compilation of References

Acharya & Chettri. (2011). Effect Of Climate Change On Birds, Herpetofauna And Butterflies In Sikkim Himalaya: A Preliminary Investigation Biodiversity of Sikkim. In Exploring and Conserving a Global Hotspot. IFS.

ADB. (2010). *Inception Report Improving Connectivity and Destination Management of Cultural and Natural Resources in the South Asia Sub-region*. package 4 India-Sikkim.

Adeyinka-Ojo, S. F., Khoo-Lattimore, C., & Nair, V. (2014). A framework for rural tourism destination management and marketing organisations. *Procedia: Social and Behavioral Sciences*, *144*, 151–163. doi:10.1016/j.sbspro.2014.07.284

Agarwal, S. (2002). restructuring seaside tourism: The resort lifecycle. *Annals of Tourism Research*, *29*(1), 25–55. doi:10.1016/S0160-7383(01)00002-0

Agrawal, V. C. (2000). *Taxonomic studies on Indian Muridae and Hystricidae (Mammalia: Rodentia)*. Records of the Zoological Survey of India, Occasional Paper No. 180.

Agrusa, J., Lema, J., Tanner, J., Afo, A., Prideaux, B., & George, B. P. (2011). Destination image of Tahiti as perceived by international tourists: A study. *Asia Pacific World: The Journal of the International Association for Asia Pacific Studies*, *2*(2), 25–39. doi:10.3167/apw.2011020207

Ahmed, Z. U., & Krohn, F. B. (1990). Reversing the United States declining competitiveness in the marketing of international tourism: A perspective on future policy. *Journal of Travel Research*, *29*(2), 23–29. doi:10.1177/004728759002900204

Airey, D. (1983). European government approaches to tourism. *Tourism Management*, *4*(4), 234–244. doi:10.1016/0261-5177(83)90001-8

Ajeya & Sangeeta. (2001). *Information Technology and Creativity to Develop Enterprises: A Case Study to Tourism in Sikkim*. National Seminar on Creativity and Innovation for Entrepreneurial Development, Raipur.

Ajzen, I., & Fishbein, M. (1980). *Understanding attitudes and predicting social behavior*. Englewood Cliffs, NJ: Prentice-Hall.

Ajzen, I. (2008). Consumer attitudes and behaviour. In Handbook of consumer psychology. New York: Lawrence Erlbaum Associates.

Akehurst, G., Bland, N., & Nevin, M. (1993). Tourism policies in the European community member states. *International Journal of Hospitality Management*, *12*(1), 33–66. doi:10.1016/0278-4319(93)90040-G

Alcock, A., Lane, S., & Grant, J. (1994). *National Ecotourism Strategy*. Canberra: Australian Government Publishing Service.

Alcock, D. (1995). Sustainable development of reef tourism. *Australian Science*, *16*, 26–27.

Aleksandrov, K. (2014). The Role of DMO for Sustainable Development of a Tourist Destination: Bulgaria Case Study. *Proceedings of 4th International Conference on Tourism & Hospitality Management*, 208-217. Retrieved May 19, 2015, from: http://jotr.eu/index.php/tourism-management/100-aleksandrov

Aleksandrov, K. (2014). The Role of DMO for Sustainable Development of a Tourist Destination: Bulgaria Case Study. *Proceedings of 4th International Conference on Tourism & Hospitality Management*. Retrieved May 19, 2015, from: http://jotr.eu/index.php/tourism-management/100-aleksandrov

Alemeida, A., & Correia, A. (2010). Tourism development in Madeira; an analysis based onthe life cycle approach. *Tourism Economics*, *16*(2), 427–441. doi:10.5367/000000010791305644

Allen, P. (2004). *Together at the table: Sustainability and sustenance in the American agrifood system*. Pennsylvania State University Press.

Almas, R., & Lawrence, G. (Eds.). (2002). *Globalization, localization and sustainable livelihoods*. Aldershot, UK: Ashgate.

Almeyda, A. M., Broadbent, E. N., Wyman, M. S., & Durham, W. H. (2010). Ecotourism impacts in the Nicoya Peninsula, Costa Rica. *International Journal of Tourism Research*, *12*(6), 803–819. doi:10.1002/jtr.797

Altieri, M. A. (1989). Agroecology: A new research and development paradigm for world agriculture. *Agriculture, Ecosystems & Environment*, *27*(1-4), 37–46. doi:10.1016/0167-8809(89)90070-4

Amir, A. F., Ghapar, A. A., Jamal, S. A., & Ahmad, K. N. (2015). Sustainable tourism development: A study on community resilience for rural tourism in Malaysia. *Procedia: Social and Behavioral Sciences*, *168*, 116–122. doi:10.1016/j.sbspro.2014.10.217

Anastasijevic, N., Anastasijevic, V., Bobic, A., Stojanovic, N., & Mesicek, M. (2009). Ecological and tourist potential of central Belgrade. *Turizam*, *13*(2), 75–83.

Anctil, A., & Blanc, D. L. (2016). An educational simulation tool for integrated coastal tourism development in developing countries. *Journal of Sustainable Tourism*, *24*(5), 783–798. doi:10.1080/09669582.2015.1091463

Andronikidis, A., Georgiou, A. C., Gotzamani, K., & Kamvysi, K. (2009). The application of quality function deployment in service quality management. *TQM J.*, *21*(4), 319–333. doi:10.1108/17542730910965047

Ankomah, P. K., & Crompton, J. L. (1990). Unrealized tourism potential: The case of Sub-saharan Africa. *Tourism Management, 11*(3), 11-27.

Anonymous. (2002). *Final Report on 20 years Perspective Plan for Sustainable Tourism Development in the State of Sikkim*. Govt. of India, Ministry of Tourism & Culture, Department of Tourism, Market Research Division, Horizon Industrial Consultancy Services, New Delhi.

Anonymous. (2014). *Summing up international student mobility in 2014*. Retrieved from http://monitor.icef.com/2014/02/summing-up-international-student-mobility-in-2014/

Anti-Secession Law. (2005). *10th National People's Congress and Chinese People's Political Consultative Conference*. Article 8. Adopted at the Third Session of the Tenth National People's Congress on March 14, 2005.

Aoki, M. (2016). Does Mitigation and adaptation technologies in rice production affect product price? Evidence from Japan. In H. Ha (Ed.), *Climate Change Impacts in Urbanizing Asia*. London: Sage Publishers.

Arahi, Y. (1998). *Rural Tourism in Japan: The Regeneration of Rural Communities*. Food & Fertilizer Technology Center.

Arellano, M., & Bond, S. (1991). Some tests of specification for panel data: Monte Carlo evidence and an application to employment equations. *The Review of Economic Studies*, *58*(2), 277–297. doi:10.2307/2297968

Arslanturk, Y., Balcilar, M., & Ozdemir, Z. A. (2011). Time-varying linkages between tourism receipts and economic growth in a small open economy. *Economic Modelling, 28*(1-2), 664–671. doi:10.1016/j.econmod.2010.06.003

Asadi, R., & Daryaei, M. (2011). Prioritization of Forms of Tourism in Iran to Formulate National Strategies. *European Journal of Scientific Research, 65*(1), 144-152.

ASEAN Secretariat and United Nation Committee of Trade and Development (UNCTAD). (2015). *ASEAN Investment Report 2013-2014: FDI Development and Regional Value Chains.* Available: http://investasean.asean.org/files/upload/AIR%202013-2014%20FINAL.pdf

ASEAN Secretariat. (2015). *ASEAN Statistics.* Available: http://www.asean.org/news/item/tourism-statistics

Ashworth, G. (1994). From history to heritage: From heritage to identity: In search of concepts and models. In G. J. Ashworth & P. J. Larkham (Eds.), *Building a new heritage: tourism, culture and identity in the new Europe* (pp. 13–30). London, UK: Routledge.

Asian Development Bank. (2014). *VIE: Urban environment and climate change adaptation project (Hoi An City, Quang Nam Province).* Hanoi, Vietnam: Asian Development Bank.

Asmusen, B., Harridge-March, S., Occhiocupo, N., & Farquhar, J. (2012). The multi-layered nature of Internet democratization of brand management. *Journal of Business Research, 66*(9), 1473–1483. doi:10.1016/j.jbusres.2012.09.010

Ateljevic, I., & Doorne, S. (2000). "Staying within the fence": Lifestyle entrepreneurship in tourism. *Journal of Sustainable Tourism, 8*(5), 378–392. doi:10.1080/09669580008667374

Ateljevic, J. (2009). Tourism entrepreneurship and regional development: Example from New Zealand. *International Journal of Entrepreneurial Behavior & Research, 15*(3), 282–308. doi:10.1108/13552550910957355

Avasthe, R.K., & Jha, A. (1999). *Mammals of Sikkim.* WWF-India.

Avieli, N. (2015). The rise and fall (?) of Hoi An, a UNESCO World Heritage Site in Vietnam. *SOJOURN: Journal of Social Issues in Southeast Asia, 30*(1), 35–71. doi:10.1355/sj30-1b

Bahuguna, A. (2004). Tourism in India: Development Perspective. *The Indian Economic Journal, 52*(1-2), 137–141.

Baidal, J. A. V. I., Sanchez, I. R., & Rebollo, J. F. B. (2013). The evolution of mass tourism destinations: New approaches beyond deterministic models in Benidorm (Spain). *Tourism Management, 34*(1), 184–195. doi:10.1016/j.tourman.2012.04.009

Balaguer, J., & Cantavella-Jordá, M. (2002). Tourism as a long-run economic factor: The Spanish case. *Applied Economics, 34*(7), 877–884. doi:10.1080/00036840110058923

Balaguer, J., & Cantavella-Jorda, M. (2004). Structural change in exports and economic growth: Cointegration and casuality. Analysis for Spain (19612000). *Applied Economics, 36*(5), 437–477. doi:10.1080/00036840410001682179

Balakrishnan, M. S. (2009). Strategic branding of destinations: A framework. *European Journal of Marketing, 43*(5/6), 611–629. doi:10.1108/03090560910946954

Balan, M., & Burghelea, C. (2015). Rural tourism and its implication in the development of the Fundata village. *Procedia: Social and Behavioral Sciences, 188*, 276–281. doi:10.1016/j.sbspro.2015.03.393

Ballman, G., Burke, J., Blank, U., & Korte, D. (1984). Toward higher quality conversion studies: Refining the numbers game. *Journal of Travel Research, 22*, 28–33.

Balmford, A., Green, J. M. H., Anderson, M., Beresford, J., Huang, C., Naidoo, R., & Manica, A. et al. (2015). Walk on the Wild Side: Estimating the Global Magnitude of Visits to Protected Areas. *PLoS Biology*, *13*(2), e1002074. doi:10.1371/journal.pbio.1002074 PMID:25710450

Bandyopadhyay, R., & Morais, D. (2005). Representative dissonance, Indias self and western image. *Annals of Tourism Research*, *32*(4), 1006–1021. doi:10.1016/j.annals.2005.02.002

Banerjee, A., Dolado, J. J., & Mestre, R. (1998). Error-correction mechanism tests for cointegration in a single-equation framework. *Journal of Time Series Analysis*, *19*(3), 267–283. doi:10.1111/1467-9892.00091

Baporikar, N., & Sokhalingam, C. P. (2010). *Strategic Management of Tourism – A Case of Oman* (1st ed.). VDM Verlag.

Baporikar, N., & Sokhalingam, C. P. (2012). Holistic Approach to Tourism Entrepreneurship: A Case of Tamil Nadu. *International Journal of Tourism and Travel*, *5*, 57–66.

Baporikar, N. (2014a). Innovation Strategies in SME: Global Perspective. In C. Machado & P. Melo (Eds.), *Effective Human Resources Management in Small and Medium Enterprises: Global Perspectives* (pp. 315–341). Hershey, PA: Business Science Reference.

Baporikar, N. (2014b). Innovation in the 21st Century Organization. In B. Christiansen, S. Yildiz, & E. Yildiz (Eds.), *Transcultural Marketing for Incremental and Radical Innovation* (pp. 339–365). Hershey, PA.

Baporikar, N. (2014c). Youth Entrepreneurship in Indian Scenario.[IJABIM]. *International Journal of Asian Business and Information Management*, *5*(2), 74–84.

Baporikar, N. (2014d). Information Strategy as Enabler of Competitive Advantage.[IJSITA]. *International Journal of Strategic Information Technology and Applications*, *5*(1), 30–41.

Baporikar, N. (2015b). Role of Entrepreneurship in Networked Indian Economy. In P. Ordóñez de Pablos (Ed.), *Technological Solutions for Sustainable Business Practice in Asia* (pp. 36–59). Hershey, PA: Business Science Reference.

Baporikar, N. (2015c). Motivating Tourism: A Case of Club Mahindra Holidays.[IJABIM]. *International Journal of Asian Business and Information Management*, *6*(2), 1–15.

Baporikar, N. (2015d). Holistic Framework for Evolving Effective Information Systems Strategy.[IJSITA]. *International Journal of Strategic Information Technology and Applications*, *6*(4), 30–43.

Baporikar, N. (2016a). Infrastructure Development as a Catalyst for Social-Economic Advancement.[IJSDA]. *International Journal of System Dynamics Applications*, *5*(4), 101–113.

Baporikar, N. (2016b). Strategic Approach to Tourism Development in Namibia.[IJSEM]. *International Journal of Sustainable Economies Management*, *5*(3), 1–12.

Baporikar, N. (2016c). Entrepreneurship Culture of SMEs in India's Tourism Sector.[IJSITA]. *International Journal of Strategic Information Technology and Applications*, *7*(2), 14–27.

Baporikar, N. (2011). Emerging Trends in Tourism Industry in Oman. In Global Hospitality and Tourism management Technologies. IGI Global.

Baporikar, N. (2015a). Effect of National Culture on Development of International Business in the Sultanate of Oman. In B. Christiansen (Ed.), Handbook of Research on Global Business Opportunities. Hershey, PA: Business Science Reference.

Barlybaev, A. A., Akhmetov, V. Y., & Nasyrov, G. M. (2009). Tourism as a factor of rural economy diversification. *Studies on Russian Economic Development*, *20*(6), 639–643. doi:10.1134/S1075700709060094

Barro, R. J., & Sala-i-Martin, X. (1992). Convergence. *Journal of Political Economy, 100*(2), 223–251. doi:10.1086/261816

Barro, R. J., & Sala-i-Martin, X. (1995). *Economic growth*. New York, NY: McGraw Hill.

Barro, R. J. (1991). Economic growth in a cross section of countries. *The Quarterly Journal of Economics, 106*(2), 407–443. doi:10.2307/2937943

Bates, C., & Bates, L. L. (2008). *Culture Shock!* Taiwan: Marshall Cavendish International Asia Pte Ltd.

Batnasan, N. (2003). Freshwater issues in Mongolia.*Proceeding of the National Seminar on IRBM in Mongolia*, 53-61.

Batra, A. (2003). Indian Tourist Sites-In the Footprints of the Buddha. *ABAC Journal, 23*(2), 46–57.

Batra, G. S., & Kaur, N. (1996). New Vistas in Reducing the Conflicts Between Tourism and the Environment: An Environmental Audit Approach. *Management Auditing Journal, 11*(4), 3–10. doi:10.1108/02686909610119985

Baum, T. (1994). The development and implementation of national tourism policies. *Tourism Management, 15*(3), 185–192. doi:10.1016/0261-5177(94)90103-1

Baum, T. (2006). Revisiting the TALC: is there an off-ramp? In R. W. Butler (Ed.), *Tourism Area Life Cycle; Conceptual and Theoretical Issues* (pp. 27–50). Clevedon, UK: Channelview Publications.

Bayer, C., & Hanck, C. (2013). Combining non-cointegration tests. *Journal of Time Series Analysis, 34*(1), 83–95. doi:10.1111/j.1467-9892.2012.00814.x

Bazneshin, S. D., Hosseini, S. B., & Azeri, A. R. K. (2015). The physical variables of tourist areas to increase the tourists' satisfaction regarding the sustainable tourism criteria: Case study of Rudsar villages, Sefidab in Rahim Abad. *Procedia: Social and Behavioral Sciences, 201*, 128–135. doi:10.1016/j.sbspro.2015.08.141

Becken, S., & Hughey, K. F. D. (2013). Linking tourism into emergency management structures to enhance disaster risk reduction. *Tourism Management, 36*, 77–85. doi:10.1016/j.tourman.2012.11.006

Beeton, S. (2004). The case study in tourism research: A multi-method case study approach. In B. W. Ritchie, P. Burns, & C. Palmer (Eds.), *Tourism research methods: Integrating theory with practice* (pp. 37–61). Cambridge, MA: CAB International.

Bel, F., Lacroix, A., Lyser, S., Rambonilaza, T., & Turpin, N. (2015). Domestic demand for tourism in rural areas: Insights from summer stays in three French regions. *Tourism Management, 46*, 562–570. doi:10.1016/j.tourman.2014.07.020

Bell, D. (2006). Variations on the rural idyll. In P. Cloke, T. Marsden, & P. Mooney (Eds.), *Handbook of rural studies* (pp. 149–160). London, UK: Sage Publications. doi:10.4135/9781848608016.n10

Benhabib, J., & Spiegel, M. (2000). The Role of Financial Development in Growth and Investment. *Journal of Economic Growth, 5*(4), 341–360. doi:10.1023/A:1026599402490

Berry, T. (2006). The predictive potential of the TALC model. In The Tourism Area Life Cycle, Conceptual and Theoretical Issues (pp. 167-175). Clevedon, UK: Channelview Publications.

Bhuiyan, M. A. H., Siwar, C., Ismail, S. M., & Islam, R. (2011). The role of government for ecotourism development: Focusing on East Coast economic region. *Journal of Social Sciences, 7*(4), 557–564. doi:10.3844/jssp.2011.557.564

Biddulph, R. (2015). Limits to mass tourism's effects in rural peripheries. *Annals of Tourism Research, 50*(1), 98–112. doi:10.1016/j.annals.2014.11.011

Biju, M. R. (2003). Eco-Tourism: Tourism of the New Millennium. *South Asian Journal of Social Political Sciences, 4*(1), 89–95.

Bird, M. (2014). *The hole in Bucharest that's become a nature reserve.* Retrieved from http://www.citymetric.com/skylines/hole-bucharest-s-become-nature-reserve-398

Bitsani, E., & Kavoura, A. (2014). Host perceptions of rural tour marketing to sustainable tourism in Central Eastern Europe. The case study of Istria, Croatia. *Procedia: Social and Behavioral Sciences, 148*, 362–369. doi:10.1016/j.sbspro.2014.07.054

Black, R. S., & Crabtree, A. (Eds.). (2007). *Quality Assurance and Certification in Ecotourism.* Wallingford, UK: CABI Publishing. doi:10.1079/9781845932374.0000

Blackburn, R. A., Hart, M., & Wainwright, T. (2013). Small business performance: Business, strategy and owner-manager characteristics. *Journal of Small Business and Enterprise Development, 20*(1), 8–27. doi:10.1108/14626001311298394

Blamey, R. K. (1995). *The Nature of Ecotourism.* Occasional Paper No 21. Canberra: Bureau of Tourism Research.

Blancas, F. J., Lozano-Oyola, M., & González, M. (2015). A European sustainable tourism labels proposal using a composite indicator. *Environmental Impact Assessment Review, 54*, 39–54. doi:10.1016/j.eiar.2015.05.001

Bora, B., & Adhikary, A. (2006). Northeast Tourism as a Gateway to Southeast Asia-Connecting Across Borders & Cultures. *International Conference on Strategic Thought in the New Age Management.* University of Jammu.

Bora, B., Adhikary, A., & Ajeya, J. (2009). *Strategic Development of Tourism in Sikkim Himalaya -An Impetuous towards Sustainable Economy.* National Seminar on Science, Technology and Development in the Himalayas, North Bengal.

Bora, B., Adhikary, A., & Ajeya, J. (2011). *Marketing of Service Sector: An Infrastructural Road Map for Sikkim Tourism.* International Conference International Conference on Infrastructure Finance, (ICIF 2010), VGSOM, IIT Kharagpur.

Bora, B., Adhikary, A., & Sikdar, S. (2006). *Northeast Tourism-The Market Beyond Border.* Kurukshetra, No.9. Ministry of Rural Development Publication.

Bora, B., Adhikary, A., & Sikdar, S. (2007). Northeast Tourism and ASEAN-Gaining Momentum in terms of Sustainable Development, Focus. *The International Journal of Management Digest, 3*(2), 7-20.

Boswijk, H. P. (1994). Testing an unstable root in conditional and structural error correction models. *Journal of Econometrics, 63*(1), 37–60. doi:10.1016/0304-4076(93)01560-9

Brahmasrene, T., & Lee, J. W. (2016). Assessing the dynamic impact of tourism, industrialization, urbanization, and globalization on growth and environment in Southeast Asia. *International Journal of Sustainable Development and World Ecology*, 1–10. doi:10.1080/13504509.2016.1238021

Bramwell, B., & Cox, V. (2009). Stage and path dependence approaches to the evolution of a national park tourism partnership. *Journal of Sustainable Tourism, 17*(2), 191–206. doi:10.1080/09669580802495782

Bramwell, B., & Lane, B. (1994). Rural tourism as a factor in rural community economic development for economies in transition. *Journal of Sustainable Tourism, 2*(1/2), 51–60.

Bramwell, B., & Lane, B. (2006). Editorial: Policy Relevance and Sustainable Tourism Research: Liberal, Radical and Post-structuralist Perspectives. *Journal of Sustainable Tourism, 14*(1), 1–5. doi:10.1080/09669580608668587

Bramwell, B., & Lane, B. (2014). The "critical turn" and its implications for sustainable tourism research. *Journal of Sustainable Tourism, 22*(1), 1–8. doi:10.1080/09669582.2013.855223

Bramwell, B. (2011). Governance, the state and sustainable tourism: A political economy approach. *Journal of Sustainable Tourism, 19*(4/5), 459–477. doi:10.1080/09669582.2011.576765

Bramwell, B. (2015). Theoretical activity in sustainable tourism research. *Annals of Tourism Research, 54*, 204–218. doi:10.1016/j.annals.2015.07.005

Brida, J. G., Coretes-Jimenez, I., & Pulina, M. (2014). Has the tourism-led growth hypothesis been validated? A Literature review. *Current Issues in Tourism.*

Briedenhann, J., & Butts, S. (2006). The application of the Delphi technique to rural tourism project evaluation. *Current Issues in Tourism, 9*(2), 171–190. doi:10.1080/13683500608668246

Briedenhann, J., & Wickens, E. (2004). Tourism routes as a tool for the economic development of rural areas – vibrant hope or impossible dream? *Tourism Management, 25*(1), 71–79. doi:10.1016/S0261-5177(03)00063-3

Brodie, J. (1995). Terrestrial runoff and the Great Barrier Reef. *Australian Science, 16*, 23–25.

Broekhuizen, H., Groothuis-Oudshoorn, C. G. M., van Til, J. A., Hummel, J. M., & Ijzerman, M. J. (2015). A review and classification of approaches for dealing with uncertainty in multi-criteria decision analysis for healthcare decisions. *PharmacoEconomics, 33*(5), 445–455. doi:10.1007/s40273-014-0251-x PMID:25630758

Brohman, J. (1996). New Directions in Tourism for Third World Development. *Annals of Tourism Research, 23*(1), 48–70. doi:10.1016/0160-7383(95)00043-7

Brooks, G. (2008). Exploiting the benefit of World Heritage Listing: Evora, Portugal and Hoi An, Vietnam. In B. Hayllar, B., T. Griffin, T., & D. Edwards (Eds.), City spaces–tourist places (pp. 341-356). Amsterdam: Elsevier.

Brown, F., & Hall, D. D. (2000). *Tourism in peripheral areas: Case studies.* Buffalo, NY: Channel View Publications.

Brown. (1968). Delphi Process: A Methodology Used for the Elicitation of Opinions of Experts. RAND. (Document No: P-3925)

Buckley, R. C. (1994). A framework for ecotourism. *Annals of Tourism Research, 21*(3), 661–669. doi:10.1016/0160-7383(94)90126-0

Buckley, R. C. (2002). Tourism ecocertification in the international year of ecotourism. *Journal of Ecotourism, 1*(2-3), 197–203. doi:10.1080/14724040208668126

Buckley, R. C. (2008). Climate change: Tourism destination dynamics. *Tourism Recreation Research, 33*(3), 354–355. doi:10.1080/02508281.2008.11081559

Buckley, R. C. (2009a). *Ecotourism: principles and practices.* Wallingford, UK: CAB International.

Buckley, R. C. (2009b). Evaluating the net effects of ecotourism on the environment: A framework, first assessment and future research. *Journal of Sustainable Tourism, 17*(6), 643–672. doi:10.1080/09669580902999188

Buckley, R. C. (2009c). Parks and tourism. *PLoS Biology, 7*(6), e1000143. doi:10.1371/journal.pbio.1000143 PMID:19564895

Buckley, R. C. (2010). *Conservation tourism.* Wallingford, UK: CAB International. doi:10.1079/9781845936655.0000

Buckley, R. C. (2011). Reconciling air travel and climate change. *Annals of Tourism Research, 38*(3), 1178–1181. doi:10.1016/j.annals.2011.01.019

Buckley, R., Cater, C., Linsheng, Z., & Chen, T. (2008). Shentai Luyou: Cross-Cultural Comparison in Ecotourism. *Annals of Tourism Research, 35*(4), 945–968. doi:10.1016/j.annals.2008.07.002

Buckley, R. (1998). Tools and indicators for managing tourism in parks. *Annals of Tourism Research*, 207–210.

Buckley, R. (2012). Sustainable tourism: Research and reality. *Annals of Tourism Research*, *39*(2), 528–546. doi:10.1016/j.annals.2012.02.003

Buhalis, D., & Law, R. (2008). Progress in information technology and tourism management: 20 years on and 10 years after the internet – the state of etourism research. *Tourism Management*, *29*(4), 609–623. doi:10.1016/j.tourman.2008.01.005

Buhalis, D. (2010). Marketing of Competitive Destinations of the Future. *Tourism Management*, *21*(1), 97–116. doi:10.1016/S0261-5177(99)00095-3

Buhrs, T. (2000). The environment and the role of the state in New Zealand. In P. A. Memon & H. Perkins (Eds.), *Environmental Planning and Management in New Zealand* (pp. 27–35). Palmerston North: Dunmore Press.

Bui, H. T., & Lee, T. J. (2015). Commodification and politicization of heritage: Implications for heritage tourism at the Imperial Citadel of Thang Long, Hanoi (Vietnam). *Austrian Journal of South-East Asian Studies*, *8*(2), 187–202.

Butler, R. W. (2011). Tourism Area Life Cycle. In C. Cooper (Ed.), *Contemporary TourismReviews* (pp. 1–33). Oxford, UK: GoodfellowPublishers Limited.

Butler, R. (2009). Tourism in the future: Cycles, waves or wheels? *Futures*, *41*(6), 346–352. doi:10.1016/j.futures.2008.11.002

Buyukozkan, G., & Berkol, C. (2011). Designing a sustainable supply chain using an integrated analytic network process and goal programming approach in quality function deployment. *Expert Systems with Applications*, *38*, 13731–13748.

Buyukozkan, G., & Cifci, G. (2013). An integrated QFD framework with multiple formatted and incomplete preferences: A sustainable supply chain application Gülc. *Applied Soft Computing*, *13*(9), 3931–3941. doi:10.1016/j.asoc.2013.03.014

Camhi, M. (1995). Industrial fisheries threaten ecological integrity of the Galapagos Islands. *Conservation Biology*, *9*(4), 715–724. doi:10.1046/j.1523-1739.1995.09040715.x

Campbell, L. M. (1999). Ecotourism in rural developing communities. *Annals of Tourism Research*, *26*(3), 534–553. doi:10.1016/S0160-7383(99)00005-5

Cancela, J., Fico, G., & Arredondo Waldmeyer, M. T. (2015). Using the Analytic Hierarchy Process (AHP) to understand the most important factors to design and evaluate a telehealth system for Parkinsons disease. *BMC Medical Informatics and Decision Making*, *15*(S3), S7. doi:10.1186/1472-6947-15-S3-S7 PMID:26391847

Caprihan, V., & Shivakumar, K. (2004, December). Eco-Tourism in India. *South Asian Journal of Social Political Sciences*, *4*(2), 80–85.

Caselli, F., Esquivel, G., & Lefort, L. (1996). Reopening the Convergence Debate: A New Look at Cross-Country Growth Empirics. *Journal of Economic Growth*, *1*(3), 363–360. doi:10.1007/BF00141044

Castley, G., Hill, W., & Pickering, C. (2008). *An Integrated Framework for developing ecological indicators of visit use of Protected Areas*. CRC.

Cater, E. A. (1993). Ecotourism in the third world: Problems for sustainable development. *Tourism Management*, *14*(2), 85–90. doi:10.1016/0261-5177(93)90040-R

Caves, R. E., & Holton, R. H. (1959). *The Canadian Economy: Prospect and Retrospect*. Cambridge, MA: Harvard University Press. doi:10.4159/harvard.9780674493704

Ceballos-Lascurain, H. (1996). *Touris, Ecotourism and Protected areas*. Gland: IUCN.

Centre for Studies in International Relations and Development (CSIRD). (2013). *9th K2K Forum- Strengthening Regional Economic Cooperation and Promoting Cultural Ties,* Report, in collaboration with Institute of Foreign Policy Studies, University of Calcutta. Retrieved on 7th March, 2016 from www.csird.org.in/rep/9th%20k2k%report.pdf

Chan, J. K. L., & Baum, T. (2007). Ecotourists perception of ecotourism experience in Lower Kinabatangan, Sabah, Malaysia. *Journal of Sustainable Tourism, 15*(5), 574–590. doi:10.2167/jost679.0

Chang, T. C. (1998). Regionalism and Tourism: Exploring Integral Links in Singapore. *Asia Pacific Viewpoint, 39*(1), 73–94. doi:10.1111/1467-8373.00054

Chang, T. (1997a). From Instant Asia to Multi-Faceted Jewel: Urban Imaging Strategies and Tourism Development in Singapore. *Urban Geography, 18*(6), 542–562. doi:10.2747/0272-3638.18.6.542

Chang, T. (1997b). Heritage as a Tourism Commodity: Traversing the Tourist–Local Divide. *Singapore Journal of Tropical Geography, 18*(1), 46–68. doi:10.1111/1467-9493.00004

Charles, R., Goeldner, J. R., & Brent, R. (2012). Toursim: Principles, Practicies, Philosophies. Hoboken, NJ: John Wiley & Sons, Inc.

Cheam, C. L., Mahmood, R., Abdullah, H., & Ong, S. C. (2013). Economic growth, tourism and selected macroeconomic variables: A triangular causal relationship in Malaysia. *Margin: The Journal of Applied Economic Research, 7*(2), 185–206.

Cheia, G. (2013). Ecotourism: Definition and concepts. *Revista de turism, North America, 15*, 56-60. Retrieved October 4, 2015, from: http://www.revistadeturism.ro/rdt/article/view/44

Chen, C. A., Lee, M. H., & Yang, Y. H. (2012). Branding Taiwan for tourism using Decision Making Trial and Evaluation Laboratory and Analytic Network Process methods. *Service Industries Journal, 32*(8), 1355–1373. doi:10.1080/02642069.2010.545881

Chen, C. F., & Chiou-Wei, S. Z. (2009). Tourism expansion, tourism uncertainty and economic growth: New evidence from Taiwan and Korea. *Tourism Management, 30*(6), 812–818. doi:10.1016/j.tourman.2008.12.013

Chen, C. L. (2010). Diversifying fisheries into tourism in Taiwan: Experiences and prospects. *Ocean and Coastal Management, 53*(8), 487–492. doi:10.1016/j.ocecoaman.2010.06.003

Chen, C. M. (2010). Role of tourism in connecting Taiwan and China: Assessing tourists perceptions of the Kinmen–Xiamen links. *Tourism Management, 31*(3), 421–424. doi:10.1016/j.tourman.2009.04.010

Chen, C.-L., & Bau, Y.-P. (2016). Establishing a multi-criteria evaluation structure for tourist beaches in Taiwan: A foundation for sustainable beach tourism. *Ocean and Coastal Management, 121*, 88–96. doi:10.1016/j.ocecoaman.2015.12.013

Chen, J. S. (2015). Tourism stakeholders attitudes toward sustainable development: A case in the Arctic. *Journal of Retailing and Consumer Services, 22*(1), 225–230. doi:10.1016/j.jretconser.2014.08.003

Chen, L., Lin, S., & Kuo, C. (2013). Rural tourism: Marketing strategies for the bed and breakfast industry in Taiwan. *International Journal of Hospitality Management, 32*, 278–286. doi:10.1016/j.ijhm.2012.07.005

Chen, L.-H., & Ko, W.-C. (2009). Fuzzy approaches to quality function deployment for new product design. *Fuzzy Sets and Systems, 160*(18), 2620–2639. doi:10.1016/j.fss.2008.12.003

Chen, M. H. (2010). The economy, tourism growth and corporate performance in the Taiwanese hotel industry. *Tourism Management, 31*(5), 665–675. doi:10.1016/j.tourman.2009.07.011

Chen, M. H. (2011). The response of hotel performance to international tourism development and crisis events. *International Journal of Hospitality Management, 30*(1), 200–212. doi:10.1016/j.ijhm.2010.06.005

Cheng, N., & Foo, N. (2012). *Templer Park under threat.* Retrieved from http://www.thestar.com.my/news/nation/2012/11/20/templer-park-under-threat/

Chettri & Bhupathy. (2009). Occurrence of *Dinodon gammiei* (Blanford, 1878) in Sikkim, Eastern Himalaya, India. *Journal of Threatened Taxa, 1*(1).

Chettri, N., Sharma, E., & Deb, D. C. (2001). Bird community structure along a trekking corridor of Sikkim Himalaya: A conservation perspective. *Biological Conservation, 102*(1), 1–16. doi:10.1016/S0006-3207(01)00092-1

Chettri, B., Acharya, B. K., & Bhupathy, S. (2011). An Overview of the Herpetofauna of Sikkim with Emphasis on Elevational Distribution Pattern and Threats and Conservation Issues: A Preliminary Investigation Biodiversity of Sikkim. In Exploring and Conserving a Global Hotspot. IFS.

Chettri, N. (2000). *Impact of habitat Disturbances on Bird and Butterfly Communities Along the Yuksom-Dzongri Trail in Khangchendzonga Biosphere Reserve* (Ph.D. dissertation). North Bengal University, India.

Chheang, V. (2013). *Tourism and Regional Integration in Southeast Asia. V.R.F. Series No. 481, Institution of Developing Economies*. Japan External Trade Organization.

Chi, C. G. Q., & Qu, H. (2009). Examining the relationship between tourists attribute satisfaction and overall satisfaction. *Journal of Hospitality Marketing & Management, 18*(1), 4–25. doi:10.1080/19368620801988891

Chiang, M. H. (2012). Tourism development across the Taiwan Strait. *East Asia, 29*(3), 235–253. doi:10.1007/s12140-012-9178-z

China. (2013). Available online May 13, 2013, http://jameskennell.files.wordpress.com/2013/04/china-tourism-policy-2013-2020.pdf

Chiu, Y. B., & Yeh, L. T. (2016). The threshold effects of the tourism-led growth hypothesis: Evidence from a cross-sectional model. *Journal of Travel Research*. doi:10.1177/0047287516650938

Chiu, Y. T. H., Lee, W. I., & Chen, T. H. (2014). Environmentally responsible behavior in ecotourism: Antecedents and implications. *Tourism Management, 40*, 321–329. doi:10.1016/j.tourman.2013.06.013

Choo, H., & Jamal, T. (2009). Tourism on organic farms in South Korea: A new form of ecotourism? *Journal of Sustainable Tourism, 17*(4), 431–454. doi:10.1080/09669580802713440

Chris, R. (2003). Recreational Tourism-Demand and Impacts (2nd ed.). Clevedon, UK: Channel View Publications.

Chung, J. Y., & Buhalis, D. (2008). Information needs in online social networks. *Information Technology & Tourism, 10*(4), 267–281. doi:10.3727/109830508788403123

Church, A., Ball, R., Bull, C., & Tyler, D. (2000). Public policy engagement with British tourism: The national, local and the European Union. *Tourism Geographies, 2*(3), 312–336. doi:10.1080/14616680050082544

Church, A. (2004). Local and regional tourism: policy and power. In A. Lew, C. M. Hall, & A. Williams (Eds.), *A companion to tourism* (pp. 555–568). Oxford, UK: Blackwell. doi:10.1002/9780470752272.ch44

Cini, F., Leone, L., & Passafaro, P. (2010). Promoting ecotourism among young people: A segmentation strategy. *Environment and Behavior, 44*(1), 87–106. doi:10.1177/0013916510389313

Clarke, J. (2000). Tourism brands: An exploratory study of the brands box model. *Journal of Vacation Marketing, 6*(4), 329–345. doi:10.1177/135676670000600404

Clemente, J., Montañés, A., & Reyes, M. (1998). Testing for a unit root in variables with a double change in the mean. *Economics Letters*, *59*(2), 175–182. doi:10.1016/S0165-1765(98)00052-4

Cohen, E., & Cohen, S. (2012). Current sociological theories and issues in tourism. *Annals of Tourism Research*, *39*(4), 2177–2202. doi:10.1016/j.annals.2012.07.009

Cole, S. (2009). A logistic tourism model – resort cycles, globalisation and chaos. *Annals of Tourism Research*, *36*(4), 689–714. doi:10.1016/j.annals.2009.07.004

Colebatch, H. (2009). *Policy*. Maidenhead, UK: McGraw-Hill.

Coles, T., Hall, C. M., & Duval, D. T. (2006). Tourism and Post-Disciplinary Enquiry. *Current Issues in Tourism*, *9*(4/5), 293–319. doi:10.2167/cit327.0

Coles, T. (2006). Enigma variations? The TALC, marketing models and the descendants of the product life cycle. In R. W. Butler (Ed.), *The Tourism Area Cycle, Conceptual and Theoretical Issues* (pp. 49–66). Channelview Publications.

Collier, A. (1989). Principles of Tourism Pitman. Academic Press.

Connelly, G. (2007). *Testing Governance - A Research Agenda for Exploring Urban Tourism Competitiveness*. Academic Press.

Cooper, C., Scott, N., & Baggio, R. (2009). Network position and perceptions of destination stakeholder importance. *Anatolia: An International Journal of Tourism and Hospitality Research*, *20*(1), 33–45. doi:10.1080/13032917.2009.10518893

Cooper, S., & Jackson, S. (1989). Destination life cycle, the Isle of Man case study. *Annals of Tourism Research*, *16*(3), 377–398. doi:10.1016/0160-7383(89)90051-0

Cooper, C. (1999), Tourism Principles and Practices. Addison Wesley Longman Publishing.

Cortes-Jimemez, I., Pulina, M., Prunera, C. R., & Artis, M. (2009). *Tourism and Exports as a Means of Growth. Working Paper 2009/10*. Research Institute of Applied Economics.

Cosma, S., Paun, D., Bota, M., & Fleseriu, C. (2014). Innovation: A useful tool in the rural tourism in Romania. *Procedia: Social and Behavioral Sciences*, *148*, 507–515. doi:10.1016/j.sbspro.2014.07.073

Cottrell, S. P., Vaske, J. J., & Roemer, J. M. (2013). Resident satisfaction with sustainable tourism: The case of Frankenwald Nature Park, Germany. *Tourism Management Perspectives*, *8*, 42–48. doi:10.1016/j.tmp.2013.05.005

Council of Agriculture Executive Yuan. (1999). *Basic Agricultural Statistics*. Retrieved October 20, 2015, from http://bulletin.coa.gov.tw

Council of Agriculture Executive Yuan. (2004). *Basic Agricultural Statistics*. Retrieved October 20, 2015, from http://bulletin.coa.gov.tw

Craik, J. (1990). A classic case of clientelism: The Industries Assistance Commission inquiry into travel and tourism. *Culture and Policy*, *2*(1), 29–45.

Dabhnet, S., Scott, N., & Ruhanen, L. (2012). Applying diffusion theory to destination stakeholder understanding of sustainable tourism development: A case from Thailand. *Journal of Sustainable Tourism*, *20*(8), 1107–1124. doi:10.1080/09669582.2012.673618

Dalkey, N., & Helmer, O. (1963). An Experimental Application of the Delphi Method to the use of experts. *Management Science*, *9*(3), 458–467. doi:10.1287/mnsc.9.3.458

Daniel, T. C. A. M., Muhar, A., Arnberger, A., Aznar, O., Boyd, J. W., Chan, K. M. A., & von der Dunk, A. et al. (2012). Contributions of cultural services to the ecosystem services agenda. *Proceedings of the National Academy of Sciences of the United States of America, 109*(23), 8812–8819. doi:10.1073/pnas.1114773109 PMID:22615401

De Mello, L. R. (1999). Foreign Direct Investment-Led Growth: Evidence from Time-Series and Panel Data. *Oxford Economic Papers, 51*(1), 133–151. doi:10.1093/oep/51.1.133

Debasish & Dilip. (2014). Assessing Impacts Through Community Perception: An Empirical Study for Sikkim. *Periodic Research, 3*(1), 118-122.

Debasish & Vivek. (2013). Purpose of Visit and Its Implication in Tourism Sector of Sikkim. *SIT Journal of Management, 3*(2), 157-172.

Deng, J., & Li, J. (2015). Self-identification of ecotourists. *Journal of Sustainable Tourism, 23*(2), 255–279. doi:10.1080/09669582.2014.934374

Deng, W. (2007). Using a revised importance–performance analysis approach: The case of Taiwanese hot springs tourism. *Tourism Management, 28*(5), 1274–1284. doi:10.1016/j.tourman.2006.07.010

Department for Business Innovation and Skills. (2011). *BIS Small Business Survey*. Sheffield, UK: Author.

Dev, K., & Walter, P. (2016). Modernisation theory, ecotourism policy, and sustainable development for poor countries of the global South: Perspectives from Nepal. *International Journal of Sustainable Development and World Ecology*.

Developments and Challenges in the Hospitality and Tourism Sector. (2010). Discussion Paper at the Global Dialogue Forum for the Hotels, Catering, Tourism Sector.

Dhami, Parks, Strager, & Conley. (2016). Suitability-sensitivity. *Journal of Ecotourismanalysis of Nature-Based Tourism Using Geographic Information Systems and Analytic Hierarchy Process*.

Di Giovine, M. A. (2009a). *The heritage-scape: UNESCO, World Heritage and tourism*. Plymouth, MA: Lexington Books.

Di Giovine, M. A. (2009b). Revitalization and counter-revitalization: Tourism, heritage, and the Lantern Festival as catalysts for regeneration in Hoi An, Vietnam. *Journal of Policy Research in Tourism. Leisure and Events, 1*(3), 208–230. doi:10.1080/19407960903204364

Diedrich, A., & Garcia-Buades, E. (2009). Local perceptions of tourism as indicators of destination decline. *Tourism Management, 30*(4), 512–521. doi:10.1016/j.tourman.2008.10.009

Dimitrovski, D. D., Todorović, A. T., & Valjarević, A. D. (2012). Rural tourism and regional development: Case study of development of rural tourism in the region of Gruţa, Serbia. *Procedia Environmental Sciences, 14*, 288–297. doi:10.1016/j.proenv.2012.03.028

Din, K. (1993). Dialogue with hosts: An educational strategy towards sustainable tourism. In V. Hitchcock & M. Parnwell (Eds.), *Tourism in South-East Asia* (pp. 327–336). London, UK: Routledge.

Ding, J.-F. (2009). Applying fuzzy quality function deployment (QFD) to identify solutions of service delivery system for port of Kaohsiung. *Quality & Quantity, 43*(4), 553–570. doi:10.1007/s11135-007-9138-7

Dissart, J. C., Aubert, F., & Truchet, S. (2009). An estimation of tourism dependence in French rural areas. In A. Matias, P. Nijkamp, & M. Sarmento (Eds.), *Advances in tourism economics* (pp. 273–294). New York, NY: Physica–Verlag/Springer. doi:10.1007/978-3-7908-2124-6_17

Doan, T. M. (2013). Sustainable ecotourism in Amazonia: Evaluation of six sites in Southeastern Peru. *International Journal of Tourism Research, 15*(3), 261–271. doi:10.1002/jtr.1866

Dodds, R., & Butler, R. W. (2010). Barriers to implementing sustainable tourism policy in mass tourism destinations. *Tourismos: An International Multidisciplinary Journal of Tourism*, *5*(1), 35–53.

Dodds, R., & Joppe, M. (2001). Promoting urban green tourism; the development of the other map of Toronto. *Journal of Vacation Marketing*, *7*(3), 261–167. doi:10.1177/135676670100700306

Dodds, R., & McElroy, J. (2008). St Kitts at a crossroads. *ARA Journal of Travel Research*, *1*(2), 1–10.

Dolgorsuren, G., Gerelchuluun, J., Puntsagsuren, C., Baldandorj, T., Bron, J., & van der Linden, W. (2013). *Intergrated water management plan of Mongolia.* Ulaanbaatar: Ministry of Environment and Green Development.

Douglas, N. (1997). Applying the life cycle model to Melanesia. *Annals of Tourism Research*, *24*(1), 1–22. doi:10.1016/S0160-7383(96)00011-4

Dredge, D., & Jenkins, J. (2007). *Tourism Planning and Policy*. Brisbane: Wiley and Sons.

Driml, S., & Common, M. (1995). Economic and financial benefits of tourism in major protected areas. *Australasian Journal of Environmental Management*, *2*(1), 19–29. doi:10.1080/14486563.1995.10648312

Dubin, R. (1976). *Theory Building in Applied Areas*. Chicago: Rand McNally.

Dwivedi, M., Shibu, T. P., & Venkatesh, U. (2007). Social software on the Internet; implications for the hotel industry. *International Journal of Contemporary Hospitality Management*, *19*(5), 415–426. doi:10.1108/09596110710757570

Dwyer, L., & Kim, C. (2003). Destination competitiveness: Determinants and indicators. *Current Issues in Tourism*, *6*(5), 369–414. doi:10.1080/13683500308667962

Dye, T. (1992). Understanding Public Policy (7th ed.). Englewood Cliffs, NJ: Prentice Hall.

Eagles, P. F. J., McCool, S. F., & Haynes, C. D. (2002). *Sustainable Tourism in Protected Areas: Guidelines for Planning and Management*. Gland, Switzerland: IUCN. doi:10.1079/9780851995892.0000

Eagles, P. F. (1995). *Key issues in ecotourism management.* Invited paper for State of Western Australia Annual Tourism Conference, Perth, Australia.

Ecotourism Society Taiwan. (2011). Retrieved January 1, 2011, from www.ecotour.org.tw

Eder, J., Smith, W. W., & Pitts, R. E. (2010). Exploring factors influencing student study abroad destination choice. *Journal of Teaching in Travel & Tourism*, *10*(3), 232–250. doi:10.1080/15313220.2010.503534

Edgell, D. Sr. (1995). A barrier-free future for tourism? *Tourism Management*, *16*(2), 107–110. doi:10.1016/0261-5177(94)00020-B

Edgell, D., Allen, M., Smith, G., & Swanson, J. (2007). *Tourism Policy and Planning: Yesterday, Today and Tomorrow*. Burlington: Butterworth Heinemann.

Edward, M., & George, B. P. (2008). Tourism development in the State of Kerala, India: A study of destination attractiveness. *European Journal of Tourism Research*, *1*(1), 16–38.

Edwards, C. (2009). *Resilient nation: How communities respond to systemic breakdown*. London, UK: Demos.

Ekinci, M. B. (2014). The Cittaslow philosophy in the context of sustainable tourism development: The case of Turkey. *Tourism Management*, *41*, 178–189. doi:10.1016/j.tourman.2013.08.013

Ekinci, Y., Sirakaya-Turk, E., & Preciado, S. (2013). Symbolic consumption of tourism destination brands. *Journal of Business Research*, *66*(6), 711–718. doi:10.1016/j.jbusres.2011.09.008

Eligh, J., Welford, R., & Ytterhus, B. (2002). The production of sustainable tourism: Concepts and examples from Norway. *Sustainable Development*, *10*(4), 223–234. doi:10.1002/sd.195

Eller, M., Haiss, P., & Steiner, K. (2005). *Financial Direct Investment in the Financial Sector: The Engine of Growth for Central and Eastern Europe?* Europalnstitut Working paper No.69. Vienna University of Economics and Business Administration.

Elliott, G., Jansson, M., & Pesavento, E. (2005). Optimal power for testing potential cointegrating vectors with known parameters for nonstationary. *Journal of Business & Economic Statistics*, *23*(1), 34–48. doi:10.1198/073500104000000307

Elliott, J. (1997). *Tourism, Politics and Public Sector Management*. London: Routledge.

Elnokaly, A., & Elseragy, A. (2013). Sustainable Heritage Development: Learning from Urban Conservation of Heritage Projects in Non Western Contexts. *European Journal of Sustainable Development, 2*, 31-54.

Emerson, R. M., Fretz, R. I., & Shaw, L. L. (2011). *Writing ethnographic field notes*. Chicago, IL: University of Chicago Press. doi:10.7208/chicago/9780226206868.001.0001

Engle, R. F., & Granger, C. W. J. (1987). Co-integration and error-correction: Representation, estimation, and testing. *Econometrica*, *55*(2), 251–276. doi:10.2307/1913236

Erbas, E. (2016). Competitive Determinance–performance Analysis. *An Illustration on Turkish Winter Tourism Destinations Tourism Analysis*, *21*(1), 93–106.

Erfani, M., Afrougheh, S., Ardakani, T., & Sadeghi, A. (2015). Tourism positioning using decision support system (case study: Chahnime–Zabol, Iran). *Environmental Earth Sciences*, *74*(4), 3135–3144. doi:10.1007/s12665-015-4365-z

Eshun, G., & Tagoe-Darko, E. (2015). Ecotourism Development in Ghana: A Postcolonial Analysis. *Development Southern Africa*, *32*(3), 392–406. doi:10.1080/0376835X.2015.1020218

Eshun, G., & Tonto, J. N. P. (2014). Community-based ecotourism: Its socio-economic impacts at Boabeng-Fiema Monkey Sanctuary, Ghana. Bulletin of Geography, 26, 67–81 doi:10.2478/bog-2014-0045

Eubanks, T. L. Jr, Stoll, J. R., & Ditton, R. B. (2004). Understanding the diversity of eight-birder sub-populations: Socio-demographic characteristics, motivations, expenditures and net benefits. *Journal of Ecotourism*, *3*(3), 151–172. doi:10.1080/14664200508668430

Eugenio-Martin, J.L., Morales, N., & Scarpa, R. (2004). Tourism and Economic Growth in Latin American Countries: A Panel Data Approach. *Nota di lavora, 26.*

European Commission, International Monetary Fund, OECD, United Nations and World Bank. (2009). *System of National Accounts 2008*. Available: https://unstats.un.org/unsd/nationalaccount/docs/SNA2008.pdf

Everett, S., & Aitchison, C. (2008). The role of food tourism in sustaining regional identity: A case study of Cornwall, South West England. *Journal of Sustainable Tourism*, *16*(2), 150–167. doi:10.2167/jost696.0

Executive Yuan. (2011). Retrieved January 12, 2014, from http://www.ey.gov.tw

Fakharyan, M., Jalilvand, M. R., Elyasi, M., & Mohammadi, M. (2012). The influence of online word of mouth communications of tourists attitudes toward Islamic destinations and travel intentions: Evidence from Iran. *African Journal of Business Management*, *6*(33), 9533–9542. doi:10.5897/AJBM12.628

Falak, S., Chiun, L. M., & Wee, A. Y. (2014). A repositioning strategy for rural tourism in Malaysia: Community's perspective. *Procedia: Social and Behavioral Sciences*, *144*, 412–415. doi:10.1016/j.sbspro.2014.07.310

Farmaki, A., Altinay, L., Botterill, D., & Hilke, S. (2015). Politics and sustainable tourism: The case of Cyprus. *Tourism Management, 47*, 178–190. doi:10.1016/j.tourman.2014.09.019

Farrell, B., & Twining-Ward, L. (2005). Seven steps towards sustainability: Tourism in the context of new knowledge. *Journal of Sustainable Tourism, 13*(2), 109–122. doi:10.1080/09669580508668481

Feder, G. (1983). On exports and economic growth. *Journal of Development Economics, 12*(1-2), 59–73. doi:10.1016/0304-3878(83)90031-7

Feenstra, R. C., Inklaar, R., & Marcel, P. (2015). The Next Generation of the Penn World Table. *American Economic Review*. Available at www.ggdc.net/pwt

Fennel, D. (2008). *Ecotourism*. New York: Routledge. doi:10.4324/9780203121108.ch31

Figgis, P. (1993). Ecotourism: Special interest or major direction. *Habitat Australia, 21*, 8–11.

Fleischer, A., & Felsenstein, D. (2000). Support for small-scale rural tourism: Does it make a difference? *Annals of Tourism Research, 27*(4), 1007–1024. doi:10.1016/S0160-7383(99)00126-7

Fleischer, A., & Pizam, A. (1997). Rural tourism in Israel. *Tourism Management, 18*(6), 367–372. doi:10.1016/S0261-5177(97)00034-4

Fleischer, A., & Tchetchik, A. (2005). Does rural tourism benefit from agriculture? *Tourism Management, 26*(4), 493–501. doi:10.1016/j.tourman.2003.10.003

Flognfeldt, T. (2001). Long-term positive adjustments to seasonality: Consequences of summer tourism in the Jotunheimen area, Norway. In T. Baum & S. Lundtorp (Eds.), *Seasonality in tourism* (pp. 109–117). New York, NY: Taylor & Francis Group. doi:10.1016/B978-0-08-043674-6.50010-6

Florez, K. C. (2013). *Tourism in Chiapas; a conversation with Hermann Bellinghausen*. Retrieved on 22nd May,2013 from http://upsidedownworld.org/main/mexico-archives-79/4208-tourism-in-chiapas-a-conversation-with-hermann-bellinghausen

Fong, V. (2016). *Smart Cities Today: Chapter Four – The Tale of Malaysia Pt. 1*. Retrieved from http://www.smartcitiesasia.com/smart-cities-malaysia/

Forum, T. (2008). *Conceptualising the value of protected areas*. Victoria University.

Fox, J., Bushley, B. R., Miles, W. B., & Shimona, A. (2003, December). *Connecting Communities and Conservation: Collaborative Management of Protected Areas in Bangladesh*. Nishorgo Support Project, Bangladesh Forest Department. East-West Center.

Fox, J., Bushley, B. R., Miles, W. B., & Shimona, A. (2008). Connecting Communities and Conservation: Collaborative Management of Protected Areas in Bangladesh. Nishorgo Support Project, Bangladesh Forest Department.

Gaddefors, J. (2005). Creating context entrepreneurial opportunities in a consumer market setting. *Journal of Enterprising Culture, 13*(3), 199–224. doi:10.1142/S0218495805000148

Galley, G., & Clifton, J. (2004). The motivational and demographic characteristics about research ecotourists: Operation Wallacea volunteers in Southeast Sulawesi, Indonesia. *Journal of Ecotourism, 3*(1), 69–82. doi:10.1080/14724040408668150

Galragchaa, P. (2010). *Management Plan for Orkhon Valley National Park (2011-2015)*. Ulaanbaatar: GIZ 454.

Gansukh, D., Navchaa, T., & Erdenetuul, S. (2012). *Orkhon Valley National Park: Tourism Management Plan (2012-2015)*. Ulaanbaatar: Ministry of Nature, Environment and Green Development.

Gantzer, H., & Gantzer, C. (1983, June). Managing Tourists and Politicians in India. Tourism Management, 118-125. doi:10.1016/0261-5177(83)90029-8

Gao, S., Huang, S., & Huang, Y. (2009). Rural tourism development in China. *International Journal of Tourism Research, 11*(5), 439–450. doi:10.1002/jtr.712

Garrod, B., & Fyall, A. (2000). Managing heritage tourism. *Annals of Tourism Research, 27*(3), 682–708. doi:10.1016/S0160-7383(99)00094-8

Gavrila-Paven, I. (2015). Tourism opportunities for valorising the authentic traditional rural space-study case: Ampoi and Mures Valleys microregion, Alba County, Romania. *Procedia: Social and Behavioral Sciences, 188*, 111–115. doi:10.1016/j.sbspro.2015.03.345

George, B. P., & George, B. P. (2004). Past visits and the intention to revisit a destination: Place attachment as the mediator and novelty seeking as the moderator. *Journal of Tourism Studies, 15*(2), 37–50.

George, H., Henthorne, T. L., & Williams, A. J. (2013). The bells within the bell curve: Destination cisitation model revisited. *Tourism Recreation Research, 38*(3), 341–348. doi:10.1080/02508281.2013.11081758

George, P. O. (2003). Strategic Management in Tourism. *South Asian Journal of Social Political Sciences, 4*(1), 86–88.

German Forum on Environment and Development. (1999). Definition of Sustainable Tourism. Author.

Gertner, D., & Kotler, P. (2004). How can a place correct a negative image? *Place Branding, 1*(1), 50-57.

Getz, D., & Carlsen, J. (2000). Characteristics and goals of family and owner-operated businesses in the rural tourism and hospitality sectors. *Tourism Management, 21*(6), 547–560. doi:10.1016/S0261-5177(00)00004-2

Getz, D., & Nilsson, P. A. (2004). Responses of family businesses to extreme seasonality in demand: The case of Bornholm, Denmark. *Tourism Management, 25*(1), 17–30. doi:10.1016/S0261-5177(03)00067-0

Ghali, M. A. (1976). Tourism and economic growth: An empirical study. *Economic Development and Cultural Change, 24*(3), 527–538. doi:10.1086/450895

Ghanian, M., Ghoochani, O. M., & Crotts, J. C. (2014). An application of European Performance Satisfaction Index towards rural tourism: The case of western Iran. *Tourism Management Perspectives, 11*, 77–82. doi:10.1016/j.tmp.2014.04.005

Ghasemi, M., & Hamzah, A. (2014). An investigation of the appropriateness of tourism development paradigms in rural areas from main tourism stakeholder's point of view. *Procedia: Social and Behavioral Sciences, 144*, 15–24. doi:10.1016/j.sbspro.2014.07.269

Ghosh, P. (1999). *Name it, India has got it, except tourists; The Rediff Business Special/Tourism in doldrums*. Retrieved from http://www.rediff.com/business/1999

Gibson, A., Dodds, R., Joppe, M., & Jamieson, B. (2003). Ecotourism in the city? Torontos green tourism. *International Journal of Contemporary Hospitality Management, 15*(6), 324–327. doi:10.1108/09596110310488168

Gilmore, A., & Simmons, G. (2007). Integrating sustainable tourism and marketing management: Can National Parks provide the framework for strategic change? *Strategic Change, 16*(5), 191–200. doi:10.1002/jsc.798

GOI. (2004). India Tourism Statistics 2004. Ministry of Tourism, Market Research Division New Delhi: GOI.

Goodwin, H., & Francis, J. (2003). Ethical and responsible tourism: Consumer trends in the UK. *Journal of Vacation Marketing, 9*(3), 271–282. doi:10.1177/135676670300900306

Gössling, S., Hall, C. M., & Scott, D. (2015). Water for Life: A Global Overview. In *Tourism and Water* (pp. 1–30). Bristol: Channel View Publications.

Gössling, S., Hall, C. M., & Weaver, D. B. (2009). *Sustainable tourism futures: Perspective on systems, restructuring and innovations*. Abingdon, UK: Routledge.

Gössling, S., Scott, D., & Hall, C. M. (2013). Challenges of tourism in a low-carbon economy. *Wiley Interdisciplinary Reviews: Climate Change*, *4*(6), 525–538. doi:10.1002/wcc.243

Government Malaysia. (2006). *Ninth Malaysia Plan 2006-2010, Economics Planning Unit*. Prime Minister's Department.

Government of India (GOI). (2002). *National Tourism Policy 2002*. New Delhi: GOI.

Government of India (GOI). (2015). *GOI - Press Release, July, 2015*. GOI.

Government of India. (2010). *India Tourism Statistics 2010*. New Delhi: Marketing Research Division, Ministry of Tourism.

Government of India. (2005). *North Eastern Region Vision 2020* (Vol. 2). Ministry of Development of North Eastern Region (MDoNER) & North Eastern Council (NEC).

Government of India. (2013). *Annual Report 2012-13*. Ministry of Tourism.

Graham, B., Ashworth, G. J., & Tunbridge, J. E. (2000). *A geography of heritage*. London, UK: Arnold.

Graham, B. (2002). Heritage as knowledge: Capital or culture? *Urban Studies (Edinburgh, Scotland)*, *39*(5-6), 1003–1017. doi:10.1080/00420980220128426

Granger, C. J. (1969). Investigating Causal Relationships by Econometrics Models and Cross Spectral Methods. *Econometrica*, *37*(3), 425–435. doi:10.2307/1912791

Granger, C. W. J. (1988). Some recent development in a concept of causality. *Journal of Econometrics*, *39*(1-2), 199–211. doi:10.1016/0304-4076(88)90045-0

Grant, M. (2004). Innovation in Tourism Planning Processes: Action Learning to Support a Coalition of Stakeholders for Sustainability. *Tourism and Hospitality Planning & Development*, *1*(3), 219–237. doi:10.1080/1479053042000306493

Greenwood, J., Williams, A. M., & Shaw, G. (1990). Policy implementation and tourism in the UK. Implications from recent tourism research in Cornwall. *Tourism Management*, *11*(1), 53–62. doi:10.1016/0261-5177(90)90008-W

Gregory, A. W., Haug, A. A., & Lomuto, N. (2004). Mixed signals among tests for cointegration. *Journal of Applied Econometrics*, *19*(1), 89–98. doi:10.1002/jae.733

Gremyr, I., & Raharjo, H. (2013). Quality function deployment in healthcare: A literature review and case study. *International Journal of Health Care Quality Assurance*, *26*(2), 135–146. doi:10.1108/09526861311297343 PMID:23534149

Gretzel, U., Fesenmaier, D., Formica, S., & OLeary, J. (2006). Searching for the future: Challenges faced by destination marketing organizations. *Journal of Travel Research*, *45*(2), 116–126. doi:10.1177/0047287506291598

Gretzel, U., Yuan, Y.-L., & Fesenmaier, D. R. (2000). Preparing for the new economy: Advertising strategies and change in destination marketing organizations. *Journal of Travel Research*, *39*(2), 146–156. doi:10.1177/004728750003900204

Grünewald, C., Schleuning, M., & Böhning-Gaese, K. (2016). Biodiversity, scenery and infrastructure: Factors driving wildlife tourism in an African savannah national park. *Biological Conservation*, *201*(September), 60–68. doi:10.1016/j.biocon.2016.05.036

Gubbi, S. (2008). Wildlife Tourism: The Great Indian Green Trick. Sanctuary Asia, 28(5), 40-44.

Gunduz, L., & Hatemi-J, A. (2005). Is the tourism-led growth hypothesis valid for Turkey? *Applied Economics Letters*, *12*(8), 499–504. doi:10.1080/13504850500109865

Guo, Y., Kim, S. S., Timothy, D. J., & Wang, K. C. (2006). Tourism and reconciliation between Mainland China and Taiwan. *Tourism Management*, *27*(5), 997–1005. doi:10.1016/j.tourman.2005.08.001

Gupta, V. (1999). Sustainable Tourism: Learning from Indian Religious Tradition. *International Journal of Contemporary Hospitality Management*, *11*(2/3), 91–95. doi:10.1108/09596119910250751

Gursoy, D., & Rutherford, D. G. (2004). Host attitudes toward tourism: An improved structural model. *Annals of Tourism Research*, *31*(3), 495–516. doi:10.1016/j.annals.2003.08.008

Gurung, C. P., & DeCoursey, M. A. (2000). Too much too fast: Lessons from Nepal's lost Kingdom of Mustang. In P. Godde, M. Price, & F. Zimmermann (Eds.), *Tourism and development in mountain regions* (pp. 239–253). Wallingford, UK: CABI Publishing.

Guzman-Parra, V. F., Quintana-García, C., Benavides-Velasco, C. A., & Vila-Oblitas, J. B. (2015). Trends and seasonal variation of tourist demand in Spain: The role of rural tourism. *Tourism Management Perspectives*, *16*, 123–128. doi:10.1016/j.tmp.2015.07.014

Hall, C. M., & Jenkins, J. M. (1995). *Tourism and Public Policy*. Routledge.

Hall, C. M., & Jenkins, J. (2004). Tourism and Public Policy. In A. Lew, C. M. Hall, & A. Williams (Eds.), *A companion to tourism* (pp. 425–540). Oxford, UK: Blackwell. doi:10.1002/9780470752272.ch42

Hall, C. M., Scott, D., & Gössling, S. (2013). The primacy of climate change for sustainable international tourism. *Sustainable Development*, *21*(2), 112–121. doi:10.1002/sd.1562

Hall, C. M. (1998). *Tourism Development, Dimensions and Issues*. Melbourne: Academic Press.

Hall, C. M. (1999). Rethinking Collaboration and Partnership: A Public Policy Perspective. *Journal of Sustainable Tourism*, *7*(3/4), 274–289. doi:10.1080/09669589908667340

Hall, C. M. (2002). Travel safety, terrorism and the media: The significance of the issue-attention cycle. *Current Issues in Tourism*, *5*(5), 458–466. doi:10.1080/13683500208667935

Hall, C. M. (2008a). *Tourism Planning: Policies, Processes and Relationships* (2nd ed.). Harlow, UK: Pearson Education.

Hall, C. M. (2008b). *Tourism Planning: Policies, processes, relationships* (2nd ed.). London: Prentice Hall.

Hall, C. M. (2010). Changing paradigms and global change: From sustainable to steady-state tourism. *Tourism Recreation Research*, *35*(2), 131–145. doi:10.1080/02508281.2010.11081629

Hall, D. R., Roberts, L., & Mitchell, M. (2003). *New directions in rural tourism*. Aldershot, UK: Ashgate.

Hall, D. (2004). Rural tourism development in southeastern Europe: Transition and the search for sustainability. *International Journal of Tourism Research*, *6*(3), 165–176. doi:10.1002/jtr.482

Hall, M., & Weiler, B. (Eds.). (1991). *Special Interest Tourism*. London: Belhaven.

Hamilton, K., & Alexander, M. (2013). Organic community tourism: A cocreated approach. *Annals of Tourism Research*, *42*, 169–190. doi:10.1016/j.annals.2013.01.015

Hannam, K., Sheller, M., & Urry, J. (2006). Editorial: Mobilities, immobilities, moorings. *Mobilities*, *1*(1), 1–22. doi:10.1080/17450100500489189

Hannam, K. (2002). Tourism and development: Globalisation and power. *Progress in Development Studies*, *2*(3), 227–234. doi:10.1191/1464993402ps039pr

Harlow, S., & Pomfret, G. (2007). Evolving environmental tourism experiences in Zambia. *Journal of Ecotourism*, *6*(3), 184–209. doi:10.2167/joe182.0

Harrison, D. (2004). Contested narratives in the domain of world heritage. *Current Issues in Tourism*, *7*(4/5), 281–290. doi:10.1080/13683500408667985

Hassan, M. K. H., & Jenggie, S. T. (2012). The impact of tourist's expenditures on Malaysian economy: An input-output analysis. *BIMP-EAGA Journal for Sustainable Tourism Development*, *1*(1), 47–54.

Haven-Tang, C., & Jones, E. (2012). Local leadership for rural tourism development: A case study of Adventa, Monmouthshire, UK. *Tourism Management Perspectives*, *4*, 28–35. doi:10.1016/j.tmp.2012.04.006

Hawkins, J. P., & Roberts, C. M. (1993). Effects of recreational scuba diving on coral reef trampling on reef-flat communities. *Journal of Applied Ecology*, *30*(1), 25–30. doi:10.2307/2404267

Hawkins, J. P., & Roberts, C. M. (1994). The growth of coastal tourism in the red sea: Present and future effects on coral reefs. *Ambio*, *23*, 503–508.

Haxton, P. (2015). *A Review of Effective Policies for Tourism Growth, OECD Tourism Papers*. Paris: OECD Publishing. doi:10.1787/23071672

Haywood, K. M. (1986). Can the tourist-area life cycle be made operational? *Tourism Management*, *7*(3), 154–167. doi:10.1016/0261-5177(86)90002-6

Headland, R. K. (1994). Historical development of Antarctic tourism. *Annals of Tourism Research*, *21*(2), 269–280. doi:10.1016/0160-7383(94)90044-2

Hegarty, C., & Przezborska, L. (2005). Rural and agri-tourism as a tool for reorganising rural areas in old and new member states: A comparison study of Ireland and Poland. *International Journal of Tourism Research*, *7*(2), 63–77. doi:10.1002/jtr.513

Henderson, J. C. (2015). Destination development and transformation: 50 years of tourism after independence in Singapore. *International Journal of Tourism Cities*, *1*(4), 269–281. doi:10.1108/IJTC-05-2015-0011

Henry, I. P., & Jackson, G. A. M. (1996). Sustainability of Management Processes and Tourism Products and Contexts. *Journal of Sustainable Tourism*, *4*(1), 17–28. doi:10.1080/09669589608667256

Herath, G., Yule, C., & Wilson, R. (2014). *Socio Economic features of Tioman Island Malaysia: Results of a Survey*. School of Business, Monash University.

Herath, G. (1995). Ecotourism development in Australia: Some relevant issues. *Annals of Tourism Research*, *24*(2), 442–446. doi:10.1016/S0160-7383(97)80012-6

Herath, G. (1996a). Ecotourism in Asia and the Pacific: potential, problems and an integrated planning model In *Proceedings of the Australian Tourism and Hospitality Research Conference. Coffs Habour: Southern Cross University*.

Herath, G. (2000). Issues surrounding entrance fees as a suitable mechanism for enhancing natural areas in Australia. *International Journal of Wilderness*, *6*, 35–39.

Herath, G. (2002). Research methodologies for planning ecotourism and nature conservation. *Tourism Economics*, *8*(1), 77–101. doi:10.5367/000000002101298007

Herath, G. (1996b). *Ecotourism and nature conservation: the use of the Safe Minimum Standard (SMS)*. Paper presented at the 40th Annual Conference of the Australian Agricultural and Resource Economics Society.

Herbert, D. (2001). Literary places, tourism and the heritage experience. *Annals of Tourism Research*, *28*(2), 312–333. doi:10.1016/S0160-7383(00)00048-7

Heston, A., Summers, R., & Aten, B. (2012). *Penn World Table Version 7.1*. Center for International Comparisons of Production, Income and Prices at the University of Pennsylvania.

Higham, J., & Luck, M. (2002). Urban ecotourism: A contradiction in terms? *Journal of Ecotourism*, *1*(1), 36–51. doi:10.1080/14724040208668111

Hjalager, A. M. (2004). Sustainable leisure life modes and rural welfare economy. The case of the Randers Fjord area, Denmark. *International Journal of Tourism Research*, *6*(3), 177–188. doi:10.1002/jtr.483

Hjalager, A. M. (2007). Stages in the economic globalization of tourism. *Annals of Tourism Research*, *34*(2), 437–457. doi:10.1016/j.annals.2006.10.006

Hjalager, A. M. (2010). A review of innovation research in tourism. *Tourism Management*, *31*(1), 1–12. doi:10.1016/j.tourman.2009.08.012

Ho, W., Dey, P.K., & Lockstrom, M. (n.d.). Strategic sourcing: a combined QFD and AHP approach in manufacturing. Supply Chain Manag., 16(6), 446–461.

Hoi An Center for Monuments Management and Conservation. (2008). *Cultural tourism and heritage management in the World Heritage Site of Ancient Town of Hoi An, Vietnam*. Bangkok: United Nations Educational, Scientific and Cultural Organization.

Holden, A., & Sparrowhawk, J. (2002). Understanding the motivations of ecotourists: The case of trekkers in Annapurna, Nepal. *International Journal of Tourism Research*, *4*(6), 435–446. doi:10.1002/jtr.402

Hong, S., Kim, S., & Kim, J. (2003). Implications of potential green tourism development. *Annals of Tourism Research*, *30*(2), 323–341. doi:10.1016/S0160-7383(02)00060-9

Hsieh, L. F., Lin, L. H., & Lin, Y. Y. (2008). A service quality measurement architecture for hot spring hotels in Taiwan. *Tourism Management*, *29*(3), 429–438. doi:10.1016/j.tourman.2007.05.009

Hsieh, T. H. L. H.-P. (2016). Indicators of sustainable tourism: A case study from a Taiwan's wetland. *Ecological Indicators*, *67*(August), 779–787.

Hsu, C. H., & Sung, S. (1997). Travel behaviors of international students at a Midwestern university. *Journal of Travel Research*, *36*(1), 59–65. doi:10.1177/004728759703600109

Hu, W., & Wall, G. (2005). Economic and environmental symbiosis in a tourism attraction: An example from Hainan, China. *International Journal of Tourism Research*, *7*(4/5), 295–310. doi:10.1002/jtr.533

Hu, Y. C., Wang, J. H., & Wang, R. Y. (2012). Evaluating the performance of Taiwan homestay using analytic network process. *Mathematical Problems in Engineering*.

Huang, L. (2008). Bed and breakfast industry adopting e-commerce strategies in e-service. *Service Industries Journal*, *28*(5), 633–648. doi:10.1080/02642060801988159

Huang, R. (2008). Mapping educational tourists experience in the UK: Understanding international students. *Third World Quarterly*, *29*(5), 1003–1020. doi:10.1080/01436590802106247

Hudson, S., & Miller, G. (2005). The responsible marketing of tourism: The case of Canadian mountain holidays. *Tourism Management, 26*(2), 133–142. doi:10.1016/j.tourman.2003.06.005

Hummelbrunner, R., & Miglbauer, E. (1994). Tourism promotion and potential in peripheral areas: The Austrian case. *Journal of Sustainable Tourism, 2*(1/2), 41–50. doi:10.1080/09669589409510682

Hussin, N. Z. (2014). Tracing the Malaysia Tourism Lifecycle and Strategy Assessment from the First Malaysia Plan to Ninth Malaysia Plan. *International Journal of Business and Social. Science*, *5*(3), 2014.

Hwang, J., & Lee, S. (2015). The effect of the rural tourism policy on non-farm income in South Korea. *Tourism Management, 46*, 501–513. doi:10.1016/j.tourman.2014.07.018

IAPPA. (2015). IAAPA Global Theme and Amusement Park Outlook.

ILO. (2010). *Development and Challenges in the tourism and hospitality sector*. Issues Paper for the Global Dialogue Forum for the Hotels, Catering & Tourism Sector. Available at http://www.ilo.org/public/english/dialogue/sectors/tourism.htm

Im, K.S., Pesaran, M.H., & Shin, Y. (2003). Testing for Unit Roots in Heterogeneous Panels. *Journal of Econometrics, 115*, 53-74.

Ingram, H., Tabari, S., & Watthanakhomprathip, W. (2013). The impact of political instability on tourism: Case of Thailand. *Worldwide Hospitality and Tourism Themes, 5*(1), 92–103. doi:10.1108/17554211311292475

Ioannides, D. (1995). A flawed implementation of sustainable tourism: The experience of Akamas, Cyprus. *Tourism Management, 16*(8), 583–592. doi:10.1016/0261-5177(95)00081-X

Iqbal, Z., Grigg, N. P., Govinderaju, K., & Campbell-Allen, N. (2014). Statistical comparison of final weight scores in quality function deployment (QFD) studies. *International Journal of Quality & Reliability Management, 31*(2), 184–204. doi:10.1108/IJQRM-06-2013-0092

Irvine, W., & Anderson, A. R. (2004). Small tourist firms in rural areas: Agility, vulnerability and survival in the face of crisis. *International Journal of Entrepreneurial Behavior & Research, 10*(4), 229–246. doi:10.1108/13552550410544204

Ivars Baidal, J. A. (2004). Tourism Planning in Spain. *Annals of Tourism Research, 31*(2), 313–333. doi:10.1016/j.annals.2003.12.001

Jaafar, M., & Maideen, S. A. (2012). Ecotourism Related Products and Activities and the economic sustainability of small and medium island chalets. *Tourism Management, 33*(3), 683–691. doi:10.1016/j.tourman.2011.07.011

Jaafar, M., Rasoolimanesh, S. M., & Lonik, K. A. T. (2015). Tourism growth and entrepreneurship: Empirical analysis of development of rural highlands. *Tourism Management Perspectives, 14*, 17–24. doi:10.1016/j.tmp.2015.02.001

Jacob, V. J., & Alles, W. S. (1987). The Kandyan gardens of Sri Lanka. *Agroforestry Systems, 5*(2), 123–127. doi:10.1007/BF00047517

Jacob, M. M. (2000). *Speech*. GOPIO Convention–2000, Zurich, Switzerland.

Jenkins, J. (2001). Editorial. *Current Issues in Tourism, 4*(2), 69–77. doi:10.1080/13683500108667882

Jha, A., & Thapa, K. (2002). *Reptiles and Amphibians of Sikkim*. Gangtok, India: WWF.

Jha, A. (2001). Information Technology and Creativity to Develop Enterprise, a Case Study of Tourism in Sikkim. *Proceedings of National Seminar supported by AICTE*.RaipurInstitute of Technology.

Jian, X., Cai, S., & Chen, Q. (2017). A study on the evaluation of product maintainability based on the life cycle theory. *Journal of Cleaner Production, 141*, 481–491. doi:10.1016/j.jclepro.2016.09.073

Jing-Ming, H. E. (2003). A Study on Rural Tourism Overseas. *Tourism Tribune*, *1*, 16.

Jithendran, K. J., & Baum, T. (2000). Human resources development and sustainability: The case of Indian tourism. *International Journal of Tourism Research*, *2*(6), 403–421. doi:10.1002/1522-1970(200011/12)2:6<403::AID-JTR239>3.0.CO;2-3

Johansen, S. (1988). Statistical analysis of cointegration vectors. *Journal of Economic Dynamics & Control*, *12*(2-3), 231–254. doi:10.1016/0165-1889(88)90041-3

Johansson, J. K. (2005). The new Brand America. *Place Branding*, *1*(2), 155–163. doi:10.1057/palgrave.pb.5990017

John, R., Smith, A., Chotipanich, S., & Pitt, M. (2014). Awareness and effectiveness of quality function deployment (QFD) in design and build projects in Nigeria. *J Facil. Manag.*, *12*(1), 72–88. doi:10.1108/JFM-07-2013-0039

Jurowski, C., Uysal, M., & Williams, D. R. (1997). A theoretical analysis of host community resident reactions to tourism. *Journal of Travel Research*, *36*(2), 3–11.

Justice, L. C. (1986). The Concept of the Urban Forest as Applied to Kuala Lumpur, Malaysia. *Journal of Arboriculture*, *12*(7), 178–181.

Kadir, N., & Karim, M. Z. A. (2012). Tourism and economic growth in Malaysia: Evidence from tourist arrivals from ASEAN-5 countries. *Economic Research Journal*, *25*(4), 1089–1100.

Kadir, N., Nayan, S., & Abdullah, M. S. (2010). The causal relationship between tourism and economic growth in Malaysia: Evidence from multivariate causality tests. *Tourism and Management Studies*, *6*, 16–24.

Kao, C. (1999). Spurious Regression and Residual Based Tests for Cointegration in Panel Data. *Journal of Econometrics*, *90*(1), 1–44. doi:10.1016/S0304-4076(98)00023-2

Kapczynski, A., & Szromek, A. R. (2008). Hypothesis concerning the development of Polish spas in the years 19492006. *Tourism Management*, *29*(5), 1035–1037. doi:10.1016/j.tourman.2007.10.001

Karan Pradyumna, P. (1989). Environment and Development in Sikkim Himalaya: A review. *Human Ecology*, *17*(2), 257-271.

Karan, P. P. (1969). The kingdom of Sikkim, Annals Map Supplement Number 10. *Annals of the Association of American Geographers*, *59*, 211–213. doi:10.1111/j.1467-8306.1969.tb00665.x

Karatzoglou, B., & Spilanis, I. (2010). Sustainable tourism in Greek islands: The integration of activity-based environmental management with a destination environmental scorecard based on the adaptive resource management paradigm. *Business Strategy and the Environment*, *19*(1), 26–38. doi:10.1002/bse.627

Kasemsap, K. (2015a). The role of marketing strategies in the tourism industry. In N. Ray (Ed.), *Emerging innovative marketing strategies in the tourism industry* (pp. 174–194). Hershey, PA: IGI Global. doi:10.4018/978-1-4666-8699-1.ch010

Kasemsap, K. (2015b). The role of ethical leadership in ethical organizations: A literature review. In C. Anyansi-Archibong (Ed.), *Contemporary issues surrounding ethical research methods and practice* (pp. 135–168). Hershey, PA: IGI Global. doi:10.4018/978-1-4666-8562-8.ch006

Kasemsap, K. (2015c). The role of medical tourism in emerging markets. In M. Cooper, K. Vafadari, & M. Hieda (Eds.), *Current issues and emerging trends in medical tourism* (pp. 89–109). Hershey, PA: IGI Global. doi:10.4018/978-1-4666-8574-1.ch007

Kasemsap, K. (2016a). Facilitating hospitality and tourism management in global business. In N. Pappas & I. Bregoli (Eds.), *Global dynamics in travel, tourism, and hospitality* (pp. 283–305). Hershey, PA: IGI Global. doi:10.4018/978-1-5225-0201-2.ch016

Kasemsap, K. (2016b). The roles of information technology and knowledge management in global tourism. In A. Nedelea, M. Korstanje, & B. George (Eds.), *Strategic tools and methods for promoting hospitality and tourism services* (pp. 109–138). Hershey, PA: IGI Global. doi:10.4018/978-1-4666-9761-4.ch006

Kasemsap, K. (2016c). Encouraging corporate social responsibility and sustainable tourism development in global tourism. In L. Guliani & S. Rizwan (Eds.), *Corporate social responsibility in the hospitality and tourism industry* (pp. 197–224). Hershey, PA: IGI Global. doi:10.4018/978-1-4666-9902-1.ch016

Kasemsap, K. (2016d). Implementing electronic commerce in global marketing. In I. Lee (Ed.), *Encyclopedia of e-commerce development, implementation, and management* (pp. 591–602). Hershey, PA: IGI Global. doi:10.4018/978-1-4666-9787-4.ch043

Kasemsap, K. (2016e). Advocating electronic business and electronic commerce in the global marketplace. In S. Dixit & A. Sinha (Eds.), *E-retailing challenges and opportunities in the global marketplace* (pp. 1–24). Hershey, PA: IGI Global. doi:10.4018/978-1-4666-9921-2.ch001

Kasemsap, K. (2016f). The roles of social media marketing and brand management in global marketing. In W. Ozuem & G. Bowen (Eds.), *Competitive social media marketing strategies* (pp. 173–200). Hershey, PA: IGI Global. doi:10.4018/978-1-4666-9776-8.ch009

Kasemsap, K. (2016g). Utilizing social media in modern business. In I. Lee (Ed.), *Encyclopedia of e-commerce development, implementation, and management* (pp. 2171–2182). Hershey, PA: IGI Global. doi:10.4018/978-1-4666-9787-4.ch156

Kassim, A. (1997). Illegal alien labour in Malaysia: Its influx, utilization, and ramifications. *Indonesia and the Malay World*, *25*(71), 50–81. doi:10.1080/13639819708729889

Kastelein, B. (2004). Urban ecotourism: impossible conundrum? Mexican cities must clean up their acts to keep tourists. *Business Mexico*, 36-42.

Kastenholz, E., Carneiro, M. J., Marques, C. P., & Lima, J. (2012). Understanding and managing the rural tourism experience: The case of a historical village in Portugal. *Tourism Management Perspectives*, *4*, 207–214. doi:10.1016/j.tmp.2012.08.009

Katircioğlu, S. T. (2009). Testing the tourism-led growth hypothesis: The case of Malta. *Acta Oeconomica*, *59*(3), 331–343. doi:10.1556/AOecon.59.2009.3.4

Katircioğlu, S. T. (2011). Tourism and growth in Singapore: New extension from bounds test to level relationships and conditional Granger causality tests. *The Singapore Economic Review*, *56*(3), 441–453. doi:10.1142/S0217590811004365

Katircioğlu, S., Fethi, S., & Caner, H. (2014). Testing the higher education-led growth hypothesis in a small island: An empirical investigation from a new version of the Solow growth model. *Quality & Quantity*, *48*(2), 729–744. doi:10.1007/s11135-012-9798-9

Kaynak, E., & Marandu, E. E. (2006). Tourism market potential analysis in Botswana: A Delphi study. *Journal of Travel Research*, *45*(2), 227–237. doi:10.1177/0047287506291595

Kerr, W. (2003). *Tourism Public Policy, and the strategic Management of Failure*. New York: Pergamon.

Keyim, P., Yang, D. G., & Zhang, X. L. (2005). Study of rural tourism in turpan, China. *Chinese Geographical Science*, *15*(4), 377–382. doi:10.1007/s11769-005-0028-4

Khalil, S., Kakar, M. K., & Waliullah, A. (2004). Role of tourism in economic growth: Empirical evidence from Pakistan economy. *Pakistan Development Review*, *46*(4), 985–995.

Khan, M. A. (2005). *Introduction to Tourism*. Anmol Publication Pvt. Ltd.

Kibicho, W. (2008). Community-based tourism: A factor- cluster segmentation approach. *Journal of Sustainable Tourism*, *16*(2), 211–231. doi:10.2167/jost623.0

Kim, D.-Y., Hwang, Y.-H., & Fesenmaier, D. R. (2005). Modeling tourism advertising effectiveness. *Journal of Travel Research*, *44*(1), 42–49. doi:10.1177/0047287505276590

Kim, H. J., Chen, M. H., & Jang, S. C. S. (2006). Tourism expansion and economic development: The case of Taiwan. *Tourism Management*, *27*(5), 925–933. doi:10.1016/j.tourman.2005.05.011

Kim, K., Uysal, M., & Sirgy, M. J. (2013). How does tourism in a community impact the quality of life of community residents? *Tourism Management*, *36*(5), 527–540. doi:10.1016/j.tourman.2012.09.005

Kim, S. S., Kim, M., Park, J., & Guo, Y. (2008). Cave tourism: Tourists characteristics, motivations to visit, and the segmentation of their behavior. *Asia Pacific Journal of Tourism Research*, *13*(3), 299–318. doi:10.1080/10941660802280448

Kim, S., & Jamal, T. (2015). The co-evolution of rural tourism and sustainable rural development in Hongdong, Korea: Complexity, conflict and local response. *Journal of Sustainable Tourism*, *23*(8-9), 1363–1385. doi:10.1080/09669582.2015.1022181

Klak, T. (2007). Sustainable ecotourism development in Central America and the Caribbean: Review of debates and conceptual reformulation. *Geography Compass*, *1*(5), 1037–1057. doi:10.1111/j.1749-8198.2007.00055.x

Kocasoy, G. (1995). Effects of tourist population pressure on pollution of coastal seas. *Environmental Management*, *19*(1), 75–79. doi:10.1007/BF02472005

Kolas, A. (2004). Tourism and the Making of Place in Shangri-La. *Tourism Geographies*, *6*(3), 262–278. doi:10.1080/1461668042000249610

Kotler, P., & Armstrong, G. (2005). *Principles of Marketing*. Available online on June 18, 2016 at http://docslide.us/documents/advertising-and-public-relations-chapter-15-priciples-of-marketing-by-philip-kotler-and-gary-armstrong-pearson.html

Krannich, R., & Petrzelka, P. (2003). Tourism and natural amenity development: Real opportunities. In D. Brown & L. Swanson (Eds.), *Challenges for rural America in the twenty-first century* (pp. 190–199). University Park, PA: Penn State University Press.

Kuala Lumpur Tourism Association (KLTA). (2012). Retrieved on 25th December, 2013 from http://www.klta.org.my/content.cfm

Kuala Lumpur Tourism Master Plan 2015-2025. (2015). *Tourism Unit*. Kuala Lumpur City Hall, Kuala Lumpur, Malaysia.

Kuentzel, W., & Heberlein, T. A. (2006). From novice to expert? a panel study of specialization progression and change. *Journal of Leisure Research*, *38*, 496–512.

Kumar, R. R., Loganathan, N., Patel, A., & Kumar, R. D. (2015). Nexus between tourism earnings and economic growth: A study of Malaysia. *Quality & Quantity*, *49*(3), 1101–1120. doi:10.1007/s11135-014-0037-4

Kuo, T.-C., Wu, H.-H., & Shieh, J.-I. (2009). Integration of environmental considerations in quality function deployment by using fuzzy logic. *Expert Systems with Applications*, *36*(3), 7148–7156. doi:10.1016/j.eswa.2008.08.029

Laarman, J. G., & Durst, P. B. (1987). *Nature travel and tropical forests (FPEI working series)*. Raleigh, NC: South Eastern Center for Forest Economics Research, North Carolina State University.

Lalib, A. W., & Williams, G. B. (1998). An intelligent maintenance model (system): An application of analytical hierarchy process and a fuzzy logic rule-based controller. *The Journal of the Operational Research Society*, *49*(S7), 745–757. doi:10.1057/palgrave.jors.2600542

Lam, C. S., & Crossley, J. (2014). Las Vegas Versus Macao as Diversified Travel Destinations. *Journal of Tourism Insights*, *5*(1), 1–26.

Lane, B., & Kastenholz, E. (2015). Rural tourism: The evolution of practice and research approaches – towards a new generation concept? *Journal of Sustainable Tourism*, *23*(8-9), 1133–1156. doi:10.1080/09669582.2015.1083997

Lane, B. (1994). What is rural tourism? *Journal of Sustainable Tourism*, *2*(1/2), 7–21. doi:10.1080/09669589409510680

Lane, B. (2009). Rural tourism: An overview. In T. Jamal & M. Robinson (Eds.), *The Sage handbook of tourism studies* (pp. 354–371). London, UK: Sage Publications. doi:10.4135/9780857021076.n20

Lane, M. B. (2010). Affirming New Directions in Planning Theory: Co-management of Protected Areas. *Society & Natural Resources*, *14*(8), 657–667. doi:10.1080/08941920118212

Lange, G. M. (2015). Tourism in Zanzibar: Incentives for sustainable management of the coastal environment. *Ecosystem Services*, *11*, 5–11. doi:10.1016/j.ecoser.2014.11.009

Lapašinskaitė, R., & Boguslauskas, V. (2015). The maintenance cost allocation in product life cycle. *The Engineering Economist*, *44*(4), 17–23.

Lask, T., & Herold, S. (2004). An observation station for culture and tourism in Vietnam: A forum for World Heritage and public participation. *Current Issues in Tourism*, *7*(4-5), 399–411. doi:10.1080/13683500408667993

Latour, B. (2005). *Resembling the social*. Oxford, UK: Oxford University Press.

Lau, P. H., Oh, S. L., & Hu, S. S. (2009). Tourist arrivals and economic growth in Sarawak. *Sarawak Development Journal*, *9*, 36–45.

Law of Mongolia on Special Protected Area. (1994). Retrieved from http://www.legalinfo.mn/law/details/479

Lawrence, M., & Dredge, D. (2007). Tourism planning and policy processes. In D. Dredge & J. A. Jenkins (Eds.), *Tourism planning and policy* (pp. 191–224). John Wiley & Sons.

Le, T. A., Weaver, D., & Lawton, L. (2015). Community-based tourism and development in the periphery/semi-periphery interface: A case study approach. In S. McCool & K. Bosak (Eds.), *Reframing Sustainable Tourism* (pp. 161–181). Springer.

Le, T. A., Bui, T. H., & Weaver, D. (2012). Community-based tourism and economic sustainability: A case study at Kim Bong wood carpentry village in Vietnam. *Proceedings of the 4th Asia-Euro Conference 2012 in Tourism, Hospitality and Gastronomy*. Subang Jaya, Malaysia: Taylor University.

Lean, H. H., Chong, S. H., & Hooy, C. W. (2014). Tourism and economic growth: Comparing Malaysia and Singapore. *International Journal of Economics and Management*, *8*(1), 139–157.

Lean, H. H., & Tang, C. F. (2010). Is the tourism-led growth hypothesis stable for Malaysia? A note. *International Journal of Tourism Research*, *12*(4), 375–378. doi:10.1002/jtr.759

Lee, C. C., & Chang, C. P. (2008). Tourism development and economic growth: A closer look at the panels. *Tourism Management*, *29*(1), 180–192. doi:10.1016/j.tourman.2007.02.013

Lee, C. C., & Chien, M. S. (2008). Structural breaks, tourism development, and economic growth: Evidence from Taiwan. *Mathematics and Computers in Simulation*, *77*(4), 358–368. doi:10.1016/j.matcom.2007.03.004

Lee, S. W., & Kim, H. J. (2010). Agricultural transition and rural tourism in Korea: Experiences of the last forty years. In G. Thapa, P. Viswanathan, J. Routray, & M. Ahmad (Eds.), *Agricultural transition in Asia* (pp. 37–64). Bangkok, Thailand: Asian Institute of Technology.

Lee, S., Graefe, A., & Li, C. (2007). The effects of specialization and gender on motivations and preferences for site attributes in paddling. *Leisure Sciences*, *29*(4), 355–375. doi:10.1080/01490400701394873

Lee, S., & Nam, S. (2005). Agro-tourism as a rural development strategy in Korea. *Journal of Rural Development*, *29*, 67–83.

Li, H., Ye, Q., & Law, R. (2013). Determinants of customer satisfaction in the hotel industry: An application of online review analysis. *Asia Pacific Journal of Tourism Research*, *18*(7), 784–802. doi:10.1080/10941665.2012.708351

Li, M., Wu, B., & Cai, L. (2008). Tourism development of World Heritage Sites in China: A geographic perspective. *Tourism Management*, *29*(2), 308–319. doi:10.1016/j.tourman.2007.03.013

Li, W., Lin, L., Shi-rong, T., Song, L., Zhao, Y., Yong, W., & Dong-dong, L. (2004). Residents' attitudes to tourism development in ancient village resorts. *Chinese Geographical Science*, *14*(2), 170–178. doi:10.1007/s11769-004-0027-x

Li, W., Zhang, Q., Liu, C., & Xue, Q. (2006). Tourism's impacts on natural resources: A positive case from China. *Environmental Management*, *38*(4), 572–579. doi:10.1007/s00267-004-0299-z PMID:16933085

Liaghati, H., Khoshbakht, K., Mahmodi, H., Koucakzade, M., & Omidvar, P. (2010). Exploring Characteristics and Profile of Urban Ecotourism (A Case Study from Tehran). *Journal of Environmental Studis*, *36*(55), 7–11.

Lim, J. (2016). *City Hall to aggressively promote KL as a destination*. Retrieved from http://www.thestar.com.my/metro/community/2016/02/20/city-hall-to-aggressively-promote-kl-as-a-destination/

Lindberg, K., Enriquez, J., & Sproule, K. (1996). Ecotourism questioned: Case studies from Belize. *Annals of Tourism Research*, *23*(3), 543–562. doi:10.1016/0160-7383(95)00074-7

Lindberg, K. (1991). *Policies for maximizing nature tourism's ecological and economic benefits*. Washington, DC: World Resources Institute.

Linstone & Turoff. (1975). The Delphi Method: Techniques and Applications. Reading, MA: Addison-Wesley.

Litvin, S. W. (2006). Revisiting Plogs model of allocentricity and psychocentricity…one more time. *The Cornell Hotel and Restaurant Administration Quarterly*, *47*(3), 245–253. doi:10.1177/0010880406289138

Liu, A. (2006). Tourism in rural areas: Kedah, Malaysia. *Tourism Management*, *27*(5), 878–889. doi:10.1016/j.tourman.2005.05.007

Liu, C. H. S., Horng, J. S., & Chou, S. F. (2015). A critical evaluation of sustainable tourism from the integrated perspective: Conducting moderated-mediation analysis. *Tourism Management Perspectives*, *16*, 43–50. doi:10.1016/j.tmp.2015.05.008

Liu, C. Z. (2002). A Study on Leisure Agriculture and Rural Development. *The Journal of Rural Development Perspectives*, *3*, 19–33.

Liu, C. Z. (2010). Rural Development and Rural Tourism in Taiwan. *Asian Journal of Arts and Sciences*, *1*(2), 211–227.

Liu, Z., Siguaw, J. A., & Enz, C. A. (2008). Using tourist travel habits and preferences to assess strategic destination positioning: The case of Costa Rica. *Cornell Hospitality Quarterly*, *49*(3), 258–281. doi:10.1177/1938965508322007

Liu, P. (2015). *Merry - go-round in Australia*. Retrieved from http://asiaweekly.com/merry-go-round-in-asia/

Loganathan, N., Ibrahim, Y., & Harun, M. (2008). Tourism development policy, strategic alliances and impact of consumer price index on tourist arrivals: The case of Malaysia. *TOURISMOS: An International Multidisciplinary Journal of Tourism*, *3*(1), 83–98.

Long, J., Vogelaar, A., & Hale, B. W. (2014). Toward sustainable educational travel. *Journal of Sustainable Tourism*, *22*(3), 421–439. doi:10.1080/09669582.2013.819877

Loureiro, S. M. C., & González, F. J. M. (2008). The importance of quality, satisfaction, trust, and image in relation to rural tourist loyalty. *Journal of Travel & Tourism Marketing*, *25*(2), 117–136. doi:10.1080/10548400802402321

Loureiro, S. M. C. (2014). The role of the rural tourism experience economy in place attachment and behavioral intentions. *International Journal of Hospitality Management*, *40*, 1–9. doi:10.1016/j.ijhm.2014.02.010

Lu, W., & Stepchenkova, S. (2012). Ecotourism experiences reported online, classification of satisfaction attributes. *Tourism Management*, *33*(3), 702–712. doi:10.1016/j.tourman.2011.08.003

Ma, M., & Hassink, R. (2013). An evolutionary perspective on tourism area development. *Annals of Tourism Research*, *41*, 89–109. doi:10.1016/j.annals.2012.12.004

MA. (2005). *Ecosystems and Human Well-being: Synthesis*. Washington, DC: Island Press.

Mac, J., & Moncuer, J. (1995). Sustainable tourism development: Managing Hawaiis unique touristic resources-Hanauma Bay. *Journal of Travel Research*, *33*(4), 51–57. doi:10.1177/004728759503300408

MacDonald, R., & Jolliffe, L. (2003). Cultural rural tourism: Evidence from Canada. *Annals of Tourism Research*, *30*(2), 307–322. doi:10.1016/S0160-7383(02)00061-0

MacFarlane, B. L. (1996). Socialization influences of specialization among birdwatchers. *Human Dimensions of Wildlife*, *1*(1), 35–50. doi:10.1080/10871209609359050

MacIntosh, R. W. (1995). *Tourism: Principles, Practices, Philosophies*. John Wiley and Sons, Inc.

MacLeod, G. (2001). New regionalism reconsidered: Globalization and the remaking of political economic space. *International Journal of Urban and Regional Research*, *25*(4), 804–829. doi:10.1111/1468-2427.00345

Madan, S., & Rawat, L. (2000). The Impact of Tourism on the Environment of Mussoorie, Garhwal Himalaya, India. *The Environmentalist*, *20*(3), 249–255. doi:10.1023/A:1006760015997

Maddala, G., & Kim, I. (1998). *Unit Roots, Cointegration, and Structural Change*. Oxford, UK: Cambridge University Press.

Magnini, V. P., Crotts, J. C., & Zehrer, A. (2011). Understanding customer delight an application of travel blog analysis. *Journal of Travel Research*, *50*(5), 535–545. doi:10.1177/0047287510379162

Maharana, R. S. C., & Sharma, E. (2000). Valuing Ecotourism In a Sacred Lake of the Sikkim Himalaya. *Journal of G.B. Pant Institute of Himalayan Environment and Development*.

Majumdar, K., & Datta, S. (2014). *Study on Mitigation Measures of Gumti Hydro Power Plant Using Analytic Hierarchy Process and Concordance Analysis Techniques*. Dubai, UAE: Academic Press.

Mak, B. (2013). The Influence of Political Ideology on the Outbound Tourism in China: 政政治思想对中国出境旅游的影响. *Journal of China Tourism Research*, *9*(1), 1–26. doi:10.1080/19388160.2013.756764

Manate, M., & Pechlaner, H. (2006). How to define, identify and monitor the decline of tourist destinations: towards an early warning system. In R. W. Butler (Ed.), *The Tourism Life Cycle, Conceptual and Theoretical Issues* (pp. 235–253). Clevedon, UK: Channelview Publications.

Manish. (2007). *Tourism Planning and Development.* Rajat Publication.

Manjulika, G. (2011). Buddhism and Deep Ecology, Buddhist Himalaya: Studies. In *Religion, History and Culture*. Namgyal Institute of Tibetology-Sikkim.

Mankiw, N. G., Romer, D., & Weil, D. N. (1992). A contribution to the empirics of economic growth. *The Quarterly Journal of Economics, 107*(2), 407–437. doi:10.2307/2118477

Mansoor, L., & Ching, O. T. (2016). *MRT project on track and well within budget.* Retrieved from http://www.nst.com.my/news/2016/02/128832/mrt-project-track-and-well-within-budget

Marker, M. A., Blanco, A., Lokanathan, S., & Verma, A. (2008). *Ecotourism in Malaysia. Project for PP5279: Cluster and National Competitiveness.* Lee Kuan Yew School of Public Policy.

Marsden, T. (2003). *The condition of rural sustainability*. Assen: Van Gorcum.

Martın, M. B. (2005). Weather, climate and tourism: A Geographical perspective. *Annals of Tourism Research, 32*(3), 571–591. doi:10.1016/j.annals.2004.08.004

Martini, A., Massa, S., & Testa, S. (2012). The role of social software for customer co-creation; does it change the practice for innovation. *International Journal of Engineering Business Management, 4*(40), 1–10.

Marzano, G., & Scott, N. (2009). Power in destination branding. *Annals of Tourism Research, 36*(2), 247–267. doi:10.1016/j.annals.2009.01.004

Mathews, H. G. (1975). International Tourism and Political Science Research. *Annals of Tourism Research, 2*(4), 195–203. doi:10.1016/0160-7383(75)90032-8

Mazumder, M. N. H., Ahmed, E. M., & Al-Amin, A. Q. (2009). Does tourism contribute significantly to the Malaysian economy? Multiplier analysis using I-O technique. *International Journal of Business and Management, 4*(7), 146–159. doi:10.5539/ijbm.v4n7p146

McAreavey, R., & McDonagh, J. (2011). Sustainable rural tourism: Lessons for rural development. *Sociologia Ruralis, 51*(2), 175–194. doi:10.1111/j.1467-9523.2010.00529.x

McCoy, P. (1982). The new national tourism policy act the state role in implementation. *Annals of Tourism Research, 9*(2), 276–279. doi:10.1016/0160-7383(82)90056-1

McDonald, J. R. (2009). Complexity science: An alternative world view for understanding sustainable tourism development. *Journal of Sustainable Tourism, 17*(4), 455–471. doi:10.1080/09669580802495709

McIntosh, A. J., & Prentice, R. C. (1999). Affirming authenticity: Consuming cultural heritage. *Annals of Tourism Research, 26*(3), 589–612. doi:10.1016/S0160-7383(99)00010-9

McKercher, B. (1995). The destination-market matrix: A tourism market portfolio analysis model. *Journal of Travel & Tourism Marketing, 4*(2), 23–40. doi:10.1300/J073v04n02_02

McKercher, B. (2005a). Are psychographics predictors of destination life cycles? *Journal of Travel & Tourism Marketing, 19*(1), 49–55. doi:10.1300/J073v19n01_05

McKercher, B. (2005b). Destinations as products? A reflection on Butlers life cycle. *Tourism Recreation Research, 30*(3), 97–102. doi:10.1080/02508281.2005.11081491

McLaughlin, M. W. (1990). *The Rand Change Agent Study Revisited: Macro Perspectives and micro Realities*. Stanford, CA: Stanford University.

Meng, Z., Wei, Y., & Yu, Y. (2011). On Life Cycle of Cultural Heritage Engineering Tourism: A Case Study of Macau. *Engineering and Risk Management, 1*, 351–357.

Miller, G., & Twining-Ward, L. (2005). *Monitoring for a sustainable tourism transition: The challenge of developing and using indicators*. Wallingford, UK: CABI Publishing. doi:10.1079/9780851990514.0000

Miller, L. (2010). *Solo women's travel surges in popularity*. Retrieved from http://gadling.com/2010/08/16/solo-womens-travel-surges-in-popularity/

Ministry of Economic Affairs. (2009). *Reaction plans for accelerating economic recovery*. Taipei.

Ministry of Transportation and Communication. (1999). Study on the effects of fewer working days on domestic tourism activities. Taipei: Statistics Bureau, MOTC.

Mishra, M., & Jha, A. (2014). Prioritizing Sectors for Economic Development in Sikkim, India. *International Journal of Asian Business and Information Management, 5*(2).

Mitchell, J., & Ashley, C. (2010). *Tourism and poverty reduction: Pathways to prosperity*. London, UK: Earthscan Publications.

Mitchell, R. E., & Reid, D. G. (2001). Community integration: Island tourism in Peru. *Annals of Tourism Research, 28*(1), 113–139. doi:10.1016/S0160-7383(00)00013-X

Mitchell, J., & Ashley, C. (2010). Tourism and Poverty Reduction. London, UK: Earthscan Publishing.

Mitra, K. (2016). *Cities, like dreams, are made of...* Retrieved from http://kindlemag.in/cities-like-dreams-made/

Miyamoto, M., Parid, M. M., Aini, Z. K., & Michinaka, T. (2014). Proximate and underlying causes of forest cover change in Peninsular Malaysia. *Forest Policy and Economics, 44*, 18–25. doi:10.1016/j.forpol.2014.05.007

MNET. (2008). *Environmental impact indicators in Mongolia*. Ulaanbaatar: Ministry of Nature, Environment and Tourism.

Mok, H. (1990). A quasi-experimental measure of the effectiveness of destinational advertising: Some evidence from Hawaii. *Journal of Travel Research, 29*(1), 30–34. doi:10.1177/004728759002900107

Molur, S., & Walker, S. (1998b). *Conservation Assessment and Management Plan for Reptiles of India. Report submitted to WWF-India/BCPP*. Coimbatore, India: Zoo Outreach Organization.

Mondal, A. K. (2003). *A Checklist of Mammals of Sikkim*. Kolkata: Zoological Survey of India.

Moore, R. L., Scott, D., & Moore, A. (2008). Gender-based differences in birdwatchers participation and commitment. *Human Dimensions of Wildlife, 13*(2), 89–101. doi:10.1080/10871200701882525

Morrison, M., & Bennett, J. (2000). Choice modelling, non-use values and benefit transfer. *Economic Analysis and Policy, 30*(1), 13–32. doi:10.1016/S0313-5926(00)50002-2

Moscardo, G. (2008). Sustainable tourism innovation: Challenging basic assumptions. *Tourism and Hospitality Research, 8*(1), 4–13. doi:10.1057/thr.2008.7

Moss, S. E., Ryan, C., & Wagoner, C. B. (2003). An empirical test of Butlers resort product life cycle: Forecasting casino winnings. *Journal of Travel Research*, *41*(4), 393–399. doi:10.1177/0047287503041004008

Mshenga, P. M., & Richardson, R. B. (2013). Micro and small enterprise participation in tourism in coastal Kenya. *Small Business Economics*, *41*(3), 667–681. doi:10.1007/s11187-012-9449-5

Mulok, D., Kogid, M., Asid, R., Lily, J., & Mansur, K. M. (2012). Tourism and economic growth linkages in Malaysia. *BIMP-EAGA Journal for Sustainable Tourism Development*, *1*(1), 3–10.

Murphy, P. E. (2013). *Tourism: A Community Approach (RLE Tourism)*. Routledge.

Mustafa, M. (2016). *Farewell to Taman Rimba Ampang as it makes way for controversial new highways.* Retrieved from http://malaysiandigest.com/features/619173-farewell-to-taman-rimba-ampang-as-it-makes-way-for-controversial-new-highways.html

Mycoo, M. (2014). Sustainable tourism, climate change and sea level rise adaptation policies in Barbados. *Natural Resources Forum*, *38*(1), 47–57. doi:10.1111/1477-8947.12033

Nagai & Nakashima. (2016). A Study on the Effects of Client Company Information on the On-Site Logistics and Processes in a Supply Chain: A New Design Approach using Quality Function Deployment. *Expert Journal of Business and Management*, *4*(1), 56–62.

Naghiu, A., Vâzquez, J. L., & Georgiev, I. (2005). Rural development strategies through rural tourism activities in Romania: Chance for an internal demand? *International Review on Public and Nonprofit Marketing*, *2*(1), 85–95. doi:10.1007/BF02893253

Nakata, N. M., Nakata, V., Keech, S., & Bolt, R. (2012). Decolonial goals and pedagogies for Indigenous studies. *Decolon Indig Educ Soc*, *1*, 120–140.

Narayan, P. K., & Narayan, S. (2006). Saving behaviour in Fiji: An empirical assessment using the ARDL approach to cointegration. *International Journal of Social Economics*, *33*(7), 468–480. doi:10.1108/03068290610673243

Narayan, P. K., & Popp, S. (2010). A new unit root test with two structural breaks in level and slope at unknown time. *Journal of Applied Statistics*, *37*(9), 1425–1438. doi:10.1080/02664760903039883

Narayan, P. K. (2005). The saving and investment nexus for China: Evidence from cointegration tests. *Applied Economics*, *37*(17), 1979–1990. doi:10.1080/00036840500278103

National Statistics Bureau. (2005). *Statistic of Social Development in R.O.C. Taipei.* Retrieved March 4, 2005, from http://www.stat.gov.tw

Navchaa, T., Amarbayasgalan, G., & Erdenetuul, S. (2015). Sustainable tourism and heritage protection in the Orkhon Valley National Park, Mongolia. *Euro-Asia Economic Forum 2015* (p. 115). Xi'an: BIT Group Global Ltd.

Nelson, C. R., & Plosser, C. R. (1982). Trends and random walks in macroeconomic time series: Some evidence and implications. *Journal of Monetary Economics*, *10*(2), 139–162. doi:10.1016/0304-3932(82)90012-5

Nelson, F. (2010). *Community rights, conservation and contested land: The politics of natural resource governance in Africa*. London: Earthscan.

Neto, F. (2003). A new approach to sustainable tourism development: Moving beyond environmental protection. *Natural Resources Forum*, *27*(3), 212–222. doi:10.1111/1477-8947.00056

Neto, F. (2003). *A New Approach to Sustainable Tourism Development: Moving Beyond Environmental Protection.* DESA Discussion Paper 29. New York: The United Nations.

Newby, P. (1994). Tourism: Support or Threat to Heritage? In G. Ashworth & P. Larkham (Eds.), *Building a New Heritage: Tourism, Culture and Identity in the New Europe* (pp. 206–228). London: Routledge.

Nguyen Thi Thu Ha. (2007). *Tourism development and the sustainable management of cultural heritage – A case study of Hoi An Ancient Town in Vietnam* (Master thesis). KDI School of Public Policy and Management.

Nissan, E., Galindo, M. A., & Méndez, M. T. (2011). Relationship between tourism and economic growth. *Service Industries Journal, 31*(10), 1567–1572. doi:10.1080/02642069.2010.485636

Njoroge, J. M. (2015). Climate change and tourism adaptation: Literature review. *Tourism & Hospitality Management, 21*, 95–108.

Noronha, F. (1999). Ten Year later, Goa Still Uneasy Over the Impact of Tourism. *International Journal of Contemporary Hospitality Management, 11*(2/3), 100–106. doi:10.1108/09596119910250977

Nowak, J. J., Sahli, M., & Cortes-Jimenez, I. (2007). Tourism, capital good imports and economic growth: Theory and evidence for Spain. *Tourism Economics, 13*(4), 515–536. doi:10.5367/000000007782696113

Nunkoo, R., Gursoy, D., & Ramkissoon, H. (2013). Developments in hospitality marketing and management: Social network analysis and research themes. *Journal of Hospitality Marketing & Management, 22*(3), 269–288. doi:10.1080/19368623.2013.753814

Nunkoo, R., & Gursoy, D. (2012). Residents support for tourism: An identity perspective. *Annals of Tourism Research, 39*(1), 243–268. doi:10.1016/j.annals.2011.05.006

Nussair, K., Erdem, M., Okumus, F., & Biligan, A. (2012). Users attitudes toward online social networks in travel. In M. Sigala, A. Christou, & U. Gretzel (Eds.), *Social Media in Travel, Tourism and Hospitality: theory, practice and cases. Ashgate Publication.*

O'Neil, P. (2007). *Essentials of Comparative Politics* (2nd ed.). Norton.

OECD. (2011a). *Towards Green Growth, Green Growth Strategy Synthesis report*. Paris: OECD.

OECD. (2014a). *New Approaches to Economic Challenges Synthesis Paper*. Available on Olis at [C (2014)41].

OECD/UNEP. (2011b). *Climate Change and Tourism Policy in OECD Countries, OECD Studies on Tourism*. OECD Publishing.

Oh, C. O. (2005). The contribution of tourism development to economic growth in the Korean economy. *Tourism Management, 26*(1), 39–44. doi:10.1016/j.tourman.2003.09.014

Okech, R. N. (2009). Developing urban ecotourism in Kenyan cities: A sustainable approach. *Journal of Ecology and Natural Environment, 1*(1), 1–6.

Okello, M. M., Wishitemi, B. E. L., & Lagat, B. (2005). Tourism Potential and Achievement of Protected areas in Kenya: Criteria and Prioritization. *Tourism Analysis, 10*(2), 151-164.

Olds, K. (1998). Urban mega-events, evictions and housing rights: The Canadian case. *Current Issues in Tourism, 1*(1), 2–46. doi:10.1080/13683509808667831

Oppermann, M. (1995). Holidays on the farm: A case study of German hosts and guests. *Journal of Travel Research, 34*(1), 63–67. doi:10.1177/004728759503400108

Orbasli, A. (2000). *Tourists in historic towns*. New York: Taylor & Francis. doi:10.4324/9780203479001

Ostrom, E. (1990). *Governing the commons: The evolution of institutions for collective action*. Cambridge University Press. doi:10.1017/CBO9780511807763

Ostrom, E. (1998). A Behavioral Approach to the Rational Choice Theory of Collective Action. *The American Political Science Review*, *92*(1), 1–22. doi:10.2307/2585925

Ostrom, E. (2005). *Understanding institutional diversity*. Princeton, NJ: Princeton Univ Pr.

Ostrom, E. (2007). A diagnostic approach for going beyond panaceas. *Proceedings of the National Academy of Sciences of the United States of America*, *104*(39), 15181–15187. doi:10.1073/pnas.0702288104 PMID:17881578

Othman, P., & Rosli, M. M. (2010). The Impact of tourism on small business performance: Empirical evidence from Malaysian Islands. *International Journal of Business and Social Sciences*, *2*, 11–20.

Othman, R., Salleh, N. H. M., & Sarmidi, T. (2012). Analysis of causal relationship between tourism development, economic growth and foreign direct investment: An ARDL approach. *Journal of Applied Sciences*, *12*(12), 1245–1254. doi:10.3923/jas.2012.1245.1254

Pal, J., Pal, M., Roy, & Mazumdar. (2016). A Study on Mitigation Measures for the Development of Neermahal Palace and Surrounding Rudrasagar Lake Area in Tripura, India using Analytic Hierarchy Process. *International Journal of Applied Engineering Research, 11*(4), 2615-2619.

Palmer, A., Koenig-Lewis, N., & Jones, L. (2013). The effects of residents' social identity and involvement on their advocacy of incoming tourism. *Tourism Management*, *38*, 142–151. doi:10.1016/j.tourman.2013.02.019

Palmeri, C. (2015). *Theme Park Growth Shifts to Asia in Business the U.S. Pioneered*. Retrieved from http://www.bloomberg.com/news/articles/2015-06-03/theme-park-growth-shifts-to-asia-in-business-the-u-s-pioneered

Papatheodorou, A. (2006). TALC and spatial implications of competition. In R. W. Butler (Ed.), *The Tourism Life Cycle: Conceptual and Theoretical Issues* (pp. 67–82). Clevedon, UK: Channelview Publications.

Paramati, S. R., Alam, M. S., & Chen, C. F. (2016). The effects of tourism on economic growth and CO2 emissions: A comparison between developed and developing economies. *Journal of Travel Research*. doi:10.1177/0047287516667848

Park, A. (2009). 'Sellinga small state to the world: Lithuanias struggle in building its national image. *Place Branding and Public Diplomacy*, *5*(1), 67–84. doi:10.1057/pb.2008.25

Park, D. B., Lee, H. J., & Yoon, Y. S. (2014). Understanding the benefit sought by rural tourists and accommodation preferences: A South Korea case. *International Journal of Tourism Research*, *16*(3), 291–302. doi:10.1002/jtr.1929

Park, D. B., Lee, K. W., Choi, H. S., & Yoon, Y. (2012). Factors influencing social capital in rural tourism communities in South Korea. *Tourism Management*, *33*(6), 1511–1520. doi:10.1016/j.tourman.2012.02.005

Parnwell, M. (2016). Heritage management and tourism development in Hoi An, Vietnam. In V. King (Ed.), *UNESCO in Southeast Asia: World Heritage Sites in comparative context*. Copenhagen: NIAS Press.

Parry, M. L., Canziani, O. F., Palutikof, J. P., van der Linden, P. J., & Hanson, C. E. (Eds.). (2007). *Climate Change 2007: Impacts, Adaptation and Vulnerability. Contribution of Working Group II to the Fourth Assessment Report of the Intergovernmental Panel on Climate Change*. Cambridge, UK: Cambridge University Press.

Passah, P. M. (2007). *Tourism as an Industry in North-Eastern Region in Ahmed Jaynal Uddin*. New Delhi: Mittal Publication.

PATA. (2015a). *Ministry of Higher Education and Tourism Malaysia Launches the Malaysia 101 Edutourism Packages to Promote Malaysian Culture*. Available online from "https://www.pata.org/ministry-of-higher-education-and-tourism-malaysia-launches-the-malaysia-101-edutourism-packages-to-promote-malaysian-culture/"

PATA. (2015b). *All posts tagged New Dimensions of Heritage and Culture Tourism*. Available online from https://www.pata.org/tag/new-dimensions-of-heritage-and-culture-tourism/

Pearce, D. G. (1998). Tourism development in Paris: Public intervention. *Annals of Tourism Research*, *25*(2), 457–476. doi:10.1016/S0160-7383(97)00096-0

Pearce, D. G. (2001). Tourism, trams and local government policy-making in Christchurch, New Zealand. *Current Issues in Tourism*, *4*(2-4), 331–354. doi:10.1080/13683500108667892

Pearlman, M. V. (1990). Conflicts and constraints in Bulgarias tourism sector. *Annals of Tourism Research*, *17*(1), 103–122. doi:10.1016/0160-7383(90)90117-A

Pearson, T. (2012). *Beautiful Venezuela: tourism with a social conscience*. Retrieved on 22nd May, 2013 from http://venezuelanalysis.com/analysis/6996

Pecchia, L., Martin, J. L., Ragozzino, A., Vanzanella, C., Scognamiglio, A., Mirarchi, L., & Morgan, S. P. (2013). User needs elicitation via analytic hierarchy process (AHP). A case study on a Computed Tomography (CT) scanner. *BMC Medical Informatics and Decision Making*, *13*(1), 2. doi:10.1186/1472-6947-13-2 PMID:23289426

Pedroni, P. (1999). Critical Values for Cointegration Tests in Heterogeneous Panels with Multiple Regressions. *Oxford Bulletin of Economics and Statistics*, *61*(s1), 653–670. doi:10.1111/1468-0084.61.s1.14

Pedroni, P. (2004). Panel Cointegration; Asymptotic and Finite Sample Properties of Pooled Time Series Tests, With an Application to the PPP Hypothesis. *Econometric Theory*, *20*(03), 597–625. doi:10.1017/S0266466604203073

Peeters, P., & Dubois, G. (2010). Tourism travel under climate change mitigation constraints. *Journal of Transport Geography*, *18*(3), 447–457. doi:10.1016/j.jtrangeo.2009.09.003

Pellegrini, T. (2007). Co-production on the web: Social softwares as a means of collaborative value creation in web-based infrastructures. *International Review of Information Ethics*, *7*(09), 1–6.

Peña, A. I. P., & Jamilena, D. M. F. (2010). The relationship between business characteristics and ICT deployment in the rural tourism sector. The case of Spain. *International Journal of Tourism Research*, *12*(1), 34–48.

Peña, A. I. P., & Jamilena, D. M. F. (2011). Market orientation adoption in rural tourism: Impact on business outcomes and the perceived value. *International Review on Public and Nonprofit Marketing*, *8*(2), 195–197. doi:10.1007/s12208-011-0068-7

Perman, R. (1991). Cointegration: An introduction to the literature. *Journal of Economic Studies (Glasgow, Scotland)*, *18*(3), 3–30. doi:10.1108/EUM0000000000151

Pesaran, M. H., Shin, Y., & Smith, R. J. (2001). Bounds testing approaches to the analysis of level relationships. *Journal of Applied Econometrics*, *16*(3), 289–326. doi:10.1002/jae.616

Phakdisoth, L., & Kim, D. (2007). The determinants of inbound tourism in Laos. *ASEAN Economic Bulletin*, *24*(2), 225–237. doi:10.1355/AE24-2C

Phan Nhu Ngoc Han. (2004). *Tourism management in Vietnam: Hoi An – A case study* (Master thesis). National University of Singapore.

Phillips, P. C. B., & Hansen, B. E. (1990). Statistical inference in instrumental variables regression with I(1) processes. *The Review of Economic Studies*, *57*(1), 99–125. doi:10.2307/2297545

Pike, S., & Page, S. J. (2014). Destination Marketing Organizations and destination marketing: A narrative analysis of the literature. *Tourism Management*, *41*, 202–227. doi:10.1016/j.tourman.2013.09.009

Pitegoff, B., & Smith, G. (2003). Measuring the return on investment of destination welcome centres: The case of Florida. *Tourism Economics*, *9*(3), 307–323. doi:10.5367/000000003101298411

Plog, S. C. (1974). Why destinations areas rise and fall in popularity. *The Cornell Hotel and Restaurant Administration Quarterly*, *14*(4), 55–58. doi:10.1177/001088047401400409

Plog, S. C. (2002). The power of Psychographics and the concept of venturesomeness. *Journal of Travel Research*, *40*(3), 244–251. doi:10.1177/004728750204000302

Plog, S. (2001). Why destinations areas rise and fall in popularity, an update of a Cornell quarterly classic. *The Cornell Hotel and Restaurant Administration Quarterly*, *42*(3), 13–24. doi:10.1016/S0010-8804(01)81020-X

Popescu, I. A., Paun, C., Nicolescu, L., & Draghici, A. (2008). Romania trying to be a European brand. *Management & Marketing-Bucharest*, (1), 61-72.

Powell, R., & Chalmers, L. (1995). *Regional Economic Impact, Gibraltar Range and Dorrigo National Parks*. Sydney: NSW National Parks and Wildlife Service.

Prabhakaran, S., Nair, V., & Ramachandran, S. (2014). Community participation in rural tourism: Towards a conceptual framework. *Procedia: Social and Behavioral Sciences*, *144*, 290–295. doi:10.1016/j.sbspro.2014.07.298

Prasad, K. G. D., Subbaiah, K. V., & Rao, K. N. (2013). Supply chain design through QFD based optimization. *Journal of Manufacturing Technology Management*, *25*(5), 712–733. doi:10.1108/JMTM-03-2012-0030

Pratt, S., McCabe, S., Cortes-Jimenez, I., & Blake, A. (2010). Measuring the effective- ness of destination marketing campaigns: Comparative analysis of conversion studies. *Journal of Travel Research*, *49*(2), 179–190. doi:10.1177/0047287509336471

Pretty, J., Adams, B., & Berkes, F. et al.. (2009). The Intersections of Biological Diversity and Cultural Diversity: Towards Integration. *Conservation & Society*, *7*(2), 100–112. doi:10.4103/0972-4923.58642

Prideaux, B. (2000). The resort development spectrum – a new approach to modelling resort development. *Tourism Management*, *21*(3), 225–240. doi:10.1016/S0261-5177(99)00055-2

Priskin, J. (2003). Issues and opportunities in planning and managing nature-based tourism in the Central Coast Region of Western Australia. *Australian Geographical Studies*, *41*(3), 270–286. doi:10.1046/j.1467-8470.2003.00234.x

Pritchard, A., & Morgan, N. J. (2001). Culture, identity and tourism representation: Marketing Cymru or Wales? *Tourism Management*, *22*(2), 167–179. doi:10.1016/S0261-5177(00)00047-9

Prosser, G. (1986). The limits of acceptable change. *Australian Parks and Recreation*, *22*, 5–10.

Prosser, G. (1995). *Tourism destination life cycles; progress, problems and prospects*. Paper to*National Tourism Research Conference*, Melbourne, Australia.

Pulido-Fernández, J. I., Andrades-Caldito, L., & Sánchez-Rivero, M. (2015). Is sustainable tourism an obstacle to the economic performance of the tourism industry? Evidence from an international empirical study. *Journal of Sustainable Tourism*, *23*(1), 47–64. doi:10.1080/09669582.2014.909447

Puri, S., & Nair, P. K. R. (2004). Agroforestry research for development in India: 25 years of experiences of a national program. *Agroforestry Systems*, *61*(1-3), 437–452. doi:10.1023/B:AGFO.0000029014.66729.e0

Putra, N. D., & Hitchcock, M. (2006). The Bali bombs and the tourism development cycle. *Progress in Development*, *6*(2), 157–166. doi:10.1191/1464993406ps134oa

Qdais & Alshraideh. (2016). Selection of management option for solid waste from olive oil industry using the analytical hierarchy process. *Journal of Material Cycles and Waste Management*, *18*(1), 177–185.

Raghavan, V. P. (2005). Economy of Eco-Tourism in Kerala. Kerala Calling, 15(2), 40-41.

Raharjo, H., Chai, K. H., Xie, M., & Bramoacher, A. C. (2010). Dynamic benchmarking methodology for quality function deployment. *Benchmarking*, *17*(1), 27–43. doi:10.1108/14635771011022307

Rahman, M. M. (2014). Trade Potential and Economic Cooperation between Bangladesh and North East India. In Developing Economic Corridors in South Asia. ADB.

Rajaratnam, S. D., Munikrishnan, U. T., Sharif, S. P., & Nair, V. (2014). Service quality and previous experience as a moderator in determining tourists' satisfaction with rural tourism destinations in Malaysia: A partial least squares approach. *Procedia: Social and Behavioral Sciences*, *144*, 203–211. doi:10.1016/j.sbspro.2014.07.288

Ramlan, M. A. B., Radam, A., Yacob, M. R., & Yahya, N. A. (2011). Willingness to pay towards the sustainability of Forest Research Institute Malaysia's (FRIM's) canopy walkway. *International Journal of Business, Management and Social. The Sciences*, *2*(3), 85–92.

Randelli, F., Romei, P., & Tortora, M. (2014). An evolutionary approach to the study of rural tourism: The case of Tuscany. *Land Use Policy*, *38*, 276–281. doi:10.1016/j.landusepol.2013.11.009

Rasul, G., & Manandhar, P. (2009). Tourism Potentials in Poverty Reduction in South Asia. *South Asia Economic Journal*, *10*(1), 187–207. doi:10.1177/139156140901000108

Ravenscroft, N., & Hadjihambi, I. (2006). The implications of Lamarckian theory for the TALC model. In R. W. Butler (Ed.), *Tourism Area Life Cycle: Conceptual and Theoretical Issues* (pp. 150–163). Cleveland, OH: Channelview Publications.

Reddy, M. V. (2008). Sustainable tourism rapid indicators for less-developed islands: An economic perspective. *International Journal of Tourism Research*, *10*(6), 557–576. doi:10.1002/jtr.700

Reduan, H. (2016). *Three environmental NGOs get go-ahead to challenge Taman Rimba Ampang closure.* Retrieved from http://www.nst.com.my/news/2016/05/147533/three-environmental-ngos-get-go-ahead-challenge-taman-rimba-ampang-closure

Reichel, A., Lowengart, O., & Milman, A. (2000). Rural tourism in Israel: Service quality and orientation. *Tourism Management*, *21*(5), 451–459. doi:10.1016/S0261-5177(99)00099-0

Reopanichkul, P., Schlacher, T. A., Carter, R. W., & Worachananant, S. (2009). Sewage impacts coral reefs at multiple levels of ecological organization. *Marine Pollution Bulletin*, *58*(9), 1356–1362. doi:10.1016/j.marpolbul.2009.04.024 PMID:19515390

Rio, D., & Nunes, L. M. (2012). Monitoring and evaluation tool for tourism destinations. *Tourism Management Perspectives*, *4*, 64–66. doi:10.1016/j.tmp.2012.04.002

Ritchie, B. W. (2003). *Managing educational tourism* (Vol. 10). Channel View Publications.

Ritchie, B., Mules, T., & Uzabeaga, S. (2008). *Visitor attraction satisfaction benchmarking project.* Sustainable Tourism CRC.

Ritchie, J. R. B., & Crouch, G. I. (2000). The competitive destination: A sustainability perspective. *Tourism Management, 21*(1), 1–7.

Ritchie, J. R. B. (1988). Consensus policy formulation in tourism. Measuring resident views via survey research. *Tourism Management, 9*(3), 199–212. doi:10.1016/0261-5177(88)90037-4

Ritchie, J. R. B., & Crouch, G. I. (2003). The Competitive Destination: A Sustainable Tourism Perspective. CABI.

Rittel, H., & Weber, M. (1973). Dilemmas in a general theory of planning. *Policy Sciences, 4*(2), 155–169. doi:10.1007/BF01405730

Roberts, L., & Hall, D. (2001). *Rural tourism and recreation: Principles to practice*. Wallingford, UK: CABI Publishing. doi:10.1079/9780851995403.0000

Robertson, C. M. (2004). Regional Tourism in South Africa: A Case of Mass Tourism in the South. *GeoJournal, 60*(3), 229–237. doi:10.1023/B:GEJO.0000034730.05992.18

Robinson, G. (1993). Tourism and tourism policy in the European community: An overview. *International Journal of Hospitality Management, 12*(1), 7–20. doi:10.1016/0278-4319(93)90038-B

Robinson, J., & OConnor, N. (2013). Ballyhoura - A Case Study of Cohesive Rural Tourism Planning in Ireland. *Tourism Planning & Development, 10*(3), 307–318. doi:10.1080/21568316.2012.747988

Rodríguez, X. A., Martínez-Roget, F., & Pawlowska, E. (2012). Academic tourism demand in Galicia, Spain. *Tourism Management, 33*(6), 1583–1590. doi:10.1016/j.tourman.2012.01.010

Rogerson, C. M. (2015). Tourism and Regional Development: The case of South Africa depressed areas. *Development Southern Africa, 3*(3), 277–291. doi:10.1080/0376835X.2015.1010713

Rowe and Wright. (1999, October). The Delphi technique as a forecasting tool: Issues and analysis. *International Journal of Forecasting, 15*(4).

Rozman, C., Potocnik, M., Pazek, K., Borec, A., Majkovic, D., & Bohanec, M. (2009). A multi-criteria assessment of tourist farm service quality. *Tourism Management, 30*(5), 629–637. doi:10.1016/j.tourman.2008.11.008

Ruhanen, L. (2013). Local government: Facilitator or inhibitor of sustainable tourism development? *Journal of Sustainable Tourism, 21*(1), 80–98. doi:10.1080/09669582.2012.680463

Ruitenbeek, J., Hewawasan, I., & Ngoile, M. (2005). *Blueprint 2050: Sustaining the marine environment in Mainland Tanzania and Zanzibar*. Washington, DC: The World Bank. doi:10.1596/0-8213-6123-6

Ruiz-Ballestros, E. (2011). Social-ecological resilience and community-based tourism; an approach from Agua Blanca, Ecuador. *Tourism Management, 32*(3), 655–666. doi:10.1016/j.tourman.2010.05.021

Russell, R., & Faulkner, B. (2004). Entrepreneurship, chaos and the tourism area lifecycle. *Annals of Tourism Research, 31*(3), 556–579. doi:10.1016/j.annals.2004.01.008

Ryan, C., Gu, H., & Zhang, W. (2009). The context of Chinese tourism: An overview and implications for research. In C. Ryan & H. Gu (Eds.), *Tourism in China: Destination, cultures and communities* (pp. 327–336). New York, NY: Routledge.

Ryan, C., Hughes, K., & Chirgwin, S. (2000). The gaze, spectacle and ecotourism. *Annals of Tourism Research, 27*(1), 148–163. doi:10.1016/S0160-7383(99)00061-4

Ryangnga, P.K. (2008). Ecotourism Prioritization: A GIS approach. *South Asian Journal of Tourism and Heritage, 1*(1).

Ryngnga, P. K. (2011). Tourism: A Trade link between India's North East and South East Asia. *South Asian Journal of Tourism and Heritage*, *4*(1), 84–89.

Saarinen, J. (2014). Critical Sustainability: Setting the Limits to Growth and Responsibility in Tourism. *Sustainability*, *6*(1), 1–17. doi:10.3390/su6010001

Sackman, H. (1974). *Delphi Assessment: Expert Opinion*. Forecasting and Group Process. R-1283-PR.

Sainaghi, R., Phillips, P., & Zavarrone, E. (2016). Performance measurement in tourism firms: A content analytical meta-approach. *Tourism Management*, *59*, 36–56. doi:10.1016/j.tourman.2016.07.002

Salifou, C. K., & Haq, I. (2016). Tourism, globalization and economic growth: A panel cointegration analysis for selected West African States. *Current Issues in Tourism*, 1–4. doi:10.1080/13683500.2016.1175421

Salleh, N. H. M., Othman, R., Hasim, M. S., & Jaafar, A. H. (2012). The pattern and the impact of Middle Eastern tourist spending on Malaysia's economy. *Jurnal Ekonomi Malaysia*, *46*(1), 53–63.

Salo, A. A., & Hamalainen, R. P. (1995). Preference programming through approximate ratio comparisons. *European Journal of Operational Research*, *82*(3), 458–475. doi:10.1016/0377-2217(93)E0224-L

Saltiel, L. (2014). Cultural governance and development in Vietnam. *University of Pennsylvania Journal of International Law*, *35*(3), 893–915.

Samad, N. (2012). *We can't help but ask the pertinent questions*. Retrieved December 26, 2013, from http://www.nst.com.my/mobile/opinion/columnist/we-can-thelp-but-ask-the-pertinent-questions-1.65614

Samsudin, P. Y., & Maliki, N. Z. (2015). Preserving cultural landscape in homestay programme towards sustainable tourism: Brief critical review concept. *Procedia: Social and Behavioral Sciences*, *170*, 433–441. doi:10.1016/j.sbspro.2015.01.004

Sattar, S. (2011). *Tourism and Development in Sikkim, Tourism and Development in Sikkim*. IIPS Mumbai.

Schendel, D., & Hitt, M. A. (2007). Introduction to volume 1. *Strategic Entrepreneurship Journal*, *1*(1/2), 1–6. doi:10.1002/sej.16

Scheyvens, R. (2011). The challenge of sustainable tourism development in the Maldives: Understanding the social and political dimensions of sustainability. *Asia Pacific Viewpoint*, *52*(2), 148–164. doi:10.1111/j.1467-8373.2011.01447.x

Schianetz, K., Kavanah, L., & Lockington, D. (2007). Concepts and tools for comprehensive sustainability assessments for tourism destinations: A comparative review. *Journal of Sustainable Tourism*, *15*(4), 369–389. doi:10.2167/jost659.0

Scott, D., Gössling, S., & Hall, C. M. (2012). International tourism and climate change. *Wiley Interdisciplinary Reviews: Climate Change*, *3*(3), 213–232. doi:10.1002/wcc.165

Sdrali, D., Goussia-Rizou, M., & Kiourtidou, P. (2015). Residents' perception of tourism development as a vital step for participatory tourism plan: A research in a Greek protected area. *Environment, Development and Sustainability*, *17*(4), 923–939. doi:10.1007/s10668-014-9573-2

Sealey, K. S., & Smith, J. (2014). Recycling for small island tourism developments: Food waste composting at Sandals Emerald Bay, Exuma, Bahamas. *Resources, Conservation and Recycling*, *92*, 25–37. doi:10.1016/j.resconrec.2014.08.008

Seema, P., Jojo, T. D., Freeda, M. S., Santosh, B., Sheetal, P., Gladwin, J., . . . Sidharth, K. (2006). *White Paper on Eco-Tourism Policy*. Center for Conservation Governance and Policy, Ashoka Trust for Research in Ecology and the Environment (ATREE).

Sequeira, T. N., & Compos, C. (2005). *International tourism and economic growth: A panel data approach*. FEEM Working Paper 141.05. Fondazione Eni Enrico Mattei.

Sezgin & Gumus. (2016). The Evaluation of Beysehir Lake National Park (Konya-Turkey) in the Framework Ecotourism. *Journal of Advanced Management Science, 4*(4).

Shah, A. (2016). *Where to go in 2016: Top 16 up-and-coming destinations*. Retrieved from http://edition.cnn.com/2015/12/22/travel/emerging-destinations-2016/

Shakya, M. (2011). Local perceptions of risk and tourism: A case study from rural Nepal. *Recreation and Society in Africa, Asia and Latin America, 1*(2), 31–64.

Shankaran. (2007). Rural tourism and Handicrafts. *Yojana, 51*(20), 29-31.

Sharma, A., & Rathore, C. K. (2015). *BIMSTEC and BCIM Initiatives and their importance for India*. Discussion Paper. Cuts International.

Sharma, P. (2015). *New Tourism Policy to Make India Incredible*. Available at: http://www.newindianexpress.com/thesundaystandard/New-Tourism-Policy-to-Make-India-Incredible/2015/05/03/article2794202.ece

Sharpley, R., & Roberts, L. (2004). Rural tourism 10 years on. *International Journal of Tourism Research, 6*(3), 119–124. doi:10.1002/jtr.478

Sharpley, R., & Sharpley, J. (1997). *Rural tourism: An introduction*. London, UK: International Thomson Business Press.

Sharpley, R. (2000). Tourism and sustainable development: Exploring the theoretical divide. *Journal of Sustainable Tourism, 8*(1), 1–19. doi:10.1080/09669580008667346

Sharpley. (2009). *Tourism development and the environment: beyond sustainability?* London: Earthscan.

Shenga, S. S. N., Mishra, S. N., Sharma, N., & Jha, A. (2015). Economic Benefits of Eco-tourism in Sikkim. *Southern Economist, 54*(6).

Shenga, S., & Jha, A. (2014). The Sikkim Ecotourism Policy - A Review. *Research Link - 121, 13*(2), 33-36.

Sheykhi, M. (2009). Domestic tourism in Iran. *Tourismos: An International Multidisciplinary Journal of Tourism, 4*(1), 109–123.

Shields, P. O. (2006). State-funded tourism marketing: The effectiveness of state travel guides for the college market. *Journal of Travel & Tourism Marketing, 20*(2), 31–49. doi:10.1300/J073v20n02_03

Sidang Dewang Negara. (2014). *Parlimen Ketiga Belas Penggal Kedua Mesyuarat Kedua*. Retrieved from https://www.cljlaw.com/files/hansard/DR/pdf/DR-09062014.pdf

Sigala, M., & Marindis, D. (2010). DMOs, e-Democracy and collaborative destination management: an implementation framework. In U. Gretzel, R. Law, & M. Fuchs (Eds.), *Information and Communication Technologies in Tourism 2010* (pp. 235–246). New York: Springer Wien. doi:10.1007/978-3-211-99407-8_20

Silva, L., & Leal, J. (2015). Rural tourism and national identity building in contemporary Europe: Evidence from Portugal. *Journal of Rural Studies, 38*, 109–119. doi:10.1016/j.jrurstud.2015.02.005

Silva, L. (2015). How ecotourism works at the community-level: The case of whale-watching in the Azores. *Current Issues in Tourism, 18*(3), 196–211. doi:10.1080/13683500.2013.786027

Simão, J. N., & Partidário, M. D. R. (2012). How does tourism planning contribute to sustainable development? *Sustainable Development, 20*(6), 372–385. doi:10.1002/sd.495

Sims, R. (2009). Food, place and authenticity: Local food and the sustainable tourism experience. *Journal of Sustainable Tourism, 17*(3), 321–336. doi:10.1080/09669580802359293

Sinclair, M. T., & Bote Gomez, V. (1996). Tourism, the Spanish economy and the balance of payments. In M. Barke et al. (Eds.), *Tourism in Spain: Critical perspectives*. Wallingford: C.A.B. International.

Singh, M. (2004). *Management of State Tourism Development Corporations*. Deep and Deep Publications Private Ltd.

Singh, R. B., & Mishra, D. K. (2004). Green tourism in mountain regions-reducing vulnerability and promoting people and place centric development in the Himalayas. *Journal of Mountain Science, 1*(1), 57–64. doi:10.1007/BF02919360

Singh, R. P., & Nachtnebel, H. P. (2016). Analytical hierarchy process (AHP) application for reinforcement of hydropower strategy in Nepal. *Renewable & Sustainable Energy Reviews, 55*(March), 43–58. doi:10.1016/j.rser.2015.10.138

Singh, S. (2001). Indian Tourism: Policy, Performance and Pitfalls. In D. Harrison (Ed.), *Tourism and the Less Developed World, Issues and Case Studies*. Oxon, UK: Cabi.

Singh, S. (2008). Destination Development Dilemma - case of Manali in Himachal Himalaya. *Tourism Management, 29*(6), 1152–1156. doi:10.1016/j.tourman.2008.02.018

Singh, S. (2011). The tourism area life cycle: A clarification. *Annals of Tourism Research, 38*(3), 1178–1187. doi:10.1016/j.annals.2011.03.005

Singh, Valene, Fish, & Ricter. (1995). *Tourism Environment- Nature, Culture and Economy.* Inter-India Publications.

Skuras, D., Petrou, A., & Clark, G. (2006). Demand for rural tourism: The effects of quality and information. *Agricultural Economics, 35*(2), 183–192. doi:10.1111/j.1574-0862.2006.00151.x

Smeral, E. (1998). The impact of globalization on small and medium enterprises: New challenges for tourism policies in European countries. *Tourism Management, 19*(4), 371–380. doi:10.1016/S0261-5177(98)00036-3

Smith, K. (2016). *Kuala Lumpur's ambitious urban rail plan starts to deliver results.* Retrieved from http://www.railjournal.com/index.php/asia/ambitious-expansion-plan-starting-to-deliver-results.html

Snieška, V., Barkauskiene, K., & Barkauskas, V. (2014). The impact of economic factors on the development of rural tourism: Lithuanian case. *Procedia: Social and Behavioral Sciences, 156*, 280–285. doi:10.1016/j.sbspro.2014.11.189

Soemarwoto, O., & Conway, G. R. (1991). The Javanese homegarden. *Journal of Farming Systems Research Extension, 2*, 95–118.

Sokhalingam, C. P., & Baporikar, N. (2011). Tourism Entrepreneurship in Tamil Nadu – A Case of Inclusive Approach, *Matrix. Business Review (Federal Reserve Bank of Philadelphia), 1*(2), 16–26.

Song, H., van der Veen, R., Li, G., & Chen, J. L. (2012). The Hong Kong tourist satisfaction index. *Annals of Tourism Research, 39*(1), 459–479. doi:10.1016/j.annals.2011.06.001

Sreekumar, T. T., & Parayil, G. (2010). Contentions and contradictions of tourism as development option: The case of Kerala, India. *Third World Quarterly, 23*(3), 529–548. doi:10.1080/01436590220138411

Stake, R. E. (1995). *The art of case study research.* Thousand Oaks, CA: Sage Publications.

Stark, J. (2015). Product lifecycle management. In *Product Lifecycle Management* (pp. 1–29). Springer International Publishing. doi:10.1007/978-3-319-17440-2_1

Steele, P. (1993). The economics of ecotourism. *Focus (San Francisco, Calif.), 9*, 4–6.

Stevenson, N., Airey, D., & Miller, G. (2008). Tourism Policy Making: The Policymakers Perspectives. *Annals of Tourism Research, 35*(3), 732–750. doi:10.1016/j.annals.2008.05.002

Su, B. (2011). Rural tourism in China. *Tourism Management, 32*(6), 1438–1441. doi:10.1016/j.tourman.2010.12.005

Su, C. S., & Sun, L. H. (2007). Taiwans Hotel Rating System A Service Quality Perspective. *The Cornell Hotel and Restaurant Administration Quarterly, 48*(4), 392–401. doi:10.1177/0010880407305836

Sugiyarto, G., Blake, A., & Sinclair, M. T. (2003). Tourism and globalization: Economic Impact in Indonesia. *Annals of Tourism Research, 30*(3), 683–701. doi:10.1016/S0160-7383(03)00048-3

Suntikul, W., & Dorji, U. (2016). Local Perspectives on the Impact of Tourism on Religious Festivals in Bhutan. *Asia Pacific Journal of Tourism Research, 21*(7), 741–762. doi:10.1080/10941665.2015.1069365

Swain, M., Brent, M., & Long, V. (1999). Annals and Tourism Evolving: Indexing 25 years of publication. *Annals of Tourism Research, 25*, 991–1014.

Swarup & Gopal. (2015). Present Pattern of Tourism – A Case Study Of Sikkim. *International Journal of Informative & Futuristic Research, 2*(11), 4128-4137.

Taghipour, H., Mohammadyarei, T., Asghari Jafarabadi, M., & Asl, H. A. (2014). *On-site or off-site treatment of medical waste: a challenge.* J Environ Health Sci Eng.

Taiwan Review. (2009, August 1). Welcoming the World. *Taiwan Review.*

Taiwan Tourism Bureau. (2011). *Regulations for the Management of Home Stay Facilities.* Taiwan Tourism Bureau.

Taiwan Tourism Bureau. (2010a). Taiwan Tourism Bureau, R.O.C. *2010 Annual Survey Report on Visitors Expenditure and Trends in Taiwan.* Retrieved January 1, 2013, from http://admin.taiwan.net.tw

Taiwan Tourism Bureau. (2010b). *Taiwan Tourism Bureau, R.O.C.* Retrieved September 12, 2013, from http://www.tbroc.gov.tw

Taiwan Tourism Bureau. (2012). *2011 Survey of Travel by R.O.C Citizens.* Retrieved January 21, 2014, from http://admin.taiwan.net.tw

Taiwan Tourism Bureau. (2013a). *Taiwan Tourism Bureau, R.O.C.* Retrieved May 20, 2013, from http://www.taiwan.net.tw

Taiwan Tourism Bureau. (2013b). *Taiwan Tourism Bureau, R.O.C.* Retrieved May 18, 2013, from http://admin.taiwan.net.tw/statistics

Tamura, K., Asano, M., & Jamsran, U. (2012). Soil diversity in Mongolia. In N. F. Norio Yamamura (Ed.), The Mongolian Ecosystem Network: Environmental Issues Under Climate and Social Changes (pp. 99-103). Springer Japan.

Tang, C. F., & Abosedra, S. (2014). Small sample evidence on the tourism-led growth hypothesis in Lebanon. *Current Issues in Tourism, 17*(3), 234–246. doi:10.1080/13683500.2012.732044

Tang, C. F., & Abosedra, S. (2016). Tourism and growth in Lebanon: New evidence from bootstrap simulation and rolling causality approaches. *Empirical Economics, 50*(2), 679–696. doi:10.1007/s00181-015-0944-9

Tang, C. F., & Abosedra, S. (2016a). Does tourism expansion effectively spur economic growth in Morocco and Tunisia? Evidence from time series and panel data. *Journal of Policy Research in Tourism. Leisure and Events, 8*(2), 127–145. doi:10.1080/19407963.2015.1113980

Tang, C. F., Cheam, C. L., & Ong, S. C. (2015). Comparing the contributions of tourism and non-tourism exports to economic growth in Malaysia. *Current Issues in Tourism*, 1–14. doi:10.1080/13683500.2015.1057108

Tang, C. F., & Chua, S. Y. (2012). The savings-growth nexus for the Malaysian economy: A view through rolling sub-samples. *Applied Economics*, *44*(32), 4173–4185. doi:10.1080/00036846.2011.587784

Tang, C. F., & Tan, E. C. (2013). How stable is the tourism-led growth hypothesis in Malaysia? Evidence from disaggregated tourism markets. *Tourism Management*, *37*, 52–57. doi:10.1016/j.tourman.2012.12.014

Tang, C. F., & Tan, E. C. (2015a). Tourism-led growth hypothesis in Malaysia: Evidence based upon regime shift cointegration and time-varying Granger causality techniques. *Asia Pacific Journal of Tourism Research*, *20*(S1), 1430–1450. doi:10.1080/10941665.2014.998247

Tang, C. F., & Tan, E. C. (2015b). Does tourism effectively stimulate Malaysias economic growth? *Tourism Management*, *46*, 158–163. doi:10.1016/j.tourman.2014.06.020

Tang, C. F., Tiwari, A. K., & Shahbaz, M. (2016). Dynamic inter-relationships among tourism, economic growth and energy consumption in India. *Geosystem Engineering*, *19*(4), 158–169. doi:10.1080/12269328.2016.1162113

Tang, C. F. (2011). Is the tourism-led growth hypothesis valid for Malaysia? A view from disaggregated tourism markets. *International Journal of Tourism Research*, *13*(1), 97–101. doi:10.1002/jtr.807

Tang, C. F. (2013a). Temporal Granger causality and the dynamic relationship between real tourism receipts, real income and real exchange rates in Malaysia. *International Journal of Tourism Research*, *15*(3), 272–284. doi:10.1002/jtr.1869

Tang, C. F. (2013b). A revisitation of the export-led growth hypothesis in Malaysia using leveraged bootstrap simulation and rolling causality techniques. *Journal of Applied Statistics*, *40*(11), 2332–2340. doi:10.1080/02664763.2013.810195

Tao, C. H., Eagles, E. F. J., & Smith, S. L. J. (2004). Profiling Taiwanese ecotourists using a self-definition approach. *Journal of Sustainable Tourism*, *12*(2), 149–168. doi:10.1080/09669580408667230

Tekken, V., & Kropp, J. P. (2015). Sustainable water management: Perspectives for tourism development in north-eastern Morocco. *Tourism Management Perspectives*, *16*, 325–334. doi:10.1016/j.tmp.2015.09.001

Teo, P., & Yeoh, B. (1997). Remaking Local Heritage for Tourism. *Annals of Tourism Research*, *24*(1), 192–213. doi:10.1016/S0160-7383(96)00054-0

Tham, S. Y., Mahmod, N. K., & Alavi, R. (2013). Assessing policies for attracting international students: Case of Malaysia. *Asia Pacific Journal of Education*, *33*(1), 112–126. doi:10.1080/02188791.2012.759536

The United Nations Database. (2013). Available online May 13, 2013, http://unctadstat.unctad.org

The World Travel & Tourism Council. (2011). *Travel & Tourism Economic Impact 2011*. Author.

Thieke, D. (2007). *Talk to me: Making public relations meaningful to business executives, Public Relations Strategist, Spring 2007*. Available online on June 15 at https://www.prsa.org/Intelligence/BusinessCase/MeasurementResources/MeasuringValueofPublicRelations/#.V2XWMpCg9aU

Thoma, M. A. (1994). Subsample instability and asymmetries in money-income causality. *Journal of Econometrics*, *64*(1-2), 279–306. doi:10.1016/0304-4076(94)90066-3

Thomas, H., & Thomas, R. (1998). The implications for tourism of shifts in British local governance. *Progress in Tourism and Hospitality Research*, *4*(4), 295–306. doi:10.1002/(SICI)1099-1603(199812)4:4<295::AID-PTH115>3.0.CO;2-0

Thomas, R., Shaw, G., & Page, S. J. (2011). Understanding small firms in tourism: A perspective on research trends and challenges. *Tourism Management*, *32*(5), 963–976. doi:10.1016/j.tourman.2011.02.003

Thomas, R. (1998). *Management of small tourism and hospitality firms*. Cassell plc.

Thompson, C. S. (2004). Host produced rural tourism: Towas Tokyo antenna shop. *Annals of Tourism Research*, *31*(3), 580–600. doi:10.1016/j.annals.2003.11.004

Tidball, K. (1988). Creating a Culture Adds to Your Bottom Line. *The Cornell Hotel and Restaurant Administration Quarterly*, *29*(1), 1–96. doi:10.1177/001088048802900118

Tien Phong. (2009). *Mat do dan so tai Hoi An cao nhat the gioi?* Retrieved from http://www.tienphong.vn/xa-hoi/mat-do-dan-so-tai-hoi-an-cao-nhat-the-gioi-171691.tpo

TIES. (2015). *The International Eco Tourism Society*. Retrieved from TIES: http://www.ecotourism.org/what-is-ecotourism

Timmermann, A. (2008). Elusive return predictability. *International Journal of Forecasting*, *24*(1), 1–18. doi:10.1016/j.ijforecast.2007.07.008

Timothy, D. J. (2003). Supranationalist Alliances and Tourism: Insights from ASEAN and SAARC. *Current Issues in Tourism*, *6*(3), 250–266. doi:10.1080/13683500308667956

Tisdell, C. (1995). Investment in ecotourism: Assessing its economics. *Tourism Economics*, *1*, 375–387.

Tomljenović, R., & Getz, D. (2009). Life cycle stages in wine tourism: A comparison of wine regions in Croatia. *Tourism Review International*, *13*(1), 31–49. doi:10.3727/154427209789130666

Tosun, C. (2001). Challenges of sustainable tourism development in the developing world: The case of Turkey. *Tourism Management*, *22*(3), 289–303. doi:10.1016/S0261-5177(00)00060-1

Tourism Bureau. (2003). *The 2002 annual report on tourism*. R.O.C.

Tourism Bureau. (2008). Welcome to Taiwan: Experience the true heart of Taiwan. *Travel in Taiwan, 28*.

Tribillion, J. (2016). *How nature turned a failed communist plan into Bucharest's unique urban park*. Retrieved from https://www.theguardian.com/cities/2016/jun/14/nature-europe-urban-protected-area-vacaresti-nature-park-romania?CMP=fb_gu

Trigau, R. (2016). *In Game of Theme Parks, Orlando rules but Asia eyes the throne*. Retrieved on 15th August, 2015 from http://www.tampabay.com/news/business/corporate/in-game-of-theme-parks-orlando-rules-but-asia-eyes-the-throne/2279234

Tripadvisor. (2016). *Hoi An Ancient Town*. Retrieved from https://www.tripadvisor.com.au/Attraction_Review-g298082-d4507121-Reviews-Hoi_An_Ancient_Town-Hoi_An_Quang_Nam_ Province.html#REVIEWS

Tsai, H. C. (2007). Agricultural Globalization and Rural Tourism Development in Taiwan. *Asia Journal of Management and Humanity Sciences*, *2*(1-4), 1–13.

Tsipidis, V. (2004). *Assessing the urban ecotourism potential of a local nature reserve: The case of Corstorphine Hill, Edinburgh, Scotland*. Ecoclub.com E-paper series, Nr.10.

Tugjamba, N., & Sereeter, E. (2013). A Research Study on the Development of the Indicators to Assess the Tourism Impacts on Protected Areas of Mongolia. *Tourism Research & Hospitality*, *2*, 3. doi:10.4172/2324-8807.1000124

Tyrrell, T., & Johnston, R. (2003). Assessing expenditure changes related to welcome center visits. *Journal of Travel Research*, *42*(1), 100–106. doi:10.1177/0047287503253907

UN Habitat, . (2014). *Hoi An – Vietnam: Climate change vulnerability assessment*. Nairobi: United Nations Human Settlements Programme.

UN. (1996). *Sustainable tourism development in small island developing states*. Report of the Secretary-General (document E/CN.17/1996/20/Add.3). New York: UN.

UN. (1999). *Tourism and sustainable development*. Report of the Secretary-General (Document No. E/CN.17/1999/5). New York: UN.

UNESCO. (2004). *World Heritage list*. Retrieved from Orkhon Valley Cultural Landscape: http://whc.unesco.org/en/list/1081

UNESCO. (2007). *Climate change and World Heritage*. Paris: United Nations Educational, Scientific and Cultural Organization. Available at: http://whc.unesco.org/en/activities/474

UNIDO. (2012). *Towards green growth through green industry development in Vietnam*. Vienna: United Nations Industrial Development Organisation.

United Nation World Tourism Organization (UNWTO). (2008). *Statistics and Tourism Satellite Account*. Available: http://statistics.unwto.org/content/tsarmf-2008

United Nations Commission for Trade and Development (UNCTAD). (2007). *FDI in Tourism: The Development Dimension*. Available: http://unctad.org/en/Docs/iteiia20075_en.pdf

United Nations Commission for Trade and Development (UNCTAD). (2012). *World Investment Report*. Available: http://unctad.org/en/PublicationsLibrary/wir2011_en.pdf

United Nations Commission for Trade and Development (UNCTAD). (2014). *World Investment Report*. Available: http://unctad.org/en/PublicationsLibrary/wir2014_en.pdf

United Nations Educational, Scientific, and Cultural Organization. (2013). Retrieved May 27, 2013, from http://www.unesco.org/new/en/unesco/about-us/who-we-are/history

United Nations Environment Programme (UNEP). (2002). *Biological Diversity and Tourism: Development of Guidelines for Sustainable Tourism in Vulnerable Ecosystems, Secretariat of the Convention on Biological Diversity*. Montreal: UNEP/CBD.

United Nations International Trade Statistics. (2008). *Trade Statistics Knowledgebase*. Available: http://unstats.un.org/unsd/tradekb/Knowledgebase/TSA-RMF-2008

United Nations. (2013). Retrieved May 27, 2013, from http://www.un.org/en/aboutun/history/index.shtml

UNWTO. (2013). *Annual reports, progress and priorities*. The World Travel and Tourism Council.

UNWTO. (2014). *Tourism highlights 2014 edition*. Madrid, Spain: United Nations World Tourism Organization.

Urry, J. (2000). Mobile sociology. *The British Journal of Sociology*, *51*(1), 185–203. doi:10.1080/000713100358499 PMID:20092503

Urry, J. (2002). *The Tourist Gaze* (2nd ed.). London: Sage.

Usha Bande. (2002). Eco-Tourism and Mountains. Yojana, 24(15), 20-24.

USTA. (2011). *The power of travel promotion*. Washington, DC: U. S. Travel Association.

van der Borg, J., Costa, P., & Gotti, G. (1996). Tourism in European Heritage Cities. *Annals of Tourism Research*, *23*(2), 306–321. doi:10.1016/0160-7383(95)00065-8

Van Doorn, J. W. M. (1982). Can Futures Research Contribute to Tourism Policy. *Tourism Management*, *3*(3), 149–166. doi:10.1016/0261-5177(82)90064-4

View Mongolia. (2016). Retrieved from http://www.viewmongolia.com/when_travel.html

Vinayak, K., & Kodali, R. (2013). Benchmarking the quality function deployment models. *Benchmarking*, *20*(6), 825–854. doi:10.1108/BIJ-07-2011-0052

Volo, S. (2010). Bloggers reported tourist experiences: Their utility as a tourism data source and their effect on prospective tourists. *Journal of Vacation Marketing*, *16*(4), 297–311. doi:10.1177/1356766710380884

Wagner, G. (2011). Going green but getting nowhere. *New York Times*, p. A29.

Waligo, V. M., Clarke, J., & Hawkins, R. (2015). Embedding stakeholders in sustainable tourism strategies. *Annals of Tourism Research*, *55*, 90–93. doi:10.1016/j.annals.2015.09.002

Wall, G. (1993). International collaboration in the search for sustainable tourism in Bali, Indonesia. *Journal of Sustainable Tourism*, *1*(1), 38–47. doi:10.1080/09669589309450699

Walmsley, D. (2003). Rural tourism: A case of lifestyle-led opportunities. *The Australian Geographer*, *34*(1), 61–72. doi:10.1080/0004918032000066155

Wang, J. C. (2009). An analysis on the development strategy of Taiwan's six new emerging industries. *Economic Outlook*, *127*, 35–38.

Wang, J. C. (2010). The strategies adopted by Taiwan in response to the global financial crisis, and Taiwans role in Asia-Pacific economic integration. *Japan and the World Economy*, *22*(4), 254–263. doi:10.1016/j.japwor.2010.06.006

Wang, L. E., Cheng, S. K., Zhong, L. S., Mu, S. L., Dhruba, B. G., & Ren, G. Z. (2013). Rural tourism development in China: Principles, models and the future. *Journal of Mountain Science*, *10*(1), 116–129. doi:10.1007/s11629-013-2501-3

Wang, P. (2003). *Financial Econometrics*. London: Routledge.

Wang, Y., & Fesenmaier, D. R. (2007). Collaborative destination marketing: A case study of Elkhart county, Indiana. *Tourism Management*, *28*(3), 863–875. doi:10.1016/j.tourman.2006.02.007

Wanhill, S. R. C. (1987). UK: Politics and tourism. *Tourism Management*, *8*(1), 54–58. doi:10.1016/0261-5177(87)90040-9

Warwick, K. (2013). *Beyond Industrial Policy: Emerging issues and new trends. OECD Science, Technology and Industry Policy Papers, No. 2*. OECD Publishing. doi:10.1787/23074957

Watson, A., & Herath, G. (1999). Research implications of the theme issues "recreation fees and pricing issues" in the public sector and societal responses to recreation fees on public lands'. *Journal of Leisure Research*, *31*, 325–334.

Weaver, D. B., & Lawton, L. J. (2007). Twenty years on: The state of contemporary ecotourism research. *Tourism Management*, *28*(5), 1168–1179. doi:10.1016/j.tourman.2007.03.004

Weaver, D. B. (2002). Hard-core eco-tourists in Lamington National Park, Australia. *Journal of Ecotourism*, *1*(1), 19–35. doi:10.1080/14724040208668110

Weaver, D. B. (2012). Organic, incremental and induced paths to sustainable mass tourism convergence. *Tourism Management*, *33*(5), 1030–1037. doi:10.1016/j.tourman.2011.08.011

Weed, M. (2006). The Influence of Policy Makers Perceptions on Sport Tourism Policy Development. *Tourism Review International*, *10*(4), 227–240. doi:10.3727/154427206779367091

Weng, C. C., & Wang, K. L. (2004). Scale and scope economies of international tourist hotels in Taiwan. *Tourism Management, 25*(6), 761–769. doi:10.1016/j.tourman.2004.06.005

Whitfield, J. (2006). A temporal analysis of conference venue refurbishment within U.K. conference sector. *Journal of Convention & Event Tourism, 8*(3), 1–19. doi:10.1300/J452v08n03_01

Whitford, M. (2009). A framework for the development of event public policy: Facilitating regional development. *Tourism Management, 30*(5), 674–682. doi:10.1016/j.tourman.2008.10.018

Wight, P. A. (2001). Eco-tourists: not a homogeneous market segment. In K. F. Backman, E. Cater, P. F. J. Eagles, & B. McKercher (Eds.), *The Encyclopedia of Ecotourism* (pp. 565–579). CAB International.

Wight, P. (1993). Sustainable tourism: Balancing economic, environmental and social goals within an ethical framework. *Journal of Tourism Studies, 4*, 54–66.

Williams, A. M., & Shaw, G. (2009). Future Play: Tourism, recreation and land use. *Land Use Policy, 265*, 5326–5335.

Wilson, G. A. (2001). From productivism to postproductivism and back again? Exploring the (un) changed natural and mental landscapes of European agriculture. *Transactions of the Institute of British Geographers, 26*(1), 77–102. doi:10.1111/1475-5661.00007

Wilson, H., & Venes, J. (2001). Factors for Success in Rural Tourism Development. *Journal of Travel Research, 40*, 132-138.

Wober, K., & Fesenmaier, D. R. (2004). A multi-criteria approach to destination benchmarking: A case study of state tourism advertising programs in the United States. *Journal of Travel & Tourism Marketing, 16*(2/3), 1–18. doi:10.1300/J073v16n02_01

Woods, M. (2005). *Rural geography: Processes, responses and experiences in rural restructuring*. London, UK: Sage Publications.

Woodside, A. G., & Dubelaar, C. (2002). A general theory of tourism consumption systems: A conceptual framework and an empirical exploration. *Journal of Travel Research, 41*(2), 120–132. doi:10.1177/004728702237412

Woodside, A. G., & King, R. I. (2001). An updated model of travel and tourism purchase-consumption systems. *Journal of Travel & Tourism Marketing, 10*(1), 3–27. doi:10.1300/J073v10n01_02

Woodside, A., & Motes, W. (1980). Image versus direct-response advertising. *Journal of Advertising Research, 20*, 31–37.

Woodside, A., & Reid, D. (1974). Tourism profiles versus audience profiles: Are upscale magazines really upscale? *Journal of Travel Research, 12*(4), 17–23. doi:10.1177/004728757401200404

World Bank. (2011). *Mongolia - Tourism sector policy note: Strengthening management of natural and cultural heritage assets to scale up tourism and stimulate local economic opportunity*. Washington, DC: World Bank. Retrieved 01 07, 2016, from http://www-wds.worldbank.org/external/default/WDSContentServer/WDSP/IB/2012/05/21/000425970_20120521123542/Rendered/PDF/686400ESW0P122080201100ENG04297547.pdf

World Bank. (2015). *World Development Indicators*. Available: http://databank.worldbank.org/data/home.aspx

World Data Atlas. (2015). *Tourism*. Retrieved from https://knoema.com/atlas/topics//tourism-indicators/number-of-arrivals

World Economic Forum. (2015). *The ASEAN Travel & Tourism Competitiveness Report 2012: Fostering Prosperity and Regional Integration Through Travel and Tourism*. Available: http://www3.weforum.org/docs/WEF_TTCR_ASEAN_Report_2012.pdf

World Health Organization. (2013). *Summary of probable SARS cases with onset of illness from 1 November 2002 to 31 July 2003*. Retrieved May 20, 2013, from http://www.who.int/csr/sars/country/table2004_04_21/en/index.html

World Tourism Organization. (2010). *United Nations World Tourism Organization Tourism Highlights, 2010 Edition.* Retrieved January 14, 2016, from http://www.unwto.org/facts/eng/pdf/highlights/UNWTO_Highlights10_en_HR.pdf

World Tourism Organization. (2012). *United Nations World Tourism Organization Tourism Highlights, 2012 Edition.* Retrieved January 14, 2016, from http://www.unwto.org/facts/eng/pdf/highlights/UNWTO_Highlights10_en_HR.pdf

World Tourism Organization. (2012a). *Open Letter to Heads of Government*. Available: http://www2.unwto.org/sites/all/files/pdf/final_golden_book_open_letter_text_0/pdf

World Tourism Organization. (2012b). *Myanmar set to rejoin UNWTO*. Available: http://media.unwto.org/en/press-release/2012-05-11/myanmar-set-rejoin-unwto

World Tourism Organization. (2013). *United Nations World Tourism Organization Annual Report 2013*. Retrieved January 14, 2016, from http://www2.unwto.org/publication/unwto-annual-report-2013

World Travel and Tourism Council. (2012). Travel and Tourism Economic Impact 2012 Taiwan. London, UK: Author.

World Travel and Tourism Council. (2015). *WTTC Data Gateway*. Available: http://www.wttc.org/datagateway/

Wray, M. (2009). Policy communities, networks and issue cycles in tourism destination systems. *Journal of Sustainable Tourism*, *17*(6), 673–690. doi:10.1080/09669580903071979

Wright, W., & Middendorf, G. (Eds.). (2008). *The fight over food: Producers, consumers, and activists challenge the global food system*. Pennsylvania State University Press.

WTO. (2009). *Handbook on Tourism Destination Branding*. Madrid: Europe-World Tourism Organization.

WTO, (2001a). *Actions in assisting developing countries to implement Agenda 21 undertaken by the World Tourism Organization since 1992*. (Document No. DESA/DSD/PC2/BP3). New York: UN.

WTO. (2001b). *The concept of sustainable tourism*. Retrieved from http://www.worldtourism.org/sustainable/ concepts.htm

WTTC. (2013). Foreword. In *Travel and Tourism Economic Impact 2013* (p. i). WTTC.

Wu, W. C., & Yang, C. Y. (2010). An empirical study on the impact of differences in bed and breakfast service quality attributes on customers' revisiting desires. *The International Journal of Organizational Innovation*, *2*(2), 223–240.

Wu, Y. Y., Wang, H. L., & Ho, Y. F. (2010). Urban ecotourism: Defining and assessing dimensions using fuzzy number construction. *Tourism Management*, *31*(6), 739–743. doi:10.1016/j.tourman.2009.07.014

Xiang, Z., & Gretzel, U. (2010). Role of social media in online travel information search. *Tourism Management*, *31*(2), 179–188. doi:10.1016/j.tourman.2009.02.016

Xiao, H., & Smith, S. L. J. (2006). Case studies in tourism research: A state-of-the-art analysis. *Tourism Management*, *27*(5), 738–749. doi:10.1016/j.tourman.2005.11.002

Xie, P. F., & Lane, B. (2006). A life cycle model for aboriginal arts performance in tourism: Perspective on authenticity. *Journal of Sustainable Tourism*, *14*(6), 545–561. doi:10.2167/jost 601.0

Xu, X. & Gursoy, D. (2014). A Conceptual Framework of Sustainable Hospitality Supply Chain Management. *Journal of Hospitality Marketing & Management*. DOI: 10.1080/19368623.2014.909691

Yang, C. C., Jou, Y. T., & Cheng, L. Y. (2011). Using integrated quality assessment for hotel service quality. *Quality & Quantity*, *45*(2), 349–364. doi:10.1007/s11135-009-9301-4

Yang, C. H., Lin, H. L., & Han, C. C. (2010). Analysis of international tourist arrivals in China: The role of World Heritage Sites. *Tourism Management*, *31*(6), 827–837. doi:10.1016/j.tourman.2009.08.008

Yasarata, M., Altinay, L., Burns, P., & Okumus, F. (2010). Politics and sustainable tourism development – can they co-exist? voices from North Cyprus. *Tourism Management*, *31*(3), 345–356. doi:10.1016/j.tourman.2009.03.016

Yin, R. K. (2009). *Case study research: Design and methods*. Thousand Oaks, CA: Sage Publications.

Yuan Control. (2004). *The survey of issues related to Ocean and Taiwan*. Taipei: Author.

Zane, B. (1997). The B&B guest: A comprehensive view. *The Cornell Hotel and Restaurant Administration Quarterly*, *38*(4), 6–75. doi:10.1016/S0010-8804(97)84308-X

Zehrer, A., Crotts, J. C., & Magnini, V. P. (2011). The perceived usefulness of blog postings: An extension of the expectancy-disconfirmation paradigm. *Tourism Management*, *32*(1), 106–113. doi:10.1016/j.tourman.2010.06.013

Zhang, R. Y., Xi, J. C., Wang, S. K., Wang, X. G., & Ge, Q. S. (2015). Village network centrality in rural tourism destination: A case from Yesanpo tourism area, China. *Journal of Mountain Science*, *12*(3), 759–768. doi:10.1007/s11629-014-3129-7

Zhao, W., Ritchie, J. R., & Echtner, C. M. (2011). Social capital and tourism entrepreneurship. *Annals of Tourism Research*, *38*(4), 1570–1593. doi:10.1016/j.annals.2011.02.006

Zhou, L. (2014). Online rural destination images: Tourism and rurality. *Journal of Destination Marketing & Management*, *3*(4), 227–240. doi:10.1016/j.jdmm.2014.03.002

Zhou, S. (2001). The power of cointegration tests versus data frequency and time spans. *Southern Economic Journal*, *67*(4), 906–921. doi:10.2307/1061577

Ziegler, J., Dearden, P., & Rollins, R. (2012). But are tourists satisfied? Importance-performance analysis of the whale shark tourism industry on Isla Holbox, Mexico. *Tourism Management*, *33*(3), 692–701. doi:10.1016/j.tourman.2011.08.004

Zografos, C., & Allcroft, D. (2007). The environmental values of potential eco-tourists: A segmentation study. *Journal of Sustainable Tourism*, *15*(1), 44–66. doi:10.2167/jost572.0

About the Contributors

Patricia Ordóñez de Pablos is a professor in the Department of Business Administration in the Faculty of Business and Economics at The University of Oviedo (Spain). She completed her education in The London School of Economics (UK). Her teaching and research interests focus on the areas of strategic management, knowledge management, organizational learning, human resource management, intellectual capital, information technologies, with special interest in Asia (Bhutan, China, Laos, Myanmar). She is Editor-in-Chief of the International Journal of Learning and Intellectual Capital (IJLIC) and International Journal of Asian Business and Information Management (IJABIM), respectively. She has edited books for IGI-Global, Routledge and Springer.

Zeyar Myo Aung holds a Masters Degree in Business Administrations specializing in the field of Human Resources Management. Key interests focus upon international tourism, human resources development, establishment of sound organizational culture for the organizations. Experienced in preparing complex multi-disciplined yet visionary strategies, reports and proposals; policy and strategic planning; product development; developing and managing work programmes, budgets and accounts; supporting and coordinating the participation and interests of different stakeholders; conceiving projects; networking; team building; working in multi-cultural teams; undertaking field and contextual research; presenting oral and written progress reports; teaching, lecturing, coaching, advising and mentoring.

***

Neeta Baporikar is currently Director/Professor (Business Management) at Harold Pupkewitz Graduate School of Business (HP-GSB), Namibia University of Science and Technology, Namibia. Prior to this she was Head-Scientific Research, with Ministry of Higher Education CAS-Salalah, Sultanate of Oman, Professor (Strategic Management and Entrepreneurship) at IIIT Pune and BITS India. With more than a decade of experience in industry, consultancy and training, she made a lateral switch to research and academics in 1995. Dr. Baporikar holds D.Sc. (Management Studies) USA, PhD in Management, University of Pune INDIA with MBA (Distinction) and Law (Hons.) degrees. Apart from this, she is also an External Reviewer, Oman Academic Accreditation Authority, Accredited Management Teacher, Qualified Trainer, Doctoral Guide and Board Member of Academics and Advisory Committee in accredited B-Schools. Reviewer for international journals, she has to her credit 5 conferred doctorates, several refereed research papers, and authored books in the area of Entrepreneurship, Strategy, Management and Higher Education.

Huong T. Bui holds a PhD in Tourism Management. She is an Associate Professor of Tourism and Hospitality at College of Asia Pacific Studies, Ritsumeikan Asia Pacific University (APU) in Japan. She has conducted a wide range of research on topics of heritage tourism, dark tourism, tourism and hospitality education, Asian tourism and mobility.

I-Ting Chen holds a PhD in Organisation and Management, a PGDip in Social Sciences Research Methods, an MSc in Tourism and Hospitality Management, all from Sheffield Hallam University, UK and a BA in Business Administration from Taiwan. I-Ting is a Business and Organizational Management Research Expert for Europe and Asia.

Amarbayasgalan Gantumur has been working as a head of the Department of Financial Management at the University of the Humanities, Mongolia, since September, 2015. He obtained BA in Economics at the National University of Mongolia, in 1999. In 2012, he completed his MSc degree in Environmental Sciences, majoring in Environmental Management and Planning, at UNESCO-IHE, The Netherlands. He has been working as a lecturer at the Mongolian Universities, since 1999. Moreover, he has been conducting research studies on investment management, environmental management, and tourism management. Amarbayasgalan Gantumur has been working as a national expert on ecosystem valuation and its cost-benefit analysis, since 2012. His research results were published in the national and international scientific journals and presented in the international conferences. He is an author of 3 textbooks on economics for university students.

Babu P. George is an Associate professor of management at Fort Hays State University, KS, USA. Service industry management is one of his areas of expertise.

Gamini Herath is the Professor of Economics at the School of Business, Monash University, Malaysia. He received his Masters in Agricultural Development Economics from the Australian National University, Canberra and Ph. D from the University of New England, New South Wales, Australia. Before joining Monash University in 2010, he worked at La Trobe University and Deakin University, in Australia. Professor Herath has published nearly 75 journal papers in highly recognized international refereed journals including: The American Journal of Agricultural Economics, Australian Journal of Agricultural and Resource Economics, Ecological Economics, Journal of Development Studies and Oxford Agrarian Studies. He has published six books; the latest, are on (a) Multi-Criteria Decision Analysis in Natural Resource Management and (b) Child Labor in South Asia published in 2006 and 2007 respectively by Ashgate Publishing Limited, England and © Institutional Aspects of Water Management by Nova Publishers, New York in 2012. He has published 17 book chapters. Prof Herath heath was a He was a visiting professor at he University of Montana USA(1999), Missouri University, Columbia USA (2004, 2008)and visiting academic to the International Food Policy Research Institute, Washington DC in 2001 and Harvard University 2015.

Ajeya Jha heads the Department of Management Studies at Sikkim Manipal Institute of Technology (SMIT) since February 2000. In addition to having post-graduate and doctoral degrees in Business Administration, he possesses graduation and post graduation in Pharmaceutical Sciences also. fellow of International Society of Management. Has a rich and diverse industrial experience of 15 years (includes launching two green-field projects), teaching 18 years and with NGO 8 months. He is the founder

Chief coordinator of Entrepreneurship Development Cell (EDC) at SMIT established with support from Department of Science and Technology, Government of India. He is an associate editor of Advances in Management, an International Journal of Management and International Journal of Biotechnology.

Kijpokin Kasemsap received his BEng degree in Mechanical Engineering from King Mongkut's University of Technology, Thonburi, his MBA degree from Ramkhamhaeng University, and his DBA degree in Human Resource Management from Suan Sunandha Rajabhat University. He is a Special Lecturer in the Faculty of Management Sciences, Suan Sunandha Rajabhat University, based in Bangkok, Thailand. He is a Member of the International Association of Engineers (IAENG), the International Association of Engineers and Scientists (IAEST), the International Economics Development and Research Center (IEDRC), the International Association of Computer Science and Information Technology (IACSIT), the International Foundation for Research and Development (IFRD), and the International Innovative Scientific and Research Organization (IISRO). He also serves on the International Advisory Committee (IAC) for International Association of Academicians and Researchers (INAAR). He has had numerous original research articles in top international journals, conference proceedings, and books on the topics of business management, human resource management, and knowledge management, published internationally.

Tuan-Anh Le is Lecturer at the School of Business and Tourism, Southern Cross University, Australia. His area of research interests covers tourism, hospitality and sustainable development. Dr Le has more than 15 years of experience in various roles as a senior HRD specialist, master trainer, tour operator, business development manager, senior researcher, advisor and consultant. He has track records in proposal development and successfully funded by various international donors e.g. the EU, ADB, UNESCO, NUFFIC, DANIDA, AECID, SNV, USAID.

Ha Luu is a senior student of Hospitality program at Duy Tan University. She is interested in tourism and biological research.

Hylmee Matahir is a Lecturer in Economics at the Faculty of Business and Management, Universiti Teknologi MARA Cawangan Sabah, Malaysia. Currently, he is doing his Ph.D. in Economics under the supervision of Chor Foon Tang at the Centre for Policy Research and International Studies (CenPRIS), Universiti Sains Malaysia.

Manjushree Mishra obtained Bachelor of Arts (1977) with distinction, Master of Arts in Analytical & Applied Economics (1979) and Bachelor in Education (1988) all from Utkal University, Bhubaneswar, India. Completed PhD in Post Reform Industrial Scenario of Sikkim with Special Reference to Hydroelectricity, Tourism, Pharmaceuticals and Tea in 2014 from Sikkim Manipal University. She has 36 years of post-graduate teaching experience in Surajmal Saha College, Puri, India and in Public Schools at (Hissar, Pune, Mussoorie, Meerut, Delhi and Jodhpur), India. Became Assistant Professor, Department of Management Sciences, Sikkim Manipal Institute of Technology in 2007. Presently serving as Associate Professor Department of Humanities and Social Sciences, Sikkim Manipal University. She has contributed number of international and national publications. Has been Resource Person in the Faculty Development Programme in Entrepreneurship (2006), for Executive Development Programs for Sikkim state Civil Service Officers 2006 and 2008 at Sikkim Manipal Institute of Technology.

Somnath Mishra earned B Tech in Mechanical Engineering from National Institute of Technology, Rourkela in 1974. Pursued M Tech in Industrial Engineering and Operations Research from Indian Institute of Technology, Kharagpur, India in 1982. Completed PhD at IIT Delhi on issues concerning Technological Forecasting Applications in Indian Context in 2004. Has 40 years of service experience with 23 years field in many prestigious posts at all levels in the Armed Forces and 17 years academic in both engineering and management at College of Military Engineering Pune, Institute of Technology Management, Mussoorie, Sikkim Manipal Institute of Technology, Manipal Institute of Technology and Sikkim Manipal University. He has executed 12 major management consultancy projects and published several papers in International and National journals/conferences. He became Pro VC in 2010 and Vice Chancellor of prestigious Sikkim Manipal University from July 2011 and continues to lead the university since then.

Ny Ngo is a senior student of Hospitality program at Duy Tan University. She is interested in art and tourism research.

Chung Nguyen is a Senior Lecturer of the University of Education - Vietnam National University, Ha Noi. He earned doctorate degree in environmental chemistry and has involved in teaching and research in environmental education and sustainable development.

Minh Nguyen is the Dean of Hospitality and Tourism Faculty at Duy Tan University, Da Nang, Vietnam. His research interest is tourism.

Ngoc Nguyen is a senior student of Hospitality Program at Duy Tan University. She is interested in tourist psychology research.

Sudipta K. Sarkar is a Senior Lecturer in Tourism with Berjaya University College of Hospitality, Malaysia. His areas of research and teaching interests are: urban ecotourism, e-tourism/IT in tourism, food tourism.

Sherap Shenga is a post graduate from School of International Studies, Jawaharlal Nehru University Delhi. Currently she is the director of Lotteries in Sikkim Government. She has served the Government of Sikkim for nearly 30 years, in various capacity in departments including Home, Tourism, Information, Land Revenue, Industries.

Eu Chye Tan is a Professor at the Department of Economics, Faculty of Economics and Administration, University of Malaya, Kuala Lumpur, Malaysia. He obtained his Ph.D in Economics from University of Warwick, United Kingdom. His research interest encompasses Development Economics, Monetary Economics and International Economics.

Chor Foon Tang earned his Ph.D. in Economics from University of Malaya and recently he is a Senior Lecturer in Economics at CenPRIS, Universiti Sains Malaysia. He won the Bright Sparks Scholarship in 2010 and the UM Excellence Award 2012 in the Category of Highest Impact Publication from the University of Malaya. Since 2014, the Research Papers in Economics (RePEc) ranked him in the Top 10% Economists in Malaysia as well as in Asia. Before joining academia, he worked in various commercial industries ranging from finance to manufacturing industries about 5 years to earn industrial experiences to understand the difference between theory and reality. His expertise and research interests primarily focus on Applied Econometrics, Applied Macroeconomics, Development Economics, Tourism Economics and Energy Economics. He is the reviewer and the editorial board member for a wide range of international and local scholarly journals. Currently, Dr. Tang has published 76 articles in both international and local scholarly journals; while 46 out of 76 articles are ISI-Web of Science (ISI-WoS) cited publication and 15 out of 76 articles are Scopus cited publications.

Hai Tran is a senior student of Hospitality program at Duy Tan University. She is interested in music, art, and tourism research.

My Tran is a senior student of Hospitality program at Duy Tan University. She is interested in music and tourism psychology research.

Xuan Tran Tran is an associate professor of the Global Hospitality and Tourism Management Department at the University of West Florida. Dr. Tran is interested in consumer behavior as it relates to Hospitality and Tourism.

Navchaa Tugjamba, professor of the University of the Humanities, Mongolia. She obtained BSc in Geography from Mongolian State University of Education, and MSc in Environmental Sciences from UNESCO-IHE, The Netherlands. Hold PhD in Education at the Mongolian State University of Education, in 2005. Navchaa Tugjamba is an educator and researcher on the ecotourism management, sustainable tourism and tourism education. She has been working in the field around 20 years. Her research results had been published in the international peer-reviewed journals and presented in the international level conferences. Also, she has been written several books and brochures on the ecotourism, tourism study and tourism education. Navchaa Tugjamba has been working as a national expert on tourism and environmental management research field for the international and national level development projects. Research interest: Ecosystem management, ecotourism management, environmental, tourism education, education for sustainable development.

Konstantin Karl Weicht is an international Organization and Management research expert. He holds a PhD in Management Studies from Sheffield Hallam University, UK, a Master of Research in Strategic Management and Innovation from the University of Salford, UK, and a Management degree in Industrial & Commercial Management from Austria. He specialises in critical ethnography, in-depth interviews, and (un)structured observation.

Index

A

activity 29, 36, 42, 44-45, 53-54, 58-59, 81, 94, 108-109, 149-150, 154-155, 159, 171, 173-174, 179-181, 185-186, 204, 213, 225-226, 251
Actor Network theory 261-263, 268
adventure tourism 107-110, 112
advertising 1-4, 7-15
Analytical Hierarchy process 101, 104-105, 107, 113
Asia 1-2, 9, 15, 25, 34-35, 41, 47, 50, 62, 77-80, 82, 84-85, 102, 150, 170, 174, 176-179, 188, 198, 204-206, 209-210, 212, 215, 217, 225-227, 229-231, 233, 235, 242, 261-264, 268
Asia and the Pacific region 204, 206, 209, 212, 215, 217

B

behavioral attitude 14
behaviour 82, 94, 173, 175, 177, 180-181, 271, 273

C

circumstances 8, 110, 159, 173, 191, 258
cointegration 121, 123, 125, 127, 188, 191-193, 235, 244, 267
collaboration 121, 150, 178, 181, 227
combined tests for cointegration 191, 193
Community Based Approaches 169
community development 79, 153, 213
comparison 107, 112-114, 125, 170, 205, 213
conservation 17, 21, 24, 26, 28, 33, 50, 55-56, 58-59, 78-80, 83-85, 87-88, 94, 103, 173, 175-176, 181-182, 251-258, 270-273, 275, 280, 284
control 1-2, 4-8, 12, 14-15, 63, 93, 152-153, 158, 176, 180-181, 212, 215, 263-264
cultural tourism 27, 79, 101, 106-111, 113, 263
culture 17, 30, 55, 57, 63, 78, 80-81, 84, 108, 121, 149-150, 153, 157, 175, 182, 205, 207, 213, 215, 227, 244, 250-251, 253-254, 261-262, 264, 268, 272-273

D

destination 1-4, 8-9, 14-15, 17, 24, 26, 28-29, 33, 35, 38, 42, 44, 47, 50, 53, 55, 58-59, 62, 76, 81-82, 89, 91, 101-103, 121, 129, 149, 159, 162, 169-183, 188, 212, 227, 231, 235, 250, 254, 256, 258, 270-271
developing countries 54-55, 61-62, 80, 154, 224-226, 230, 233, 250-251, 274
development 1-2, 12, 15, 17-18, 22, 24-29, 31, 34-35, 46-51, 53-63, 76-82, 84-85, 89, 94-95, 102-104, 120, 149-159, 162-163, 169-181, 183-185, 203-218, 225-226, 230, 233-236, 239, 245, 249, 251-258, 261-265, 268, 271-273, 277

E

economic growth 35, 53, 55-56, 61, 63, 79, 120-123, 125-129, 157-159, 178-179, 188-195, 197-198, 203, 205-206, 209, 224-225, 227, 233-236, 238, 243-245, 253, 258, 264, 271
Ecosystem services 24-26, 31, 33
ecotourism 18, 25-26, 29, 48-49, 56, 76-77, 79-80, 83-84, 103, 105, 113, 173-185, 213, 256, 270, 272-273, 275, 280
eco-tourism principle 277
eco-tourists 174-175, 179-183, 185, 270
educational tourism 120-123, 125-129, 184
employment 34, 37-38, 49, 55, 59-63, 76-83, 89, 94, 149, 154, 157, 159, 226, 229-230, 273
environment 2-3, 8-9, 15, 17-19, 21, 25-26, 28-29, 31, 33, 35, 54-55, 57, 61-62, 76-84, 86, 88, 91, 94-95, 102-103, 109, 158, 173-177, 179-182, 184, 206, 213, 215-216, 218, 225-227, 230, 250, 257, 271-272, 278

F

facilities 56, 58-59, 61-62, 76, 94, 109, 114, 150, 155, 163, 173, 215-216, 224, 271-272, 274-275, 282, 284

financial benefits 270-275, 280-281, 284
foreign direct investment 224, 236-238, 249

G

George-Henthorne-Williams model 182
government 21, 35-36, 46, 50-51, 56-57, 59, 80, 82-83, 85, 94-95, 101, 103-104, 114, 120-121, 150-158, 162, 169, 178-179, 203-204, 206-210, 212-214, 216-217, 224-227, 229, 236-238, 243-244, 251, 253-255, 257, 262, 264, 270, 273, 275-277, 281
Granger causality 120-121, 124, 126-128, 188-189, 191-192, 194-198, 235-237

H

heritage tourism 250-251, 258

I

income 6, 36-37, 55, 59, 61, 63, 76-78, 81, 85, 89, 105-107, 109, 111-113, 183, 209-210, 215, 226, 230, 237-238, 243, 254-256, 273
India 34-39, 42, 45-51, 80, 101-102, 149-152, 155-157, 159-160, 162-163, 178, 272-273
insights 150, 180, 185, 273

K

Kharkhorin 22, 33
Kuala Lumpur 173-179, 182-186

L

long-run relationship 123, 125, 193, 225, 236-237, 239
low-impact facilities 271-272, 274-275, 282, 284

M

Malaysia 77-80, 84-86, 120-123, 125, 127-129, 173-174, 177-180, 182-183, 185, 188-191, 193-195, 197-198, 227, 230, 233, 239, 243-244, 261-268
motivation 173, 215, 225, 254, 274
mountainous region 18

N

natural resources 20-21, 36, 63, 76, 103, 175, 227, 272-273
nature tourism. 273
New Taiwan Dollar 204
Non-Governmental Organisations (NGOs) 169
Northeast 102, 205, 227, 233

O

Orkhon Valley 17-18, 22, 25, 31, 33
Orkhon Valley National Park (OVNP) 17, 22, 31, 33

P

places 40, 61-62, 102, 108, 129, 149, 156, 185, 212, 226, 263, 283
pleasure 76, 181, 183
PLOG'S DESTINATION LIFE CYCLE MODEL 170, 175
policy 18, 28-29, 34, 47, 51, 54, 56, 58, 61, 63, 79, 88-89, 93-94, 102-104, 106, 110, 114, 121-122, 128-129, 149-160, 162-163, 169, 189, 194, 197-198, 208, 211, 216, 225, 227-228, 230, 244-245, 254, 258, 264, 270-271, 273, 275-276, 278, 282-284
Policy Cycle 152, 169
Policy Implementation 153, 169
Policy Instruments 169
positive experience 80, 82, 279
public 1-4, 7-10, 12, 14-15, 28, 30-31, 37, 53, 55, 57, 59, 83-84, 129, 150-151, 153-156, 158, 169, 184-185, 210, 212, 227, 236, 251, 253, 283
public relations 1-4, 7-10, 12, 14-15, 251

Q

Quality Function Deployment 101-102, 104, 106, 111, 114

R

religious tourism 27, 101-102, 106-110, 112, 114
Republic of China 204-205, 207-208, 210-212
rural hotels 204-205, 208, 214-216, 218
rural tourism 53-63, 76, 84, 153, 162, 203-204, 206, 212-218, 273

S

services 2, 12, 24-27, 29, 31, 33, 55, 58-59, 61, 76, 82, 85, 102, 150-152, 158, 163, 181, 213, 215-216, 218, 224, 226, 230-231, 235, 244-245, 255-258, 263, 272
small hotels 203, 205, 213-214, 216
social norms 1-2, 4, 14

spiritual beliefs of the Indigenous 270-272, 274-275, 282-284
Stakeholders 26-29, 51, 57-58, 60, 76-77, 82-83, 93, 103, 121, 153, 169, 227, 251, 258
sub-region 35, 47, 49-51
sustainability 34, 42, 45, 50-51, 54, 57, 60, 62-63, 76-77, 79-80, 82-83, 94, 106, 111, 149, 175-176, 180, 184, 217, 226, 250-252, 258, 274, 280
sustainable 17-18, 24, 26, 31, 33, 53-63, 76-85, 93-95, 102-104, 153, 157, 174-175, 183-184, 215, 217, 225-226, 233, 236, 244, 251, 256, 272-274
sustainable development 26, 53-58, 60, 62, 76, 78-80, 82, 84, 94-95, 102, 104, 157, 175, 184, 251
sustainable tourism 17, 24, 26, 31, 33, 53-57, 59-63, 76-85, 93, 95, 103, 217, 233
synthesis 170-171, 181, 183

T

tourism 1-3, 8-10, 12, 15, 17-22, 24-29, 31, 33-37, 39-40, 42, 44-51, 53-63, 76-86, 88-91, 93-95, 101-114, 120-123, 125-129, 149-160, 162-163, 169-181, 183-185, 188-195, 197-198, 203-218, 224-240, 242-245, 250-258, 261-268, 271-275, 277, 279-280
tourism carrying capacity 17-18, 24, 26, 31, 33
tourism development 1-2, 17-18, 22, 24, 26-28, 31, 34-35, 46-51, 54-56, 58, 60-61, 63, 77-78, 80, 82, 84-85, 150, 152-153, 156-158, 163, 169, 179-180, 183, 203-213, 215-218, 234-236, 245, 251-252, 256-258, 261-265, 268, 272-273
tourism impacts 24, 26, 33, 89, 175
Tourism in the Protected Area 17, 21, 24, 33
Tourism Planning for Conservation 33
tourism policy 18, 106, 150-160, 162, 169, 275
tourism receipts 189, 227, 234, 261, 264-268
tourism-led growth hypothesis 188, 224-225, 227, 233-236, 242-244

U

United Nations 79, 149, 204, 210-211, 226, 239, 265
urban ecotourism 173-177, 181, 183-184

V

value 14, 25-28, 50, 61, 82, 110, 114, 123, 125, 154, 156, 159, 174-175, 181-182, 191, 195, 204, 209, 216, 231, 249, 267, 274, 277, 279, 281, 284
variance decomposition 120-121, 127-128
Vector Auto Regressive 261-262
Vietnam 1-2, 4-6, 85, 211, 227, 230, 239, 243, 250-252, 254, 256-258
visit intention 1-4, 7-10, 14

W

wealth 21, 55, 225, 274
wildlife tourism 101, 107-110, 112-114
World Heritage 22, 33, 211, 250-253, 257-258
World Tourism Organization 78, 80, 149, 204, 226-227
World Travel and Tourism Council 203

www.ingramcontent.com/pod-product-compliance
Lightning Source LLC
LaVergne TN
LVHW060416300926
849162LV00006B/1440